QUATTRO® PRO

User's Guide

BORLAND INTERNATIONAL, INC. 1800 GREEN HILLS ROAD
P.O. BOX 660001, SCOTTS VALLEY, CA 95066-0001

PRINTED IN THE USA.
10 9 8 7 6 5 4 3

R4

C O N T E N T S

T A B L E S

F I G U R E S

This book is one in a set of three QUATTRO PRO manuals:

- *Getting Started* tells you how to get Quattro up and running, and includes a hands-on tutorial that introduces you to Quattro's basic features. It also contains chapters geared specifically toward novice users, users upgrading from earlier versions of Quattro, and users switching over to Quattro from Lotus 1-2-3.

- Use the *@Functions and Macros* manual after you're more familiar with the program. It includes alphabetic descriptions of Quattro's @functions, macro commands, and menu-equivalent macro commands.

- This book, the *User's Guide*, is your major source of information about the program as you learn to use it. It goes into thorough detail about each area of Quattro.

If you purchased a network package, you also have the *Network Administrator's Guide*, which contains all the information you need to run Quattro on a local area network.

Before you begin this book, be sure to read *Getting Started*.

What's in this manual

This guide is divided into six parts:

Part 1: Quattro basics
- **Chapter 1, "Quattro: An overview,"** describes some of the operations used throughout Quattro, such as choosing a command from a menu.

- **Chapter 2, "The pull-down menus,"** introduces each selection on the menu bar.

- **Chapter 3, "Entering data,"** explains how to enter labels, numbers, and formulas into your spreadsheet, how to edit entries, and how to use Quattro @functions to help calculate data in your spreadsheet.

- **Chapter 4, "Printing,"** covers the details of printing Quattro spreadsheets and graphs to a printer, a file, or a screen preview: setting margins and page lengths, printer setup strings, and so on.

Part 2: Making changes

- **Chapter 5, "Changing data in your spreadsheet,"** covers the kinds of changes you can make to specific parts of the spreadsheet—from moving data to performing a global search and replace operation.

- **Chapter 6, "Changing the style of your spreadsheet,"** describes how to change the way your spreadsheet displays data: formatting blocks of data, setting fonts, adjusting column widths, drawing lines, and shading blocks of the spreadsheet.

- **Chapter 7, "Setting options,"** shows you how to change options that affect the current spreadsheet only, such as the default column width, and options that affect the overall system, such as the display colors for the spreadsheet.

Part 3: Files and windows

- **Chapter 8, "Working with spreadsheet files,"** explains how to access files and display them in open windows, as well as how to retrieve spreadsheet files, save them in a file for future use, and perform several other file operations.

- **Chapter 9, "Manipulating windows,"** describes how to best use windows in Quattro, both by arranging up to 32 open windows in customized onscreen configurations and by splitting a single spreadsheet window into two.

- **Chapter 10, "Using the File Manager,"** explains how to use Quattro's File Manager. With it, you can display, open, sort, rename, move, copy, and delete files. It also tells you how to move in and out of directories in the directory tree.

- **Chapter 11, "Linking spreadsheets,"** explains how to use spreadsheet links to pass information between spreadsheets. With links, you can copy or move data directly from one spreadsheet to another, or use formulas in one spreadsheet that reference cells in other spreadsheets.

- **Chapter 12, "Advanced file tools,"** covers importing data created with other programs and exporting data for use with other programs, merging existing spreadsheets together, extracting portions of one spreadsheet into a separate file, and parsing labels into separate columns.

■ **Chapter 13, "Building graphs,"** describes the ten different kinds of Quattro graphs and how to create and save them. It also covers how to insert graphs directly into your spreadsheet.

■ **Chapter 14, "Customizing graphs,"** explains how to use graph customization commands to change how Quattro displays your graph.

■ **Chapter 15, "Annotating your graph,"** covers graph customization features that let you add text, arrows, lines, rectangles, round rectangles, polygons, polylines, and ellipses to your graph.

■ **Chapter 16, "Using macros,"** tells you how to create macros to automate printing, formatting, and other Quattro operations.

■ **Chapter 17, "Using Transcript,"** explains how to use the Transcript utility to protect against mistakes and power failures, audit spreadsheet changes, and create macros.

■ **Chapter 18, "Using Quattro as a database manager,"** tells you how to set up all or part of your spreadsheet like a database. It describes how to search through and sort information in a database and set up your database for data entry. It also covers linking to an external Paradox database file.

■ **Chapter 19, "Working with statistics and analyzing data,"** covers advanced mathematics features like regression analysis, matrix arithmetic, sensitivity analysis, and linear programming.

■ **Appendix A, "Help and hints,"** offers solutions to common questions and misunderstandings.

■ **Appendix B, "A DOS primer,"** offers basic information on using the DOS operating system.

■ **Appendix C, "Networking with Quattro,"** describes how one person at a time can use Quattro on a local area network. See the *Network Administrator's Guide* for information about multiuser access in a networked version.

■ **Appendix D, "Quattro keys and indicators,"** defines all possible mode and status indicators that can appear on your screen and explains the cursor-movement, function, and other special keys in Quattro.

■ **Appendix E, "Printer setup strings,"** lists ASCII character codes used to give setup commands to Epson, IBM, and HP LaserJet printers. It also describes how to translate codes used by other printers.

- **Appendix F, "Working with fonts,"** contains information about Quattro's special fonts and how font building works.
- **Appendix G, "ASCII codes,"** is an ASCII table listing decimal and hexadecimal codes for each ASCII character.
- **Appendix H, "Error messages,"** lists and describes all possible error messages that might occur in Quattro and offers solutions.
- **Appendix I, "123-compatible menu tree commands,"** lists commands on the 123-compatible menus and their corresponding commands on the standard Quattro menus.
- **Appendix J, "Menu maps,"** illustrates the Quattro menu tree, broken up according to the chapters of this manual.
- **Glossary** gives definitions of key words used in this manual and in Quattro.

1-2-3

If you're using the 123-compatible menu tree, pay attention to the instructions next to the "lotus" icons (like this one). You'll find special information about performing the operation using the 123-compatible menu commands. If you don't see this symbol, you don't have to worry about what command to use—the 123-compatible command name is the same as the Quattro name. You can also use the table in Appendix I to look up the corresponding Quattro command for any command in the 123-compatible menus.

Typefaces and icons in this book

All typefaces in this manual were produced by Borland's word-processing program, Sprint, and output on a PostScript typesetter. Their uses are as follows:

`Monospace type`	This typeface represents text displayed on your screen or anything you must type.
Italics	Italics are used for emphasis and to introduce a new term; all new terms are defined in the Glossary.
Keycap	This special typeface indicates a key on your keyboard. It often indicates a particular key you should press—for example, "Press *Esc* to cancel a menu."

When menu commands appear in full (the name of the command as it appears on the menu, preceded by the command names used to get to it), the keystrokes you press to execute the command are shown in bold. For example, to execute the /Options I International I Currency command, you'd press */OIC*.

This book documents Quattro features using commands on the standard Quattro menu tree.

A lotus icon sets apart equivalent commands in the 123-compatible menus.

A mouse icon sets apart special instructions for mouse users.

▶ An arrow next to a command on a displayed menu means that you may choose it to display another menu. You might also see keyboard shortcuts displayed on the menu. To widen or narrow a menu, press the Expand key (+) or the Contract key (-).

Supported equipment

The next two sections cover both necessary and optional equipment supported by Quattro.

Necessary equipment

Here's what you'll need to run Quattro:

- **Computer.** Quattro is designed to run on the IBM XT, AT, PS/2, and fully compatible computers.
- **Operating system.** Quattro runs on DOS 2.0 or later.
- **Memory.** To run Quattro, you'll need at least 512K of random-access memory (RAM); we recommend 640K of RAM.
- **Disk drive.** Your computer must have a hard disk with at least 3Mb of disk space available; we recommend 4Mb of free disk space.

Optional equipment

You don't need the following equipment to run Quattro, but each option does enhance its features:

- **Graphics card.** If you want to display or annotate graphs, you need a graphics card and a display capable of high-resolution graphics (a color monitor is not necessary). You can still build and print graphs without a graphics card, however. Quattro supports the following graphics cards:

- IBM Color/Graphics Adapter
- Hercules (monochrome) Graphics Card
- IBM Enhanced Graphics Adapter (color or monochrome)
- IBM Video Graphics Array (color or monochrome)
- IBM 3270/PC and 3270/AT with APA
- AT&T 6300 640x400
- MCGA (IBM Model 30)
- IBM 8514 Graphics Adapter

■ **Expanded memory card.** You can add expanded memory cards to your computer to increase the amount of data it can "memorize," so you can work with larger spreadsheets or more spreadsheets at one time. Quattro works with any LIM 3.2 or 4.0 card, including the following:

- Intel Above Board
- AST RAMpage!
- Quadram Liberty
- STB Memory Champion

Quattro automatically detects and uses expanded memory. You can alter what Quattro uses expanded memory for with the /Options I Other I Expanded Memory command (see page 200).

■ **Mouse.** Quattro works with mice that are compatible with the Microsoft Mouse interface. These include the Microsoft Mouse (bus and serial), Mouse Systems Mouse (with the MSMOUSE driver), and the Logitech Mouse.

■ **Printer.** You can run Quattro with dot matrix, daisy wheel, laser, or PostScript printers. See the README file for a complete list of supported printers.

■ **Math coprocessor.** Quattro automatically detects and uses any coprocessor installed in your computer.

How to contact Borland

As a Borland customer, you have full access to Borland technical support for help with any problems you can't solve yourself. To register for this support, be sure to fill out and mail in the registration card that you'll find inside the box Quattro came in.

The quickest and easiest way to contact Borland is to log on to Borland's Forum on CompuServe: Type GO BORAPP from the main CompuServe menu. Leave your questions or comments there for the support staff to process.

If you prefer (or if you don't subscribe to CompuServe), write a letter detailing your comments and send it to:

Technical Support Department: QUATTRO PRO
Borland International
1800 Green Hills Road
P.O. Box 660001
Scotts Valley, CA 95066-0001, USA

You can also telephone our Technical Support department at 408-438-5300. Please note that you must be a registered owner to receive telephone support; be sure to send in your license statement. Whichever method you use to contact Borland, you need to provide the information listed below. If you're calling Borland, be sure to have this information at hand *before* you call:

- Quattro version number and serial number
- computer make, model number, and amount of RAM
- operating system and version number
- graphics card type
- contents of your CONFIG.SYS and AUTOEXEC.BAT files
- any RAM-resident programs loaded when the problem occurred (such as SideKick, SuperKey, Lightning, or a RAM disk)

P A R T

1

Quattro basics

1

Quattro: An overview

This chapter introduces you to some of the basic procedures involved in using Quattro. It tells you how to

- use specific keys and a mouse with Quattro
- use Quattro menus to issue commands
- create "shortcuts" to execute menu commands with one keystroke
- get onscreen help about whatever you're doing
- use the *Esc* key to cancel a menu or prompt
- specify a new default directory
- enter data into the spreadsheet and make changes to it
- save and retrieve spreadsheet files
- switch to a different display mode
- access DOS from within the spreadsheet
- exit Quattro

After reading this chapter, you should be able to build a simple spreadsheet with Quattro.

The Quattro screen

The Quattro screen has four distinct areas: the menu bar, the spreadsheet area, the input line at the top, the status line at the bottom, and the mouse palette at the right. The following figure shows a typical spreadsheet screen:

Figure 1.1
A spreadsheet screen

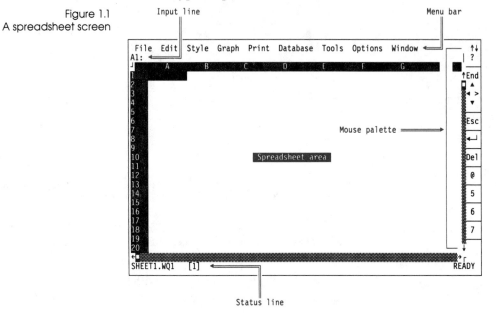

"Using the Quattro menus" on page 25 describes how the menu bar works. See "The mouse palette" on page 22 for a description of the mouse palette. The next three sections discuss the spreadsheet area, the input line, and the status line.

The spreadsheet area

The spreadsheet area takes up most of your display screen. It is the area where you open spreadsheet and File Manager windows and make changes to your spreadsheets.

Quattro shows only part of the spreadsheet in a window at a time. To view other areas, you can *scroll* the spreadsheet, using either the scroll bars (see page 13) or the cursor-movement keys (see page 16).

The spreadsheet itself is a rectangular grid made up of columns (identified by letters) and rows (identified by numbers). Each intersection of a column and a row makes up a *cell*, which is where you enter data.

The following figure shows the various components that make up the Quattro spreadsheet:

Figure 1.2
The parts of a Quattro
spreadsheet

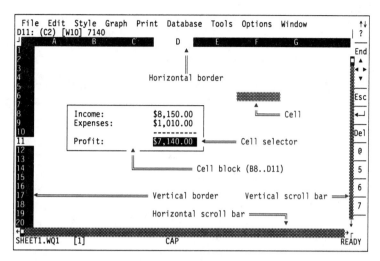

- **The horizontal border** is a row of letters that identifies each column of cells in the spreadsheet (256 in all). It titles columns as A-Z, then AA-AZ, BA-BZ and so on, up to IA-IV. It shows the column containing the cell selector in reverse video on a monochrome screen and in a contrasting color on a color screen.

- **The vertical border** is a column of numbers (1-8192) that identifies each row of cells in the spreadsheet. It shows the row containing the cell selector in reverse video or in a contrasting color, depending on your monitor.

- **A cell** is a box in the spreadsheet in which you can enter data. Each cell is identified by an *address* determined by the column and row that contain it. For example, the cell in the upper left corner of the spreadsheet is A1. The letter and number that make up the cell address are the cell's *coordinates*.

- **The cell selector** is the highlighted rectangle that indicates the current cell. This is the cell that will be affected by your next action, such as entering a value. You can move the selector to any cell in the spreadsheet.

- **A cell block** is a rectangular group of cells identified by the cell addresses of two opposite corners—usually the upper left and bottom right cells (in the preceding figure, B8 and D11). You use blocks in commands and formulas to act on several cells at once.

- **Scroll bars** appear along the bottom and right edge of each spreadsheet window. On both the vertical and horizontal scroll bars, a *scroll box* indicates the current position of the cursor relative to the portion of the spreadsheet that contains data. To move to a different part of the spreadsheet, drag the scroll box along the scroll bar, then release.

Messages pertaining to any errors that occur while you're working, such as "Syntax Error," appear in a box over the spreadsheet. Appendix H, "Error messages," explains all error messages.

 See page 21 for information about how to use a mouse to manipulate windows.

The input line

When you highlight a cell, the input line at the top of the spreadsheet screen displays information about the current cell. The following figure shows typical information on the input line in Ready mode:

Figure 1.3
The input line in Ready mode

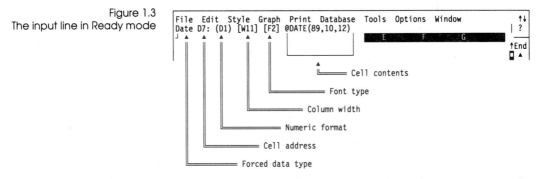

In Ready mode, the input line displays the following types of information about the current cell:

■ **Forced data type** (if any). When you set the cell to accept only label or date entries (with /**Database** I **Data Entry**), Quattro displays Label or Date before the address. If the cell selector is inside an inserted graph, Quattro displays Graph.

■ **Address**, as defined by the intersection of a column and row; for example, A10.

■ **Numeric format** (if set to override the spreadsheet default). This appears as the format's initial followed by its precision (or date format number). For example, (C2) stands for Currency format with two decimal places.

- **Column width** (if different from the default). This appears as a *W* in brackets followed by the set width. For example, [W14] indicates a column width of 14 characters.

- **Font type** (if different from Font 1, the default). This appears as [F#], with # being the number of the font between two and eight.

- **Contents**. The data in the cell appears as you typed it, not as Quattro displays it in the spreadsheet. For example, if the data appears as $1,290 in the cell, it displays as 1290 on the input line in Ready mode (or status line in Edit mode) because you don't include the dollar sign and comma when you enter the value.

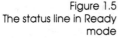
Edit

If you press *F2* and start typing, you're in Edit mode. The current cell information that appeared on the input line in Ready mode moves to the status line at the bottom of the spreadsheet. The input line in Edit mode shows [Enter] and [Esc] mouse buttons and the data you're editing or entering in that cell. If the current entry is longer than your screen is wide, the input line drops down and overlaps the spreadsheet. Any block name references on the input line change to cell block coordinates in Edit mode. When you finish, Quattro writes it into the current cell.

The following figure shows the input line in Edit mode:

Figure 1.4
The input line in Edit mode

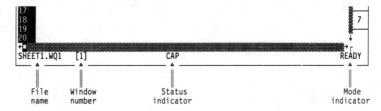

The status line

In Ready mode, the bottom line of the spreadsheet screen (the status line) displays information about the current state of the program.

The following figure shows typical information on the status line:

Figure 1.5
The status line in Ready mode

- **File name** shows the name of the current spreadsheet file. If you haven't yet loaded or saved a spreadsheet, it shows the file name as SHEET# (where # is the number of the current window).

■ **Window number** displays the number of the current window. Quattro assigns the numbers in the order in which the windows are opened.

■ **Status indicator** displays current status conditions in the program. For example, CAP indicates that the *Caps Lock* key is on.

■ **Mode indicator** shows the current mode the spreadsheet is in; for example, MENU indicates that a menu is displayed.

When you highlight a menu command, Quattro replaces the file name display with a brief description of the command.

You can also display the current date and time on the status line with the /**Options** I **Other** I **Clock** command (see "Clock display" in Chapter 7).

For a table that describes each possible mode and status condition, see Appendix D, "Quattro keys and indicators."

Edit

If you press *F2* to enter Edit mode or begin typing in a cell, the status line changes. The information about the current cell that Quattro displays on the input line moves to the status line. (See the figure at the start of the previous section for an illustration of the current cell information that appears on the input line in Ready mode.)

A tour of your keyboard

Certain keys on your keyboard have special meaning in Quattro. The *cursor-movement keys* on the right side of your keyboard let you move to different areas of the screen. The *function keys*, on the left or top of your keyboard (*F1* and up), automate Quattro commands. Both of these key groups are discussed in the following sections. These and other special keys are also described in Appendix D, "Quattro keys and indicators." You can also refer to the Quick Reference Guide that came with your Quattro package.

Cursor-movement keys

The Quattro cursor-movement keys let you

■ move around a spreadsheet

■ position the cursor within a cell entry during Edit mode

- highlight menu items
- page through help screens

In a menu, you can use the cursor-movement keys to highlight different menu items. The ↑ and ↓ keys move you up and down in the menu. → and ← take you to adjacent menus if you are in the first level of menus pulled down from the menu bar. *Home* takes you to the first item on the menu; *End* takes you to the last.

 With help information displayed (press *F1*), use the arrow keys to highlight options on the help screen. When you press *Enter*, Quattro displays another help screen with details about the option you chose.

In a spreadsheet, the cursor-movement keys have the most varied capabilities. The arrow keys move the cell selector around the spreadsheet. *PgUp* and *PgDn* scroll the spreadsheet up and down one screenful at a time. In addition, you can use key combinations to move to more exact areas of the spreadsheet. For example, press *End* then → to go to the rightmost edge of the current block of data.

Table 1.1 describes the effect of each cursor-movement key in a Quattro spreadsheet.

Key	Description
←	Moves left one cell.
→	Moves right one cell.
↑	Moves up one cell.
↓	Moves down one cell.
Ctrl ← or *Shift-Tab*	Moves left one screen.
Ctrl → or *Tab*	Moves right one screen.
PgUp	Moves up one screen.
PgDn	Moves down one screen.
Home	Moves to upper left cell (A1).
End	Must be used with another cursor-movement key.
End-Home	Moves to lower right corner of the non-blank part of the spreadsheet.
End ↑	If the current cell contains an entry, moves up to the next non-blank cell beneath an empty one. If the current cell is blank, moves up to the next non-blank cell.
End ↓	If the current cell contains an entry, moves down to the next non-blank cell above an empty one. If the current cell is blank, moves down to the next non-blank cell.
End →	If the current cell contains an entry, moves right to the next non-blank cell followed by an empty one. If the current cell is blank, moves right to the next non-blank cell.
End ←	If the current cell contains an entry, moves left to the next non-blank cell preceded by an empty one. If the current cell is blank, moves left to the next non-blank cell.
F5 (GoTo)	Moves to any cell you specify by cell address.

When you enter data in a cell, you can use a cursor-movement key instead of *Enter* to enter the item *and* move the cell selector in the indicated direction. For example, if you type an entry with the selector in cell B6, then press ↓ , Quattro writes the entry into cell B6 and moves the selector to cell B7.

The GoTo key takes you to whatever cell in the spreadsheet you specify. When you press *F5*, Quattro prompts you for a cell address. Enter any valid address. When you press *Enter*, the selector moves to that cell. For example, to go to cell B10, press *F5*, then type B10 and press *Enter*.

Some of the cursor-movement keys work differently in Edit mode (see "Editing entries" on page 48).

Taking a quick look

To momentarily view a different part of the spreadsheet and then return to your original position, use the GoTo key, then cancel the command with *Esc*. In other words,

1. Press the GoTo key (*F5*). Quattro prompts you for a cell address.

2. Instead of typing in a cell address (as you normally would with *F5*), use the cursor-movement keys to take you to the area you want to view. (Don't press *Enter*.)

3. When you're ready to return to your original place, press *Esc*. Quattro cancels the GoTo command and returns you to the cell that was current when you initiated the command.

Using the End key

The *End* key is very useful when used with other cursor-movement keys. You can use it to move quickly to the corners of the current block of data, or to move across an expanse of blank cells to the next block of data.

You'll find the *End* key especially useful in *pointing* out a block of cells in response to a command prompt; for example, to indicate a block of cells to move. (See page 71 for more information about pointing out blocks.)

The following figure demonstrates how the *End* key works from various positions in a spreadsheet:

Figure 1.6
How the End key works

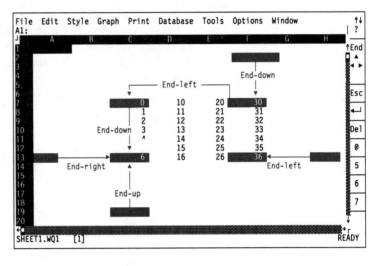

Function keys

The function keys on the left or top of your keyboard (labeled *F1* and up) perform often-used Quattro commands with one simple keystroke. Some of the keys have more than one function; to access further functions, hold down the *Alt, Ctrl,* or *Shift* key, then press the function key.

The Quattro package includes templates that you place over the function keys to show each key's special function. One is designed for keyboards that group the function keys at the left side of the keyboard. The other is for keyboards with the function keys at the top of the board.

For a table describing each of the function keys as well as other special keys, see Appendix D, "Quattro keys and indicators." You can also refer to the Quick Reference Guide that came with your Quattro package.

Change your mind? The Esc key

In Quattro, the *Esc* key is the all-purpose "uh-oh" key. It can't reverse mistakes you've already made, but it does let you back out of mistakes before it's too late.

Suppose that, while editing or replacing a cell entry, you decide you'd rather keep the old entry. Press *Esc* and the original entry returns—*as long as you press Esc before you press Enter.*

Similarly, if you choose a menu command that displays a prompt and decide not to carry out the command, *Esc* cancels the command. With menus displayed, you can press *Esc* to exit the current menu and return to the previous menu or the spreadsheet.

General rule You can interrupt any sequence that ends with *Enter* by pressing *Esc* before you press *Enter*.

Press *Ctrl-Break* to return immediately to the spreadsheet from within Help or menus, just as if you had pressed *Esc* enough times to return to Ready mode.

To reverse mistakes you've already made, such as deleting a block or erasing a spreadsheet, use the /Edit I Undo command (see "Undoing a change" in Chapter 5).

Using a mouse

A *mouse* is a hand-operated pointing device attached to your computer. The mouse has up to three buttons that send signals to the computer when you press them, just as pressing keys on a keyboard does. Quattro uses only the left and rightmost buttons. In Quattro, you can optionally use a mouse to perform many tasks, such as choosing a menu command or selecting a cell.

  The mouse icon means special instructions for mouse users. Quattro automatically detects a mouse.

If you have a mouse (and your mouse software is loaded), a *pointer* appears on your screen. (Initially, the pointer is a highlighted rectangle, like a block cursor, but if you set your screen's display mode to graphics—see page 33—the pointer becomes an arrow.) To control the pointer, roll the mouse across your desktop or mouse pad.

Remember The tip of the pointer (or the middle of the box pointer) is what you need to position.

Basic techniques

There are six fundamental actions you need to know when using a mouse with Quattro.

Figure 1.1
Six basic mouse techniques

Technique	Action
Point	Move the mouse pointer to a specific area onscreen.
Click	Quickly press and release the left button.
Double-click	Quickly press and release the left button twice in succession.
Hold down	Hold down a button while you do something else; for example, hold down the rightmost button while you click the left to extend a block.
Drag	Press the left button and hold it down while you move the pointer.
Release	Let up on the left button after dragging.

Use these techniques to perform the following general functions with a mouse:

■ **Select an item or activate an area.** For example, you can click to choose a command from a menu, activate a different part of the screen, or select a button on the mouse palette.

■ **Point out a cell block.** Many Quattro commands work on a block of cells. You can use the mouse to drag through the block of cells to select them so you can work on them. See page 71 for more information about pointing out blocks.

■ **Move a boundary.** You can drag to adjust the width of a column, to resize a window, or to reposition a window.

■ **Accept or cancel cell entries and edits or file name entries in a prompt box.** Click the [Enter] and [Esc] buttons on the input line for cell entries and edits, and in the file-name prompt box for file name entries. See Chapter 8 for more on responding to file-name prompts. You will also see prompt boxes with [Enter] and [Esc] buttons when you choose certain commands that require you to enter a value, such as /Edit I Fill or /Graph I Customize Series I Bar Width.

The mouse palette

To the right of the Quattro screen is a column of boxes, called a mouse *palette*.

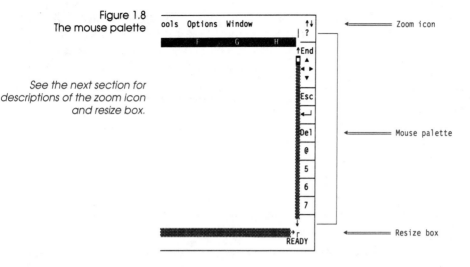

Figure 1.8
The mouse palette

See the next section for
descriptions of the zoom icon
and resize box.

When you're using your mouse to choose menu commands, point out cell blocks, and so forth, you'll find it much easier to use the mouse palette for some things, rather than switching over to the keyboard.

Here are the components of the mouse palette, starting from the top:

- The **help icon (?)** displays help screens. Click it instead of pressing *F1*.

- The **arrows**, which appear under the word "End" on the second button of the mouse palette, function just like the arrow keys on your keyboard after you press the *End* key: They move quickly to the end of an area in the indicated direction. (See page19 for details on how the *End* key works.)

- **Esc** duplicates the *Esc* key.

- ↵ duplicates the *Enter* key.

- **Del** duplicates the *Del* key.

- **@** displays a list of @function commands. Click it instead of pressing *Alt-F3*.

- The three buttons labeled 5, 6, and 7 are assigned to the {BEEP} macro command by default, but you can reassign them to execute your own macros.

All the mouse buttons except the help icon and the "End" arrows are user-definable. Use the /Options | Mouse Palette command to customize them any way you prefer (see "Customizing your mouse palette" in Chapter 7).

More mouse shortcuts

In addition to the mouse palette, Quattro offers a convenient mouse icon on the menu bar, as well as boxes and bars in the spreadsheet area:

- A **zoom icon** on the menu bar. Click it to zoom or unzoom the active window to or from full-screen display.

- A **close box** in the top left corner of a window. Click it to close the file and window.

- **Scroll bars** along the bottom and right edge of each spreadsheet window. On both the vertical and horizontal scroll bars, a *scroll box* indicates the current position of the cursor relative to the portion of the spreadsheet that contains data. To move to a different part of the spreadsheet, drag the scroll box along the scroll bar, then release.

- A **resize box** in the lower right corner of a window. To change the size of a window, just drag the resize box until the window is the size you want and release. To *reposition* a window, drag any window border.

The following figure points out these screen elements:

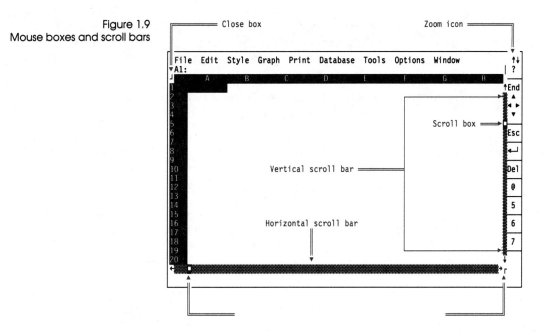

Figure 1.9
Mouse boxes and scroll bars

Using the Quattro menus

A menu is a list of commands or options. To initiate commands in Quattro, you call up a menu or sequence of menus and choose items. All Quattro menus branch from the menu bar. To activate the Quattro menu bar from the keyboard, press the forward slash key (/).

Once you activate a menu, you can choose a command from it using either of these methods:

- Use the arrow keys to highlight the command you want and press *Enter*.
- Type the key letter of the command you want (the letter that is highlighted or in a different color in the command name).

 If you have a mouse, just click the command you want.

All menu commands that bring up another menu are indicated with an arrowhead (▶) after the command name. Any function key or *Ctrl*-key combination that's assigned to a command is also shown on the menu.

Esc To exit a menu without choosing a command, press *Esc*. This returns you to the previous menu or, if you press it while the menu bar is active, removes the menu and returns you to the spreadsheet.

Ctrl Break To return to the spreadsheet directly from a menu, press *Ctrl* and *Break* at the same time.

When you choose a command from a menu, Quattro might ask you for information. For example, the /Edit I **Move** command asks you for a block of cells to move. Usually, a default value is given with the prompt. (The /Edit I **Move** command default is the current cell.) To accept the default value in answer to the prompt, press *Enter*. To enter a different cell block, type it in or point to a different block (see page 71). If the default value is text, you can press *Esc* to clear it and enter a new value or press *F2*, the Edit key, to edit the existing value. (Once you're in Edit mode, *Esc* clears the entry.) To remove the prompt without entering a value, press *Esc* twice. (See "Responding to file-name prompts" in Chapter 8 for details about the file-name prompt box.)

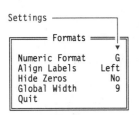 Click the [Enter] and [Esc] buttons on the input line or on the mouse palette to accept or cancel entries in a cell or in response to a prompt.

If there's a particular menu command you use often in your work, you can store that command sequence in a special key, called a *shortcut*. Then, instead of using the menus to choose the command each time, you can simply press the shortcut key. See "Creating shortcuts," which follows shortly.

Changing menu width

Some commands on Quattro menus have *settings* associated with them. Quattro shows these settings (if any) on the right side of each menu.

```
Settings ─────────────┐
  ╔═══ Formats ═══╗   │
  ║               ▼   ║
  Numeric Format   G
  Align Labels  Left
  Hide Zeros      No
  Global Width     9
  Quit
```

To remove the settings from a menu display and shrink the menu's width, press the Contract key (the minus key on the numeric keypad). To return settings to a menu display, press the Expand key (the plus key on the numeric keypad). For example, the expanded /**Options** I Formats menu shows the current spreadsheet defaults.

Creating shortcuts

Shortcuts work for any menu command.

As you become more familiar with Quattro, you'll find there are certain commands you use more than others, but you may have to work your way through several menus to get to some of them. You can make it easier to use your favorite commands by creating *shortcuts* for them. You can then execute the assigned command in a single keystroke.

To create a shortcut,

1. Activate the menu and highlight the command you want to abbreviate.
2. Hold down *Ctrl* and press *Enter*. Quattro prompts you for a key to assign the command to.
3. Hold down *Ctrl* and press any alphabetic key.

Quattro stores the command with that *Ctrl*-key combination and returns to Ready mode. Quattro displays the shortcuts you create next to the commands on the menus.

To execute an assigned shortcut, hold down *Ctrl* and press the assigned key. Quattro must be in Ready mode for your shortcuts to work.

To save the shortcuts you've created for use from now on, choose /**Options** | **Update**. Quattro saves shortcuts with the menus you used to create them. So if you switch to a different menu tree, you'll have to create new shortcuts.

To remove a shortcut you've created, highlight the shortcut's command on the menu, press *Ctrl-Enter*, then press *Del* twice.

Quattro comes with certain shortcuts preassigned (see Table 1.2). You can reassign these keys if you like (except for *Ctrl-D*, which lets you enter dates in the spreadsheet).

Table 1.2
Preassigned shortcuts

Shortcut	Command
Ctrl-A	/Style I Alignment
Ctrl-C	/Edit I Copy
Ctrl-D *	Date prefix
Ctrl-E	/Edit I Erase Block
Ctrl-F	/Style I Numeric Format
Ctrl-G	/Graph I Fast Graph
Ctrl-I	/Edit I Insert
Ctrl-M	/Edit I Move
Ctrl-N	/Edit I Search & Replace I Next
Ctrl-P	/Edit I Search & Replace I Previous
Ctrl-R	/Window I Move/Size
Ctrl-S	/File I Save
Ctrl-T	/Window I Tile
Ctrl-W	/Style I Column Width
Ctrl-X	/File I Exit

* Not reassignable

See Appendix D for a list of Quattro's function-key shortcuts, which are not reassignable.

Getting help

[F1]
Help

Whenever you're in Quattro, you can press the Help key, *F1*, to get instant assistance. A window of information pertinent to what you're doing is displayed over the current screen. For example, if you press *F1* with a menu option highlighted, the help system displays a description of that option.

When you press the Help key from within a general area of Quattro, such as Ready mode in a spreadsheet, Quattro displays the Help Topics screen. This screen lists several different areas you can display help about. Highlight the area you're interested in and press *Enter*. Quattro then displays a more specific help screen.

Usually, several screens of related information are available for each topic. If the help screen is one of a series, Next or Previous appears at the bottom of the screen; choose Next to see the next screen in the series, or Previous to review the previous one. Areas that offer further information appear in bold as *keywords* on the screen. Related topics are listed in the bottom area of the screen. Use the arrow keys to highlight the topic for which you want more information, then press *Enter* to display the related screens.

Once you're inside the help system, choose Help Topics to return to the Help Topics screen. Choose Menu Topics to display a screen of menu descriptions. To return immediately to the spreadsheet from any level of help, press *Esc*.

 To exit help using a mouse, click the status line or the help window to return to the spreadsheet.

If Quattro displays an error message in the middle of the screen, press *F1* to display an explanation of it. You can also review short descriptions of error messages that appear onscreen by pressing *F1* and choosing Error Messages from the Help Topics screen. For more details on any error message, see Appendix H, "Error messages."

You can also refer to Appendix A, "Help and hints," if you encounter problems while working with Quattro. This appendix offers solutions to common Quattro questions and misunderstandings.

Setting the default directory

The default directory setting tells Quattro where to look for and store spreadsheet files when you haven't specified any other directory. If you don't set this option, Quattro uses the current drive and directory. If you want to keep your spreadsheet files in a different directory than the program files, change the default directory:

1. Choose /**Options** | **Startup** from the menu bar.

2. Press *D* to choose **Directory**.

3. Quattro prompts you for a directory with the current directory shown as the default. Edit the existing directory path, or press *Esc* and enter a new path. Then press *Enter*.

4. To save the new directory as the directory default, choose **Update** from the **Options** menu.

Caution! If you don't update the defaults after changing directories, the original directories will be in effect next time you use Quattro.

 If you're using the 123-compatible menu trees, choose /**Worksheet** | **Global** | **Default** | **Directory**.

Regardless of the default directory, you can always access any directory on your disk. Simply include the directory path as part of the file name you specify when saving or retrieving a file.

Entering and editing data

To enter information in the spreadsheet, move the cell selector to the cell you want and type in the entry. The characters you type appear on the input line above the spreadsheet. The cursor, shown as a highlighted rectangle, shows you where the next character will appear. If you make a mistake while typing, simply press *Backspace* to erase the character, then type the correct one.

When the entry is complete, press *Enter* or any of Quattro's cursor-movement keys ($\rightarrow$, $\leftarrow$, *PgUp*, and so on). Quattro writes the value into the current cell, erasing any previous entry. If you entered the data by pressing a cursor-movement key, the cell selector moves in the appropriate direction.

Important! If you enabled the Undo command (with /Options | Other | Undo), you'll be able to bring back entries you accidentally overwrite. Just press */EU* or the Undo key, *Alt-F5*.

If Quattro finds an error (such as incorrect formula syntax) in your entry, it beeps, displays an error message, and automatically enters Edit mode with the cursor positioned near the problem.

In Edit mode, use $\rightarrow$ and $\leftarrow$ to position the cursor anywhere in the entry. You can then insert new characters, or use *Del* to remove erroneous ones. When you've corrected the error, press *Enter* to enter the item again.

Once you've entered data in a cell, you can always go back and change the entry. Simply highlight the cell with the cell selector, then either reenter the data or press *F2* (Edit), make the desired changes, and press *Enter*. "Editing entries," on page 48, discusses editing entries in detail.

To highlight a cell using a mouse, just click the cell.

You can enter four different kinds of information in a spreadsheet cell:

- **numbers**, such as 3987 or 0.39225
- **text**, called *labels*, such as ADDRESS, John Henry, or '1989 PROJECTIONS (the apostrophe at the beginning tells Quattro to accept 1989 as text)
- **dates** (preceded by *Ctrl-D*), such as 3/15/89 or 6/21
- **formulas**, such as 4982+5233 or +C3*B23. Formulas can reference data stored in other cells to calculate new values.

Each type of cell entry is described in detail in Chapter 3.

If you want, you can force a cell or block of cells to accept only labels or dates (see Chapter 18).

To delete a recorded entry, highlight the cell and press *Del*, or use the /Edit | Erase Block command (see Chapter 5).

Saving and retrieving spreadsheets

You can save the data you've entered in a spreadsheet in a disk *file*. Later, you can access the spreadsheet by retrieving the file it's stored in.

To save a new, unnamed spreadsheet in a disk file,

1. Choose /File | Save. Quattro prompts you for the name you want to give the file and displays a list of files existing in the default directory.
2. Enter a file name or choose one from the displayed list. You can use up to eight letters or numbers. Quattro automatically attaches the default extension to the file (initially, .WQ1).
3. Press *Enter*.

To save an existing, previously named spreadsheet,

1. Choose /File | Save.
2. Quattro displays a menu with three options: **Cancel, Replace,** and **Backup.**
3. Press *R* to overwrite the existing file. Press *B* to rename the existing file with the .BAK file-name extension, then save the new file. Press *C* to cancel the command.

To save the current spreadsheet to another file name,

1. Choose /File I Save **As**. Quattro will prompt for a file name just as it does when you choose /File I Save for an unnamed spreadsheet.
2. Enter a file name or choose one from the displayed list. You can use up to eight letters or numbers. Quattro automatically attaches the default extension to the file (initially .WQ1).
3. Press *Enter*. If you choose a file name that already exists, Quattro offers the same three options it does with /File I Save: Cancel, **R**eplace, and **B**ackup. Proceed as described in the previous list of instructions.

Caution! If you exit Quattro without saving the current spreadsheet, all your work will be lost. Always save before you leave the program or turn off the computer.

If you're entering a lot of data in a spreadsheet, it's a good idea to save your work periodically. That way, if something happens to your system memory (such as a power failure), you'll lose only what you entered since your last save. The Transcript utility, however, protects against data loss (see Chapter 17).

After you've saved a spreadsheet in a file, you can bring it back up onscreen any time by retrieving it:

1. Choose /File I **R**etrieve.
2. If you haven't saved the data currently in the spreadsheet, Quattro asks if you want to lose your changes. Choose **N**o to go back and save the changes, or choose **Y**es to discard changes and continue.
3. Quattro prompts you for the name of the file you want and displays a list of spreadsheet files in the default directory.
4. Choose a file from the list, or type in the exact name (including the directory and file-name extension if different from the default).

The file you specify is immediately displayed in the Quattro spreadsheet.

You can also retrieve spreadsheet files created with other programs and save spreadsheets for use with other programs. (For more information about working with spreadsheet files, see Chapter 8).

Note   If privacy is a concern, you can assign a password to your spread-sheet when you save it. Then no one will be able to retrieve the file without first supplying the correct password (see Chapter 8).

You can also retrieve files with the File Manager. With the File Manager, you can peruse files on an entire disk with ease and open several files at the same time. See Chapter 10 for full details.

Setting display mode

Normally, Quattro uses an 80x25 character (or text) mode for displaying your spreadsheets. In text mode, your screen can display only ASCII characters such as letters, special characters, and lines. If you have an EGA or VGA display adapter, Quattro also offers a graphics display mode. In graphics display mode, your screen uses tiny dots to create a display, so it's not limited to any specific character set. It can display all kinds of graphics. It's like the difference between a daisy wheel printer (that prints only characters) and a graphics printer.

Note   Graphics display mode is not available without an EGA or VGA display adapter.

In graphics display mode, Quattro makes the following display changes:

- If you have a mouse, Quattro displays the pointer as an arrowhead rather than as a block.

- If you insert a graph in your spreadsheet, you'll be able to see it just as it appears when you press *F10*. (In character mode, inserted graphs are indicated only by highlighting.)

- Quattro displays some menus as *galleries* rather than conventional text menus. A gallery is simply a graphic representation of options. For example, in graphics mode the /Graph I Graph Type command displays a gallery of images depicting different types of graphs.

To change screen display mode, choose /Options I Display Mode. Quattro displays a list of different screen modes available for your computer. The Display Mode menu for an EGA graphics card offers the following display modes:

```
┌─ Display Mode ─┐
│ A. 80x25       │
│ B. Graphics Mode │
│ C. EGA: 80x43  │
└────────────────┘
```

■ **80x25** is the standard character mode.

■ **Graphics Mode** uses graphics mode for spreadsheet area display.

■ **EGA: 80x43** displays 43 lines on the screen to display more of the spreadsheet area.

 Most mouse software supports only the three display modes listed here. If you choose a display mode not supported by your mouse, Quattro displays a "Mouse not supported for this display mode" message and disables your mouse.

Once you've chosen a display mode, Quattro uses it immediately. If you want to use that display mode as the new default, choose /Options I Update to store the setting with Quattro.

Caution! Depending on the type of computer you have, graphics mode may slow down operation somewhat. If this is the case, you can use character mode as the default and switch to graphics mode to view graphs inserted in your spreadsheet.

Accessing DOS

When you're working in Quattro, you can access the operating system (DOS) without having to exit the program:

1. Choose /File I Utilities I DOS Shell. The spreadsheet disappears and the DOS prompt appears.

2. Work within DOS for as long as you want. You can even go into another program, as long as it fits into system memory.

3. When you're ready to return to Quattro, type EXIT on the DOS command line and press *Enter*. The spreadsheet reappears exactly as you left it.

Note that it is essential that you return to Quattro and exit properly when you end your work session.

Your DOS manual describes the commands available to you within DOS.

 If you're using the 123-compatible menus, choose /System I OS.

Exiting Quattro

When you're finished working with Quattro,

1. Choose /File Exit. If your spreadsheet contains data that you haven't yet saved, an exit confirmation menu asks "Lose your changes and Exit?" and gives you three choices: **No, Yes,** and **Save & Exit.**
2. Choose **Yes** to discard changes and exit Quattro. Choose **Save & Exit** to store your data in a file, then exit Quattro. **No** cancels the exit and returns you to the spreadsheet.

When you exit Quattro, the spreadsheet disappears and the DOS prompt returns. To return to Quattro, you can reload the program by typing *Q* and pressing *Enter.*

File Exit

Ctrl-X is the default shortcut for the /File | Exit command.

1-2-3

If you're using the 123-compatible menus, choose /**Quit** instead of /File | Exit. Quattro always displays a confirmation menu when you exit, regardless of whether data might be lost. This is for compatibility with Lotus 1-2-3.

2

The pull-down menus

All Quattro commands are accessed through the menu bar that appears across the top of the Quattro screen:

Figure 2.1
The menu bar

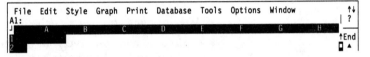

Each of the commands on the menu bar displays another menu, which is called a *pull-down menu* because you pull it down from the menu bar. Each pull-down menu accesses a different branch of the Quattro command tree.

This chapter briefly describes the pull-down menus associated with each menu bar command. Further chapters detail the commands on these menus.

File

```
╒══════ File ══════╕
│                  │
│ New              │
│ Open             │
│ Retrieve         │
│                  │
│ Save     Ctrl-S  │
│ Save As          │
│ Close            │
│ Close All        │
│ Erase            │
│                  │
│ Directory        │
│ Workspace     ▶  │
│ Utilities     ▶  │
│ Exit     Ctrl-X  │
│                  │
╘══════════════════╛
```

The /File command brings up the File menu, which you can use to open, close, save, and retrieve files and windows, access DOS, open a File Manager window, and exit Quattro.

- **New** opens up a new spreadsheet file and window.

- **Open** opens up a window and calls up an existing file.

- **Retrieve** lets you display a spreadsheet stored in a file, replacing the current spreadsheet.

- **Save** lets you save the current spreadsheet in a file.

- **Save As** saves a file under another name.

- **Close** closes the current file and window.

- **Close All** closes all open files and windows.

- **Erase** removes the current spreadsheet from system memory, leaving you with a blank, unformatted spreadsheet. You can use this command to clear the spreadsheet (*after saving your work*) to begin a new file.

- **Directory** lets you override the default startup directory.

- **Workspace** lets you save your current setup of multiple windows and spreadsheets in a file for future use, or load a saved workspace into Quattro.

- **Utilities** lets you access DOS, open a File Manager window, or set file compression options.

- **Exit** puts away the Quattro program and returns you to DOS. If your spreadsheet contains data that you haven't saved, Quattro asks if you want to save it first.

All File menu commands (except Exit) are described in Chapter 8, "Working with spreadsheet files." Exit is described on page 35.

The File Manager also lets you work with files, as well as directories. This feature is covered in Chapter 10, "Using the File Manager."

Edit

```
══════ Edit ══════
Copy          Ctrl-C
Move          Ctrl-M
Erase Block   Ctrl-E
Undo
─────────────────────
Insert        Ctrl-I ▶
Delete               ▶
─────────────────────
Names                ▶
Fill
Values
Transpose
Search & Replace     ▶
```

The /Edit command brings up the Edit menu, which you can use to adjust data in your spreadsheet. Most of the Edit menu commands affect a block of cells you specify within the spreadsheet. The block can be a single cell or any rectangular group of cells.

- **Copy** duplicates the contents of a cell block and writes them one or more times into another area of the spreadsheet.

- **Move** moves a cell block from one part of the spreadsheet to another.

- **Erase Block** deletes the contents of a cell block.

- **Undo** lets you reverse certain kinds of operations, such as moving, copying, or deleting a block, erasing a spreadsheet, deleting block or graph names, and more. Undo must be enabled *before* you use it (/Options I Other I Undo I Enable).

- **Insert** adds one or more blank rows or columns into the spreadsheet.

- **Delete** removes one or more specified rows or columns from the spreadsheet.

- **Names** lets you assign names to cell blocks for easier and more accurate reference. You can also use this command to modify and delete block names.

- **Fill** enters a sequence of numbers in a cell block.

- **Values** converts all formulas in a given block to their end values.

- **Transpose** reverses the arrangement of data within a block so that data displayed in rows is displayed in columns and vice versa.

- **Search & Replace** lets you search through the spreadsheet for all instances of a certain label or value and change them automatically.

All of the Edit menu commands are covered in Chapter 5, "Changing data in your spreadsheet."

Style

```
╔══════════ Style ══════════╗
║ Alignment        Ctrl-A ► ║
║ Numeric Format   Ctrl-F ► ║
║ Protection              ► ║
╟───────────────────────────╢
║ Column Width     Ctrl-W   ║
║ Reset Width               ║
║ Hide Column             ► ║
║ Block Widths            ► ║
╟───────────────────────────╢
║ Line Drawing              ║
║ Shading                 ► ║
║ Font                    ► ║
║ Insert Break              ║
╚═══════════════════════════╝
```

The /Style command brings up the Style menu, which you can use to change the appearance of your spreadsheet. The changes you make with it are stored with individual cells.

- **Alignment** lets you change the way entries in a block are aligned: left, right, center, or according to the alignment default in effect for that spreadsheet.

- **Numeric Format** lets you display numbers and dates in different formats and hide cell entries from view.

- **Protection** lets you disable overall spreadsheet protection (set with the /Options I Protection command) for individual blocks of cells. You also use this command to return protection to a block.

- **Column Width** lets you adjust the width of a column.

- **Reset Width** returns a column to the default column width.

- **Hide Column** temporarily removes one or more columns from the screen display. You also use this command to display hidden columns.

- **Block Widths** lets you automatically set the width of each column in a block to a given width, the default width, or individual widths automatically determined by the longest entry in each column.

- **Line Drawing** lets you draw single, double or thick lines and boxes around cell blocks in the spreadsheet.

- **Shading** lets you shade areas of the spreadsheet in grey or black.

- **Font** lets you change the print-time font for characters in the spreadsheet.

- **Insert Break** inserts a hard page break at the row containing the cell selector. The row must be a blank row.

All of the Style menu commands are covered in Chapter 6, "Changing the style of your spreadsheet."

Graph

```
══════ Graph ══════

Graph Type        ▶
Series            ▶
Text              ▶

Customize Series  ▶
X-Axis            ▶
Y-Axis            ▶
Overall           ▶

Insert
Hide
Name              ▶
View
Fast Graph   Ctrl-G
Annotate
Quit
```

The /Graph command brings up the Graph menu, which you can use to create, view, annotate, and save graphs using data from spreadsheets. You can choose from several types of graphs, including line graphs, bar graphs, column graphs, and pie charts.

■ **Graph Type** lets you choose from ten basic types of graphs.

■ **Series** lets you specify up to six sets of spreadsheet values to plot on the graph's y-axis and one set of values to label or plot on the x-axis.

■ **Text** lets you add a main title, a subtitle, axis titles, and a legend to the graph. It also lets you change the size, typestyle, and color of the titles.

■ **Customize Series** lets you change the way series of values are represented in the graph: the colors, marker symbols, and fill patterns used to show each series; whether each series is shown as a line, markers, both, or neither in a line graph; and the legend titles and position. You can also use this command to assign a different graph type to a series, plot a series on a second y-axis, explode pie slices, and reset block assignments to the series.

■ **X-Axis** lets you adjust the scale and display of the x-axis.

■ **Y-Axis** lets you adjust the scale and display of the y-axis (and a secondary y-axis if your graph has one).

■ **Overall** lets you display the graph with a three-dimensional effect, add and alter grids on the graph, and change colors used to display the overall graph.

■ **Insert** lets you insert a named graph or the current graph directly into the spreadsheet.

■ **Hide** lets you remove an inserted graph.

■ **Name** lets you store a graph with the current spreadsheet, display a named graph, delete one or all graph names, and display a series of named graphs with an individually timed interval for each.

■ **View** displays the current graph on the screen. Press any key to return to the Graph menu.

■ **Fast Graph** automatically creates a graph using any block of data you select.

- **Annotate** lets you draw on your graph, adding descriptive text, lines, arrows, and geometric shapes.

- **Quit** returns you to the spreadsheet.

Graph menu commands are discussed in Chapter 13, "Building graphs," Chapter 14, "Customizing graphs," and Chapter 15, "Annotating your graph."

Print

```
━━━━━ Print ━━━━━
Block
Headings             ▶

Destination          ▶
Layout               ▶
Format               ▶

Adjust Printer       ▶
Spreadsheet Print
Graph Print          ▶
Quit
```

The /**Print** command brings up the **Print** menu, which you can use to print both spreadsheets and graphs.

- **Block** lets you specify the area of the spreadsheet you want to print.

- **Headings** lets you specify blocks of the spreadsheet to be printed as headings at the top and/or left of each page as headings.

- **Destination** lets you send your spreadsheet either to a printer or to a disk file for future use. You can also use it to specify high-quality printing and to preview a printed spreadsheet onscreen.

- **Layout** lets you change the margins or page length of your spreadsheet and enter printer setup commands, headers, and footers. You can specify printing with or without page breaks, enter printer setup strings, and choose either portrait or landscape mode. You can also return all print commands to their default settings.

- **Format** lets you print a list of individual cell contents and formatting information instead of the usual spreadsheet format.

- **Adjust Printer** displays a menu with commands to advance the paper in the printer and set the top-of-page indicator.

- **Spreadsheet Print** begins printing the current spreadsheet to the specified graphics printer, to a text printer, to a disk file, or to the Screen Previewer.

- **Graph Print** lets you set the destination, margins, and dimensions for your graph. It also prints the current graph, either to the printer, to a disk file, or to a screen preview.

- **Quit** returns you to the spreadsheet.

All **Print** menu commands are discussed in Chapter 4, "Printing."

Database

```
╔══════ Database ══════╗
║ Sort              ▶ ║
║ Query             ▶ ║
║ Restrict Input      ║
║ Data Entry        ▶ ║
╚═════════════════════╝
```

The /Database command brings up the **Database** menu, which you can use to work with data in your spreadsheet that's set up like a database—in other words, data that can sensibly be divided into rows of related data (records) and columns of categorized data (fields).

- **Sort** lets you specify the order in which you want information displayed in your database.

- **Query** lets you search through your database for specific data. Optionally, you can copy the data you find to another part of the spreadsheet or delete it.

- **Restrict Input** lets you set up the spreadsheet like a form for easy data entry.

- **Data Entry** lets you limit the type of data permitted in a block of cells to values or dates only.

All **Database** menu commands are discussed in Chapter 18, "Using Quattro as a database manager."

Tools

```
╔══════ Tools ══════╗
║ Macro           ▶ ║
║ Reformat          ║
║                   ║
║ Import          ▶ ║
║ Combine         ▶ ║
║ Xtract          ▶ ║
║ Update Links    ▶ ║
║                   ║
║ Advanced Math   ▶ ║
║ Parse           ▶ ║
║ What-If         ▶ ║
║ Frequency         ║
╚═══════════════════╝
```

The /Tools command displays the **Tools** menu, which contains commands more experienced spreadsheet users might need.

- **Macro** lets you create and execute macros. A *macro* is a set of one or more commands that you can execute with a single command. You can also delete macros and specify the current spreadsheet as a macro library, which Quattro will use to look for macros from within other spreadsheets.

- **Reformat** rearranges the text entered in long labels so that it fills the specified block.

- **Import** lets you retrieve a text file and automatically translate it into spreadsheet format.

- **Combine** lets you merge two blocks or spreadsheet files together.

- **Xtract** lets you copy part of a Quattro spreadsheet into a separate file.

- **Update Links** offers options for working with linked spreadsheets. You can use it to open linked spreadsheets, update values linked to closed spreadsheets, switch links from one spreadsheet to another, and delete links to specific spreadsheets.

- **Advanced Math** lets you invert or multiply a data matrix, perform regression analysis on data to show how one variable is affected by others, and perform linear programming on a data model.

- **Parse** lets you break down long labels into separate cell entries. It's used to translate text files created with other programs.

- **What-If** lets you perform a sensitivity analysis to see how data is affected by changing one or more values.

- **Frequency** breaks down a block of values in ranges and creates a table that shows how many values fall within each range.

The Advanced Math, What-If, and Frequency commands are covered in Chapter 19, "Working with statistics and analyzing data." Macro is described in Chapter 16, "Using macros." Reformat is covered in Chapter 5, "Changing data in your spreadsheet." The Update Links menu is discussed in Chapter 11, "Linking spreadsheets." Parse, Import, Combine, and Xtract are covered in Chapter 12, "Advanced file tools."

Options

```
════ Options ════
Hardware          ▶
Colors            ▶
International     ▶
Display Mode      ▶
Startup           ▶
Mouse Palette     ▶
Graphics Quality  ▶
Other             ▶
─────────────────
Update
─────────────────
Formats           ▶
Recalculation     ▶
Protection        ▶
Quit
```

The /Options command displays the Options menu, which contains commands that let you change default settings both for the current spreadsheet and for the overall system. The first section of the menu lists commands that affect the system and can be updated with the Update command. The last section lists commands whose settings are stored with the current spreadsheet only.

- **Hardware** lets you specify information about your computer screen and the printer you'll be using to print spreadsheets. It also shows your system's memory use and any coprocessor.

- **Colors** lets you change the colors and/or attributes used to display all parts of Quattro.

- **International** determines the standards for displaying currency, punctuation, date, and time.

- **Display Mode** lets you change the mode Quattro uses to display spreadsheets and menus on your screen. Normally,

Quattro uses 80x25 character mode. You can switch to a more condensed display or, if you have an EGA or VGA display adapter, to a graphics mode that allows you to view graphics within the spreadsheet.

- **Startup** lets you specify default information that Quattro uses to start up the program, such as the default extension to be added to spreadsheet files, the default directory, the default menu tree, and the name of a file to be retrieved automatically when you load Quattro.

- **Mouse Palette** lets you redefine the functions of the mouse palette buttons that display along the right edge of your screen if you have a mouse and the mouse software is loaded.

- **Graphics Quality** allows you to choose between draft-quality fonts with faster display and printing and presentation-quality fonts with a pause for building new font files when you display and print.

- **Other** lets you enable or disable the Undo command, change clock display, specify when to redraw the screen during macro execution, tell Quattro how to use your expanded memory, and specify how to access Paradox files on a local area network.

- **Update** stores the current system command settings as defaults to be used with all new spreadsheets.

- **Formats** determines the standard spreadsheet numeric format, label alignment, zero display, and column width.

- **Recalculation** determines the order of formula calculation, the number of iterations, and whether formulas are calculated automatically (either in the foreground or in the background) or only when you press the Calc key (*F9*). It also lets you track circular references.

- **Protection** lets you enable or disable cell protection for your entire spreadsheet. When enabled, you can't make changes to cell entries, unless protection has been disabled for the cell with /Style | Protection.

- **Quit** returns you to your spreadsheet.

All **Options** menu commands except **Display Mode** are described in Chapter 7, "Setting options." **Display Mode** is discussed on page 33.

Window

```
╔═══════ Window ═══════╗
  Zoom
  Tile          Ctrl-T
  Stack
  Move/Size     Ctrl-R
  ─────────────────────
  Options              ▶
  ─────────────────────
  Pick
╚═════════════════════╝
```

The /Window command displays the **Window** menu, which contains commands that let you open windows and alter the ways Quattro displays them.

■ **Zoom** expands the active window to full screen. If it already fills the screen and other windows are open, it shrinks the window back to what it was before, redisplaying the other windows.

■ **Tile** displays all open windows on the screen at once.

■ **Stack** arranges each open window as one full layer and displays the top line of each (showing the name of the spreadsheet or directory it contains).

■ **Move/Size** lets you change the size and/or position of the active window onscreen.

■ **Options** lets you split the active window into two *panes*, so you can view two parts of your spreadsheet at once. You can also use window options commands to lock certain rows and/or columns on your screen so they don't scroll and to display a spreadsheet in a coded "map" mode.

■ **Pick** displays a list of all open windows. The window you choose becomes the active (topmost) one.

The **Window** menu commands are described in Chapter 9, "Manipulating windows." File Manager windows are covered in detail in Chapter 10, "Using the File Manager."

3

Entering data

Although entering data in a spreadsheet is simple and straight-forward, Quattro offers numerous options in this area. For example, you can include prefixes in text entries (labels) that specify alignment. When you want to reference a cell in a formula, you can type its block coordinates, point to it, or enter a block name. You can also force a cell or block of cells to accept only labels or only dates.

This chapter describes how to enter both values and labels into the spreadsheet, how to build formulas to calculate values, and how to edit existing spreadsheet data. It also covers some of the general skills you'll rely on consistently when you use Quattro:

For information about moving and copying data, see Chapter 5.

- specifying blocks of cells for use in formulas or with commands
- "pointing" with the cell selector or with a mouse to specify cell blocks
- naming blocks for future reference
- using choice lists to review and/or enter @functions, macro commands, and block names

Entering data

When you load Quattro, a blank spreadsheet appears ready for data entry. Quattro gives it the default file name of SHEET1, which you can change when you save the spreadsheet.

To enter data in a spreadsheet cell, use the cursor-movement keys to move the cell selector to it and type the entry. The characters you type appear on the input line above the spreadsheet. Use the *Backspace* key to erase mistakes as you type.

When you press *Enter* or one of the cursor-movement keys, Quattro writes the data into the highlighted cell. If the entry is a formula, Quattro automatically evaluates it and displays the results. If any other cells in the spreadsheet contain formulas referencing the current cell, Quattro recalculates them. (See page 58 for more information about entering formulas.)

If you set /Options | Recalculation | Mode to Manual, Quattro won't recalculate formulas affected by the new data until you press the Calc key, *F9*. (See page 207 for more information on the Recalculation menu.) You can also use the Calc key to calculate a value before you enter it. For example, if you type 8*9 on the input line, then press *F9*, Quattro replaces the formula with the result, 72. The formula used to calculate the value is erased.

Quattro automatically enters Edit mode if it discovers a problem with your entry, such as an illegal character. It won't accept the entry until you've corrected the problem. To cancel the entry, press *Esc*.

Editing entries

Once you've written an entry into a cell (by pressing *Enter*), you can *erase* it by simply moving the selector to it and pressing *Del*. You can *alter* its contents in either of two ways:

- Move the cell selector to the cell and enter a new value. When you press *Enter* or any of the cursor-movement keys, the new value replaces the old. (To avoid accidental deletion, Quattro doesn't erase an entry if you just select it and press *Enter*.)
- Make changes to the existing entry using Edit mode.

Edit

In Edit mode, you can insert or delete characters in an entry without retyping the whole thing. Begin by moving the cell selector to the cell you want to change. Then press the Edit key (*F2*) to enter Edit mode. The EDIT indicator appears on the status line, and the contents of the current cell appear (as they were entered) on the input line. You can use the cursor-movement keys to move the cursor to any part of the entry. *Backspace* deletes characters to the left of the cursor.

When you first enter Edit mode, Quattro also automatically enters Insert mode and inserts any characters you type at the cursor. To write over existing characters, press the *Ins* key to enter Overwrite mode. (The OVR mode indicator appears on the status line.) Press *Ins* again to return to Insert mode.

Any entry displayed on the input line appears as you typed it in, which is not necessarily how Quattro displays it in the cell. For example, if a cell contains a formula that produces a value, you edit the formula, not the value. If the cell contains a number, you edit the actual number (as you entered it), regardless of the numeric format.

To edit an entry using a mouse, click the cell to move the cell selector there, then click the input line. To move the edit cursor, click where you want to position it. After editing, click the [Enter] button on the input line to enter the entry and exit Edit mode. To discard your changes instead of entering them, click the [Esc] button on the input line.

Table 3.1 shows the functions of certain keys in Edit mode.

Table 3.1
Special keys in Edit mode

Key	Function
Esc	Erases the contents of the input line. If you press it again, it discards any changes you made to the cell and exits Edit mode.
Enter	Enters the data and exits Edit mode.
←	Moves the cursor one space to the left.
→	Moves the cursor one space to the right.
Backspace	Deletes the character to the left of the cursor.
Ins	Toggles between Insert and Overwrite modes. (Insert mode is the default.)
Del	Deletes the character at the cursor position.
Ctrl-	Deletes all characters from the cursor to the end of the entry.
Ctrl-Backspace	Erases the contents of the input line.
Tab or *Ctrl* →	Moves the cursor five spaces to the right.
Shift-Tab or *Ctrl* ←	Moves the cursor five spaces to the left.

Table 3.1: Special keys in Edit mode (continued)

Key	Function
Home	Moves the cursor to the first character in the cell.
End	Moves the cursor to the last character in the cell.
↑	Enters the data, exits Edit mode, and moves selector up one cell, *unless* the cursor follows an operator at the end of the entry. If it does, Quattro enters Point mode, so you can input cell references by pointing to them (see page 71).
↓	Enters the data, exits Edit mode, and moves selector down one cell, *unless* the cursor follows an operator at the end of the entry. If it does, Quattro enters Point mode.
PgDn	Enters the data, exits Edit mode, and moves selector down one screen "page" or screenful, *unless* the cursor follows an operator at the end of the entry. If it does, Quattro enters Point mode.
PgUp	Enters the data, exits Edit mode, and moves selector up one screen "page," *unless* the cursor follows an operator at the end of the entry. If it does, Quattro enters Point mode.
F2 (Edit)	Toggles to display an indicator on the status line that tells you what type of data you're editing—either value or label.

For a complete list of key functions, both in and out of Edit mode, see the Quick Reference Guide or Appendix D, "Quattro keys and indicators."

Note Quattro records none of the changes you make until you press *Enter*, ↑, ↓, *PgUp*, or *PgDn*. Until then, you can press *Esc* to remove the changes and return the cell to the way it was before. After that, you can press *Alt-F5* to undo your changes (if you enable the Undo command with /**O**ptions I **O**ther I Undo).

In Edit mode, you can also use pointing and choice lists to help you correct an entry. See "Pointing out cell blocks" and "Using a choice list," both later in this chapter.

Data types

There are two basic types of data you can enter in a spreadsheet: labels and values.

- A *label* is a text entry such as "Total."
- A *value* is any value entered either as a number, a date, or a formula that calculates a number. Formulas usually use numbers you've entered in other cells to calculate a value, such as the difference between the numbers in two cells or the total of values in a column. You can also use special @functions and numeric values in formulas.

Note You can force a cell or block of cells to accept only labels or dates with the /Database I Data Entry menu (see Chapter 18).

Quattro determines the data type of a cell entry by the first character you type. It then replaces the READY indicator on the status line with LABEL for text or VALUE for numbers, dates, or formulas. After you enter the data, the READY mode indicator reappears. The following figure shows a spreadsheet with four types of cell entries: numbers, formulas, dates, and labels. The number, formula, and date are all value entries.

Figure 3.1
Different types of data in a spreadsheet

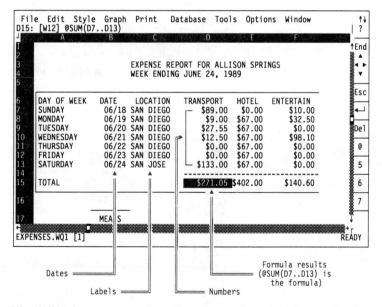

The following sections describe how to enter labels and the different kinds of numeric values (numbers, formulas, and dates).

Labels

A label is a text cell entry used for descriptive information, such as a column or row heading, or for textual data, such as a name or address. It can begin with any letter or punctuation mark other than the following:

/ + – $ (@ # .

Although you can include numbers *within* labels, labels themselves are not usually used in numeric calculations. If you want to *start* a label with a number, see page 53.

When you begin typing a label, the LABEL mode indicator appears on the status line. When you press *Enter*, Quattro writes the label into the cell, and the mode indicator returns to READY.

Label alignment

When you enter a label in a cell, Quattro positions it according to the spreadsheet's default alignment. This default is initially left, but you can change it to right or centered with the /**O**ptions | Formats | **A**lign Labels command (see Chapter 7).

The following figure shows three labels in a spreadsheet aligned left, right, and centered:

Figure 3.2
Label alignment

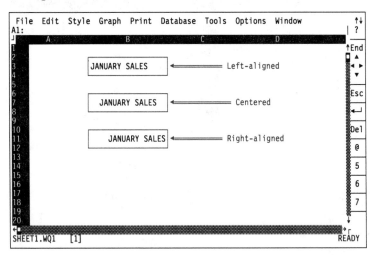

If you want to align a label differently than the alignment default, you can precede the label with a *label-prefix character*, either when entering it or by editing it. The label-prefix character is one of three special punctuation marks that tell Quattro how to align labels (Table 3.2).

Table 3.2
Label-prefix characters

Label-prefix character	Alignment
' (apostrophe)	Left-justified
" (quotation mark)	Right-justified
^ (caret)	Centered

Quattro does not display label-prefix characters in the spreadsheet, but they do appear on the input line when you select a label cell.

To use one of the label-prefix characters as a punctuation mark at the beginning of a label rather than a prefix, precede it with another label prefix indicating the alignment you want. For example, to enter the label

"Harry" Harrison

and align it with the left side of the cell, enter or edit the label as follows:

```
'"Harry" Harrison
```

If you want to change alignment for several labels at once, you can use the /Style | Alignment command (see Chapter 6).

Including numbers in labels

As long as the label *begins* with a letter or punctuation mark, you can include numbers with no special prefix. To enter a label that *begins* with a number, such as 145 Howard Ave., precede it with a label prefix (Table 3.2). Otherwise, Quattro perceives it as an illegal value entry (values cannot contain text), beeps, displays an error message, and goes into Edit mode so you can correct it.

Some numeric entries cause problems if you don't enter them as labels. For example, the phone number 458-1233 appears as -775 in the spreadsheet because Quattro interprets it as a formula; it subtracts 1233 from 458. And Quattro displays value entries in the current numeric format, so that zip codes might appear as decimal numbers or percentages. In cases like these, you need to precede the entry with a label prefix, so that Quattro treats the numbers as labels.

Phone numbers and zip codes

If there are a number of cells in which you expect to enter telephone numbers or zip codes, you may want to predefine those cells as labels with the /Database I Data Entry command (see "Restricting the type of data entry" in Chapter 18). Then you won't need to include the label prefix each time you enter a phone number or zip code.

Repeating characters

You can automatically repeat one or more characters across the width of a cell by preceding the character(s) with a backslash (\). For example, to fill a cell with hyphens, type

\-

To begin a label with a backslash without repeating the characters after it, precede the backslash with a label-alignment prefix.

Note   When you repeat the hyphen character across the width of more than one cell, a slight gap appears between one cell and the next when you print the contents of those cells on a graphics printer. For a smooth, unbroken line, use the /Style I Line Drawing command (see page 160).

Labels wider than one cell

Labels can be up to 254 characters long. When you enter a label that exceeds the width of the cell, Quattro automatically displays the "spillover" text in blank cells to the right. When the label runs into a cell that contains an entry, Quattro truncates it, but still stores the entire label entered. In other words, only characters that fit in the cell(s) appear.

When you edit a label, you see the entire entry on the input line above, even if it doesn't all fit in the spreadsheet cell. If necessary, the input line drops down into the spreadsheet window to make room for the entry.

To edit a label that spills over into other cells, you must highlight the first, or leftmost, cell. Only then does the entry appear on the input line, letting you know it is the cell that actually contains the entry.

To fully display a lengthy entry, you can widen the column containing it (see Chapter 6).

Numbers

Numbers are a type of value entry. When you begin typing a number, the VALUE mode indicator appears on the status line. When you press *Enter*, Quattro enters the number and aligns it with the right side of the cell. To change alignment, use the /Style | Alignment command (see Chapter 6).

Although entering numbers in a cell is fairly straightforward, there are several rules to keep in mind:

- A number entry basically contains only numerals (0 to 9), although you can include a leading negative (-) or positive (+) sign or a dollar sign ($), or follow a number with a percent sign (%). You can use a single decimal point.
- Don't use parentheses to indicate a negative number. Use a minus sign (-) instead. However, if you change the numeric format to Currency or Financial, negative numbers appear in parentheses.
- Never include commas in your numbers. You can later display them automatically by changing the numeric format.
- Don't include spaces in the entry.
- Never substitute a lowercase *l* ("el") for 1 (one) nor an uppercase *O* ("oh") for 0 (zero).

You can use scientific notation (for example, 2.35E+8) to enter a number. If the calculated number fits in the cell (and the numeric format makes it possible), Quattro displays it in full.

With the /Edit | Fill command, you can enter a sequence of numbers automatically (see Chapter 5).

Length

Like a label, a number can also be longer than a cell is wide. If a number doesn't fit in the current cell, however, it won't run into adjacent cells as labels do. Instead, it displays either in scientific notation or as a row of asterisks (*********), depending on the cell's numeric format. The number appears in full if you widen the column sufficiently with the /Style | Column Width command (see Chapter 6).

Numeric format

You can choose from ten different formats for displaying numbers. The formats do not change the number itself, only how Quattro displays it. For example, the Fixed format limits the number of decimal places displayed. The original number, however, is still stored in Quattro, and this complete number is what Quattro uses in all calculations.

The initial default format for numbers is General, which displays numbers just as you enter them. These are your format choices:

- **Fixed** limits the number of decimal places displayed.

- **Scientific** translates numbers into scientific notation.

- **Currency** displays numbers as the specified currency (dollars, pounds, yen, and so on). To choose the default currency, choose /Options I International I Currency.

- **,** (financial) inserts commas every three digits.

- **+/-** translates numbers into a horizontal bar graph. Each integer translates into a symbol: + for each positive integer, – for each negative, and . (a period) for zero.

- **Percent** displays numbers as percentages.

- **Date** displays numeric values as dates or time in the chosen format.

- **Text** (show formulas) displays formulas entered, not their calculated results.

- **Hidden** suppresses display of entries. The Hidden format affects label entries as well as value entries. All other formats affect only values (including dates and formulas).

If you want to specify a new default format, use the /Options I Formats I Numeric Format command (see Chapter 7). You can also change the way numbers in individual cells or blocks of cells are displayed with the /Style I Numeric Format command (see Chapter 6). That section also includes detailed information on each of the numeric formats.

Dates and times

Dates   Another type of value entry is a date. To enter dates in most spreadsheet programs, you need to use a special date @function, such as @DATE, then set the numeric format for that cell to **Date**. Quattro greatly simplifies the use of dates by allowing you to use a shortcut.

Date

To enter a date, hold down *Ctrl* and press *D*, then enter a date in any of the following formats:

- DD-MMM-YY (04-Oct-89)
- DD-MMM (04-Oct, assumes current year)
- MMM-YY (Oct-89, assumes first day of the month)
- the Long International date format—MM/DD/YY (10/04/89)
- the Short International date format—MM/DD (10/04, assumes current year)

The first three options, which require alphabetic characters to indicate the month, are always permitted. The other two work only when the International date format is MM/DD/YY or MM/DD. (MM/DD/YY is the default Long International date format, and MM/DD the default Short International.)

Quattro's International date formats are numbers only. If you prefer a different International date format, use the /**Options** I International I **Date** command to switch to any of the three alternate formats:

- DD/MM/YY (DD/MM)
- DD.MM.YY (DD.MM)
- YY-MM-DD (MM-DD)

You can choose only one as the default setting for an entire spreadsheet. The International date format you choose on the /**Options** I International I **Date** menu changes the effect of the Long and Short International commands on the /**Style** I **Numeric Format** I **Date** menu. The three date formats that require alphabetic characters to indicate the month are unaffected. Once you choose an International date format, all dates you enter with numeric characters only must follow that format.

Tip   If you forget to press *Ctrl-D* before entering the date, Quattro will calculate the date as a formula. You need to delete the entry and start again, preceding the date with *Ctrl-D*.

You can change the date format to any of those listed in this section with the /**Style** l **Numeric Format** command (see Chapter 6) or the /**Options** l **Formats** l **Numeric Format** command (see Chapter 7).

You can use date values in spreadsheet calculations. For example, subtracting 10/1/89 from 10/8/89 would result in a value of 7.

You can also enter date values using any of the date @functions: @DATE, @DATEVALUE, @DAY, @DAYOFWEEK, @MONTH, @NOW, @TODAY, and @YEAR. Date functions are fully described in *@Functions and Macros*. These functions return a date serial number. To display a serial number as a date, choose /**Style** l **Numeric Format** l **Date** and pick a date format (see page 149).

To force a cell or cell block to accept only date entries, use the /**Database** l **Data Entry** command (see Chapter 18).

If you're using the 123-compatible menus, choose /**Range** l **Data Entry** l **Date** to allow only dates in a block. To display values in a block in date format, choose /**Range** l **Format** l **Date**. To change global display format to date, choose /**Worksheet** l **Global** l **Format** l **Date**.

Times   You can enter time values using any of the time @functions: @HOUR, @MINUTE, @NOW, @SECOND, @TIME, and @TIMEVALUE. Time functions are fully described in *@Functions and Macros*. These functions return a date serial number. To display a date serial number as a time, choose /**Style** l **Numeric Format** l **Date**, then choose **Time** and pick a time format (see page 149).

Formulas

Another way to enter a value in a cell is with a *formula*. Formulas let you take advantage of one of Quattro's most powerful and time-saving features: automatic calculation.

Quattro instantly calculates all kinds of information for you. Using data entered in the spreadsheet, it can total columns of figures, calculate monthly profit, even determine the future value of an investment. And if the figures involved are changed, Quattro automatically recalculates the formula.

Quattro formulas are like any basic algebraic formula. They combine *values* and *operators* to calculate a single end value, as in the formula in the following figure:

Figure 3.3
How Quattro formulas work

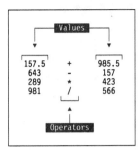

You can use actual numbers or the block coordinates for one or more cells that contain numbers. For example,

+A1 – A2

tells Quattro to subtract the value in cell A2 from the value in cell A1.

Note To enter a value that begins with a nonnumeric character, precede it with a plus sign so that Quattro knows the entry is a value and not a label.

The result is displayed in the cell, just as if you had typed it in. The formula appears on the input line when the cell is selected and on the status line when you're editing the entry.

Formulas can be up to 254 characters long. You can include spaces between operators and values, but Quattro deletes them automatically. A formula must begin with one of the following characters:

0 1 2 3 4 5 6 7 8 9 . + – (@ # $

To begin a formula with a letter, such as for a cell block or text entry, precede it with a plus sign (+). Otherwise, Quattro interprets the entry as a label instead of a value and does not calculate the formula.

By default, Quattro aligns the results of formulas with the right side of the cell (unless the result is a string value, in which case the result is left-aligned). To change alignment, use the /Style l **Alignment** command (see Chapter 6).

Formula values

Values in a formula can be any of the following:

- numbers (for example, 948, –84, 43.23)
- text surrounded by double quotation marks (for example, "PROFIT" or "Dear Mr.")
- block coordinates for other cells that contain either values or labels (for example, B12, G29)
- cell block names (for example, EXPENSES)
- Quattro @functions; for example, @SUM(B1..B24)

When you use a coordinates for a cell as a value, Quattro refers to the value contained in that cell. For example, the formula B6+C1 adds the values in those two cells and displays the result.

Quattro @functions are a set of standard formula commands used to simplify complex calculations. For example, @SUM totals values of specified cells, while @DATE calculates and enters the current date. @functions are described on page 67. The individual @function commands are described in Chapter 1 of *@Functions and Macros*.

Operators

Operators are fully described in Chapter 1 of @Functions and Macros.

Formulas use *operators*, or mathematical symbols, to express a relationship between two or more values; for example, C5-D12. Often formulas contain several operators, as in

+C5 – D12 + F24 * 0.123

The result of a formula depends on the order in which Quattro performs the arithmetic operations. Quattro assigns each operator a *precedence* and performs the operations in order of precedence. For example, because multiplication has greater precedence than addition,

5 + 1 * 3 = 8, *not 18*

Quattro performs operations with equal precedence from left to right.

Table 3.3 lists the operators allowed in Quattro formulas and the precedence assigned to each. Operators with the highest precedence (7) are performed first.

Table 3.3
Quattro operators

Operator	Description	Precedence
&	String combination	1
#AND# #OR#	Logical AND, logical OR	1
#NOT#	Logical NOT	2
= <>	Equal, not equal	3
< >	Less than, greater than	3
<=	Less than or equal	3
>=	Greater than or equal	3
− +	Subtraction, addition	4
* /	Multiplication, division	5
− +	Negative, positive	6
^	To the power of (exponentiation)	7

You can override the precedence of operators by including parentheses in your formula. Any operation surrounded by parentheses is given highest priority.

Using parentheses

To ensure that Quattro evaluates a formula in the order you want, use parentheses to enclose the portion you want calculated first. You can nest parentheses inside other parentheses; Quattro calculates the innermost part first. For example,

$4 * 2 + 3 = 11$
$4 * (2 + 3) = 20$
$(4*2) + (3 + 5) * 4 = 40$
$((4*2) + (3 + 5)) * 4 = 64$

If you include no parentheses, Quattro performs the calculations in the order (precedence) shown in Table 3.3.

Types of formulas

Quattro works with three different kinds of formulas: arithmetic, text, and logical.

Arithmetic formulas

Arithmetic formulas, such as +B3*1.3, calculate numeric values. These are the most commonly used formulas. They can use most of the @functions and accept any of the following operators:

$- + * / ^ = < > <= >= <>$

Text formulas Text formulas are any formulas that have a textual result. For example, +C4&" Review" enters the value in cell C4 and adds a space and the word *Review*. Text formulas include those created with string functions or an @IF function that results in a text string (Chapter 1 of *@Functions and Macros* has details on @functions). Text formulas accept any of the following operators:

& < > <= >= = <>

Concatenation of text strings

A concatenated string generally has three parameters:

- A + (plus sign) identifies the string as a formula.
- The **constant** is the part of the formula that will not change; it is surrounded by quotation marks.
- The **variable** is the part of the formula that is concatenated to the constant. Precede it with an ampersand (&) to append it to the constant and follow it with another ampersand if more information is added (concatenated) to the end of the string. The variable must be a valid text string. Use the @STRING function if the variable is not a text string; @STRING converts a variable to a string.

Example 1: +"Book"&" Review"

This example concatenates the text string "Book" to the text string " Review"; the result is *Book Review*. In this example, the plus sign denotes a formula and "Book" and " Review" are both constants.

Example 2: +C4&" Review"

This formula adds a space and the text *Review* to the contents of cell C4. If C4 contains the label 'Book, the result of the formula is *Book Review*. Since what C4 contains might change at any time, the contents are referenced as a variable. " Review" is the only constant in the formula. In this example, we assume that cell C4 contains a label. The next example shows how to change the formula if C4 contains a value.

Example 3: +@STRING(C4,0)&" Review"

This example is similar to Example 2, except that the @STRING function is used to translate a value in C4 into a string for the purposes of the formula. If cell C4 contained the value 4, the result would be *4 Review*.

Example 4: +"{IF "&@CELLPOINTER("address")&"=0}"

This example tests the contents of the current cell to see if they equal zero. The text formula is an example of concatenation within a macro. In this case, "{IF " is the constant, followed by an ampersand and the variable @CELLPOINTER("address"). Note the second ampersand; anything that follows a concatenated field must be concatenated to the formula. The second concatenated field, which is a second constant, is "=0}". The formula breaks down into the following parts:

+

The plus sign denotes a formula.

"{IF "
The first constant. Note that it is surrounded by quotation marks.

&@CELLPOINTER("address")
This is the variable in the formula. The @function will return a text string (the current address of the cell selector). Notice the ampersand, which specifies that the text string returned by @CELLPOINTER is to be concatenated to the previous string (the first constant).

&"=0}"
The second constant. Note that it is surrounded by quotation marks. This string is to be concatenated to variable in the formula, so it too is preceded by an ampersand. So if the current cell is A4, the text formula in this example returns the text string "{IF A4=0}" for use in a macro.

Logical formulas
Logical formulas are true/false statements concerning values in other cells; for example, +C3<10. Quattro checks the spreadsheet to see if the statement is true or not. If true, it enters a 1 in the cell; if false, it enters a 0. In some cases, you can specify different values to be entered depending on the condition. For example, the following formula could be used to calculate an employee's eligibility for a bonus:

@IF(COMMISSION>1000 #AND# EXPENSES<300,100,0)

If commission is greater than $1,000 and expenses are less than $300, Quattro enters 100 in the cell; otherwise, it enters 0.

Logical formulas accept any of the following operators:

< > <= >= <> = #NOT# #AND# #OR#

If a logical formula results in a textual value, such as

@IF(C3>10,"Profit","Loss")

it is also considered a text formula.

Pointing in formulas

Suppose you are in the middle of building a formula, and you forget the address of a cell you want to include. There's no need to abandon the entry to search for the address. Quattro has an easier way, called *pointing*.

Pointing lets you enter a cell address in a formula by moving the cell selector to the cell you want to include.

For example, to enter the formula +B3*(B4-B5) into cell B6 by pointing,

1. Move the cell selector to cell B6.
2. Press + to begin the formula.
3. Press ↑ until the cell selector is in cell B3. (The mode indicator changes to POINT.) The address of the current cell is displayed on the input line as you move the selector.
4. Press the asterisk key (*). Quattro enters an asterisk after "+B3" and returns the selector to the entry cell, B6.
5. Press the open parenthesis key, (.
6. Move the cell selector to cell B4.
7. Press the minus key (-).
8. Move the cell selector to cell B5.
9. Press the close parenthesis key,).
10. Press *Enter.* Quattro writes the formula into the entry cell and clears the input line.

Quattro automatically enters the cell addresses into the formula you point to. All you need to enter are the operators and punctuation.

 If you have a mouse, you can point out cell references in a formula. Just click the cell you want to reference.

You can also enter *blocks* of cells by pointing to them. For more information on pointing, see page 71.

Relative vs. absolute addresses

Quattro keeps excellent track of the cells you refer to in formulas:

- If you move the cells specified in a formula to another place in the spreadsheet or to another spreadsheet, Quattro automatically adjusts the reference in the formula.
- If you move a formula from one cell to another, the cell references in the formula remain unchanged.
- If you insert a column or row within a specified block, Quattro automatically increases the block specified in the formula to include it.
- If you delete a column or row within a specified block, Quattro automatically decreases the block specified in the formula (*unless* you delete a column or row that contains one of the corner cells, in which case ERR appears in the formula's cell).
- If you copy a block of cells that includes a formula *and* the cells referenced in the formula, Quattro updates the formula to reference the new cell locations (even if you've copied the cells to a different spreadsheet).

This last characteristic can save you a great deal of time when you replicate sections of a spreadsheet. However, it can also cause complications when you choose to copy a formula without copying the cells it references. For details, see page 115.

Recalculation

By default, Quattro calculates formulas in a spreadsheet when you enter them, and recalculates them each time you change the data involved. Quattro offers three options for formula recalculation:

- **Background** (the default) recalculates between keystrokes so you never have to pause for recalculation.
- **Automatic** pauses operation momentarily while Quattro recalculates formulas.
- **Manual** recalculates the formulas only when you press the Calc key, *F9*.

To change the recalculation setting for a spreadsheet, use the /Options | Recalculation | Mode command (see Chapter 7). This changes the recalculation mode for the current spreadsheet only and stores the setting with the spreadsheet.

When recalculation is set to **Manual**, Quattro still calculates formulas when you enter or edit them, but not when values in the cells they reference change. For example, with the formula +A1 + B2, if you change the value in B2, Quattro doesn't update the formula. When you add or change data in the spreadsheet, the CALC mode indicator appears on the status line. You can then initiate recalculation manually by pressing the Calc key, *F9*.

Note   The CALC mode indicator on the status line tells you that data has been added or changed, and Quattro has not recalculated the spreadsheet. To recalculate a single cell in Manual recalculation mode, select the cell, press Edit (*F2*), and then press *Enter*.

Adding comments to entries

Quattro includes a special *cell notation* feature that lets you attach notes or comments to a cell. These comments don't appear in the spreadsheet, nor do they interfere with the spreadsheet data in any way. You can use them to add helpful information about a cell entry, such as a description of a macro or a note about how a figure was calculated.

You can add comments to value, formula, and date entries. Simply type a semicolon (;) after the regular entry and enter your comment. The semicolon and all characters after it are stored with the cell but are not displayed in the spreadsheet. You can see the cell entry and the comment on the input line when the cell is high-lighted. To store a comment in an empty cell, just type a plus sign (+) to flag the entry as a value, then enter two double quotation marks, a semicolon, and the comment.

Cell notation doesn't appear in a printed spreadsheet, unless you set the /Print | Format command to **Cell-Formulas** (see page 99).

Entering special characters

As well as all the characters on your keyboard, you can enter any ASCII character in a spreadsheet or graph. This includes inter-national characters such as ñ and á, mathematical symbols like √, and even special symbols such as ¶ and ♣.

To enter a special symbol in a spreadsheet cell or in graph text, hold down the *Alt* key and use the numeric keypad (on the right side of your keyboard) to enter the decimal code for the character. Appendix G lists all ASCII characters and the decimal and hexadecimal codes for each. For example, to enter £, hold down the *Alt* key and type 156 on the numeric keypad.

Note   If you have any RAM-resident programs like SuperKey loaded, hold down *Shift-Alt* instead of *Alt* and type the decimal ASCII character code.

Using @functions

Quattro provides many built-in functions—called *@functions* because they are always preceded by an "at" sign—that perform advanced calculations and return values. @functions are special commands that you enter in spreadsheet cells, either alone or within formulas.

This section describes

- the different types of @functions and what they're used for
- the syntax for @function statements
- the arguments used within @functions
- how to create @function statements

Refer to Chapter 1 of *@Functions and Macros* for a table that lists and briefly describes each Quattro @function by category, and for detailed information on each @function.

Types of functions

Quattro @functions can be divided into eight categories:

- **Mathematical** functions are used in more complex mathematical formulas; for example, to determine the trigonometric sine or square root.
- **Statistical** functions perform mathematical operations on a group of values; for example, to find the average value in a block of cells.
- **String** functions manipulate character strings or labels; for example, to insert characters in the middle of a string.

- **Miscellaneous** functions perform a variety of calculations; for example, to return the value in a specified position in a lookup table.
- **Logical** functions are used mostly in conditional statements, where the results are based on the validity of a logical expression, such as +A3>0.
- **Financial** functions primarily calculate investments and cash flow; for example, to determine annuity and mortgage payments.
- **Date and time** functions calculate dates and times. For example, @NOW returns the current date or time (depending on the numeric format).
- **Database statistical** functions perform mathematical calculations on records in a database; for example, to find the maximum value in a field.

Although each category of functions is used for a different purpose, they all share the same basic format and construction.

Function syntax

As with spreadsheet formulas, it's important to enter functions in the proper format, or *syntax*. All Quattro functions have the same basic syntax:

@FUNCTION(*Argument1, Argument2, …*)

A function's syntax must meet the following rules:

- There is always a leading @.
- You can enter the function name in either uppercase or lowercase letters.
- You must enclose the required arguments following the function name in parentheses. (Functions that don't require arguments don't need parentheses.)
- When there are multiple arguments, you must separate them with commas. (You can change the argument separator to a semicolon or period instead of a comma with the /Options | International | Punctuation command; see page 189).
- If the function syntax specifies a certain order for arguments, you must enter them in that order.

- There must be no spaces between @ and the function name. There may be spaces between arguments, parentheses, and the function name, but Quattro deletes them.
- You can "nest" functions inside other functions. For example, @INT(@SUM(A2..A10)).

Each function must use a separate set of parentheses, however.

Note You can add notes or comments to your @function statements; just type a semicolon at the end and enter your comment. (See page 66.)

Arguments in functions

Argument is a generic term for the information required by the function. Most functions need at least one argument. The type of information required depends on the specific function. There are three general types of arguments:

- numeric values
- cell blocks
- strings

Most arguments require one of these types of values. Some accept a combination or a choice of types. For example, @SUM accepts a block in combination with numeric values.

The values required by each function are described in the "Entering arguments in functions" section in Chapter 1 of *@Functions and Macros*.

Function statements

A *function statement* is the complete command string, including arguments and punctuation. You enter a function statement in a spreadsheet cell just as you would any other value: Highlight the cell with the cell selector and type the entry. When you press *Enter*, the result of the function is entered in the cell. If the result is a numeric value, it becomes a value entry. If the result is a string, it becomes a label entry.

If you enter any part of the function statement incorrectly, Quattro beeps, enters Edit mode, displays a message saying "Syntax error," and moves the cursor to the part of the function statement causing the problem.

You can use more than one @function in a single statement. For example,

@ROUND(@AVG(C14..F24),2)

You can nest as many functions as you like in a statement (up to 254 characters).

This is called *nesting* functions. The more complex the statement, however, the more difficult it will be to debug should there be problems. It's best to break down complex function statements into several smaller statements, which you can reference with a final statement. The smaller pieces will make it easier to pinpoint an error, and will be available for use with other formulas, thereby increasing memory efficiency.

There are four Quattro features that can assist you in constructing function statements:

Functions

- The **Functions key** (*Alt-F3*) displays the @functions choice list. You can choose a function from the list to enter it on the input line (see page 76).

- The **@ button** on the mouse palette also displays the @functions choice list.

- **Block Names** make it easier to reference blocks of cells. Once you've assigned a name to a block, you can reference it by name instead of by its block coordinates (see page 127).

- **Pointing** lets you insert cell references in a function statement by pointing to them, either with the cell selector or a mouse pointer (see page 71).

Specifying cell blocks

Many formulas that include @functions (and many menu commands as well) operate on more than one cell at once. Rather than entering the coordinates of each cell involved, you can specify a *block* of adjacent cells by entering a *range of cells*. This saves not only time, but spreadsheet space as well. For example, to total the values in a column, you could type

@SUM(A1..A7)

instead of

A1+A2+A3+A4+A5+A6+A7

A cell block is any rectangular group of cells on the spreadsheet. The following figure shows a few examples:

Figure 3.4
Examples of cell blocks

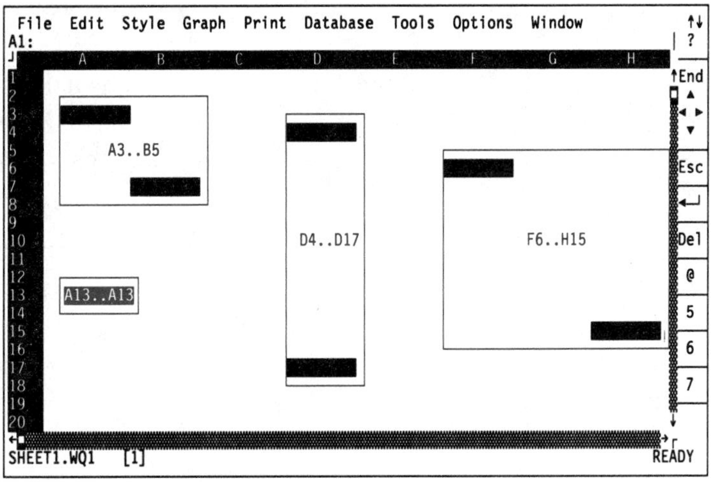

```
 File   Edit   Style   Graph   Print   Database   Tools   Options   Window          ↑↓
A1:                                                                                  | ?
J        A         B         C         D         E         F         G        H     ↑End
1                                                                                     ▲
2                                                                                   ◄  ►
3     ▬▬▬▬▬▬                                                                          ▼
4
5          A3..B5
6                                                                                   Esc
7              ▬▬▬▬▬▬
8                                                                                    ↵
9
10                                        D4..D17              F6..H15              Del
11
12                                                                                   @
13   ┌─────────┐
     │A13..A13 │                                                                     5
14   └─────────┘
15                                                                                   6
16
17                                                                                   7
18                           ▬▬▬▬▬▬
19
20
←□                                                                                  →
SHEET1.WQ1   [1]                                                              READY
```

To specify the cell coordinates of a block, enter the address of the top left cell (the *anchor cell*), followed by one or two periods (..) and the address of the bottom right cell. For example, the block

F6..H15

refers to the rightmost block of cells shown in the previous figure. (You can actually enter the coordinates of any two cells that are in opposite corners in any order. However, Quattro will translate the address into the top left cell of the block followed by the bottom right.)

Caution!   If you delete a row or column containing a specified block's coordinate cell or move data into a coordinate cell, the block reference becomes ERR, and the formula itself results in ERR. This is meant to prevent you from accidentally erasing data referenced by a formula. To reverse the move, press the Undo key (*Alt-F5*, if enabled) immediately afterward. Or, to restore the cell reference, edit the formula and replace ERR with the cell reference.

You can also specify a cell block by pointing it out or by entering the name you've assigned a block. Pointing is detailed in the next section. Block names are covered on page 127.

Pointing out cell blocks

An easy way to specify a cell block, either within a formula or in response to a command prompt, is to *point* it out with the cell selector. This is a very simple process—once you use it, you may never want to type in coordinates again.

To point out a single cell, move the selector to it and press *Enter* or enter an operator, comma, or close parenthesis.

To point out a multiple-cell block using the keyboard,

1. Move the cell selector to one corner of the block you want to specify.
2. Press the Period key (.) to *anchor* the block, if necessary.
3. Move the selector to the opposite corner of the block. Quattro highlights the block as you extend it.
4. Press *Enter* or enter an operator, comma, or close parenthesis.

With a little practice, you can use a mouse with ease and speed to point out single cells and cell blocks.

- To point out a single cell, click it.
- To point out a multiple-cell block with a mouse, drag from one corner of the block to the opposite corner and release. Quattro highlights the entire block. Or, click one corner of the block, move to the opposite corner, and hold down the right button of the mouse while you click the left.

Note If the block you want to point to is in a different spreadsheet window, activate the window first by clicking it, then point out the block.

The following sections discuss each step involved in pointing: entering Point mode, anchoring the first cell of a block, extending the block, exiting Point mode, and confirming entries. See also "EXT mode: A shortcut" on page 75, which describes how to select a block without entering Point mode.

Entering Point mode

You can enter Point mode in two situations:

- in response to a command prompt
- while entering a formula

When Quattro prompts you for a cell block, it offers a default block. Usually this is the current cell; when appropriate, it is the last block previously specified with the command. To accept the default block, just press *Enter*. To specify a different block, press any of the cursor-movement keys to begin pointing.

If you're typing in a formula and want to point out a block, make sure the formula is ready to accept a block. (The cursor must be after a mathematical operator [+ – / *], an open parenthesis [(], or a comma [,]. Otherwise, if you press a cursor-movement key, Quattro will enter the formula in the cell and return to Ready mode.) Press any cursor-movement key to begin pointing. To begin a formula by pointing out a cell reference, type +, then point.

To point out a cell or block of cells while you are editing a formula, the cursor must be at the end of the entry and must also be preceded by a mathematical operator, an open parenthesis, or a comma.

Note   If you have multiple windows open, you can press the Next Window key, *Shift-F6*, to enter Point mode and jump to the next window. If the window is split into two panes, you can press the Pane key, *F6*, to enter Point mode and jump into the other pane. See Chapter 9 for more about manipulating windows.

Anchoring the first cell of a block

To specify a cell as the first corner of a block, you need to *anchor* the cell. This tells Quattro that the cell is the first coordinate of the block.

To anchor the first cell of a block, move the selector to it and press the Period key (.) or the Select key (*Shift-F7*). (If you press *Esc* before you anchor a block, the selector returns to the cell that was current when you began pointing, and the reference disappears from the input line.)

Note   If you're pointing in response to a command prompt, Quattro usually provides an anchor for you, using as a default either the current cell or the first cell of the last block specified with the command. If the default is anchored, it appears after the prompt as a block (such as A1..A1). If it's unanchored, the current cell appears as a single cell address (A1).

To "unanchor" a cell, press *Esc*. You can then move the selector out of the current cell without extending the block.

To unanchor a cell *and* return to the cell that was current when you began pointing, press *Backspace*.

Extending the block

Once a cell is anchored, either by you or by Quattro, moving the selector away from the anchor *extends* the block. The anchor remains as the first coordinate of the block, and the selector indicates the last coordinate. Everything between the two is highlighted.

To specify the block you want to use, move the selector to the far end of the block until everything you want to include is highlighted.

End To indicate an entire filled block, use the *End* key in conjunction with the arrow keys to speed up block extension. For example, in the following figure, the quickest way to get from the anchor to the opposite end of the block is to press *End* ↓ to move to cell C8, then *End* → to move to cell F8. If you press *End* and an arrow key from within a filled cell, Quattro moves the selector in the direction of the arrow until it reaches a blank cell. It stops the selector immediately before the blank cell.

Figure 3.5
Using the End key to extend
a block

The End key can help you point out the corners of a block.

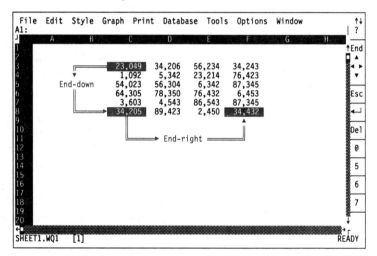

If you change your mind after anchoring and extending a block, press *Esc* or *Backspace* to remove the highlighting and unanchor the first cell. *Esc* returns the selector to the cell that was the anchor. *Backspace* returns the selector to the cell that was current when you first began pointing.

To extend the selection from a different corner of the highlighted block, press the Period key (.). This moves you counterclockwise around the corners.

Exiting Point mode	The block you pointed out on the spreadsheet is indicated by coordinates on the input line. The pointing process is not complete, however, until you *exit* Point mode, thereby entering the highlighted block as a response or cell reference.

To exit Point mode and enter the highlighted block in response to a prompt, just press *Enter*.

To enter a block in a formula (and exit Point mode), press any character key, such as an operator or comma. Quattro remains in Edit or Value mode. To enter the block in the formula *and* enter the formula in the cell (returning to Ready mode), press *Enter*. You can then add to or finish editing the formula.

If the character you enter creates an invalid formula, Quattro beeps, displays an error message, and places you in Edit mode so you can correct it. For example, suppose you press *Enter* after pointing out the block in the following formula:

@SUM(A1..C10

Quattro would then refuse the entry because it requires a close parenthesis. If you were pointing out a cell in a different spreadsheet, Quattro jumps back to the original spreadsheet window.

Confirming an existing entry

When you initiate a command that requires a block, Quattro often follows the prompt with a default block. To use the default block, simply press *Enter*. To erase the block and show the current cell as the anchor, press *Backspace*. To erase the block and use the top left cell of it as the anchor, press *Esc*.

If you can't see the entire block onscreen, and you want to check it out to make sure it's what you want, use the Period key (.) to move around the corners of the block. This actually shifts the anchor from corner to corner, clockwise or counterclockwise, depending on the direction you selected the block. If the block is what you wanted, press *Enter* to confirm the block. If it wasn't exactly what you wanted, use the cursor-movement keys to adjust the block from any corner.

Ext mode: A shortcut

If you prefer, you can select a block of cells *before* you choose a menu command that operates on a block.

To select a block using the keyboard,

1. Move the cursor to one corner of the block you want to select.
2. Press *Shift-F7* (the Select key). The EXT indicator appears on the status line.
3. Move to the opposite corner of the block. Quattro highlights the block as you extend it.
4. Choose the menu command you want to operate on the block; for example, /**Print** | **Block**. When you choose the command, Quattro automatically accepts the block you selected using *Shift-F7* without displaying a prompt. If the menu command is one that prompts for two blocks, such as the source and destination blocks that /**Edit** | **Copy** requires, Quattro automatically accepts the block you selected using *Shift-F7* as the first block (the source) and immediately prompts you for the second block (the destination).

To select a block using a mouse,

1. Click one corner of the block.
2. Move the pointer to the opposite corner of the block.
3. Hold down the right button while you click the left. Quattro highlights the block you selected.
4. Choose the menu command you want to operate on the block; this works exactly the same as described in step 4 of the previous list.

Using a choice list

It's easier to enter data if you use *choice lists* to display your options. You can select an option from a choice list to enter it on the input line.

Choices

To display a choice list, use the *F3* function key. You can display three types of choice lists with this key:

■ **Block Names** (*F3*) displays a list of all existing block names for the current spreadsheet. To display the coordinates alongside each block name, press the Expand key (+ on the numeric keypad). To remove the coordinates from the list, press the Contract key (- on the numeric keypad). Within the names list, you can use *F3* to toggle between displaying the list full screen and in a choice list window.

The Choices key, F3, has different purposes depending on where you are. In Ready mode, *F3* activates the menu bar. In a list of block or file names, *F3* zooms the window. To use *F3* to display the block names list, the edit cursor must be at a place in a formula or prompt where pointing out a block is permitted. Wherever pointing out a cell or block of cells is possible, you can also press the Choices key, *F3*, to choose from a list of block names.

■ **Macros** (*Shift-F3*) displays a menu of macro command categories. Choose a category to display all the macro commands within it.

■ **Functions** (*Alt-F3*) displays a list of all Quattro @functions.

Choice lists not only remind you of your current options or command syntax; you can also use them to enter parts of a formula or macro, or to answer a command prompt. With a choice list displayed, use the ↑ and ↓ keys to highlight the choice you want. Then press *Enter*. Quattro automatically writes the item on the input line, at the cursor position.

C H A P T E R

4

Printing

After an introduction to the **Print** menu, this chapter is divided into two sections. The first, "Printing a spreadsheet," discusses how to

Before printing a graph or spreadsheet, you may need to change your default printer setting. See page 176 · for details.

- include headings on each page of a printed spreadsheet
- print to a disk file or preview onscreen
- print headers and footers on each page
- print with or without page breaks
- change margins
- print special effects such as lines, boxes, and shaded cells
- use setup strings to give commands to your printer
- print in landscape mode
- print a list of spreadsheet cell contents, as opposed to data in spreadsheet format

The second section, "Printing a graph," describes how to

- send your graph to a disk file
- display a page preview of your printed graph
- specify the dimensions and layout of your graph
- print more than one graph per page
- print a graph in landscape mode
- print your graph to a special file for use with another program

Creating and customizing graphs is covered in chapters 13, 14, and 15.

The Print menu

```
╔══════ Print ══════╗
║ Block             ║
║ Headings        ▸ ║
║                   ║
║ Destination     ▸ ║
║ Layout          ▸ ║
║ Format          ▸ ║
║                   ║
║ Adjust Printer  ▸ ║
║ Spreadsheet Print ║
║ Graph Print     ▸ ║
║ Quit              ║
╚═══════════════════╝
```

To print either a spreadsheet or a graph, choose /Print to display the Print menu. Only two commands on the Print menu affect graph printing: Adjust Printer and Graph Print. The rest apply to spreadsheets only.

- **Block** lets you specify the area of the spreadsheet you want to print.

- **Headings** lets you specify blocks of the spreadsheet to be printed at the top and/or left of each page as headings.

- **Destination** lets you send your spreadsheet either to a printer or to a disk file. You can also use it to specify graphics printing and to preview your printed spreadsheet.

- **Layout** lets you change the margins or page length for the spreadsheet and enter printer setup commands, headers, and footers, as well as specify printing with or without page breaks or horizontally. You can also return all print commands to their default settings.

- **Format** lets you print a list of individual cell contents and formatting information instead of the usual spreadsheet data.

- **Adjust Printer** displays a menu with commands to advance the paper in the printer and set the top-of-page indicator.

- **Spreadsheet Print** begins printing the specified block of the current spreadsheet, either to the specified printer, to a disk file, or to an onscreen preview.

- **Graph Print** provides all the options for printing the current graph, either to a printer, to a disk file, or to an onscreen preview.

- **Quit** or *Esc* returns you to the spreadsheet.

Quattro saves **Block**, **Heading**, and **Layout** print settings with the spreadsheet for use next time you print it.

Note The Style menu contains commands that add presentation-quality special effects to a spreadsheet. You can use it to switch type fonts, shade areas of the spreadsheet, and draw lines and boxes. Chapter 6 covers Style menu commands in detail.

1-2-3 If you're using the 123-compatible menus, choose /Print and then choose either **Printer**, **File**, **Binary File**, **Graphics Printer**, or **Screen Preview** to display the menu of print options, which is identical for each of these destinations.

Printing a spreadsheet

When you've completed a spreadsheet, you can print it (or any part of it) using the commands on the **Print** menu. With these commands, you can quickly print a simple list of figures or create a sophisticated multi-page report, embellished with headers, footers, and page numbers.

The basic procedure

The basic procedure is as follows:

1. With the spreadsheet you want to print displayed, choose **/Print**.
2. Choose **Block** and specify the block of cells you want to print.
3. If you want to change any of the print settings (for example, adjust page margins, add headers and footers, or print to a disk file instead of the printer), set the appropriate print commands.
4. Turn the printer on and choose **Ad**just Printer | **Align** to adjust the paper alignment.
5. When all the print defaults and options are set as you want them, you're ready to print. For highest-quality output, choose **Graphics Printer** as your print destination. Choose **S**pread-sheet Print. A WAIT mode indicator appears on the right end of the status line while Quattro sends the data to the printer or file.

   If there is a problem with the printer (for example, if it's turned off or is out of paper), an "I/O error" warning appears on the status line and a confirmation menu offers two choices: **Abort** or **Continue**. Choose **Abort** to halt the command, or correct the situation and choose **Continue**.
6. If you are printing to a text printer, choose **Ad**just Printer | **Form Feed** to advance the printer to the top of the form after printing is complete.
7. When printing is complete, choose **Q**uit or press *Esc* to return to the spreadsheet.

Since Quattro saves most printer commands with your file, printing a spreadsheet for a second time is usually much easier. In most cases, you simply choose /**Print** | **Spreadsheet Print** to begin printing.

To abort printing before it's complete, press the *Ctrl* and *Break* keys at the same time. Depending on the size of your printer's memory buffer, printing may continue for a while before stopping.

For information about fonts and spreadsheet printing, read "Choosing a font" in Chapter 6, the "Printing" and "Fonts" sections in Appendix A, and Appendix F, "Working with fonts."

The following sections describe specifying the block to print, adjusting the printer, choosing a print destination, adding column and row headings, and defining page layout.

Specifying the block to print

Before you can print your spreadsheet, you must specify the exact cell block you want to print:

1. Choose /**Print** | **Block**. The menu disappears temporarily and Quattro prompts you for a cell block.
2. Enter the cell block's coordinates or block name, or point out the block using the direction keys (move the selector to one corner, press the Period key, move to the opposite corner, and press *Enter*).

Quattro prints everything in the block you specify. If a cell's contents spill over into adjacent cells, be sure to include the spillover cells in the print block; otherwise, only part of the entry will be printed.

Quattro stores the /**Print** | **Block** command setting with the spreadsheet when you save the file. To remove the setting, choose /**Print** | **Layout** | **Reset**, then choose **Print Block**.

1-2-3

If you're using the 123-compatible menus, choose /**Print** | (pick print destination) | **Range**.

The following figure shows how a spreadsheet appears when printed. Notice that blank rows appear in the printout because they are within the spreadsheet's data block.

Figure 4.1
A printed spreadsheet

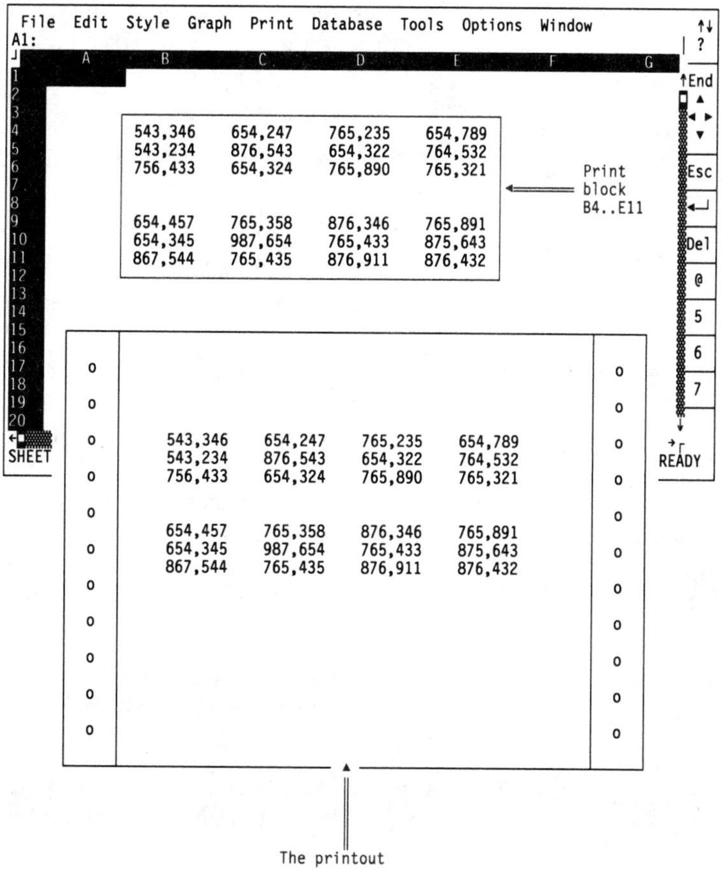

Figure 4.1
A printed spreadsheet

The printout

Adjusting the printer

Before you begin printing (unless you're printing to disk), make sure your printer is turned on and ready ("online"). If the paper in your text printer isn't properly positioned, you can use the Adjust Printer menu commands to reposition it.

When you choose /Print | Adjust Printer, Quattro displays the Adjust Printer menu.

┌─ Adjust Printer ─┐
│ Skip Line   │
│ Form Feed   │
│ Align   │
└──────────────────┘

- **Skip Line** moves the paper in the printer forward one line.
- **Form Feed** moves the paper in the printer forward to the top of the next page.

■ **Align** tells Quattro to assume that the current position of the paper in the printer is correct; that is, printing will begin at the top of the page. It also resets the line counter.

To ready the printer, you can use the Skip Line and Form Feed commands to line up the top of a page with the printer's print-head.

When the paper is properly aligned, use the **Align** command to set the "Top of Page." This resets Quattro's line counter, which determines the placement of page breaks, headers, footers, and margins. If you adjust the printer paper without choosing the **Align** command afterwards, your printout could appear misaligned.

The **Align** command also resets the page number to one. If, for instance, you print the same job more than once, or print more than one job in succession, you should choose /Print | Adjust Printer | **Align** between each **Spreadsheet Print** command to start each print job on page one. This is especially important if you have included a # symbol in your header or footer to number the pages consecutively (see page 93).

When printing is complete, you can use the Form Feed command to move the paper forward one page; this is necessary only when you are printing to a text printer.

Note   If you choose Skip Line or Form Feed after printing spreadsheet data to disk, Quattro adds a blank line or group of lines to the end of the file.

1-2-3   If you're using the 123-compatible menus, choose /Print | (pick print destination) | Line, Page, or Align instead of /Print | Adjust Printer | Skip Line, Form Feed, or Align.

Specifying print destination

The /Print | Destination menu lets you specify where the printout of your spreadsheet goes.

```
===== Destination =====
—Draft-Mode Printing—
 Printer
 File
—Final-Quality Printing—
 Binary File
 Graphics Printer
 Screen Preview
```

■ **Printer**, the default, is a simple text printer option. It prints a spreadsheet *without special effects* on your default printer when you choose **Spreadsheet Print**. You cannot use this option to print a graph or special effects (such as shading, line-drawing, or an inserted graph) in a spreadsheet.

- **File** sends the spreadsheet to a disk file as if it were printing to a text printer. The data is stored in ASCII format, including all print information, such as headings and layout settings.
- **Binary File** sends the spreadsheet to a disk file as if it were printing to your default graphics printer. For example, if your graphics printer were a PostScript printer, Quattro would create a PostScript file.
- **Graphics Printer** prints your spreadsheet on the printer specified as the default graphics printer with the /Options | Hardware | Printers | Default Printer command (see Chapter 7). This printer option will include any special graphics effects, such as line-drawing, shading, or an inserted graph.
- **Screen Preview** displays your spreadsheet on the screen as it will appear when printed on the default graphics printer.

Printing to a text file

If you want to save a spreadsheet for future printing, or to use with another program (for example, a word-processing program like Sprint), you can "print" it to a text file on your disk.

To print a spreadsheet to a text file,

1. Choose /**Print** | **Destination** | **File**. Quattro prompts you for a file name. If you're saving to a floppy disk, make sure to specify the correct drive.
2. Adjust any print settings you want, such as the block to print or margins.
3. Choose **S**preadsheet Print to print your spreadsheet to a disk file as if it were printing to a text printer.
4. If you want to save another block of data at the end of the file, specify the new block and choose **S**preadsheet Print again. You can save as many spreadsheet blocks as you like in the same file.
5. When Quattro finishes writing to the file, choose **Q**uit to exit the menu. Quattro appends the .PRN extension and closes the disk file.

1-2-3

If you're using the 123-compatible menus, choose /**Print** | **File** | **Go** to print to a text file.

You can print a .PRN file at any time from DOS. You can also use it with other programs—word processors, for example.

To print a spreadsheet .PRN file from DOS, use the DOS PRINT command:

```
PRINT filename.PRN
```

You can also use the DOS FIND, SORT, and TYPE commands with the file.

Printing to a binary file

To print a spreadsheet with final-quality graphics to a disk file, choose /**Print** I **Destination** I **Binary File**, then choose **Spreadsheet Print**. Quattro writes your data to a .PRN file using all the settings for your default graphics printer.

To print a binary file from DOS, you must use the DOS COPY command with the /B parameter:

```
COPY filename.PRN /B LPT1
```

This sends a binary file (/B) to the LPT1 printer port. If your printer is connected to a different port (such as COM1 or PRN), specify it instead of LPT1.

1-2-3

If you're using the 123-compatible menus, choose /**Print** I **Binary File** I **Go** to print to a file with final-quality graphics.

PostScript printers

PostScript printers offer a wide array of printing fonts. If you want to take advantage of these fonts in your printed spreadsheet file, specify a PostScript printer as your default graphics printer with /**Options** I **Hardware** I **Printers** I **Default Printer** (see Chapter 7). Then, when you choose /**Style** I **Font** I **Edit Font** I (pick font number) I **Typeface**, you'll see additional PostScript fonts. If you choose them, they won't show up onscreen (Quattro will use a stand-in font instead), but Quattro will use them to print your spreadsheet to a binary file.

Screen preview

Before you print a spreadsheet, you can use the Screen Previewer to view it onscreen as it will appear when printed on the default graphics printer. Except for minor differences in the selection of fonts, the preview display should match the printed output exactly. To preview your spreadsheet, choose /**Print** I **Destination** I **Screen Preview**, align the printer, and then choose **Spreadsheet Print**. Quattro displays your spreadsheet full screen, using the margins, fonts, orientation, and print specifications you selected.

The following figure shows a preview of a spreadsheet with two inserted graphs: a piece of clip art created with the Graph

Annotator and an area graph. The 200% display on the status line indicates the current zoom level. A zoom box (see the explanation under Guide, which follows shortly) represents the area visible onscreen in zoomed mode.

Figure 4.2
A previewed spreadsheet

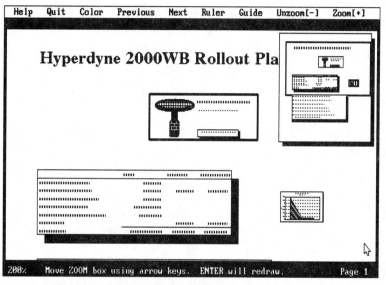

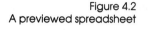 If you're using the 123-compatible menus, choose /Print | Screen Preview | Go to print to the screen.

You'll sometimes notice a "Now building font" message when you preview or print your spreadsheet with /Options | Graphics Quality set to Final. See Appendix F for information about working with fonts.

The Screen Previewer menu bar contains the following commands:

- **Help** calls up Screen Previewer help.

- **Quit** or *Esc* returns you to the Print menu.

- **Color** lets you switch to a different color set. The Screen Previewer initially displays your output in colors it judges to be appropriate to both your screen and printer. To switch to any one of the following color sets, press /C or click **Color** with a mouse:

    - A set for color screens, where the main body of the previewed page appears in monochrome. This is appropriate for a system with a color screen and a monochrome printer.

- A set for color screens with a color printer.
- A monochrome set with the page displayed black on white. This is appropriate for normal black-and-white monitors.
- A reversed monochrome set. This is appropriate for many plasma and LCD displays.

■ **Previous** and **Next** move forward or backward to the following or preceding page of your print job, if it has multiple pages.

■ **Ruler** overlays a one-inch grid on the previewed spreadsheet. This allows you to see the exact layout of the spreadsheet on the printed page so you can make exact modification to the page layout. Choose **Ruler** again to toggle the grid off.

■ **Guide**, in a zoomed view, displays a miniature page in the upper right corner of the Screen Previewer. The page guide has an outline around the zoomed area (a *zoom box*) that represents the area on the screen. Move the zoom box around the page guide with the arrow keys or a mouse to view a different part of the spreadsheet (or graph). **Guide** is a toggle that is on by default; press *Del* or choose **Guide** to remove it, and press *Ins* or choose **Guide** again to restore it.

■ **Unzoom [-]** removes the enlargement added with **Zoom**.

■ **Zoom [+]** allows you to enlarge (zoom) the display. There are three levels of zoom:

- 100% displays the whole page.
- 200% displays half a page at twice the size.
- 400% displays one-eighth of a page at four times the size.

Check the status line for the current level of zoom. By zooming the screen, you can focus on details in a particular area of a specific page. Move the zoom box in the page guide to focus on a different area.

To choose a command from the Screen Previewer menu bar, you can do any of the following:

■ Press the first letter of the command.

■ Click the command name with a mouse.

■ Press / to activate the menu bar, move to a command with ← or →, and press *Enter*.

If the spreadsheet is larger than a single page, you can press *PgDn* to view the next page. *PgUp* displays the previous page.

If you have a mouse, click any Screen Previewer command to choose it, or drag the zoom box in the page guide to view different areas of the spreadsheet.

The following table lists keys you can use in the Screen Previewer:

Table 4.1
Special keys in the Screen
Previewer

Key	Effect
Esc	Exits the Screen Previewer (same as /**Q**uit).
F1	Displays online help (same as /**H**elp).
PgUp	Displays the previous page (same as /**P**revious).
PgDn	Displays the next page (same as /**N**ext).
↑	Scrolls the zoomed display up.
↓	Scrolls the zoomed display down.
→	Scrolls the zoomed display right.
←	Scrolls the zoomed display left.
Home	Displays the top of a zoomed page.
End	Displays the bottom of a zoomed page.
Enter	Redisplays the zoomed area.
Del	Removes the page guide when a page is zoomed.
Ins	Redisplays the page guide for a zoomed display.

Headings

The **Headings** command lets you print specific columns or rows from the spreadsheet on each page. When you choose this command, Quattro displays a menu with two options: **L**eft Heading and **T**op Heading. Left headings print along the leftmost column of the page. Top headings print at the top of each page, below any specified headers (see the following figure).

Figure 4.3
Headings printed on pages

```
o                                                                          o
      --------------------------------------------------------------
o     INVOICE #   PURCHASE DATE   SALESREP   ACCOUNT #    AMOUNT       o
      --------------------------------------------------------------
o                                                                          o
          1         03/01        Nancy        15684     $1,432.56
o         2         03/01        Jane         16029     $1,722.13      o
          3         03/01        Bob          16374     $2,011.70
o         4         03/01        Ron          16719     $2,301.27      o
          5         03/02        Sally        17064     $2,590.84
o                                                                          o
```

*Use the **Headings** command
with large spreadsheets to
include row or column
headings on each page.*

```
o    o                                                                     o
     o    --------------------------------------------------------------
o    o    INVOICE #   PURCHASE DATE   SALESREP   ACCOUNT #    AMOUNT   o
     o    --------------------------------------------------------------
o    o       47         03/11        Jane         21894     $3,383.93  o
     o       48         03/12        Bob          22239     $3,673.50
o    o       49         03/12        Ron          22584     $2,401.49  o
     o       50         03/12        Bob          22929     $2,691.06
o    o       51         03/12        Jane         23274     $2,980.63  o
     o       52         03/13        Ron          23619     $3,270.20
o    o       53         03/13        Nancy        23964     $3,559.77  o
     o       54         03/13        Jane         24309     $3,849.34
o    o       55         03/14        Bob          15684     $4,138.91  o
     o       56         03/14        Ron          16029     $4,428.48
o    o       57         03/14        Sally        16374     $1,784.45  o
     o       58         03/15        Sally        16719     $2,074.02
o    o       59         03/15        Jane         17064     $2,363.59  o
     o       60         03/15        Bob          17409     $2,653.16
o    o       61         03/16        Nancy        17754     $2,942.73  o
     o       62         03/16        Nancy        18099     $3,232.30
o    o       63         03/16        Ron          18444     $3,521.87  o
     o       64         03/16        Bob          18789     $1,432.56
o    o       65         03/17        Jane         19134     $1,722.13  o
     o       66         03/17        Ron          19479     $2,011.70
o    o       67         03/17        Nancy        19824     $2,301.27  o
     o       68         03/18        Ron          20169     $2,590.84
o    o       69         03/18        Bob          20514     $2,880.41  o
     o       70         03/18        Jane         20859     $3,169.98
o    o       71         03/19        Bob          21204     $3,459.55  o
     o       72         03/19        Ron          21549     $3,749.12
o    o       73         03/19        Sally        21894     $4,038.69  o
     o       74         03/19        Sally        22239     $4,328.26
o    o       75         03/20        Jane         22584     $1,532.78  o
     o       76         03/20        Bob          22929     $1,822.35
     o       77         03/20        Nancy        23274     $2,111.92  o
     o       78         03/21        Nancy        17064     $2,401.49
     o       79         03/21        Ron          17409     $2,691.06  o
     o       80         03/21        Bob          17754     $4,680.15
     o       81         03/22        Jane         18099     $1,356.94  o
     o       82         03/22        Ron          18444     $1,646.51
     o       83         03/22        Nancy        18789     $1,936.08  o
     o       84         03/22        Ron          19134     $2,225.65
     o       85         03/23        Bob          19479     $2,515.22  o
     o                                                                     o
```

If you specify a column or row as a heading, and it is already part of the print block, it appears twice. Be sure to exclude the headings from the print block. For example, if you've specified cells A2..G2 as headings and want to print all data under them down to row 30, specify A3..G30 as your print block.

To set print headings,

1. Choose /Print I Headings.
2. Choose **Left Heading** or **Top Heading**. Quattro prompts you for a cell block.
3. Specify the address of any cell in the column (for a left heading) or row (for a top heading).
4. Press *Enter*.

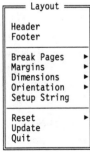

If you're using the 123-compatible menus, choose /Print I (pick print destination) I Options I Borders I Cols (or Rows).

Quattro stores the headings you specify with the spreadsheet when you save it. To remove the settings for both headings, use the **Reset** command. Choose /Print I Layout I Reset, then choose **Headings**.

Layout options

To make it as easy as possible to print spreadsheet files, Quattro uses the most common defaults for its print options. It prints your spreadsheet with automatic page breaks on $8\frac{1}{2}$x11-inch paper with approximately $\frac{1}{2}$-inch margins.

You can change these settings to print with different dimensions. You can also use other Layout menu commands to specify optional settings, such as margins, headers, footers, page orientation, hard page breaks, and printer setup strings.

```
==== Layout ====
Header
Footer
────────────
Break Pages   ▶
Margins       ▶
Dimensions    ▶
Orientation   ▶
Setup String
────────────
Reset         ▶
Update
Quit
```

When you choose /Print I Layout, Quattro displays the Layout menu.

- **Header** lets you specify text to be added to the top of each printed spreadsheet page.

- **Footer** lets you specify text to be added to the bottom of each printed spreadsheet page.

- **Break Pages** lets you print a spreadsheet without page breaks, headers, or footers.

- **Margins** lets you specify four margins for the printed page and the page length. The default settings leave approximately $\frac{1}{2}$-inch margins on all sides of $8\frac{1}{2}$x11-inch paper.

- **Dimensions** lets you specify layout dimensions in inches or centimeters rather than character size, the default.

- **Orientation** lets you print the spreadsheet vertically (portrait) or horizontally (landscape).
- **Setup String** lets you send print codes to the printer.
- **Reset** returns the print block, headings, and layout commands to their default settings.
- **Update** saves the current Layout settings as the new defaults.
- **Quit** returns you to the Print menu.

Quattro stores all Layout menu settings with the current spreadsheet. Page layout settings, like all other Print commands, revert to the defaults when you exit Quattro or open a new file. To change the default Layout values for all new spreadsheets, choose /Print | Layout | Update (see page 99). To reinstate the last saved default settings, choose /Print | Layout | Reset (see page 98).

Headers and footers

Headers and footers are lines of text that print at the top and bottom of each page of a printed spreadsheet. They can each contain one line, up to 254 characters.

To enter a header or footer,

1. Choose /Print | Layout | Header or Footer. Quattro prompts you for a line of text.
2. Type the text you want to use as the footer or header. Use *Backspace* or any of the editing keys to correct mistakes as you type.
3. Press *Enter*.

Quattro enters the header or footer, which appears at the top or bottom of each page. *Quattro automatically separates headers and footers from the text of a page with two blank lines.* Unless you specify otherwise, headers and footers are left-aligned. To change or delete a header or footer, choose the command again and delete the entry or edit it.

1-2-3

If you're using the 123-compatible commands, choose /Print | (pick print destination) | Options | Header (or Footer).

Important!

If you set Break Pages to **Yes** (see the following section), Quattro automatically allows three lines for a header and three for a footer, even if you did not specify any header or footer text to print. One line is allowed for the header or footer text, and the other two are for spacing. For example, if you normally can print 66 lines on a page with a length of 66 lines, Quattro can print only

60 lines of the spreadsheet print block because of the three lines it allows for a header and the three lines is allows for a footer. One way to print more lines per page is to set **Break Pages** to **No**. In this example, you could print a full 66 lines on the page, but you would not be able to have a header or footer.

Quattro offers three special characters for use in headers and footers:

(number sign) enters the current page number.

@ enters the current date (as determined by your computer's calendar).

| (a vertical bar character) determines the position of the text: left, right, or center.

The last character, |, works like a tab, with the first tab centering the text and the second aligning it right. To enter a vertical bar character (|) on most keyboards, hold down the *Shift* key and press the Backslash key (\). You can use | between text to align parts of a header or footer differently. Quattro allows up to two | characters in a header or footer line. Table 4.2 shows examples.

Table 4.2
Aligning headers and footers

Entry	Results		
`Budget Report`	Budget Report		
`|Budget Report`		Budget Report	
`||Budget Report`			Budget Report
`Budget Report||Page #`	Budget Report		Page 3
`@|Budget Report|Page #`	16-Jan-90	Budget Report	Page 3

Printing without page breaks

By default, Quattro recognizes hard page breaks—inserted in a spreadsheet either with the /**Style** | **Insert Break** command or by typing in the characters |::—and automatically inserts additional page breaks where necessary.

You can tell Quattro not to insert page breaks, but instead print the data in one continuous stream, recognizing only hard page breaks. To print without page breaks,

1. Choose /**Print** | **Layout** | **Break** Pages.

2. Choose **No**. This setting prints the spreadsheet without "soft" page breaks, headers, or footers. This is useful for quick print-

outs or for printing to a disk file where hard page breaks are recognized.

To return to using page breaks, set **Break Pages** back to **Yes**.

If you're using the 123-compatible menus, choose **/Print** | (pick print destination) | **Options** | **Other** | **Unformatted**. To return to printing with page breaks, choose **/Print** | (pick print destination) | **Options** | **Other** | **Formatted**.

How Quattro breaks pages

If your spreadsheet won't fit across one page, Quattro fits as many columns as it can on the first page, then starts a new page where it continues printing more rows of the same columns, printing as many pages as necessary to reach the last row of the spreadsheet. Then Quattro goes back to the first row of the spreadsheet and picks up at the column where it left off, printing as many columns as it can fit on a page until it reaches the last row of the spreadsheet, and so on until the entire spreadsheet is printed. You can combine the pages to create one large spreadsheet.

When you're printing a spreadsheet with an inserted graph to a graphics printer, the graph might break at the same column as the rest of the data in the spreadsheet. So, part of the graph prints with the block of columns that fit on one page, and the rest of the graph prints on the page where the rest of the columns appear.

To print a wide spreadsheet with fewer breaks, you can set the **Orientation** command to Landscape to print it horizontally (see page 97).

Changing the margins and page length

Default margin and page length settings leave ½-inch margins on all sides of a spreadsheet printed on 8½x11-inch paper (see Figure 4.4 on page 95).

If you're using wide paper or a font size larger than 10 characters per inch, you'll need to change the right margin. You can change the other margins to best present your spreadsheet—to center a small spreadsheet on the page, for example.

Figure 4.4
A printed spreadsheet with
standard margins

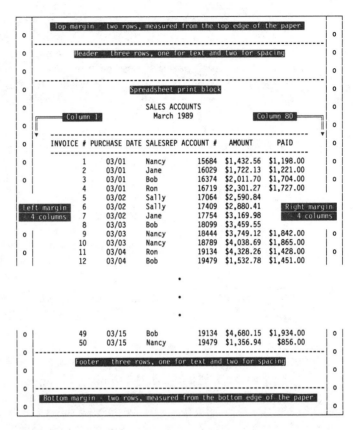

To change any of the margin settings,

1. Choose /**Print** I **Layout** I **Margins**.
2. Specify the setting you want to change.
3. Enter a new value.
4. To return to the **Print** menu, press *Q* twice.

If you're using the 123-compatible menus, choose /**Print** I (pick
print destination) I **Options** I **Margins**.

```
┌── Margins ──┐
│              │
│ Page Length  │
│ Left         │
│ Top          │
│ Right        │
│ Bottom       │
│              │
│ Quit         │
└──────────────┘
```

- **Page Length** (1-100) determines the number of lines printed on each page. The default, 66, is the correct setting for a dot-matrix printer that prints 6 lines per inch (the standard setting) on 11-inch paper. If your printer is set to a different lines-per-inch value, if your paper is a different length, or if it is a laser printer, change this setting accordingly. For example, the page length setting for a laser printer should be 60 because a laser printer can only print on 10 inches of an 11-inch page. To calculate the page length, multiply the lines-per-inch value by the number of printable inches on a page. The number of printable lines on a page is unaffected by headers, footers, or top or bottom margins.

- **Left** (0-254) determines the amount of space to leave between the left edge of the paper and the first column of data. The default, 4, leaves 4 character spaces, or about $\frac{1}{2}$ inch. Depending on the width of your spreadsheet, you may want to lengthen or shorten this margin.

- **Top** (0-32) determines the number of blank lines to leave at the top of each page. The default, 2, leaves approximately $\frac{1}{2}$ inch. If you include a header in your printout, it prints underneath this margin with two blank lines between it and the spreadsheet data.

- **Right** (0-254) determines the amount of space to leave for a right margin. This value is the number of spaces between the *left* edge of the paper and the beginning of the right margin, like the margin settings on a typewriter. The default, 76, begins the right margin at the 76th character space, leaving an approximately $\frac{1}{2}$-inch margin when 10-pitch characters are printed on $8\frac{1}{2}$-inch paper.

  If you're using wide paper, compressed or proportional print, or a different pitch, Quattro will be able to fit more characters on a line, so you'll want to increase your right margin accordingly. Compressed print on $8\frac{1}{2}$-inch paper can print as many as 120 characters on a line, depending on your printer. You may need to experiment to find the best setting for your printer. (See "Setup strings" for information on using printer commands, such as compressed print.)

- **Bottom** (0-32) determines the number of blank lines to leave at the bottom of each page. The default, 2, leaves approximately $\frac{1}{2}$ inch. If you include a footer in your printout, it is printed above this margin with two blank lines between it and the spreadsheet data.

To store the new settings as defaults, choose /Print I Layout I Update.

Note When printing spreadsheets, Quattro assumes a character size of $\frac{1}{10}$ of an inch horizontally and $\frac{1}{6}$ of an inch vertically and uses this to measure margins and page length. So for a 1-inch margin, specify 10, and for an 11-inch page length, specify 66. If you prefer to use inches or centimeters for measurement, use the /Print I Layout I Dimensions command (see page 91).

Changing page orientation

Normally, Quattro prints spreadsheets upright. With the /Print I Layout I Orientation command, you can print your spreadsheet horizontally.

```
┌─ Orientation ─┐
│               │
│ Portrait      │
│ Landscape     │
└───────────────┘
```

To change page orientation,

1. Choose /Print I Layout I Orientation.
2. Choose **Landscape** to print horizontally or **Portrait** to print vertically.

In order to print a spreadsheet in landscape mode, the /Print I Destination command must be set to **Graphics Printer** (see page 84). Otherwise, Quattro ignores the orientation setting.

 If you're using the 123-compatible menus, choose /Print I (pick print destination) I **Options** I **Direction**.

Setup strings

Printers often require special codes to invoke certain functions, such as compressed or letter-quality printing. The **Setup String** command lets you send such codes to your printer.

A *setup string* is a sequence of characters interpreted by the printer as one or more commands. Appendix E lists ASCII translations of codes used by popular printers. If you're using a printer that isn't listed, refer to its manual for the specific print commands (*Esc-X*, *Esc-G*, and so on). Then use the procedure described in Appendix E to translate the commands into ASCII codes (for example, \015 tells an IBM or Epson printer to use compressed print).

To enter a setup string,

1. Choose /**Print** I **Layout** I **Setup String**. Quattro prompts you for the string you want to send.
2. Type as many commands as you like (up to 39 characters). Do not use spaces to separate commands.

3. Press *Enter*. Quattro will send the setup string to the printer each time you choose **Spreadsheet Print**.

You can also embed setup strings in your spreadsheet by entering them in the first cell of a blank row. (If the row is not blank, Quattro does not print data following the string.) The row must not be part of a heading. Precede the string with two vertical bar characters (| |); for example, | |\015\0272. Embedded setup strings have greater flexibility because you can specify different codes for different areas of your spreadsheet. For example, you can specify column headings to be printed in bold type, then return to normal typeface for the rest of the spreadsheet.

If your printer offers compressed type, you can use setup strings in combination with other print settings to make wide spreadsheets fit on standard-sized paper. To print 132 characters per line on paper 8½ inches wide, set the right margin to 132 and enter \015 with the **Setup String** command to compress type (if you have an IBM or Epson printer). To print 254 characters on paper 14 inches wide, set the right margin to 254 and enter \015 with the **Setup String** command to compress type.

1-2-3

If you're using the 123-compatible menus, choose /**Print** | (pick print destination) | **Options** | **Setup**.

Resetting print options

To return the spreadsheet settings to the last saved default values,

1. Choose /**Print** | **Layout** | **Reset**.
2. Choose the area you want to reset from the menu Quattro displays.

```
┌─ Print Reset ─┐
│               │
│ All           │
│ Print Block   │
│ Headings      │
│ Layout        │
└───────────────┘
```

- **All** returns all spreadsheet print commands to their last saved default values.
- **Print Block** clears the setting for the /**Print** | **Block** command.
- **Headings** erases the cell block coordinates entered for the **Top** and **Left Heading** commands.
- **Layout** returns all commands on the Layout menu and submenus to their default settings, except for **Header** and **Footer**.

Note A /**Print** | **Layout** | **Reset Layout** command cannot undo a /**Print** | **Layout** | **Update** command. To return to the defaults in effect before updating, you must reenter the settings individually.

If you're using the 123-compatible menus, choose /**Print** | (pick print destination) | **Clear**.

Changing layout defaults

Quattro automatically saves all page layout settings with the current spreadsheet. The next time you retrieve that spreadsheet, the settings will be the same as they were when you saved the file.

If you want to save your page layout settings with the system configuration file, to be used as the settings for *all* new spread-sheets, use the Update command on the Layout menu.

When you choose /**Print** | **Layout** | **Update**, Quattro saves the current page layout settings as the new defaults. Any changes you made to the system defaults (on the **Options** menu) are saved as well. If there are defaults you've changed, but don't want updated, change them back to the initial default before choosing **Update**.

Caution! The /**Print** | **Layout** | **Update** command permanently erases the previous default settings from the Layout menu. Be sure you really want to replace those settings before using this command.

 If you're using the 123-compatible menus, choose /**Worksheet** | **Global** | **Default** | **Update**.

Changing the print format

The /**Print** | **Format** command offers two options. The default, **As Displayed**, prints data exactly as it appears onscreen.

The second option, **Cell-Formulas**, prints data in an entirely different format. It lists the contents of each cell, one per line, exactly as they appear on the input line when you highlight a cell. It includes each cell's address, format and width (if different from the default), and contents as entered, as well as any comments you've added to the regular cell contents (see page 66). When you print a spreadsheet in the **Cell-Formulas** format, Quattro ignores all other print formatting information (hard page breaks, footers, borders, and so on).

The following figure shows two printouts. The first is printed with the default, **As Displayed**. The second is printed with the Cell-Formulas option.

Figure 4.5
Two printout formats

```
Block (A1..B8) printed
with "As Displayed" option
```

```
Block (A1..B8) printed
with "Cell-Formulas" option
```

```
Budget for June
------------------------
Food                $108
Rent                $355
Car pmt             $292
Fun                 $200
========================
TOTAL               $955
```

```
A1: [W13] 'Budget for June
A2: [W13] \-
B2: \-
A3: [W13] 'Food
B3: (C0)  108
A4: [W13] 'Rent
B4: (C0)  355
A5: [W13] 'Car pmt
B5: (C0)  292
A6: [W13] 'Fun
B6: (C0)  200
A7: [W13] /=
B7: /=
A8: [W13] 'TOTAL
B8: (C0)  @SUM(B3..B6)
```

To print a list of cell contents,

1. Choose /**Print** I **Format** I **Cell-Formulas**.

2. Choose **S**preadsheet Print.

To return to regular spreadsheet format, choose /**Print** I **Format** I
As Displayed.

If you're using the 123-compatible menus, choose /**Print** I (pick
print destination) I **Options** I **Other** I **Cell-Formulas**.

Printing a graph

The Graph Print menu

```
===== Graph Print =====

Destination          ▶
Layout               ▶
Go
Write Graph File     ▶
Name
Quit
```

Procedures for printing a graph are similar to those for printing
spreadsheets, but the commands are separate. All commands that
affect graph printing appear on the /**Print** I **Graph Print** menu.

- **Destination** lets you specify where to send your graph: to the
  default graphics printer, to a disk file, or to the Screen
  Previewer.

- **Layout** contains all the commands that affect the page layout of
  a graph.

- **Go** sends your graph to the specified print destination.

- **Write Graph File** saves your graph in a special file to use with
  another program.

- **Name** changes the current graph to a different named graph, just as /Graph | Name | Display does, but does not display the graph onscreen.
- **Quit** returns you to the **Print** menu.

1-2-3 If you're using the 123-compatible menus, choose /**Print** | **Chart Print**.

The basic procedure

The basic procedure for printing a graph is as follows:

1. Display the spreadsheet containing the graph and make sure the current graph is the one you want to print.

2. Choose /**Print** | **Graph Print**.

3. If you want to change any of the graph print settings (for example, adjust graph size, change the margins, or print to a disk file instead of the printer), set the appropriate **Graph Print** commands.

4. Turn the printer on and adjust the paper alignment (if necessary) using the **Adjust Printer** commands (see page 83).

5. When you're ready to begin printing your graph, choose **Graph Print** | **Go**.

   A WAIT mode indicator appears on the right end of the status line while Quattro sends the data to the printer or file.

   If there is a problem with the printer (for example, if it's turned off or is out of paper), an "I/O error" warning appears on the status line and a confirmation menu offers two choices: **Abort** or **Continue**. Choose **Abort** to halt the command, or correct the situation and choose **Continue**.

6. When printing is complete, choose **Quit** or press *Esc* to return to the **Print** menu.

Ctrl Break   To abort printing before it's complete, press the *Ctrl* and *Break* keys at the same time. Depending on the size of your printer's memory buffer, printing may continue for awhile before stopping.

Graph printing messages

When you choose **Go** from the **Graph Print** menu, Quattro will sometimes display a message on the screen.

For example, Quattro might need to build fonts before printing (assuming the graph was created with one or more Bitstream fonts). While it builds the font files, you will see a "Now building font" message. After font building has finished, the message "Now printing (Ctrl-Break to stop)" appears. Quattro may also need to build fonts while preparing a screen preview, and then again for zooming purposes in the Screen Previewer. For more information about font building, see Appendix F, "Working with fonts."

If, for any reason, you would prefer to turn off font building, choose /Options | Graphics Quality | Draft to switch from final mode to draft mode (see Chapter 7).

Specifying print destination

The /Print | Graph Print | Destination menu lets you specify where the printout of your graph goes.

```
╔══ Destination ══╗
║ File            ║
║ Graphics Printer║
║ Screen Preview  ║
╚═════════════════╝
```

- **File** sends the graph to a disk file as though it were printing to the default graphics printer.

- **Graphics Printer** prints your graph on the printer specified as the default graphics printer with the /Options | Hardware | Printers | Default Printer command (see Chapter 7).

- **Screen Preview** displays your graph on the screen as it will appear when printed on the default graphics printer.

The following sections describe the **File** and **Screen Preview** options.

Printing to a file

If you want to save a graph for future printing, you can "print" it to a disk file.

To print a graph to a disk file,

1. Choose /Print | Graph Print | Destination | File. Quattro prompts you for a file name. If you're saving to a floppy disk, make sure to specify the correct drive.

2. Choose Graph Print | Go.

   Quattro now goes through the motions of printing to the default graphics printer; however, instead of actually sending bytes to a printer, it sends them to a disk file.

3. If you want to save another graph at the end of the file, make that graph current and choose **Graph Print | Go** again. You can save as many graphs as you like in the same file.

4. When Quattro finishes writing to the file, choose **Quit** to exit the menu.

To send a disk file to the printer from DOS, you must use the DOS COPY command:

```
COPY filename.PRN /B LPT1
```

This sends a binary file (/B) to the LPT1 printer port. If your printer is connected to a different port (such as COM1 or PRN), specify it instead of LPT1.

PostScript printers   PostScript printers offer a wide array of printing fonts. If you want to take advantage of these fonts in your printed graph file, specify a PostScript printer as your default graphics printer with the **/Options | Hardware | Printers | Default Printer** command (see Chapter 7). Then, when you choose **/Graph | Text | Font** (text area) **| Typeface**, you'll see additional PostScript fonts. If you choose them, they won't show up onscreen (Quattro will use a stand-in font instead), but Quattro will use them to print your graph.

Screen preview

Before you print a graph, you can use the Screen Previewer to view it onscreen as it will appear when printed on your default graphics printer. Just choose **/Print | Graph Print | Destination | Screen Preview**, then choose **Graph Print | Go**. Quattro displays your graph full screen, with the layout, fonts, page orientation, and other print specifications you selected. Press *G* (or click Guide on the menu bar) to display the page guide in zoom mode. The page guide shows you what part of your graph or spreadsheet is currently displayed with an outlined zoom box (see the following figure). To view a different area, move the zoom box with the arrow keys or a mouse.

Figure 4.6
A previewed graph

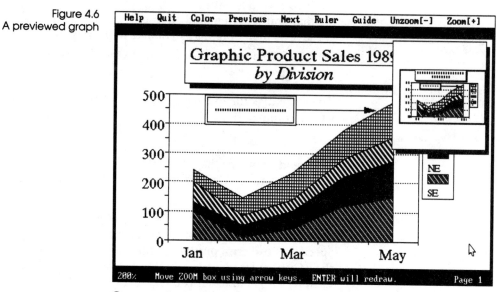

Once you're in the Screen Previewer, screen preview options are the same for spreadsheets and graphs. See "Screen preview" on page 86 for information.

Layout options

With the /Print I Graph Print I Layout menu, you can change the layout of a graph on the page. This includes changing the paper margins, graph size, page orientation, and aspect ratio.

```
┌─── Layout ───┐
│              │
│ Left Edge    │
│ Top Edge     │
│ Height       │
│ Width        │
│              │
│ Dimensions ►│
│ Orientation ►│
│ 4:3 Aspect ►│
│              │
│ Reset      ►│
│ Update       │
│ Quit         │
└──────────────┘
```

If you don't see the current settings, press +.

- **Left Edge** lets you specify how far from the left edge of the paper the graph should begin printing. The default is zero.

- **Top Edge** lets you specify how far from the top edge of the paper the graph should begin printing. The default is zero.

- **Height** lets you specify the height of the graph. The default is six inches.

- **Width** lets you specify the width of the graph. The default is eight inches.

- **Dimensions** lets you specify layout dimensions in inches (the default) or centimeters.

- **Orientation** lets you print the graph vertically (portrait) or horizontally (landscape). The default is **Portrait**.

- **4:3 Aspect** preserves the default 4:3 aspect ratio of a graph so no distortion occurs when you print it, view it onscreen, or insert it into a spreadsheet, no matter what dimensions you assign to it.
- **Reset** reinstates the last saved graph layout settings.
- **Update** saves the current graph layout settings as the new defaults.
- **Quit** returns you to the current Graph Print menu.

Once you've adjusted all your graph print options, you can print the current graph by choosing **Go** from the **Graph Print** menu.

Graph margins

The **Left Edge** and **Top Edge** commands tell Quattro where to begin printing the graph. Quattro then tries to fill the space allotted. If you want to print a graph with a larger left or top margin, increase these settings accordingly.

The **Height** and **Width** commands tell Quattro to print a graph with particular dimensions, which affects the size of the right and bottom margins. For example, if you're printing on paper $8\frac{1}{2}$ inches wide, and you want to leave 2-inch margins on both sides of the page, specify 2 inches with the **Left Edge** command and $4\frac{1}{2}$ inches with the **Width** command.

By default, Quattro measures margins and dimensions for graphs in inches. You can change this default with the **/Print | Graph Print | Dimensions** command.

You can specify any width from 1 to 8 inches and any height from 1 to 10 inches. If you specify a width or height outside of these ranges, Quattro defaults to full size. By default, Quattro preserves the 4:3 aspect ratio of a graph unless you set **/Print | Graph Print | Layout | 4:3 Aspect** to **No**. When you set the **4:3 Aspect** command to **Yes**, Quattro compresses or expands the graph to fit whatever dimensions you specify. See the next section for more about the aspect ratio of a graph.

Preserving a graph's shape

By default, Quattro reproduces a given graph so that its height and width are always in a ratio of four to three. Its proportions stay the same regardless of **Layout** menu settings when you print it, view it, preview it, or insert it in a spreadsheet. This is the "natural" look of the graph, matching what you see when you view or annotate. For best results, especially with annotated graphs, you should leave **4:3 Aspect** set to **Yes**.

If you want your graph to stretch to fit the dimensions you've assigned to it and not necessarily keep the same proportions, set /Print I Graph Print I Layout I 4:3 Aspect to **No**. When you turn the default aspect ratio off, you allow Quattro to distort the shape of your graph to fit the margins you've chosen or the block you've specified in a spreadsheet. With **4:3** Aspect set to **No**, a graph fits as exactly as possible into a given layout or spreadsheet block. With the default aspect ratio on, Quattro determines the largest 4:3 shape that fits inside the allocated space and uses that. For example, the following figure shows a graph inserted into block C1..F20 of a spreadsheet with **4:3** Aspect set to **Yes**. Notice how the graph preserves its height to width ratio of four to three, even though the block is not the same shape.

Figure 4.7
A graph inserted with 4:3
Aspect on

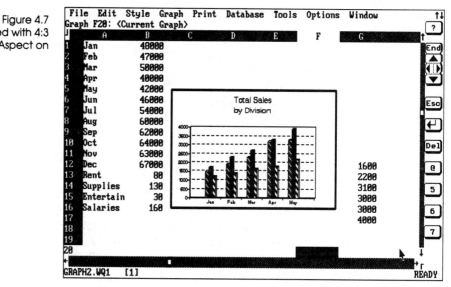

In the following figure, **4:3** Aspect has been set to **No** and the *F9* key pressed to repaint the screen. Notice how the inserted graph stretches itself to fill the C1..F20 block.

Figure 4.8
A graph inserted with 4:3
Aspect off

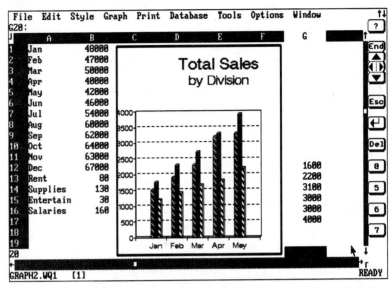

Another example: Suppose your graph has a specified width of 2 inches and a height of 8 inches. With **4:3** Aspect set to **No**, Quattro produces a long, skinny graph. With **4:3** Aspect set to **Yes**, the same layout settings result in a graph with a width of 2 inches and a height of 1½ inches, because these are the largest values that fit into the prescribed space with the correct aspect ratio. Another example is a graph with a width of 8 inches and a height of 2 inches. With the default aspect ratio on, Quattro produces a graph with a width of 2.66 inches and a height of 2 inches, which preserves the 4:3 aspect ratio.

Changing page orientation

Just as with a printing a spreadsheet, you can print a graph either in portrait orientation (vertically) or landscape orientation (horizontally). Choose **/Print I Graph Print I Layout I Orientation** and choose either **Portrait** or **Landscape**.

The following figures show the difference in graph layout between portrait and landscape mode:

Portrait:

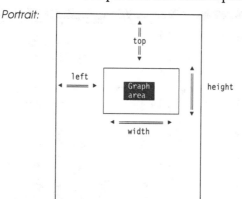

Landscape:

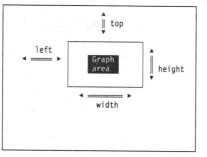

Writing to a special file

If you want to use your graph with another program, save it in a special file with the /Graph | Graph Print | Write Graph File command. When you choose this command, Quattro displays a menu with three options.

- **EPS File** stores the graph in an encapsulated PostScript file, which you can use with many word-processing programs, including Borland's Sprint.

- **PIC File** stores the graph in a file for future printing with Lotus 1-2-3.

- **Quit** returns you to the **Graph Print** menu.

See page 103 for information about graph files and PostScript printers.

P A R T

2

Making changes

5

Changing data in your spreadsheet

The data you enter into a spreadsheet is never final. You can
always add information or change existing data. This chapter
describes the changes you can make in a spreadsheet using the
Edit menu.

The Edit menu

```
┌──────── Edit ────────┐
│ Copy          Ctrl-C │
│ Move          Ctrl-M │
│ Erase Block   Ctrl-E │
│ Undo                 │
├──────────────────────┤
│ Insert        Ctrl-I ▶│
│ Delete               ▶│
├──────────────────────┤
│ Names                ▶│
│ Fill                 │
│ Values               │
│ Transpose            │
│ Search & Replace     ▶│
└──────────────────────┘
```

To access commands on the **Edit** menu, choose /Edit from the
menu bar.

- **Copy** duplicates the contents of a cell block and writes them
  one or more times into any area of the spreadsheet you specify.

- **Move** transfers a cell block from one part of the spreadsheet to
  another.

- **Erase Block** deletes the contents of a cell block.

- **Undo** lets you reverse certain kinds of operations, such as
  moving, copying, or deleting a block, erasing a spreadsheet,
  deleting block or graph names, and more.

- **Insert** places one or more blank rows or columns into the
  spreadsheet.

- **Delete** removes one or more rows or columns from the
  spreadsheet.

- **Names** lets you assign names to cell blocks for easier and more accurate reference. You can also use this command to modify and delete block names and create a table of existing names.
- **Fill** enters a sequence of numbers in a cell block.
- **Values** converts all formulas in a given block to their end values.
- **Transpose** reverses the arrangement of data within a block so that data displayed in rows is displayed in columns and vice versa.
- **Search & Replace** lets you search through the spreadsheet for all instances of a certain label or value and change them automatically.

You can also copy and move blocks from one spreadsheet to another. The destination spreadsheet, however, must be open.

To exit the Edit menu without choosing a command, press *Esc* to reactivate the menu bar or press *Ctrl-Break* to return to the spreadsheet.

Specifying a cell block

A *block* is any rectangular group of spreadsheet cells (including a single cell). Most of the Edit menu commands work on a given block of cells. When you choose a command, Quattro asks you to specify the cell block to be affected and presents a default block, which is either the current cell or the last block the command was used with. You can press *Enter* to operate on the default block or specify another block using one of the following methods:

- Enter the coordinates for two cells in opposite corners (usually the top left and bottom right cells), separated by one or more periods; for example, A3..C10.

We discuss naming blocks on page 127.

- Enter the name of a cell block you previously named with the /Edit | Names | Create command.
- Press *F3* to see a choice list of block names and choose one from the list.
- Use the cursor-movement keys or a mouse to point out the block, highlighting it on the screen.

For details on pointing, see "Pointing out cell blocks" on page 71.

Shift	F7

Select

You can also specify a block of cells for a command to work on *before* you choose the command—either by selecting the block with the Select key (*Shift-F7*) or by pointing out the block with a mouse.

To select a block with the Select key,

1. Move the cell selector to a corner cell of the block.
2. Press the Select key (*Shift-F7*). Quattro displays the EXT (extend block) indicator on the status line.
3. Move to the opposite corner of the block.

With the block selected, choose the command you want to work on that block. To cancel the selection without using a command on it, press *Esc*.

To select a block in EXT mode using a mouse, click one corner of the block, move to the opposite corner, and hold down the right button while you click the left.

Note   If you're working with multiple spreadsheets, you can specify a block within a different spreadsheet to use commands on (except for the /Edit | Search & Replace command). For more information on working with multiple spreadsheets, see Chapter 9, "Manipulating windows."

Copying a block

The /Edit | Copy command duplicates the contents of one or more cells. You can use it to do the following actions, either within one spreadsheet or from one spreadsheet to another:

- copy one cell to many cells
- copy one block to another block
- copy one column to many columns
- copy one row to many rows

To copy a block of cells,

1. Choose /Edit | Copy. Quattro prompts you for the block you want to copy (the *source block*). The default block is the current cell.

Press F3 at the prompt for a list of existing block names.

2. Press *Enter* to copy the contents of the current cell, or specify a different block. Quattro now prompts you for a destination.

3. If you want to copy the block to a different spreadsheet, open that spreadsheet or press *Shift-F6* until it's active (or press *Alt-n*, where *n* is the number of the window you want to jump to). (See page 123 for more information on passing data between spreadsheets.)

4. Specify the upper left corner cell of the block you want to copy the data to. Or, if you want to place copies of the source block into adjacent rows or columns, specify a block of cells.

Quattro copies the data in the source block to the destination block. It copies any cell-formatting information as well; for example, alignment, display format, or cell protection. The contents of the source block are unaffected.

 Ctrl-C is the default shortcut for the /Edit I Copy command.

Copy   You can undo a Copy command by choosing /Edit I Undo (or pressing *Alt-F5*) as long as you enabled the Undo command before the copy operation took place. See "Undoing a change" later in this chapter for details.

To copy a block of data *and* transpose the columns and rows of the block, use the /Edit I Transpose command (see the end of this chapter).

To copy a block of data *without* copying any of the formulas that calculated the data, use the /Edit I Values command (see "Converting formulas to their values" later in this chapter).

1-2-3   If you're using the 123-compatible menu trees, choose /Copy.

Copying in reverse

You can copy a block of data from another part of the spreadsheet or from another spreadsheet to the *current* area (instead of the other way around):

1. Choose /Edit I Copy.

2. Press *Esc* to delete the current cell coordinates from the input line.

3. If the data is in another spreadsheet window, press *Shift-F6* until it's active (or press *Alt-n*, where *n* is the number of the window you want to jump to).

4. Move the selector to point out the block you want to copy.

5. Press *Enter.* The selector returns to its original position on the input line, and Quattro prompts you for the destination block.

6. Press *Enter.*

Quattro copies the block to your original position in the spreadsheet.

Copying formulas

If you copy a cell block containing both a formula and any cells referenced by that formula, Quattro automatically updates the formula to reference the new cell positions. This is very helpful when you want to duplicate parts of a spreadsheet, or when you want to copy a formula to, say, add the figures in each column. But things aren't so simple when you want the references outside the copy block to remain the same.

Normally, cell references in a formula are considered *relative*. This means that Quattro keeps track of each cell reference by remembering its position in relation to the formula cell, *not* by its address. The difference between relative and absolute cell addresses is much like the difference between these two directions to a house:

- "Go to the next corner, turn left, go two more blocks, turn right, and stop at the second house on the left."
- "Go to the blue house on the corner of Clinton and Darwin: 319 Clinton St."

The first set of directions is valid only from the point at which you received it. Try using it from a different direction and you'll probably get lost. The second set of directions, though not as explicit, will always get you to the same house.

For example, if you enter the formula +B3+C2 in cell B2, Quattro would interpret it (during copying) as "Add the value in the cell directly below this one to the value in the cell to the right." If you copy all three cells as a block to another part of the spreadsheet, the formula is still valid and doesn't need adjusting. But if you copy the formula alone to cell H6, the formula changes to H7+I6 and evaluates to zero, which probably isn't what you intended (see the following figure).

Figure 5.1
Copying a formula and its
cell references

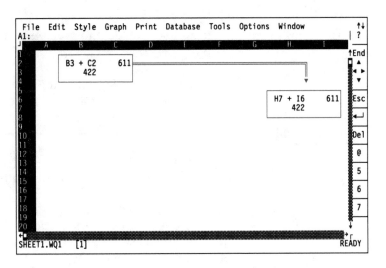

*B2..C3 has moved to H6..I7.
Notice that Quattro has
adjusted the formula to
reflect the positions of the
data cells relative to the
formula cell's position.*

Absolute addresses

If you *don't* want Quattro to adjust your cell references when you copy a formula, specify the cells in a formula as *absolute*. An absolute cell reference always refers to the original cell address, regardless of where the formula is copied to.

You can specify all or part of a cell address as absolute. Simply insert a dollar sign ($) before the coordinate you want to remain fixed. For example,

- $B$6 makes both coordinates of address B6 absolute.
- $B6 locks the address into column B, but lets the row coordinate be relative.
- B$6 locks the address into row 6, but allows the column coordinate to be relative.

Look at the example in the previous figure: If you copy the formula in cell B2 to H6, Quattro makes the following adjustments to the formula given these specifications:

+$B$3+C2	→	+$B$3+I6
+$B3+C2	→	+$B7+I6
+B$3+C2	→	+H$3+I6

F4
Abs

The Abs key (*F4*) makes inserting dollar signs in an address very easy. After entering an address in a formula, press *F4* once to make the whole address absolute. Press it again to make only the row absolute, again to make only the column absolute, and a fourth time to make the entire address relative again. Table 5.1 shows the effects of pressing the Abs key (*F4*).

Number of times pressed	Cell reference
starting reference	B6
1	$B$6
2	B$6
3	$B6
4	B6

You can use the Abs key (*F4*) when entering or editing a formula. You can also use it in Point mode without disturbing the position of the cell selector.

Cell blocks are also relative, whether they are named or not. You can specify a named block as absolute by preceding its name with a dollar sign. You cannot, however, use a block name to make that block partially absolute. To specify a named block as partially absolute, you have to refer to the block by its coordinates.

Whether a reference is absolute or relative, you can copy only the *value* of a formula without copying the formula or replace a formula with its calculated value. Use the /Edit | Values command (see "Converting formulas to their values" later in this chapter).

Making multiple copies of cells

You can make multiple copies of cells in a single column or row using a single copy operation. Simply extend the destination block to include more than one row or column.

For example, to enter a line of hyphens across a row (see the following figure), you could fill the first cell in the row with hyphens (enter \-), then use the /Edit | Copy command to enter hyphens in the rest of the cells in the row. Simply specify the block of cells you want as the destination block.

This is an easy way to enter many similar formulas in one sweep. For example, to produce a total at the end of each column of the spreadsheet shown in the following figure, you could enter

    B18

as the source cell, and

    C18..E18

as the destination cells. Because the formula in B18 contains *relative* cell references, Quattro adjusts them to reference similar cells in each column.

Figure 5.2
Copying a formula into
several cells

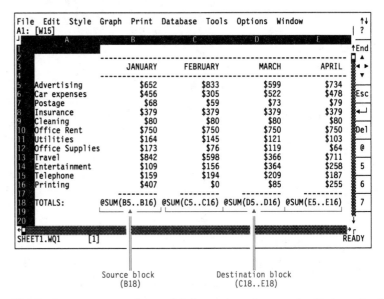

Similarly, you can make multiple copies of several cells in a single row or column. For example, to copy the column headings in row 3 into rows 4, 5, and 6, enter

    B3..E3

as the source block, and

    B4..E6 **or** B4..B6

as the destination block (specifying the first column of the block is sufficient). Quattro then copies the headings three times, as shown in the following figure:

Figure 5.3
Making multiple copies of
headings

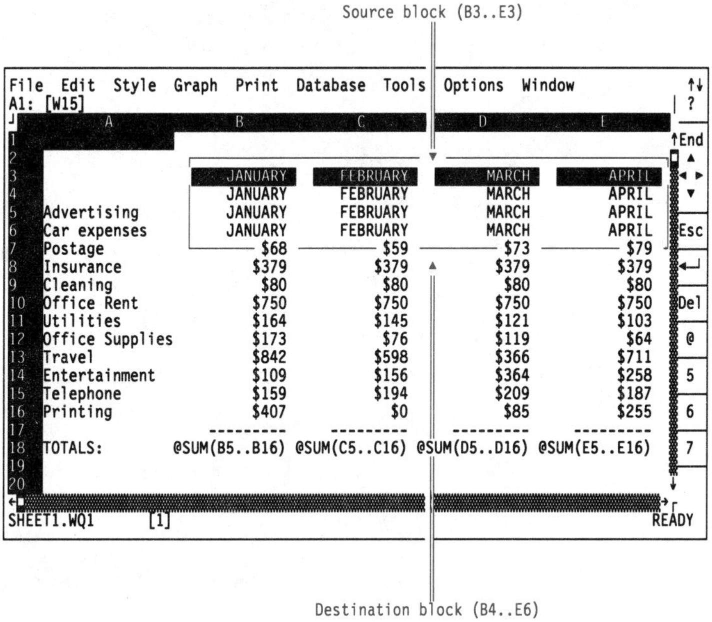

Source block (B3..E3)

```
 File  Edit  Style  Graph  Print  Database  Tools│ Options  Window            ↑↓
A1: [W15]                                                                    │ ?
┌─────────────A──────────B──────────C──────────D──────────E──────────┐  ↑End
1│                                                                    │      ▲
2│                                                                    ▼     ◄ ►
3│                    JANUARY    FEBRUARY     MARCH      APRIL                ▼
4│                    JANUARY    FEBRUARY     MARCH      APRIL
5│ Advertising        JANUARY    FEBRUARY     MARCH      APRIL              Esc
6│ Car expenses       JANUARY    FEBRUARY     MARCH      APRIL
7│ Postage               $68         $59        $73        $79              ←┘
8│ Insurance            $379        $379     ▲ $379       $379
9│ Cleaning              $80         $80        $80        $80
10│ Office Rent          $750        $750       $750       $750             Del
11│ Utilities            $164        $145       $121       $103
12│ Office Supplies      $173         $76       $119        $64              @
13│ Travel               $842        $598       $366       $711
14│ Entertainment        $109        $156       $364       $258              5
15│ Telephone            $159        $194       $209       $187
16│ Printing             $407          $0        $85       $255              6
17│
18│ TOTALS:        @SUM(B5..B16) @SUM(C5..C16) @SUM(D5..D16) @SUM(E5..E16)   7
19│
20│
└─────────────────────────────────────────────────────────────────────┘
SHEET1.WQ1        [1]                                            READY
```

Destination block (B4..E6)

Moving a block

You can move blocks
between open spreadsheets
(see page 123).

The /Edit I **Move** command moves the contents of a block of cells
from where it is to another part of the spreadsheet or to a different
spreadsheet. Quattro overwrites any existing data in the new
location.

To move a block of cells,

1. Choose /Edit I **Move**. Quattro prompts you for the block you
   want to move. The default block is the current cell.

2. Press *Enter* to move the contents of the current cell, or specify a
   new block of cells. Quattro now prompts you for a destination.
   If you want to move the block to a different spreadsheet, press
   Shift-F6 until you're in that spreadsheet (or *Alt-n*, where *n* is the
   number of the window you want to jump to).

Press F3 at the prompt for a
list of existing block names.

3. Specify the upper left corner cell of the block you want to
   move the data to.

Quattro moves the data in the source block to the cells in the
destination block and automatically adjusts any affected formulas

in the spreadsheet. Along with the data, it moves any cell-formatting information, such as alignment or numeric format, from the cells in the source block.

1-2-3

If you're using the 123-compatible menus, choose /**Move** instead of /Edit I **Move**.

Move

Ctrl-M is the default shortcut for the /Edit I **Move** command.

The next three sections describe certain side effects that can occur when you move data from one place to another, into a referenced cell, or to and from established blocks.

Effects on formulas

If you move a cell that contains a formula, its cell references remain intact, regardless of whether they are absolute or relative. Quattro adjusts the cell references only when you copy a formula. (We discuss absolute and relative addresses on page 116.)

If you move a formula into another spreadsheet without moving the cells it references, Quattro automatically links the two spread-sheets so the formula still references the same cells in the original spreadsheet. If you move the formula back to the first spread-sheet, Quattro removes the links.

If you move a cell that is individually referenced by a formula, Quattro automatically updates the formula to reference the new location, even if you've specified the reference as absolute. For example, if you move the contents of cell B4 to B6, Quattro automatically revises any formula referencing B4 to reference B6. If you move B4 into cell B6 of a spreadsheet named TAX, the formula's reference changes to [TAX]B6.

If you move a cell that is contained within a block referenced by a formula, the formula still references the same block. However, if you move any of the block's corner cells, the block is extended or contracted to reflect the new location. For example, if A30 contains the formula @SUM(B4..F12), and you move the data in B6, the formula in A30 remains the same. If you move the data in cell F12 to D14, however, the formula changes to @SUM(B4..D14). (See Figure 5.5 on page 122.) The exception to this is if you move a corner cell into another spreadsheet. In this case, references to the block aren't affected.

User's Guide

Effects on cell references

If you move data into a cell that has been explicitly referenced by a formula or block name, the reference becomes invalid. This includes both references to single cells and to coordinates used to define a block. Quattro replaces all references to the block in formulas with ERR, and therefore the cell displays ERR. If you named the block, Quattro shows the block coordinates for it in the block names list as ERR. Because ERR values indicate an error, they can't be used in calculations. This protects you from accidentally writing over a cell referenced by a formula.

For example, in the following figure, cells C5..D8 are referenced by the formula in cell F5. When you move the contents of A3 to C5, the formula in F5 becomes @SUM(ERR) and displays ERR in the cell. The block names list would also show INPUT as ERR. If you moved data into cell C8 or D5, there would be no problem: Although they are corner blocks, they are not used as *coordinates* to define the block (C5 and D8 are the coordinates).

Figure 5.4
Moving data to a block
coordinate

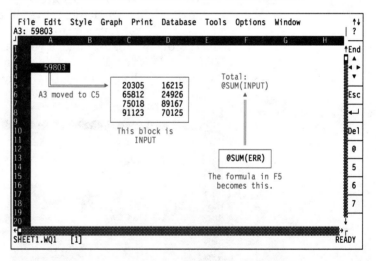

This feature ensures that formulas do not display the wrong values if you accidentally move data into their reference cells. The ERR values are easy to spot, and you can immediately correct them.

To reverse a move operation that has caused errors, use the Undo command (*/EU* or *Alt-F5*) immediately after the move. Undo must be enabled *before* you use it. You cannot salvage the formulas by using /Edit | **Move** command again to move the data back to where it was.

If you need to move data into a cell that is referenced by a formula or named, use the /Edit | **Copy** command, then erase the original data. The /Edit | **Copy** command will not turn cell or block references into ERR.

If you've performed other operations since the move, use the Transcript utility to undo it (see Chapter 17, "Using Transcript").

Effects on blocks

If you move an established block (a block that you have named or referenced within a formula) to a new location, Quattro automatically updates the block name or reference to reflect the new location. If you move only part of an established block, however, complications can arise.

The critical cells of any block are the *coordinate cells* (the upper left and lower right cells). If you move either one of these cells, the block extends (or contracts) to use the address of the new location as a coordinate. For example, if you define the block PRINT2 as B4..F12 and move cell F12 to D14, the new block for PRINT2 automatically changes to B4..D14. Figure 5.5 illustrates this.

Figure 5.5
Moving the coordinate of an established block

Moving the contents of F12 to D14 redefines the block.

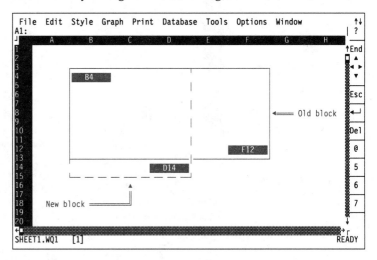

Moving any of the non-coordinate cells of a block anywhere except to the coordinate cells doesn't affect the block's definition or any references to it. If you move data into one of the coordinate cells of an established block, the references to the block display ERR (see the previous section, "Effects on cell references").

Passing data between spreadsheets

Although you can work in only one window at a time, there are many commands that let you jump back and forth between windows. For example, you can use the /Edit I Copy command to copy data from one spreadsheet to another. All commands that prompt you for a cell block allow you to specify a block in a different spreadsheet (except /Edit I Search & Replace I Block).

To reference a block in a different spreadsheet, you can point to the block or type in the reference:

■ To point to a cell block in a different spreadsheet, activate the spreadsheet first, then point out the block as you would normally. When you press *Enter*, Quattro puts you back in the original spreadsheet. The input line shows the spreadsheet name in brackets followed by the block coordinates or name.

■ To type in a block reference in another spreadsheet, precede the block coordinates or name with the spreadsheet's name in square brackets; for example, [TAX]A1..G10.

The most common way to pass data between spreadsheets is by moving or copying data.

To move or copy a block of data *to* another spreadsheet,

1. Choose /Edit I Copy or /Edit I Move. Quattro prompts you for the block you want to copy or move (the source block).

2. Press *Enter* to copy or move the contents of the current cell, or specify a different block. Quattro prompts you for a destination.

Next window

3. Type in the destination block coordinates or name, preceded by the spreadsheet's file specification; for example,

    [TAXES]B6..G10

If the spreadsheet is in a different directory, include the directory path as well; for example,

    [\QUATTRO\TAX]BLOCKNAME

Or, go into the spreadsheet you want to copy or move the data to, and position the cell selector in the top left cell of the destination block.

4. Press *Enter*. Quattro copies or moves the data into the destination spreadsheet and returns to the source spreadsheet.

1-2-3

If you're using the 123-compatible menus, choose /**C**opy or /**M**ove.

If you move formulas into a different spreadsheet without moving the cells they reference along with them, Quattro automatically inserts links to the references so that they refer to the same cells in the original spreadsheet.

Tip   If you have a set of formulas, macros, or spreadsheet headings that you use often, you can copy them into a separate file to use as a spreadsheet template. Then, when you want to create a new spreadsheet, you can just copy the template and begin with that. (See Chapter 8 for more information.)

To copy or move a block of data *from* another spreadsheet,

1. Choose /**Edit** I **C**opy or /**Edit** I **M**ove. Quattro prompts you for the block you want to copy or move (the source block).

2. Type in the source block coordinates or name, preceded by the spreadsheet's file specification; for example,

    `[\QUATTRO\BUDGET]TOTALS`

    Or, go into the spreadsheet you want to copy or move the data from and use the selector to point out the source block.

3. Press *Enter*. The selector returns to its original position on the input line, and Quattro prompts you for the destination block.

4. If necessary, move the selector to the top left corner of the new location or type in the cell's address, then press *Enter*.

1-2-3

If you're using the 123-compatible menus, choose /**C**opy or /**M**ove.

When you copy data between spreadsheets, it's always easier to use block names instead of coordinates. If there are blocks you expect to copy into several spreadsheets, name them first with the /**Edit** I **N**ames I **C**reate command.

You can also use the /**Tools** I **C**ombine command to copy data from another spreadsheet (see Chapter 12). You can use this command to insert data directly (overwriting any existing data), subtract values in another spreadsheet from existing values, or add values from another spreadsheet to existing values.

Erasing a block

To erase the data within a single cell, simply move the cell selector to it and press *Del*. To erase the contents of a *block* of cells, use the /Edit I Erase Block command:

1. Choose /Edit I Erase Block. Quattro prompts you for the block you want to erase. The default block is the current cell.
2. Specify the block you want to erase and press *Enter*. If you want to erase a named block, press *F3* at the prompt for a list of block names and choose the name from the list.

The contents of the specified block disappear. However, the format and alignment specifications remain with the blank cell.

Erase Block

Ctrl-E is the default shortcut for the /Edit I Erase Block command.

Another way to delete a block of data is to select the block first (using the Select key, *Shift-F7*), then press *Del*.

To erase a block of data with a mouse, just point out the block, then press *Del*.

If you accidentally erase a block of data, use the **Undo** command (*/EU* or *Alt-F5*) to bring it back. Undo must be enabled *before* you use it. Undo reverses the last operation you did. To undo an operation you did earlier, use the Transcript utility (see Chapter 17, "Using Transcript").

1-2-3

If you're using the 123-compatible menus, choose /Range I Erase.

If /Options I Protection is set to Enable, you won't be able to erase any block unless all its cells have been explicitly unprotected with /Style I Protection I Unprotect (see Chapters 6 and 7).

To delete entire rows or columns of the spreadsheet, use the /Edit I Delete command (see the end of this chapter).

To delete the contents of an entire spreadsheet, choose /File I Erase (see Chapter 8). Quattro erases all the data within that file, leaving an empty file open. To delete a spreadsheet file, use the File Manager utility (see Chapter 10).

Undoing a change

Quattro comes with a special Undo command (/Edit I Undo or *Alt-F5*) that you can use to reverse certain kinds of operations *after* you've carried them out. Before you can use the Undo command, you must enable it:

1. Choose /Options I Other I Undo.
2. Choose Enable.
3. If you want the Undo command enabled from now on, press *Esc*, then choose Update from the Options menu.

Note An error message displays if you choose /Edit I Undo or press *Alt-F5* without first enabling the Undo command.

Enabling the Undo command (/Edit I Undo or *Alt-F5*) slows down Quattro's operation slightly, but it will be well worth it when you need to undo a major mistake, like erasing the spreadsheet.

Undo

Alt-F5 is the default shortcut for the /Edit I Undo command.

The /Edit I Undo command cannot undo every operation Quattro performs, but it can reverse the following types of operations:

- changes to spreadsheet entries, including new entries and deletions
- named graph deletions
- block name deletions
- retrieving files
- erasing spreadsheets

To undo named graph and block name deletions, Quattro must be in Ready mode (without a menu displayed).

You can't undo changes to command settings, format settings, File Manager file manipulations or deletions, or spreadsheet style commands such as line-drawing, fonts, and shading.

Undo always works on the last "undo-able" operation, no matter how long ago you performed it. For example, suppose you use /Edit I Erase Block to delete a cell block, then make several block formatting changes. Suddenly you realize you deleted the wrong data. You can still use Undo to reverse the /Edit I Erase Block command and retrieve your data.

You can also use the Transcript utility to undo operations you performed at any time during the current session. With Transcript, you can rerun entire work sessions or parts of sessions, omitting the part you want to undo (see Chapter 17).

Tip The Undo command is handy for checking out the effects of a change before committing to it. For example, if your spreadsheet calculates your company's net profit, you could experiment with the effects of changing an influencing factor, such as salaries or rent. Each time you make a projected change, choose /Edit | Undo or press *Alt-F5* to bring the spreadsheet back to its previous state.

 If you're using the 123-compatible menu trees, choose /Worksheet | Global | Default | Other | Undo to enable the Undo command, and /Worksheet | Undo to use it.

Using named blocks

If there's a block you expect to refer to later, either within a formula or macro or in response to a command prompt, you can make it easier to reference the block by assigning a name to it, such as JANSALES. You can then refer to the block by name instead of entering the coordinates or pointing out the block. Although this is a completely optional feature, it has several important advantages:

- Names are usually easier to remember than block coordinates.
- If you move the contents of a named block elsewhere in the spreadsheet or to another spreadsheet, Quattro still associates the name with the same data, regardless of the new block coordinates.
- Referencing block names instead of block coordinates in a formula can make the formula much easier to read and to understand. For example, the formula *Price – Cost* makes immediate sense, whereas you'd have to study the spreadsheet to know what B15 – D8 is about.
- Using block names increases accuracy. If you make a typing error in a block name reference, Quattro doesn't accept the name. If you make an error in typing block coordinates, you operate on the wrong block. This can be crucial in commands like /Edit | Erase Block.
- When you link to another spreadsheet, you won't need to go into the other spreadsheet to find the block coordinates.

- It's easier to reference a block in another spreadsheet when you've named the block. Just precede the block name with the spreadsheet name in square brackets.
- If you ever intend to reference a block within a macro, giving it a block name is highly recommended for accuracy.

You can assign a name to any block in the spreadsheet, from a single cell to the entire spreadsheet. Once you've named a block, Quattro stores the name and recalls it each time you load that spreadsheet file. It's a good idea to name critical cell blocks as you build a spreadsheet, then always reference the names instead of the block coordinates. Consider the following formula used to calculate the monthly payment on a house:

@PMT(B3,B4/B6,B542B6)

Unless you've memorized the format for the @PMT function, it's hard to make much sense of this formula. However, if you named each of the cells involved according to its contents, the formula would be much easier to read:

@PMT(PRICE,INTEREST/MONTHS,TERM42MONTHS)

Not only would you be less likely to make mistakes while entering the formula, but any problems with the formula would be easier to pinpoint.

Caution! If you delete the contents of or move data into a named block's coordinate cell(s), the block becomes invalid. Any formulas referencing the named block display ERR to indicate that the formulas no longer reference the data they used to.

Referencing a block name

To reference a named block, you can type the block name or choose it from a choice list of existing block names for the current spreadsheet. To display this choice list while editing a formula or when Quattro prompts for a block, press *F3*. Use the arrow keys to scroll through the list. To enter a block name from the list on the input line, simply highlight it on the list and press *Enter*. To display the list while entering or editing a formula, the cursor must be to the right of an operator or open parenthesis. For example, in the formula

$\boxed{\text{F3}}$
Choices

+C742@SUM(B6..D19)

you can display a block names list after typing +, *, or ((open parenthesis). You can also enter a block name by typing it.

To expand the names list to include block coordinates, press the Expand key (+ on the numeric keypad). Press the Contract key (– on the numeric keypad) to remove coordinates. Press *F3* again to "zoom" the names list to full screen or shrink it back down.

The Names menu

To assign, delete, and create a table of block names, use the /Edit I Names command, which brings up the **Names** menu.

- **Create** assigns a name to a block of cells.
- **Delete** removes an assigned block name.
- **Labels** automatically assigns block names to single cells using adjacent labels.
- **Reset** deletes all assigned block names.
- **Make Table** creates a table of existing block names and their coordinates and writes it into a block of the spreadsheet.

If you're using the 123-compatible menus, choose /**Range** I **Name**.

Keep the following guidelines in mind when naming blocks:

- Block names can be up to 15 characters long.
- Use any keyboard characters (*A* to *Z*, 0 to 9, punctuation marks, and special characters such as #, $, or %).
- Avoid using operator characters (+, –, *, and /) and spaces, especially at the end of the name, since these characters could be misinterpreted in a formula.
- Uppercase and lowercase letters are equivalent; in other words, *INPUT* is the same as *input*. Quattro always uses uppercase letters to display block names in formulas.

Block names can define overlapping areas. For example, the following group of block names is acceptable:

COMPANY   A1..C10
ADDRESS   A3..C4
TOTALS   A10..M10

Aside from the restrictions of system memory, there is no limit to the number of block names you can assign to a spreadsheet.

Caution!   Although it's possible to assign more than one name to the same block, this isn't advised. Since changing the coordinates of a named block updates all references to that block (whether referenced by that name or not), Quattro may update references that you don't want changed. For example, if cell C9 has two names, BOB and TOM, and you reassign BOB to D1, TOM also changes to D1. To change the name of a block, you must delete the name, then assign a new name to the block.

The next five sections describe the options on the **Names** menu.

Naming a block   You can create any number of block names for a spreadsheet. Quattro stores the block names with the spreadsheet in which they were created.

To assign a name to a block of cells,

1. Choose /**Edit** | **Names** | **Create**. Quattro prompts you for a block name and displays a scrollable list of existing block names for the spreadsheet.
2. Enter a block name that isn't included on the list. Quattro prompts you for the coordinates of the block you're naming and shows the current cell as the default.
3. Press *Enter* to name the current cell or specify a new block.

To change the block assigned to an existing block name, choose /**Edit** | **Names** | **Create** and choose the name from the displayed list. Then specify the new block you want to use for the name.

 If you're using the 123-compatible menus, choose /**Range** | **Name** | **Create**.

To change the name of a block, delete the existing block name first, then assign the new name to the block.

Deleting a block name   You can delete a block name without affecting the spreadsheet block itself. Quattro converts any formulas referencing the name to reference the block's coordinates; their results are unchanged.

For example, if a formula references a block named TOTAL, like @SUM(TOTAL), and you delete TOTAL from the list of block names, the formula adjusts to reference the cell coordinates of the block, like this—@SUM(B1..B20).

To delete a block name,

1. Choose /Edit | Names | Delete. Quattro prompts you for the block name to delete and displays a list of existing names.
2. Choose a block name from the list, or type a name in.

If you're using the 123-compatible menus, choose /Range | Name | Delete.

Note If you delete a block name by accident, use the Undo command (*/EU* or *Alt-F5*) immediately afterward to restore it. Undo must be enabled *before* you use it. If you've performed other operations that can't be undone in the meantime, use the Transcript utility to bring back the name (see Chapter 17, "Using Transcript").

To delete the data stored *within* a block, use the /Edit | Erase Block command (see page 125).

To delete *all* block names, use the /Edit | Names | Reset command (see the next section).

Deleting all block names The /Edit | Names | Reset command deletes *all* block names in your spreadsheet.

To delete all block names,

1. Choose /Edit | Names | Reset.
2. Press *Y* to choose Yes from the "Delete all named blocks?" confirmation menu.

If you're using the 123-compatible menus, **Reset** immediately deletes your block names without displaying any confirmation menu. This is compatible with Lotus 1-2-3.

Although choosing /Edit | Names | Reset immediately deletes all block names in the spreadsheet from memory, the spreadsheet itself is not affected. Quattro simply alters any formulas that reference named blocks so that they refer to the coordinates of the blocks instead of the names.

Note If you use this command accidentally, use the Undo command (*/EU* or *Alt-F5*) immediately afterward to reverse the command. Undo must be enabled *before* you use it. If you've performed other operations that can't be undone in the meantime, use the Transcript utility to bring back the names (see Chapter 17, "Using Transcript").

To delete one or more individual block names, use the /Edit I Names I Delete command (see page 130).

With the /Edit I Names I Labels command, you can tell Quattro to use the label next to a cell for the cell's block name. It automatically gives a name to each individual cell in a given block using adjacent labels. This is especially useful if you have one or more cells that are identified by labels next to them, as in a data entry form.

To assign names to cells using adjacent labels,

```
Labels
Right
Down
Left
Up
```

1. Choose /Edit I Names I Labels.

2. Choose the option that reflects the position of the cells you want to name in relation to the labels. For example, if the blocks you're naming are below the labels, choose **Down**. Quattro then prompts you for the block of labels to use as names.

3. Specify the block containing the *labels*, not the blocks to be named.

Quattro uses each label in the specified block (up to 15 characters) as a name for an adjacent cell. It ignores any numeric values in the block; you can only use labels as block names.

Block names assigned with the /Edit I Names I Labels command remain in memory until deleted. Subsequent changes to the labels themselves do not affect the block names.

If you're using the 123-compatible menus, use /**Range** I **Name** I **Labels**.

The following figure shows a group of values used to calculate the monthly payment on a loan. To assign the labels next to the values as block names, you would specify **Right** as the block position, then specify cell block B2..B5.

Figure 5.6
Using labels to name single-
cell blocks

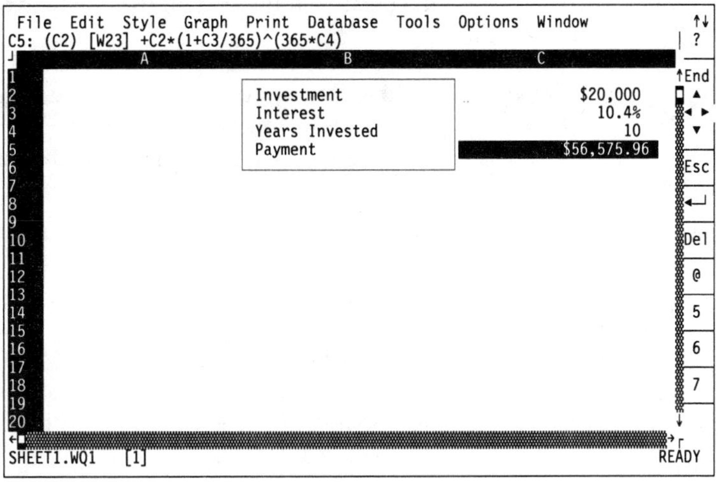

```
 File  Edit  Style  Graph  Print  Database  Tools  Options  Window      ↑↓
C5: (C2) [W23] +C2*(1+C3/365)^(365*C4)                                  | ?
⌐          A                    B                       C        ⌐
1                                                                       ↑End
2                     Investment                  $20,000              □ ▲
3                     Interest                      10.4%              ◄ ► 
4                     Years Invested                  10              ▼
5                     Payment                    $56,575.96
6                                                                       Esc
7                                                                       ↵
8
9                                                                       Del
10
11                                                                      @
12
13                                                                      5
14
15                                                                      6
16
17                                                                      7
18
19
20                                                                      ↓
←□                                                              →⌐
SHEET1.WQ1    [1]                                                    READY
```

*Quattro will name each cell
in the C2..C5 block after the
labels in the B2..B5 block to
the right. For example, the
block name for C2 will be
INVESTMENT.*

Before you use the /Edit I Names I Labels command, it's a good
idea to carefully check over the labels you want to use. If there are
duplicate labels or labels that duplicate preexisting block names,
Quattro overwrites previous assignments. Press *F3* in Edit mode
or after an operator or open parenthesis to display a list of block
names. Press *F3* again to expand the list to full view. The Expand
and Contract keys (+ and –) toggle a display of block coordinates
for each name, whether you're in full view or not.

Note   If there are leading or trailing spaces within a label, Quattro
includes them in the block name. For example, a name that
appears to be "INPUT" may have been accidentally entered as
"INPUT   " (with three trailing spaces). Therefore, check your
labels and edit them, if necessary, before you use them to name
cells.

You can also use the **Assign Names** command on the /**Database** I
Query menu to automatically assign names to the cells in the first
row of a database, using the field names (see Chapter 18).

Making a table of
named blocks

To view a list of named blocks while you're editing or entering a
formula, or when Quattro prompts you for a cell block, press *F3*,
then press the Expand key (+) to see each cell's coordinates. The
Contract key (-) removes the coordinates display. Press *F3* again to
zoom the block names list to full screen. You can also create a
table that lists the same information as a permanent part of your
spreadsheet.

To create a table that shows the blocks you've named,

1. Move the selector to the top left cell of the block you want to use for the table. Be sure there's plenty of empty space in the area you specify. Quattro overwrites any data that exists in the cells you use to display the table.

2. Choose /Edit | Names | Make Table. Quattro prompts you for a block, with the current cell shown as the default.

3. Press *Enter* to use the current cell as the upper left corner cell of the table, or specify a different cell.

Quattro instantly creates a two-column table in the specified area (see the following figure). The first column lists block names alphabetically. The second column indicates the corresponding block coordinates.

Figure 5.7
Table of named blocks

```
 File  Edit  Style  Graph  Print  Database  Tools  Options  Window        ↑↓
 F5:                                                                        | ?
 J        F      G        H        I       J       K        L
 5                                                                         ↑End
 6                                                                          ▲
 7                                                                         ◄ ►
 8                                                                          ▼
 9
 10                     APRIL          E4                                  Esc
 11                     AUG            I4
 12                     DEC            M4                                   ◄┘
 13                     FEBRUARY       C4
 14                     JANUARY        B4                                  Del
 15                     JULY           H4
 16                     JUNE           G4                                   @
 17                     MARCH          D4
 18                     MAY            F4                                   5
 19                     NOV            L4
 20                     OCT            K4                                   6
 21                     SEP            J4
 22                     TOTAL          N4                                   7
 23
 24
 SHEET1.WQ1      [1]                     CAP                             READY
```

Quattro doesn't automatically update a named block table. If you add, change, or delete block names, you must re-create the table to reflect the changes.

 If you're using the 123-compatible menus, choose /**Range** | **Name** | **Table**.

Filling a block with sequential values

With the /**Edit** | **Fill** command, you can automatically fill a cell block with a sequence of values. You can use this command to automatically enter invoice numbers, account numbers, purchase-order numbers, and even dates.

When you choose /Edit I Fill, Quattro prompts you sequentially for four things:

- a cell block to fill with numbers
- a start value
- a step (interval) value
- a stop value

You can supply all three values as formulas as well as numbers.

Quattro fills the block with values until either it reaches the stop value or the block is full. For example, if you specify A1..A10 as the fill block, 2 as the start value, 2 as the step, and 30 as the stop value, Quattro will stop with number 20, since that is the end of the block (see the following figure).

The following figure shows a two-column block (D7..E11) filled with the same sequence of values. When you specify more than one column as the fill block, Quattro begins in the upper left corner and writes numbers down the column, then moves to the top of the next column.

Figure 5.8
Two blocks filled with values

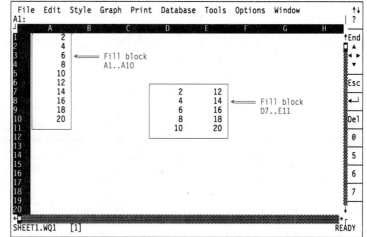

To fill a block with sequential values,

1. Choose /Edit I Fill. Quattro prompts you for a block.
2. Indicate the block you want to fill with values. Quattro prompts you for a start value and offers a default value of 0.

If the Fill command was used earlier, you may see different start, step, and stop values.

3. Press *Enter* to start the sequence with 0, or enter another value. Quattro prompts you for a step value and offers a default value of 1.

4. Press *Enter* to display every value in the sequence, or enter another number. A step value of 2 displays every other value; 3 displays every third value, and so on. Quattro prompts you for a stop value and offers a default value of 8192.

5. Press *Enter* to display all values in the series up to 8192 or until the cell block is filled, or enter another number.

Quattro enters the values in the cells specified as the fill block. If there are more cells than values, it won't fill the entire block. If there are more values than cells, it won't enter all possible values.

If you're using the 123-compatible menus, choose /**D**ata | Fill.

You can generate values in either descending or ascending order. To indicate descending order, enter the high number as the start value, the low number as the stop value, and a negative number as the step value. For example, the values

Start = 20
Step = –2
Stop = 10

create the following series of numbers:

20, 18, 16, 14, 12, 10

To generate dates with the /Edit | Fill command, just press *Ctrl-D,* then enter the dates in a valid date format. Make sure the stop value is higher than the date serial numbers you want to fill the block with. Quattro fills the block with dates shown as date serial numbers. To display the values as dates, use /**S**tyle | **N**umeric Format | **D**ate to change the block's display format. You can also use date @functions with Fill. (See page 57 for more information on working with dates.)

Converting formulas to their values

Formulas require much more memory than simple values. Quattro conserves memory used for formulas by storing only a single copy of duplicate formulas. You can conserve even more memory by converting formulas you no longer need to their end results. This is a good idea if you've used many different formulas to build an area of your spreadsheet and no longer need the formulas themselves for continued calculations.

The /Edit | Values command lets you copy the *values* calculated by formulas without copying the formulas. You can copy these values to another part of the spreadsheet or copy them over the formulas that computed them, then remove the formulas themselves from the spreadsheet.

To copy formula values,

1. Choose /Edit | Values. Quattro prompts you for the source block and shows the current cell as the default block.

2. Indicate the block you want to copy. Quattro prompts you for the destination block. Again, the current cell is the default.

3. To replace the formulas in the specified block with their values, specify the same block as the source block. To copy the values of the formulas in the source block to another part of the spreadsheet, specify the top left corner cell of the block you want them copied to. (The formulas in the source block remain intact.)

Quattro immediately copies the formula values to the destination block. If the source and destination blocks are the same, it permanently replaces all formulas in the block.

1-2-3

If you're using the 123-compatible menus, choose /Range | Value.

Caution!   If you copy formula values to a block that already contains entries, the values will replace the existing entries, and any calculations relying on those cells will use the new values.

To copy formulas *and* their values to another part of the spreadsheet, use the /Edit | Copy command (see page 113).

To convert a single formula to its resulting value, simply select the cell containing it, press the Edit key (*F2*), then the Calc key (*F9*), then *Enter*. The result of the formula becomes the new entry in the cell.

To copy the values of all or part of a spreadsheet into a separate file, use the Values option with the /File | Extract command (see Chapter 12).

Searching for and replacing data in a block

Quattro's /Edit | Search & Replace command lets you alter numerous cell entries instantaneously. It automatically searches through a block for the value or string you specify, then replaces each match it encounters with the new value. It also gives you an easy way to find a specific entry.

You can use Search & Replace on numbers and formulas, as well as labels.

```
┌══ Search & Replace ══┐
│ Block                │
│ Search String        │
│ Replace String       │
│─Options──────────────│
│ Look In            ▶ │
│ Direction          ▶ │
│ Match              ▶ │
│ Case Sensitive     ▶ │
│ Options Reset        │
│──────────────────────│
│ Next         Ctrl-N  │
│ Previous     Ctrl-P  │
│ Quit                 │
└──────────────────────┘
```

Choose /Edit | Search & Replace to display the Search & Replace menu.

- **Block** specifies the block to search through for the given value. If you don't specify a block, Quattro searches through the entire spreadsheet.

- **Search String** lets you enter a string, value, or formula to search for.

- **Replace String** lets you enter a string with which to replace instances of the search string.

- **Look In** determines how Quattro treats formulas during its search: The **Formula** setting looks in the formulas themselves (including cell references, operators, block names, and values), and the **Value** setting looks at the formulas as displayed in the spreadsheet. A third option, **Conditions**, lets you enter a condition as the search string; for example, B13>500. Quattro looks for all values that meet the condition instead of the label B13>500. When entering a condition, use the coordinates of the current cell as the beginning of the condition, or a question mark to look in all cells; for example, ? = 100.

- **Direction** specifies searching by row or column. The default, **Row**, searches the given block from the current cell either forward or backward, row by row.

- **Match** specifies whether the search string must be a whole cell entry or any part of a cell entry. The default, **Part**, searches for partial cell entries as well as whole. For example, if *cat* were the search string, **Part** would find *catamaran* and *scatter* as well as *cat*.

- **Case Sensitive** determines whether Quattro searches for strings whose capitalizations exactly match that of the search string. The default, **Any Case**, searches for strings regardless of capitalization. For example, if the search string were *HARPER*,

Any Case would find *Harper, harper,* and *HaRpEr* as well as *HARPER.*

■ **Options Reset** removes any entries you've placed in **Search String, Replace String,** and any of the **Options,** and resumes the default settings.

■ **Next** begins the search from the current cell to the bottom right corner of the specified block.

■ **Previous** begins the search from the current cell to the top left corner of the specified block.

■ **Quit** exits the **Search & Replace** menu and returns to the spreadsheet.

To replace one string of characters with another,

1. Choose /Edit I Search & Replace.

2. Choose **Block,** then specify the block you want to search through.

3. Choose **Search String** and enter the string of characters you want to search for.

4. Choose **Replace String** and enter the character string you want to replace the search string with.

5. By default, Quattro searches the entries as they appear on the input line (for example, the formula you entered rather than the resulting value). If you want to search for the formula as displayed in the spreadsheet instead, choose **Look In,** then choose **Values.** If you want to use a condition as the search string, choose **Look In I Conditions.**

6. By default, Quattro searches the given block row by row, beginning with the current cell. To search column by column, choose **Direction,** then **Column.**

7. By default, Quattro looks for your search string in any part of a cell entry. To specify looking for the search string as a whole cell entry only, choose **Match,** then **Whole.**

8. By default, Quattro looks for your search string regardless of capitalization. To search for strings that match exactly the capitalization of the search string as you entered it, choose **Case Sensitive,** then **Exact Case.**

9. To begin the search from the current cell forward, choose **Next.** To search from the current cell backward, choose **Previous.** Quattro looks through the given block for your

search string. It stops at the first match it finds and displays the prompt menu.

```
┌─ Replace this string? ─┐
│                        │
│ Yes                    │
│ No                     │
│ All                    │
│ Edit                   │
│ Quit                   │
└────────────────────────┘
```

10. Press *Y* to replace the string, *N* to leave it as is, *A* to replace this string and all others without further prompting, *E* to enter Edit mode so you can make changes to the current string then continue with the replace operation, or *Q* to abort the operation without changing the current string.

Next

Ctrl-N is the default shortcut for the /Edit I Search & Replace I Next command.

Ctrl P
Previous

Ctrl-P is the default shortcut for the /Edit I Search & Replace I Previous command.

1-2-3

If you're using the 123-compatible menus, choose /Range I Search & Replace.

You can also use the /Database I Query command to search through a database spreadsheet. For more information, see Chapter 18.

Reformatting text entries in a block

You can store all kinds of information, including text, in your spreadsheet. The /Tools I Reformat command provides the most important features of a word-processing program: adjustable "margins" and paragraph reformatting. With it, you can enter text as a long label or a series of labels, then reorganize the text as a paragraph, taking up as many cells or columns as you specify.

Reformat makes it easy to include instructions, memos, and descriptive text in your spreadsheet. However, it is not a word processor. To manipulate large areas of text, you might want to use an actual word-processing program. You can save text from the spreadsheet in a text file by printing it to a disk file, then use the file with a word-processing program such as Sprint (see page 85). You can also load files created with other programs into the spreadsheet with the /File I Import command. (To break down long labels into two or more cells, use the /Tools I Parse command; see Chapter 12.)

For example, the following figure shows a paragraph of text entered as three long labels in cells A1 through A4. Although Quattro displays the text across eight columns, you actually enter it only in column A. Because the cells to the right are empty, the text spills over into them for display only.

Figure 5.9
Text entered as long labels

```
File  Edit  Style  Graph  Print  Database  Tools  Options  Window    ↑↓
A20:                                                                  | ?
 ┘      A      B      C      D      E      F      G      H
1  The Reformat command opens up all kinds of possibilities for your  ↑End
2  spreadsheet. With it, you can enter long labels, then reformat them to  ▲
3  fill the space you want filled. The Reformat command works like a mini  ◄ ►
4  word-processor.                                                      ▼
5
6                                                                     Esc
7
8                                                                      ◄┘
9
10                                                                    Del
11
12                                                                     @
13
14                                                                     5
15
16                                                                     6
17
18                                                                     7
19
20
 ←                                                                   →┌
SHEET1.WQ1    [1]                                                    READY
```

The text you see is entered in Column A only.

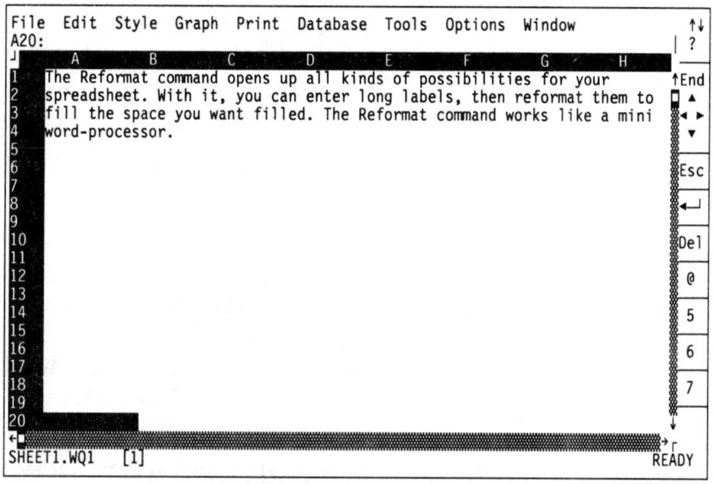

The following figure shows the same text reformatted to fit into four columns: A through D. Because the "margins" are narrower, the display takes up more rows (now 1 through 9). Note that the text is still "contained" only in Column A, even though it spills over into B, C, and D.

Figure 5.10
The same text justified within
four columns

```
File  Edit  Style  Graph  Print  Database  Tools  Options  Window    ↑↓
A1: 'The Reformat command opens up all                               | ?
 ┘      A      B      C      D      E      F      G      H
1  The Reformat command opens up all                                  ↑End
2  kinds of possibilities for your                                     ▲
3  spreadsheet. With it, you can enter                                ◄ ►
4  long labels, then reformat them to                                  ▼
5  fill the space you want filled.
6  The Reformat command works like                                   Esc
7  a mini word-processor.
8                                                                      ◄ ┘
9
10                                                                    Del
11
12                                                                     @
13
14                                                                     5
15
16                                                                     6
17
18                                                                     7
19
20
 ←                                                                   →┌
SHEET1.WQ1    [1]                                                    READY
```

The text is still stored only in Column A.

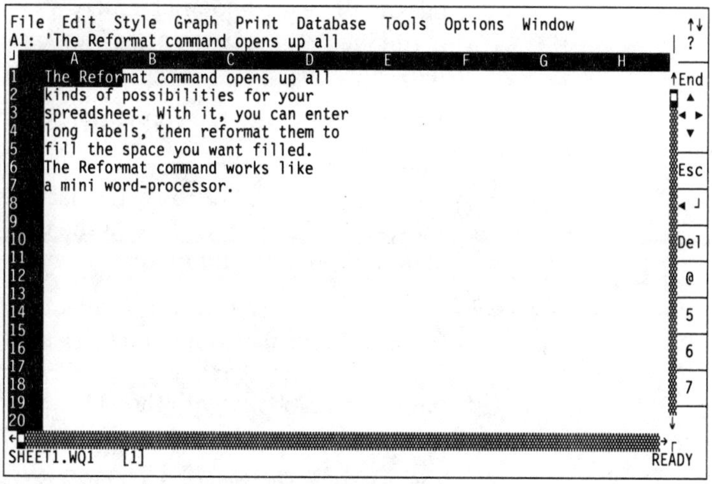

To reformat text in a block of cells,

1. Enter the text you want to reformat in one or more cells of the same column. You can include up to 254 characters in a single

cell. The cells containing the text to be justified must be adjacent (no blank cells between them) and must begin in the same column.

2. If any of the cells you intend to reformat are protected, turn off default protection temporarily (choose /Style | Protection | Unprotect to unprotect the block). You cannot reformat a protected cell. (Protection is discussed on pages 153 and 210.)

3. Move the cell selector to the cell containing the first label to be reformatted.

4. Choose /Tools | Reformat. Quattro prompts you for a block.

5. Specify the columns and/or rows where you want the reformatted text to appear. If you specify columns within the current row only, the text fills up as many rows as necessary to display the text within those columns. If you specify both columns and rows, Quattro reformats the text within the block, putting any extra text in the last row.

6. If you turned off protection before reformatting, turn it back on again (choose /Style | Protection | Protect).

Quattro reformats the text to fit the space you indicated, breaking sentences as necessary. If a word is longer than the column width, Quattro truncates it or runs it into the cell to the right (if empty). If you specify the reformat block by indicating the first row only, be sure there are enough blank rows underneath for the reformatted text. If the destination block contains data, an error message appears.

If you're using the 123-compatible menus, choose /Range | Justify.

Remember, even though Quattro may display the reformatted text in several columns or rows, the data is actually *stored* in the leftmost cells of each row. To edit the text, you need to go to these cells and press the Edit key (*F2*).

Caution! If any of the cells in your reformat block are protected, the /Tools | Reformat command causes an error. Before you reformat a block that may contain protected cells, turn off spreadsheet protection globally with the /Options | Protection | Disable command.

Once you've reformatted a label, you can reverse the command if you need to with the Undo key (*Alt-F5*, if enabled). You can also reformat the text so that it fills the same space as it did before (although some of the line breaks may change).

The /Tools I **Reformat** command works only on existing text. You cannot reformat an empty block, then enter the data.

Inserting columns and rows

With the /Edit I **Insert** command, you can easily insert blank columns and rows anywhere in the spreadsheet.

To insert one or more columns or rows,

1. Move the cell selector to any cell in the column to the right of where you want to insert a column or to the row below where you want to insert a row.
2. Choose /Edit I Insert.

3. Choose **Rows** to insert one or more rows, or **Columns** to insert one or more columns. Quattro prompts you for the insert location and shows the current cell as the default.
4. Press *Enter* to insert a single column to the left of the current cell or a single row above the current cell, or enter a different cell block. To insert more than one column or row at a time, extend the given block accordingly. For example, to insert three columns to the left of cell C3, enter the block C3..E3; the data in cell C3 moves to cell F3 and so on. To insert two rows above cell C3, enter the block C3..C2.

Quattro inserts the new columns or rows and assigns the inserted cells the spreadsheet's defaults for alignment, display format, and column width.

Ctrl-I is the default shortcut for the /Edit I Insert command.

Insert

If you insert a column or row within the boundaries of a named block or a block referenced by a formula, Quattro automatically adjusts the block to include the new column or row.

Note

Quattro will not insert a column or row if there is data written near the last column (column IV) or last row (row 8192) that would be pushed "over the edge" of your spreadsheet. Instead, it displays an error message. You can delete the data near the edge or move it inward, then try again.

Caution!

If inserting columns pushes a named block or cell reference over the edge, it becomes ERR.

If you're using the 123-compatible menus, choose /**Worksheet** I **Insert** I **Column** or /**Worksheet** I **Insert** I **Row**.

Deleting columns and rows

With the /**Edit** I **Delete** command, you can delete columns and rows anywhere in the spreadsheet.

To delete one or more columns or rows,

1. Move the cell selector to any cell in the column or row you want to delete.
2. Choose /**Edit** I **Delete**.

3. Choose **Rows** to delete one or more rows or **Columns** to delete one or more columns. Quattro prompts you for the columns or rows to delete and shows the current cell as the default.
4. Press *Enter* to delete the column or row containing the selector. To delete more than one column or row at a time, extend the given block accordingly. For example, to delete columns C, D, and E, enter the block C3..E3.

If you're using the 123-compatible menus, choose /**Worksheet** I **Delete** I **Column**.

Caution! If the deleted column or row was within the boundaries of a named block or a block referenced by a formula, Quattro automatically adjusts the block. If a cell in the deleted column or row is a coordinate cell (a corner cell used to define the block), the block becomes invalid and any formulas or names referencing the block show ERR. Any formulas that reference an individual cell within a deleted column also appear as ERR.

To delete the contents of a column or row without deleting the actual column itself, use the /**Edit** I **Erase Block** command (see page 125).

Transposing columns and rows

A typical spreadsheet contains column headings, row headings, or both, with related data underneath the column headings or to the right of the row headings. Whichever way you choose to set up your spreadsheet, you can reverse the placement of data in columns and rows with the /Edit I Transpose command.

The following figure shows a spreadsheet with the same data arranged two ways: one with column headings and the other with row headings. The Transpose command switches either block from one arrangement to the other.

Figure 5.11
The results of transposing
data

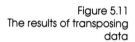

```
 File  Edit  Style  Graph  Print  Database  Tools  Options  Window        ↑↓
A1: 'Phone                                                             |  ?
J        A          B         C        D        E        F      G      H  ___
1     Phone       $159                                                  ↑End
2     Travel      $456    ◄══════════ Row headings                      □ ▲
3     Postage     $68                                                   ◄ ►
4     Rent        $750                                                    ▼
5
6                                                                       Esc
7                      Column headings
8                              ||                                        ↵
9
10                             ▼                                        Del
11
12            Phone    Travel   Postage   Rent                           @
13            $159     $456     $68       $750
14                                                                       5
15
16                                                                       6
17
18                                                                       7
19
20
←□                                                                      ↓
SHEET1.WQ1    [1]                                                      READY
```

The /Edit I Transpose command copies part of a spreadsheet to another area *and* transposes the columns and rows. You cannot replace an entire cell block with transposed data; you must copy it (with the Transpose command) to a different part of the spreadsheet first.

Caution!   You cannot successfully transpose formulas that contain relative cell references. If you do, the formulas become inaccurate. You can make the references absolute before transposing the data, but the formulas will continue to reference the original cells, not the transposed copies. The best way to rearrange columns and rows that contain formulas is to use the /Edit I Move command (see page 119).

To copy and transpose data,

1. Choose /Edit I Transpose. Quattro prompts you for the source block.

2. Specify the block you want to transpose. Quattro prompts you for the destination cell.

3. Indicate the upper left cell of the block to which you want to copy the transposed data. This cannot be a cell within the source block—you will disarrange the data if you do not choose a cell outside the source block.

Quattro copies the data to the specified area, rearranging the columns and rows. The original data remains the same.

If you're using the 123-compatible menus, choose /Range | Transpose.

Caution! If data exists in the block you specify as the destination block, Quattro overwrites it with the new data. Remember that the transposed data can be a different shape than the original, so you might want to first copy it to an area far from other data, then move it again if necessary.

6

Changing the style of your spreadsheet

Quattro lets you display your spreadsheet data in many ways. For example, you can use line-drawing, shading, and special fonts to add graphic touches to the spreadsheet, adjust column widths, and temporarily hide columns from view. You do all this with the **Style** menu.

This chapter discusses each of the **Style** menu commands, organized as they appear on the menu:

- "Changing data display" describes how to change alignment, numeric format, and protection options for blocks of cells.
- "Working with columns" discusses how to change column widths and temporarily remove columns from the screen.
- "Presentation-quality options" describes how to draw lines and boxes around cell blocks, shade areas of the spreadsheet, change type fonts, and insert page breaks. It also discusses how to use bullet codes to print bulleted lists in the spreadsheet.

The Style menu

```
┌───────── Style ─────────┐
│ Alignment      Ctrl-A ► │
│ Numeric Format Ctrl-F ► │
│ Protection            ► │
├─────────────────────────┤
│ Column Width   Ctrl-W   │
│ Reset Width             │
│ Hide Column           ► │
│ Block Widths          ► │
├─────────────────────────┤
│ Line Drawing            │
│ Shading               ► │
│ Font                  ► │
│ Insert Break            │
└─────────────────────────┘
```

The **Style** menu contains commands you can use to change the display of your data.

- **Alignment** lets you change the way Quattro aligns entries in a block: left, right, center, or according to the alignment default in effect for that spreadsheet.

- **Numeric Format** allows you to display numbers and dates in different formats and hide cell entries from view.

- **Protection** lets you disable overall spreadsheet protection (set with the /Options | Protection command) for individual blocks of cells. You can also use this command to return protection to a block.

- **Column Width** adjusts the width of a column.

- **Reset Width** returns a column to the default column width.

- **Hide Column** temporarily removes one or more columns from the screen display. You can also use this command to return hidden columns to display.

- **Block Widths** lets you automatically set the widths of all columns in a block—to a specified width, to the default width, or to varying widths depending on the longest entry in each column.

- **Line Drawing** draws single, double, or thick lines and boxes around blocks in the spreadsheet.

- **Shading** adds grey or black shading to areas of the spreadsheet.

- **Font** lets you assign different type fonts to blocks of the spreadsheet. Quattro uses these fonts to print spreadsheet characters in different typefaces, styles, colors, and point sizes.

- **Insert Break** inserts a hard page break code (| ::) above the current row.

Changing data display

The first three commands on the **Style** menu affect how Quattro displays data within a given cell block. With them, you can realign data in a block, change the format used to display values and dates in a block, and remove spreadsheet protection from a block.

Aligning blocks of data

When you enter data in a cell, Quattro automatically aligns it according to the default alignment setting: left for labels and right for values and dates. With the /Style I Alignment command, you can change the way data is aligned within a given block of cells. (To change the global alignment setting for labels in a spreadsheet, use the /Options I Formats I Align Labels command—see "Global label alignment" in Chapter 7.)

To realign values, dates, or labels in a block of cells,

1. Choose /Style I Alignment.

2. The initial setting, **General**, right-aligns values and dates, and aligns labels according to the /Options I Formats I Align Labels setting. Choose **Left** to align data to the left, **Right** to align data to the right, or **Center** to center data. Quattro prompts you for the cell block you want to realign and shows the current cell as the default block.

3. Press *Enter* to align only the current cell, or specify a different cell block.

Alignment

Ctrl-A is the default shortcut for the /Style I Alignment command.

You can also align labels differently than the default by entering or editing a label-prefix character (see "Label alignment" on page 52).

1-2-3

If you're using the 123-compatible menus, choose /Range I Alignment.

Block numeric format

Numbers are entered and stored in a Quattro spreadsheet as a series of numerals; for example, 295842.42949 and –0.45611. They can have up to 16 significant digits. A significant digit is any integer that is not a leading zero; decimals, commas, dollar signs, and percent signs do not count as part of the total. For example, the number 1.23 has three significant digits. The number .000123 also has three significant digits because the leading zeroes do not count.

When you enter a number in a cell, Quattro automatically displays it according to the default numeric format setting.

Initially, this setting is **General**, which displays numbers more or less as you enter them. You can change this to any of ten other numeric formats, including formats that add commas, dollar signs, percent signs, or other characters to your original number.

Quattro stores dates you enter in a spreadsheet (either with *Ctrl-D* or a date @function) as numbers that equal the number of days between the date and December 30, 1899. Quattro uses this date serial number for calculations but displays the date in the global numeric format.

To calculate the Julian day from the date number, add 2415017.5 to the date number. In Quattro, days start at midnight, but Julian days start at noon. Add the .5 portion of the number 2415017.5 to make up for the time (half a day) between midnight and noon.

Important! Numeric format doesn't affect the way Quattro stores numbers or dates, only the way it displays them. For example, some formats limit the number of decimal places that appear on your screen. This does not diminish the accuracy of Quattro calculations, which still rely on the stored number (up to 16 significant digits). This stored number is also what Quattro displays on the input line when you select a cell or on the status line when you press *F2*.

With the /Style I Numeric Format command, you can override the default numeric format to change the way Quattro displays dates or numbers in a given spreadsheet block. (To change the global numeric format for the spreadsheet, use the /Options I Formats I Numeric Format command—see "Global display format" in Chapter 7.)

To change the format of numbers or dates in a block,

1. Choose /Style I Numeric Format. The **Numeric Format** menu appears.

```
┌─ Numeric Format ─┐
│                  │
│ Fixed            │
│ Scientific       │
│ Currency         │
│ ,                │
│ General          │
│ +/-              │
│ Percent          │
│ Date           ▶ │
│ Text             │
│ Hidden           │
│ Reset            │
└──────────────────┘
```

2. Choose the format in which you want Quattro to display numbers or dates in this block. (Table 6.1 describes each of these options.)

3. If the format you chose allows a variable number of decimal places, Quattro prompts you for the number of decimal places you want displayed. Press *Enter* to use the default precision setting (2), or enter another number (0-15). Remember that this setting is for display only; Quattro still uses the full number as stored for calculations.

4. If you chose **Date**, you must choose a specific date format, or choose **Time** and choose a specific time format.

5. When you've specified all the format details, Quattro prompts you for the block to be modified. Press *Enter* to change the format of the current cell only, or specify a different block.

Quattro immediately adjusts the display of numbers or dates within the specified block. The Hidden format is the only format option that affects label entries in the block. Any numbers you now enter in the block will appear in the chosen format.

Numeric Format

Ctrl-F is the default shortcut for the /Style | Numeric Format command.

If you're using the 123-compatible menus, choose /**Range** | **Format.**

If the format you choose creates a number too long to be displayed in the current column, a string of asterisks appears in the cell. You can redisplay the number by widening the column (see "Setting column width" later in this chapter).

When you select a cell formatted with the /Style | Numeric Format command, the format is indicated in parentheses on the input line. The first letter of the format name appears next to the number of decimal places specified. For example, (C2) indicates the Currency format with two decimal places. (For date formats, the code shows *D* followed by the date format number.)

Caution! Although it is tempting to preformat large areas of the spreadsheet in your planned format, doing so consumes quite a bit of memory space. It is much more efficient to format only the cells you are currently using. Or better yet, change the global numeric format to the format you use the most (see "Global display format" in Chapter 7).

Table 6.1 describes each of the format choices listed on the **Numeric Format** menu.

Table 6.1: Examples of numeric formats

Format	Description	Examples
Fixed	Displays no more than the specified number of decimal places. Leading zeros appear.	46, 0.56, –34.00
Scientific	Uses scientific notation. Allows only one digit in the integer portion of the number.	2.35E+2, 4.76E+9
Currency	Displays numbers as currency, in the format specified with the /Options I International command (see "Currency" in Chapter 7).	$3,467.00, 35, ($56.24)
, (comma)	Separates thousands with commas, and shows negative numbers in parentheses. This is also known as the Financial format.	15,120.25, (2,456)
General	Displays numbers basically as entered (suppressing trailing or leading zeros). If too long to fit current cell, they are rounded (if fractional) or translated into scientific notation.	456.9452, –365 0.41, 1.955E+6
+/-	Transforms values into a horizontal bar graph. Each integer translates into a symbol: + for each positive integer, – for each negative integer, and . for zero.	+ + + – – – – . . .
Percent	Displays numbers as percentages.	13.40%, –56.44%
Date	Displays numbers as dates or time in the format you choose:	
	Date DD-MMM-YY DD-MMM MMM-YY Long International (see page 57) Short International (see page 57)	09-Apr-89 09-Apr Apr-89 04/09/89, 89-09-04, 04.09.89 04/09, 04.09, 09-04
	Time HH:MM:SS AM/PM HH:MM AM/PM Long International (see page 191) Short International (see page 191)	11:31:28PM 05:15AM 15:23:55, 15.23.55, 15,23,55 14:56, 14.56, 14,56, 14h56m
Text	Displays formulas instead of their results. Displays numbers entered in the block in General format. This is also known as the Show Formulas format.	B6*C3, @SUM(B1..B10)
Hidden	Suppresses display of both value and label entries. Entries still appear on the input line when the cell is selected.	
Reset	Returns the numeric format for this block to the default format (specified with the /Options I Formats I Numeric Format command). Redisplays entries hidden with the Hidden format.	

To display a value as a time, you must first choose **Date**, then **Time**, then the time format you want.

You can enter a date directly in date format when you precede it with the date prefix *(Ctrl-D)*. If you enter dates using the @DATE, @DATEVALUE, or @NOW function (described in *@Functions and Macros*), you must reformat the cells with the **Date** command. Otherwise, Quattro displays the results as a date serial number.

If you've hidden cell contents with the **Hidden** command, you may want to use the protection commands to prevent the cells' entries from being accidentally overwritten (see the following section).

Quattro rounds numbers off to the specified decimal place in the case of Fixed, Scientific, Currency, Comma, Percent, and +/- formats. The **General** command rounds off fractional numbers as necessary to fit in the cell. The original numbers (as entered) still appear on the input line when you select the cells that contain them, and it is these numbers that Quattro uses in all calculations.

The format you assign to a cell stays with the cell, even if you delete its contents. If you move the contents, however, the format moves with the data and is removed from the original cell. If you copy a formatted cell, the copy takes on the format of the original cell.

Protecting cell blocks

The /**Options** | **Protection** setting (see "Protection options" in Chapter 7) lets you enable or disable overall spreadsheet protection. When spreadsheet protection is enabled, no changes can be made to the spreadsheet. You can, however, remove protection from individual blocks of cells with /**Style** | **Protection**.

To remove protection from a block of cells,

```
┌─ Protection ─┐
│              │
│ Protect      │
│ Unprotect    │
│              │
└──────────────┘
```

1. Choose /**Style** | **Protection**.
2. Choose **Unprotect**. Quattro prompts you for a cell block.
3. Press *Enter* to remove protection from the current cell only, or enter a different block.

Cells explicitly unprotected with the /**Style** | **Protection** command display U on the input line when you select them.

When a cell is protected, you cannot edit, replace, or delete its entry. Nor can you delete a column or row that contains a protected cell. You *can*, however, erase the entire spreadsheet, even if it contains protected cells.

To return protection to a block of cells,

1. Choose /**Style** | **Protection**.

2. Choose **Protect**.

3. Press *Enter* to protect the current cell only, or specify a different block.

Protected cells display PR on the input line when you select them.

1-2-3   If you're using the 123-compatible menus, choose /**Range** | **Protect** or **Unprotect**.

Note   When you disable spreadsheet protection with the /**Options** | **Protection** | **Disable** command, no spreadsheet cells are protected, even those you protected individually with the /**Style** | **Protection** command.

With default spreadsheet protection enabled, you will still be able to move the cell selector around the entire spreadsheet, but you can make changes only to the cells that have been unprotected. To restrict movement of the selector to unprotected cells only, use the /**Database** | **Restrict Input** command (see "Restricting the type of data entry" in Chapter 18).

Working with columns

```
Column Width   Ctrl-W
Reset Width
Hide Column          ▶
Block Widths         ▶
```

The middle group of commands on the **Style** menu affect columns. You can use these commands to change the column width of a single column or of all columns in a block and to temporarily remove columns from display.

Setting column width

All columns in a spreadsheet start out the same width. Initially, this is nine spaces, but you can change the default column width with the /**Options** | **Formats** | **Global Width** command.

Three commands on the **Style** menu let you adjust the width of individual columns or all columns in a block: **Column Width**,

Reset Width, and **B**lock Widths. Column Width affects the current column. **R**eset Width returns the current column back to the default column width. **B**lock Widths affects all columns in a block.

Column width and the default font

The point size of Font 1, which serves as the default font for your spreadsheet, directly affects how wide Quattro makes columns. Because Quattro measures column width in terms of character spaces (1 to 254), a larger point size results in a wider column. A column set up to hold five 72-point characters is much wider than a column set up to hold five 6-point characters.

So, if the width of your columns seems too narrow when you print and text is truncated, check the size of Font 1. See page 164 for information about choosing or redefining Quattro fonts.

Adjusting individual columns

The /**S**tyle | **C**olumn Width command lets you adjust individual columns to any width between 1 and 254 spaces. This not only lets you make room for lengthy entries, but you can fit more on the screen by customizing columns to the exact widths needed.

To adjust a column's width,

1. Move the cell selector to the column whose width you want to change.
2. Choose /**S**tyle | **C**olumn Width. Quattro prompts you for a column width and shows the current column width as the default.
3. Type a number from 1 to 254, *or* press ← or → to widen or narrow the current column onscreen until it's the width you want.
4. Press *Enter*.

The specified column immediately adjusts to the new width. When you select a cell in a column whose width has been adjusted, the new width appears in brackets (for example, [W18]) on the input line.

To resize a column using a mouse, drag the column letter right to widen the column or left to narrow it, then release.

Ctrl W
Column Width

Ctrl-W is the default shortcut for the /**S**tyle | **C**olumn Width command.

1-2-3

If you're using the 123-compatible menus, choose /**W**orksheet | **C**olumn | **S**et Width.

If your spreadsheet window is split into two panes, column width changes affect the current pane only (see "Splitting a window" in Chapter 9). If you change column width in the right or bottom pane, Quattro discards the changes when you close that pane. If you want the width changes stored with the spreadsheet, make them in the top or left pane.

Resetting column width

To return an adjusted column to the spreadsheet's default width, use the /**Style** I **Reset Width** command:

1. Move the cell selector to the column you want to adjust.
2. Choose /**Style** I **Reset Width**.

Quattro immediately resets the column to the default column width, and the column will respond to all subsequent default changes.

 If you're using the 123-compatible menus, choose /**Worksheet** I **Column** I **Reset Width**.

To reset the width of all columns in a given block, use the /**Style** I **Block Widths** I **Reset Width** command (see "Resetting the width of a group of columns" later in this chapter).

Tip If you want to easily spot columns whose widths have been individually adjusted, you can temporarily make the default width very narrow or very wide. Quattro doesn't change the widths of the columns you adjusted with the /**Style** I **Column Width** command, so they stand out from the others. After you've made the desired changes to those columns, you can return the default width to its previous setting.

Setting a column's width to the default width with the /**Style** I **Column Width** command is not the same as resetting the width. A column won't be affected when you change the default width until you reset it with /**Style** I **Reset Width** command or /**Style** I **Block Widths** I **Reset Width**.

Adjusting all columns in a block

The /**Style** I **Block Widths** command lets you set the width of all columns in a block. When you choose this command, Quattro displays the **Block Widths** menu.

```
┌─ Block Widths ─┐
│                │
│ Set Width      │
│ Reset Width    │
│ Auto Width     │
└────────────────┘
```

■ **Set Width** sets the width of all columns in a block to a given width.

- **Reset Width** returns all columns in a block to the current global width.
- **Auto Width** automatically adjusts the width of each column according to each column's longest entry.

1-2-3 If you're using 123-compatible menus, choose /**Range** I **Column**.

Specifying one width for a group of columns

To change all columns in a block to one width,

1. Choose /**Style** I **Block Widths** I **Set Width**.
2. Specify the block of columns to adjust (you can select just one row of the block). Quattro prompts you for the column width.
3. Type any number from 1 to 254, or use the → or ← keys to indicate the width onscreen.
4. Press *Enter*.

Quattro adjusts each column included in the block to the width you specify.

1-2-3 If you're using the 123-compatible menus, choose /**Range** I **Column** I **Set Width**.

To set the size of more than one adjoining column, first select a block of cells intersecting the columns first (either with the Select key—*Shift-F7*—or a mouse), then resize one of the columns with /**Style** I **Column Width**, as described on page 155. Quattro sets all columns to the width of the column you resized.

Resetting the width of a group of columns

To reset the width of all columns in a block,

1. Choose /**Style** I **Block Widths** I **Reset Width**. Quattro prompts you for the block to adjust.
2. Specify the block you want to affect.

Quattro resets the width of all columns in the block to the default value. Initially, the default column width is nine, but you can change this with the /**Options** I **Formats** I **Global Width** command.

1-2-3 If you're using the 123-compatible menus, choose /**Range** I **Column** I **Reset Width**.

Adjusting columns according to existing entry lengths

To automatically adjust the column width according to entry length,

1. Choose /Style | Block Widths | Auto Width. Quattro prompts you for the number of extra spaces you want between columns.
2. Enter a number between 0 and 40. Quattro adds the number you enter to the width of each column's longest entry to figure the column's width. Quattro then prompts you for the block of columns you want to adjust.
3. Specify the block you want to affect. If you specify a single-row block, Quattro will examine the row and all cells below it, looking for the longest entry. If you specify more than one row, Quattro will look only within the given block for entry lengths.

Quattro adjusts the columns accordingly.

Tip   If a column you're adjusting contains a long entry that spills over into blank cells to the right, and you *don't* want the column adjusted to that cell entry's length, specify a multi-row block that stops short of the cell. If necessary, you can use the /Style | Block Widths | Auto Width command again, this time specifying a block that begins underneath the spillover entry.

1-2-3   If you're using the 123-compatible menus, choose /Range | Column | Auto Width.

Hiding columns

Occasionally, you may want to temporarily remove columns of data from the screen, retaining only pertinent information onscreen. The /Style | Hide Column command lets you hide columns from view without losing the data they contain. You can later redisplay the columns with the same command.

To hide columns from view,

```
┌─ Hide ─┐
│ Hide    │
│ Expose  │
└─────────┘
```

1. Move the cell selector to any cell in the column you want to hide.
2. Choose /Style | Hide Column.
3. Choose Hide from the menu Quattro displays.

4. Quattro prompts you for the column(s) you want to hide. The current cell is shown as the default.

5. If you want to hide more than one column in a row, extend the block to include at least one cell in each column you want hidden.

6. Press *Enter.*

Quattro immediately removes the specified columns from view. Columns to the right of the hidden columns move left to fill in the empty space, but Quattro doesn't change their associated letters. In other words, if you hide column B, the columns onscreen are labeled A, C, D, and so on.

Note As with column width changes, if your screen is divided into two window panes (see "Splitting a window" in Chapter 9), hidden or exposed columns affect the current window only. If you want the changes retained when you close the second window, make them in the top or left pane.

While a column is hidden, Quattro still keeps track of the data contained in it. Any formulas that rely on data in the hidden column are still accurate.

When you print a spreadsheet, any columns hidden from view are not included in the printout.

If you use the /Tools I Xtract command to save part of a spreadsheet that includes hidden columns (see "Extracting part of a spreadsheet" in Chapter 12), Quattro saves the hidden columns in the new file, although they will still be hidden from view when you retrieve the file.

To return one or more hidden columns to the screen,

1. Choose /Style I Hide Column I Expose. All hidden columns temporarily return to the screen with asterisks (*) next to their column letters.

2. Specify any cell in the column you want to redisplay. To redisplay more than one column, indicate a block of cells that includes those columns. (You can include columns that weren't hidden in the group.)

Quattro continues to display the columns you specified (without the asterisks) and removes other hidden columns from view.

Quattro momentarily displays hidden columns during a few specific operations, such as /Edit l Move and /Edit l Copy, so you can place or access data in these columns. For example, when you choose /Edit l Move, Quattro displays the entire spreadsheet with asterisks next to column headings that you have hidden. You can then move data into or out of the hidden columns. When the operation is complete, Quattro again removes hidden columns from the display.

 If you're using the 123-compatible menus, choose /Worksheet l Column l Hide and /Worksheet l Column l Display instead of /Style l Hide Column.

Presentation-quality options

The last group of commands on the **Style** menu let you refine your spreadsheet before printing. You can draw lines and boxes, add shading, change the font, and insert page breaks. The following sections describe each of these options.

Drawing lines in a spreadsheet

The /Style l Line Drawing command lets you draw single, double, or thick lines and boxes around data. The following figure shows a spreadsheet embellished with lines and boxes:

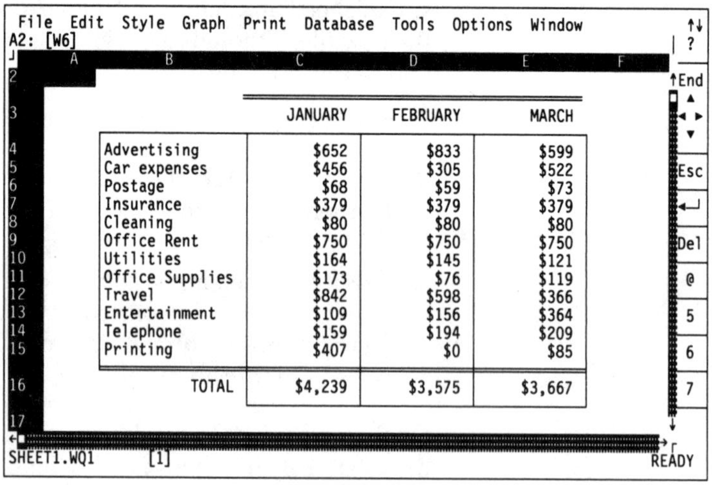

Figure 6.1
A spreadsheet with lines and boxes

		JANUARY	FEBRUARY	MARCH
	Advertising	$652	$833	$599
	Car expenses	$456	$305	$522
	Postage	$68	$59	$73
	Insurance	$379	$379	$379
	Cleaning	$80	$80	$80
	Office Rent	$750	$750	$750
	Utilities	$164	$145	$121
	Office Supplies	$173	$76	$119
	Travel	$842	$598	$366
	Entertainment	$109	$156	$364
	Telephone	$159	$194	$209
	Printing	$407	$0	$85
	TOTAL	$4,239	$3,575	$3,667

File Edit Style Graph Print Database Tools Options Window
A2: [W6]

SHEET1.WQ1   [1]   READY

To draw lines in a cell block,

1. Choose /Style | Line Drawing.

2. Quattro prompts you for the block you want to draw lines around. When you specify the block, Quattro displays a menu of different placement options for the drawn lines.

```
Placement:

All
Outside
Top
Bottom
Left
Right
Inside
Horizontal
Vertical
Quit
```

- **All** puts a box around the block you specify and draws vertical and horizontal lines between all cells in the block to produce a grid.

- **Outside** draws a box around the border of the block you specify.

- **Top** draws a horizontal line on top of the first row of the block.

- **Bottom** draws a horizontal line below the last row of the block.

- **Left** draws a vertical line along the left border of the block.

- **Right** draws a vertical line along the right border of the block.

- **Inside** draws vertical and horizontal lines between all cells in the block.

- **Horizontal** draws lines between each row in the block.

- **Vertical** draws lines between each column in the block.

- **Quit** returns to the spreadsheet without making any changes.

3. Choose a command from the menu of line placement options. Quattro displays a menu of line type options.

```
Line types:

None
Single
Double
Thick
```

4. Choose **Single** to draw a single line, **Double** to draw a double line, or **Thick** to draw a thick band. **None** removes any lines previously set with that option.

5. Quattro returns you to the menu of placement options so you can add other lines to the block. Press *Esc* to specify a different block for line drawing, or choose **Quit** to exit the menus and return to the spreadsheet.

Tip To change the screen color of drawn lines, use the /Options | Colors | Spreadsheet | Drawn Lines command (see "Spreadsheet colors" in Chapter 7).

You can use any combination of options to draw lines and boxes. For example, suppose you wanted to draw a double-lined border around a cell block, and single vertical lines between the columns in the block:

1. Choose /**Style** | **Line Drawing**.
2. Enter the block you want to draw a box around.
3. Choose **Outside** as the line placement, then **Double** as the line type.
4. Now choose **Vertical** as the line placement and **Single** as the line type.

   Quattro draws vertical lines between the columns in the cell block and a double line around the border.

If you're using the 123-compatible menus, choose /**Range** | **Output Style** | **Line Drawing**.

To remove lines and boxes, choose the option that produced the the line(s) or box(es), then choose **None** as the line type. To remove *all* lines and boxes from a block, choose **All** as the line placement option (regardless of what combination of options created the lines), then choose **None** as the line type.

Note   When you print a spreadsheet with drawn lines in draft mode, the lines appear as +, –, and | . To print lines smoothly, set the /**Print** | **Destination** setting to **Graphics Printer**. For more information, see page 84.

Shading areas of a spreadsheet

The /**Style** | **Shading** command lets you shade areas of the spreadsheet in grey or black. You can use it to set up a data entry form, shading either the cells used to enter data or those not used. The following figure shows a sample spreadsheet enhanced with shading:

Figure 6.2
A spreadsheet with shading

```
 File  Edit  Style  Graph  Print  Database  Tools  Options  Window       ↑↓
 A1:                                                                      |  ?
└         A         B          C            D               E       F    ↑End
 1                                                                        ▪  ▲
 2                         Daily Sales Totals                                ◄ ►
 3                                                                           ▼
 4
 5            DATE     DEPARTMENT   DEPT. NUMBER     TOTAL SALES          Esc
 6            -----------------------------------------------------
 7            01-Jun   TV/Stereo         1100   ▓▓▓▓▓▓▓▓▓▓▓▓▓           ↵
 8                     Housewares        1200   ▓▓▓▓▓▓▓▓▓▓▓▓▓
 9                     Appliances        1300   ▓▓▓▓▓▓▓▓▓▓▓▓▓          Del
10            02-Jun   TV/Stereo         1100   ▓▓▓▓▓▓▓▓▓▓▓▓▓
11                     Housewares        1200   ▓▓▓▓▓▓▓▓▓▓▓▓▓          @
12                     Appliances        1300   ▓▓▓▓▓▓▓▓▓▓▓▓▓
13            03-Jun   TV/Stereo         1100   ▓▓▓▓▓▓▓▓▓▓▓▓▓          5
14                     Housewares        1200   ▓▓▓▓▓▓▓▓▓▓▓▓▓
15                     Appliances        1300   ▓▓▓▓▓▓▓▓▓▓▓▓▓          6
16            04-Jun   TV/Stereo         1100   ▓▓▓▓▓▓▓▓▓▓▓▓▓
17                     Housewares        1200   ▓▓▓▓▓▓▓▓▓▓▓▓▓          7
18                     Appliances        1300   ▓▓▓▓▓▓▓▓▓▓▓▓▓
19            05-Jun   TV/Stereo         1100   ▓▓▓▓▓▓▓▓▓▓▓▓▓
20                     Housewares        1200   ▓▓▓▓▓▓▓▓▓▓▓▓▓
 ←                                                                       ►
 SHEET1.WQ1      [1]                    CAP                         READY
```

To shade an area of a spreadsheet,

```
┌ Shading ┐
│ None    │
│ Grey    │
│ Black   │
└─────────┘
```

1. Choose /**Style** | **Shading**.

2. Choose **Grey** to print shading in grey, **B**lack to shade in black, or **None** to remove shading from a block.

3. Specify the cell or block you want to shade.

Quattro displays both black and grey shading as black and grey on your screen by default. Grey shading appears only in the part of the cell not occupied by data; behind the data itself, the shading is black. On a monochrome screen, black shading appears as bold. To change the onscreen shading color, use the /**Options** | **Colors** | **Spreadsheet** | **Shading** command (see "Spreadsheet colors" in Chapter 7).

If you use shading in combination with line drawing, the shading can sometimes overlap lines (for example, if you box a cell, then shade it). When you print the spreadsheet, however, shading lines up correctly with the lines.

Note   To print shaded cells in the spreadsheet, use the /**Print** | **Destination** | **Graphics Printer** command to specify graphics printing; otherwise, the shaded cells won't print. For more information, see page 84.

1-2-3   If you're using the 123-compatible menus, choose /**Range** | **Output Style** | **Shading**.

Choosing a font

With the /Style | Font command, you can change the typeface, style, color, and point size used to print characters in your spreadsheet. You can use up to eight different fonts in a spreadsheet, and you can redefine any of the available fonts by adjusting its typeface, style, size, and color. The fonts are used for printing only and don't appear on your screen (except during a screen preview).

To assign a font to a block,

1. Choose /Style | Font. Quattro displays a menu of eight popular fonts, plus the **Edit Fonts** and **Reset** commands.
2. Choose the font you want to use. (To use fonts other than those listed, use **Edit Fonts** to alter available fonts. See the next section.)
3. Specify the block you want to assign the font to.

 If you're using the 123-compatible menus, use /Range | Output Style | Font.

By default, Quattro uses Bitstream Dutch 12-point black, or whatever you've edited the first font selection to be. An easy way to change the font for *all* spreadsheet cells except those to which you've explicitly assigned a font is to edit Font 1 (see the next section).

Font changes won't show up on your screen, but Quattro uses them when you print. To print using anything other than the default font, you must have the /Print | Destination command set to **Graphics Printer** (see page 84). To view the font change on your screen, use the /Print | Destination | Screen Preview command (see page 84).

To change fonts used in graph text, see "Setting font options" in Chapter 13.

Redefining installed fonts

The default options on the /Style | Font menu give you a good assortment of text fonts to choose from. However, these options reflect only a portion of the available typefaces, point sizes, colors, and styles. Although you can have only eight defined text fonts at a time, you can alter any of the predefined fonts to suit your own style.

Note   The font defined in the first slot (Font 1) is the default font, and Quattro uses it for any part of the spreadsheet that isn't assigned a specific font. Quattro also uses the default font to calculate standard column width and row height. So if you redefine Font 1, be sure to use the typeface, size, style, and color you want for the overall graph.

To redefine any of the fonts shown on the Font menu,

1. Choose /Style | Font. Quattro displays a list of eight predefined fonts and the Edit Fonts and Reset commands.

2. Choose Edit Fonts.

```
Typeface     ▶
Point Size   ▶
Style        ▶
Color        ▶
Quit
```

3. Choose the font slot you want to redefine. Quattro displays the menu of the characteristics you can redefine for that font: typeface, point size, style, and color.

4. To use a different typeface for the font, choose Typeface, then choose any of the listed selections. (Figure 6.3 shows how the typefaces appear when printed. See Appendix F for details on the different typefaces available.)

5. To change the size of the font, choose Point Size, then choose any of the standard sizes offered.

6. To change the font style, choose Style, then choose any of four possible styles: Bold, Italic, Underlined, and Reset. (Reset returns the font to regular style.)

Note   Bold and Italic are available with only a few typefaces. Specifically, you can only use bold with Bitstream Dutch and Bitstream Swiss, and you can only use italic with Bitstream Dutch, Bitstream Swiss, Bitstream Courier, and Roman. You can specify using these styles with other typefaces, but they won't take effect in printing.

7. To change the color assigned to the font, choose Color, then choose an available color. Remember that spreadsheet fonts affect printed output, not screen display, so this setting works only if you have a color printer.

8. When you're done making adjustments, choose Quit to return to the Edit Fonts menu where you'll see your new definition of that font slot.

To reset all fonts to the default settings, choose /Style | Font | Reset.

Note   If you choose a printer-specific font from the **Typeface** menu, you won't be able to adjust the size or style of the font (see "Printer-specific fonts" in Appendix F).

When you redefine a font using a high-quality Bitstream typeface (Dutch, Swiss, and Courier), Quattro needs to create a new font file before it can display or print the font. It may pause to do this when you go into the Screen Previewer or begin printing. Once created, though, Quattro can access the file without pausing. For more information on building font files, see Appendix F. If you prefer to turn font building off until you are ready to print your final draft, set the /Options l Graphics Quality command to **Draft** (see page 198).

Important!   In order to create a new Bitstream font file, Quattro requires 125K bytes of free memory.

1-2-3   If you're using the 123-compatible menus, choose /**Range** l **Output Style** l **Font** l **Edit Fonts**. Choose a font, then choose the font characteristic you want to change.

The following figure shows the standard typefaces available with Quattro:

Figure 6.3
Standard Quattro typefaces

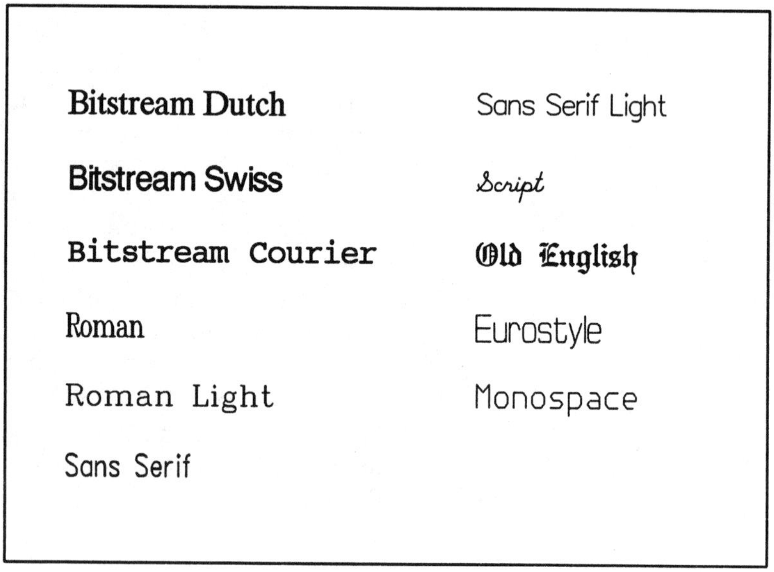

Bitstream Dutch	Sans Serif Light
Bitstream Swiss	*Script*
Bitstream Courier	𝕺𝖑𝖉 𝕰𝖓𝖌𝖑𝖎𝖘𝖍
Roman	Eurostyle
Roman Light	Monospace
Sans Serif	

Adding bullet characters

A design option that isn't on the **Style** menu is the *bullet* feature. This is a special code that prints bullet characters of various styles in your spreadsheet. You simply type the following code where you want the bullet to appear:

```
\bullet #\
```

where # represents the number of the bullet character you want to use.

Important! Add a label-prefix character to the bullet code if it is the first thing you are entering in a spreadsheet cell; without it, Quattro interprets the string as something you want to repeat across the cell. The bullet character numbers are as follows:

0 box
1 filled box
2 checked box
3 check
4 shadowed box
5 shadowed checked box
6 filled circle

When you print the spreadsheet, Quattro inserts the appropriate bullet character in place of the code. To see the bullet character on the screen, set the **/Print | Destination** command to **Screen | Preview** and then choose **/Print | Spreadsheet Print**.

1-2-3
If you're using the 123-compatible menus, choose **/Print | Screen Preview | Go**.

The following figure shows all of Quattro's bullets, which you can use both in your spreadsheets and in graphs:

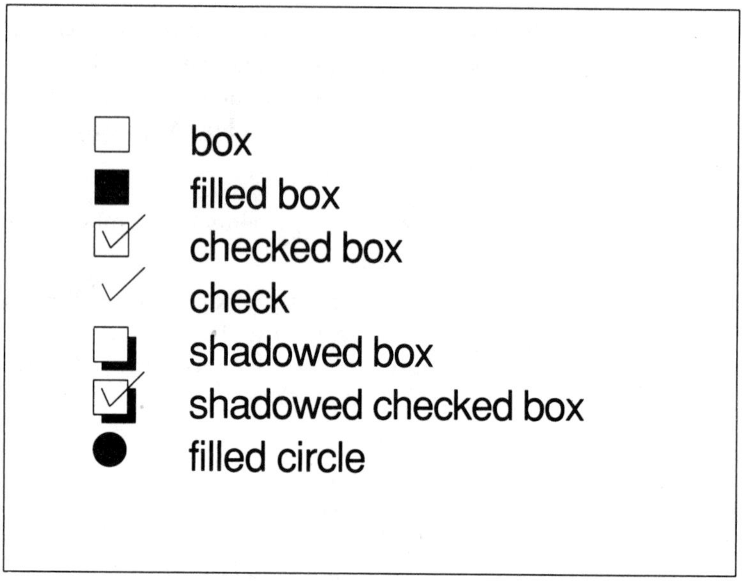

Figure 6.4
Quattro's bullet characters

☐ box
■ filled box
☑ checked box
✓ check
☐ shadowed box
☑ shadowed checked box
● filled circle

See "Graph text," beginning on page 344, for information about including bullets in graph text; no label-prefix character is necessary in the bullet syntax for graph text. "Creating design elements" on page 400 discusses how to add bullets to a text element in the Graph Annotator.

Inserting page breaks

Quattro automatically inserts page breaks where needed as specified by the /Print | Layout | Margins | Page Length command (see page 94). You can also specify *hard page breaks* as well. You insert hard page breaks manually; Quattro stores them with the spreadsheet, and they remain until deleted from your spreadsheet.

There are two ways to create hard page breaks:

- Type them into the spreadsheet.
- Use the /Style | Insert Break command.

To type a page break into the spreadsheet,

1. Move the selector to the first cell in the row of the print block where you want to begin a new page.

2. Choose /Edit | Insert | **R**ows and press *Enter* to insert a blank row above the current cell.

3. Type | :: (a vertical bar and two colons) and press *Enter*. This enters two colons at the beginning of the row, indicating a page break.

To insert a page break using the menus,

1. Move the selector to the first cell in the row at which you want to begin a new page.

2. Choose /**S**tyle | **I**nsert Break.

🌸
1-2-3
If you're using the 123-compatible menus, choose /**W**orksheet | **P**age Break.

The following figure shows a spreadsheet with two page breaks inserted:

Figure 6.5
Two page breaks in a
spreadsheet

```
File   Edit   Style   Graph   Print   Database   Tools   Options   Window        ↑↓
A1:                                                                            |  ?
 J      A          B           C          D           E            F           ↑End
1                                                                              □ ▲
2                        1989 BUSINESS EXPENSES                                ◄ ►
3                                                                                ▼
4                    Salaries    Insurance   Travel   Entertainment   Supplies
5       04-Oct       $58,600     $1,800      $1,989          $560     $1,999
6       11-Oct       $58,600     $1,800      $2,007          $599     $2,022    Esc
7       18-Oct       $58,600     $1,800      $2,406          $609     $2,032
8       25-Oct       $58,600     $1,800      $2,450          $621     $2,087    ↵
9    ::
10      01-Nov       $58,600     $1,800      $2,494          $633     $2,142    Del
11      08-Nov       $58,600     $1,800      $2,538          $645     $2,197
12      15-Nov       $58,600     $1,800      $2,582          $657     $2,252    @
13      22-Nov       $58,600     $1,800      $2,626          $669     $2,307
14      29-Nov       $76,000     $1,800      $2,670          $681     $2,362    5
15   ::
16      06-Dec       $76,000     $1,800      $2,714          $693     $2,417    6
17      13-Dec       $76,000     $1,800      $2,758          $705     $2,472
18      20-Dec       $76,000     $1,800      $2,802          $717     $2,527    7
19      27-Dec       $76,000     $1,800      $2,846          $729     $2,582
20
SHEET1.WQ1      [1]                                                         READY
```

7

Setting options

There are two kinds of options you can set in Quattro:

- **System options** affect the entire Quattro program. They determine things like the display colors for the program and the directory where Quattro stores your spreadsheets. You can change system options temporarily or store them with the program so they're used from now on. The stored, or *updated*, settings remain in effect until you change them again.

- **Global options** determine overall defaults for the current spreadsheet. For example, the /Options I Formats I Numeric Format command sets the default display formats for the spreadsheet, which you can then override for a block with the /Style I Numeric Format command. Quattro stores global options with the spreadsheet and uses them each time you load it. Between spreadsheets, however, Quattro reverts to the original settings for these options.

One system option not discussed in this chapter is Display Mode; see "Setting display mode" on page 33.

The Options menu

```
═══ Options ═══
Hardware          ▶
Colors            ▶
International     ▶
Display Mode      ▶
Startup           ▶
Mouse Palette     ▶
Graphics Quality  ▶
Other             ▶
─────────────────
Update
─────────────────
Formats           ▶
Recalculation     ▶
Protection        ▶
Quit
```

You can change both global and system options with commands on the **Options** menu. The first group of commands on this menu deals with system options, which you can save as new defaults with the **Update** command. The last group of commands deals with global options, which affect individual spreadsheets.

Caution: /Options I Update saves *all* updatable default settings, even those set in other menus, such as the /Print I Layout and /Options I Display Mode defaults.

- **Hardware** lets you specify information about your computer screen and the printer you'll be using to print spreadsheets, as well as any special fonts you want to use. It also shows your system's memory use, expanded memory (EMS), and any coprocessor.

- **Colors** lets you change the display colors and intensities of the spreadsheet, menus, and File Manager.

- **International** determines the standards for displaying currency, punctuation, date, and time.

- **Display Mode** lets you change the mode Quattro uses to display spreadsheets and menus on your screen. Normally, Quattro uses 80x25 character mode. You can switch to a more condensed display or to a graphics mode that lets you view graphics within the spreadsheet. See "Setting display mode" on page 33 for information.

- **Startup** lets you specify default information that Quattro uses to start up the program, such as the default extension it should add to spreadsheet files and the name of an autoload file.

- **Mouse Palette** lets you redefine the functions of the mouse palette buttons that display along the right edge of your screen.

- **Graphics Quality** lets you choose between draft-quality fonts with faster display and printing and presentation-quality fonts; with the latter, Quattro pauses to build new font files when you display and print.

- **Other** lets you enable or disable the /Edit I Undo command (*Alt-F5* is the default shortcut for Undo). You can also change the clock display, specify when to redraw the screen during macro execution, tell Quattro how to use expanded memory (if available on your computer), and set options to access Paradox files on a local area network.

- **Update** makes the current option settings permanent by storing them in the Quattro resource files, RSC.RF and QUATTRO.MU.

- **Formats** determines the standard spreadsheet display format, label alignment, zero display, and column width.

- **Recalculation** determines the order of formula calculation, the number of iterations, and whether formulas are calculated automatically (either in the foreground or in the background) or only when you press the Calc key (*F9*). It also lets you track circular cell references.

- **Protection** lets you protect your spreadsheet from any changes being made to it.

- **Quit** returns you to the spreadsheet.

To override global options for specific blocks of the spreadsheet (for example, to use a different display format or to alter the width of an individual column), use the **S**tyle commands (see Chapter 6, "Changing the style of your spreadsheet").

Hardware options

The **Hardware** menu contains information about your system that you specified during installation. It also displays information about your system's memory and coprocessor (if one is installed on your computer). You can use it to change settings for your computer screen or printer(s) without having to exit Quattro and run the installation program again.

Choose /Options | **Hardware** to display the Hardware menu.

- **Screen** lets you specify information about your computer screen, overriding Quattro's automatic screen detection. You can also use it to configure your own video driver and to adjust your screen's aspect ratio, which Quattro uses to display pie charts.

- **Printers** lets you specify the type of printer(s) you'll use. You can specify up to two printers. You can also use this command to set special font options.

- **Normal Memory** displays the number of bytes of available system memory (RAM).

- **EMS** displays the number of bytes of available expanded memory (if any). Quattro automatically detects and uses expanded memory. To alter how much of your EMS Quattro uses for spreadsheets, use the /Options Other Expanded Memory command described later in this chapter.

- **Coprocessor** displays the type of math coprocessor (if any) used by your computer (8087, 80287, or 80387). This is detected and used automatically.

Once you've set the /Options I Hardware commands to reflect your system's configuration, press *Esc* and choose **Update** from the **Options** menu to make the settings permanent (see "Updating the system options" later in this chapter).

Use caution when you choose /Options I **Update** because it saves *all* default settings.

1-2-3
If you're using the 123-compatible menus, choose /**Worksheet** I **Global** I **Default** I **Hardware**.

Screen options

During installation, Quattro automatically detects one of the following types of screens and loads a special file, called a *driver file*, that contains information about your screen:

AT&T 400 Line	IBM 3270 PC
CGA	IBM 8514/A
EGA	MCGA
Hercules	VGA

If you're using a nonstandard screen type, you may need to specify information about the screen with the /Options I Hardware I Screen command. You can also use this command to change the resolution or aspect ratio used for displaying graphs, or to specify a second screen for graphs.

```
===== Screen =====

Screen Type           ►
Resolution            ►
Aspect Ratio
CGA Snow Suppression  ►
Quit
```

When you choose /Options I Hardware I Screen, the Screen menu appears.

- **Screen Type** lets you specify a different screen driver for displaying graphs. This can be a second screen attached to your computer, or one that you switch to for displaying graphs. When you choose this command, Quattro displays a list of screen types. Choose the type you'll be using for graphs.

- **Resolution** lets you change the resolution of your screen.

- **Aspect Ratio** lets you adjust your screen so that it displays a perfect circle (used for displaying pie charts).
- **CGA Snow Suppression** lets you prevent the screen from flickering when you scroll, which is sometimes a problem with CGA screens.
- **Quit** returns you to the **Options** menu.

Caution! After you make changes to the screen defaults, choose /**Options** | **Update** to save the changes. Otherwise, the original defaults take effect next time you use Quattro.

Note If you have a black-and-white screen with a color graphics card, Quattro treats it as if it were color and translates the colors into shades of black and white. Some of the shades may be hard to distinguish onscreen. To switch to black and white display, choose **Black** & White from the /**Options** | **Colors** | **Palettes** menu.

The following sections describe how to switch your screen to a different resolution and adjust the aspect ratio used by your screen to display graphs.

Setting the resolution

If you have a color monitor, you can change the resolution of Quattro graphs with the **Resolution** command. Choose **Resolution** from the /**Options** | **Hardware** | **Screen** menu to display a menu listing the modes available for your particular screen type. (If you don't have a color monitor, no options are listed.)

The initial default for each screen type is the highest resolution available. If you have a CGA monitor, Quattro uses black-and-white display for graphs to attain higher resolution.

Choose the mode you want to use. It becomes effective when you leave the menu. If you want to use the new resolution from now on, choose **Update** from the **Options** menu.

1-2-3
If you're using the 123-compatible menus, choose /**Worksheet** | **Global** | **Default** | **Hardware** | **Resolution**.

Adjusting the aspect ratio

Different monitors have different *aspect ratios*, which is the ratio of the screen's width to its height. In order to display a perfect circle on your screen (as is needed for a pie chart), Quattro needs to know the aspect ratio of your particular screen. In most cases, Quattro estimates this accurately. But, if pie charts appear slightly elongated on your screen, you can use the **Aspect Ratio** command to adjust the display.

When you choose **Aspect Ratio** from the /**Options** | **Hardware** | **Screen** menu, Quattro displays a circle on your screen. Use ↑ and ↓ to expand or contract the circle's height until it appears to be perfectly round. Then press *Enter*. Quattro then uses the new aspect ratio to display pie charts.

Caution! Be sure to update this setting with /**Options** | **Update** after adjusting the ratio if you want to use it as the new default.

If you're using the 123-compatible menus, choose /**Worksheet** | **Global** | **Default** | **Hardware** | **Aspect Ratio**.

Defining printers

When you installed Quattro, you specified information about the printer(s) you use to print spreadsheets and graphs. With the /**Options** | **Hardware** | **Printers** command, you can make changes to those specifications without running the install program again. This command displays the **Printers** menu.

```
═══ Printers ═══
1st Printer       ▶
2nd Printer       ▶
Default Printer   ▶

Plotter Speed     ▶
Fonts             ▶
Auto LF           ▶
Single Sheet      ▶
Quit
```

- **1st Printer** lets you specify information about your primary printer.

- **2nd Printer** lets you specify information about a second printer.

- **Default Printer** lets you choose between the primary and second installed printers for your default printer.

- **Plotter Speed** prompts you for the speed at which you want to run your color plotter. The default value, 0, results in the fastest speed allowed by your plotter, or whatever speed your plotter is set to; otherwise, 1 is the slowest speed and 9 the fastest. A setting of 2 is recommended for printing on transparencies. As your pens age, you may want to reduce speed to improve print quality.

- **Fonts** allows you to specify any LaserJet font cartridges you're using and turn off automatic scaling for fonts in graphs.

- **Auto LF** specifies whether your printer automatically inserts a carriage return and linefeed character at the end of each line. The initial default is **No**. If you don't know whether your printer has automatic linefeed, check your printer's manual or print some sample text. If your printout appears double spaced, change this to **Yes**; if it prints everything on one line without advancing, change this to **No**.

- **Single Sheet** specifies whether you'll be using continuous-feed paper. The initial default expects continuous-feed paper. If you'll be using single sheets of paper, set this to **Yes**.

■ **Quit** returns you to the **O**ptions menu.

1-2-3

If you're using the 123-compatible menus, choose /**W**orksheet I **G**lobal I **D**efault I **H**ardware I **P**rinters.

Graphics Printer options

During installation, you specified information about one or two printers for use with Quattro. To make changes to those specifications, use the **1**st Printer or **2**nd Printer commands. Both take you to the same menu.

```
╔══ 1st Printer ══╗
║ Type of Printer ▶║
║ ─Make────────────║
║ ─Model───────────║
║ ─Mode────────────║
║ Device          ▶║
║ Baud Rate       ▶║
║ Parity          ▶║
║ Stop Bits       ▶║
║ Quit             ║
╚══════════════════╝
```

■ **Type of Printer** lets you set the make, model, and mode of your printer. Once set, they're displayed in the lines below this command.

■ **Device** displays a list of possible printer connections: Parallel 1 or 2, Serial 1 or 2, and the DOS devices LPT1 through LPT4 and EPT. The default is Parallel 1. If you choose a serial device, Quattro uses the printer setup established by DOS to determine baud rate, parity, and number of stop bits. If you've already set up your computer to work with this printer, you won't need to adjust these settings. If not, you may need to use the **B**aud Rate, **P**arity, and **S**top Bits commands (see below). If anything needs adjusting, it's usually the baud rate.

■ **Baud Rate** specifies the baud rate (110 to 19200) at which Quattro will communicate with your serial printer. The initial default, Leave As Is, uses the baud rate set by the most recent DOS MODE command.

■ **Parity** specifies the type of parity your serial printer uses. You can set this to **O**dd, **E**ven, **N**one, or Leave As Is. The initial default, Leave As Is, uses the parity set by the DOS MODE command.

■ **Stop Bits** specifies how many stop bits are used at the end of each transmitted byte. You can set this to **1** Bit, **2** Bits, or Leave As Is. The initial default, Leave As Is, uses the number of stop bits set by the DOS MODE command.

■ **Quit** returns you to the **P**rinters menu.

To make changes to your primary printer specifications,

1. Choose /**O**ptions I **H**ardware I **P**rinters.
2. Choose **1**st Printer.
3. Choose **T**ype of Printer.
4. Choose the make of your printer (or the make closest to it) from the displayed list.

5. Choose the model of your printer.

6. Choose the mode of your printer.

7. Choose **Device.** Then specify the device connection to which this printer is attached.

8. If you specified a serial device, you may need to specify baud rate, parity, and stop bits. By default, Quattro uses the settings established by DOS for these commands. If you want to change any of them, choose the command and enter a new value.

9. To specify information about a second printer, press *Esc* and choose **2nd Printer.** Repeat the last six steps.

When you've specified information about your printers, press *Esc* three times to return to the **Options** menu and choose **Update.** This stores the information for future use.

Note If you switch printers, Quattro remembers the first typeface setting you chose and prints in that typeface or the closest matching face. However, the **Typeface** menu reflects only the fonts available for the currently selected printer. See Appendix F for more information about fonts.

To send a graph or spreadsheet with high-quality graphics like lines and shading to your graphics printer, use the /**Print** I **Destination** I **Graphics Printer** command (see page 84).

PostScript printer modes

When you specify that your printer is a PostScript printer, Quattro offers two printing modes: **Normal** and **Use Patterns.** The mode you pick affects how printed graphs appear. If you choose **Normal,** any fill patterns in your graphs print as shaded areas. If you choose **Use Patterns,** the graphs print a little more slowly, but the fill patterns in your printed graph look the same as when you display or preview your graph.

The Default Printer option The **Default Printer** command tells Quattro which of your two defined printers to use. You can use this command to switch easily between two printers or print modes. Quattro uses the settings for the default printer when you print to disk, to a graphics printer, or to the Screen Previewer.

Choose /**Options** I **Hardware** I **Printers** I **Default Printer** to display the **Default Printer** menu.

```
┌─ Default Printer ─┐
│                   │
│ 1st Printer       │
│ 2nd Printer       │
└───────────────────┘
```

See the previous section, "Graphics printer options," for a description of how to change the specifications of your installed **1st** or **2nd Printer.**

After you've changed the default printer, choose /**Options** | **Update** to make the changes permanent.

Caution! If you choose /**Options** | **Update,** you'll update *all* default settings.

 If you're using the 123-compatible menus, use /**Worksheet** | **Global** | **Default** | **Printer.**

Font options

Quattro comes with several Bitstream typefaces that you can use to build fonts for printing spreadsheet text or printing and displaying graph text. Quattro also lets you use additional Bitstream typefaces that are available separately or come with application programs. To use the additional Bitstream fonts, you must first "load" them into Quattro. This copies the font files and reformats them for Quattro's use, giving them a .SFO file-name extension.

Note Quattro includes its own installation program for Bitstream fonts, BSINST.EXE. See Appendix F for information. Use it instead of the installation procedure documented in your Bitstream manual.

```
┌═══ Fonts ═══┐
│             │
│ LaserJet Fonts  ►│
│ Autoscale Fonts ►│
└─────────────┘
```

Quattro includes two other font options. Choose /**Options** | **Hardware** | **Printers** | **Fonts** to display the Fonts menu.

■ **LaserJet Fonts** lets you tell Quattro which cartridge fonts you have installed in your LaserJet printer. Specify which set of fonts (if any) is in the left cartridge and which is in the right.

■ **Autoscale Fonts** lets you override Quattro's automatic font-scaling option. Quattro works hard to make your graphs look good, no matter how large or small the space in which you choose to display them. By default, Quattro reduces point sizes as a function of the portion of the screen (or sheet of paper) allocated for the graph. The less vertical space allocated for the graph, the smaller the autoscaled point size of graph text. If you prefer that Quattro not automatically scale fonts, set **Autoscale Fonts** to **No.**

If **Autoscale Fonts** is set to **No,** eight points is the smallest font size Quattro generates. To allow Quattro to create font sizes smaller than eight points, **Autoscale Fonts** must be set to **Yes.**

See page 164 for information about choosing spreadsheet fonts. See page 347 for details about choosing fonts for graph text. "Choosing font quality," on page 198, explains how to switch between a draft-quality mode that builds no new font files and a final-quality mode that builds new font files as necessary.

Color options

The color combinations that Quattro displays on a color monitor are carefully chosen to enhance readability. However, since colors are often a matter of personal preference, Quattro lets you adjust the colors used in each part of the program.

```
═══ Colors ═══
Menu            ▶
Desktop         ▶
Spreadsheet     ▶
Conditional     ▶
Help            ▶
File Manager    ▶
Palettes        ▶
Quit
```

When you choose /Options ┃ Colors, Quattro displays the Colors menu.

■ **Menu** determines the display colors of the command menus.

■ **Desktop** sets colors for error and status messages on the screen. It also lets you change the ASCII characters used to fill in the screen background and shading.

■ **Spreadsheet** determines the colors in spreadsheet windows.

■ **Conditional** lets you specify different colors for spreadsheet values that meet certain conditions.

■ **Help** lets you change the display colors of the help system.

■ **File Manager** lets you change the colors in a File Manager window.

■ **Palettes** lets you restore the default colors for a display in color, monochrome, or black and white with a CGA video adapter.

■ **Quit** returns you to the Options menu.

After you've changed any of the colors, press *Esc* and choose Update from the Options menu to make the changes permanent.

Caution! Choose /Options ┃ Update only when you want to save *all* default settings.

 If you're using the 123-compatible menus, choose /**Worksheet** ┃ **Global** ┃ **Default** ┃ **Colors**.

Menu colors

The /Options | Colors | Menu command lets you change the display colors of menus onscreen: the menu frame, the banner, the first letters of the menu items, and so forth.

Choose /Options | Colors | Menu to display the **Menu** menu.

- **Frame** determines the color of the box around the Quattro menus.
- **Banner** sets the color of the menu name.
- **Text** is the color for menu items (all but the first letter).
- **Key Letter** sets the color of the first letter of each menu item.
- **Highlight** determines the color of the highlight bar used to choose menu items.
- **Settings** is the color for the command settings in the menu.
- **Explanation** sets the color for the menu command description at the bottom of the screen.
- **Drop Shadow** determines the color of the shadow under the menu frame.

  To remove the menu shadow from display, choose Drop Shadow from the /Options | Colors | Menu menu, then choose Empty (for a monochrome screen), or choose the color in the top left corner of the palette (for a color screen).
- **Mouse Palette** affects the color of the mouse palette on the right of the spreadsheet screen.
- **Shadow** determines the ASCII character used to create menu shadows.
- **Quit** returns you to the Colors menu.

To change the color for an item listed on this menu,

1. Choose the area you want to change. A color palette appears, displaying every color or hue available. (If you have a monochrome screen, you'll see a menu of display attributes.)
2. Use the arrow keys to highlight the color or option you want to use. Then press *Enter* to choose it. The color palette (or menu) disappears and Quattro immediately displays the item in its new color.
3. Change the color of another item, or save the new color as the default (see the next step).

4. If you want to save the colors you chose as the new defaults, press *Q* twice to return to the **Options** menu and choose **Update**, or press */OU* if you've exited the menus.

Caution!   /**Options** | **Update** saves *all* default settings.

 You can use a mouse to choose a color from the color palette. Just click the color combination you want.

 If you're using the 123-compatible menus, choose /**Worksheet** | **Global** | **Default** | **Colors** | **Menu**.

Desktop colors

```
═══ Desktop ═══
─Colors─────────
 Status
 Highlight-Status
 Errors
 Background
─Fill Characters─
 Desktop
 Quit
```

The /**Options** | **Colors** | **Desktop** menu lets you set color options for the Quattro *desktop*, the part of the screen not filled with a spreadsheet window. This includes the status line and the screen background. You can also specify the characters to use for background shading and the mouse pointer.

Quattro displays the **Desktop** menu when you choose /**Options** | **Colors** | **Desktop**.

- **Status** determines the color for the file name, date and time (if any), and standard indicators on the status (bottom) line.

- **Highlight Status** sets the color for the WAIT and ENTER indicators on the status line.

- **Errors** is the color for error messages on the screen.

- **Background** lets you change the color underneath spreadsheet or directory windows. This color is revealed only when you shrink a window smaller than the screen and no other windows are underneath it.

- **Desktop** determines the ASCII character used to display the background color when no windows are displayed; for example, when you've resized a spreadsheet window to fill only half the screen.

- **Quit** returns you to the **Colors** menu.

Press *Ctrl-Break* to return directly to the spreadsheet.

The steps necessary to change desktop colors and save them as the new defaults are the same as for menu colors (page 181).

 If you're using the 123-compatible menus, choose /**Worksheet** | **Global** | **Default** | **Colors** | **Desktop**.

Spreadsheet colors

The /Options I Colors I Spreadsheet menu lets you change the colors of parts of the spreadsheet screen. Choose /Options I Colors I Spreadsheet to display the **Spreadsheet** menu.

```
╔═ Spreadsheet ═╗
║ Frame         ║
║ Banner        ║
║ Cells         ║
║ Borders       ║
║ Titles        ║
║ Highlight     ║
║ Graph Frames  ║
║ Input Line    ║
║ Unprotected   ║
║ Labels        ║
║ Shading       ║
║ Drawn Lines   ║
║ Quit          ║
╚═══════════════╝
```

- **Frame** determines the color that boxes, or frames, each spreadsheet window.
- **Banner** lets you change the color for spreadsheet banners, used to display spreadsheet names when more than one spreadsheet window is on the screen.
- **Cells** sets the color for cells in the spreadsheet.
- **Borders** determines the color of the box around the spreadsheet and the column and row borders.
- **Titles** sets the color for locked titles.
- **Highlight** lets you change the highlight color for the current cell.
- **Graph Frames** determines the frame color for any graph you insert in the spreadsheet.
- **Input Line** sets the color for data on the input line at the top of the screen.
- **Unprotected** lets you change the color for cells in the spreadsheet whose protection status has been explicitly changed with the /Style I Protection I Disable command.
- **Labels** specifies the color to use for label entries.
- **Shading** determines the fill color for cells shaded with the /Style I Shading command.
- **Drawn Lines** affects the color of lines drawn on a spreadsheet with /Style I Line Drawing.
- **Quit** returns you to the Colors menu.

The steps necessary to change spreadsheet colors and save them as the new defaults are the same as for menu colors (page 181).

 If you're using the 123-compatible menus, choose /Worksheet I Global I Default I Colors I Spreadsheet.

To vary the display colors for cells based on the values contained in them, use the Conditional command (see the next section).

Conditional colors

The /Options | Colors | Conditional menu lets you change the color of specific types of data displayed in your spreadsheet: ERR values, labels, values above or below a specified range, and so forth. You can use it to highlight specific values in your spreadsheet. For example, you could display all negative values in red or all values greater than 1000 in green.

```
╔══════ Conditional ══════╗
║ On/Off               ▶  ║
║ ERR                     ║
║ Smallest Normal Value   ║
║ Greatest Normal Value   ║
║ Below Normal Color      ║
║ Normal Cell Color       ║
║ Above Normal Color      ║
║ Quit                    ║
╚═════════════════════════╝
```

Choose /Options | Colors | Conditional to display the Conditional menu.

■ **On/Off** tells Quattro whether to use the conditional colors set with this menu. It has two options: Enable and Disable. **Disable** is the initial default.

■ **ERR** specifies the color to use for ERR and NA values generated by formula errors.

■ **Smallest Normal Value** and **Greatest Normal Value** let you set up a range of values to be considered normal, which will display in the normal cell color. You can then specify different colors for values within the range, above the range, and below the range.

■ **Below Normal Color** specifies the color to use for values below the number indicated with **S**mallest Normal Value.

■ **Normal Cell Color** specifies the color to use for values within the range set up with **S**mallest Normal Value and **G**reatest Normal Value.

■ **Above Normal Color** specifies the color to use for values above the number indicated with **G**reatest Normal Value.

■ **Quit** returns you to the Colors menu.

To set up conditional colors,

1. Choose /Options | Colors | Conditional.
2. Choose **S**mallest Normal Value and enter the lowest value you want included in the range.
3. Choose **G**reatest Normal Value and enter the highest value you want included in the range.
4. Choose **O**n/Off, then Enable to turn on conditional colors.
5. Choose the type of value you want affected (ERR, **B**elow Normal Color, Normal Cell Color, or **A**bove Normal Color).

6. Choose the color combination you want to use from the displayed color palette (or menu, if you have a monochrome screen).

 You can use a mouse to choose a color from the color palette. Just click the color combination you want.

7. To change the color used for another type of data, choose the type from the Conditional menu and choose a color from the palette or menu.

8. If you want to use the new colors next time you work with Quattro, press *Q* twice and choose Update from the Options menu.

Quattro uses the new conditional colors immediately. To turn off conditional colors, choose /Options | Colors | Conditional | On/Off | Disable.

Quattro saves the On/Off, Smallest Normal Value, and Greatest Normal Value settings with each spreadsheet. If you want to save all conditional settings as the new defaults, press *Q* twice and choose Update from the Options menu, or press */OU* if you've exited the menus.

Note Spreadsheet display is faster when conditional colors are disabled. For quick display response, disable conditional colors when they're not necessary.

1-2-3 If you're using the 123-compatible menus, choose /Worksheet | Global | Default | Colors | Conditional.

Help colors

```
┌─── Help ───┐
│ Frame      │
│ Banner     │
│ Text       │
│ Keywords   │
│ Highlight  │
│ Quit       │
└────────────┘
```

The Help menu lets you change the colors of help information on your screen when you press *F1*. When you choose /Options | Colors | Help, the Help menu appears.

- **Frame** determines the color for the box, or frame, around the help window.

- **Banner** specifies the color of the name of the help screen.

- **Text** sets the color of general text in the help screen.

- **Keywords** lets you change the color of key words, or words that you can choose to display more information.

- **Highlight** determines the color of the help cursor used to select key words.

- **Quit** returns you to the Colors menu.

The steps necessary to change help colors and save them as the new defaults are the same as for menu colors (page 181).

If you're using the 123-compatible menus, choose /**W**orksheet | **G**lobal | **D**efault | **C**olors | **H**elp.

File Manager colors

The File Manager menu lets you change the colors for file information in the File Manager. Choose /**O**ptions | **C**olors | **F**ile Manager to display the File Manager menu.

You can also display this menu from within the File Manager. Choose /**F**ile | **U**tilities | **F**ile Manager. Quattro displays a File Manager window. Now choose /**O**ptions | **C**olors | **F**ile Manager. Quattro displays the File Manager menu, a duplicate of the menu accessed with the /**O**ptions | **C**olors command in a spreadsheet window.

```
╒═ File Manager ═╕
│                │
│ Frame          │
│ Banner         │
│ Text           │
│ Active Cursor  │
│ Inactive Cursor│
│ Marked         │
│ Move           │
│ Copy           │
│ Quit           │
│                │
╘════════════════╛
```

- **Frame** determines the color of the box around the File Manager window.

- **Banner** sets the color of the name of the directory at the top of the File Manager window.

- **Text** specifies the color of the text in the File Manager window.

- **Active Cursor** specifies the color of the cursor or highlight in the active pane.

- **Inactive Cursor** lets you change the color of selections outside the current pane. For example, when you're in the control pane, the currently selected file has the inactive cursor color.

- **Marked** determines the color of data you have marked in the File Manager window with the Select key, *Shift-F7*.

- **Move** sets the display color of file names you have selected for moving in the File Manager window with the Move key, *Shift-F8*.

- **Copy** sets the display color of file names you have selected for copying in the File Manager window with the Copy key, *Shift-F9*.

- **Quit** returns you to the Colors menu.

The steps necessary to change File Manager colors and save them as the new defaults are the same as for menu colors (page 181).

If you're using the 123-compatible menus, choose /**W**orksheet | **G**lobal | **D**efault | **C**olors | **F**ile Manager.

Reinstating
default colors

After you've made changes to any of the colors used, you can reinstate the original default colors for either monochrome or color screens.

To override any color changes you've made, even after updating the defaults, choose /Options | Colors | Palettes. The Palettes menu appears.

To reinstate default colors,

1. Choose /Options | Colors | Palettes.
2. Specify your screen type. Choose **Monochrome** to reinstate original default colors for a monochrome screen. Choose **Color** to reinstate colors for a color screen. Choose **Black & White** to reinstate colors for a black-and-white monitor with a color graphics card (CGA), such as a Compaq.
3. If you want to erase all color changes you've made and use the original default colors as the new defaults, press *Esc* twice and choose **Update** from the **Options** menu.

Note   If you have a black-and-white monitor with a color graphics card, you can switch to the **Black & White** palette for better display.

   If you're using the 123-compatible menus, choose /**Worksheet** | **Global** | **Default** | **Colors** | **Palettes**.

International options

International settings determine standards for displaying currency, punctuation, dates, and time. This not only affects the display of values in the spreadsheet, but also how Quattro displays the date and time on the status line and how you enter arguments in @functions.

The initial defaults are set to display the formats standard for the United States. If you are using Quattro in another country, or are doing business with another country, you can change these settings to suit your requirements.

The international defaults determine your display *options*, not the display itself. To actually *set the display* of a cell value as a date, time, or currency value, use the /Style | Numeric Format command (see page 149) or the /Options | Formats | Numeric Format command (see "Formatting options" later in this chapter).

Choose /Options | International to display the menu of international defaults.

```
┌ International ┐
│              │
│ Currency     │
│ Punctuation ▶│
│ Date        ▶│
│ Time        ▶│
│ Quit         │
└──────────────┘
```

- **Currency** lets you specify the character(s) to indicate currency. You can display the characters before or after the value. The initial default displays the dollar sign ($) before the value.

- **Punctuation** determines the characters used to separate thousands, show the decimal point in numbers, and separate arguments in functions and macros. The initial default uses a comma to separate thousands and arguments and a period as a decimal point; for example, 1,234.56.

- **Date** determines the date format used as the Long and Short International options on the /Style | Numeric Format | Date and /Options | Formats | Numeric Format | Date menus. MM/DD/YY or MM/DD is the initial default.

- **Time** sets the time format used as the International option on the /Style | Numeric Format | Date | Time and /Options | Formats | Numeric Format | Date | Time menus. HH:MM:SS is the initial default.

- **Quit** returns you to the spreadsheet.

Press *Esc* to back out of the International menu to the Options menu.

To make permanent the changes you made to the International settings, choose Update from the Options menu.

Caution! Choosing /Options | Update saves *all* default settings.

1-2-3 If you're using the 123-compatible menus, choose /Worksheet | Global | Default | Other | International.

Currency

When you use the currency numeric format, either as the global format or as the format for a specific block, Quattro initially displays values as dollars, with a preceding dollar sign. You can change the currency format to display other types of currency with the /Options | International command. This command lets you change the character(s) used as a currency symbol, and lets you position the characters after or before the currency value.

To display a different type of currency, such as yen or pounds,

1. Choose /Options I International I Currency.

2. Quattro prompts you for the character(s) to use as a currency symbol. You can use any character or character combination, including special ASCII characters.

   To enter an ASCII character not on your keyboard, hold down the *Alt* key and use the numeric keypad to enter the ASCII number for that character. See Appendix G for the ASCII character codes.

3. When you press *Enter*, Quattro displays a menu with two items: **Prefix** and **Suffix**. Choose **Prefix** to display the symbol before the value (as in $100). Choose **Suffix** to display the symbol *after* the value (as in 500F).

4. To store the new currency format as the default (to be used whenever **Currency** is chosen as the display format), press *Esc* and choose **Update** from the **Options** menu.

 If you're using the 123-compatible menus, choose /Worksheet I Global I Default I Other I International I Currency.

Punctuation

Punctuation settings specify the punctuation characters used to do three things:

- designate a decimal point in numbers
- separate arguments in @function statements and in macro commands
- separate thousands in numbers (display only)

```
═══ Punctuation ═══
A.  1,234.56  (a1,a2)
B.  1.234,56  (a1.a2)
C.  1,234.56  (a1;a2)
D.  1.234,56  (a1;a2)
E.  1 234.56  (a1,a2)
F.  1 234,56  (a1.a2)
G.  1 234.56  (a1;a2)
H.  1 234,56  (a1;a2)
```

Normally, a period is used for a decimal point, commas are used to separate thousands, and either commas or semicolons work as argument separators. You can also choose from seven other punctuation combinations.

When you choose **Punctuation** from the /Options I International menu, the **Punctuation** menu appears.

Each option shows the punctuation marks used to mark thousands and the decimal place, followed by the punctuation mark used to separate arguments in @functions and macros (a1,a2).

Note Regardless of the punctuation setting, semicolons are always accepted as argument separators.

To change the punctuation characters,

1. Choose /**Options** | International | **Punctuation**.
2. Specify the combination of punctuation characters you want to use. The last four options specify that a blank space be used to separate thousands in numbers.
3. To store the punctuation combination as the new default, press *Esc* twice and choose **Update** from the **Options** menu.

If you're using the 123-compatible menus, choose /**Worksheet** | Global | Default | Other | International | **Punctuation**.

International date format

The /**Options** | International | **Date** command does not directly determine how Quattro displays dates in the spreadsheet. Rather, it determines the *international date format* given as an *option* for date display. When you choose **Date** from the /**Options** | Formats | Numeric Format menu, both short and long versions of this format appear as optional date formats. To set the actual display of dates in your spreadsheet, use the /**Style** | Numeric Format | Date command (see page 149).

Initially, the Long and Short International date formats are MM/DD/YY and MM/DD. The short format is simply a truncated version (month and day only) of the format you choose for long. To change the international date format,

```
====== Date ======
A. MM/DD/YY  (MM/DD)
B. DD/MM/YY  (DD/MM)
C. DD.MM.YY  (DD.MM)
D. YY-MM-DD  (MM-DD)
```

1. Choose /**Options** | International | **Date**.
2. Specify one of the four options listed on the **Date** menu.
3. The format you pick appears (in both long and short form) when you choose the /**Options** | Formats | Numeric Format | Date menu. Quattro uses the long version of the format as the international clock option (see "Clock display" later in this chapter).
4. To store the date format you chose as the new default, press *Esc* twice and choose **Update** from the **Options** menu.

If you're using the 123-compatible menus, choose /**Worksheet** | Global | Default | Other | International | **Date**.

International time format

The /Options I International I Time command specifies the *international time format*. Both short and long versions of this format are listed as optional time formats when you choose Time from the /Options I Formats I Numeric Format I Date menu. To set the actual display of times in your spreadsheet, use /Style I Numeric Format (see page 149) or /Options I Formats I Numeric Format (see "Global display format" later in this chapter).

Initially, the Long and Short International time formats are HH:MM:SS and HH:MM. The short format is simply a truncated version of the format you choose for long. To change the format for international time,

1. Choose /Options I International I Time.

2. Specify one of the four options listed on the Time menu. All international time settings use 24-hour formats (000-2359).

```
====== Time ======
A. HH:MM:SS  (HH:MM)
B. HH.MM.SS  (HH.MM)
C. HH,MM,SS  (HH,MM)
D. HHhMMmSSs (HHhMMm)
```

3. Quattro lists the format you choose on the /Options I Formats I Numeric Format I Date I Time menu and uses it as the international clock setting (see "Clock display" later in this chapter).

4. To store the date format you chose as the new default, press *Esc* twice and choose Update from the Options menu.

If you're using the 123-compatible menus, choose /Worksheet I Global I Default I Other I International I Time.

Startup options

```
====== Startup ======
Directory
Autoload File
Startup Macro
File Extension
Beep           ▸
Menu Tree      ▸
Quit
```

The Startup menu includes information that Quattro references each time it is loaded. When you choose /Options I Startup, Quattro displays the Startup menu.

- **Directory** specifies the default directory where Quattro stores spreadsheet files.

- **Autoload File** specifies the name of a spreadsheet file that Quattro loads automatically each time you enter Quattro.

- **Startup Macro** specifies the name of a macro that Quattro will execute automatically (if it can locate it) each time you retrieve a spreadsheet.

- **File Extension** specifies the default file-name extension that Quattro uses as the default for spreadsheet files.

- **Beep** determines whether Quattro beeps when you make an error. The initial default is **Yes**. To turn off the beeps, set this command to **No**.

- **Menu Tree** lets you specify a different menu structure to use with Quattro.

- **Quit** returns you to the **Options** menu.

Once you've set the startup options the way you want them, be sure to press *Esc* and choose **Update** from the **Options** menu.

Caution! /**O**ptions | **U**pdate saves *all* default settings.

The default directory

When you first load Quattro, the current disk drive and/or directory is used as the default directory for all Quattro files. This is the directory Quattro automatically checks for spreadsheet files when no other directory is specified.

The /**O**ptions | **S**tartup | **D**irectory command lets you specify a different directory for storing your Quattro spreadsheet files. To specify a new default directory,

1. Choose /**O**ptions | **S**tartup | **D**irectory.
2. Quattro prompts you for a path name. Enter the path, including the drive letter, of the directory you want to store you data files in. For example,

   `C:\QUATTRO\FILES`

   stores your data files in a subdirectory called FILES in the QUATTRO directory on your hard disk.
3. To save the new directory as the default, press *Esc*, then choose **Update** from the **Options** menu.

 If you're using the 123-compatible menus, choose /**W**orksheet | **G**lobal | **D**efault | **D**irectory.

Quattro stores spreadsheet and other data files in the default directory when you don't indicate a different directory or drive. It also displays the contents of this directory when you are retrieving or storing a file. You can override this directory with any **File** menu command simply by preceding the file name you specify with a different directory path (see "Responding to file-name prompts" in Chapter 8).

Note You can also temporarily change the directory Quattro goes to with the /File | Directory command (see "Overriding the default directory" in Chapter 8). Any changes to the default directory, however, automatically update the setting of the /File | Directory command.

Tip If you enter a period (.) at the /Options | Startup | Directory prompt, you can load Quattro from any directory on your hard disk and make that directory the default for the current work session. Be sure to choose /Options | Update after you change the /Options | Startup | Directory setting to make it the new default. You might want to set up your default directory with a period if you have several data directories in which you work for an equal amount of time. That way, you can always move to the directory where the files you want to work in are stored and start Quattro with that directory as the default.

Autoload options

With the next two **Startup** menu options, you can specify the following items to be loaded automatically when you load Quattro:

- a spreadsheet file
- a macro

Each time you load Quattro, it checks to see if there's a spreadsheet file with the name specified as the autoload name. If so, it retrieves the file automatically. Quattro then looks for a macro with the specified autoload macro name. If it finds one, it executes the macro.

After you've changed autoload defaults, be sure to choose /Options | Update to save them.

Caution! /Options | Update saves *all* default settings.

Autoload file Initially, the default autoload file is QUATTRO.WQ1. Each time you load Quattro, it looks for a file in the default directory named QUATTRO.WQ1 and retrieves it automatically if it exists.

You can change this default to a file with a different name. To autoload a different file,

1. Choose /**O**ptions I **S**tartup I **A**utoload File. Quattro prompts you for a file name and shows the current autoload file as the default.

2. Edit the existing name or type in a new one. If you want to automatically load a file in a different directory, specify the directory path with the file name.

3. Press *Esc* to return to the **O**ptions menu and choose **U**pdate. Otherwise, the new file name will be discarded when you exit Quattro.

If you're using the 123-compatible menus, choose /**W**orksheet I **G**lobal I **D**efault I **F**iles I **A**utoload File.

Note   You can also automatically retrieve a spreadsheet or workspace file when you load Quattro by specifying the file name with the Quattro load command at the DOS prompt. For example,

    Q MYWORK

loads a spreadsheet called MYWORK. If you want to retrieve a saved workspace of files and windows called YEARLY, just type Q YEARLY. (See "Retrieving a file from the command line" in Chapter 8 for details.)

Autoload macro

Initially, the default startup macro is \0. This means that, every time you retrieve a spreadsheet file, Quattro looks for a macro named \0 and executes it automatically if it exists.

You can change this default to a macro with a different name. Just choose /**O**ptions I **S**tartup I **S**tartup Macro and enter any macro name.

After you specify a new startup macro, return to the **O**ptions menu (press *Esc*) and choose **U**pdate. Otherwise, the new macro name will be discarded when you exit Quattro.

Caution!   /**O**ptions I **U**pdate saves *all* default settings.

You can use the startup macro with an autoload file to load a special application automatically when you start Quattro.

You can also load a macro automatically with a spreadsheet by specifying the names of both on the DOS command line when you load Quattro; for example,

    Q FILENAME MACRO

(see "Retrieving a file from the command line" in Chapter 8 for details).

If you're using the 123-compatible menus, choose /**Worksheet** I **Global** I **Default** I **Files** I **Startup Macro**.

Command-line options Quattro has a few command-line options that you can specify when you load Quattro, just as you can specify a file or macro name. The syntax is as follows:

Q *<filename> <macroname> <⁄options>*

/D   Loads Quattro with a specific .RF (defaults) file other than RSC.RF. Be sure to specify the directory path to the .RF file, if not the same as the directory from which you are loading Quattro.

/I   Loads Quattro with autodetection of screen hardware enabled. This is the same as the /**Options** I **Hardware** I **Screen** I **Screen Type** I **Autodetect Driver** command.

The three following command-line options force Quattro to load with a specific color palette. These are the same as the /**Options** I **Colors** I **Palettes** I **Color**, **Monochrome**, and **Black & White** commands:

/IC   Forces Quattro to load with a color palette.
/IM   Forces Quattro to load with a monochrome palette.
/IB   Forces Quattro to load with a black-and-white palette.

/E   Loads Quattro with LIM 4.0 EMS disabled and 3.x enabled. Use this option if you suspect that your EMS board is not completely 4.0-compatible.

/X   Enables 386 extended-memory code-swapping.

Default file extension

The /**Options** I **Startup** I **File Extension** command specifies the default extension for spreadsheet files. If you don't specify an extension with file commands, Quattro assumes this extension. The initial default is .WQ1, which stores files in Quattro format.

To specify a different default file-name extension,

1. Choose /**Options** I **Startup** I **File Extension**.

2. Enter a three-letter extension preceded by a period.

3. If you want to use the new extension from now on, press *Esc* and choose **Update** from the **Options** menu.

If you're using the 123-compatible menus and defaults, the initial default file extension is .WK1, which stores spreadsheets in a 123-compatible format. This format doesn't include some of the features exclusive to Quattro—for example, inserted graphs. Unless you expect to be swapping files frequently between Quattro and Lotus 1-2-3, it's best to change this back to the Quattro extension, .WQ1. Choose /**Worksheet** | **Global** | **Default** | **Files** | **Startup** | **Extension**.

To store files for use with another program, specify the file-name extension that the program uses as a default (see "Translating files" in Chapter 8).

Setting the computer's beep

Normally, when you make an error in Quattro (for example, if you enter a formula with the wrong syntax), Quattro causes your computer to beep. If you find the beep annoying, you can turn it off with the beep option.

To set the beep option,

1. Choose /**Options** | **Startup** | **Beep**.

2. Choose **No** to keep Quattro from beeping on errors. Choose **Yes** to return error beeps.

3. If you want the new setting to be permanent, press *Esc* to return to the **Options** menu and choose **Update**.

If you're using the 123-compatible menus, choose /**Worksheet** | **Global** | **Default** | **Other** | **Beep**.

Using a different menu tree

A menu tree is the structure of the menus that contain Quattro commands. Quattro comes with three different menu trees:

- **QUATTRO.MU**, the standard Quattro menu tree, is the one documented here.

- **123.MU**, the 123-compatible menu tree, is used if you specify 123-compatibility when you install Quattro. You can also load

Quattro with the 123-compatible menu tree from the command line with the Q123 command.

- **Q1.MU** uses the structure of the menus in earlier versions of Quattro with new commands added on. You can use it to ease your transition between versions, but the new menu structure is definitely recommended.

To switch to a different menu tree,

1. Choose /Options | Startup | Menu Tree.
2. Quattro displays a list of available menu tree files. Choose the one you want to use.
3. Quattro switches immediately to that menu tree. If you want to use the menu tree you've specified the next time you load Quattro, be sure to choose

   - /Options | Update in the QUATTRO.MU menu tree.
   - /Default | Update in the Q1.MU menu tree.
   - /Worksheet | Global | Default | Update in the 123.MU menu tree.

Note   When you change menu trees, you also change system defaults; for example, the file-extension default changes to .WK1 when you are in the 123-compatible menu tree. You must set your defaults for each menu tree you use.

1-2-3

If you're using the 123-compatible menus, choose /Worksheet | Global | Default | Files | Menu Tree.

See Chapter 4 in *Getting Started*, "Quattro for Lotus 1-2-3 users," for more information about working with the 123-compatible menus and other compatibility issues.

Customizing your mouse palette

The Quattro mouse palette appears at the right edge of your screen. (See page 22 for information on how to use the palette.) Seven of the mouse palette buttons are user-assignable, so you can make them perform any Quattro function you choose.

To assign a special function to one of these assignable buttons,

1. Choose /Options | Mouse Palette.

2. Choose the button(s) you want to customize by selecting **1st Button**, **2nd Button**, and so on. Only the help icon (?) and the "End" arrows are not user-assignable.

3. A menu of text and macro assignment appears for each button you choose. For example, if you choose **5th Button**, you'll see that the **Text** (the label on the button in the mouse palette) is "5," and the **Macro** assigned to it is {BEEP}. This means that, when you click on the button that reads "5" on the mouse palette, your computer will beep.

4. Choose **Text** and enter any three characters you want to appear as the label for that button. For example, { } might stand for "Macros" (since macros require braces around them).

5. Choose any macro command you want the button to execute (refer to Chapter 2 of *@Functions and Macros* for a complete list of macros). For example, a mouse button assigned to the {MACROS} macro will display a list of Quattro macros, just as pressing the Macros key (*Shift-F3*) does.

If you're using the 123-compatible menus, choose /**W**orksheet | **G**lobal | **D**efault | **M**ouse Palette.

Choosing font quality

When you redefine a font using a Bitstream typeface (Dutch, Swiss, and Courier), Quattro needs to create a new font file before it can display or print the font. By default, the /**O**ptions | **G**raphics Quality command is set to Final. This means that Quattro pauses to build separate Bitstream font files as necessary when you go into the Screen Previewer or the Graph Annotator, display a graph, or begin printing. This takes a little time; however, once Quattro creates a font file, it can access it without pausing. For more information about building font files, see Appendix F.

If you prefer that Quattro not build new Bitstream font files until you have finished working, set /**O**ptions | **G**raphics Quality to Draft. In Draft mode, Quattro substitutes Hershey fonts for any Bitstream fonts it hasn't yet built. Occasionally, the font substitution can cause minor changes between the viewed and printed forms of a graph or spreadsheet. When you're ready to print your final draft, choose /**O**ptions | **G**raphics Quality | Final to turn on font building before you print.

Other options

```
====== Other ======
Undo              ▶
Macro             ▶
Expanded Memory   ▶
Clock             ▶
Paradox           ▶
```

The /Options ∣ Other command displays a menu with miscellaneous system options.

- **Undo** lets you enable or disable the Undo command (*/EU* or *Alt-F5*), which reverses the last "undo-able" operation.

- **Macro** lets you specify which parts of the screen to redraw during macro execution.

- **Expanded Memory** lets you tell Quattro how to use any expanded memory you may have.

- **Clock** determines the format, if any, Quattro uses to display the current date and time on the status line.

- **Paradox** lets you set options to access Paradox files on a local area network.

If you're using the 123-compatible menus, choose /**Worksheet** ∣ **Global** ∣ **Default** ∣ **Other**.

The Undo key

The /**Options** ∣ **Other** ∣ **Undo** command lets you enable or disable the /**Edit** ∣ **Undo** command (shortcut, *Alt-F5*). If enabled, you can use Undo to immediately reverse the effects of an operation. For example, if you accidentally delete a block of spreadsheet data, just press *Alt-F5* to bring it back.

To enable or disable the Undo key,

1. Choose /**Options** ∣ **Other** ∣ **Undo**.
2. Choose **Enable** or **Disable**.
3. If you want to save the new setting, press *Esc* and choose **Update** from the **Options** menu.

While enabled, the Undo command slows down Quattro's operation slightly. If program speed is crucial to you, you can always disable this key and use the Transcript utility to undo operations.

If you're using the 123-compatible menus, choose /**Worksheet** ∣ **Global** ∣ **Default** ∣ **Other** ∣ **Undo**.

For details on the Undo key, including the types of operations it can reverse, see page 126. For information on using Transcript to reverse operations, see Chapter 17, "Using Transcript."

Macro redraw

With the /**Options** I **Other** I **Macro** command, you can tell Quattro which parts of the screen to redraw during macro execution. The initial setting, **Both**, suppresses redrawing of both spreadsheet windows and menus (panels), including the status line and the input line, until execution is over. This speeds up macro execution, since Quattro doesn't have to stop and draw each of these items used in the macro. You can also suppress redrawing the spreadsheet window alone, or turn off redraw suppression altogether, so that Quattro redraws both menus and windows during macros.

To change the redraw macro setting,

1. Choose /**Options** I **Other** I **Macro**.
2. Choose **Both** to suppress redrawing of both spreadsheet windows and menus (panels); choose **Panel** to suppress redrawing of menus, the status line, and the input line; choose **Window** to suppress redrawing windows only; or choose **None** to redraw everything during macros.
3. If you want to use this redraw setting from now on, press *Esc* and choose **Update** from the **Options** menu.

 If you're using the 123-compatible menus, choose /**Worksheet** I **Global** I **Default** I **Other** I **Macro**.

Expanded memory

If your computer has expanded memory (EMS), Quattro automatically detects it and uses it to store spreadsheets. Expanded memory allows you to load and work with unusually large spreadsheets, or with many spreadsheets at once. However, because it requires Quattro to shuffle data in and out of system memory, using expanded memory to store all spreadsheet information does slow down performance somewhat. Quattro attempts to balance program speed and memory space by storing only *part* of your spreadsheets (the actual data) in available EMS. To tip this balance in either direction, specify different EMS use with the /**Options** I **Other** I **Expanded Memory** command:

■ If you're working with a very large spreadsheet and are running out of system memory, you can tell Quattro to store both spreadsheet data *and* formatting data in EMS.

■ If you usually use fairly small spreadsheets and don't usually need EMS, you can speed up computer access time by telling Quattro to store less in EMS (format data only) or none at all.

```
┌─ Expanded Memory ─┐
│                   │
│ Both              │
│ Spreadsheet Data  │
│ Format            │
│ None              │
└───────────────────┘
```

To change what's stored in expanded memory,

1. Choose /**Options** | **Other** | **Expanded Memory**.

2. Choose **Format** to store only spreadsheet formatting information; choose **Both** to store both spreadsheet data and format; choose **None** to not use expanded memory; or choose **Spreadsheet Data** to return to storing cell data.

3. If you want to use this option setting from now on, press *U* to choose **Update** from the **Options** menu.

If you're using the 123-compatible menus, choose /**Worksheet** | **Global** | **Default** | **Other** | **Expanded Memory**.

Note   You must close all windows and then reload them to benefit from changing the Expanded Memory option.

Clock display

With the /**Options** | **Other** | **Clock** command, you can display the date and time on the status line. When you choose this command, you get a menu with three options.

```
┌──── Clock ────┐
│               │
│ Standard      │
│ International │
│ None          │
└───────────────┘
```

The initial default for this command is **None**, which doesn't display the clock. You can change this setting to **Standard**, which displays the date and time in standard format (DD-MMM-YY and HH:MM AM/PM). Or you can choose **International**, which displays date and time in the Long International formats specified with the /**Options** | **International** | **Date** and **Time** commands (see page 190 and following).

To change the spreadsheet's date and time display,

1. Choose /**Options** | **Other** | **Clock**.

2. Choose an option from the Clock menu. Quattro immediately displays the date and time in the new format.

3. If you want to use the new clock format from now on, choose /**Options** | **Update**.

If you're using the 123-compatible menus, choose /**Worksheet** | **Global** | **Default** | **Other** | **Clock**.

Quattro updates the time displayed on your screen every 60 seconds. If the time or date displayed is incorrect, you need to update your computer's internal clock. You can do this without leaving Quattro with the /File I Utilities I DOS Shell command.

Accessing Paradox files

Quattro automatically translates Paradox files into spreadsheets and lets you use the /Database I Query command with untranslated Paradox files. If you're working on a local area network, you need to set some options to tell Quattro where to look for Paradox files. Use the /Options I Other I Paradox command to specify these network options:

- **Network Type** lets you specify the type of local area network you have.

```
 Paradox
Network Type ▶
Directory
Retries
Quit
```

- **Directory** lets you specify the directory where you keep the PARADOX.NET file.

- **Retries** lets you specify a timed interval (in seconds) that Quattro should wait between trying to open the same locked file again.

Note For the option you choose to take effect, you must choose /Options I Update, then exit and reenter Quattro.

For details on how to translate Paradox files into spreadsheets, see page 233. To find out how to query an untranslated Paradox database file, see page 487.

Updating the system options

When you make a change to any of the Quattro system options, that change remains in effect until you exit Quattro. When you reload Quattro, the previous settings take effect.

If you want to make your new settings permanent, choose /Options I Update. Quattro stores the new settings in the Quattro resource files and uses them each time you load Quattro.

To restore the original defaults, copy the original resource files (RSC.RF and QUATTRO.MU) from your distribution disks.

1-2-3

If you're using the 123-compatible menus, choose /Worksheet I Global I Default I Update instead of /Options I Update. If you load Quattro with the Q123 command (see 196), Quattro stores any default changes you update in the resource files for the 123-compatible menus instead of the standard Quattro resource files.

Remember /Options I Update updates *all* system defaults. If there are some defaults you want to change only temporarily, set these *after* you've made and updated changes you want to save.

/Options I Update affects only system options, not global options (Format, Recalculation, and Protection). When you retrieve a spreadsheet, Quattro uses the global option settings in effect when the file was last saved.

Note If you choose /Print I Layout I Update to update your print layout settings, Quattro also updates *all* system default settings (see page 99 for details).

Formatting options

```
══ Formats ══
Numeric Format ▶
Align Labels   ▶
Hide Zeros     ▶
Global Width
Quit
```

The /Options I Formats command lets you change settings that affect the global, or default, display of data in your spreadsheet. Choose /Options I Formats to display the Formats menu.

- **Numeric Format** determines the global format for numbers, dates, and time.

- **Align Labels** determines global label alignment.

- **Hide Zeros** determines whether zero values are displayed.

- **Global Width** determines the default column width.

- **Quit** returns you to the Options menu.

Press *Esc* to back out of the Formats menu to the Options menu.

You can override the **Numeric Format**, **Align Labels**, and **Global Width** settings locally with the associated /**Style** menu commands, which affect blocks. You can also override /**Style** I Alignment by including a label prefix with a label.

Quattro sets and stores global formatting options with individual spreadsheets. You can't use the /Options I Update command to update these settings for use with all spreadsheets.

 If you're using the 123-compatible menus, choose /**Worksheet** I **Global**. On the Global menu, Format is the equivalent of **Numeric Format**, Label Prefix is the equivalent of **Align Labels**, Zero is the equivalent of **Hide Zeros**, and Column Width is the equivalent of **Global Width**.

Global display format

The /**O**ptions | Formats | Numeric Format command determines the default format for numbers, dates, or time in your spreadsheet. This is the format that Quattro uses if you don't specify another for a block with the /**S**tyle | Numeric Format command (see page 149).

Initially, the default display format is set to **General**. This displays numbers more or less as you enter them (unless they don't fit within the current column, in which case Quattro translates them into scientific notation).

To change the global display format,

```
┌─ Numeric Format ─┐
│                  │
│ Fixed            │
│ Scientific       │
│ Currency         │
│ ,                │
│ General          │
│ +/-              │
│ Percent          │
│ Date           ▶ │
│ Text             │
│ Hidden           │
└──────────────────┘
```

1. Choose /**O**ptions | Formats | Numeric Format. Quattro displays the **Numeric Format** menu.

2. Choose the format you want to use most often in the spreadsheet. If the format you choose allows a variable number of displayed decimal places, you will then need to specify a number between 0 and 15. Regardless of the number of decimal places displayed, Quattro stores the number originally entered or calculated (up to 15 significant digits) and uses it in calculations.

3. If you choose **Date**, Quattro displays another list, showing specific date formats and **Time**. If you choose **Time**, another list of possible time formats appears.

Quattro changes all existing entries in your spreadsheet to reflect the new format and stores the new setting with the spreadsheet. All subsequent entries will use the new format, except those formatted as a block with the /**S**tyle | Numeric Format menu.

Note   If you've split your screen into two windows, only the current window is affected by changes to the global display format. The other window shows the spreadsheet with the original formats. When you close the second window, the default format set in the top or left window is used. (Display formats set locally with the /**S**tyle | Numeric Format menu affect *both* windows, however.)

1-2-3   If you're using the 123-compatible menus, choose /**W**orksheet | Global | Format.

For further details on each of these display formats, see page 149. That section also describes how to assign a different display format to a specific block of cells.

Global label alignment

The /**Options** I **Formats** I **Align Labels** command determines the general alignment of labels in the spreadsheet (left, right, or centered). Initially, **Align Labels** is set to **Left**, which aligns labels flush with the left sides of their cells.

You can align labels differently by preceding them with label-prefix characters (see page 52) or by using the /**Style** I **Alignment** command (see page 149).

If you intend for most of the labels in your spreadsheet to be either right-aligned or centered, specify this with the default alignment setting.

To change the label alignment setting,

1. Choose /**Options** I **Formats** I **Align Labels**.
2. Specify **Right**, **Left**, or **Center**. Quattro stores the new label alignment setting with the current spreadsheet only.

Quattro will align all labels you subsequently enter according to the new setting (unless you precede them with a different label-prefix). Unlike the /**Options** I **Formats** I **Numeric Format** menu settings, existing entries are not affected. To alter the alignment of existing entries, you must use the /**Style** I **Alignment** command (or change the label's prefix).

Value entries (including the results of @VALUE functions) are always right-aligned and are not affected by label alignment settings.

If you're using the 123-compatible menus, choose /**Worksheet** I **Global** I **Label Prefix**.

Global display of zeros

Initially, Quattro displays all values in the spreadsheet, even when they equal zero. The /**Options** I **Formats** I **Hide Zeros** command lets you suppress the display of any cell entry whose value equals *exactly* zero, whether it was entered directly or calculated with a formula (a value such as .004 will display as 0 if decimal precision is 2 or less, even if zero suppression is active, because it is not actually 0). Quattro will show the zero values (or formulas resulting in them) on the status line, however, when you select the cells containing them and press *F2* to enter Edit mode.

To suppress display of zero values,

1. Choose /**O**ptions I Formats I Hide Zeros.
2. Choose Yes.

Zero suppression does not remove the zero values from the spreadsheet. They remain in memory, even though they are hidden, and return when you reset the Hide Zeros default to No.

Caution! When zero suppression is on, it is very easy to accidentally write over cells that contain formulas.

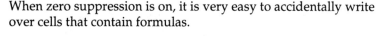 If you're using the 123-compatible menus, choose /**W**orksheet I Global I Zero.

Global column width

When a blank Quattro spreadsheet first appears, all its columns are the same width (nine characters wide). You can adjust the width of all columns in a spreadsheet at once by changing the Global Width setting.

To change the default column width for the current spreadsheet,

1. Choose /**O**ptions I Formats I Global Width.
2. Type the value you want to use as the default column width.
3. Press *Enter.*

The global column width is stored with the current spreadsheet, regardless of whether you update the option settings. It returns to the original default of nine for new spreadsheets.

The /Options I Formats I Global Width command doesn't affect columns that have been individually adjusted with /Style I Column Width or the commands on the /Style I **B**lock Widths menu. Before those columns can be affected by a change in the global width, you must return them to the global column width with the /Style I **R**eset Width command (see page 154).

Note If your screen is split into two windows, only the current window is affected by changes to the global column width (or columns adjusted individually with the /Style | Column Width command). The other window will show the spreadsheet with the original column widths. When you close the second window, Quattro retains the column widths of the top or left window.

 If you're using the 123-compatible menus, choose /Worksheet | Global | Column Width.

Recalculation options

```
┌─ Recalculation ─┐
│                 │
│ Mode          ▶ │
│ Order         ▶ │
│ Iteration       │
│─Circular Cell─  │
│ Quit            │
└─────────────────┘
```

Recalculation refers to how Quattro updates formula results when you change cell values those formulas depend on. When you choose the /Options | Recalculation command, the Recalculation menu appears.

- **Mode** specifies whether Quattro pauses to calculate formulas when necessary, calculates them automatically between keystrokes, or calculates formulas only when you press the Calc key (*F9*).

- **Order** determines the sequence in which Quattro calculates formulas in a spreadsheet.

- **Iteration** determines how many times Quattro recalculates formulas in the spreadsheet before calculation is considered complete.

- **Circular Cell** is a display-only command. It lists the address of the first cell (if any) that contains a formula with a reference that eventually refers back to itself, either directly or indirectly. Because it lists only one cell, it's not an accurate way to check circular references, but instead is just an indicator of their existence. You can use the /Window | Options | Map View command to easily audit all cells that contain circular references (see "The map view" in Chapter 9).

- **Quit** returns you to the Options menu.

Recalculation mode

Recalculation time is greatly minimized by Quattro's method of intelligent recalculation, which recalculates only those formulas that have been changed. (Many spreadsheet programs recalculate all formulas in the spreadsheet whenever a change is made.)

To change Quattro's recalculation mode,

1. Choose /**Options** I **Recalculation** I **Mode**.
2. Choose one of three modes of recalculation:

   - **Background**, the default mode, recalculates formulas between keystrokes in the "background." It does not interrupt your work and performs recalculation automatically.
   - **Automatic** also recalculates formulas automatically but pauses until recalculation is finished.
   - **Manual** recalculates the formulas you enter or edit but does not recalculate the formulas whose references change until you press the Calc key, *F9*.

3. Quattro stores this setting with the current spreadsheet only.

When you set /**Options** I **Recalculation** I **Mode** to **Manual**, Quattro still calculates formulas when you enter or edit them, and displays the resulting value. It does not, however, automatically recalculate formulas whose references change. For example, if you enter +B3-C16 in a cell, Quattro displays the resulting value. Quattro continues to display that same value, even if you change the values contained in B3 or C16.

F9
Calc

If any formula in the spreadsheet needs to be recalculated, the CALC indicator appears at the bottom right of the screen to remind you that the spreadsheet is not entirely accurate. Press the Calc key (*F9*) to recalculate all formulas that need it. Formulas are recalculated as necessary, and the CALC indicator disappears.

To recalculate a single cell,

1. Select the cell.
2. Press Edit (*F2*), then *Enter*. (This works only if the formula is not dependent on other formulas.)

Either Background or Automatic is the recommended recalculation mode, since both ensure that your spreadsheet data is always accurate. Manual mode is most appropriate as a temporary break from recalculation while you adjust crucial cells. You should then return to Background or Automatic mode for increased accuracy and spreadsheet speed. If Quattro is in Background mode, and you want to pause briefly to finish recalculation, press *F9*, the Calc key.

In Background mode, Quattro will always finish recalculation before saving, extracting, or printing the spreadsheet. You never need worry about ending up with a "half-calculated" spreadsheet.

 If you're using the 123-compatible menus, choose /Worksheet | Global | Recalculation | Automatic, Manual, or Background.

Order of recalculation

Normally, Quattro recalculates a spreadsheet in Natural order, which means that, before a formula is calculated, each cell it references is recalculated first, to ensure accuracy.

To reset the recalculation order,

1. Choose /Options | Recalculation | Order.
2. Specify Natural, Rowwise, or Columnwise. Quattro stores this setting with the current spreadsheet only.

In the Columnwise option, recalculation starts in cell A1 and proceeds down column A, ignoring formulas in other columns. When A is finished, recalculation continues in B1, and on down column B. This continues through to the end of the spreadsheet (column IV).

Rowwise recalculation also starts in cell A1, but the recalculation proceeds by rows, starting at 1 and continuing through row 8192.

Before natural recalculation was introduced, the only orders available were rowwise and columnwise. These orders are maintained as options for Quattro, even though they are rarely used and are not recommended.

Columnwise and rowwise recalculation are provided for special purposes, such as for circularly linked formulas that solve a problem or attain a goal. For more information, refer to popular literature on spreadsheet problem-solving. If you're not engaged in a problem-solving situation such as this, always use natural recalculation order.

 If you're using the 123-compatible menus, choose /Worksheet | Global | Recalculation | Columnwise or Rowwise.

Number of iterations

Many complex formulas, such as those involving financial calculations and complicated engineering problems, require multiple evaluations to attain an acceptable degree of accuracy. These formulas are therefore deliberately constructed to contain *circular references*, references that eventually refer back to the original formula. For such applications, Quattro allows you to set the number of iterations, or cycles of recalculation, it should perform each time the spreadsheet is recalculated.

To change the iteration default,

1. Choose /Options | Recalculation | Iteration.
2. Enter any number up to 255 iterations. For each iteration, Quattro recalculates all cells with circular references.

Note If you have specified either a columnwise or rowwise order of recalculation, you should set the number of iterations to at least two. Otherwise, the spreadsheet may be inaccurate.

If Quattro can't find any circular references in the spreadsheet and recalculation order is set to Natural, the iteration count is ignored.

1-2-3 If you're using the 123-compatible menus, choose /Worksheet | Global | Recalculation | Iteration.

Protection options

A completed spreadsheet represents hours, days, or even weeks of work—work that you could all too easily destroy with an erroneous /Edit | Erase Block command or an overwritten formula. The /Options | Protection command lets you protect your work by disallowing changes to the spreadsheet.

To enable or disable protection for all cells in a spreadsheet except those that have been explicitly "unprotected,"

1. Choose /Options | Protection.
2. Choose Enable to turn on global spreadsheet protection. Quattro protects all cells in the spreadsheet, unless you explicitly unprotect a block with the /Style | Protection | Unprotect command (see page 153).

```
┌─ Protection ─┐
│ Enable       │
│ Disable      │
└──────────────┘
```

3. Choose **Disable** to remove *all* protection from the spreadsheet. Quattro ignores the status of cell blocks explicitly protected or unprotected with /**Style** I **Protection** commands until you exit Disable mode.

4. To protect *part* of your spreadsheet, set /**Options** I **Protection** to Enable, then use /**Style** I **Protection** I **Unprotect** to remove protection from the cells you want to allow changes to.

If you're using the 123-compatible menus, choose /**Worksheet** I **Global** I **Protection**.

When default protection is enabled, protected cells display PR on the input line when selected. Whether or not default protection is enabled, unprotected cells display U on the input line when selected.

You cannot delete a column or row that contains a protected cell. You *can*, however, permanently erase a protected spreadsheet from disk with the File Manager /**Edit** I **Erase** command. Use caution when you choose /**Edit** I **Erase** in the File Manager; the Undo command will not recover a file deleted this way.

Quattro saves default protection status with the spreadsheet. When you protect a spreadsheet, it remains protected until you unprotect it.

To protect or unprotect cells individually or as blocks, use the /**Style** I **Protection** command (see page 153).

To prevent unauthorized access to a spreadsheet, assign a password to the spreadsheet file (see "Assigning a password to a file" in Chapter 8).

3

Files and windows

214

8

Working with spreadsheet files

Quattro stores the information you enter in a spreadsheet in system memory, called RAM (random access memory). However, RAM is temporary. When you turn off the computer or exit Quattro, or if there is a power outage, all data stored in RAM is erased.

In order to use a spreadsheet again at a later time, you must save it on either a floppy or hard disk. Each spreadsheet you save is stored in a *file* with a unique name. Once you've saved a spreadsheet in a file, you can access it at any time by loading it into a *spreadsheet window*. You can have up to 32 spreadsheet windows open at once, each containing a different spreadsheet. The windows can share the screen or can be arranged in layers that you display one at a time.

You can even load spreadsheet files created with other popular programs, or store Quattro files for use with other programs; Quattro translates the files automatically.

Note   Quattro's virtual memory manager, VROOMM™, makes it possible to load and work with extra large spreadsheets (even those similar programs can't handle) without taking away from program performance. If your computer has expanded memory (EMS), you can use it to work with even larger spreadsheets (see page 200 for how to specify what Quattro loads into EMS).

This chapter describes how to

- open and close a spreadsheet window
- load a file into a window
- remove a spreadsheet from a window
- save a spreadsheet in a file
- save an arrangement of windows and files as a *workspace*, which you can load later
- assign a password to a file so unauthorized people can't access it
- change the default directory where Quattro stores spreadsheet files
- create a spreadsheet skeleton, or *template*, that you can use as a foundation for creating new spreadsheets
- save and retrieve files in different program formats, such as Lotus 1-2-3 or Paradox

For details on working with windows, see Chapter 9, "Manipulating windows."

For information on how to use the File Manager to work with files, see Chapter 10, "Using the File Manager."

The File menu

```
═════ File ═════
New
Open
Retrieve

Save        Ctrl-S
Save As
Close
Close All
Erase

Directory
Workspace      ▶
Utilities      ▶
Exit        Ctrl-X
```

You can access most file functions with the /File command, which brings up a menu with the following commands:

- **New** overlays the existing window with a new blank spreadsheet window so you can create a new file.
- **Open** overlays the existing window with a new spreadsheet window *and* loads the file you specify into the window.
- **Retrieve** lets you display a spreadsheet stored in a file, replacing the current spreadsheet.
- **Save** saves the current spreadsheet in a file, using the existing file name.
- **Save As** lets you save the current spreadsheet under a different file name.
- **Close** removes any data from the current window and puts away the window.
- **Close All** closes all open files and windows.

- **Erase** removes the current spreadsheet from memory, leaving you with a blank, unformatted spreadsheet. You can use this command to clear the spreadsheet window (*after saving your work*) to begin a new file.
- **Directory** lets you specify a temporary directory path.
- **Workspace** lets you save your current setup of multiple windows and spreadsheets in a file for future use, or load a saved workspace into Quattro.
- **Utilities** accesses miscellaneous file utilities that let you access DOS, open a File Manager window, and set file-compression options.
- **Exit** puts away the Quattro program and returns you to DOS. If your spreadsheet windows contain data that you haven't saved, Quattro asks if you want to save the files first.

This chapter covers all the File menu commands except three. **Exit** is discussed on page 35. Two **Utilities** options, **DOS Shell** and **File Manager**, are discussed elsewhere: DOS Shell on page 34, and File Manager in Chapter 10, "Using the File Manager."

Responding to file-name prompts

Most File menu commands require the name of a file to work on. When you choose one of these commands, Quattro prompts you for a file name.

There are two types of file prompt displays. One includes a list of all spreadsheet files in the default directory (see the following figure). This is the initial prompt display for most File commands. You can choose a name from the list or type one in.

Figure 8.1
A typical file list

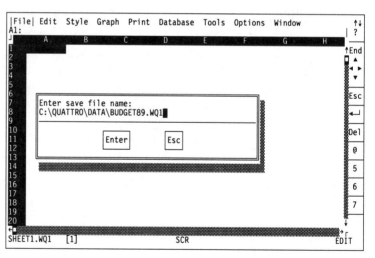

The other file prompt display is a simple *prompt box*, which contains the prompt, a default file name, and two mouse buttons (see the following figure). This display appears when the prompt default already includes a name, or when you begin to type a name.

Figure 8.2
A file-name prompt box

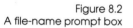

The file-name prompt box contains two buttons for use with a mouse: [Enter] and [Esc]. Click these buttons instead of pressing the *Enter* and *Esc* keys.

The simplest way to respond to either file prompt is to type in the name of the file you want and press *Enter*. Quattro offers numerous options, however, for entering file names and directories. For example, you can

■ choose any file name from the list to enter it as the response.

■ choose a subdirectory from the list to display a list of files in that directory.

■ press *Backspace* with a list displayed to show files in the parent directory.

■ press *Spacebar* to edit the existing file name.

■ display a list of files in any directory by pressing *Esc* twice to erase the path name, entering a different path name, and pressing *Enter*.

■ display a list of files that match any wildcard you type. For example, *.PRN displays a list of all text files in the directory. 87*.WQ? displays a list of all spreadsheets with names beginning with 87. An asterisk looks for any number of characters in its position. A question mark looks for any single character in its position.

■ press *F3* to expand the file list to fill the screen, showing numerous file names at once.

■ press + (plus) on the numeric keypad to display file information about the files in the list.

 To choose a file name with a mouse, double-click it.

Table 8.1 details the effects of different actions on file prompts—both in a file list and a prompt box.

Table 8.1: Effects of keys pressed in a file prompt display

Key pressed	Within a file list	Within a prompt box
Ctrl-Backspace	Removes default prompt and file list.	Clears default prompt.
Esc	Removes list, erases wildcard from prompt line.	Erases path name. If file name appears as default, replaces it with a wildcard and displays file list.
Backspace	Displays a list of all files in the parent directory.	Deletes character to left of cursor, or if file name appears as default, beeps.
Begin Typing	Removes list and replaces wildcards with what you type.	Adds characters you type to the prompt line. If file name appears as default, replaces it.
Spacebar	Highlights next file in the list.	Adds a space to the prompt line.
Enter	Enters the file name highlighted on the list. If a directory name is highlighted, displays a list of all files in that directory.	Adds the file-name wildcard after the directory path and shows a list of all files in that directory. If a file name is shown, enters it.
F2	Prompts "Search for: *". Type the first letter(s) of the file you want Quattro to search for and highlight it on the list.	
F3	Expands the file list to full screen so you can see all your files at once. Press F3 again to shrink it back.	
+ (keypad)	Displays status information with file names—one file per row.	
– (keypad)	Removes status information from file list, showing names only.	

If no default is shown after the prompt (not even a directory), *Esc* removes the prompt and returns to the menu, and *Enter* adds the current directory path to the prompt line and shows a list of all files in the directory.

Accessing files

Once you've saved spreadsheet data in a file, you can redisplay it at any time by loading it into a window. You can also load files created with other spreadsheet programs; Quattro translates them automatically.

The first three commands on the File menu let you open a window and/or load a file into a window:

- **New** opens a new, blank spreadsheet window, overlaying existing windows.
- **Open** opens a new window *and* loads the file you specify into it. Any existing spreadsheet data is still accessible.
- **Retrieve** loads a file into the current window and replaces any existing data.

Another window-related command, /File | Erase, clears any data and formatting information from the current window, allowing you to begin a new file.

The following sections describe how these four options work.

Opening a new window

When you first load Quattro, it displays one spreadsheet window, which fills the screen. You can use this window to create new spreadsheets or to display existing ones. If you want to create a new spreadsheet without putting away the current spreadsheet, use the /File | New command. Quattro opens a blank window, covering up existing windows. It names the window SHEET#, where # is the number of windows you've opened since loading Quattro. You can change the name when you save the file.

You can have up to 32 open windows at a time, with different spreadsheets in each. Each window you open is assigned a number (shown in brackets on the status line when it's active and on the top of the frame when it's visible), according to the order in which you opened it. Each new window overlays other open windows. However, even though they are out of sight, they remain open and accessible via the **Window | Pick** command.

Opening a window and a file

To work with another existing spreadsheet *without putting away the current spreadsheet*, use the /File | **Open** command:

1. Choose /File | **Open**. Quattro prompts you for a file name and displays a list of existing spreadsheet files in the default directory.
2. Choose the spreadsheet file you want to load into the new window.

Quattro displays the window in the size and position that file was last viewed in.

Note You can also use the File Manager to open a single file or set of files at once (see Chapter 10, "Using the File Manager").

Retrieving a file into a window

If you want to load an existing spreadsheet file into the current window, use the /File | Retrieve command. This command erases any data in the current window, then fills it with the specified spreadsheet data.

To retrieve a spreadsheet file into the current window,

1. Choose /File | Retrieve.

   If your current window contains unsaved data, Quattro prompts, "Lose your changes?" Choose No to go back and save changes, or Yes to continue.

   Quattro prompts you for the name of a file and displays a list of spreadsheet files in the default (or overriding) directory.

2. Enter a file name or choose one from the displayed list (highlight it and press *Enter*).

3. If the file has been assigned a password, Quattro prompts you for it. Type the password and press *Enter*. If the password is incorrect, Quattro displays an error message and aborts the command.

When a spreadsheet is retrieved, it replaces any existing data on the screen. The spreadsheet window takes on the size and position of the window the file was saved in. For example, if the spreadsheet window was in the left half of the screen when you saved the file, the window you retrieve the file in moves to the left half of the screen.

To retrieve a file that was created with a different program, include the file-name extension when you retrieve it (see "Translating files" later in this chapter).

To retrieve a saved workspace, use the /File | Workspace | Restore command (see page 229).

Retrieving a file from the command line

When you first load Quattro (by typing Q *Enter* from the DOS prompt), you can specify a spreadsheet or workspace file to be retrieved at the same time.

To load a specific spreadsheet or workspace file, type Q, followed by a space and the name of the file you want to retrieve; for example,

```
Q BUDGET
```

To load a file from a directory other than the default directory, include the path name with the file name; for example,

```
Q C:\COMPANY\BUDGET
```

loads both Quattro and the BUDGET file in the COMPANY directory on the hard disk at the same time. If it can't find the directory or the file you specify, Quattro opens a new file by that name.

See page 229 for more information about saving and restoring workspaces.

To invoke a macro from the command line, include its name after the Q command and a file name. For example,

```
Q BUDGET \number
```

loads Quattro, retrieves the BUDGET spreadsheet or workspace file, and invokes a macro named \NUMBER. For more information about macros, see Chapter 16, "Using macros."

Automatically retrieving a file

When you start Quattro from DOS without specifying a particular file name for it to retrieve, a blank spreadsheet is normally displayed. However, if your default directory contains an autoload file, this file is retrieved automatically.

An *autoload file* is a spreadsheet file specified with the Autoload File command on the /**Options** I **Startup** menu (see "Startup options" on page 191). Initially, this default is QUATTRO.WQ1, and any spreadsheet file named QUATTRO is loaded automatically when no other is specified. However, you can change this default to any file name you like.

 If you're using the 123-compatible menus, choose /**Worksheet** I **Global** I **Default** I **Files** I **Autoload File**.

This feature lets you immediately display the spreadsheet you use most often. If you use a *template* to create spreadsheets (a spreadsheet you've created with the basic parameters you use most often), you can display it automatically instead of the blank spreadsheet. (For more information, see "Creating custom spreadsheet templates" later in this chapter.)

Clearing a window to start a new file

To erase all data from the current spreadsheet window so you can create a new spreadsheet without opening another window, use the /File | Erase command. This command deletes all spreadsheet data and returns all column widths, numeric formats, and other settings to their default values.

To clear the current spreadsheet window,

1. If the current window contains data you want to save, store it in a file first: use /File | Save or /File | Save As.

2. Choose /File | Erase. If the current window contains data you haven't saved yet, Quattro displays a confirmation menu asking, "Lose your changes?"

3. If you want to save your data, choose No, save the spreadsheet (see the following section), then choose /File | Erase again. If you don't mind losing your changes, choose Yes.

Quattro clears the current spreadsheet window, and you can start fresh.

1-2-3

If you're using the 123-compatible menus, choose /Worksheet | Erase. Quattro always displays the Erase confirmation menu, regardless of whether data may be lost.

Note If the Undo key (*Alt-F5*) is enabled, you can use it to bring back a spreadsheet you accidentally erase. Undo reverses the last operation. To bring back a spreadsheet you erased earlier, use the Transcript utility (see Chapter 17, "Using Transcript").

If you want to put away the spreadsheet file *and* close the window, use the /File | Close command (see "Closing windows" later in this chapter). If you want to replace the current window contents with another spreadsheet, use the /File | Retrieve command (see page 222). To erase only *part* of a spreadsheet, use the /Edit | Erase Block command (see page 125) or the /Edit | Delete command (see page 144).

Tip   An alternative to beginning a new spreadsheet with a blank screen is to create a spreadsheet file that contains default settings and skeletal data standards for your spreadsheet files. Then, instead of using the /File I New command, you can simply retrieve this file each time you want to build a new spreadsheet. See "Creating custom spreadsheet templates" later in this chapter for more information.

Saving files

There are two file commands you can use to save a spreadsheet in a file:

- **Save As** lets you assign a name to a spreadsheet and then save it, or save a spreadsheet under a different name.
- **Save** saves the spreadsheet under the current name.

Save

Ctrl-S is the default shortcut for the /File I Save command.

You can protect your spreadsheet from unauthorized access by assigning a password when you save it. See "Assigning a password to a file" later in this chapter.

If you haven't saved the spreadsheet before, or if you want to store it in a different file, use the Save As command:

1. Choose /File I Save As. Quattro prompts you for a file name and shows the default directory path. The current file name and path are used as the default.

2. To use the default file name, press *Enter*. To use a different file name, enter a new name, or press *Spacebar* or *F2* and edit the existing name, or press *Esc* to display a list of files in the default directory. If you don't specify a file-name extension, Quattro automatically adds the default extension (initially .WQ1). (If you specify a different extension, you'll have to include it each time you're prompted for a file name.)

```
┌─ File Already Exists ─┐
│                       │
│ Cancel                │
│ Replace               │
│ Backup                │
└───────────────────────┘
```

3. If the file name you enter already exists, Quattro displays an overwrite warning menu.

4. Choose the option you want:

- **Cancel** interrupts the command and returns you to the spreadsheet; you can then save the spreadsheet under a different file name.

- **Replace** overwrites the existing file.

- **Backup** makes a copy of the existing file, giving it a .BAK file-name extension. To retrieve the backup file later, include the .BAK extension with that name.

Quattro saves the spreadsheet in the specified directory, and also saves the position and size of the spreadsheet window, so that when you retrieve the file, it's displayed just as it was when you saved it. The spreadsheet data remains on your screen, and you can continue working on it.

Once you've named your spreadsheet, you can store changes you make to it with the /File | Save command. Quattro assumes you want to save the file under the same name.

Although the Transcript utility backs up your work in case of a power failure or accident (see Chapter 17), it's still a good idea to save your spreadsheet periodically as you work.

When you save a spreadsheet, Quattro stores the data in the spreadsheet with formatting information, including display format, label alignment, column width, protection, and recalculation mode. Zero display is not saved. Quattro also saves any graphs and named blocks and the current /File | Directory setting with the spreadsheet. System defaults such as hardware and color settings are *not* stored with individual spreadsheets; a spreadsheet assumes the current setting for these defaults the next time it's retrieved.

Note   If you're saving to a floppy disk that doesn't have enough room for the spreadsheet, Quattro displays an error message. Press *Esc*, insert a new disk, and try again. If you don't have a preformatted disk, you can use the /File | Utilities | DOS Shell command to return to DOS and format one without having to exit Quattro.

If there still isn't room, try using a .WQ! extension to compress the file (see the section on using SQZ! to compress a file, which follows shortly).

To save a Quattro spreadsheet file for use with another program, such as Paradox, Reflex, Lotus 1-2-3, or dBASE, include the program's data file extension with the file name when you save it (see "Translating files" later in this chapter for details).

Assigning a file name

File names can be up to eight characters long and can consist of both letters and numbers. You can enter file names using either upper- or lowercase letters. Do not use spaces in a file name. You can, however, use the underscore character (_) to simulate spaces, for example, 87_SALES.

When you name a file, use a name that will help you remember what is in the file, such as BUDGET or TAXES. If you have several similar files, you can differentiate between them by adding dates (BUDGET86 or TAXES615). If you share a disk with other people, it's a good idea to begin each of your file names with your initials. This ensures that all your files will be displayed together, since Quattro sorts file names alphabetically. You can also use wild-cards to display only your files; for example, JM*.* displays only files beginning with *JM*.

Caution! If the name you give a file is more than eight characters long, Quattro truncates it. This will cause problems if the first eight characters of two file names are the same. For example, SPREADSHEET1 and SPREADSHEET2 would both be truncated to SPREADSH, and saving one would overwrite the other.

Unless you're saving your file for use with another program, it's best if you don't include an extension with the file name. Quattro then adds the default extension (initially .WQ1) automatically and you won't have to include it when you retrieve the file later. (To change the default extension, see page 195.)

Using SQZ! to compress a file

Quattro provides a built-in feature, SQZ!, which allows you to compress ("squeeze") spreadsheet files for more efficient storage. This is particularly helpful if you're storing large spreadsheets on a floppy disk or telecommunicating files over a modem. When you retrieve the file, Quattro automatically expands it to its original size and form.

To use SQZ!, all you have to do is include a special file-name extension when you save the file:

- .WKZ compresses files from earlier versions of Quattro.
- .WQ! compresses QUATTRO PRO spreadsheet files.

- .WK$ compresses Lotus 1-2-3 .WKS files.
- .WK! compresses Lotus 1-2-3 .WK1 files.

Quattro compresses the file as it saves it.

There are a few options you can set for the SQZ! function. To change them, choose /File | Utilities | SQZ!. Quattro displays the SQZ! menu.

```
════ SQZ! ════
Remove Blanks
Storage of Values
Version
Quit
```

- **Remove Blanks** specifies whether to store blank cells. Normally, Quattro stores both blank cells that have been preformatted and blank labels with the spreadsheet. To save space, you can delete blank labels and formatting for blank cells by setting this default to **Yes**. The blank cells will be removed permanently from the spreadsheet, so keep this default set to **No** if you want to retain preformatting for blank cells.

- **Storage of Values** specifies how to store spreadsheet values. Normally, Quattro stores both formulas and their resulting values with a spreadsheet. To save space, you can set the Storage of Values default to **Remove** to erase the resulting values. Quattro automatically recalculates the formulas when you retrieve the file. To save values up to 7 significant digits (instead of the usual 15), set this default to **Approximate**. The initial setting, Exact, stores both formulas and their exact resulting values.

Note   If you plan to use your spreadsheet with another product (Reflex, for example), do not use the **Remove** setting with a compressed file. The other program will need the formula results in order to translate the data correctly.

- **Version** lets you specify the version of SQZ! you want to use: SQZ! or SQZ! Plus. Use SQZ! Plus unless you want to share files with someone who is using SQZ! 1.x with Lotus 1-2-3 or Symphony. (SQZ! Plus in Quattro is fully compatible with SQZ! Plus and SQZ! v.1.5 for Lotus 1-2-3.)

- **Quit** returns you to the spreadsheet.

Assigning a password to a file

When you save a spreadsheet file, you can protect it from unauthorized access by giving it a password. That password must then be supplied before the file can be retrieved.

To assign a password to a spreadsheet,

1. With the spreadsheet displayed, choose /File | Save **As**. Quattro prompts you for a file name.
2. Type the name of the file, followed by a space and the letter *P*.
3. Press *Enter*. Quattro prompts you for a password.
4. Type the password you want to give the file. You can use up to 15 characters. The characters you type are shown on the screen as square bullets (■ ■ ■) so they are hidden from curious bystanders.
5. Press *Enter*. Quattro asks for verification, just in case you made a typographical error.
6. Type the password again, and press *Enter*. If the password differs at all from the first one you typed, Quattro displays an error message and aborts the command.

1-2-3 If you're using the 123-compatible menus, choose /File | **Save** then follow steps 2 through 6 in this section.

A file that has been assigned a password is said to be *encrypted*. To retrieve an encrypted file, supply the correct password.

Caution! If you forget the password you assign to a file, you won't be able to access it. For this reason, it's important to record your passwords when you create them—either on paper or in another encrypted file.

Saving and retrieving workspaces

The arrangement of windows and files in Quattro is called a *workspace*. The workspace includes the position and size of all windows and the files contained in each window. If, after creating a workspace that includes various files and windows, you want to leave Quattro but don't want to have to build your workspace all over again when you return, use the /File | Workspace command to save it.

To save a workspace,

1. Choose /File | **Workspace** | **Save**. Quattro prompts you for a name to give the workspace.
2. Type a valid file name. Don't include a file-name extension; Quattro automatically includes the .WSP extension for workspace files.

3. Press *Enter.*

Quattro stores the exact placement of all open windows and the files displayed in each. (Quattro doesn't prompt you to save data in the windows; use **Save** or **Save As** for this.)

To retrieve a workspace,

1. Choose /**File** | **Workspace** | **Restore**. Quattro displays a list of existing workspace files.
2. Choose the file you want from the list, or type in a name and press *Enter.*

Quattro replaces any existing windows with the windows stored in the workspace file, then retrieves the appropriate file for each.

To load Quattro and restore a workspace at the same time, include the name of the workspace after Q on the DOS command line. For example, to load Quattro and restore the SALES workspace, type Q SALES and press *Enter.*

Note   If you have a workspace *and* a spreadsheet file with the same name, Quattro will load the file, not the workspace.

Quattro always retrieves the latest saved version of files when you retrieve a workspace. If you leave the workspace and save a file that is included in the workspace, Quattro will retrieve the updated version of the file when you choose /**File** | **Workspace** | **Restore**.

Closing windows

When you're through working with a window, you can put it away by closing it. To close the current window,

1. Choose /**File** | **Close**. (If the window contains data you haven't saved yet, Quattro asks if you want to lose your changes. To save the file, press *N*, then choose /**File** | **Save** or **Save As**.)
2. Quattro closes the window, revealing any windows underneath, and replaces it with the window that was underneath it. If it was the last open window, the screen appears blank except for the status line, mouse palette, and an abbreviated **File** menu with five available options:

   - **New** (to open a blank spreadsheet in a new window)
   - **Open** (to open an existing spreadsheet in a new window)

- Utilities (to shell to DOS, open a File Manager window, or compress a file)
- Workspace (to load a workspace—see page 229)
- Exit (to exit to DOS)

If you're using the 123-compatible menus, choose /View | Close.

To close all open windows and exit Quattro, choose /File | Exit. For each window that contains unsaved changes, Quattro asks if you want to lose your changes. If you choose Save & Exit, Quattro prompts you for confirmation at each unsaved spreadsheet and then exits to DOS. If you choose Yes, Quattro closes the spreadsheet without saving and exits to DOS. No aborts the Exit command.

If you have a mouse, click the close box in the upper left corner of a window to close it.

Overriding the default directory

The default directory is the disk drive and directory specified with the /Options | Startup | Directory command; it's where Quattro stores spreadsheet files.

When you use a file command, Quattro displays a list of files in the default directory. Unless you specify otherwise, spreadsheet files are saved in the default directory, and Quattro looks there when you choose /File | Retrieve to retrieve a file.

You can always override the default directory by specifying a different one when Quattro prompts you for a file name. You can also access a different directory with the /File | Directory command. When you specify a directory with /File | Directory, files in that directory are displayed each time you initiate a File menu command within that spreadsheet.

Quattro preserves the specified path name when you save the spreadsheet. Quattro reverts to the default directory when you save other spreadsheets. This lets you access different directories without having to reset the default directory or include a path name with file names.

The File Manager also lets you access a different directory or set of directories. For detailed information about the File Manager, see Chapter 10, "Using the File Manager."

To change the default directory temporarily,

1. Choose /File I Directory. Quattro prompts for a directory path name.
2. Either edit the existing default, or press *Esc* to erase it, then enter the path name for the directory you want. If the disk drive differs from the current directory, include the drive designation, too.

Quattro uses the new directory until you specify another one with /File I Directory, change the default directory, or exit Quattro. As with the default directory, you can always override the temporary directory by specifying a directory when Quattro prompts you for a file name.

When you change the default directory with the /Options I Startup I Directory command (see page 192), the /File I Directory command is automatically set to the same directory. Changing the temporary directory does not affect the /Options I Startup Directory command setting, however.

For more information on using subdirectories, see Appendix B, "A DOS primer."

Creating custom spreadsheet templates

After you've worked with Quattro for a while, you may find certain traits typical of your spreadsheets: macros you use repeatedly, standard column widths or numeric formats, and so on. You can save yourself the time required to set up standard spreadsheets by creating spreadsheet *templates*.

A spreadsheet template is like a structural skeleton that you can use as a base for your spreadsheet. You can store in it whatever defaults you wish. If you've already set up one spreadsheet with the formatting defaults and customized structure you prefer, just erase the data you've entered and save the file under a different name (with /File I Save As). When you retrieve the template, much of your initial work will be done for you. Just add your data and save the file under a different name.

You may want to create several types of spreadsheet templates— for example, one for a monthly budget, another for expense reports. The templates can simply be forms you need to fill out.

Translating files

Quattro lets you save spreadsheets for use with other programs, such as Lotus 1-2-3, and automatically translates files created with other programs when you retrieve them.

Table 8.2 shows the types of files Quattro can translate, the extensions used for each, and the translator file required for each.

Table 8.2
Files Quattro can translate

Extension	Program
.WKS	Lotus 1-2-3, version 1A
.WK1	Lotus 1-2-3, version 2.01
.WKE	Lotus 1-2-3, educational version
.WRK	Symphony, version 1.2
.WR1	Symphony, version 2.0
.WKQ	Earlier versions of Quattro
.WQ1	QUATTRO PRO
.WKP	Surpass
.DB	Paradox
.DB2	dBASE II
.DBF	dBASE III, III+, and IV
.RXD	Reflex, version 1
.R2D	Reflex, version 2
.WK$	SQZ (Lotus 1-2-3, version 1A)
.WK!	SQZ (Lotus 1-2-3, version 2.01)
.WR$	SQZ (Symphony, version 1.2)
.WR!	SQZ (Symphony, version 2.0)
.WKZ	SQZ (earlier versions of Quattro)
.WQ!	SQZ (QUATTRO PRO)
.DIF	VisiCalc
.SLK	Multiplan

To save a file for use with one of the above programs, just include the appropriate extension when you save it. For example, to save the spreadsheet MYFILE for use with Symphony, specify the file name as MYFILE.WRK.

To retrieve a file created by one of the above programs, just include the file's extension when you retrieve it. Quattro translates it for you. It converts the database field names to spreadsheet labels that serve as column headings and automatically names the cells underneath each name (just as if you had used the **Assign Names** command).

Because Quattro's virtual memory manager, VROOMM™, is superior to those used by other spreadsheet and database programs, you should be able to load even larger spreadsheets than you could in other programs, without any loss of program performance. If you have expanded memory (EMS), you can use it to store some or all of your spreadsheet data, extending your maximum spreadsheet size even further (see page 200 for how to specify what Quattro loads into EMS).

Note   dBASE II and dBASE III use the same file-name extension (.DBF) but different file formats. To save files in dBASE II format, use the .DB2 extension, then change the extension to .DBF before retrieving the file in dBASE II. To retrieve dBASE II files in Quattro, however, use the .DBF extension.

You can also combine files and extract files in different program formats (see "Combining files" and "Extracting part of a spreadsheet" in Chapter 12).

When you save a Quattro spreadsheet in Paradox, Reflex, or dBASE format, a translator menu appears with three options.

```
View Structure
Write
Quit
```

- **View Structure** shows you how Quattro intends to format the file. Choose **V**iew Structure to display a list of field names based on the data in the first row of the spreadsheet. If the first row of the spreadsheet contains data that is invalid as a database field name—for example, numbers or spaces—Quattro uses the spreadsheet column letters to represent the field names when you view the structure. To change the field type, field size, or name of a field, choose it from the list and enter the correct information. To remove a field from the file being translated, highlight it on the list and press *Del*.

- **Write** translates the file to Paradox, Reflex, or dBASE format.

- **Quit** returns to the spreadsheet

Note   When you have added special Quattro features like linking or presentation-quality graphics to a spreadsheet file, you may see a warning message when you attempt to save that file to another file format. The warning states what feature will be lost when Quattro translates the file. If you don't want to lose the feature, save the spreadsheet as a .WQ1 file.

9

Manipulating windows

A *window* is a rectangular area onscreen that displays information. In Chapter 8, you learned how to open and close spreadsheet windows. In Chapter 10, you learn how to open and close File Manager windows. This chapter describes the mechanics of working with windows, including how to

- get into the window you want to work with
- expand a window to fill the whole screen, overlaying any other open windows
- arrange all open windows onscreen at once

For information about copying or moving data between spreadsheet windows, see page 111.

- show all open windows in layers, producing a three-dimensional, stacked effect
- change the size or position of a window
- lock specific spreadsheet rows or columns in place so they stay onscreen when you scroll
- split a window into two panes so you can view two parts of the same spreadsheet
- display a spreadsheet in a condensed "map mode" so you can see more onscreen at once

For information on how to reference data in another spreadsheet, see Chapter 11, "Linking spreadsheets."

What is a window?

In Quattro, there are two types of windows you can open to work with data or files: spreadsheet windows and File Manager windows. You can have up to 32 windows open at once, some sharing the screen and some overlaying others.

By opening multiple windows, you can work with several spreadsheets at once. This is helpful not only for working on related spreadsheets simultaneously, but also for quickly jumping back and forth between projects without losing your place in each.

The following figure shows three windows sharing the Quattro screen:

Figure 9.1
The screen split into three windows

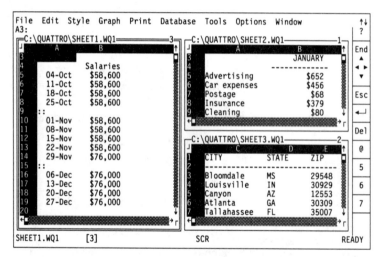

You can arrange open windows however you want. Some may share the screen; some may completely fill the screen, hiding others. Quattro arranges the hidden windows in layers, like a stack of papers on your desk that you can shuffle through.

The following figure shows a three-dimensional picture of a set of open windows. You can see how the windows are layered. Because the Quattro screen is two-dimensional, you see usually only the top layer. (You can use the /Window | Stack command to produce a three-dimensional effect, however. See the section "Stacking windows" on page 240.)

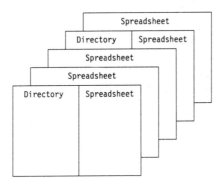

Figure 9.2
How open windows can be
layered

The Window menu

```
┌──── Window ────┐
│ Zoom           │
│ Tile     Ctrl-T│
│ Stack          │
│ Move/Size Ctrl-R│
├────────────────┤
│ Options       ►│
├────────────────┤
│ Pick           │
└────────────────┘
```

Each time you open a spreadsheet window, Quattro overlays the other window(s) with the new one. Access open windows individually by moving through the layers, or use the commands in the **Window** menu to change the way windows appear onscreen.

- **Zoom** expands the active window to fill the screen. If it already fills the screen and other windows are open, it shrinks the window back to what it was before and redisplays the other windows.

- **Tile** displays all open windows on the screen at once.

- **Stack** arranges open windows in layers and displays the top line of each (showing the name of the spreadsheet or directory list it contains).

- **Move/Size** lets you change the size or position of the active window on the screen.

- **Options** lets you split the active window into two *panes*, so you can view two parts of your spreadsheet at once. It also lets you lock specified columns or rows on the screen, remove the column and row borders from the screen, and display data in a condensed "map" mode.

- **Pick** displays a list of open windows. The window you choose becomes the active one.

Activating a window

When you have multiple windows open, you can only work in one at a time. This is called the *active* window, indicated by a double-line border.

There are three ways to activate an open window:

- Press the Next Window key, *Shift-F6*, to move into the next window (in the sequence in which they were created). If the window is underneath other windows, it moves to the top.
- Choose the /**Window** I **Pick** command, or press the Pick Window key, *Shift-F5*. Quattro displays a list of currently open windows, including the file contained in it and the window number. When you choose a window from the list, Quattro activates it.
- Hold down the *Alt* key and press the number of the window you want to move into. (The active window number appears in brackets on the status line, and each window's number appears in the top right corner of the window.) Quattro activates and displays that window. If you press *Alt-0*, Quattro displays the Pick Window list.

 To activate a window with a mouse, click any part of it.

If you're using the 123-compatible menus, choose /**View** I **Pick**.

1-2-3

Zooming in on a window

If the active window takes up only part of the screen, you can "zoom" in on it for a closer look. Quattro fills the screen with the active window (temporarily overlaying the others), so you have more room for the work you're doing.

To zoom in on a window,

1. Make sure the window is active. If not, use *Shift-F6*, *Alt #* (where # is the window number you want to zoom), or /**Window** I **Pick** to make it active.
2. Choose /**Window** I **Zoom** or press the Zoom key, *Alt-F6*.

 If you have a mouse, click the zoom icon in the upper right corner of the screen to zoom or unzoom a window.

To return the window to its previous size and position, and redisplay the windows it shared the screen with, choose /Window | Zoom or press *Alt-F6* again.

If you're using the 123-compatible menus, choose /View | Zoom.

The following figure shows the window that appeared on the left of the screen in Figure 9.1 "zoomed" to full screen:

Figure 9.3
A "zoomed" window

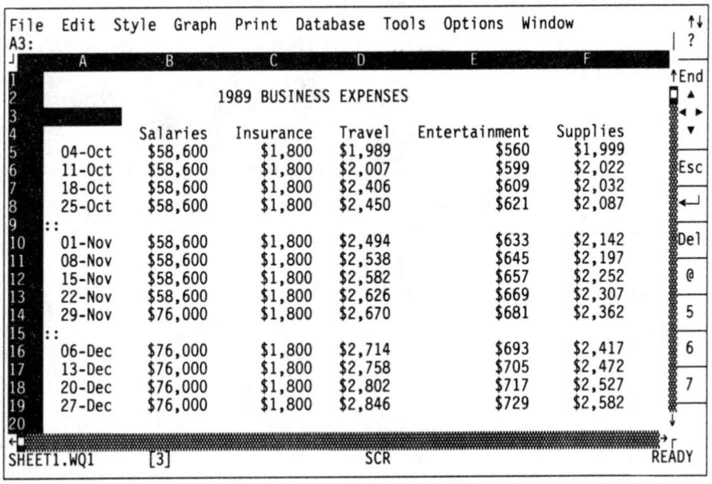

```
File  Edit  Style  Graph  Print  Database  Tools  Options  Window        ↑↓
A3:                                                                        | ?
J     A        B          C        D          E            F             ↑End
1                                                                         □ ▲
2                         1989 BUSINESS EXPENSES                          □ ◄ ►
3
4              Salaries  Insurance  Travel  Entertainment  Supplies         ▼
5     04-Oct   $58,600   $1,800    $1,989         $560    $1,999
6     11-Oct   $58,600   $1,800    $2,007         $599    $2,022         Esc
7     18-Oct   $58,600   $1,800    $2,406         $609    $2,032
8     25-Oct   $58,600   $1,800    $2,450         $621    $2,087         ↵
9     ::
10    01-Nov   $58,600   $1,800    $2,494         $633    $2,142         Del
11    08-Nov   $58,600   $1,800    $2,538         $645    $2,197
12    15-Nov   $58,600   $1,800    $2,582         $657    $2,252         @
13    22-Nov   $58,600   $1,800    $2,626         $669    $2,307
14    29-Nov   $76,000   $1,800    $2,670         $681    $2,362         5
15    ::
16    06-Dec   $76,000   $1,800    $2,714         $693    $2,417         6
17    13-Dec   $76,000   $1,800    $2,758         $705    $2,472
18    20-Dec   $76,000   $1,800    $2,802         $717    $2,527         7
19    27-Dec   $76,000   $1,800    $2,846         $729    $2,582
20
SHEET1.WQ1      [3]                        SCR                          READY
```

Arranging open windows as tiles

To view all open windows at once, choose the /Window | Tile command. Quattro divides the screen into *tiles*, with a window in each tile. It repositions and resizes the windows as necessary, giving the windows equal room on the screen (when possible).

Ctrl-T is the default shortcut for the /Window | Tile command.

The following figure shows nine spreadsheets arranged onscreen with the /Window | Tile command:

Figure 9.4
Tiled windows

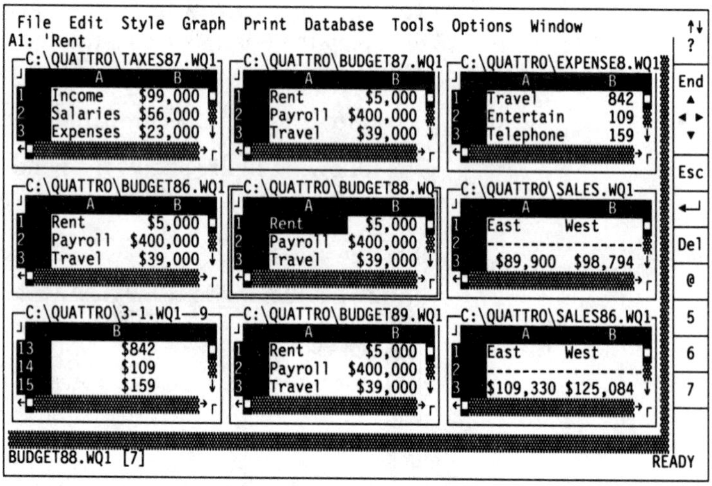

```
 File  Edit  Style  Graph  Print  Database  Tools  Options  Window        ↑↓
A1: 'Rent                                                                   ?
┌C:\QUATTRO\TAXES87.WQ1┐ ┌C:\QUATTRO\BUDGET87.WQ1 ┌C:\QUATTRO\EXPENSE8.WQ1┐
J       A       B         J      A       B         J      A       B        End
1  Income    $99,000 ▢   1  Rent     $5,000 ▢    1  Travel      842       ▲
2  Salaries  $56,000 ▒   2  Payroll $400,000 ▒   2  Entertain   109  ▒   ◄ ►
3  Expenses  $23,000 ↓   3  Travel  $39,000 ↓    3  Telephone   159  ↓    ▼
←■            →  ┌       ←■            →  ┌       ←■            →  ┌
                                                                          Esc
┌C:\QUATTRO\BUDGET86.WQ1 ┌C:\QUATTRO\BUDGET88.WQ┐ ┌C:\QUATTRO\SALES.WQ1─┐
J       A       B         J      A       B         J      A       B        ↵
1  Rent      $5,000 ▢    1  Rent     $5,000 ▢    1  East     West       
2  Payroll $400,000 ▒    2  Payroll $400,000 ▒   2  -------------------  Del
3  Travel  $39,000 ↓     3  Travel  $39,000 ↓    3  $89,900  $98,794 ↓
←■            →  ┌       ←■            →  ┌       ←■            →  ┌       @
┌C:\QUATTRO\3-1.WQ1─9┐   ┌C:\QUATTRO\BUDGET89.WQ1 ┌C:\QUATTRO\SALES86.WQ1┐ 5
J       B               J      A       B         J      A       B
13        $842 ▢        1  Rent     $5,000 ▢    1  East     West      ▢   6
14        $109 ▒        2  Payroll $400,000 ▒   2                     ▒
15        $159 ↓        3  Travel  $39,000 ↓    3  $109,330 $125,084 ↓   7
←■            →  ┌       ←■            →  ┌       ←■            →  ┌

▓▓▓▓▓▓▓▓▓▓▓▓▓▓▓▓▓▓▓▓▓▓▓▓▓▓▓▓▓▓▓▓▓▓▓▓▓▓▓▓▓▓▓▓▓▓▓▓▓▓▓▓▓▓▓▓▓▓▓▓▓▓▓▓▓▓▓▓
 BUDGET88.WQ1 [7]                                                    READY
```

/Window | Tile displays as many as 32 windows on the screen at once. Although this doesn't allow you to see much of the spreadsheets, it works well as a window directory, which you can then use to zoom in on windows.

If you're using the 123-compatible menus, choose /View | Tile.

Stacking windows

The /Window | Stack command rearranges all open windows in layers. The top line of each layer is revealed so you can see the name of the spreadsheet or directory list it contains and the window number. Stacking creates a three-dimensional effect, so you can see what's underneath the layer you're working on.

The following figure shows a Quattro screen with stacked windows:

Figure 9.5
Stacked windows

```
┌──────────────────────────────────────────────────────────────────┬───┐
│ File  Edit  Style  Graph  Print  Database  Tools  Options  Window │ ↑↓│
│ A1:                                                                │ ? │
│ ▓▓┌─C:\QUATTRO\BUDGET89.WQ1──────────────────────────────────6┐  ├───┤
│ ▓▓│┌─C:\QUATTRO\EXPENSE8.WQ1────────────────────────────────5┐│  │End│
│ ▓▓│┌─C:\QUATTRO\SALES.WQ1──────────────────────────────────4┐││  │ ▲ │
│ ░┌─C:\QUATTRO\EXPENSE.WQ1═══════════════════════════════════1═││  │◄ ►│
│ J │  A       B         C         D         E          F    1│ │  │ ▼ │
│ 1 │                                                          ▓ │  ├───┤
│ 2 │               1989 BUSINESS EXPENSES                     ▓ │  │Esc│
│ 3 │                                                          ▓ │  ├───┤
│ 4 │         Salaries  Insurance  Travel  Entertainment  Supplies▓│ │ ↵ │
│ 5 │ 04-Oct  $58,600   $1,800    $1,989       $560      $1,999 ▓ │  ├───┤
│ 6 │ 11-Oct  $58,600   $1,800    $2,007       $599      $2,022 ▓ │  │Del│
│ 7 │ 18-Oct  $58,600   $1,800    $2,406       $609      $2,032 ▓ │  ├───┤
│ 8 │ 25-Oct  $58,600   $1,800    $2,450       $621      $2,087 ▓ │  │ @ │
│ 9 │ ::                                                       ▓ │  ├───┤
│ 10│ 01-Nov  $58,600   $1,800    $2,494       $633      $2,142 ▓ │  │ 5 │
│ 11│ 08-Nov  $58,600   $1,800    $2,538       $645      $2,197 ▓ │  ├───┤
│ 12│ 15-Nov  $58,600   $1,800    $2,582       $657      $2,252 ▓ │  │ 6 │
│ 13│ 22-Nov  $58,600   $1,800    $2,626       $669      $2,307 ▓ │  ├───┤
│ 14│ 29-Nov  $76,000   $1,800    $2,670       $681      $2,362 ▓ │  │ 7 │
│ 15│ ::                                                        │ │  │   │
│ ◄─▓▓▓▓▓▓▓▓▓▓▓▓▓▓▓▓▓▓▓▓▓▓▓▓▓▓▓▓▓▓▓▓▓▓▓▓▓▓▓▓▓▓▓▓▓▓▓▓▓▓▓▓▓▓▓▓▓→ ┌ │  │   │
├──────────────────────────────────────────────────────────────────┤   │
│ EXPENSE.WQ1  [1]                                          READY    │   │
└──────────────────────────────────────────────────────────────────┴───┘
```

 If you have a mouse, you can easily activate layers of a stacked set of windows. Just click the top line of the window you want to work with. Quattro moves the window to the top of the stack. To activate a layer whose title line is overlaid by another window, click the window's left border.

 If you're using the 123-compatible menus, choose /View I Stack.

Changing window size and position

When you display more than one window onscreen, Quattro divides the available space more or less equally between windows. You can fine-tune both the size and position of windows with the /Window I Move/Size command. This command lets you do two things:

- change the width or height of a window
- move a window anywhere on the screen

⎡Ctrl⎤ ⎡R⎤
Move/Size

Ctrl-R is the default shortcut for the /Window I Move/Size command.

To change the position of a window,

1. Make sure the window you want to move is active. If not, use /Window I Pick, *Shift-F6,* or *Alt* # (where # is the number of the window you want to move) to make it active.

2. Choose /Window I Move/Size. Quattro displays a MOVE indicator in the top left corner of the window.

3. Use the arrow keys to move the window: → and ← move the outline horizontally, and ↑ and ↓ move it vertically.

4. When the window is in the position you want, press *Enter*.

 To move a window with a mouse, drag any border of the window until the window is where you want it, then release.

In Move/Size mode, you can also use the following key commands (instead of arrow keys) to resize or reposition the window:

T (top) moves the window to the top half of the screen.
B (bottom) moves the window to the bottom half of the screen.
L (left) moves the window to the left half of the screen.
R (right) moves the window to the right half of the screen.
Z (zoom) zooms the window so it fills the screen.

To change the size of a window,

1. Make sure the window you want to resize is active. If not, use /Window I Pick, *Shift-F6*, or *Alt #* (where # is the number of the window you want to move) to make it active.

2. Choose /Window I Move/Size. Quattro displays the MOVE indicator in the active window.

3. Press the *Scroll Lock* key. The MOVE indicator changes to SIZE.

4. Use the arrow keys to adjust the window's outline on the screen: → and ← adjust the outline's width, and ↑ and ↓ adjust the height.

5. When the window is the size you want, press *Enter*.

 To resize a window using a mouse, drag the resize box in the bottom right corner of the window until the window is the size you want, then release.

If you're using the 123-compatible menus, choose /View I Move/Size.

Note To change the size *and* position of a window, use the *Scroll Lock* key to switch between Move and Size mode. With *Scroll Lock* on, the arrow keys change the size of a window. With *Scroll Lock* off and the *Shift* key held down, the arrow keys also resize a window. *Num Lock* and *Shift* both toggle from Move to Size mode and vice versa, but only *Scroll Lock* changes the onscreen indicator. Don't press *Enter* until the window is both the size and position you want.

Window options

The /Window | Options command offers a menu of commands you can use to adjust the active window's display:

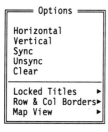

- **The first group** of commands lets you divide a window into two panes that you can scroll separately.

- **Locked Titles** lets you freeze certain rows or columns on your screen as titles. The titles stay put, even when you scroll the rest of the spreadsheet.

- **Row & Col Borders** lets you remove or redisplay the borders at the top and left of each spreadsheet window. (The borders identify columns and rows.)

- **Map View** condenses the spreadsheet display into columns that are one-character wide with codes to represent types of cell entries.

Splitting a window

By using multiple windows, you can view different spreadsheets at the same time, but you can't load the same spreadsheet into different windows. To view different parts of the *same* spreadsheet, split the spreadsheet window into two *panes*. The panes can be side by side (vertical) or one on top of the other (horizontal). The following figure shows a window split horizontally:

Figure 9.6
A spreadsheet window split horizontally

```
 File   Edit   Style   Graph   Print   Database   Tools   Options   Window        ↑↓
A1:                                                                               |  ?
J          A          B          C          D          E          F           
1                                                                              ↑End
2                        1989 BUSINESS EXPENSES                                  ▮  ▲
3                                                                              ◄  ►
4                 Salaries   Insurance   Travel   Entertainment   Supplies        ▼
5      04-Oct      $58,600     $1,800    $1,989          $560       $1,999
6      11-Oct      $58,600     $1,800    $2,007          $599       $2,022      Esc
7      18-Oct      $58,600     $1,800    $2,406          $609       $2,032
8      25-Oct      $58,600     $1,800    $2,450          $621       $2,087      ⏎
9      01-Nov      $58,600     $1,800    $2,494          $633       $2,142
           A          B          C          D          E          F          Del
1                                                                               @
2                        1989 BUSINESS EXPENSES
3                                                                               5
4                 Salaries   Insurance   Travel   Entertainment   Supplies
5      04-Oct      $58,600     $1,800    $1,989          $560       $1,999
6      11-Oct      $58,600     $1,800    $2,007          $599       $2,022      6
7      18-Oct      $58,600     $1,800    $2,406          $609       $2,032
8      25-Oct      $58,600     $1,800    $2,450          $621       $2,087      7
9      01-Nov      $58,600     $1,800    $2,494          $633       $2,142
10     08-Nov      $58,600     $1,800    $2,538          $645       $2,197      ↓
EXPENSE.WQ1   [1]                                                             READY
```

Opening a second window pane

You can open a second pane at any place in the spreadsheet. The window is divided at the row or column containing the current cell.

To split the active window into two panes,

1. Move the cell selector to the row or column at which you want the window to be split.
2. Choose /**Window** | **Options**.
3. Choose **Horizontal** to split the window horizontally at the row containing the selector. Choose **Vertical** to split the window vertically at the column containing the selector.

Pane

The menu disappears and the window is split into two panes. The *current pane* is the one containing the cell selector. To move into the other pane, press the Pane key, *F6*.

To use a mouse to activate a different pane, click the pane you want.

Some display changes you make to the spreadsheet in the current pane do not affect the other pane:

- locked titles
- hidden or exposed columns
- column width
- default display format

For example, if you change column widths (either default or specific) in one pane, the previous widths remain in the other. And if you change default display format in one pane, the previous format remains in the other. (The /**Style** | **Numeric Format** command affects both window panes, however.) When you return the window display to one pane, Quattro retains format changes only if they were made in the top or left pane.

1-2-3

If you're using the 123-compatible menus, choose /**Worksheet** | **Window** | **Horizontal** or **Vertical**.

Unsynchronizing the window panes

When you first split the window into two panes, the panes are *synchronized*, which means that when you scroll in one pane, the other scrolls automatically. You can change this so that each pane works independently of the other. This lets you view one part of the spreadsheet in one pane, while you scroll to another part in the other.

To synchronize or unsynchronize your window panes,

1. Choose /**Window** I **Op**tions (either before or after splitting the window).
2. Choose **Unsync** to be able to scroll the panes independently, or choose **S**ync to return synchronization.

 If you're using the 123-compatible menus, choose /**Worksheet** I **Window** I **S**ync or **Unsync**.

Closing the second window pane

To remove the second pane from the window, choose /**Window** I **Op**tions I **Clear**. The pane on the bottom or right disappears, and the other pane again takes up the entire spreadsheet area.

 If you're using the 123-compatible menus, choose /**Worksheet** I **Window** I **Clear**.

Any column width changes, locked titles, or columns that were hidden or revealed in the top or left pane remain in effect.

Locking rows and columns

When your spreadsheet contains more than one screenful of information, you must scroll the spreadsheet, using the cursor-movement keys, to display different sections. Often, you will want your row or column headings to stay onscreen while you scroll.

The /**Window** I **Op**tions I **Locked Titles** command lets you lock specific rows and/or columns of the spreadsheet onscreen as *titles*. When you scroll the spreadsheet, the titles remain fixed onscreen while the rows beneath (or columns to the right) scroll as usual.

This command is most often used to lock headings in place on the screen, but you can use it to freeze any part of the spreadsheet.

To lock titles onscreen,

1. Scroll the spreadsheet so that the column(s) or row(s) you want to use as titles are visible at the far left or at the top of the screen. You will not be able to adjust the position of the titles after they are frozen.

2. Move the cell selector to the row below or column to the right of the section you want to lock. (All rows above the cell selector and/or all columns to the left will also be frozen.) To lock both the top and left parts of the screen, position the selector in the top left cell of the part you want to remain scrollable.

┌─ Locked Titles ─┐
│   │
│ Horizontal   │
│ Vertical   │
│ Both   │
│ Clear   │
└─────────────────┘

3. Choose /Window I Options I Locked Titles. The Locked Titles menu appears.

4. Choose Horizontal to lock all rows above the cell selector, Vertical to lock all columns to the left, or Both to lock both rows above and columns to the left.

Any previous /Window I Locked Titles command is cleared, and Quattro locks the specified columns or rows in place as titles.

To unlock titles without specifying new ones, choose /Window I Options I Locked Titles I Clear.

1-2-3 If you're using the 123-compatible menus, choose /Worksheet I Titles.

The following figure shows a spreadsheet with column headings locked as titles. The data underneath the headings has been scrolled to reveal the bottom part of the spreadsheet.

Figure 9.7
A spreadsheet with locked titles

```
 File  Edit  Style  Graph  Print  Database  Tools  Options  Window        ↑↓
B32: [W13]                                                            | ?
 J        A            B           C           D           E
 1                                                                    ↑End
 2                                                                    □ ▲
 3                       Yearly Expense Report                        ◄ ►
 4                                                                    ▼
 5                    JANUARY    FEBRUARY     MARCH       APRIL
 6                                                                    Esc
19 Lunches               $80         $80         $80         $80
20 Commissions          $750        $750        $750        $750      ←┘
21 Legal Services       $164        $145        $121        $103
22 Accountant           $173         $76        $119         $64      Del
23 Typing               $842        $598        $366        $711
24 Dues                 $109        $156        $364        $258      @
25 Printing             $159        $194        $209        $187
26                 ----------------------------------------------     5
27 TOTAL             $4,239      $3,575      $3,667      $4,078
28                                                                    6
29
30                          ══════ Locked titles                     7
31
32
SHEET1.WQ1     [1]                                               READY
```

To view expense figures for June through December, you could also lock column A, then scroll right. To do so, you would move the selector to cell B6, then choose /Window I Locked Titles I Both (choosing Vertical would cancel the previous Horizontal setting).

F5
GoTo

You cannot move the cell selector inside a spreadsheet title while Quattro is in Ready mode. You can, however, use the GoTo key, *F5*, to access the cells in the locked titles. When you press *F5*, you'll be able to move the selector to any cell in the spreadsheet, either by pointing or by specifying a cell address or block name. If you access cells within a title, the titles are duplicated onscreen. The following figure shows the example above with the cell selector in cell B5. The block of column headings locked as titles (A1..E6) is duplicated above row 7.

Any changes you make to the duplicate cells are automatically reflected in the frozen titles.

Figure 9.8
Highlighting a cell within a title

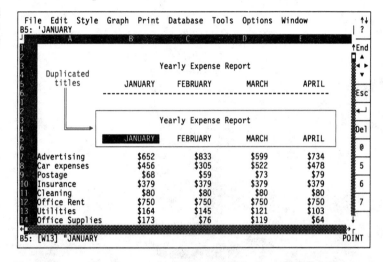

To remove a duplicate column, press *Tab,* then *Shift-Tab.* To remove a duplicate row from the screen, press *PgDn,* then *PgUp.* To remove both duplicate columns and rows from the screen, press *End-Home* to go to the bottom right, then *Home.*

Note   As with hidden and widened columns, locked titles affect the current pane only. If the window is divided into two panes, locked titles will be retained in the spreadsheet *only* if you created them in the top or left pane.

Removing borders

The row and column borders are the highlighted lines at the top and left of the spreadsheet that identify the columns and rows. The column border identifies columns as A, B, C … IV. The row border identifies rows as 1, 2, 3 … 8192. The intersection of the row and column borders is what defines the address of a cell.

If you don't need the row and column borders (for example, if your spreadsheet is set up as a form for data input), you can remove them from the screen.

To remove or restore row and column borders,

1. Choose /**Window** | **Options** | **Row & Col Borders**.
2. Choose **Hide** to remove spreadsheet borders. To redisplay spreadsheet borders, set this command back to **Display**.

If you're using the 123-compatible menus, choose /**Worksheet** | **Window** | **Row & Col Borders**.

The following figure shows two spreadsheets, one with borders and one without:

Figure 9.9
Spreadsheets with and
without borders

With borders

```
 File  Edit  Style  Graph  Print  Datab se  Tools  Options  Window       ↑↓
A3: [W15]                                                                   ?
┌─C:\QUATTRO\EXPENS89.WQ1─────────────────── ▼ ──────────────────2─┐
│J         A              B           C           D           E      ↑│ End
│11  Utilities          $164        $145        $121        $103    ■│  ▲
│12  Office Supplies     $173         $76        $119         $64     │ ◀ ▶
│13  Travel             $842        $598        $366        $711      │  ▼
│14  Entertainment      $109        $156        $364        $258      │
│15  Telephone          $159        $194        $209        $187     │ Esc
│16  Printing           $407          $0         $85        $255    ▼│
│17                  ---------   ---------   ---------   ---------    │  ↵
│◀■                                                            ▶ r   │
└───────────────────────────────────────────────────────────────────┘ Del
┌─C:\QUATTRO\YEARLY.WQ1═══════════════════════════════════════════1─┐  @
│                      Yearly Expense Report                     ↑│
│                                                                 ■│  5
│              JANUARY     FEBRUARY      MARCH       APRIL         │
│            ---------------------------------------------------   │  6
│Advertising    $652        $833        $599        $734          │
│Car expenses   $456        $305        $522        $478          │  7
│Postage         $68         $59         $73         $79          │
│Insurance      $379        $379        $379        $379         ▼│
│◀■                                                            ▶ r │
└───────────────────────────────────────────────────────────────────┘
 YEARLY.WQ1    [1]                         ▲                     READY
```

Without borders

Note Row and column borders don't show up on a printed spreadsheet, regardless of the /**Window** | **Options** | **Row & Col Borders** setting.

The map view

The /**Window** | **Options** | **Map View** command displays the spreadsheet in the current window (or pane) in Map mode, which is something like an aerial view of your data. It condenses the spreadsheet into cells that are one character wide, and in place of data shows one-character codes that indicate the type of data in each cell. This gives you an overall picture of your spreadsheet and is especially useful for checking data types and tracking linked formulas or circular cells.

You can use the map view in a split window to show the complete spreadsheet in one pane, and the map view of the spreadsheet in another pane.

To display the map view of a spreadsheet, choose /Window | Options | Map View | Yes. To return to regular display, set this command back to No.

The following figure shows a spreadsheet in two panes of a window. The right pane uses regular spreadsheet display, and the left pane displays the map view of the spreadsheet.

Figure 9.10
Two views of a spreadsheet

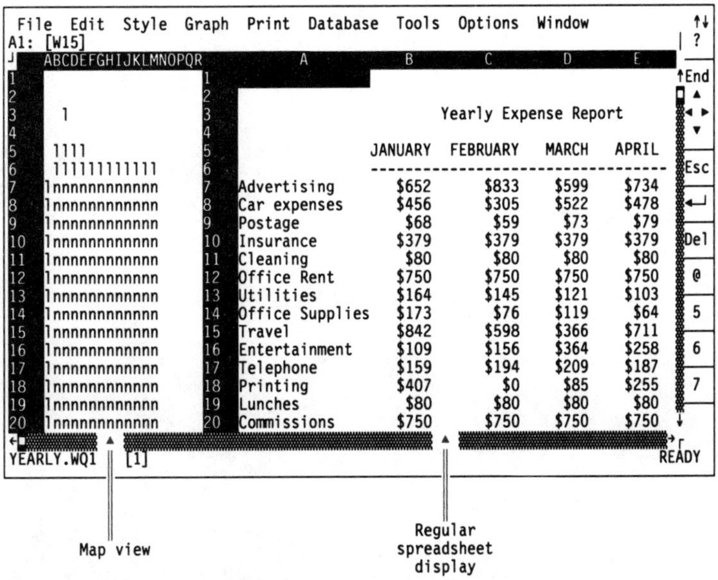

Map view

Regular
spreadsheet
display

Quattro identifies cell data in a map view with the following codes:

l label
n number
+ formula
− link formula
c circular cell
g inserted graph

You can use the map view in conjunction with the /Edit | Search & Replace command to search for any of the data identifiers shown. Just make sure the /Edit | Search & Replace | Look-In command is set to **Values**, then enter the code to look for as the search string. This makes it easy, for example, to search through a large spreadsheet for cells containing circular references.

If you're using the 123-compatible menus, choose /**Worksheet** | **Window** | **Map** View.

10

Using the File Manager

Quattro's File Manager works with DOS to give you easy access to files. You can use it to work with spreadsheet files or any other files located on either your hard disk or a floppy disk.

With the File Manager, you can

- Display a list of files in any directory or disk drive and open a file by choosing its name.
- Use wildcards to filter the file list; for example, *.WQ1 to display only Quattro spreadsheet files.
- Sort a file list by name, extension, size, DOS order, or timestamp.
- Apply a negative filter to show all files except those specified in the filter; for example, [*.WQ1] to show all files *except* Quattro spreadsheet files.
- Display a directory tree that shows the structure of all directories on your disk. You can move in and out of directories in the tree, change the display size of the tree, and use the GoTo key (*F5*) to search through the tree for the file you specify.
- Move or copy a file from one directory to another.
- Rename files.
- Delete files from the disk.

The File Manager window

The File Manager works within a File Manager window. This window displays only file names and subdirectories. To open a File Manager window, choose /File | Utilities | File Manager. Quattro displays the File Manager window in the position of the last open File Manager window (see the following figure). It contains information about files in the current directory or the directory displayed in the window when you last used it.

1-2-3

If you're using the 123-compatible menus, choose /System | File Manager. Once you're in the File Manager, all of the menus are identical to the Quattro menus.

Figure 10.1
A File Manager window

```
File  Edit  Sort  Tree  Print  Options  Window                          ↑↓
                                                                         ?
┌C:\QUATTRO\DATA\═══════════════2═   ▓═E═══════F═══════G═══════H══▓
                                   ↑                                    End
      Drive:  C                    ▓                                     ▲
   Directory: \QUATTRO\DATA\       ▓                                    ◄ ►
      Filter: *.*                  ▓                                     ▼
   File Name: █                    ▓
                                   ▓                                    Esc
   ..                             
   BUDGET87  WQ1      1,441    3-07-89▓                                  ↵
   BUDGET88  WQ1      1,441    3-07-89▓
   BUDGET89  WQ1      1,441    3-07-89▓                                 Del
   EXPENSE8  WQ1      1,441    3-07-89▓
   SALES86   WQ1      1,441    3-07-89▓                                  @
   SALES87   WQ1      1,441    3-07-89▓
   SALES88   WQ1      1,441    3-07-89▓                                  5
   SALES89   WQ1      1,441    3-07-89▓
   TAXES87   WQ1      1,441    3-07-89▓                                  6
   TAXES88   WQ1      1,441    3-07-89▓
   THREE     WSP      2,520    3-07-89▢                                  7
   TRAFFIC   WQ!      3,004    1-30-89↓
   <more>                          
C:           [2]                                                      READY
```

The File Manager window is divided into three sections called *panes*.

- The top pane, called the *control pane*, contains prompts that let you specify a different disk drive and directory, filter the list of files, and enter a file name to look for or open.

- Below the control pane is the *file list pane*, which contains a list of files and subdirectories in the specified directory.

- With the /Tree | Open command, you can activate a third pane, called the *tree pane*, which displays a graphic representation of the directories on the specified drive (see "The directory tree pane" later in this chapter).

Note   The function-key assignments in a File Manager window are not
the same as in a spreadsheet window. For example, in a spreadsheet window, *F9* is the Calc key; in a File Manager window, *F9*
rereads the files in the directory from disk. See page 254 for a list
of window keys in the File Manager. Page 259 lists special keys in
the control pane; page 263, the file list pane; and page 267, the tree
pane.

A pane must be active before you can work in it. The active pane
has an active cursor in it. To activate another pane, press the Pane
key, *F6,* or the *Tab* key.

When first displayed, the File Manager window takes up half the
screen. To give more room to the directory, choose the /**Window** |
Zoom command or press the Zoom key, *Alt-F6.* Quattro expands
the File Manager window to fill the screen. To "unzoom" the
directory, press *Alt-F6* or */WZ* again.

You can have two or more File Manager windows open at the
same time. To open a second File Manager window, just choose
/**File** | **Utilities** | **File Manager** again. The new File Manager
window covers up the existing one if the current window is
zoomed. Otherwise, the second window opens next to the active
File Manager window. If two File Manager windows are already
open, the third window overlays the inactive window, leaving the
active one displayed.

To move between File Manager windows, use the Next Window
key, *Shift-F6* (or *Alt #*, where # is the number of the window you
want to jump to). You can use the /**Window** | **Move/Size**
command to resize or reposition the windows. For more
information on working with multiple windows, see Chapter 9,
"Manipulating windows."

Note   Any modifications you make to the File Manager window become
the new default settings. The next time you open the File
Manager, the window display will be as you last specified.

To close the active File Manager window, choose /**File** | **Close**. To
return to the spreadsheet you were working on without closing
the File Manager windows, press the Next Window key, *Shift-F6.*
Quattro temporarily removes the directories from display. You
can redisplay the last-used File Manager window at any time with
Shift-F6.

Moving around in File Manager windows

Special window key combinations make it easy to move around in a File Manager window or switch from one window to another. Refer to Table 10.1 for a list of window keys you can use in a File Manager window.

Key	Name	Action
Shift-F5 or *Alt-0*	Pick Window	Displays a list of open windows so you can activate a different window (same as /**Window** I **Pick**).
F6 or *Tab*	Pane	Activates the next File Manager window pane in the following order: control pane, file list pane, tree pane. The active pane has a double-line border.
Shift-Tab		Activates the control pane and moves the cursor to the File Name prompt. (Can be used for macros to put the File Manager window pane and cursor in a known state.)
Shift-F6	Next Window	Activates the next open File Manager or spreadsheet window.
Alt-F6	Zoom Window	Zooms an open window to full screen and back again. If the window is already expanded, shrinks it again (same as /**Window** I **Zoom**). If you zoom a window with a directory tree pane open at the botton, the tree pane moves to the right.
Alt #		Jumps to window number #. The window number appears on the top edge of each frame, and on the status line for an active window.

The File Manager menus

When you're in a File Manager window, you have access to a different set of menus. When you press the Slash key (/), Quattro activates the File Manager menu bar (see the following figure). This menu contains a subset of the usual menu commands, with some new ones added.

Figure 10.2
The File Manager menu bar

```
File  Edit  Sort  Tree  Print  Options  Window                    ↑↓
                                                                    ?
╒═C:\QUATTRO\DATA\═══════════════2═╕   E      F      G      H
```

■ **File** lets you create a new window or close the active one, update the directory display, create a directory, save a particular configuration of open windows, access DOS, and more.

■ **Edit** lets you copy, move, rename, duplicate, or erase files from the displayed directory.

■ **Sort** lets you reorder the list of files by name, timestamp, extension, size, or DOS order.

■ **Tree** lets you display the directory tree in a pane below or to the right of the file list, resize the tree pane, and close the tree pane.

■ **Print** displays a menu for printing selected files. This menu has most of the functionality of the standard spreadsheet **Print** menu.

■ **Options** lets you switch the file list display between names only and names and file status. You can also specify the directory initially displayed in a File Manager window and reset many system options such as text printer and screen colors.

■ **Window** lets you adjust the windows displayed onscreen. You can use it to resize, reposition, and expand the current window, or move to a different window.

Each of these menu options except /**Window** is discussed in full later in the chapter. The **Window** menu is the same as in a spreadsheet window (minus the /**Window** | **Options** command) and is covered in Chapter 9, "Manipulating windows."

The control pane

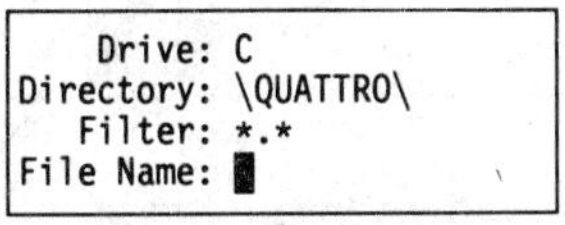

```
┌─────────────────────┐
│      Drive: C        │
│ Directory: \QUATTRO\ │
│    Filter: *.*       │
│ File Name: █         │ \
└─────────────────────┘
```

The control pane of the File Manager window contains the following prompts: Drive, Directory, Filter, and File Name. Initial settings for these prompts show the current drive and directory, with a file filter of

　　　.

(which shows all files). The File Name prompt is blank. You can change any of the prompt settings to look at different files.

To change a control setting,

1. Press *F6* (if necessary) until the control pane is active.
2. Use the ↑ and ↓ arrow keys to move the cursor bar to the setting you want to change.
3. Press *Esc* to erase the entire entry, or press *Backspace* to erase one character at a time.
4. Type the new setting.
5. Press *Enter*, ↑, or ↓ to enter the setting.

The following sections describe each prompt in detail.

The Drive prompt

The Drive prompt contains a letter indicating the disk drive currently being viewed. In most cases, this will be *C* or *D* to indicate a hard disk drive. You can change it to *A* or *B* to view files on a floppy disk drive. If you have a RAM disk or are connected to a local-area network disk, enter the correct letter for the disk.

The Directory prompt

The Directory prompt contains the name of the directory currently displayed. To view the contents of a different directory, enter the directory name at this prompt. Be sure to precede each subdirectory in the path name with a backslash (\).

You can also change the directory from within the file list pane. If you want to see one of the subdirectories included on the list, just choose it. If you want to see the currently displayed directory's parent, choose the .. (root directory) item.

Note The tree pane also permits you to change directories. If you have a tree open, use the arrow keys in the tree pane to move to a new directory, or click the directory name with a mouse.

The Filter prompt

The Filter prompt lets you restrict the files shown in the file list pane. This setting accepts DOS wildcards:

* takes the place of any number of characters.
? takes the place of one character.

The default, *.*, displays all files. To narrow down the files listed, you can change the filter to exclude unwanted files. For example, TAX*.* displays all file names beginning with *TAX* and ending with any extension. Q*.WQ1 displays a list of Quattro spreadsheet files with names beginning with *Q*.

You can also specify a *negative filter* to display all files *except* those that meet the filter specifications. To indicate a negative filter, enclose the wildcard specification with brackets ([ ]). For example, to display a list of all files except those beginning with *TAX*, enter the following specification:

    [TAX*.*]

You can combine filter specifications to create one filter up to 63 characters long. Just separate the specifications with commas. For example, type

    .WQ1,[TAX.*]

in the Filter prompt to display all Quattro spreadsheet files whose names do not begin with *TAX*. Or, type

    .WQ1,.WK1,[TAX*.*]

to display all Quattro files (*.WQ1) and 1-2-3 files (*.WK1) that do not begin with *TAX*.

The Filter prompt limits the files displayed in the File Manager window, but it doesn't prevent you from accessing unlisted files. You can always type in the name of a file at the File Name prompt, regardless of whether it's shown in the list.

Table 10.2 lists sample filters and their effects.

Table 10.2
File filter examples

Filter	Meaning
.	Display all files.
*.WQ1	Display only files ending with extension .WQ1.
[*.WK?]	Display all files, except those ending with extension .WKS, .WKQ, WK1, or any other file extension beginning with .WK.
SS*.*,[*.WQ1]	Display all files beginning with SS, except those ending with extension .WQ1.

The directory filter remains in effect until you change it, even if you change directories. To erase the filter you've set and change it to *.*, highlight the Filter prompt and press *Esc*, then *Enter*.

The File Name prompt

When you first open the File Manager window, the control pane is active and the blank File Name prompt is highlighted. You can use the File Name prompt to

■ open a spreadsheet file

■ look for a file that's stored somewhere on your disk

To open a spreadsheet file, type the name at the File Name prompt and press *Enter*. Quattro removes the File Manager window and displays the spreadsheet. You can enter the name of any file in the displayed directory, even if it's filtered out of the list. If Quattro doesn't find a file by that name in the directory, it creates a new spreadsheet with that name and displays it.

F5
GoTo

To look for a file anywhere on the specified drive, type in the file name and press the GoTo key, *F5*. Quattro searches through every directory on the disk until it finds a file with that name, then changes the file list to show the directory that contains it, with the file name you specified highlighted. If there are other files with the same name, press *F5* again to move to the next.

If you don't know the exact name of the file you're looking for, you can use wildcards to search for near matches. For example, JANE*.WQ1 looks for any Quattro spreadsheet file whose name begins with *JANE* and stops at the first one it finds. To highlight the next matching file name, press *F5* again. File-name wildcards follow the same rules as in filters (see page 256).

Table 10.3 lists the functions of many keystrokes you can use in
the control pane of a File Manager window. See Table 10.1 on
page 254 for a list of window function keys you can use in the File
Manager's control pane.

Table 10.3
Special keys in the control
pane

Key	Name	Action
F2	Rename	Prompts for a new file name, and renames the current file list selection to the file name you specify (same as /Edit I **Rename**).
F5	GoTo	Searches the specified drive for the file name (or combination of wildcard characters) typed at the File Name prompt.
Esc	Escape	Clears the entry at the prompt. When you move the highlight bar away from the prompt and make no new entry, Quattro restores the original entry.
Del	Delete	Deletes the character to the left of the cursor.
Enter	Enter	Moves the cursor to the blank File Name prompt or, if the cursor is at the File Name prompt, opens the file or subdirectory highlighted on the file list.
Home	Home	Moves the cursor to the beginning of the prompt entry.
End	End	Moves the cursor to the end of the prompt entry.

The file list pane

The file list pane lists all files and subdirectories that pass through
the given filter in the specified drive and directory. File names are
listed first, followed by subdirectory names, in alphabetical order.
The following figure shows a close-up of a file list pane. It lists
files in rows. The first column shows file names, the second shows
file-name extensions, and the third shows file size (in number of
bytes). The last two columns show the date and time the file was
last altered.

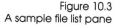

Figure 10.3
A sample file list pane

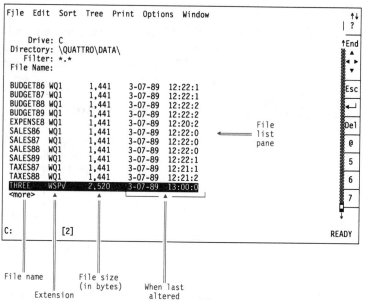

File name
Extension
File size
(in bytes)
When last
altered

The check mark you see at the bottom of the file list in this figure indicates your cursor position in the file list. This is useful if you have a display that uses inverse video to show both the highlight bar and files that have been selected. With the black-and-white palette, for example, the check mark position is the only way to tell where the cursor is in a block of selected file names.

If there are more files in the directory than will fit in the pane, Quattro displays a <more> indicator at the bottom of the list. Press *PgDn* to display the next pageful of names or *End* to display the end of the list.

A directory status line at the end of the list shows

- the number of files in the directory
- the number of files displayed in the file list
- how many bytes have been used
- the total number of bytes available

You can change the file list display to show only names and extensions with the /Options I File List I Wide View command (see "Changing the file list display," which follows shortly). This allows room for more file names on the list.

Note Table 10.4 on page 263 contains a list of special keys you can use in the file list pane.

Reordering files

By default, Quattro lists all files and subdirectories in the file list in alphabetical order.

- **Name** sorts file names and subdirectories in the file list alphabetically by name, then extension.
- **Timestamp** sorts file names and subdirectories chronologically according to their *timestamp*, which shows when the file was last modified. The oldest file is listed first. This command sorts by date and time, even when the /Options | File List command is set to **Wide View**.
- **Extension** sorts the file list alphabetically, first by extension, then file name.
- **Size** sorts file names and subdirectories by DOS size (in bytes). The smallest file appears first in the list. This command sorts by size, even when you've suppressed size display from the file list (with /Options | File List | Wide View).
- **DOS Order** sorts file names in the same order that the DOS command DIR would list them (usually in the order of original creation).

To change the order of the file list,

1. Choose /Sort.
2. Choose the sort order you want from the list.

When you choose **Name** or **DOS Order**, Quattro also re-sorts subdirectories listed in the tree pane.

Changing the file list display

The /Options | File List command determines the way Quattro displays files in the file list.

To change the file list display,

1. Choose /Options | File List.
2. Choose Full View, the default, to display file names one per line, with size and timestamp information to the right of the

name. Choose **Wide** to display file names and extensions only, in as many columns as will fit.

The following figure shows two File Manager windows, side by side. The file list on the left is set to display status information for each file. The one on the right is set to **Wide** View.

Figure 10.4
The two file list display options

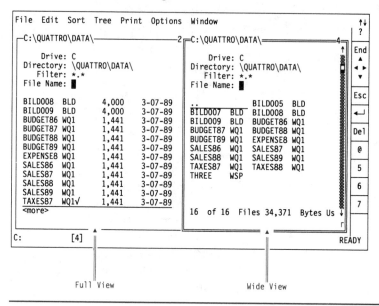

Full View   Wide View

Changing the directory default

The /Options I Startup I Directory setting determines which directory is displayed when you first open a File Manager window.

To change the directory displayed at startup,

1. Choose /Options I Startup I Directory.
2. Choose **Previous** (the default) to display the last directory you looked at in your last Quattro session. Choose **Current** to show the directory tree you were in when you loaded Quattro.

Displaying different directories

If the file you want isn't in the directory shown in the file list, you can access different directories by choosing subdirectories or the .. (root directory) item in the file list.

To display files in one of the subdirectories listed in the file list pane (indicated by a backslash after the directory name), just move the cursor bar to it and press *Enter*. The Directory prompt changes to show the subdirectory name and the file pane changes to list files in that subdirectory.

To move out of the current directory and into its parent directory (the directory in which it is stored), press *Home* to highlight the .. (root directory) item at the top of the file list pane, then press *Enter*. Quattro bumps you back one level in the directory and displays file names and subdirectories in the parent directory.

Special keys in the file list pane

Table 10.4 lists the functions of many keystrokes you can use in the file list pane of a File Manager window. See Table 10.1 for a list of window function keys you can use in the File Manager.

Table 10.4
Special keys in the file list pane

Key	Name	Action
F2	Rename	Lets you rename the current (highlighted) file (same as /Edit I **Rename**).
Shift-F7 or +	Select	Selects the current (highlighted) file in the list so you can open, move, copy, or delete it. If the file is already selected, unselects it.
Alt-F7	All Select	Selects all files in the list for moving, copying, or deleting. If some files on the list are already selected, unselects those files.
Shift-F8	Move	Moves the selected files into the paste buffer, removing them from the list.
Del	Delete	Deletes the selected files or the highlighted file from the disk.
F9	Calc	Reads the disk and refreshes the file list pane (same as /File I **Read Dir**).
Shift-F9	Copy	Copies the selected files into the paste buffer for copying to another directory or disk, keeping them on the list.
Shift-F10	Paste	Inserts the files in the paste buffer at the cursor position in the current directory's file list.
Esc	Escape	Returns all selected files to normal, then activates the control pane and moves the cursor to the File Name prompt.

Table 10.4: Special keys in the file list pane (continued)

Key	Name	Action
Enter	Enter	Opens selected files or the file at the cursor. If the highlight bar is on the .. (root directory) item, moves to the parent directory. If the highlight bar is on a subdirectory, moves to the subdirectory.
Home	Home	Moves the highlight bar to the .. (root directory) item.
End	End	Moves the highlight bar to the end of the file list.
PgUp	Page Up	Moves the file list display up one screen.
PgDn	Page Down	Moves the file list display down one screen.

The directory tree pane

By choosing subdirectories or the .. (root directory) item, you can get to any file stored on your disk. But if you expect to traverse many directories, or if you're not sure what files are in your directories, it's better to use the directory tree, which you can display in a third tree pane.

The tree pane lists all directories and subdirectories on your disk in alphabetical order. Move the cursor around the tree to display different directory contents in the file list pane.

To work with the tree pane, choose /Tree.

- **Open** displays the directory tree for the specified disk.
- **Resize** lets you change the size of the tree pane in relation to the size of the file list pane.
- **Close** removes the tree pane from the File Manager window.

The following figure shows a sample directory tree in the File Manager window:

Figure 10.5
A directory tree

```
 File  Edit  Sort  Tree  Print  Options  Window                              ↑↓
⌐                                                              ┌─SAMPAPP      | ?
  └  Drive: H                                                  ├─SAMPLE      ↑─
  Directory:  \NFILES\QUATTRO\PROF\PROGRAM\                    └─TOOLKIT     ■End
      Filter:  *.*                                          ├─PS             ▪ ▲
  File Name: ▮                                               ├─PUG           ▪ ▼
                                                             ├─PWB           ◄ ►
  ..                                                         ├─QRG           ▪Esc
  123      CMP    135,142    7-04-86    1:23:01             ├─RUNTIME        ▪
  123      MNU     49,159    7-16-89   15:47:00             ├─SQL            ▪←┘
  123      MU     200,304    7-28-89   18:15:07             ├─TEST           ▪
  123      RF       1,448    7-28-89   16:40:26             ├─TRIAL          ▪Del
  123      SET     40,303   12-31-87   10:44:00             ├─UGMAN          ▪
  BOLD     CHR     14,670    6-05-89   14:43:26             └─VPSADDLE       ▪ @
  CGMGEN   BGI      7,598    7-26-89   14:24:13           ├─REFLEX           ▪
  COUR     SFO     26,130    7-26-89   14:24:13           ├─PSFONTS          ▪ 5
  COURI000 FON      4,951    7-15-89   10:57:13           ├─QUATTRO          ▪
  COURI001 FON      4,108    7-15-89   11:04:12           └─FONTS            ▪ 6
  COUR_000 FON      4,036    7-15-89   11:02:16           ├─SKPLUS           ▪
  DTBI     SFO     25,474    7-26-89   14:24:13           ├─SUPERKEY         ▪ 7
  DUT      SFO     27,680    7-26-89   14:24:13           ├─PARADOX3         ▪
  DUTB     SFO     26,952    7-26-89   14:24:13           ├─REF              ↓
  DUTI     SFO     26,296    7-26-89   14:24:13           ├─START          ┌
  <more>                                                                   READY
  H:            [2]
```

The tree appears on the right
when the window is zoomed.
Otherwise, it appears below
the file list.

Displaying the tree

To display the directory tree, choose the /Tree I Open command. Quattro opens a *tree pane* below or to the right of the file list pane in the File Manager window. If the File Manager window is zoomed to fill the entire screen, the tree appears to the right of the file list. If the window occupies only part of the screen, the tree appears below the file list.

The root directory is shown at the far left, with subdirectories to the right and below it. Quattro highlights the current directory on the tree. If there are more directories on your disk than fit in the tree pane, use the cursor-movement keys to scroll the list. To display files in a different directory, use the cursor-movement keys to move the highlight bar. As you move the bar, the Directory prompt changes to show the name of the highlighted directory, and the file list changes to display the files in that directory.

F6

Pane

You can access the directory tree only when the tree pane is active (which it is when you first display it). To activate different File Manager panes, use the Pane key, *F6*.

If you have a mouse, click any directory name on the directory tree to move to that directory. To zoom the active File Manager window to full size, click the zoom icon at the far right edge of the menu bar. When you zoom the window, the tree moves from below the file list to the right of the file list. Click the zoom icon again to toggle the window back to its former size and position. To resize the window, drag the resize box in the lower right corner of the window. If you resize the window to full size, the tree moves from below the file list to the right of the file list.

Changing the tree's size

When you first display a directory tree, Quattro divides the available File Manager window space equally between the file list pane and the tree pane. Depending on what you're doing and the size of the file list, you may want to give more or less space to the tree pane.

To change the size of the tree pane,

1. Choose /Tree | **R**esize. Quattro prompts you for a percentage.
2. Enter the percentage of the window you want to use to display the tree.
3. Press *Enter*.

The following figure shows a zoomed File Manager window with a tree pane sized at 80%.

Figure 10.6
The tree pane resized

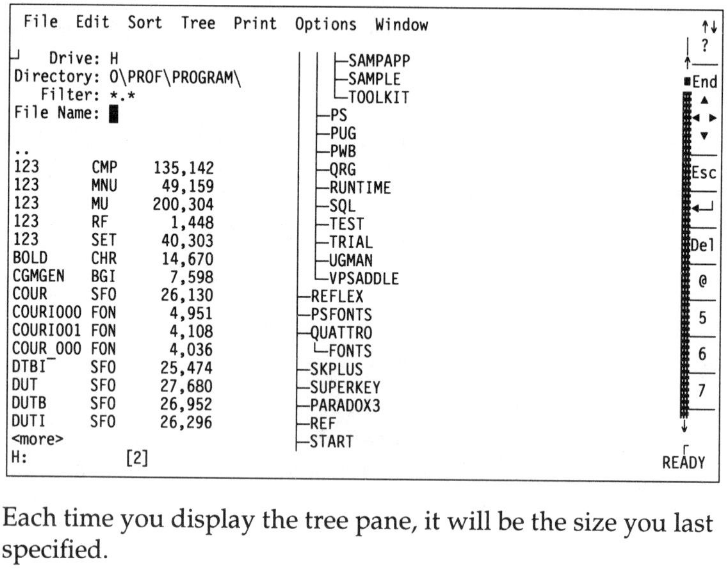

```
┌─────────────────────────────────────────────────────────────┐ ↑↓
│ File  Edit  Sort  Tree  Print  Options  Window              │ │ ?
│┘   Drive: H                          ├─SAMPAPP               │ ↑
│Directory: O\PROF\PROGRAM\            ├─SAMPLE                │ ■End
│    Filter: *.*                       └─TOOLKIT               │ ▲
│File Name: █                          ├─PS                    │ ◄ ►
│                                      ├─PUG                   │ ▼
│ ..                                   ├─PWB                   │
│123      CMP    135,142               ├─QRG                   │ ■Esc
│123      MNU     49,159               ├─RUNTIME               │
│123      MU     200,304               ├─SQL                   │ ◄┘
│123      RF       1,448               ├─TEST                  │
│123      SET     40,303               ├─TRIAL                 │ Del
│BOLD     CHR     14,670               ├─UGMAN                 │
│CGMGEN   BGI      7,598               └─VPSADDLE              │ @
│COUR     SFO     26,130             ├─REFLEX                  │
│COURIO00 FON      4,951             ├─PSFONTS                 │ 5
│COURIO01 FON      4,108             ├─QUATTRO                 │
│COUR 000 FON      4,036             └─FONTS                   │ 6
│DTBI     SFO     25,474           ├─SKPLUS                    │
│DUT      SFO     27,680           ├─SUPERKEY                  │ 7
│DUTB     SFO     26,952           ├─PARADOX3                  │
│DUTI     SFO     26,296           ├─REF                       │ ↓
│<more>                            ├─START                     │
│H:          [2]                                               │ READY
└─────────────────────────────────────────────────────────────┘
```

Each time you display the tree pane, it will be the size you last specified.

Special keys in the tree pane

Table 10.5 lists the keystrokes that let you select, delete, open, and refresh the display of file and directory names in the tree pane.

Table 10.5
Special keys in the tree pane

Key	Name	Action
Esc	Escape	Returns all selected files to normal, then activates the control pane and moves the cursor to the File Name prompt.
Del	Delete	Deletes all selected files or the highlighted file in the file list.
F9	Calc	Reads the disk and refreshes the tree pane (same as /File | **Read** Dir).

Removing the directory tree

If you're going to be working in the same directory, you can give more space to the file list by closing the tree pane. Choose /**Tree** | **Close**. Quattro removes the directory tree and expands the file list pane to fill its space.

Printing in the File Manager

The /**Print** menu lets you print parts of the File Manager window. When you choose this command, Quattro displays a tailored **Print** menu, similar to the one accessed within a spreadsheet (see Chapter 4, "Printing").

```
═══ Print ═══
Block              ▶
Destination        ▶
Page Layout        ▶
Reset              ▶
Adjust Printer     ▶
Go                 ▶
Quit
```

The main difference is that the /**Print** | **Block** command gives you three options: Files, Tree, or Both.

The default option is Files, which prints a list of all files in the file list pane, even those you have to scroll to display. To print the directory tree, choose **Tree**. To print the file list followed by the directory tree, choose **Both**.

To print the current file information in a File Manager window,

1. If you need to, check the settings for your default printer on the /**Options** | **Hardware** | **Printers** menu (see page 176).
2. Choose /**Print** | **Block**.
3. Choose **File** to print the file list, **Tree** to print the directory tree, or **Both**.

4. Choose **Destination** and set it to either **Printer** or **File**. Set any other print options you want.

5. Choose **Go** to send it either to the printer or to a file.

For more information on print commands, see Chapter 4.

Working with files

```
╔════ Edit ════╗
║ Select File  ║
║ All Select   ║
╟──────────────╢
║ Copy         ║
║ Move         ║
║ Erase        ║
║ Paste        ║
╟──────────────╢
║ Duplicate    ║
║ Rename       ║
╚══════════════╝
```

With the File Manager, you can move, copy, rename, or delete files on your disk without accessing DOS. Choose /Edit to display the File Manager Edit menu.

- **Select File** marks the highlighted file on the file list so that it stays marked even when you move the highlight bar away. You can use this command when you want to select a group of file names.

- **All Select** marks all files on the file list, or if any files are already selected, it *unselects all files.*

- **Copy** marks the file names you have selected and places the file names in the paste buffer. You can then move to any other directory and paste the files there.

- **Move** marks the file names you have selected and places the file names in the paste buffer. You can then move to any other directory and paste the files there.

- **Erase** deletes the selected files from the disk.

- **Paste** inserts the files whose names are currently in the paste buffer in the current directory.

- **Duplicate** lets you copy *and* rename a file, storing the copy in the same or a different directory. This is the same as a DOS COPY command.

- **Rename** lets you change the name of a file.

Table 10.4 on page 263 lists special keys used in the file list pane for moving around in the pane, and for renaming, moving, copying, opening, and deleting files.

Selecting files

The first step to moving, copying, or deleting files is to select the files you want to work on. You do this with the Select and All Select keys, (*Shift-F7* and *Alt-F7*), or the /Edit I Select File and /Edit I **All** Select commands. The Plus key (+) works the same as *Shift-F7*.

First, display the directory you want to work with in the File Manager window and activate the file pane. To select an individual file in the list, move the cursor bar to the file name and choose /Edit I Select File or press *Shift-F7* or +. To select all files in the list, choose /Edit I All Select or press *Alt-F7*. To unselect a selected file, highlight it and choose /Edit I Select File or press *Shift-F7* again. To unselect all selected files in the list, choose /Edit I All Select or press *Alt-F7*.

You can use the **All** Select command in conjunction with the Filter prompt (page 256) to select a specific group of files in the directory. Go to the control pane and set the filter to show only the files you want to work with. Then go into the file list pane and choose /Edit I **All** Select or press *Alt-F7*.

Opening files

To open a spreadsheet file and display it in a new spreadsheet window, just highlight the file name on the list and press *Enter*. Quattro removes the File Manager window from view and displays the spreadsheet, overlaying any existing spreadsheet windows.

To open several spreadsheet files at once, use the /Edit I Select command, *Shift-F7*, or the Plus key (+) to select each file on the file list, then press *Enter*. Quattro opens a new spreadsheet window for each and loads the files.

 To open a file using a mouse, double-click the file name. To open more than one file at one time, click each file name you want to open. Then double-click any of the selected file names or press *Enter*.

Note Remember that you can also open a file from within the File Manager window by entering a name at the control pane's File Name prompt and pressing *Enter*. The name you enter doesn't have to be one of those displayed in the list, but it does have to be in the displayed directory. Otherwise, Quattro creates a new file with that name.

Copying files

To copy one or more files to a different directory,

1. Use the Plus key (+) or *Shift-F7* to select the file(s) you want to copy on the file list. If you have a mouse, click the file name.
2. Choose /Edit | **Copy** or press the Copy File key, *Shift-F9*. Quattro changes the color of the file names you have selected for copying; if you have a monochrome monitor, they appear in bold. Quattro stores the names of the selected files in temporary memory, called a *paste buffer*.
3. Move to the directory to which you want to copy the files (choose a subdirectory or .., or use *Shift-F6*, the Next Window key, to move to a different File Manager window).
4. Choose /Edit | **Paste** or press the Paste key, *Shift-F10*. Quattro copies the selected files and inserts them in the current file list, positioning them according to the current sort order.

Warning! Quattro's **Copy** command, like the DOS COPY command, will overwrite a file by the same name in a different directory without a warning message.

Moving files

To move one or more files to a different directory,

1. Use the Select key, + or *Shift-F7*, to select the files you want to move on the file list. If you have a mouse, click the file name.
2. Choose /Edit | **Move** or press the Move key, *Shift-F8*. Quattro changes the color of the file names you have selected for moving; if you have a monochrome monitor, they appear in bold. Quattro stores the names of the selected files in the paste buffer.
3. Move to the directory you want to store the files in (choose a subdirectory or .., or use *Shift-F6* to move to a different File Manager window).
4. Choose /Edit | **Paste** or press the Paste key, *Shift-F10*. Quattro removes the files you selected from the previous directory and inserts them in the current file list.

If you use two windows to move files between directories, you'll be able to see more clearly how the files are removed from one directory and added to another.

Deleting files

To delete a file from the file list,

1. Move the cursor bar to the file name. (To delete two or more files from the list, use the Select key, + or *Shift-F7*, to select the files.)
2. Press *Del* or choose the /Edit I Erase command. Quattro displays the prompt: "Are you sure you want to delete this file?"
3. Press *Y* to choose **Yes** and delete the highlighted file.

If you've deleted all the files from a directory, you can delete the directory itself. Just highlight the name of the directory on the parent's file list and choose /Edit I Erase or press *Del*.

 If you have a mouse, click the file(s) you want to delete and press *Del*.

Duplicating files

To make a copy of a file and give the copy a different name, use the /Edit I **Duplicate** command:

1. Highlight the file you want to duplicate on the file list (or type its name at the File Name prompt).
2. Choose /Edit I **Duplicate**. Quattro asks you for a name for the new file.
3. Type the name you want to give the new file. To store the duplicate in a different directory, include the directory path with the file name.
4. Press *Enter*. Quattro creates a copy of the highlighted file, giving it the specified name or location.

Renaming files

To change the name of a file, use the /Edit I **Rename** command:

1. Highlight the file on the list (or enter its name at the File Name prompt).

2. Choose /Edit | **Rename** or press the Rename key, *F2.* Quattro prompts you for the new name.

3. Type the new name you want for the file. To move the file to a different directory as you rename it, include the directory path with the file name.

4. Press *Enter.* Quattro renames the highlighted file and moves it if you specified a different location.

Note   When you rename a spreadsheet file, it's essential to keep the same file-name extension. The extensions give Quattro information about the contents of the file. For example, Quattro knows that a Quattro spreadsheet file always ends in .WQ1.

The File menu

```
┌──── File ────┐
│              │
│ New          │
│ Open         │
│ Close        │
│ Close All    │
│──────────────│
│ Read Dir     │
│ Make Dir     │
│──────────────│
│ Workspace  ▶ │
│ Utilities  ▶ │
│ Exit         │
│              │
└──────────────┘
```

The File menu accessed from within a File Manager window contains some familiar commands and some new ones.

- **New** opens a new window and spreadsheet file.
- **Open** opens a new window and loads in an existing file.
- **Close** closes the current window.
- **Close All** closes all open files and windows.
- **Read Dir** reads and redisplays the files on the current directory.
- **Make Dir** creates a new directory or subdirectory with the name and location you supply.
- **Workspace** lets you save the current setup of windows in a file, or retrieve a saved workspace setup.
- **Utilities** accesses file utilities that let you access DOS, open another File Manager window, or set file-compression options.
- **Exit** puts away Quattro and returns you to DOS (see page 35).

Updating the file list

The /File | **Read Dir** command rereads the files on the specified directory and updates the file list accordingly. Use this command when you've inserted a new disk in a floppy drive, or when someone else has added files to the directory on a local area network.

The Calc key, *F9,* performs the same function as /File | **Read Dir**. In effect, it "recalculates" the directory display.

Creating a new subdirectory

With the /File | Make Dir command, you can add a new subdirectory to your disk.

To make a new directory,

1. Choose /File | Make Dir. Quattro prompts you for a directory name.

2. Enter a name, adhering to standard DOS rules for subdirectory names. If you want to store the subdirectory somewhere other than in the displayed directory, include a directory path with the name.

3. Press *Enter* to create the new directory.

For details on how DOS uses directories and subdirectories, see Appendix B, "A DOS primer."

File Manager options

```
╔══ Options ══╗
║             ║
║ Hardware  ▶ ║
║ Colors    ▶ ║
║ Beep      ▶ ║
║ Startup   ▶ ║
║ File List ▶ ║
║ Display Mode ▶ ║
║ Update      ║
╚═════════════╝
```

When you choose /Options from the File Manager menu, Quattro displays an adjusted Options menu, listing some of the same system options available within a spreadsheet window and two options that deal directly with File Manager windows.

■ **Hardware** lets you redefine your printer or screen settings. For details, see page 173.

■ **Colors** lets you change the display colors for the File Manager and other areas. For details, see page 180.

■ **Beep** determines whether Quattro beeps when you make an error. The initial default is **Yes**. To turn off the beeps, set this command to **No**.

■ **Startup** lets you load a new menu tree and choose between a File Manager display of the directory you were in when you last used Quattro, or the directory you just loaded Quattro from (see page 262).

■ **File List** makes the File Manager display just the file names in the file list, in several columns, or in a single column that includes size, date, and time information for each file (see page 261).

- **Display Mode** lets you change the mode Quattro uses to display spreadsheets and menus on your screen. Normally, Quattro uses 80x25 text mode. If you have an EGA or VGA, you can switch to a graphics display mode that allows you to view graphics within the spreadsheet (see page 33).

- **Update** stores the current option settings as the new defaults. This command also stores any changes you've made to the spreadsheet window **O**ptions menu.

11

Linking spreadsheets

By creating *links* between spreadsheets, you can look at and work with data in different spreadsheets. This lets you access and keep current figures in one or more files. People commonly use links to consolidate several related spreadsheets into one spreadsheet that shows totals.

A spreadsheet link is simply a formula reference to a cell or block within another spreadsheet. The reference is *live*, which means that if referenced spreadsheets are open, Quattro automatically updates the link formula when the referenced data changes, just as it would if all the data were in the same spreadsheet.

The following figure shows one spreadsheet linked to two others. Check the top of each spreadsheet window for the name of the file it contains. SALES.WQ1, the spreadsheet that contains the link, is the *primary* spreadsheet because its values depend on two other spreadsheets. OCTSOUTH.WQ1 and OCTNORTH.WQ1, the spreadsheets referenced by the link, are the *supporting* spreadsheets.

Figure 11.1
A linked spreadsheet

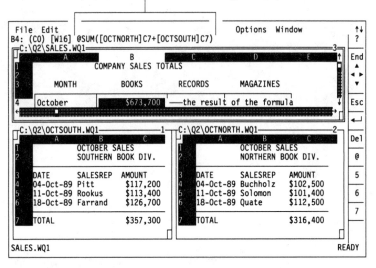

Formula that calculates the sum of C7 in two supporting spreadsheets

Note The primary spreadsheet must be a Quattro .WQ1 or .WQ! file. The supporting spreadsheets can be in any spreadsheet format that Quattro can read.

This chapter describes how to

For information about linking Quattro spreadsheets to Paradox, Reflex, or dBASE database files, see Chapter 18.

- create spreadsheet links either by typing them in or using Point mode
- use "3-D consolidation" to link to all open spreadsheets at once
- set up a "link library" for easy referencing and updating
- link to unloaded spreadsheets
- update the current spreadsheet based on link values in one or more closed supporting spreadsheets
- automatically switch all links to one spreadsheet over to another spreadsheet
- link several spreadsheets to one "year-to-date" spreadsheet that combines figures from the others
- break down a large spreadsheet into several more manageable ones

Why use links?

By linking spreadsheets that deal with the same type of information, you can increase Quattro's power and flexibility. There are many good reasons to use spreadsheet links:

- **To share information.** By linking pertinent information in different spreadsheets, you can minimize the amount of information you need to enter. Since Quattro automatically updates primary formulas when you make a change, you can be sure your information is up to date. And by using one formula for several spreadsheets, you save disk space.

- **To simplify a complex problem.** Rather than trying to build one giant, complex spreadsheet, you can break down the information into separate spreadsheets. You can link data calculated in those spreadsheets to an overview spreadsheet. This keeps the individual spreadsheets small and specialized so they're easy to work with. You can also use the specialized spreadsheets as building blocks for other applications.

- **To divide work among several people.** If you use several linked spreadsheets for a single application, you can easily divide the application's work among several people. This is especially useful if you're using a local area network because changes that one person makes to a supporting file are immediately reflected in other files. (For more information about using Quattro on a local area network, see Appendix C and the *Network Administrator's Guide*.)

- **To build models too large for memory.** No matter how much memory you have, sooner or later you'll tackle a problem that requires more. By dividing an application over several spreadsheets and accessing only the linked values from unloaded spreadsheets, you can build linked models that are much larger than the memory capacity of your computer.

- **To add flexibility to spreadsheets.** By creating what-if models based on interchangeable spreadsheet components, you can quickly switch supporting components using the /Tools | Update Links command.

- **To access information in a database file.** Rather than translating a Paradox, Reflex, or dBASE file into a Quattro spreadsheet each time you want to access data in it, you can use linking with the /Database | Query command to extract only the information you need. (See "Querying an outside database" in Chapter 18 for information.)

For examples of spreadsheet links, see "Spreadsheet linking examples" at the end of this chapter.

Creating a spreadsheet link

The difference between a spreadsheet link and a normal block reference is that the link reference includes a spreadsheet name. The spreadsheet name precedes the block reference and is enclosed in square brackets; for example, [BUDGET88]A15..F45.

There are three ways to create a spreadsheet link:

- Type in the link reference as a block address preceded by a spreadsheet name in square brackets, such as

  `[BUDGET.WQ1]F6`

  This tells Quattro to get the value in cell F6 in the BUDGET.WQ1 spreadsheet.

- Point to the block in the other spreadsheet, just as you would point to a block in the current spreadsheet.

- Use a special "3-D" link character (an asterisk) to create a link to all open spreadsheets at once. For example, @SUM([*]F6) adds the values stored in cell F6 of every open spreadsheet.

Typing link references

To type in a link reference as all or part of a formula, use the following format:

  +[filespec]block

The plus sign is needed only if the reference is the first item in a cell entry (otherwise, Quattro regards the reference as a label). *Block* is any valid cell address, block, or block name (A1..Q25 in the following example), and *filespec* includes up to four parts:

$$[C:\backslash QUATTRO\backslash BUDGET.WQ1]A1..Q25$$

| | | | |
| Drive Name | Path Name | File Name | Extension |

- **Drive name** is a letter that identifies the disk drive containing the file. This is necessary *only* if the spreadsheet you're referencing is stored on a different disk drive; otherwise, leave it out.

- **Path name** is a list of directories leading to the one containing the referenced spreadsheet. Each directory is preceded by a backslash. This is necessary *only* if the spreadsheet is in a different directory than the current spreadsheet; otherwise, leave it out.

- **File name** is the file's name.

- **Extension** is a three-letter suffix separated from the file name by a period (.). It is necessary *only* if the referenced spreadsheet file has a different extension than the current spreadsheet; otherwise, leave it out.

For example, in the link reference

[C:\QUATTRO\TAXES\SCHEDC.WK1]

C: is the drive letter, \QUATTRO\TAXES is the directory path, SCHEDC is the file name, and .WK1 is the file-name extension.

You can enter all alphabetic characters in *filespec* in either upper- or lowercase. Don't include blank spaces in any part of the reference. Below are some examples of valid link references:

+[MYFILE.WQ1]A1

@SUM([C:\QUATTRO\MYFILE]A1..A8192)

+[MYFILE]SALARIES

Tip   In most cases, you'll only need to enter the file name of the supporting spreadsheet. In fact, you should make a point of keeping all your linked spreadsheets in the same directory and use the same extension for each. That way, you'll never need to enter more than a file name for link references. And should you move the linked spreadsheets to a different directory, you won't need to edit the references.

Pointing out link references

When entering formula references, it's often easier to point to a cell or block rather than enter the address. You can use Point mode to point out linked references as well. This not only can save time, but also ensure accuracy; you can be sure you're referencing the right address and file name.

To enter a link reference using Point mode,

1. If the spreadsheet you want to reference isn't open, use /File |
   Open to open it first.

2. At the proper place in a formula or macro command, or in
   response to a command prompt, activate the spreadsheet you
   want to reference. (If the reference is the beginning of a
   formula you're entering in a cell entry, type a plus sign first.)
   You can display the spreadsheet in one of three ways:

   ■ Hold down the *Alt* key and press the number of the spread-
     sheet window (as shown in the top right corner of the
     window).

   ■ Press *Alt-0* or *Shift-F5* to display a list of open spreadsheet
     files, then choose one from the list.

   ■ Press the Next Window key, *Shift-F6*, until you're in the
     spreadsheet you want to reference.

   If part of the spreadsheet you want to link to is displayed
   onscreen, click that window to activate it.

3. Move the cell selector to the cell you want to reference. If you
   want to reference a block, move to one corner of the block,
   press the Period key (.) to anchor the selection, and move to
   the opposite corner (*or*, if the block is named, press *F3* and
   select one of the listed block names).

   To select a block with a mouse, drag from one corner of the
   block to the opposite corner, then release.

4. Press *Enter*, or if the reference is within a formula or macro
   command, enter the next character.

Quattro moves the cursor to its original place in the primary
spreadsheet. It enters the block or cell you pointed to on the edit
line, automatically including the linking file name.

Linking to open spreadsheets automatically

If you're consolidating information from several spreadsheets that
all have the same layout, you can use Quattro's 3-D link feature to
create links to all of them. Simply use /File | **Open** to load the
primary spreadsheet and all of its supporting spreadsheets.
(Unload any irrelevant files.) To reference corresponding values
in all of the spreadsheets, use the 3-D link code [*] in place of the
spreadsheet names in the linking syntax. For example,

@SUM([*]A1)

adds up the values in cell A1 in all of the supporting spreadsheets and puts the results in the cell containing the formula.

@AVG([*]B3..C10)

finds the average of all values in block B3..C10 of each open spreadsheet.

You can limit the open spreadsheets that Quattro automatically links to by including wildcard combinations in the 3-D link code. These wildcard codes are standard DOS wildcards. A question mark (?) stands for any single character, and an asterisk (*) stands for any number of characters. Table 11.1 shows some examples of 3-D link codes and what they do.

Table 11.1
Sample 3-D link codes

Link code	Effect
[]	Looks first in the active spreadsheet, then in all open spreadsheets.
[*]	Links to all open spreadsheets.
[AB*]	Links to all open spreadsheets with names beginning with *AB*.
[A*B]	Links to all open spreadsheets with names beginning with *A* and ending in *B*.
[A?B]	Links to all open spreadsheets with three-character names beginning with *A* and ending in *B*.
[AB???]	Links to all open spreadsheets with five-character names beginning with *AB*.

For a detailed example of linking to all open spreadsheets, see Example 2 later in this chapter.

Indirect references

If you often use certain spreadsheet blocks in linking, you can simplify referencing by storing the link references in named blocks—either in the current spreadsheet or in a separate one. For example, if you often reference the total of cells A1..A10 in the BUDGET spreadsheet, you could use /Edit | Names | Create to name a cell in your current spreadsheet TOTAL. In the cell you named TOTAL, enter the link formula @SUM([BUDGET]A1..A10).

Then whenever you want to reference the total of cells A1..A10 in the BUDGET spreadsheet, just use the TOTAL block name.

Link libraries

You can create a spreadsheet that contains nothing but link references to other spreadsheets. Such a spreadsheet is called a *link library*. By assigning each reference location a block name, you can use the library's block names to indirectly link to other spreadsheets.

For example, suppose you have a link library called LIB that lists common link references (see block B8..B16 in the following figure). The library contains a block named EXPENSES (cell B8), which you've referenced in several spreadsheets with the link [LIB]EXPENSES. This EXPENSES block in turn references the EXPENSES block in a spreadsheet called JANUARY. But now you want to look at February expenses. Instead of editing each link in all the spreadsheets that reference the block named EXPENSES in LIB, just go to cell B8 in LIB and change the +[JANUARY]EXPENSES link to +[FEBRUARY]EXPENSES. All links to [LIB]EXPENSES now reference the EXPENSES block in a spreadsheet called FEBRUARY.

Figure 11.2
A link library

Note how the links in block B8..B16 appear as values in the spreadsheet. You can see the actual link for B8 on the input line.

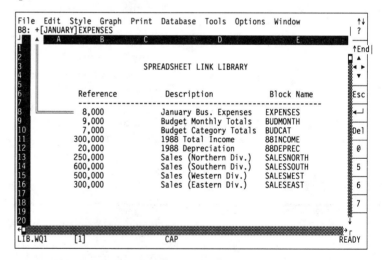

The following figure illustrates the indirect link from SHEET1 to JANUARY. SHEET1 references a block in LIB, which in turn references a block in JANUARY.

Figure 11.3
An indirect link

SHEET1.WQ1 (contains a reference to [LIB]EXPENSES)

LIB.WQ1 (cell B8 is named EXPENSES and contains a reference
to [JANUARY]EXPENSES)

JANUARY.WQ1 (contains a block named EXPENSES)

Moving and copying link formulas

When you copy a formula that contains a link reference, cell
addresses in the link reference are adjusted like any other cell
address. In other words, relative addresses are changed to
reference *position*, while absolute addresses stay the same.

When you copy a link formula from one spreadsheet to another,
the file link remains, even if you copy it into the spreadsheet it
references. However, if you *move* a link formula into the spreadsheet it references, Quattro removes the link, leaving only the
block reference.

If you move a formula to another spreadsheet without moving the
cells it references, Quattro automatically creates links to the
original spreadsheet and treats the references as absolute, even if
they weren't specified as such. For example, to create the spreadsheet shown in the following figure, block B6..B8 was copied to
C6..C8 of another spreadsheet, and B11..B13 was moved to
another spreadsheet. Look at the effects. For the copy operation,
Quattro has copied the cell references themselves as you'd expect,
but the linking portion didn't adjust. For the move operation,
Quattro inserted or removed links so that the spreadsheet
referenced remains the same. Quattro treated the cell reference as
though it were absolute, even if it wasn't.

Figure 11.4
Moving and copying links

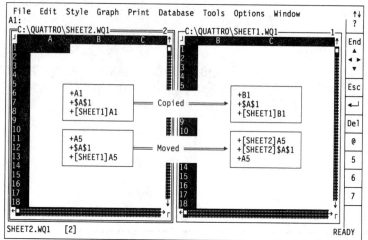

If you move a cell or block in a supporting spreadsheet, any link references to it in loaded primary spreadsheets are adjusted accordingly. However, link references in *unloaded* spreadsheets will not be updated. You can avoid this problem by using block names in link references whenever possible. Each time you load a primary spreadsheet, Quattro automatically updates any block names that have been moved.

Loading a linked spreadsheet

When you load a file that contains links in its formulas or named blocks, Quattro checks to see if all its supporting spreadsheets are loaded. If not, a menu with three linking options pops up:

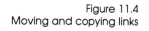

- **Load Supporting** automatically loads all supporting spreadsheets. If those spreadsheets also contain links to unloaded spreadsheets, Quattro loads those spreadsheets, too, until supporting spreadsheets *at all levels* are open.

- **Update Refs** accesses linked values in unloaded supporting spreadsheets without loading them. This takes up much less memory space than loading spreadsheets, so numerous spreadsheets can be handled. If, after choosing this option, you decide you want to open the unloaded files, use the /Tools I Update Links I Open command (see "Supporting spreadsheets" later in this chapter).

■ **None** temporarily replaces links to closed supporting spreadsheets with the value NA (not available). This option is useful for quickly examining or editing large spreadsheets when you don't need the links for calculation. It saves the time required to update values and the memory required to load supporting spreadsheets. If you later want to replace the NA placeholders with the actual link values, use /Tools | Update Links | Refresh to update values, or /Tools | Update Links | Open to load the supporting spreadsheets (see "Updating spreadsheet link values" later in this chapter). You can use these commands anytime, not just when you first open a spreadsheet.

Linking to unloaded spreadsheets

A spreadsheet doesn't have to be open for you to create a link to it. You can type in a link reference to an unloaded spreadsheet. You can also choose the **Update Refs** option (mentioned in the previous section) when you open a primary spreadsheet to load only the *linked values* from supporting spreadsheets, leaving the spreadsheets themselves closed. This can be very useful if you're working with a large network of linked spreadsheets that won't all fit into memory, or if you want to quickly view or edit a spreadsheet.

Linking unloaded spreadsheets has one disadvantage: You cannot update unloaded files.

Suppose you have three spreadsheets that are linked: spreadsheets A, B, and C. Spreadsheet A is dependent on values in spreadsheet B. Spreadsheet B is dependent on values in spreadsheet C, and spreadsheet C is dependent on spreadsheet A. So the spreadsheets pass values in a circular fashion (see the following figure). You're working in spreadsheet A and the other spreadsheets are closed. You change values in spreadsheet A that affect spreadsheet C. Those values in turn affect spreadsheet B and should be passed back to spreadsheet A. But because spreadsheets B and C are closed, their values don't get updated, and the values that spreadsheet A gets from spreadsheet B are now inaccurate.

Figure 11.5
Spreadsheets linked in a
circular fashion

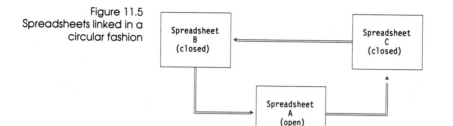

If you used the /Tools | Update Links | Refresh command to update link values, the data would still be inaccurate because files B and C haven't been updated since you made the changes: They still contain inaccurate results. The only way you can be sure your results are current in a case like this is to have all three spreadsheets open at once.

Note If you're working on spreadsheet A on a local area network and someone else is working on supporting spreadsheet B or C, choose /Tools | Update Links | Refresh after that person saves or closes B or C to update the links in spreadsheet A.

You can avoid this problem altogether by structuring your linked spreadsheets hierarchically, with links that only flow one way. Then you can work on the spreadsheets one at a time. As long as you start with the spreadsheet that's top in the hierarchical structure and proceed downward (choosing **Update Refs** for each spreadsheet you open), the spreadsheet values will always be correct (see the following figure):

Figure 11.6
Spreadsheets linked
hierarchically

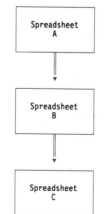

The Update Links menu

```
╔═ Update Links ═╗
║ Open           ║
║ Refresh        ║
║ Change         ║
║ Delete         ║
╚════════════════╝
```

To display a menu of commands that relate directly to spreadsheet linking, choose /Tools I Update Links.

- **Open** lets you open one or more supporting spreadsheets that are linked to the current spreadsheet.
- **Refresh** updates data in the current spreadsheet based on data in unopened supporting spreadsheets.
- **Change** lets you switch over all links that reference one supporting spreadsheet to another.
- **Delete** removes all link references to one or more supporting spreadsheets.

Supporting spreadsheets

If your current spreadsheet is dependently linked to one or more closed spreadsheets, you can use the **O**pen command on the /Tools I Update Links menu to open one or more of the supporting spreadsheets:

1. Choose /Tools I Update Links I Open. Quattro displays a choice list of unopened supporting spreadsheets for the current spreadsheet.
2. Select each spreadsheet you want to open. To select a spreadsheet, highlight its name and press the Select key, *Shift-F7*. Quattro shows a check mark in front of each selected spreadsheet name. To unselect any spreadsheet on the list, press *Shift-F7* again. To select (or unselect) all spreadsheets on the list, press the All Select key, *Alt-F7*.
3. Press *Enter*. Quattro opens all spreadsheets you selected on the list. The current spreadsheet remains active.

If all supporting spreadsheets are already open, or if the current spreadsheet contains no links, Quattro displays an error message when you choose /Tools I Update Links I Open.

Updating spreadsheet link values

If you're working with a spreadsheet that is dependently linked to closed spreadsheets, you can use the /Tools I Update Links I Refresh command to access values in the supporting spreadsheets. This command is similar to the **Update Refs** option offered when you first open a primary spreadsheet, except that you can use it any time, not just when you open the spreadsheet, and you can specify which spreadsheets to update values from.

Use the /Tools I Update Links I Refresh command after you've chosen the None option (offered on the menu for linked spreadsheets when you open the primary spreadsheet) to update referenced values from specific spreadsheets.

To update link values from one or more supporting spreadsheets,

1. Choose /Tools I Update Links I Refresh. Quattro displays a choice list of unopened supporting spreadsheets for the current spreadsheet and prompts "Pick one or more spreadsheets."

2. Select each spreadsheet you want to access values from. To select a spreadsheet, highlight its name and press the Select key, *Shift-F7*. Quattro shows a check mark in front of each selected spreadsheet name. To unselect any spreadsheet on the list, press *Shift-F7* again. To select (or unselect) all spreadsheets on the list, press the All Select key, *Alt-F7*.

3. Press *Enter*. Quattro reads linked values from the specified spreadsheets into the current spreadsheet.

If all supporting spreadsheets are already open, or if the current spreadsheet contains no links, Quattro displays an error message when you choose /Tools I Update Links I Refresh.

Tip   The /Tools I Update Links I Refresh command is especially useful when you're working on a local area network. While you're working on one spreadsheet, others may be working on supporting spreadsheets (which remain closed to you). If people announce over the network when they save or close a file, all those with spreadsheets linked to a primary spreadsheet can use /Tools I Update Links I Refresh to access those updated values.

Changing spreadsheet links

The /Tools I Update Links I Change command unlinks your spreadsheet from one supporting spreadsheet and links it to another. This is especially useful after you've renamed a spreadsheet.

To switch over links from one spreadsheet to another,

1. Choose /Tools | Update Links | Change. Quattro displays a choice list of supporting spreadsheets for the current spreadsheet.

2. Highlight the supporting spreadsheet whose linkage you want to change and press *Enter*. Quattro prompts you for a spreadsheet name.

3. Type the name of the new supporting spreadsheet and press *Enter*. Or, to edit the existing name, press *Spacebar* to enter Edit mode and make the necessary changes.

Note The new supporting spreadsheet must have the same layout as the previous supporting spreadsheet because the same relative cells will be referenced. If it doesn't, the formulas that reference linked cells may show error messages.

If the current spreadsheet contains no links, Quattro displays an error message when you choose /Tools | Update Links | Change.

Deleting spreadsheet links

The Delete command on the **Update Links** menu cancels the link between your primary spreadsheet and one or more supporting spreadsheets:

1. Choose the /Tools | Update Links | Delete command. Quattro displays a choice list of supporting spreadsheets for the current spreadsheet.

2. Select each spreadsheet you want to delete links to. To select a spreadsheet, highlight its name and press the Select key, *Shift-F7*. Quattro shows a check mark in front of each selected spreadsheet name. To unselect any spreadsheet on the list, press *Shift-F7* again. To select (or unselect) all spreadsheets on the list, press the All Select key, *Alt-F7*.

3. Press *Enter*. Quattro replaces all link references to the selected spreadsheets with an ERR value, but doesn't remove any formulas containing the ERR values. You can edit them to replace the ERR values with valid references.

Spreadsheet linking examples

The following sections provide two typical linking examples. The first breaks down a large spreadsheet into several smaller ones. The second links several monthly expenses spreadsheets to one yearly spreadsheet. See page 356 for an example of using links to create a graph that references data from different spreadsheets.

Example 1

You can use linking with the /Edit I Move command to break a large spreadsheet down into several smaller ones.

For example, suppose you have a spreadsheet that you've used to calculate estimated taxes. On part of the spreadsheet, you have income information. On another part, you list salaries and commissions. Elsewhere on the same spreadsheet, you list monthly business expenses. And finally, you have a section that calculates your estimated taxes based on other information in the spreadsheet. You could break this spreadsheet down into four separate spreadsheets and use linking in the final one (the one that calculates taxes) to access information in the others.

To break down a large spreadsheet, use the following general procedure:

1. Create and open as many new blank spreadsheets as you need. For example, if you want to break your current spreadsheet into three spreadsheets, create two new ones.
2. Save each new spreadsheet with a unique name.
3. Choose /Window I Tile to arrange all the windows onscreen. Activate the window containing your large spreadsheet.
4. Choose /Edit I Move. Quattro prompts you for the block you want to move.
5. Point out (or enter the cell address of) the block of data you want to move into a new spreadsheet. Quattro prompts you for a destination.
6. Type in the name of the destination spreadsheet surrounded by brackets and followed by a cell address; for example, [INCOME]A1. Or, move into one of the blank spreadsheets and point out the block you want to move the data to.
7. Press *Enter*.

8. Repeat the preceding steps for each block of data you want to move into a new spreadsheet.

If a block move contains formulas that reference cells outside of the block, Quattro automatically creates links so they still refer to the same data.

Example 2

A common use of spreadsheet linking is to merge values from individual spreadsheets into one spreadsheet that shows totals—for example, linking monthly spreadsheets to a year-to-date spreadsheet. The links you create are "live," so that as you enter or change data in the monthly spreadsheets, the year-to-date spreadsheet is kept current (as long as both spreadsheets are open).

Say, for example, that you want to create a set of expense account spreadsheets. You want twelve monthly spreadsheets and one year-to-date spreadsheet. Begin by setting up the skeleton of the first monthly spreadsheet (see the following figure). Include headings and formulas that total monthly expenses. Make any format changes you want, then save the spreadsheet under the name JANEXP.

Figure 11.7
A monthly expenses
spreadsheet

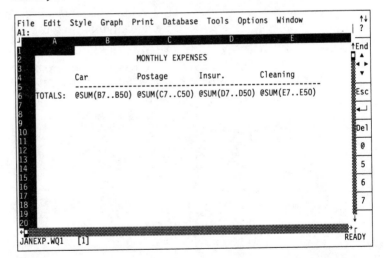

Next, make 11 copies of the JANEXP file. You could name them FEBEXP, MAREXP, and so on. The easiest way to do this is with the File Manager's /Edit | Copy command (see "Duplicating files" on page 271).

Now create the year-to-date spreadsheet (see the following figure). Set up the headings as shown and format the spreadsheet as you like (changing column widths, display format, and so on). Enter the formulas with the 3-D link code to add up expense totals from each monthly spreadsheet. For example, in cell B6 enter the formula @SUM([*]B6) to total the values in cell B6 in all open spreadsheets.

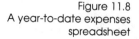

Figure 11.8
A year-to-date expenses spreadsheet

Cells B6..E17 show the formulas you would enter in the spreadsheet.

```
File  Edit  Style  Graph  Print  Database  Tools  Options  Window       ↑↓
A1: [W16]                                                               | ?
┘           A              B            C            D            E
1                                                                     ↑End
2                    Yearly Expense Report                            ▲
3                                                                     ◄ ►
4                                                                     ▼
5
6      Car expenses     @SUM([*]B6)                                   Esc
7      Postage          @SUM([*]C6)
8      Insurance        @SUM([*]D6)
9      Cleaning         @SUM([*]E6)                                   ↵
10     Office Rent      @SUM([*]F6)
11     Utilities        @SUM([*]G6)                                   Del
12     Office Supplies  @SUM([*]H6)
13     Travel           @SUM([*]I6)                                   @
14     Entertainment    @SUM([*]J6)
15     Telephone        @SUM([*]K6)                                   5
16     Printing         @SUM([*]L6)
17     Advertising      @SUM([*]M6)                                   6
18
19     TOTAL            @SUM(B6..B17)                                 7
20
←
YEAREXP.WQ1  [1]                                                    READY
```

Now when you input data into any of the monthly spreadsheets, they're automatically reflected in the year-to-date spreadsheet.

Note   You can also use the /Tools | Combine command to total values from two or more spreadsheets, but this command doesn't *link* the spreadsheets. In other words, /Tools | Combine combines the files once and the results are static—not updated like link values.

12

Advanced file tools

In addition to the standard file functions on the File menu, the Tools menu offers four commands for use with files:

- **Import** lets you retrieve a text file and automatically translate it into spreadsheet format.

See Chapter 11 for information about linking files with the /Tools | Update Links command.

- **Combine** lets you merge two spreadsheet files together.
- **Xtract** lets you copy part of a Quattro spreadsheet into a separate file.
- **Parse** lets you break down long labels (such as those created by importing a text file) into separate columns.

This chapter describes each of these special file tools. Other items on the Tools menu include

- Macro (described in Chapter 16, "Using macros")
- Reformat (described on page 140)
- Update Links (described in the previous chapter)
- Advanced Math, What-If, and Frequency (described in Chapter 19, "Working with statistics and analyzing data")

Importing a file

The /Tools | Import command copies a text file into the current spreadsheet in much the same way that the /Tools | Combine command copies in a spreadsheet file.

A *text file* consists of plain text with a minimum of formatting. The /Tools | Import command converts a text file into a spreadsheet file.

Note   There's no need to import spreadsheet or database files created with Paradox, Reflex, Lotus 1-2-3, dBASE, or Symphony. These files are translated automatically when you retrieve them (see page 233).

```
┌══════════ Import ══════════┐
│                            │
│ ASCII Text File            │
│ Comma & "" Delimited File  │
│ Only Commas                │
│                            │
└────────────────────────────┘
```

Choose /Tools | Import to display the Import menu.

- **ASCII Text File** lets you import a plain, unformatted text file. Quattro automatically converts the data into a single column of labels. Each line in the file becomes a label.

- **Comma & " " Delimited File** lets you import a file that uses commas and quotes to separate text in rows. The delimiters are used to set up columns in the spreadsheet.

- **Only Commas** imports a file delimited only with commas. Only Commas uses quotes optionally to enclose text that includes a comma.

The first two options are described in detail later in this section.

To import a file,

1. Move the cell selector to the upper left corner of the block in which you want to place the imported file.

2. Choose /Tools | Import.

3. Choose the appropriate option. Quattro prompts you for a file name and displays a list of all files with the .PRN extension in the default data directory. You can display *all* files by changing the file name default to *.* and pressing *Enter*, or display files with a .TXT extension by changing it to *.TXT. To display files in a different directory, press *Esc* and enter a different directory path, then press *Enter*.

4. Choose or enter the name of the file you want to import.

The text file is copied into the current spreadsheet beginning with the current cell.

1-2-3   If you're using the 123-compatible menus, choose /File | Import | Text instead of ASCII Text File, or /File | Import | Numbers instead of Comma & " " Delimited File.

ASCII text files

ASCII text files are straight, unformatted text, such as a letter or mailing list written with a word processor. When you import an ASCII text file, you should first remove any special formatting characters such as bold, underlining, or centering. Make sure none of the lines are longer than 254 characters.

Quattro enters each line in an ASCII text file as a label in the first column of the indicated block (using columns to the right for spillover display only). The long labels can then be broken up into a more usable format with the /Tools | Parse menu (see "Breaking down long labels" later in this chapter). Any blank lines in the imported file become empty labels.

The following figure shows an ASCII text file imported into a spreadsheet:

Figure 12.1
How Quattro imports an
ASCII text file

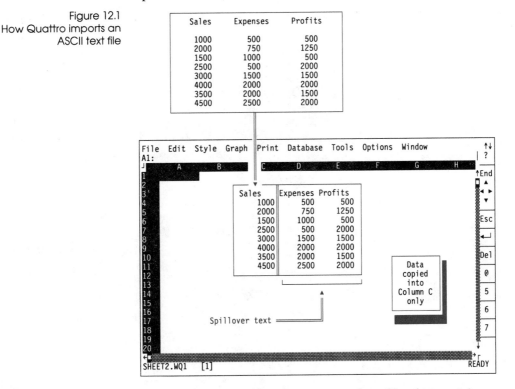

Caution! Many word-processing programs produce files that contain special characters that you may not be able to see. For example,

WordStar inserts soft carriage returns at the end of each line. Characters such as these may produce unwanted results. If your word processor has an option for creating straight ASCII files, use it to create the file you intend to import.

Files with commas and quotes

A comma-and-quote delimited file is a text file with the following format: Data is entered in rows, much like the rows of a spreadsheet, and groups or types of data are separated (or delimited) on each line with commas. Text strings are surrounded by quotation marks.

When Quattro imports a comma-and-quote delimited file, it adheres to the following rules:

- Each group of data is stored in a separate cell.
- Data groups surrounded by quotes are stored in the spreadsheet as labels.
- Data groups that are strictly numbers become value entries.

The following figure shows a comma-and-quote delimited file imported into a spreadsheet:

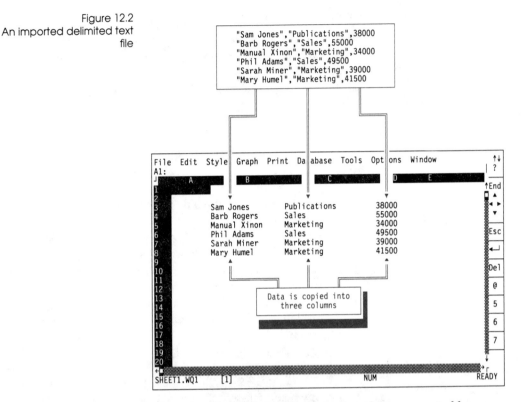

Figure 12.2
An imported delimited text file

Many form letter data files, including those generated by WordStar's MailMerge, are delimited with commas and quotes.

Combining files

The /**Tools** I **Combine** command lets you copy all or part of an existing spreadsheet file into any area of the current spreadsheet. Unlike /**File** I **Retrieve**, it does not erase the current spreadsheet; it affects only the portion of the spreadsheet covered by the inserted block.

Tip   It's easier to use links when you want to reference the data in different spreadsheets than to actually combine the files. We provide the **Combine** command for macro compatibility, but we recommend that you read the previous chapter for information about using Quattro's powerful spreadsheet links.

Combine options let you

- copy the combine file "as is" into the specified block, replacing any existing values. This is the same as using the /Edit I Copy command.
- add the values from the combine file to the existing values in the block.
- subtract the new values from present values in the block.

These options are discussed in detail later in this section.

To combine files,

1. If you intend to combine only *part* of a file with the current one, make sure you know the exact block you want to use— either the block name or the cell coordinates. You may need to retrieve the file first and make note of this.

2. Display the spreadsheet file you want to add to and place the cell selector in the top left cell of the block in which you want to insert the combine file. Make sure you have enough space to the right and below so that cell entries won't be overwritten unexpectedly.

3. Choose /Tools I Combine to display the Combine menu:

4. Choose the appropriate option:

- **Copy** inserts the exact contents of the file.
- **Add** adds the new values to the existing values.
- **Subtract** subtracts the new values from the existing values.

5. Quattro displays a submenu. Choose File to copy the entire file into the existing one. Choose Block to copy a specified block of the file.

6. If you chose Block, Quattro prompts you for a cell block. Enter a block address or name. (Because the block names are from another file, you can't display a list of the names.)

7. Quattro prompts you for the name of the file to combine and displays a list of spreadsheet files in the default data directory. Type or choose a file name. You can specify a different directory by pressing *Esc* twice, then typing a new directory path. When you press *Enter*, a list of files in the new directory is displayed. To combine a file created with another program, include the extension with the name (see "Translating files" on page 233 for more information).

If you're using the 123-compatible menus, choose /File | Combine, Copy, **Add**, or **Subtract**, then choose Entire File instead of File and Named Range instead of **Block**.

Quattro copies the contents and format settings (such as numeric format) of the specified file or block into the current spreadsheet. If you *copied* the data, Quattro also copies cell display settings, such as line-drawing and shading. It deletes any named blocks in the file being copied to avoid confusion (it converts references to them into cell ranges). For details on the mechanics of entering a file name, refer back to page 217.

Caution! /Tools | Combine overwrites any protected cells in the block you specify for combining data.

To copy or move a block of cells directly from one spreadsheet to another without overwriting, adding, or subtracting values, use the /Edit | Copy or /Edit | Move command. If you copy formulas into a different spreadsheet, Quattro automatically changes the references so they refer to relative cells in the new spreadsheet. If you *move* formulas into a different spreadsheet, Quattro automatically inserts links to the original cells in the source spreadsheet. See "Passing data between spreadsheets" on page 123 for details on moving and copying blocks. Chapter 11, "Linking spreadsheets," explains how to use spreadsheet links within formulas to permanently link values between spreadsheets so that Quattro will automatically update them when you make changes.

Copying data

The Copy option for the /Tools | Combine command copies data directly from a file into the current spreadsheet. The data is inserted beginning at the position of the cell selector. If you specify the entire file, Quattro only copies the block that contains data.

For example, suppose you have a file called HEADINGS that you use to set up headings for your spreadsheets:

Figure 12.3
A headings file

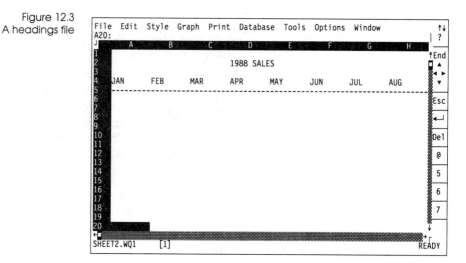

To insert these headings in the spreadsheet shown in the following figure, you would move the cell selector to cell A1, choose /Tools | Combine, choose Copy, then File. When Quattro prompts you for a file name, enter HEADINGS. The headings are added to the top of the file (see Figure 12.5). The data underneath the headings is not overwritten because Quattro only copies the block that contains data (A1..M5) into the spreadsheet.

Figure 12.4
A spreadsheet lacking
headings

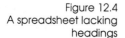

Figure 12.5
The spreadsheet with
headings added

```
File  Edit  Style  Graph  Print  Database  Tools  Options  Window        ↑↓
A1: [W10]                                                                 | ?
J        A         B         C         D         E         F       G
1                                                                       ↑End
2                               1988 SALES                              ■ ▲
3                                                                       ◄ ►
4   JAN       FEB       MAR       APR       MAY       JUN       JUL        ▼
5  --------------------------------------------------------------------
6   $450,334  $463,942  $477,550  $491,158  $504,766  $518,374  $531,982  Esc
7   $451,468  $465,076  $478,684  $492,292  $505,900  $519,508  $533,116
8   $452,602  $466,210  $479,818  $493,426  $507,034  $520,642  $534,250  ↵
9   $453,736  $467,344  $480,952  $494,560  $508,168  $521,776  $535,384
10  $454,870  $468,478  $482,086  $495,694  $509,302  $522,910  $536,518  Del
11  $456,004  $469,612  $483,220  $496,828  $510,436  $524,044  $537,652
12  $457,138  $470,746  $484,354  $497,962  $511,570  $525,178  $538,786  @
13  $458,272  $471,880  $485,488  $499,096  $512,704  $526,312  $539,920
14  $459,406  $473,014  $486,622  $500,230  $513,838  $527,446  $541,054  5
15  $460,540  $474,148  $487,756  $501,364  $514,972  $528,580  $542,188
16  $461,674  $475,282  $488,890  $502,498  $516,106  $529,714  $543,322  6
17  $462,808  $476,416  $490,024  $503,632  $517,240  $530,848  $544,456
18                                                                        7
19
20
SHEET2.WQ1      [1]                                              READY
```

With the /Tools I Combine I Copy command, Quattro copies
formulas as is. However, if they reference cells outside of the
block being copied, they may be inaccurate. If you want to copy
the formula *values* instead of the formulas themselves, use the
/Tools I Xtract I Values command to copy them to another file first
(see "Extracting part of a spreadsheet" later in this chapter).

Adding data

The **Add** option for the /Tools I Combine command combines
values in the inserted block with existing values in that area of the
spreadsheet and displays the sum. Quattro first converts any
formulas involved to their resulting values.

/Tools I Combine I **Add** is most useful for combining files for a
cumulative total; for example, to compile year-to-date figures
from monthly spreadsheets. The figure on the following page
shows three spreadsheets with monthly expense figures.

Figure 12.6
Three monthly spreadsheets

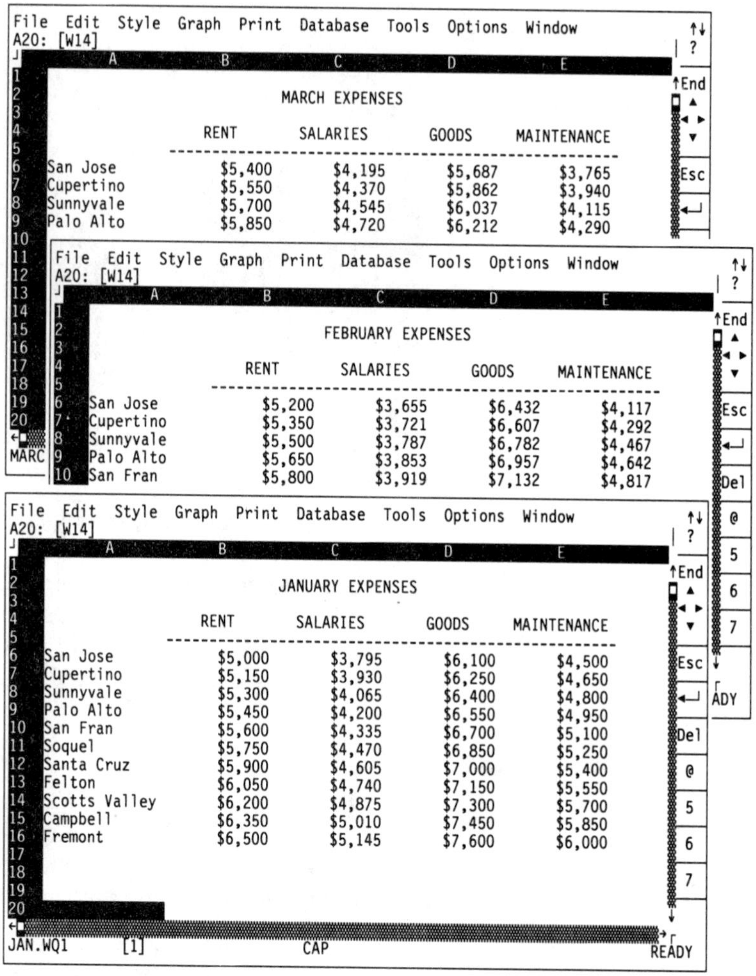

```
File  Edit  Style  Graph  Print  Database  Tools  Options  Window        ↑↓
A20: [W14]                                                                | ?
      A          B           C            D          E                   ↑End
                                                                          ▲
                      MARCH EXPENSES                                    ◄ ►
                                                                          ▼
             RENT       SALARIES      GOODS      MAINTENANCE
           ------------------------------------------------------        Esc
San Jose     $5,400     $4,195       $5,687      $3,765
Cupertino    $5,550     $4,370       $5,862      $3,940                    ↵
Sunnyvale    $5,700     $4,545       $6,037      $4,115
Palo Alto    $5,850     $4,720       $6,212      $4,290
```

```
File  Edit  Style  Graph  Print  Database  Tools  Options  Window        ↑↓
A20: [W14]                                                                | ?
       A          B           C            D          E                  ↑End
                                                                          ▲
                      FEBRUARY EXPENSES                                 ◄ ►
                                                                          ▼
              RENT       SALARIES      GOODS      MAINTENANCE
            ------------------------------------------------------
San Jose      $5,200     $3,655       $6,432      $4,117                 Esc
Cupertino     $5,350     $3,721       $6,607      $4,292
Sunnyvale     $5,500     $3,787       $6,782      $4,467                   ↵
Palo Alto     $5,650     $3,853       $6,957      $4,642
San Fran      $5,800     $3,919       $7,132      $4,817                  Del
```

```
File  Edit  Style  Graph  Print  Database  Tools  Options  Window        ↑↓       @
A20: [W14]                                                                | ?
        A          B           C            D          E                 ↑End      5
                                                                          ▲
                      JANUARY EXPENSES                                  ◄ ►       6
                                                                          ▼
               RENT       SALARIES      GOODS      MAINTENANCE                      7
             ------------------------------------------------------
San Jose       $5,000     $3,795       $6,100      $4,500                Esc ↓
Cupertino      $5,150     $3,930       $6,250      $4,650
Sunnyvale      $5,300     $4,065       $6,400      $4,800                  ↵  ADY
Palo Alto      $5,450     $4,200       $6,550      $4,950
San Fran       $5,600     $4,335       $6,700      $5,100                 Del
Soquel         $5,750     $4,470       $6,850      $5,250
Santa Cruz     $5,900     $4,605       $7,000      $5,400                  @
Felton         $6,050     $4,740       $7,150      $5,550
Scotts Valley  $6,200     $4,875       $7,300      $5,700                  5
Campbell       $6,350     $5,010       $7,450      $5,850
Fremont        $6,500     $5,145       $7,600      $6,000                  6

                                                                          7


JAN.WQ1     [1]                    CAP                          READY
```

You can retrieve one, place the cell selector at cell A1, and combine each of the other files with /Tools | Combine | Add, so that a cumulative spreadsheet is created showing year-to-date expense totals.

Figure 12.7
Totals created with the Add
option

```
File  Edit  Style  Graph  Print  Database  Tools  Options  Window        ↑↓
A1: [W14]                                                                 | ?
         A            B           C           D           E              ↑End
 1                                                                        ▲
 2                         MARCH EXPENSES                                 ◄ ►
 3                                                                        ▼
 4                    RENT      SALARIES      GOODS    MAINTENANCE
 5               --------------------------------------------------       Esc
 6   San Jose      $15,600     $11,645      $18,219    $12,382
 7   Cupertino     $16,050     $12,021      $18,719    $12,882            ↵
 8   Sunnyvale     $16,500     $12,397      $19,219    $13,382
 9   Palo Alto     $16,950     $12,773      $19,719    $13,882
10   San Fran      $17,100     $12,948      $19,894    $14,057            Del
11   Soquel        $17,550     $13,324      $20,394    $14,557
12   Santa Cruz    $18,000     $13,700      $20,894    $15,057            @
13   Felton        $18,450     $14,076      $21,394    $15,557
14   Scotts Valley $18,900     $14,452      $21,894    $16,057            5
15
16                                                                        6
17                  Original labels remain
18                                                                        7
19
20
MARCH.WQ1    [1]                         CAP                          READY
```

Before you use the /**Tools** I **Combine** I **Add** command, place the cell selector where you want the upper left corner of the inserted data to be (in the example, this would be cell B1.) Data will be added to values below or to the right of the selector.

1-2-3 If you're using the 123-compatible menus, choose /**File** I **Combine** I **Add**.

If you add an entire file, Quattro adds all cells that contain values. If you specify a block to add, Quattro adds exactly that block.

When adding spreadsheet values, make sure both spreadsheets or blocks are set up similarly; for example, with headings in the same position. The incoming data will assume the cell formats (display format, column width, and so on) of the current spreadsheet.

Caution! Accuracy is very important when adding combined values. If the cell selector is one cell off when you combine the files, the combined data may be useless. For this reason, it's a good idea to save the current spreadsheet before combining data. Then, if you don't get the results you want, you can retrieve the file as it was before the combine operation.

When you add values with the /**Tools** I **Combine** I **Add** command, Quattro follows these rules:

■ In the current spreadsheet, cells that contain labels, formulas, ERR, or NA are not altered by the incoming data.

- Value entries in the affected block of the current spreadsheet are replaced by the sum of the original and incoming values.

- When adding incoming values to those existing in the spreadsheet, Quattro converts all incoming formulas to their end values and interprets labels and blank cells as zero.

Subtracting data

The **Subtract** option for the /**Tools** | **Combine** command subtracts values in a specified block or file from existing values in the current spreadsheet. It has the same requirements and rules as the **Add** option.

Subtract is often used to break down a file that has been combined with the /**Tools** | **Combine** command. For example, after combining the monthly spreadsheets, such as those shown in Figure 12.6, you might want to pull out certain months to see how their absence affects the total.

1-2-3

If you're using the 123-compatible menus, choose /**File** | **Combine** | **Subtract**.

Extracting part of a spreadsheet

The /**Tools** | **Xtract** command lets you save part of a spreadsheet in a separate file. This command copies, or *extracts*, a specified block of the spreadsheet to a different file, leaving the original file intact. Extracting is useful for breaking down a large spreadsheet into more manageable pieces. You can then work on those pieces separately or combine them with other spreadsheets.

Tip   It's easier to open a blank spreadsheet in a new window with /**File** | **New** and copy a block of data to it with /**Edit** | **Copy** than to extract the block. We provide the **Xtract** command for macro compatibility, but we recommend that you read Chapter 9 for information about working with multiple windows in Quattro.

/**Tools** | **Xtract** is much like /**Edit** | **Copy** with two major differences:

- **Xtract** includes an option to copy *values only*, which means that only the resulting values of formulas are copied—not the formulas themselves.

■ Xtract saves all the spreadsheet's block names, named graphs, and defaults along with the specified block. Some of the block names or graphs may not be meaningful if they refer to cells or blocks that were not included in the extracted block. You can delete them, reassign them, or ignore them.

If you want to extract only the data in a spreadsheet block (including formulas), use the /Edit I Copy command to copy the data into a different spreadsheet (see page 123).

The /Tools I Xtract menu has two options: Formulas and Values. Formulas saves an exact copy of the block, including formulas. Values converts all formulas in the block to their end values before saving it.

When the Formulas option is used, formulas are updated to reference cells relative to their new positions, even if they are absolute. (Absolute formulas retain their absoluteness for the new spreadsheet after their initial adjustment.) If the formulas being saved reference cells outside the block being saved, problems can arise. In this case, it's best to use the Values option. Or convert those individual formulas to their results with the /Edit I Values command (see page 136).

To extract part of a spreadsheet,

1. Choose /Tools I Xtract. The Xtract menu appears.
2. Choose Formulas to save the block exactly as is. Choose Values to save the resulting values of formulas instead of the original formulas.

3. Quattro prompts you for a file name and displays a list of files in the default data directory.
4. Choose a file from the list, or type in a new name. If you want to save the extracted data for use with another program, include the appropriate extension (see page 233). For details on the mechanics of entering a file name, refer back to page 217.
5. If the file name you enter already exists, Quattro displays the same overwrite warning menu as when you choose /File I Save As (see page 225). Choose Cancel to halt the extract operation, Replace to overwrite the existing file with the extracted block, or Backup to create a backup copy of the existing file with the extension .BAK.

6. Quattro prompts you for a cell block. To indicate the block you want to extract, either type the cell coordinates or a block name, or point to the block using the direction keys, then press *Enter*.

If you're using the 123-compatible menus, choose /**File** | **Xtract**.

The extracted block is placed in the new spreadsheet beginning at cell A1, regardless of its position in the original file.

If you include the file-name extension used by a different program, Quattro automatically translates the spreadsheet data into a file for use with that program. In order for the extracted data to work with the program, however, the extracted block must be set up in a way that makes sense to the program. For example, if you are extracting to a database file in a program like Reflex, the block should list related data in columns, which are interpreted as fields, and with column headings, which are interpreted as field names, such as that in the following figure:

Figure 12.8
Data set up for extracting to
a database file

```
 File   Edit   Style   Graph   Print   Database   Tools   Options   Window          ↑↓
 A20: [W16]                                                                          | ?
 J           A                 B                   C           D         E    |
 1  NAME             HOME ADDRESS          CITY          STATE     ZIP        ↑End
 2  -----------------------------------------------------------------------    ▲
 3  Sally Rogers     5843 Old County Rd.   Bloomdale     MS        29548       ◄ ►
 4  Bill Rivers      990 Middlefield St.   Louisville    IN        30929        ▼
 5  Sandy Marks      224 Handley Dr.       Canyon        AZ        12553
 6  Cindy Klein      155 Miguel St.        Atlanta       GA        30309      Esc
 7  Denise Miller    829 Powers Dr.        Tallahassee   FL        35007
 8  Mark Taylor      399 Glenview Way      Harrisburg    PA        13099       ↵
 9  Kate Hill        8398 Inlet Rd.        Fort Worth    TX        50294
10                                                                            Del
11
12                                                                             @
13
14                                                                             5
15
16                                                                             6
17
18                                                                             7
19
20
                                                                              ↓
 SHEET2.WQ1        [1]                         CAP                            READY
```

Breaking down long labels

After you've imported a text file to the spreadsheet, you may need to break down or *parse* the data into individual cells. Imported ASCII files most often require parsing because Quattro interprets each line of text as a single label.

The following figure shows an imported ASCII text file. Although the spreadsheet appears to contain data in several columns, the text in each row is actually entered only in column A, as you can see by the input line. The columns to the right are used only to display the spillover of column A.

Figure 12.9
An imported ASCII text file

```
File  Edit  Style  Graph  Print  Database  Tools  Options  Window        ↑↓
A3: [W16] 'Sally Rogers     5843 Old County Rd.    Bloomdale     MS      295|  ?
J          A                    B                 C          D       E
1  NAME              HOME ADDRESS            CITY           STATE   ZIP      ↑End
2  --------------------------------------------------------------------           ▲
3  Sally Rogers      5843 Old County Rd.     Bloomdale      MS      29548    ◄ ►
4  Bill Rivers       990 Middlefield St.     Louisville     IN      30929    ▼
5  Sandy Marks       224 Handley Dr.         Canyon         AZ      12553
6  Cindy Klein       155 Miguel St.          Atlanta        GA      30309    Esc
7  Denise Miller     829 Powers Dr.          Tallahassee    FL      35007
8  Mark Taylor       399 Glenview Way        Harrisburg     PA      13099    ←┘
9  Kate Hill         8398 Inlet Rd.          Fort Worth     TX      50294
10                                                                           Del
11
12                                                                           @
13
14                                                                           5
15
16                                                                           6
17
18                                                                           7
19
20
←□▮▮▮▮▮▮▮▮▮▮▮▮▮▮▮▮▮▮▮▮▮▮▮▮▮▮▮▮▮▮▮▮▮▮▮▮▮▮▮▮▮▮▮▮▮▮▮▮→
SHEET2.WQ1        [1]                       CAP                       READY
```

To turn this file into a useful database file, you need to break down each row, or label, into individual *fields*. In this example, the first column could be the Name field, the second the Address field, the third the City field, and so on. The /Tools | Parse menu lets you break down labels with minimum effort (see "Setting up a database" in Chapter 18).

You can also use /Tools | Parse to break down data in a regular spreadsheet; for example, to turn a Name column into two columns—one for first name and one for last.

Choose /Tools | Parse to display the Parse menu.

- **Input** lets you specify the block containing the label entries to be parsed.

- **Output** lets you specify the cell block you want the parsed data to be copied to.

- **Create** inserts a format line above the current cell. This line indicates how Quattro will break down the labels into separate cells.

- **Edit** lets you alter the parsing format suggested by Quattro.

- **Go** begins the parsing procedure.

- **Reset** erases all menu settings.

- **Quit** returns you to the spreadsheet.

Press *Esc* to back out of the Parse menu to the Tools menu.

The basic procedure for parsing a file is as follows:

1. Use **Create** and **Edit** to set up one or more format lines to indicate how you want the labels broken up.
2. Use **Input** to specify the column containing the labels to be parsed, including the format line.
3. Use **Output** to specify the block you want to copy the parsed labels to.
4. Choose **Go**.

1-2-3

If you're using the 123-compatible menus, choose /Data | Parse | Format Line | Create and Edit instead of /Tools | Parse | Create and Edit, choose /Data | Parse | Input Column instead of /Tools | Parse | Input, and choose /Data | Parse | Output Range instead of /Tools | Parse | Output.

Input and output blocks

Before you can parse data, you need to tell Quattro which block of data to parse and where to copy the parsed data. You do this by assigning cell blocks with the Input and Output commands on the /Tools | Parse menu.

The input block is the spreadsheet column that contains the text you want to parse and the format line(s) used to parse it. (Remember that your labels are contained in a single column, even though they may be displayed across several.) To specify the input block, choose /Tools | Parse | Input, then indicate the block you want to parse. Be sure to include all format lines. When you press *Enter*, Quattro returns to the Parse menu.

The output block is the block of cells you want to copy the parsed data to. To specify the output block, choose /Tools | Parse | Output. You can specify the output block in either of two ways: by the top left cell or by the entire block.

In either case, Quattro uses whatever space is required for the parsed data, overwriting cells if necessary. To be on the safe side, you may want to first copy the parsed data to another part of the spreadsheet. Then, when you've obtained the results you want, replace the original data with /Edit I Move.

To clear both of the parsing blocks, choose /Tools I Parse I Reset.

When you've assigned both parsing blocks and have set up the format lines, you can begin parsing. Choose /Tools I Parse I Go. Quattro displays the WAIT mode indicator while it completes the parsing. When the parsing is complete, Quattro enters the parsed data in the output block.

If you're using the 123-compatible menus, choose /Data I Parse I Reset instead of /Tools I Parse I Reset and /Data I Parse I Go instead of /Tools I Parse I Go.

Format lines

A *format line* begins with a unique prefix, a vertical bar (I), and stretches across the length of the text below it. It uses the following special symbols to indicate how to translate text into separate fields:

    I begins a format line.
    V begins a value cell entry.
    L begins a label cell entry.
    T begins a time value translated into a serial number.
    D begins a date value translated into a serial number.
    > continues an entry.
    * indicates blank spaces that can be filled in by longer entries underneath the first.
    S tells Quattro to skip (delete) the character in this position (this symbol can only be entered by editing the format line).

When you create a format line, Quattro bases the format line on the first row of data, using these symbols to indicate parsing. You can edit the line to parse the labels differently, and you can insert additional format lines to parse specific areas differently.

Creating a format line   To create a format line, position the cell selector at the first cell containing a label to be parsed and choose **Create** from the /Tools I Parse menu. Quattro creates and inserts a format line above the current cell. It contains parsing directions for the entire block based on the first label.

If you're using the 123-compatible menus, choose /Data I Parse I Format Line I Create.

The following figure shows a format line inserted in cells A1..E1 above the imported text file shown earlier:

Figure 12.10
An initial format line

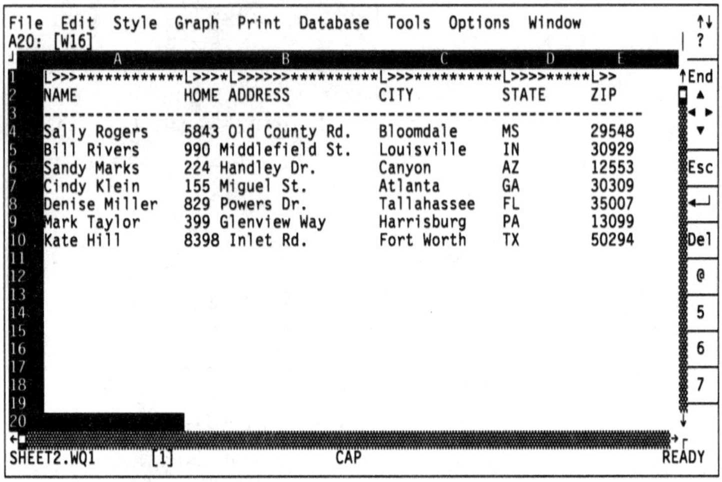

```
File  Edit  Style  Graph  Print  Database  Tools  Options  Window         ↑↓
A20: [W16]                                                                | ?
J          A              B              C           D        E
1  L>>>***********L>>>*L>>>>>***********L>>>***********L>>>>>****L>>      ↑End
2  NAME           HOME ADDRESS        CITY           STATE    ZIP          ▲
3  ------------------------------------------------------------------    ◄ ►
4  Sally Rogers   5843 Old County Rd.  Bloomdale      MS       29548        ▼
5  Bill Rivers    990 Middlefield St.  Louisville     IN       30929
6  Sandy Marks    224 Handley Dr.      Canyon         AZ       12553     Esc
7  Cindy Klein    155 Miguel St.       Atlanta        GA       30309
8  Denise Miller  829 Powers Dr.       Tallahassee    FL       35007      ↵
9  Mark Taylor    399 Glenview Way     Harrisburg     PA       13099
10 Kate Hill      8398 Inlet Rd.       Fort Worth     TX       50294     Del
11
12                                                                         @
13
14                                                                         5
15
16                                                                         6
17
18                                                                         7
19
20
SHEET2.WQ1      [1]                        CAP                        READY
```

The format line shown here breaks the first label up into six cells—one for each word in the label. Because each word begins with a letter, each becomes a separate label entry. In this case, the format line needs to be edited because Quattro has divided the address field into two fields: Home and Address.

Editing format lines

To edit a format line, make sure the cell selector is in the first cell of the format line, then choose /Tools | Parse | Edit. Quattro enters Format mode, which is similar to Edit mode, except that you can edit the format line directly within the spreadsheet, not just on the edit line. The FRMT mode indicator appears in the bottom right corner of the screen.

1-2-3

If you're using the 123-compatible menus, choose /Data | Parse | Format Line | Edit.

In Format mode, you can use the same edit keys you use in Edit mode to make changes to the format line. Quattro automatically places the spreadsheet in Overwrite mode (OVR) so that you can replace characters without misaligning the rest of the line. You can't move from the format line while editing it, but you can use ↑, ↓, PgUp, and PgDn to scroll the text underneath it.

When you're finished, press Enter. (To discard any changes you made, press Esc twice instead.)

The next figure shows the same format line as Figure 12.10 after editing. The address field is now presented as one field, Home Address.

Figure 12.11
An edited format line

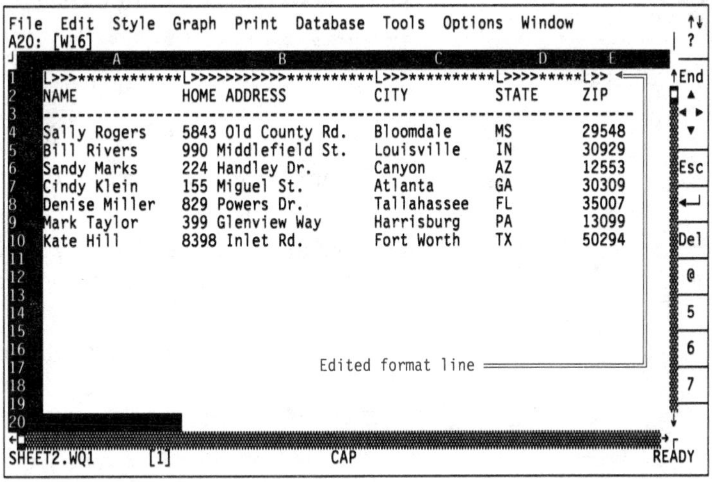

```
File  Edit  Style  Graph  Print  Database  Tools  Options  Window          ↑↓
A20: [W16]                                                              |  ?
⌐         A              B              C            D         E
I L>>>**********L>>>>>>>>>>**********L>>>>*******L>>>>****L>>  ◄─       ↑End
2 NAME            HOME ADDRESS       CITY         STATE     ZIP            ▲
3 ─────────────────────────────────────────────────────────              ◄ ►
4 Sally Rogers    5843 Old County Rd. Bloomdale    MS       29548         ▼
5 Bill Rivers     990 Middlefield St. Louisville   IN       30929
6 Sandy Marks     224 Handley Dr.     Canyon       AZ       12553       Esc
7 Cindy Klein     155 Miguel St.      Atlanta      GA       30309
8 Denise Miller   829 Powers Dr.      Tallahassee  FL       35007       ↵
9 Mark Taylor     399 Glenview Way    Harrisburg   PA       13099
10 Kate Hill      8398 Inlet Rd.      Fort Worth   TX       50294       Del
11                                                                       @
13
14                                                                       5
15
16                                                                       6
17                          Edited format line
18                                                                       7
19
20
SHEET2.WQ1    [1]                      CAP                            READY
```

When the format line is correct, all you need to do is specify input and output blocks, then choose Go to begin the parsing.

Using more than one format line

In some cases, you'll need to use more than one format line to parse a file. For example, in the following figure, the initial format line makes little sense. It uses only the spreadsheet title to base parsing on.

Figure 12.12
The initial format line for a
spreadsheet

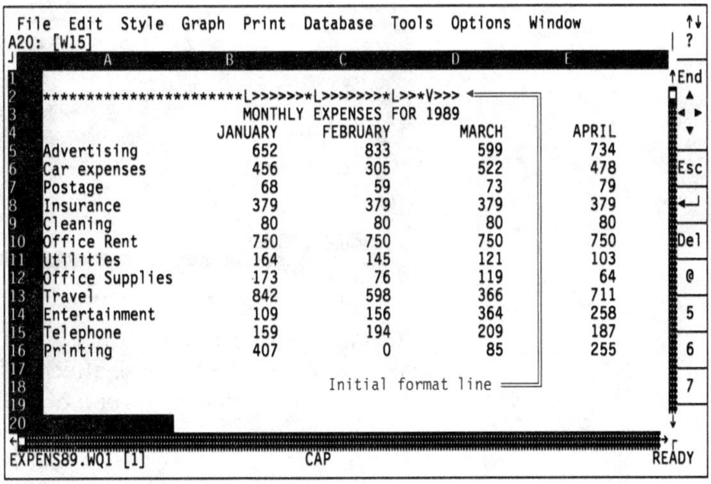

```
File  Edit  Style  Graph  Print  Database  Tools  Options  Window          ↑↓
A20: [W15]                                                              |  ?
⌐         A              B              C            D         E
I                                                                      ↑End
2 **********************L>>>>>>*L>>>>>>>*L>>*V>>>  ◄─                     ▲
3               MONTHLY EXPENSES FOR 1989                                ◄ ►
4               JANUARY   FEBRUARY       MARCH        APRIL              ▼
5 Advertising      652        833         599          734
6 Car expenses     456        305         522          478            Esc
7 Postage           68         59          73           79
8 Insurance        379        379         379          379            ↵
9 Cleaning          80         80          80           80
10 Office Rent     750        750         750          750            Del
11 Utilities       164        145         121          103
12 Office Supplies 173         76         119           64             @
13 Travel          842        598         366          711
14 Entertainment   109        156         364          258             5
15 Telephone       159        194         209          187
16 Printing        407          0          85          255             6
17
18                   Initial format line                               7
19
20
EXPENS89.WQ1 [1]                      CAP                             READY
```

Figure 12.13 shows the same spreadsheet with two more format lines. The original format line has been edited to keep the spreadsheet title based in one cell, which will spill over into adjacent cells. The second and third format lines were entered without editing.

To make the same adjustments,

1. Move the selector to cell A2 and choose /Tools I Parse I Edit.
2. Change the format line to show arrows extending from the first *L* to the end of the label.
3. Move to cell A4 and choose /Tools I Parse I Create. Another format line is added above the headings, correctly interpreting each heading as a label.
4. Move to cell A6 and choose /Tools I Parse I Create again. Another format line is created above the data, correctly interpreting the numbers as values and the row headings as labels.

1-2-3 If you're using the 123-compatible menus, choose /Data I Parse I Format Line I Edit and Create.

Figure 12.13
A spreadsheet with three
format lines

```
File  Edit  Style  Graph  Print  Database  Tools  Options  Window        ↑↓
A20: [W15]                                                               | ?
J         A           B           C           D           E
1                                                                      ↑End
2  ********************L>>>>>>>>>>>>>>>>>>>>>>>                         ▲
3                     MONTHLY EXPENSES FOR 1989                        ◄ ►
4  ********************L>>>>>>>*****L>>>>>>>*****L>>>>*******L>>>>      ▼
5                     JANUARY    FEBRUARY     MARCH       APRIL
6  L>>>>>>>>>>*********V>>********V>>********V>>********V>>            Esc
7  Advertising           652         833         599         734
8  Car expenses          456         305         522         478      ↵
9  Postage                68          59          73          79
10 Insurance             379         379         379         379      Del
11 Cleaning               80          80          80          80
12 Office Rent           750         750         750         750      @
13 Utilities             164         145         121         103
14 Office Supplies       173          76         119          64      5
15 Travel                842         598         366         711
16 Entertainment         109         156         364         258      6
17 Telephone             159         194         209         187
18 Printing              407           0          85         255      7
19
20
EXPENS89.WQ1 [1]                    CAP                         READY
```

You can insert as many format lines in your spreadsheet as necessary. Each format line affects all the text below it down to the next format line or the end of the input block.

4

Graphs

13

Building graphs

With a few well-placed keystrokes, Quattro can turn numeric spreadsheet data into a graph, often revealing information not immediately apparent in a table of numbers.

Quattro can create many different types of graphs:

- Line
- Bar
- XY
- Stacked Bar
- Pie
- Area
- Rotated Bar
- Column
- High-Low
- Text

You create a graph using commands on the **Graph** menu; most importantly, the **Series** command tells Quattro which data in your spreadsheet to graph. You can view your graph at any point in the building process with the /**Graph** I **View** command or the Graph key, *F10.*

Once you've completed a graph, you can print it on a printer or plotter, or save it for future use. You can even insert a graph directly in your spreadsheet, alongside the numbers it represents. This makes it easy to create sophisticated reports showing both text and graphics on the same page.

Graph

From within the spreadsheet, you can always view the latest graph instantly by pressing the Graph key, *F10*. The graph display automatically reflects any changes you've made to spreadsheet values.

Note

To see graphs onscreen, your computer must have graphics capability; for example, an EGA board. Even if you don't have a graphics board, you can still build graphs and print them on a graphics printer.

This chapter describes

- how to create a basic Quattro graph
- the different graph types and what they're best used for
- adding text to a graph
- storing graphs with a spreadsheet and displaying previously saved graphs
- inserting a graph in the spreadsheet

The next two chapters, "Customizing graphs" and "Annotating your graph," describe how to fine-tune the graph you've created. To print a graph, refer back to "Printing a graph" in Chapter 4.

What is a graph?

A graph is a visual representation of numeric information. Graphs offer a fresh perspective on the data stored in your spreadsheets. For example, the bar graph in the following figure shows a dip in sales in April with a rising trend since May:

Figure 13.1
A bar graph showing sales
trends

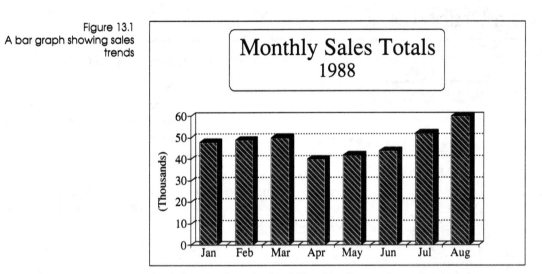

And the pie chart in the following figure shows how each monthly sales total contributes to the whole:

Figure 13.2
A pie chart showing
percentages

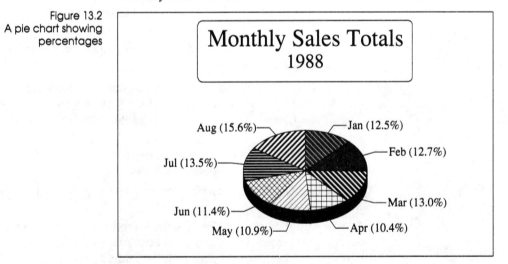

Often a graph will uncover a trouble spot or pinpoint the beginning of a new pattern. You can then return to the spreadsheet data for a look at the data behind such areas.

Graphs help both with analyzing past or present data and with visualizing future situations. Just as you can set up a database to create what-if scenarios (see "Performing a sensitivity analysis" in Chapter 19), you can use graphs to help foresee future directions.

The Graph menu

When you choose /Graph, Quattro displays the **Graph** menu.

```
 ═══ Graph ═══
Graph Type    ▶
Series        ▶
Text          ▶
─────────────────
Customize Series ▶
X-Axis        ▶
Y-Axis        ▶
Overall       ▶
─────────────────
Insert
Hide
Name          ▶
View
Fast Graph  Ctrl-G
Annotate
Quit
```

- **Graph Type** lets you choose the basic graph type.
- **Series** lets you specify up to six blocks of data to plot on your graph and one block of data to use as labels for the x-axis.
- **Text** lets you add text to the graph, as well as change the typestyle, size, and color of that text.
- **Customize Series** lets you embellish your graph with an array of options, including changing marker symbols, colors, and fill patterns, and using a different graph type or y-axis scale for an individual series.
- **X-Axis** contains options related to the x-axis, including scaling and adjusting tick marks.
- **Y-Axis** contains options related to the y-axis, including scaling and tick marks.
- **Overall** lets you add a three-dimensional effect to a graph, set grid options, and change graph colors for the overall graph.
- **Insert** lets you paste a graph directly into your spreadsheet.
- **Hide** removes a graph from the spreadsheet.
- **Name** lets you store one or more graphs with the current spreadsheet, display a graph previously stored with the spreadsheet, delete one or all named graphs, and display a graph for a timed interval.
- **View** displays the current graph. To return to the **Graph** menu, press any key except the Slash key (/).
- **Fast Graph** automatically creates a basic graph out of the block of data you specify.
- **Annotate** activates the Graph Annotator, which lets you add text, arrows, lines, and geometric shapes to your graph as you would previously with an independent graphics package.
- **Quit** returns you to the spreadsheet.

This chapter describes commands in the first and last sections of the **Graph** menu (except **Annotate**). The next chapter, "Customizing graphs," covers the **Customize Series**, **X-Axis**, **Y-Axis**, and **Overall** commands. The **Annotate** command is covered in Chapter 15, "Annotating your graph."

Business graphics terminology

If you've never worked with business graphs before, there are several terms you may not be familiar with:

Axis. Most graphs contain two axes: the x-axis runs horizontally along the bottom of the graph; the y-axis runs vertically at the left. The intersection of a point on each axis represents the data point.

Data Point. A single spreadsheet value displayed in a graph.

Fill Pattern. The geometric pattern (for example, crosshatching) that fills bars in a bar graph or slices in a pie or column chart. Typically, Quattro assigns each series a different fill pattern.

Font. A typestyle for graph text, such as Roman or Sans Serif.

Label. In a spreadsheet, a label is a text entry. In a graph, labels are spreadsheet entries (of any type) that you assign to the graph to define plotted values.

Legend. A key displayed to the right or beneath a graph that specifies the colors, marker symbols, or fill patterns for each series graphed.

Logarithmic. A method of scaling graphs in which each major division of the scale represents 10 times the value of the previous division. Logarithmic (or log) scaling is best suited to widely varying, positive data.

Plotter. A machine that prints (usually colored) graphs on paper or transparency film, using mechanically-driven pens.

Scale. The range of values associated with an axis.

Series. A set of cell values plotted sequentially on a graph. Each cell value is represented by a data point on the graph.

Tick Marks. Scale indicators placed at regular intervals along an axis.

The basics of creating a graph

The general procedure for building a graph is as follows:

1. Choose the type of graph you want to create (for example, a line graph or pie chart).

2. Specify the spreadsheet data to be plotted. For most graph types, you can specify up to six series of data and a block of spreadsheet labels to define the x-axis.

3. Add any titles, legends, or other text you want to the graph.

4. View the graph. (You may want to try different graph types to see which best displays your data.)

5. Use customizing commands to perfect the graph (change colors, fill patterns, and so forth).

6. Use graph annotation tools to embellish your graph with text, arrows, and geometric shapes.

7. When you're satisfied, print the graph or save it for future use.

Of course, each of these steps includes many options and a little experimentation will give you the exact result you want. The rest of this chapter gives you all the details you need to create and save a basic graph.

Graph types

Quattro can build many types of graphs, and—with few limitations—you can change the graph type at any time. If you don't choose a type, Quattro creates a stacked bar graph by default.

Most graphs position data relative to two yardsticks: the x-axis and the y-axis. The x-axis is the horizontal line at the bottom of a graph. This axis shows progression of values and often represents time (days, weeks, quarters, and so on). The data plotted on the graph determines the y-axis values, which serve as reference points for the placement of bars, lines, and markers on the graph.

Exceptions to this general graph layout include the pie chart, which illustrates values as a percentage of a circular whole; the column chart, which shows values as a percentage of a column; the rotated bar graph, which switches positions of the x- and y-axes; and the XY graph, which lets you scale the x-axis with values from a series.

Figure 13.3 shows four different graphs created by plotting the same series in the sample spreadsheet (shown in Figure 13.4).

Figure 13.3
Different graphs plotting the same information

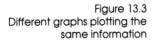

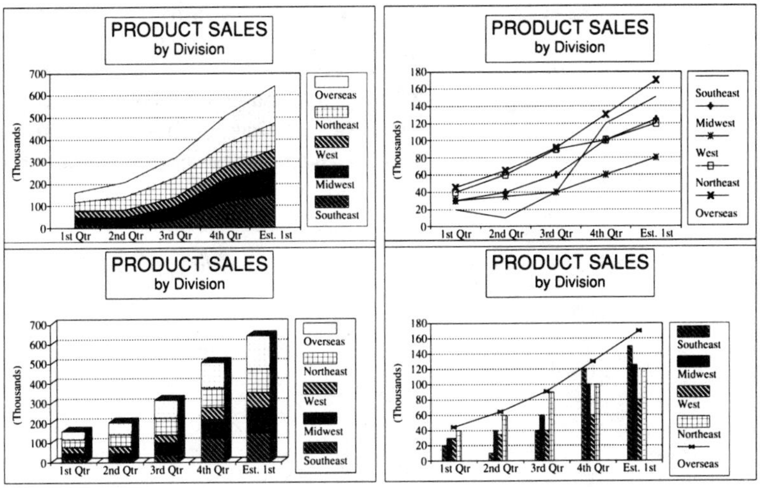

Figure 13.4
The spreadsheet used to create sample graphs

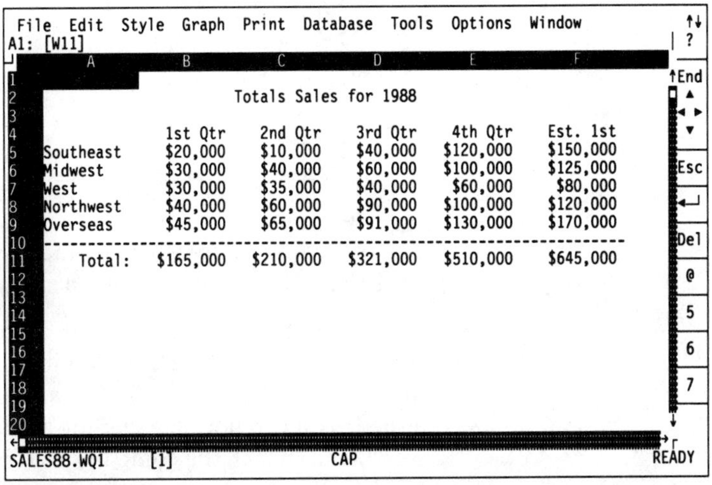

	1st Qtr	2nd Qtr	3rd Qtr	4th Qtr	Est. 1st
Southeast	$20,000	$10,000	$40,000	$120,000	$150,000
Midwest	$30,000	$40,000	$60,000	$100,000	$125,000
West	$30,000	$35,000	$40,000	$60,000	$80,000
Northwest	$40,000	$60,000	$90,000	$100,000	$120,000
Overseas	$45,000	$65,000	$91,000	$130,000	$170,000
Total:	$165,000	$210,000	$321,000	$510,000	$645,000

The following sections describe each available graph type. Later in the chapter, "Choosing a graph type" tells how to choose a type of graph and explains which graph types are best suited for presenting certain kinds of information. For information on how to combine certain different graph types in one graph, see "Overriding the graph type" in Chapter 14.

Line

The line graph is the most common type of business graph. It connects each value in a series with a line. If there's more than one series, Quattro uses a separate line for each. A line graph plots values from left to right, in the order in which they appear in the spreadsheet.

A line graph makes it easy to see dips and rises in a set of numbers. For this reason, line graphs are often used to plot data over time, both to review patterns and predict trends.

Figure 13.5
A single series plotted on a
line graph

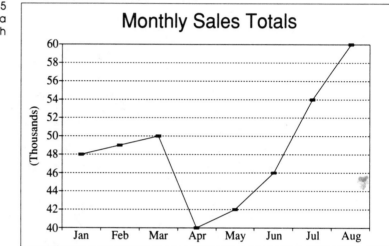

The preceding figure is a line graph showing monthly sales totals for 1989. Low spring sales and a rising trend are clearly shown.

By plotting two or more series in a line graph, you can compare different sets of data. The following figure shows the same information as the last, but with the sales figures for the previous year added. You can now see that the sales dip in spring is an expected trend, and in fact, the company is doing better this year than ever before.

Figure 13.6
A line graph with multiple
series

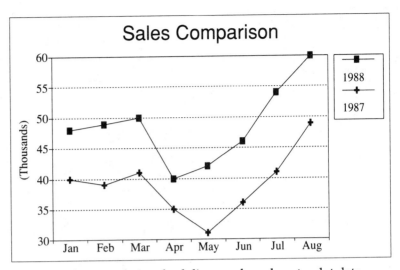

Initially, a line graph uses both lines and markers to plot data.
With the /Graph | Customize Series | Markers & Lines | Formats
command, you can specify using lines or markers only to
represent individual series or the entire graph (see "Changing
marker and line format" in Chapter 14).

Bar

A bar graph uses vertical bars, extending upward from the x-axis,
to indicate magnitude. Each bar represents a value in a series, and
Quattro determines each bar's height by that value, plotted
according to the scale given on the y-axis.

When you plot more than one series, the bars for each appear side
by side, and Quattro assigns each series a different fill pattern or
color. Quattro determines bar width by the number of values
plotted (the more values plotted, the narrower the bars), and by
the /Graph | Customize Series | Bar Width setting (see "Changing
bar width" in Chapter 14).

Bar graphs are usually used to compare the values of different
items at specific points in time. The following figure shows a bar
graph charting yearly sales for each region over five years. The
contrast between bar colors and patterns emphasizes the
difference between totals for each region.

Figure 13.7
A bar graph

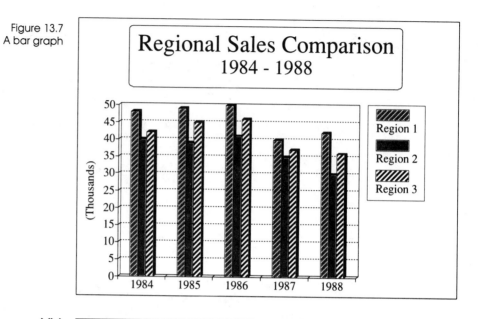

XY

An XY graph looks superficially like a line graph but is actually very different: It plots values against two numeric axes, rather than just the usual y-axis.

Usually, XY graphs are used to show the relationship between two or more blocks of data. For example, imagine a spreadsheet that shows units sold and advertising expenses over a six-month period. You could create an XY graph showing the progression of units sold in relation to advertising expenses by assigning units sold to the x-axis and advertising expenses to the y-axis.

The next figure shows such a graph. The x-axis shows how many units were sold, and Quattro automatically scales the y-axis to show advertising expenses. Each point represents both units sold and advertising spent for each month. The extent to which the plotted points lie in a straight line represents the degree of correlation between the two series. In this graph, you can see a clear correlation between advertising and sales.

Figure 13.8
Profits and advertising
expenses shown on an XY
graph

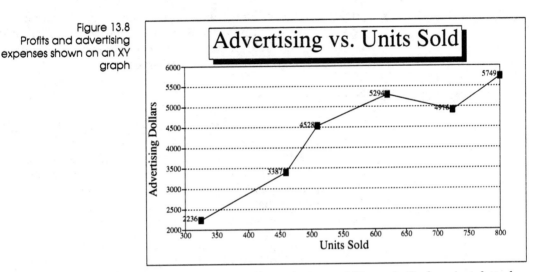

You can plot up to six series on an XY graph. Each series plotted shows the relationship between the values in the series and those on the x-axis. The following figure is the same as the previous one, but with two more factors added—training and promotion:

Figure 13.9
Three series plotted on an XY
graph

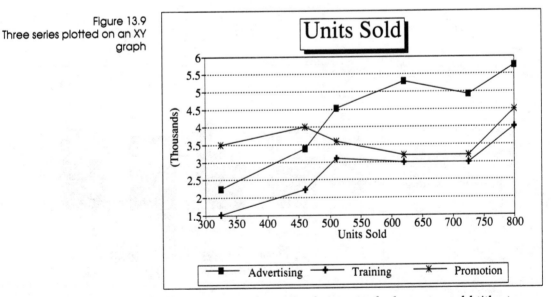

To define the information being graphed, you can add titles to both the x- and y-axes (see "Graph text" later in this chapter).

An XY graph uses lines only to show values. You can add markers to show the individual values in a series with the /Graph I Customize Series I Markers & Lines I Formats command (see "Changing marker and line format" in Chapter 14).

Stacked bar

A stacked bar graph uses bars to indicate values but, like an area graph (see "Area" later in this chapter), it stacks corresponding values of each series vertically, showing cumulative values. Quattro plots the first series on the bottom of the graph, and stacks each progressive series on top of the previous one. This shows not only the total reached by the combined values, but the relationship between each value and the whole.

The following figure shows the number of subscriptions sold each month for each of four regions. The top of each bar reflects the total number of subscriptions sold per month. By comparing the sizes of bar sections created by each series, you can see that, in general, subscription sales are highest in the Northeast and lowest in the South.

Figure 13.10
A stacked bar graph

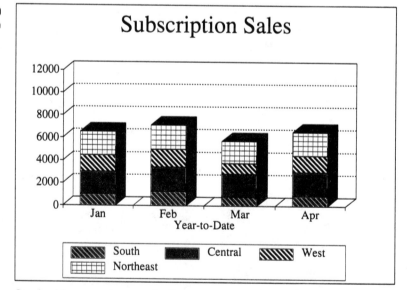

Stacked bar graphs are similar to area graphs in that they show cumulative totals, but they focus more on the individual points on the x-axis rather than showing collective trends.

Pie

A pie chart uses a circle, or *pie*, to show the relative contribution of each value to the whole.

Note   By its nature, a pie chart represents a single series, so be aware when creating pie charts that Quattro always uses the data in the first series. You can use a second series to explode, shade, or color the slices, in addition to the menu commands that perform those functions (see "Using a second series" in Chapter 14).

The following figure shows total expenses for 1989. It's clear that salaries are the largest expense.

Figure 13.11
A pie chart

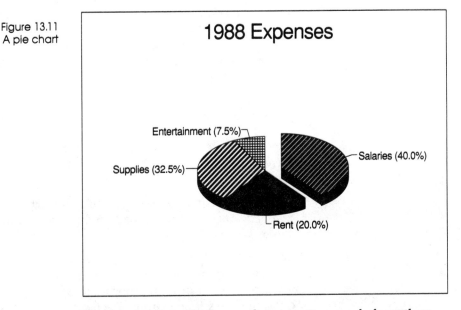

Quattro automatically figures the percentages and places them next to each slice. To add additional text, such as the labels describing the expense categories in the previous figure, use /Graph | Series | X-Axis Series (see "Labeling the x-axis" later in this chapter). You can further alter the appearance of a pie chart by "exploding" (pulling out) slices for emphasis or changing the color or pattern assigned to slices. You can also display the actual values instead of percentages. (See "Customizing a pie or column chart" in Chapter 14.)

Note A pie chart cannot display negative numbers. Quattro converts any negative values in the first series to positive.

If a pie chart appears oblong on your screen, you can adjust it with the /**O**ptions | **H**ardware | **S**creen | **A**spect Ratio command (see page 175).

Area

An area graph, like a line graph, uses lines to represent values. But, like a stacked bar graph, it plots cumulative rather than individual values. In other words, it plots the first series as usual along the x-axis, then stacks the second series on top of the first, so that the points graphed represent the total of the corresponding values from both series. It then places the third series on top of the first two, and so forth. The area beneath each line is filled with a different color or pattern to dramatize the difference between series.

Area graphs are often used to show how each series affects the performance of the whole over time. Although only the first line plotted is an accurate pattern (a dip in a further series might appear as a rise if values under it are high), the size of the area corresponding to each series represents its contribution to the whole.

The top line of an area graph not only shows the total of all values graphed, it also reveals the pattern created by averaging the values in each series.

The following figure is an area graph showing monthly sales for each of four divisions of a company. The top line shows total sales for all four. You can see that, even though sales for the southern division were very low in April, sales for the other three divisions were high enough to keep the graph from dipping that month.

Figure 13.12
An area graph

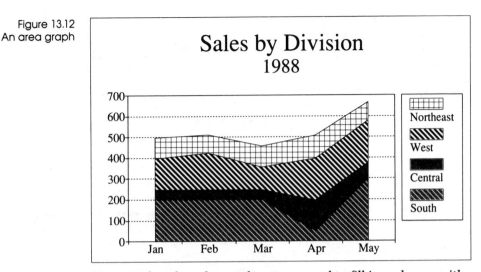

You can alter the colors and patterns used to fill in each area with the **C**olors and **P**atterns commands on the **/**Graph **| C**ustomize Series menu (see "Changing series display colors" in Chapter 14).

Rotated bar

A rotated bar graph is identical to a standard bar graph except that it reverses the positions of the x- and y-axes, extending the bars horizontally from left to right.

Like a standard bar graph, this graph type is used to compare and contrast values. The repositioning of axes is primarily a matter of presentation preference, although it does allow for longer x-axis labels.

The following figure shows a rotated bar graph that plots fund-raising figures. The left-to-right presentation adds a goal-oriented focus.

Figure 13.13
A rotated bar graph

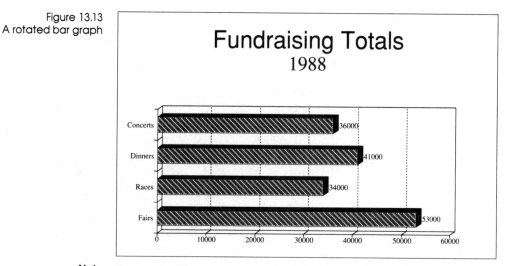

Fundraising Totals
1988

Note   For rotated bars, menu entries referring to the x-axis now refer to the vertical axis, and vice versa. For example, in a rotated bar graph, the y-axis title prints at the bottom of the screen.

Column

A column graph or *chart* is similar to a pie chart in that it shows the values in a single series as percentages of the whole. Instead of slicing up a circle, it stacks slices vertically on a rectangular column.

The main advantage of column graphs over pies is that column graphs allow more room to label individual sections. The following figure shows the same total business expenses as the pie chart shown previously, with section labels:

Figure 13.14
A column graph

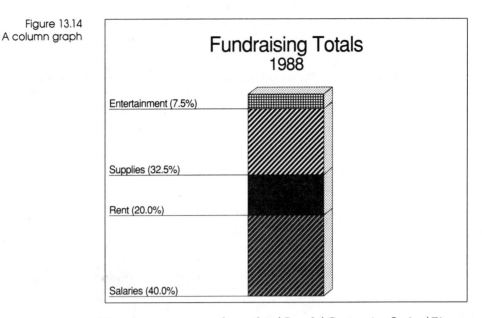

You can use commands on the /Graph | **Customize Series** | **Pies** menu to change how Quattro displays values in the column graph and to change colors and patterns used for each section of the column (see "Customizing a pie or column chart" in Chapter 14). You can also use a second series to change the color or pattern of the slices, in addition to the **Pies** menu commands that perform these functions (see "Using a second series" in Chapter 14).

Note   Like a pie chart, a column graph cannot display negative numbers. Quattro converts any negative values in the first series to positive.

High-low (open-close)

The usual purpose of high-low (open-close) graphs is to track daily stock prices. High-low graphs assume that you have two series: one showing the highest price a stock reached each day and one showing the lowest price. You may also have two other series: one showing opening price for each day and the other showing closing price.

A high-low graph uses the first two series to create a set of vertical lines—one for each pair of daily values. Quattro positions the top of each line to show the high daily value on the y-axis and the bottom shows the low value. If you assign third and fourth series (the opening and closing prices), Quattro uses them to place tick marks on the vertical lines: a line protruding left for the opening (third series) value and a line protruding right for the closing (fourth series) value.

You can also plot a fifth and sixth series on a high-low graph. If included, they produce horizontal lines, like those in a typical line graph, across the vertical lines. Use them to plot additional information, such as average daily price or standard deviation. If you prefer, you can display these series as bars instead of lines with the /Graph | Customize Series | Override Type command (see "Overriding the graph type" in Chapter 14).

The following figure shows a high-low graph tracking a stock's price over three years. It includes tick marks for opening and closing values.

Figure 13.15
A high-low graph

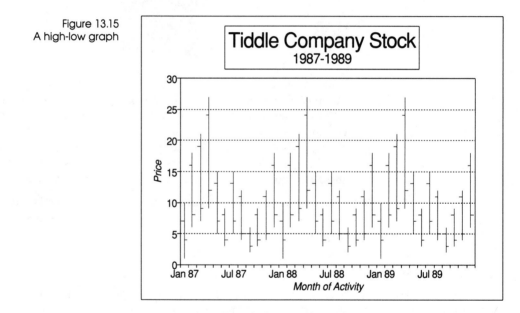

Another use for high-low graphs is to plot experimental data; for example, temperatures recorded over time. The vertical lines can show the high and low values recorded for each day. You could use the additional tick marks to represent average and median values. With experiments producing standard error values, the vertical lines could represent the range of values that fall within the experimental error.

Text

Text graphs really aren't graphs at all in the strict sense of the word; they're blank screens on which you can draw using Quattro's graph annotation tools. Described in detail in Chapter 15, the Annotator lets you add text (in various fonts and styles), as well as geometric shapes (including lines, arrows, rectangles, and ellipses). Applications for text graphs include "bulleted" presentation slides and organization charts.

The following figure shows a flow chart created with a text graph and graph annotation:

Figure 13.16
An annotated text graph

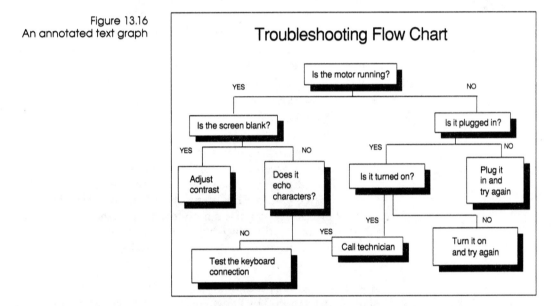

For more information on text graphs, see Chapter 15.

Choosing a graph type

The type of graph you choose usually depends on the analysis you want to perform. Think about what it is you want to illustrate. Total sales dollars for each division of a company? The number of products produced each month of a year? The ratio of personnel expense to other classes of expense? How hours worked affect productivity?

Certain types of graphs are best suited for plotting certain types of data:

- **Line graphs** are best for showing progression of values over a period of time—to track sales, for example. Use them to help illuminate patterns and trends over time.

- **Bar graphs** (including rotated bar) are good for comparing values of different items at specific points in time—for example, to contrast monthly commissions for each sales representative.

- **Stacked bar and area graphs** show the relationship between individual values and the total—for example, how total sales are divided between regions. Because area graphs use lines to track values, they better show the patterns created over time.

- **Pie and column charts** compare the individual values within a single series and show how they affect the whole—for example, how yearly expenses break down into categories. Use them to focus on the individual values in a single series.

- **XY graphs** plot values in one series against those in another—to show the relationship between salary and length of employment, for example.

- **High-low graphs** display vertical lines that represent the difference between corresponding values in two series. You can add tick marks to pinpoint values within the range created by the first two values. Though most often used in tracking daily stock prices, you can use a high-low graph whenever you want to compare the difference between pairs of values. If you use a third or fourth series to create tick marks, their values must fall between the corresponding values in the first two series.

If you don't specify a graph type, Quattro automatically creates a stacked bar graph. You can switch to a different graph type at any time. In fact, you'll probably want to experiment with different graph types to see how Quattro best displays your data.

To choose a graph type,

```
┌─ Graph Type ─┐
│ Line         │
│ Bar          │
│ XY           │
│ Stacked Bar  │
│ Pie          │
│ Area         │
│ Rotated Bar  │
│ Column       │
│ High-Low     │
│ Text         │
└──────────────┘
```

1. Choose /Graph | Graph Type. Quattro displays a menu of graph types.

   If your screen is in graphics mode (set with /Options | Display Mode), Quattro displays the graph type selections in a pictorial gallery.

2. Choose a graph type. If you've already assigned values to the graph, you can immediately choose View to see how the graph displays your data.

You can also use the /Graph | Customize Series | Override Type command to combine different graph types in one graph (see "Overriding the graph type" in Chapter 14).

 If you're using the 123-compatible menus, choose /Graph | Type.

Creating an instant graph

The easiest way to build a simple, unadorned graph is with the Fast Graph command. This command takes a block of data in your spreadsheet and divides it logically to create a graph. The way Quattro divides the data depends on the dimensions and contents of the block.

When a block contains more rows than columns, Quattro

- plots each column (up to six) as a single series
- creates x-axis labels using the labels in the first column (if it contains labels)
- creates a graph legend using the labels in the first row (if it contains labels)

When a block contains more columns than rows, Quattro

- plots each row (up to six) as a single series
- creates x-axis labels using the labels in the first row (if it contains labels)
- creates a graph legend using the labels in the first column (if it contains labels)

To create a fast graph,

1. Choose /Graph | Graph Type and choose the type of graph you want to create. If you don't do this, Quattro defaults to a stacked bar graph.
2. Choose /Graph | Fast Graph. Quattro prompts you for the block of data to graph.
3. Specify your spreadsheet data, either by pointing out the block or typing its coordinates. Include any headings for the columns or rows of values.

4. Quattro displays the graph on the screen. Press any key to return to the spreadsheet.

1-2-3

If you're using the 123-compatible menus, use the /Graph | Instant Graph command.

Caution! Blank columns and rows in your block of data can create series of zero values that throw off your graph. Delete them before you point out the block at the Fast Graph command prompt.

The following figure shows a block of spreadsheet data (A1..F5) that will become an instant graph. The block contains more columns than rows, so Quattro plots each row as a series. The first row of the block contains labels, so Quattro uses the labels in that row (B1..F1) to create x-axis labels. The first column of the block contains labels, so Quattro uses the labels in that column (A2..A5) to create a graph legend.

Figure 13.17
The spreadsheet block

```
 File  Edit  Style  Graph  Print  Database  Tools  Options  Window            ↑↓
 A1: [W15]                                                                       ?
        A           B       C       D       E       F       G
                                                                              ▯End
 1                 Jan     Feb     Mar     Apr     May                          ▲
                                                                              ◄ ►
 2   Southeast     100      10      40     120     150                          ▼
 3   Northeast      30      40      60     100     125
 4   West           70      35      40      60      80                        Esc
 5   Midwest        40      60      90     100     120
                                                                               ↵
 6   Total         240     145     230     380     475
 7                                                                            Del
 8
 9                                                                             @
10
11                                                                             5
12
13                                                                             6
14
15                                                                             7
16
 INSTANT.WQ1   [2]                                                          READY
```

The following figure shows the instant graph that Quattro created with the block of spreadsheet data shown in the previous figure. The graph type is stacked bar, the default.

Figure 13.18
The instant graph

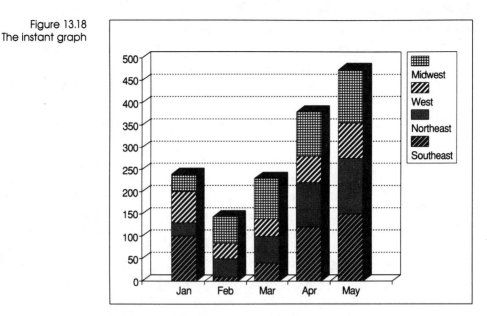

Fast Graph is a good way to begin a graph when the data is set up as Quattro expects it. You can then use other graph commands to elaborate on it: adding titles, repositioning the legend, rescaling an axis, and so on.

If your spreadsheet data isn't set up in the default manner—for example, if you want to plot columns of data and Fast Graph divides your data into rows—you can reach the same end with the following commands:

- Use /Graph I Series I Group to divide a block of values into up to six graph series (you specify whether it's divided by rows or columns), or assign each series individually with /Graph I Series commands (see page 338).

- Create a legend using the /Graph I Text I Legends command: Use text in your spreadsheet or type in your own (see page 346).

- Label the x-axis with spreadsheet text using the /Graph I Series I X-Axis Series command (see page 341).

Assigning values to a graph

The most important step in building a graph is telling Quattro just what numbers you want plotted. For most graph types, you can specify up to six sets, or *series*, of values with the /Graph | Series command. You'll also use this command to label the x-axis.

When you choose /Graph | Series, Quattro displays the **Series** menu.

```
===== Series =====

1st Series
2nd Series
3rd Series
4th Series
5th Series
6th Series
X-Axis Series
Group        ▶
Quit
```

- **1st-6th Series** let you specify up to six series from the current spreadsheet to plot on the graph. Quattro assigns each series a unique fill pattern, color, or marker symbol.
- **X-Axis Series** lets you specify a block of spreadsheet labels or values to display along the graph's x-axis as *tick labels*. These labels help define the data plotted. (For an XY graph, you use this command to provide scaling information for the x-axis.)
- **Group** lets you specify a block of spreadsheet values that Quattro will divide into separate series for the graph—either one column or one row per series.
- **Quit** returns you to the Graph menu.

If you're using the 123-compatible menus, you'll assign blocks of data to the first to sixth series in your graph with the **A-F** commands on the **Graph** menu. The /Graph | **X** command specifies the block of labels or values to use as x-axis labels.

Defining each series

In choosing which data to plot, keep the following points in mind:

- Any labels in a block you assign to a numbered series are translated into zeroes, which could throw off your graph. (You can use labels in the x-axis series, however.)
- There should be no blank cells within the series block.
- Although there is no limit to the number of values allowed in a series, the more values graphed, the more crowded the graph will be, and the more slowly it will display and print.
- You can assign up to six data series for every graph except for pie and column charts, which graph only a single series.
- When plotting more than one series, make sure each series has the same number of values.

The following figure shows a simple bar graph charting two series:

Figure 13.19
A bar graph with two series

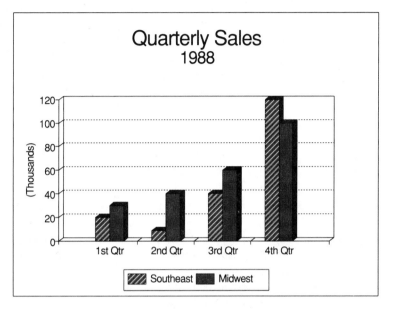

To define series for a graph:

1. Choose /Graph I Series. Quattro displays the **Series** menu.

2. Choose **1st** Series from the menu. The menu temporarily disappears and Quattro prompts you for a cell block. If any block was previously assigned, it appears as the default and is highlighted.

3. Enter the coordinates of the block containing the values you want to plot first. The easiest way to do this is by "pointing" out the block. Use the direction keys to move the cell selector to the first value you want to use. (If you're editing an existing series, you may need to unanchor the selector first by pressing *Backspace* or *Esc.*) Press the Period key (.) to anchor the selection. Use the direction keys to extend the selection until the entire block you want is highlighted. Then press *Enter.*

   To point out a block with a mouse, drag from one corner of the block to the opposite corner, then release.

4. Now, or at any time during the graph-building process, you can view the graph-in-progress by pressing *F10*, the Graph key. The graph fills the screen. To return to the **Graph** menu,

press any key (except the forward slash key, which activates the Graph Annotator).

5. If you want to plot more than one series, enter them in the same way: Choose **2nd Series** and assign a cell block; choose **3rd Series** and assign a cell block, and so on. You can assign up to six series. (Pie and column charts recognize only the first.)

6. You might want to try different graph types to see how they display this information. You can change the type with the /Graph | Graph Type command.

If you're using the 123-compatible menus, choose /Graph | **A** instead of /Graph | Series | **1st Series**, /Graph | **B** for /Graph | Series | **2st Series**, and so on.

Note The block you assign to a series doesn't have to be in the same spreadsheet you're creating the graph in. You can use linking to reference cells in another spreadsheet. If the spreadsheet's open, just choose /Graph | Series, then activate that spreadsheet window and point out the block. If it's not open, you can still reference it by entering the block coordinates preceded by the spreadsheet name (and directory if different) in square brackets; for example,

[\SALES\BUDGET]A4..A15

For details on how to work with more than one open spreadsheet, see Chapter 9, "Manipulating windows." For an example of creating a graph using data from different spreadsheets, see "Using links to build a graph" later in this chapter.

To clear a block assignment from a series without specifying a new block, choose /Graph | **Customize Series** | **Reset**, then choose that series from the displayed menu.

If you're using the 123-compatible menus, choose /Graph | **Reset**.

Assigning a series group

If the data you want to plot on a graph is stored in adjacent columns or rows of the spreadsheet, you'll find it faster to assign several series at once with the /Graph | Series | Group command. This command is similar to Fast Graph (see page 335), except that it doesn't assign x-axis labels or legends. Your data block must contain values only. It also gives you the option of dividing your block into columns or rows of data.

To assign series in a group,

1. Choose /Graph | Series | Group.

2. Choose **Columns** if each series is in a column, **Rows** if each is in a row. Quattro then prompts you for a block.

3. Specify the block containing the series group. Quattro carves the block into separate series: one series per column (if you choose **Column**) or one series per row (if you chose **Row**).

If you're using the 123-compatible menus, choose /Graph | **Group**.

The following figure shows how the **Group** command would break up a spreadsheet block into columns:

Figure 13.20
Dividing a block of columns
into separate series

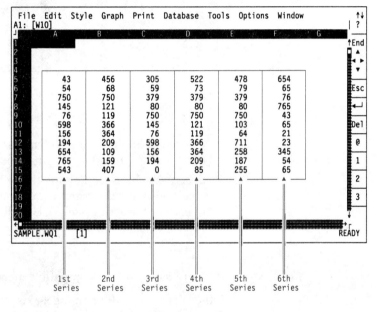

Labeling the x-axis

The x-axis is the horizontal line at the bottom of most graph types. Unlike the y-axis, it generally has no numeric meaning and is simply used to place labels, from left to right, in the order in which they appear in the spreadsheet. With the /Graph | Series | X-Axis Series command, you can use spreadsheet entries, either text or numeric, to label this axis as a way to identify the series plotted on it. The exception to this is XY graphs, which are discussed in the next section.

Figure 13.21 shows months as the x-axis labels on a bar graph.

Figure 13.21
X-axis tick labels

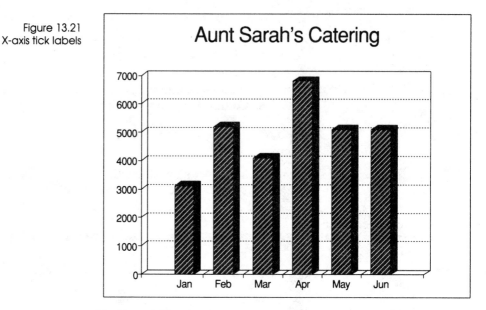

To assign tick labels to the x-axis,

1. Choose /**Graph** I **Series** I **X-Axis Series**. The menu disappears and Quattro prompts you for a block.

2. Specify the block containing the cells you want to serve as labels. Usually, these are row or column headings that pertain to each of the series plotted. Use either labels or values.

3. Press *V* to view the graph, then press any key to return to the menu.

If you're using the 123-compatible menus, choose /**Graph** I **X**.

If the labels don't all fit on the x-axis, they overlap each other. You can adjust the arrangement of tick labels with **X**-Axis menu commands (see "Adjusting ticks on the axis" in Chapter 14) or reduce the point size of labels with /**Graph** I **Text** I **Font** I **Data & Tick Labels** to fit more on the axis (see "Setting font options" later in this chapter).

XY graphs: The exception

In an XY graph, you assign numeric values to both the x- and y-axes. Quattro uses these values to scale each axis, then plots the relationship between the two sets of values on the graph. If you assign further series, Quattro plots them in relation to the x-axis values.

The following figure shows an XY graph plotting the relationship between employee age and salary. The highest salary is shown for age 57.

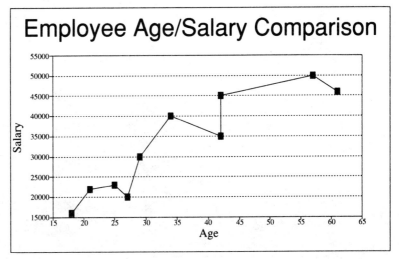

Figure 13.22
An XY graph showing age and salary of employees

To create an XY graph,

1. Choose /Graph I Series I **X**-Axis Series to assign values to the x-axis.

2. Choose /Graph I Series I **1st** Series to assign values to the y-axis. Use additional series commands (**2nd** through **6th**) to plot further values against the same x-axis.

1-2-3 If you're using the 123-compatible menus, choose /Graph I **X** to assign x-axis values and /Graph I **A-F** to assign y-axis values.

To help identify the graph, you'll probably want to add titles to both the x- and y-axes. Titles are discussed next.

Graph text

A few words go a long way in clarifying a graph. Quattro lets you add a main title, a subtitle, a title for each axis, and a legend. You can control the color, size, and font used for each area.

The following figure shows examples of each type of graph text:

Figure 13.23: Graph text

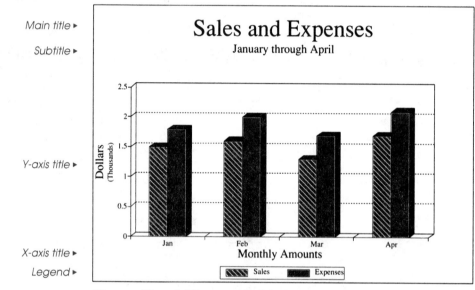

Choose / **Graph | Text** to display the **Text** menu.

- **1st Line** lets you specify the first line of the main title displayed above the graph.

- **2nd Line** lets you specify the second line of the main title. It is displayed below the first line of the title in smaller type.

- **X-Title** lets you specify text to be displayed beneath the x-axis.

- **Y-Title** lets you specify text to be displayed vertically to the left of the y-axis.

- **Secondary Y-Axis** lets you specify text to be displayed vertically to the right of a second y-axis.

- **Legends** lets you create a graph legend that defines the lines, markers, or fill patterns used to plot each series.

- **Font** lets you change the typeface used to display text in the graph, as well as the point size, color, and style (bold, italic, and underlined). See "Setting font options" later in this chapter.

■ **Quit** returns you to the Graph menu.

Use the /Graph | Text command to add text to your graph beyond what already exists in your spreadsheet.

To create x-axis labels, use the /Graph | Series | **X**-Axis Series command to specify a block of labels or values in your spreadsheet (see page 341).

To create data labels inside a graph, use the /Graph | Customize Series | Interior Labels command to specify a block of labels or values in your spreadsheet to appear in the graph as labels for the data points in each series (see "Labeling points on a graph" in Chapter 14).

The following sections describe how to enter titles and choose different fonts, sizes, colors, and styles for the titles, legends, and other graph text.

Creating titles

To add or change an existing title,

1. Choose /Graph | Text. Quattro displays the Text menu.
2. Choose the title line you want to add or change. 1st Line and 2nd Line display text above the graph; **X**-Title displays text below the x-axis; **Y**-Title displays text to the left of the y-axis, and **Secondary Y**-Axis displays text to the right of a second y-axis.
3. Quattro prompts you for the title's text, showing any previous entry as the default. Press *Esc* to erase a previous entry. Type in your new entry (up to 39 characters), or edit the existing one using the cursor-movement keys or *Backspace*.

Tip To use a cell entry as the title, type a backslash (\) followed by the cell's address. For example, \C4 enters whatever is written in cell C4.

To include any of Quattro's seven available bullet characters in your title, use the \bullet #\ syntax described on page 167. You can use bullets in any graph title except the y-axis or secondary y-axis.

To erase a title without replacing it, choose it from the Text menu, press *Esc*, and then press *Enter*.

1-2-3

If you're using the 123-compatible menus, choose / Graph |
Options | Titles | First and Second to define the first and second
lines of a graph, **X**-Axis and **Y**-Axis for the x- and y-axis titles
(respectively), and **2**nd Y-Axis for a secondary y-axis title.

Creating a legend

Like the legend of a road map, a graph legend is an area that
assists the viewer in understanding the meaning of the colors,
patterns, or markers the graph contains. Quattro can display a
legend either just beneath the graph or to the right as shown:

Figure 13.24
Graph legends

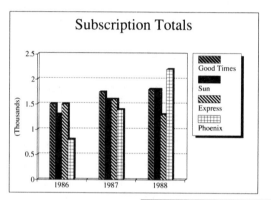

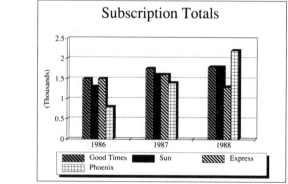

To add a legend to a graph,

1. Choose / Graph | Text | Legends. Quattro displays the Legends
   menu, which offers you six graph series to choose from and a
   Position command.

2. Choose the series you want to define in the legend. Quattro prompts you for legend text.

3. Enter text that helps define the series corresponding to that number. Although you can enter up to 19 characters per series definition, it's best to keep the legend text short to leave plenty of room for the graph.

4. Repeat the last two steps for each series plotted in your graph.

5. By default, Quattro positions the legend to the right of the graph. If you want to move it below the graph, choose Position. Quattro displays a list of positions.

6. Choose **Bottom**.

Note   To remove a legend from a graph without resetting the legend series commands, choose / Graph | Text | Legends | Position | None.

Tip   To use a cell entry as a legend, type a backslash (\) followed by the cell's address. For example, \C4 enters whatever is written in cell C4.

To include any of Quattro's seven available bullet characters in your legend, use the \bullet #\ syntax described on page 167.

1-2-3   If you're using the 123-compatible menus, choose / Graph | Options | Legend.

Setting font options

With the / Graph | Text | Font command, you can change the way Quattro displays text in the graph.

Choose / Graph | Text | Font to display a menu of graph text items.

- **1st Line** changes the font of the first line of the main graph title.

- **2nd Line** changes the font of the second line of the main graph title.

- **X-Title** changes the font of the x-axis title.

- **Y-Title** changes the font of the titles for the two y-axes (both primary and secondary).

- **Legends** changes the font of text in a graph legend.

- **Data & Tick Labels** changes the font of labels and scaling information.

- **Quit** returns you to the Text menu.

Choose any of these commands to display a menu that lists font options for that graph text item.

```
Typeface      ▶
Point Size    ▶
Style         ▶
Color         ▶
Quit
```

■ **Typeface** determines the typeface Quattro uses to display the text.

■ **Point Size** determines the size of the text in points.

■ **Style** lets you choose the bold or italic version of the typeface or underline the text. If you don't choose a style, Quattro assumes you want the regular version of the typeface.

■ **Color** lets you change the display color of the text.

■ **Quit** returns you to the Font menu.

The following sections describe each of these options.

Using a different typeface

Quattro initially displays all graph titles in the default typeface, which is Bitstream Swiss. Half the fun of designing a graph is experimenting with different fonts, and Quattro offers an array of typefaces to choose from. See Appendix F for details on the different typefaces available in Quattro.

Note   The Bitstream Dutch typeface is equivalent to Times Roman, and Bitstream Swiss is equivalent to Helvetica.

To change the font of a title or other graph text,

1. Choose / Graph I Text I Font. Quattro displays a menu of different graph text items.

2. Choose the text you want to change the typeface of. Quattro displays a menu of font options.

3. Choose Typeface. Quattro displays the Typeface menu.

4. Choose the typeface you want to use for the text.

5. To see how the typeface you chose looks in the graph, press the Graph key, *F10.* Then press any key (except /) to return to the menu.

1-2-3

If you're using the 123-compatible menus, choose / Graph I Options I Titles I Typeface, choose a text item, then choose Typeface.

Quattro supports the internal fonts of two popular series of printers: PostScript and LaserJet. If your installed printer is one of these, the Typeface menu lists special fonts available only for your printer under the standard Quattro typefaces. When you display a graph that uses these printer-specific fonts, Quattro substitutes a reasonable facsimile, but of course, uses the real thing for printing.

LaserJet LaserJet typefaces are preset to specific sizes and styles. If you choose one of these, you won't be able to change the title's point size or style.

Sometimes, when printing, previewing, or annotating your graph, Quattro displays a "Now building font" message. When you use a Bitstream font that Quattro hasn't used before, it needs to create a new font file before it can display or print the font. It may pause to do this when you display or print a graph. Once created, though, Quattro can access the font file without pausing. For more information on building font files, see Appendix F. You also have the option to turn off font building any time (see "Font options" in Chapter 7).

Important! In order to create a new Bitstream font file, Quattro requires 125K bytes of free memory.

Figure 6.3 on page 166 shows each standard Quattro typeface.

Changing text size
Quattro initially displays the first line of the main title in 36-point type, the subtitle in 24-point, and all other text in 18-point type. The size is measured in *points*, which is a unit of measurement used in typography. One point is equal to 1/72nd inch. You can set text to be from 6 to 72 points in size.

To change the size of a title,

1. Choose /Graph | Text | Font. Quattro displays a menu of different graph text items.
2. Choose the text you want to change the size of. Quattro displays a menu of font options.
3. Choose Point Size. Quattro displays a menu of point sizes.
4. Choose the size you want for the text.
5. To check your choice, press the Graph key, *F10*. Then press any key (except /) to return to the menu.

If you're using the 123-compatible menus, choose /Graph | Options | Titles | Typeface, choose a text item, then choose Point Size.

Setting the font style

The font you choose for a title or other graph text shows up in regular print. You can change this to display the font as bold, italic, or underlined with the Style command.

To display a font in bold, italic, or underlined,

1. Choose /Graph | Text | Font. Quattro displays a menu of different graph text items.

2. Choose the text you want to change the style of. Quattro displays a menu of font options.

3. Choose **Style** to display a menu of text style options.

4. Choose the style you want for the text.

   Note: Bold and Italic styles are available with only a few typefaces. Specifically, you can use bold only with Bitstream Dutch and Bitstream Swiss, and you can use italic only with Bitstream Dutch, Bitstream Swiss, Bitstream Courier, and Roman. You can specify using these styles with other typefaces, but they won't take effect in printing.

5. To see the effects of the style setting, press the Graph key, *F10.* Then press any key (except /) to return to the menu.

To return the font of a title or text to regular print, choose /Graph | Text | Font, choose the title or text you want to change, then choose **Style | Reset.**

If you're using the 123-compatible menus, choose /Graph | Options | Titles | Typeface, choose a text item, then choose **Style.**

The following figure shows titles in the Bitstream Dutch typeface using different style settings:

```
┌═══ Style ═══┐
│ Bold        │
│ Italic      │
│ Underlined  │
│ Reset       │
│ Quit        │
└─────────────┘
```

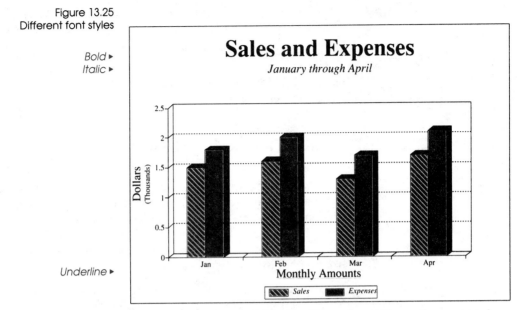

Figure 13.25
Different font styles

Bold ▶
Italic ▶

Underline ▶

Note Not all styles are available for all typefaces. If you choose a style that isn't available for the current typeface, Quattro uses the regular style for that typeface.

Changing the colors of graph text If you have a color screen, you can change the colors used to display titles and other graph text on the screen. If you don't have a color screen, you can use these same commands to affect how the graph will be printed on a color printer.

To change the color of graph titles and text,

1. Choose /Graph | Text | Font. Quattro displays a menu of different graph text items.

2. Choose the text you want to change the color of. Quattro displays a menu of font options.

3. Choose Color. Quattro displays a menu of all available colors. (If you have a color monitor and Quattro is set to graphics display mode, a gallery of actual colors appears. Otherwise, a menu of color names appears.)

4. Choose the color you want for the text.

5. To see the text in the new color, press the Graph key, *F10*. Then press any key (except /) to return to the menu.

If you're using the 123-compatible menus, choose /Graph |
Options | Titles | Typeface, choose a text item, then choose **Color.**

Caution! 123-compatible files with .WK1 and .WKS file-name extensions
don't include graph color information. If you save a graph with
such a file extension, it will revert back to default graph colors
when you retrieve it.

Storing and displaying named graphs

When you save a spreadsheet with the /File | Save or Save **As**
command, Quattro automatically saves the last graph you created
(the "current graph") with the file. You can associate and save
more than one graph with a spreadsheet with the /Graph | Name
command. All graphs you save with a file can be retrieved again
from within that same spreadsheet.

To name graphs and work with named graphs, use the /Graph |
Name command. This displays the **Name** menu.

- **Display** replaces the current graph with a named graph.
- **Create** names the current graph and stores it with the
  spreadsheet.
- **Erase** deletes a named graph.
- **Reset** deletes all named graphs with the current spreadsheet.
- **Slide** lets you display a named graph for a specified number of
  seconds.

The following sections describe how to use these commands to
name graphs, load named graphs, and erase named graphs. See
"Inserting graphs in the spreadsheet" later in this chapter for
details on how to insert named graphs in the spreadsheet.

Saving graph specifications

To save the current graph specifications,

1. Choose /Graph | Name | Create. Quattro prompts you for a
   name to give the graph and displays a list of existing graph
   names for that spreadsheet.
2. Enter a graph name (up to 15 characters) and press *Enter.* If the
   graph name already exists, Quattro overwrites it.

Quattro saves the graph settings under the name you specified. You can retrieve the settings any time the spreadsheet used to build the graph is active. The named graph reflects the data currently in the spreadsheet. You will also be able to insert the graph into the spreadsheet in which it was built.

Note Graphs saved with /Graph | Name | Create cannot be used with spreadsheets other than the one they were created in. (To save a graph for future printing, apart from a spreadsheet, use the /Print | Graph Print | Destination command. (See page 84 for more information.)

Displaying a named graph

You can use the **Display** command to make a previously saved graph the current graph. Because it overwrites the current graph settings with the saved settings, make sure that you save the current graph first if you might want to use it again.

To display a previously saved graph,

1. Choose /Graph | Name | Display. Quattro prompts you for the name of the graph you want to retrieve and displays a list of existing named graphs in your default directory.
2. Choose a graph name from the list or type in a name.

Quattro retrieves and displays the graph you asked for.

Another way to display a named graph, if it has been inserted in a spreadsheet, is to position the cursor in the block it occupies and press *F10*, the Graph key.

If you're using the 123-compatible menus, choose /Graph | Name | Use.

Deleting named graphs

When you don't expect to use a named graph again, it's a good idea to delete it to keep it from cluttering up both your disk and the list of named graphs; you'll also free up some memory.

To delete a single named graph,

1. Choose /Graph | Name | Erase.
2. Choose the graph name from the list or type in a name.

If you're using the 123-compatible menus, choose /Graph | Name | Delete.

To delete *all* saved graphs, choose /Graph | Name | Reset, then choose Yes from the displayed confirmation menu.

To remove the current graph settings, choose /Graph | Customize Series | Reset | Graph.

Slide shows

With the /Graph | Name | Slide command, you can tell Quattro to retrieve a series of named graphs and display them onscreen for a specified number of seconds, returning afterward to the spreadsheet.

To display a graph or a series of graphs momentarily,

1. Prepare two columns side by side in your spreadsheet, away from the main body of data. The first column contains the names of graphs you want to display for a timed interval, and the second column contains an integer that represents the duration of the interval in seconds for each graph. The second column is optional; Quattro defaults to a value of 0 (zero) if you omit the second column. A value of 0 means "Display the graph until any key is pressed."

2. Choose /Graph | Name | Slide. Quattro prompts for a slide show block.

3. Enter the block coordinates for the two columns you prepared in step 1.

Tip To create "title slides" to introduce graphs in a slide show, use the annotation tools to create a text graph. See "Annotating a text graph" in Chapter 15.

Inserting graphs in the spreadsheet

With the /Graph | Insert command, you can insert a named graph or the current graph directly into your spreadsheet. Just like graphs displayed full view, the inserted graph is "live"; as you change data affecting the graph, Quattro automatically redraws the graph to reflect the updated data.

Note In order to display graphs in a spreadsheet, you must have an EGA or VGA display adapter, and Quattro must be in graphics mode. Otherwise, the inserted graph appears as highlighting only.

If the graph you insert uses Bitstream fonts and /Options | Graphics Quality is set to Final, Quattro builds any new Bitstream fonts necessary for screen display. If /Options | Graphics Quality is set to Draft, Quattro uses Hershey fonts instead of building new Bitstream fonts. (See page 198 for more information about choosing font quality.)

To insert a named graph or the current graph in the spreadsheet,

1. If you have an EGA or VGA, make sure your screen is set to graphics mode: Choose /Options | Display Mode, then choose **B**, Graphics Mode. If you don't have an EGA or VGA, skip to the next step.

2. Choose /Graph | Insert. Quattro prompts you for the name of the graph to insert and displays a list of existing named graphs.

3. Specify the graph to insert. To insert the current graph, choose <Current Graph>. Quattro prompts you for the block in which to insert the graph.

4. Point out the block in the spreadsheet, or enter the coordinates of the block.

If you don't have an EGA or VGA or you are working in text mode, press F10 with your cursor in the inserted graph block to view the inserted graph.

Quattro draws the graph in the given block using a 4:3 height-to-width ratio; for example, four-inches wide by three-inches high. If the block you specified has different proportions, the graph floats in blank space. If you *don't* want Quattro to float the graph, but would rather the graph be stretched to fill the space, set the 4:3 Aspect command on the /Print | Graph Print | Layout menu to **No** (see page 105).

Note If the graph you insert has too many points for Quattro to fit into the space you allot, Quattro displays the error message "Graph too complex." If you adjust settings for an inserted graph and those adjustments cause an error, you'll see the general error message "Graph error" in the graph block. To see a more explicit message, put the cursor in the inserted graph block and press *F10* to display the graph full screen.

See Figure 4.7 on page 106 for an example of a graph inserted in a spreadsheet.

To print the inserted graph with the spreadsheet data, just include it in the block you specify for printing and be sure to choose /Print | Destination | Graphics Printer before you choose Spreadsheet Print.

See "How Quattro breaks pages" on page 94 for information about page breaks and inserted graphs. When you specify a block for the inserted graph, keep in mind that a block might not print with the same size or dimensions as the onscreen display. For example, with a standard printer that prints 6 lines per inch and 10 characters per inch, and Quattro's default font and column width, the block A1..A6 translates to about one square inch, although A1..A6 does not appear square onscreen.

An inserted graph isn't necessarily the graph Quattro displays when you press *F10* or choose /Graph | View. The current graph command settings may reflect an entirely different graph. To change the settings for the inserted graph, move the cell selector into the block containing the graph, then choose /Graph. The settings for the graph commands now reflect the inserted graph. The input line displays the graph name and whatever changes you make to those commands affect the inserted graph only.

It's possible to insert up to eight different graphs in a spreadsheet. The graph command settings reflect whatever graph contains the cell selector. If the cell selector isn't in one of the graphs, the commands reflect, as always, the current graph.

To remove a graph from a spreadsheet,

1. Choose /Graph | Hide. Quattro prompts you for the name of the graph you want to remove.
2. Quattro removes the graph from the spreadsheet, revealing blank cells underneath.

Using links to build a graph

As mentioned before, any series you plot on a graph doesn't have to be in the same spreadsheet in which you're building the graph. You can use linking to access series in any spreadsheet. In fact, you can build a graph with series from many different spreadsheets. Whether the supporting spreadsheets are loaded or not, the graph will plot accurate data that Quattro updates to reflect any changes to the spreadsheets.

Linking in a graph works just like linking elsewhere. To assign a series stored in a different spreadsheet, choose /Graph | Series, then move to that spreadsheet and point out the series block or type in the block preceded by the spreadsheet name in square brackets.

You can also link to labels in other spreadsheets. Suppose you wanted to title your graph with a label that is located in cell A1 of a spreadsheet called TAXES. First, create the link in any cell of the spreadsheet in which you are creating the graph. Find an empty cell (let's use B30 as an example) and type +[TAXES]A1. Then, choose /Graph | Text | 1st Line and enter \B30 at the "First title line" prompt. Quattro will use the contents of B30 as your graph title. Since B30 contains a link to a label in the other spreadsheet, Quattro will use that label to title your graph.

The following figure shows the Quattro screen divided up into four windows. Three of the windows contain sales spreadsheets for different divisions of the same company. The fourth window contains an inserted graph that uses links to plot sales totals from each of the spreadsheets. With a workspace set up like this, you can move in and out of each of the spreadsheets and make changes, seeing instantly the effects of those changes on the graph.

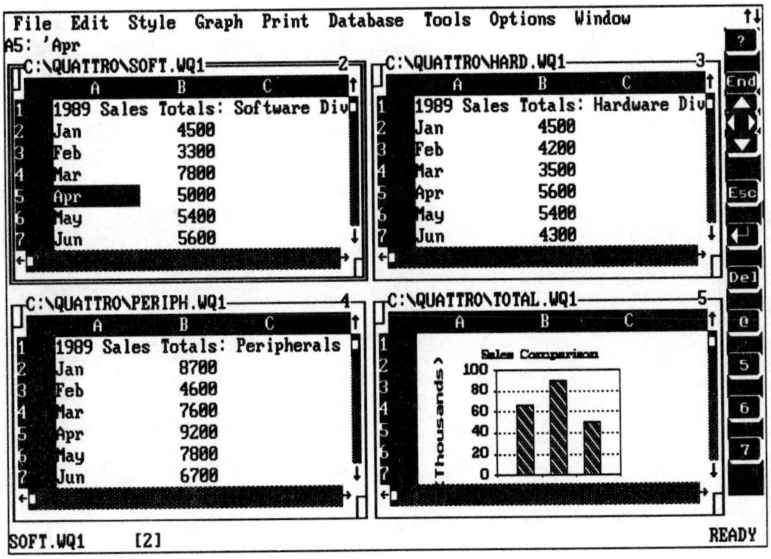

Figure 13.26
A graph linked to three spreadsheets

358

14

Customizing graphs

In the last chapter, you learned how to build a basic graph. Because a basic graph relies to a great extent on default values for various options, it may not look exactly like you want it to. Quattro offers a range of commands for fine-tuning graphs.

There are four commands on the Graph menu that deal with customizing graphs:

- **Customize Series** lets you change the colors, markers, or fill patterns used to represent each series in the graph. You can also use this command to display a series in a different graph type, label individual points in a graph, and change the bar width.
- **X-Axis** lets you adjust the scale and display of the x-axis.
- **Y-Axis** lets you adjust the scale and display of both the primary and secondary y-axes.
- **Overall** lets you add or remove the three-dimensional graph effect, adjust grids, and change colors of the overall graph.

This chapter describes how to use each of these commands to create a fully customized business graph. The next chapter, "Annotating your graph," describes how to use annotation tools to add text, arrows, lines, and other shapes to your graph.

Customizing series display

Quattro automatically assigns each series in your graph a unique color as well as a fill pattern (for bar graphs) or marker symbol (for line graphs). You can change the colors, patterns, and symbols used with commands on the **Customize Series** menu. You can also add interior labels to define specific points in a graph, and assign an "override graph type" to a series to display it differently.

Choose /**Graph** | **Customize Series** to display the **Customize Series** menu.

```
┌─ Customize Series ─┐
│                    │
│ Colors           ▶ │
│ Fill Patterns    ▶ │
│ Markers & Lines  ▶ │
│ Bar Width          │
│                    │
│ Interior Labels  ▶ │
│ Override Type    ▶ │
│ Y-Axis           ▶ │
│ Pies             ▶ │
│ Update             │
│ Reset            ▶ │
│ Quit               │
└────────────────────┘
```

- **Colors** lets you change the color of a series.

- **Fill Patterns** lets you change the patterns for each series on a bar or area graph.

- **Markers & Lines** lets you change the style of lines and marker symbols for each series on a line or XY graph. It also lets you display a series without markers, with markers only (no lines), or with neither.

- **Bar Width** allows you to adjust the width of the bars in bar, stacked bar, and rotated bar graphs.

- **Interior Labels** lets you use spreadsheet entries to label individual points in a graph. Quattro places these labels either centered over, above, below, to the right of, or to the left of each data point on a line graph (unlike the x-axis labels, which always appear beneath the x-axis). On a bar graph, a label always appears above the top of the bar.

- **Override Type** lets you assign a specific type of graph to a given series. It overrides the graph type chosen with the /**Graph** | **Graph Type** command.

- **Y-Axis** lets you plot a series using a second y-axis.

- **Pies** lets you change the fill pattern or color for each slice of a pie chart or each section of a column chart. You can also explode specific pie slices and display percentages, currency, or actual values next to each pie slice or column section.

- **Update** saves any changes you have made to general graph settings, like graph type or outlines, as the new defaults.

■ **Reset** lets you remove one or more series from a graph by resetting its spreadsheet block assignment. This also erases any customization settings assigned to the series. If you reset the entire graph, Quattro returns general graph commands to their last saved defaults.

■ **Quit** returns you to the **Graph** menu.

Changing series display colors

By default, Quattro assigns each series a different color. If you like, you can change the color associated with a series with the /Graph I Customize Series I Colors command:

1. Choose /Graph I Customize Series I Colors. Quattro displays a menu of the six series and their current color assignments. Press the Expand key (+) if you don't see the current assignments.

2. Choose the series for which you want to assign a new color. A menu appears that lists the color options available. The current color for that series is highlighted. (If your screen is set to graphics with the /Options I Display Mode command, Quattro displays a pictorial gallery of colors instead of a menu.)

On a monochrome display, all non-black colors appear white.

3. Choose the color you want to represent the series. Quattro returns to the menu of graph series.

4. If you want to change the colors of other series, choose that series, then choose the color you want for it.

1-2-3

If you're using the 123-compatible menus, choose /Graph I Options I Range Customize I Colors.

To make the changed series color assignments the new defaults, choose /Graph I Customize Series I Update.

Note   123-compatible files with .WK1 and .WKS file-name extensions don't include graph color information. If you save a graph with such a file extension, it will revert back to default graph colors when you retrieve it.

For more information about the colors available with different screen modes, see page 175.

Changing fill pattern

In bar graphs, Quattro fills all bars in a series with the same pattern; this helps identify the series each bar belongs to.

You can change the fill pattern for each series with the **Fill Patterns** command:

```
┌─ Fill Patterns ─┐
│ A - Empty        │
│ B - Filled       │
│ C - - - - - -    │
│ D - Lt ///       │
│ E - Heavy //     │
│ F - Lt \\\       │
│ G - Heavy \\     │
│ H - +++++        │
│ I - Crosshatch   │
│ J - Hatch        │
│ K - Light Dots   │
│ L - Heavy Dots   │
│ M - Basketweave  │
│ N - Bricks       │
│ O - Cobblestones │
│ P - Stitch       │
└─────────────────┘
```

1. Choose /**Graph** I **Customize Series** I **Fill Patterns**. Quattro displays a menu of the six series and their current fill pattern assignments. Press the Expand key (+) if you don't see the current assignments.

2. Choose the series for which you want to change the fill pattern. Quattro displays a menu of available patterns. The current fill pattern for that series is highlighted.

   If your text screen is set to graphics (with the /**Options** I **Display Mode** command), Quattro displays a gallery of fill patterns instead of a menu.

3. Choose the fill pattern you want to represent the series. Quattro returns to the menu of graph series.

4. If you want to change the fill patterns used for another series, choose it, then choose the pattern you want for it.

To change the patterns Quattro uses for slices of a pie chart (or sections of a column graph), use the /**Graph** I **Customize Series** I **Pies** I **Patterns** command (see "Changing fill patterns for slices" later in this chapter).

 If you're using the 123-compatible menus, choose /**Graph** I **Options** I **Range Customize** I **Fill Patterns**.

To make the changed fill pattern settings the new defaults, choose /**Graph** I **Customize Series** I **Update**.

Customizing markers and lines

Quattro uses *markers* to indicate individual data points in a line or XY graph and connects the points with *lines*. For each series, it uses a different marker symbol and a different type of line. You can customize both markers and lines with the /**Graph** I **Customize Series** I **Markers & Lines** command.

- **Line Styles** lets you change the pattern used in the lines of line graphs.
- **Markers** lets you change the marker symbol used for each series plotted.
- **Formats** specifies whether to display both lines and markers, markers only, lines only, or neither.
- **Quit** returns you to the **C**ustomize Series menu.

Changing line styles

Quattro uses different styles of lines (solid, dashed, and so forth) to differentiate between series in a line or XY graph. If you like, you can change the line style assigned to each series.

To change line style for a series,

1. Choose /**G**raph I **C**ustomize Series I **M**arkers & Lines.
2. Choose Line Styles. Quattro displays a menu of the six series and their current line style assignments. Press the Expand key (+) if you don't see the current assignments.

```
┌══ Line Styles ══┐
│ Solid           │
│ Dotted          │
│ Centered        │
│ Dashed          │
│ Heavy Solid     │
│ Heavy Dotted    │
│ Heavy Centered  │
│ Heavy Dashed    │
└─────────────────┘
```

3. Choose the series you want to change line styles for. Quattro displays a menu of available styles. The current line style for that series is highlighted.

   If your screen display mode is set to graphics (with /**O**ptions I Display Mode), Quattro displays a pictorial gallery of line styles instead of a menu.

4. Choose the line style you want to represent the series. Quattro returns to the menu of graph series.
5. If you want to change the line style used for another series, choose that series, then choose the line style you want for it.

1-2-3 If you're using the 123-compatible menus, choose /**G**raph I **O**ptions I **F**ormat I **L**ine Styles.

To make the changed line style setting the new default, choose /**G**raph I **C**ustomize Series I **U**pdate.

Changing the marker symbols

If you don't like the marker Quattro uses to indicate a series, you can change it. To change marker symbols for a graph,

1. Choose /**G**raph I **C**ustomize Series I **M**arkers & Lines.
2. Choose Markers. Quattro displays a menu of the six series and their current marker symbol assignments. Press the Expand key (+) if you don't see the current assignments.

```
┌─────── Markers ───────┐
│                       │
│ A - Filled Square     │
│ B - Plus              │
│ C - Asterisk          │
│ D - Empty Square      │
│ E - X                 │
│ F - Filled Triangle   │
│ G - Hourglass         │
│ H - Square with X     │
│ I - Vertical Line     │
│ J - Horizontal Line   │
│                       │
└───────────────────────┘
```

3. Choose the series for which you want to assign a new marker. Quattro displays a menu of available marker symbols. The current marker for that series is highlighted.

   If your screen display mode is set to graphics (with /Options | Display Mode), Quattro displays a pictorial gallery of marker symbols instead of a menu.

4. Choose the marker you want to represent the series. Quattro returns to the menu of graph series.

5. If you want to change the marker symbol used for another series, choose it, then choose the marker you want for it.

1-2-3 If you're using the 123-compatible menus, choose /Graph | Options | Format | Markers.

To make the changed marker symbol setting the new default, choose /Graph | Customize Series | Update.

Changing marker and line format

The /Graph | Customize Series | Markers & Lines | Formats command lets you change how Quattro displays lines and markers in a line or XY graph. When you choose this command, Quattro displays a menu of the six graph series plus a Graph command to change the entire graph. When you choose any option, Quattro displays the Formats menu:

```
┌─ Formats ─┐
│           │
│ Lines     │
│ Symbols   │
│ Both      │
│ Neither   │
│           │
└───────────┘
```

■ **Lines** removes data point markers from a line or XY graph. This creates a cleaner graph that focuses on the pattern created by the values rather than the values themselves.

■ **Symbols** uses markers to indicate data points, but doesn't connect the markers with lines. The absence of lines makes it easier to view values that are not in any specific order and sometimes reveals interesting groupings of data.

■ **Both** is the default. It plots data using both markers to show individual values and lines to connect all values in a series.

■ **Neither** displays neither lines nor symbols to indicate a series. It's a good way to temporarily remove a series from a graph without having to respecify the series block to bring it back. You can also use this option in conjunction with interior labels to plot a series with labels instead of markers or lines. (See "Labeling points on a graph" later in this chapter.)

To change marker and line format in your graph,

1. Choose /Graph | Customize Series | Markers & Lines.

2. Choose Formats.

3. Choose the series you want to change the format of or **Graph** to change the entire graph.

4. Choose **Lines**, **Symbols**, **Both**, or **Neither**.

If you're using the 123-compatible menus, choose / **Graph** I **Options** I **Format** I **A-F** or **Graph** for the entire series.

To make the changed marker and line format setting the new default, choose / **Graph** I **Customize Series** I **Update**.

The following figure shows a line graph that plots three series. The first series is set to display in both lines and markers. The second shows markers only, and the third shows only lines.

Figure 14.1
A line graph with different
marker and line formats

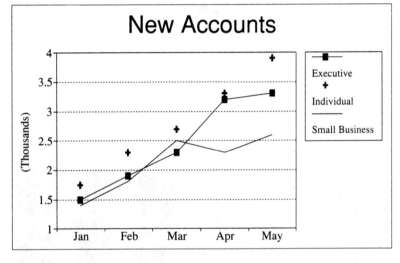

Changing bar width

When Quattro draws a bar graph, it divides up the amount of space on the x-axis evenly between the bars and adjusts the bar width accordingly. So the more values you plot, the less space Quattro allows for each bar.

Initially, Quattro uses 60 percent of the allotted axes space to actually draw the bar. The other 40 percent is left blank, giving a fairly wide space between bars. In other words, if the bars are 6 millimeters wide, Quattro leaves 4 millimeters of space between each bar.

You can adjust the percentage of space Quattro uses to calculate bar width with the **Bar Width** command:

1. Choose /Graph I **Customize Series** I **Bar Width**.
2. Quattro prompts you for a percentage.
3. Enter any number between 20 and 90. The larger the number, the wider the bars will be.

1-2-3 If you're using the 123-compatible menus, choose /Graph I **Options** I **Range Customize** I **Bar Width**.

To make the changed bar width setting the new default, choose /Graph I **Customize Series** I **Update**.

Labeling points on a graph

The Interior Labels command lets you use data in your spreadsheet to label the individual points on a graph. Figure 14.2 shows a graph with interior labels added to the second series.

Figure 14.2
Interior labels help clarify a graph

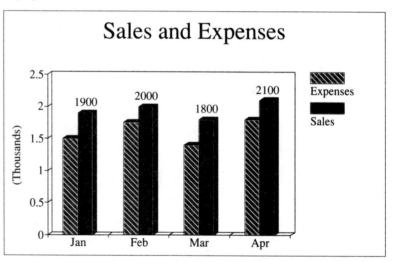

To label points on a graph,

1. Choose /Graph I **Customize Series** I **Interior Labels**. Quattro displays a menu of six graph series.
2. Choose the series for which you want to assign labels. Quattro prompts you for a cell block. Specify the cells you want to use to label the data points.

Position

Center
Left
Above
Right
Below
None

3. Quattro displays a menu of positions for the labels.

4. Choose the option that best suits your graph. Center places the labels directly on the points graphed (except on bar graphs, in which they are placed above the bars). None removes the labels from display. You can then redisplay them without having to redefine the source.

5. To see the labels displayed in the graph, press *F10*. To then return to the menu, press any key except the forward slash (/).

The cells you specify as interior labels should reflect the values entered in that series. The block can contain either values or labels. To display the exact value of the point (as done in Figure 14.2), use the same block you assigned to the series.

1-2-3

If you're using the 123-compatible menus, choose / **Graph** I **Options** I **Data Labels**, choose the series letter, then specify the spreadsheet data to label this series and the position for the labels.

Note Interior labels will not appear on area, pie, or column graphs. On bar graphs, interior labels always appear above the bars. On rotated bar graphs, the labels always appear to the right. On stacked bar graphs, only labels for the last (top) series are shown.

Overriding the graph type

By combining lines and bars in a graph, you can call attention to one series. For example, the following figure shows two series graphed as lines, and a third graphed as bars:

Figure 14.3
A graph with combined
graph types

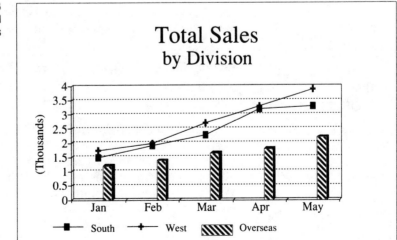

Combined graph types work best when the values in each series graphed represent different types of information and do not overlap much.

To override the existing graph type for an individual series,

1. Choose /Graph | Graph Type and choose one of the graph types that can be overriden: Line, Bar, or XY. Quattro uses the graph type you choose as the default for any series not assigned another type.

2. Choose /Graph | Customize Series | Override Type. Quattro displays a menu of six graph series.

3. Choose the series you want to assign an overriding graph type to. Quattro displays the Override Type menu for that series.

```
┌─ #th Series ─┐
│              │
│ Default      │
│ Bar          │
│ Line         │
│              │
└──────────────┘
```

4. If the overall graph type is bar, choose Line to plot the series with a line. If the overall type is line, choose Bar to plot the series as bars.

5. Press *F10* if you want to see how the combined types look.

6. Repeat the procedure as necessary to assign overriding graph types to other series. Quattro displays any series without an override graph type in the type originally chosen with the /Graph | Graph Type command.

Note   When combining graph types, try to display the series with the lowest range of values as bars. Otherwise, the bars will cross over the lines and make it harder to read the graph.

To reset a series so that it displays in the overall graph type, choose /Graph | Customize Series | Override Type, choose the series number, then choose Default.

1-2-3   If you're using the 123-compatible menus, choose /Graph | Options | Range Customize | Override Type.

Plotting a series on a second y-axis

Normally, the data points from each series in a graph are positioned relative to the y-axis. Occasionally it's useful to compare different series against two different axes; for example, if you're comparing two series with a wide difference in magnitude. With the /Graph | Customize Series | Y-Axis command, you can create a second y-axis to the right of a line, bar, or XY graph and use that axis to plot some of the graph.

To plot a series on a second y-axis,

1. Choose /Graph | Customize Series | Y-Axis. Quattro displays a menu of six possible graph series.
2. Choose the series you want to plot on a second y-axis. Quattro displays a menu with two choices: **Primary Y-Axis** and **Secondary Y-Axis**.
3. Choose **Secondary Y-Axis**. Quattro creates a separate y-axis to the right of the graph and bases its scale solely on the values within that series.
4. If there are other series you want to plot on the second y-axis, repeat the procedure as necessary for those series. Each time you assign another series to the second y-axis, Quattro rescales the axis to include values in that series. Quattro plots any series not assigned to the secondary y-axis on the primary y-axis.
5. Press *F10* if you want to see how the graph looks with the new axis.

To plot a series you've assigned to the second y-axis back on the first y-axis, choose /Graph | Customize Series | Y-Axis, choose the series number, then choose **Primary Y-Axis**.

If you're using the 123-compatible menus, choose /Graph | **Options** | **Range Customize** | **Y-Axis**.

Once you've created a second y-axis, you can change its format and scale with the /Graph | Y-Axis | 2nd Y-Axis command, just as you use /Graph | Y-Axis to format and scale the primary y-axis (see "Scaling and formatting an axis" later in this chapter for details).

The following figure compares monthly profit with gross sales. Because gross sales values are so much higher than profit figures, they're plotted on a secondary y-axis. This allows you to view both sets of figures in the same graph and compare the monthly progress of each.

Figure 14.4
A graph with two y-axes

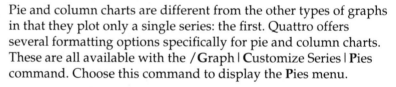

Customizing a pie or column chart

Pie and column charts are different from the other types of graphs in that they plot only a single series: the first. Quattro offers several formatting options specifically for pie and column charts. These are all available with the /Graph | Customize Series | Pies command. Choose this command to display the Pies menu.

```
═══ Pies ═══
Label Format  ►
Explode       ►
Patterns      ►
Colors        ►
Tick Marks    ►
Quit
```

- **Label Format** specifies the display format for labeling pie or column slices.

- **Explode** lets you pull out, or *explode*, one or more specific slices of the pie. This command is for pie charts only.

- **Patterns** specifies the fill patterns for each pie or column slice.

- **Colors** specifies the colors for each pie or column slice.

- **Tick Marks** lets you remove tick marks (lines connecting labels to slices) from a pie or column chart, or return them if they've been removed.

- **Quit** returns you to the **Customize Series** menu.

Note If you have a second series assigned, it may affect the colors, patterns, and explosion of pie or column slices (see "Using a second series" later in this chapter). If you don't want this to happen, remove the second series assignment with /Graph | Customize Series | Reset.

The following sections describe these options for pie and column charts.

Changing label format   By default, Quattro labels each slice of a pie or column chart with the percentage that section contributes to the whole. (If x-axis tick labels are assigned, these appear next to the percentages. See the next figure.)

Figure 14.5
A pie chart showing
percentages

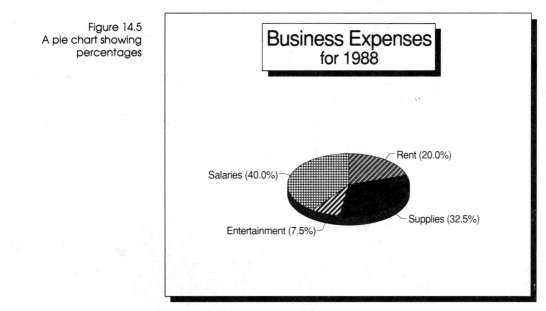

To change the format of these labels,

1. Choose /**Graph** I **Customize Series** I **Pies** I **Label Format**. Quattro displays the Label Format menu.

- **Value** displays the cell entries exactly as shown in the spreadsheet.
- **%** shows the percentage of each value in relation to the whole pie or column.
- **$** shows the spreadsheet values preceded by a dollar sign.
- **None** removes the labels from the chart entirely.

2. Specify the format you want to use. The Label Format command does not affect labels assigned to the chart with the /**Graph** I **Series** I **X-Axis Series** command. If assigned, these appear alongside the other labels. To display both spreadsheet values and percentages, specify the spreadsheet values with

the /**Graph** I **Series** I **X-Axis Series** command and leave the
Label Format command set to %.

 If you're using the 123-compatible menus, choose /**Graph** I
Options I **Range** Customize I **Pies** I **Label Format**.

To make the changed label format setting the new default, choose
/**Graph** I **Customize Series** I **Update**.

Exploding pie slices There may be one or more slices of your pie chart to which you'd
like to draw attention. You can do this by "exploding" individual
slices. This pulls the slice slightly away from the center. The
following figure shows a pie chart with two slices exploded:

Figure 14.6
A pie chart with exploded
slices

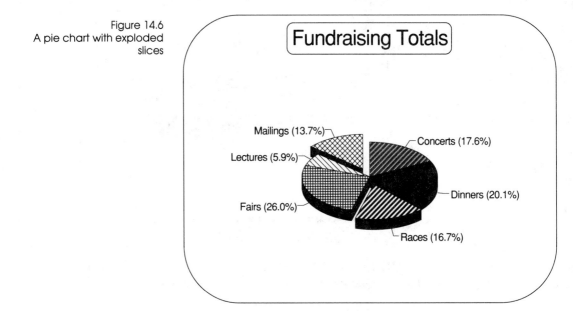

To explode pie slices,

1. Choose /**Graph** I **Customize Series** I **Pies** I **Explode**. Quattro
   displays the Explode menu, which lists nine slices.
2. Choose the slice you want to explode. The first slice begins at
   12:00 (straight up) and proceeds clockwise. Quattro displays
   two options: **Explode** and **Don't Explode**.
3. Choose **Explode** to pull the slice away from the pie.
4. Repeat the last two steps for any other slices you want to
   explode.

To return a slice to its original position, choose /Graph |
Customize Series | Pies | Explode, choose the slice number, then
choose **Don't Explode**.

If you're using the 123-compatible menus, choose /Graph |
Options | **Range Customize** | **Pies** | **Explode**.

You can also explode pie slices the way Lotus 1-2-3 does, by
entering 100 (or 101 through 107) in the corresponding slot in the
second series (see "Using a second series" later in this chapter).

Changing fill patterns for slices

By default, Quattro assigns a pattern to each slice of a pie or
column chart, but you can change the pattern of any slice in the
chart.

To change the patterns used for pie or column slices,

1. Choose /Graph | Customize Series | Pies | Patterns. Quattro
   displays a menu of nine slices.
2. Choose the slice you want to change the pattern of. If your pie
   or column chart contains more than nine slices, Quattro
   repeats the patterns. In other words, slice 10 will have the
   same pattern as slice 1, slice 11 will be the same as 2, and so
   on. Quattro displays a menu of available fill patterns.

   If your text screen is set to graphics (with the /Options |
   Display Mode command) and you have a color monitor,
   Quattro displays a pictorial gallery of fill patterns instead of a
   menu.
3. Choose the pattern you want to fill the slice with. The menu or
   gallery disappears.
4. If you want to change the patterns of other slices, choose the
   corresponding slice commands and choose new patterns for
   each.

If you're using the 123-compatible menus, choose /Graph |
Options | **Range Customize** | **Pies** | **Patterns**.

You can also change the color and pattern of pie slices the way
Lotus 1-2-3 does, by entering numbers between 0 and 8 in a
second series block (see "Using a second series" later in this
chapter).

To make the changed slice fill pattern assignments the new
defaults, choose /Graph | Customize Series | Update.

Changing the color of slices

Quattro also assigns different colors to the individual slices of a pie or column chart. You can change the color assigned to any slice in your pie or column chart:

1. Choose /**Graph** | **Customize Series** | **Pies** | **Colors**. Quattro displays a menu of nine slices.

2. Choose the slice you want to change the color of. If your pie or column chart contains more than nine slices, Quattro repeats the colors. In other words, slice 10 will have the same color as slice 1, and so on. Quattro displays a menu of available colors.

   If your screen is set to graphics (with the /**Options** | **Display Mode** command) and you have a color monitor, Quattro displays a pictorial gallery of colors instead of a menu.

3. Choose the color you want to assign to the slice.

4. If you want to change the colors of other slices, choose the corresponding slice commands and choose new colors for each.

To make the changed slice color assignments the new defaults, choose /**Graph** | **Customize Series** | **Update**.

To change the color of other parts of the chart, such as the background, slice outlines, or text, use /**Graph** | **Overall** | **Background Color**, /**Graph** | **Overall** | **Grid** | **Grid Color**, or /**Graph** | **Text** | **Font** | (pick text item) | **Color** (page 351). See "Changing graph background color" and "Changing grid color" later in this chapter.

1-2-3

If you're using the 123-compatible menus, choose /**Graph** | **Options** | **Range Customize** | **Pies** | **Colors**. Also, 123-compatible files with .WK1 and .WKS file-name extensions don't include graph color information. If you save a graph with such a file extension, it reverts back to default graph colors when you retrieve it.

You can also change the color and pattern of pie slices the way Lotus 1-2-3 does, by entering numbers between 0 and 8 in a second series block (see the next section).

User's Guide

Using a second series

In addition to using the /Graph | Customize Series | Pies commands to explode, color, and fill individual slices, you can use spreadsheet values to perform these functions. If a pie chart contains an active second series (assigned with /Graph | Series | 2nd Series), then the value in each cell of the second series controls the display of each corresponding slice in the first series. You can customize column charts the same way, except for exploding slices, which works only on pie charts.

A value of 0 through 8 determines the color and pattern Quattro assigns to the slice. For example, if the second value in the second series is 5, then the second slice will display with the pattern and color determined by the sixth pick on the /Graph | Customize Series | Pie | Patterns and Colors menus, respectively. (By default, this is cross-hatched magenta.)

Note that the order of the patterns on Quattro's **Patterns** menu is not the same as the order of Lotus 1-2-3 patterns 1-7.

Exploding a slice requires adding 100 to the pattern/color value. For example, consider this set of values for series 2.

0 4 2 107 3

The fourth wedge of this five-slice pie will be exploded; the colors and patterns used for each slice will be the first, fifth, third, eighth, and fourth picks, respectively, on the /Graph | Customize Series | Pies | Colors and Patterns menus.

These second series values "wrap" every nine counts; that is, a value of 9 has the effect of a 0, 10 has the effect of 1, 11 is the same as 2, and so on. Similarly, 109 equals 100, 110 equals 101, and so on. Using the second series this way lets you explode more then nine slices of a pie chart. In addition, it's possible to use formulas that cause a given slice to take on a certain color only when some other criteria are met.

Caution!

Even if you don't intend to use this feature, be aware of the effect of the second series on pie and column charts, especially when you change graph types, because the accidental application of random values to slice color and pattern assignment is seldom pleasing.

Removing tick marks

By default, Quattro draws tick marks from each slice of a pie or column chart to its label. If your chart contains only a handful of slices, chances are it's pretty clear which label defines which slice. If you prefer, you can remove the tick marks with the **Tick Marks** command:

1. Choose /**Graph** I **Customize Series** I **Pies** I **Tick Marks**.
2. Choose **No**.

To return the tick marks to the chart, set this command back to **Yes**.

If you're using the 123-compatible menus, choose /**Graph** I **Options** I **Range** Customize I **Pies** I **Tick Marks**.

If you want the changed tick mark setting to be the new default, choose /**Graph** I **Customize Series** I **Update**.

Updating graph defaults

The **Update** command on the **Customize Series** menu saves the current general graph settings as the new defaults. General graph settings include default background color, outline options, color and fill pattern assignments for series 1-6 and pie/column chart slices 1-9, axis scaling options, and so on.

If you're using the 123-compatible menus, choose /**Graph** I **Options** I **Range** Customize I **Update**.

Resetting series assignments

To remove one or more series and their customization settings from a graph (or reset *all* graph settings), use the /**Graph** I **Customize Series** I **Reset** command.

To reset block and customization settings for a series,

1. Choose /**Graph** I **Customize Series** I **Reset**. Quattro displays a menu of six series, plus a **Graph** command.
2. Choose the series you want to reset. Choose **Graph** to reset every series in the graph.

Tip   The /Graph | Customize Series | Reset | Graph command is an easy way to erase the current graph and start fresh with your last saved settings.

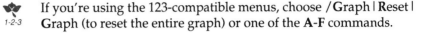 If you're using the 123-compatible menus, choose /Graph | Reset | Graph (to reset the entire graph) or one of the **A-F** commands.

Scaling and formatting an axis

Most graphs can have up to three different axes:

- The *x-axis* is the bottom line of the graph along which values are plotted.
- The *y-axis* is the vertical line on the left side of the graph. It contains a range of numbers, or *scale*, against which a series is plotted. When you create a graph, Quattro automatically scales the y-axis to include the highest and lowest values among all the series.
- The *second y-axis* appears on the right side of the graph only if you've assigned series to it with /Graph | Customize | Series | Y-Axis | (pick series) | Secondary Y-Axis. Quattro scales this axis automatically to reflect the series assigned to it.

Note   In a rotated bar graph, the x-axis and y-axis switch places, so the x-axis appears at the left and the y-axis at the bottom of the graph.

You can adjust the scale and format of any of these axes with the following commands:

- /Graph | X-Axis
- /Graph | Y-Axis
- /Graph | Y-Axis | 2nd Y-Axis

All these commands display a similar menu with minor differences. The **Y-Axis** menu contains every command on the **X-Axis** menu except **Alternate Ticks** and has one additional command: **2nd Y-Axis**. **2nd Y-Axis** displays the same menu as **Y-Axis**.

```
┌────── X-Axis ──────┐
│                    │
│ Scale            ▶ │
│ Low                │
│ High               │
│ Increment          │
│ Format of Ticks  ▶ │
│ No. of Minor Ticks │
│ Alternate Ticks  ▶ │
│ Display Scaling  ▶ │
│ Mode             ▶ │
│ Quit               │
│                    │
└────────────────────┘
```

■ **Scale** lets either you or Quattro determine the graph's numeric scale. When set to **M**anual, you can specify the exact range you want. You can adjust the scale of the y-axis of a graph or the x-axis of an XY graph.

■ **Low** lets you specify the low end of the graph's scale. (Manual scaling only.)

■ **High** lets you specify the upper end of the graph's scale. (Manual scaling only.)

■ **Increment** lets you specify the distance between ticks along the axis. For example, if **Low** is set to 0, **High** to 500, and Increment to 100, Quattro will draw ticks at every hundredth value: 0, 100, 200, 300, 400 and 500 (manual scaling only).

■ **Format of Ticks** lets you change the format used to display numeric tick labels on the y-axis of a graph or the x-axis of an XY graph.

■ **No. of Minor Ticks** lets you skip some of the axis tick labels. For example, if you specify 3 with this command, Quattro displays the first label in the series, skips the next three (showing *minor ticks*—that is, ticks alone—instead), displays one, replaces the next three with ticks alone, and so on.

■ **Alternate Ticks** displays labels on two levels, alternating levels for each item. This makes the display more readable when the labels are crowded.

■ **Display Scaling** determines whether or not Quattro displays the scale measurement ("thousands," "millions," and so on) next to the axis if the axis plots consistently large values.

■ **Mode** lets you switch to a logarithmically scaled axis.

■ **Quit** returns you to the **Graph** menu.

The following sections describe how to use these commands to adjust the scale of an axis and change how Quattro displays tick labels along an axis.

If you're using the 123-compatible menus, choose / **Graph** | **Options** | **Scale** | **X-Scale**, **Y-Scale**, or **2nd Y-Scale**. On these axes-scaling menus, choose **Automatic** or **Manual** instead of **S**cale, **Lower** instead of **High**, **Indicator** instead of **Display Scaling**, **Tick Increment** instead of **Increment**, **Scaling Mode** instead of **M**ode, and **Draw Alternating Ticks** instead of **Alternate Ticks**.

Adjusting the axes scale

When Quattro draws a graph, it automatically adjusts the axes scale to best fit the range of numbers assigned to the axes. You can change this scale, however, to fine-tune a graph or to zoom in on a specific area.

To adjust the scale of the y-axis of a graph or the x-axis of an XY graph,

1. Choose /Graph | X-Axis, /Graph | Y-Axis, or /Graph | Y-Axis | 2nd Y-Axis.
2. Choose Scale. A menu appears with two options: Automatic and Manual.
3. Choose Manual. Quattro returns you to the axis menu.
4. Choose Low. Quattro prompts you for a number to use as the low end of the scale, with zero shown as the default.

The x-axis scale can be adjusted on XY graphs only.

5. Enter the first number you want to appear on the axis. If you want all your values to appear on the graph, make sure this number is less than the lowest number assigned to the axis.
6. Choose High. Quattro prompts you for a number to use as the upper end of the scale, with zero shown as the default.
7. Enter the last number you want to appear on the axis. Again, if you want all your values to appear on the graph, make sure this number is more than the highest number assigned to the axis.
8. Choose Increment. Quattro prompts you for an increment number, with zero shown as the default.
9. Enter the number of the interval you want between tick marks on the axis. Quattro adds tick marks from the Low value to the High value based on the Increment value. If you leave this value at 0, Quattro determines the increments automatically.

You may need to experiment with changing your graph's scale before you find the range that best suits your graph. You need to be careful not to specify too great a scale range. Otherwise, your graph might appear compressed beyond readability.

Adjusting ticks on the axis

Quattro marks off each incremental value on an axis with a tick mark—a short line below or next to the axis, usually labeled. (To label the x-axis, use the /Graph | Series | X-Axis Series command; see page 341.) There are two ways you can change tick labeling:

- Change the numeric format of tick labels on the y-axis of a graph or the x-axis of an XY graph.
- Skip some tick labels, substituting small unlabeled tick marks—minor ticks—at regular intervals.

For an x-axis, you can use a third option to adjust tick labels:

- Stagger tick labels on two levels to allow more room for each label.

The following sections describe these three options.

Format of ticks

The Format of Ticks command lets you change the display format of tick labels on the y-axis of a graph or the x-axis of an XY graph:

1. Choose /Graph | X-Axis, /Graph | Y-Axis, or /Graph | Y-Axis | 2nd Y-Axis.

```
═══ Format ═══
Fixed
Scientific
Currency
,
General
+/-
Percent
Date
Text
Hidden
```

2. Choose Format of Ticks. Quattro displays a menu identical to that displayed with the /Style | Numeric Format command.

3. Choose the format you want for your tick labels. (To set the format to Time, choose Date, then Time.) For most formats, you'll also need to specify precision or style. Table 6.1 on page 152 describes each available format.

4. If you want to use this format as the default for all graphs, choose Update.

The /Graph | X-Axis | Format of Ticks command affects the x-axis of an XY graph only. To change the format of labels assigned to the x-axis in other types of graphs, go into the spreadsheet and change the display format of the x-axis series block with the /Style | Numeric Format command.

If you're using the 123-compatible menus, choose /Graph | Options | Scale | (pick axis) | Format.

Number of minor ticks If the labels you use to define ticks along the x-axis don't all fit onscreen, they overlap. To avoid this problem, you can use the **No. of Minor Ticks** command to replace some of the labels with minor tick marks.

On a y-axis, Quattro automatically inserts labels (numbers) where they fit. You can use the **No. of Minor Ticks** command to display fewer numbers, replacing some with tick marks.

The following figure shows a graph that skips every other x-axis tick label:

Figure 14.7
A graph with skipped labels

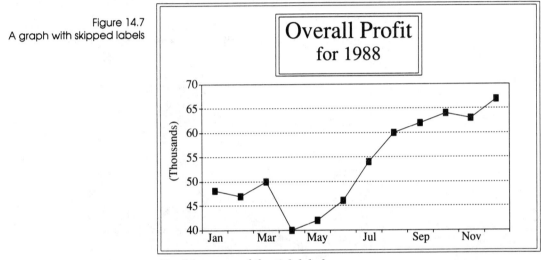

To skip some of the tick labels,

1. Choose /Graph | X-Axis, /Graph | Y-Axis, or /Graph | Y-Axis | 2nd Y-Axis, depending on the axis you want to adjust.

2. Choose **No. of Minor Ticks**. Quattro prompts you for a number.

3. Enter the number of labels you want to skip over. (To display every other label, enter 1; to display every third label, enter 2; and so on.)

4. To redisplay all axis labels, choose the command again and enter 0.

The **No. of Minor Ticks** command affects all types of graphs except pie and column charts.

Once you've set the **Y-Axis | No. of Minor Ticks** command to something other than 0, you override Quattro's automatic placement of ticks on the y-axis. If you later add more values, or resize the graph or y-axis labels, the labels could overlap. To reset tick placement, set this command back to 0.

If you're using the 123-compatible menus, choose **/ Graph | Options | Scale |** (pick axis) **| No. of Minor Ticks**.

Alternating ticks   Another solution to x-axis tick labels that won't all fit on the screen is to display them on two levels with the **Alternate Ticks** command.

Figure 14.8 shows a graph with alternated x-axis labels.

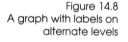

Figure 14.8
A graph with labels on
alternate levels

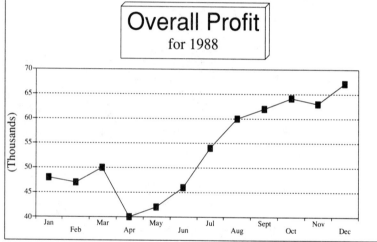

*Alternate Ticks is available
only for the x-axis.*

To display tick labels on alternate levels,

1. Choose **/ Graph | X-Axis | Alternate Ticks**.
2. Choose **Yes** to alternate the labels.

To return x-axis labels to the same line, set this command back to **No**.

Alternated labels do not affect pie or column charts.

If you're using the 123-compatible menus, choose **/ Graph | Options | Scale |** (pick axis) **| Draw Alternating Ticks**.

Scaling display

Quattro automatically scales each axis to fit the range of values in the series assigned to it. If the series contains large numbers, Quattro divides tick labels by 1000 or 10,000 and indicates the multiplier next to the axis.

Figure 14.9
The y-axis scaling display

The word "Thousands" next to the y-axis indicates that the numbers on the y-axis scale should be multiplied by 1000—so that 10 represents 10,000, 20 represents 20,000, and so on.

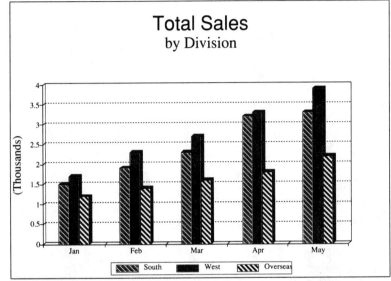

To remove the scaling label from the screen,

1. Choose /Graph l X-Axis, /Graph l Y-Axis, or /Graph l Y-Axis l 2nd Y-Axis.
2. Choose **Display Scaling**.
3. Choose **No**.

To return scaling to the screen, set this command back to **Yes**.

1-2-3 If you're using the 123-compatible menus, choose /Graph l **Options** l **Scale** l (pick axis) l **Indicator**.

Note Scaling display occurs on the x-axis only for XY graphs.

Logarithmically scaling an axis

In a logarithmically scaled axis, each major division of the axis represents 10 times the value of the previous division. This type of scale is useful when you're plotting series with wide ranges in magnitude.

The following figure shows two graphs that plot the same data. The first uses the y-axis scale Quattro set up automatically. In the second, the y-axis is logarithmically scaled. With the logarithmic axis, you can see more clearly the range of values in the series.

Figure 14.10
A logarithmic graph versus a
standard graph

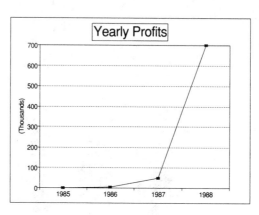

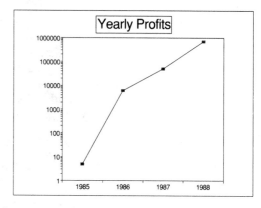

To logarithmically scale an axis,

1. Choose /Graph | X-Axis, /Graph | Y-Axis, or /Graph | Y-Axis | 2nd Y-Axis.

2. Choose **Mode**.

3. Choose **Log**.

To return the axis back to standard scaling, set this command to **Normal**.

If you're using the 123-compatible menus, choose / Graph | Options | Scale | (pick axis) | Scaling Mode.

Note It's impossible to logarithmically scale negative or zero values. If your graph's y-axis scale begins with 0, set the scale manually to begin at 1 (or 10 or .00001 or any positive number) first. You must also adjust the upper end of the graph scale.

Customizing the overall graph

Certain customization features such as grids and background color affect the entire graph. These are available through the / Graph | Overall command. Choose this command to display the Overall menu.

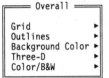

- **Grid** changes the color, pattern, and style of grid lines on the graph.

- **Outlines** adjusts the frame used to box titles, legends, and the overall graph.

- **Background Color** changes the color behind the graph.

- **Three-D** determines whether a graph displays with a three-dimensional effect.

- **Color/B&W** lets you switch between color and black-and-white displays to see how your graph will print in black and white.

Adjusting grid lines

When first created, most graphs include horizontal dotted lines extending from each y-axis tick mark. These lines are called *grid lines*, and they make it easier to pinpoint values. You can add horizontal and vertical grid lines to your graph, or remove them entirely. You can change the pattern, thickness, and color of these grid lines, as well as the outline color of the graph legend, main title, and the overall graph itself. You can also change the color used to fill the grid.

To change a graph's grid lines, choose / Graph | Overall | Grid. The Grid menu appears.

- The **Horizontal, Vertical, Both,** and **Clear** commands change the position of the grid lines.
- **Grid Color** changes the color used for grid lines.
- **Line Style** changes the pattern used to create the lines.
- **Fill Color** changes the color used behind the grid lines.
- **Quit** returns you to the Graph menu.

Changing grid type

With the first four commands on the Grid menu, you can change the position of grid lines on your screen (horizontal or vertical).

To change the position of grid lines in your graph, choose Horizontal to create grid lines from the y-axis only, **V**ertical to create grid lines from the x-axis only, and **B**oth to create grid lines from both axes. Choose **C**lear to remove grid lines altogether.

If you're using the 123-compatible menus, choose / **Graph** | **O**ptions | **G**rid | **H**orizontal, **V**ertical, **B**oth, or **C**lear.

If you want the changed grid settings to be the new defaults, choose /**Graph** | **C**ustomize Series | **U**pdate.

The following figure shows a graph with both horizontal and vertical grid lines:

Figure 14.11
A graph with grid lines

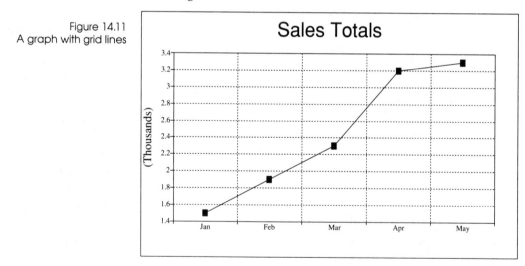

Changing grid color

To change the color used to display grid lines on your screen,

1. Choose /**Graph** | **Overall** | **Grid** | **Grid** Color. Quattro displays a menu of the colors available for your screen. (If you've set your screen to graphics mode with the /**Options** | **Display** Mode command and you have a color monitor, Quattro displays a pictorial gallery of colors instead of a menu.)

2. Choose the color you want to use.

Note The **Grid** Color command controls a number of graph elements including the color of outlines around the main title, the graph legend, bars, pie and column slices, areas, and the overall graph itself.

1-2-3 If you're using the 123-compatible menus, choose /**Graph** | **Options** | **Grid** | **Grid** Color.

Changing grid line style To change the line pattern used to create grid lines,

```
Line Style
Solid
Dotted
Center
Dashed
Heavy Solid
Heavy Dotted
Heavy Center
Heavy Dashed
```

1. Choose /**Graph** | **Overall** | **Grid** | **Line** Style. Quattro displays a menu of line styles. (If you've set your screen to graphics mode with the /**Options** | **Display** Mode command, Quattro displays a pictorial gallery of line styles instead of a menu.)

2. Choose the line style you want to use for the grids.

Figure 14.12 shows a graph with dashed horizontal grid lines.

Figure 14.12
A graph with dashed
horizontal grid lines

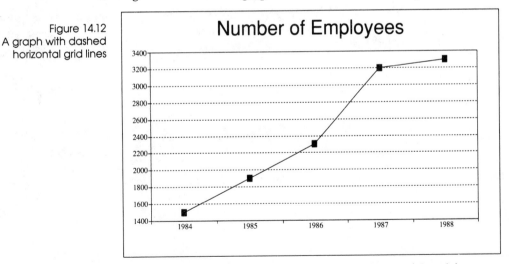

1-2-3 If you're using the 123-compatible menus, choose /**Graph** | **Options** | **Grid** | **Line** Style.

Changing grid fill color   The /Graph | Overall | Grid | Fill Color command lets you change the color behind the grid lines. You pick a color the same way as with /Graph | Overall | Grid | Grid Color (see page 386).

If you're using the 123-compatible menus, choose /Graph | Options | Grid | Fill Color.

Adjusting graph outlines

By default, Quattro doesn't draw boxes, or *outlines*, around the graph or its titles. It does, however, create a box outline around graph legends by default. You can add or adjust outlines to the graph, titles, and the legend with the **Outlines** command on the /Graph | Overall menu.

To adjust graph outlines,

1. Choose /Graph | Overall | Outlines. Quattro displays a menu of the three different outlines you can add or adjust.

2. Choose **Titles** to adjust the outline around the main title (both lines). Choose **Legend** to adjust the outline around the graph legend (created with /Graph | Text | Legend). Choose **Graph** to change the outlines around the entire graph, including any legend. Quattro displays a menu of outline types.

3. Choose the option you want for that outline. **None** removes the outline altogether.

The following figure shows a graph and its titles and legends with 3-D outlines:

Figure 14.13
A graph with 3-D outlines

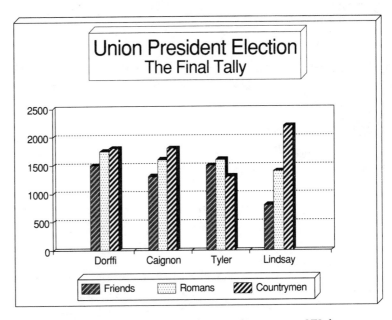

See page 371 for examples of shadow outlines, page 372 for examples of round rectangle outlines, and page 381 for examples of double-line outlines.

Note   To change the *color* of these outlines, as well as grid lines, bar outlines, area outlines, and pie and column slice outlines, use the /**Graph** | **Overall** | **Grid** | **Grid Color** command (see page 386).

1-2-3

If you're using the 123-compatible menus, choose /**Graph** | **Options** | **Overall** | **Outlines**.

If you want the changed outline settings to be the new defaults, choose /**Graph** | **Customize Series** | **Update**.

Changing graph background color

To change the color for the background area outside of a graph, choose /**Graph** | **Overall** | **Background Color**. Quattro displays a menu of colors. Highlight the color you want to use and press *Enter*. (To change the background color *inside* a graph, use /**Graph** | **Overall** | **Grid** | **Fill Color**.)

If you've set your screen mode to graphics (with the /**Options** | **Display Mode** command) and you have a color monitor, Quattro displays a pictorial gallery of colors instead of a menu of color names.

1-2-3 If you're using the 123-compatible menus, choose /Graph | Options | Overall | Background Color.

If you want the changed background color to be the new default, choose /Graph | Customize Series | Update.

Note On a monochrome display, all non-black colors appear white.

Three-dimensional graphs

By default, Quattro creates most graphs with a three-dimensional effect. To add or remove the three-dimensional effect from a graph,

1. Choose /Graph | Overall | Three-D.
2. Choose **No** to remove the effect. To return it, set this command back to **Yes**.

If the three-dimensional effect would make your graph impossible to read (such as a bar graph with numerous bars or a pie chart with fifty or more slices), Quattro displays and prints the graph in one dimension, regardless of the Three-D setting. Also, some printers and plotters print one dimension only.

1-2-3 If you're using the 123-compatible menus, choose /Graph | Options | Overall | 3D.

If you want the changed three-dimensional setting to be the new default, choose /Graph | Customize Series | Update.

The following figure shows two bar graphs, one with the three-dimensional effect and one without it:

Figure 14.14
Graphs with and without
three dimensions

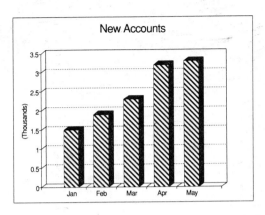

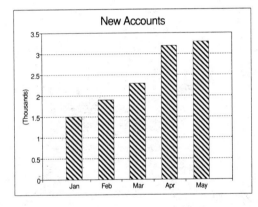

15

Annotating your graph

Once you've created and customized your graph, you can use Quattro's Graph Annotator to add descriptive elements to it. Figure 15.1 shows a graph embellished with annotation.

Figure 15.1
An annotated graph

You need a graphics card to display or annotate graphs.

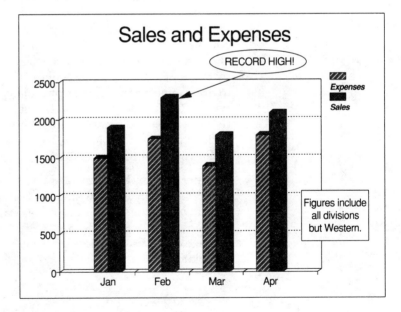

With graph annotation, you can

- insert boxed or floating text to help describe the graph
- add arrows or lines to point out areas on the graph

- use different shapes to enclose text or graph points
- fully customize annotation design elements—change their colors, patterns, size, and style
- draw custom pictures, logos, symbols, and so forth
- "link" an annotation element with a point in the graph so that, when the graph changes to reflect new values, the element moves along with it
- copy or move design elements from one graph to another
- use a text graph type (a blank graph screen) to create bulleted lists, flow charts, and freehand graphics
- resize or move the graph title, legend, or graph itself
- customize the graph directly; for example, change text fonts, grid color, and background color

The Annotator screen

All graph annotation takes place within Quattro's Graph Annotator (see the following figure). To activate the Annotator, press the Slash key (/) while viewing a graph or choose / Graph | Annotate. If you want to add annotation to an existing graph that is not the current graph, first choose the graph you want to edit by name with the / Graph | Name | Display command. If you want to draw annotation elements on a blank screen, first set the graph type to **Text** or remove any series assignments from the graph (with / Graph | Customize Series | Reset). (If no series are assigned to the graph, Quattro automatically sets the graph type to **Text** when you enter the Annotator.)

Note   The function-key assignments in the Graph Annotator are not the same as in a spreadsheet window. For example, in a spreadsheet window, *F7* is the Query key; in the Graph Annotator, *F7* activates Proportional Resize mode. See "Graph Annotator keys," starting on page 408, for a complete list of special keys in the Graph Annotator.

Figure 15.2
The Graph Annotator

Toolbox ▶

Draw Area ▶
(where the graph is)

Property Sheet ▶
(with Clipboard menu)

Gallery ▶
(empty box at far right)

Status Box ▶

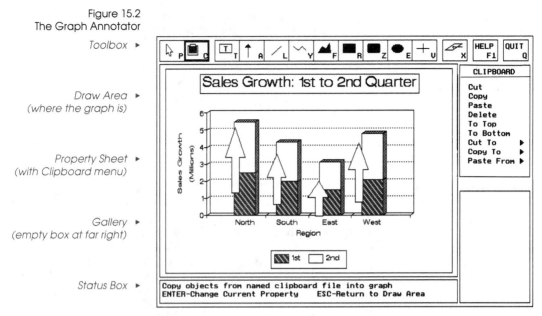

There are five parts to the Graph Annotator:

- The **Draw Area** contains the graph, titles, and legend. Use this area to create, move, resize, delete, and copy annotation design elements.

- The **Toolbox** contains an array of symbols, or *icons*, you can use to create elements, get help, enter Edit mode, and exit the Annotator. To activate it, press the Slash key (/). To return to the Draw Area without choosing an icon, press *Esc*. To create an element in the Draw Area, choose it from this gallery. Quattro then moves you into the Draw Area so you can draw the element.

- The **Property Sheet** lists the adjustable properties available for the current element type. For example, when you highlight a line element, the Property Sheet lists Color and Style. Use this menu to adjust the properties of a given element in the Draw Area, either before creating it or while editing it. To activate the Property Sheet, press *F3*. To return to the Draw Area without choosing a command, press *Esc*.

- The **Gallery** displays available options for the property highlighted on the Property Sheet. For example, when you highlight a Color property, this gallery displays the different colors available for your computer. Quattro activates the Gallery automatically when you choose a property command.

- The **Status Box** at the bottom of the Annotator screen is where Quattro displays instructions, keyboard shortcuts, and menu command descriptions.

 To activate a different area of the Annotation screen with a mouse, just click that area.

Annotating complex graphs

The more data points and series your graph contains, the longer Quattro takes to draw it. Since the Annotator redraws your graph every time you make a change, you might find annotating a complex graph rather cumbersome. To avoid this problem, Quattro analyzes the current graph when you activate the Annotator. If it would take a long time to draw, Quattro minimizes its display to show only the graph outline, the axes, and grid lines.

In many cases, the minimized display is sufficient for your annotation needs. You can resize and move the graph, create text elements, draw shapes, and so forth. When you reach a point where you need to see the rest of the graph for exact placement of elements, press the Graph key (*F10*). Quattro then redraws the graph in full.

The Toolbox

The Annotator Toolbox (Figure 15.3) always appears at the top of the Annotator screen. You can use it to create and modify annotation design elements, display help text, and exit the Annotator.

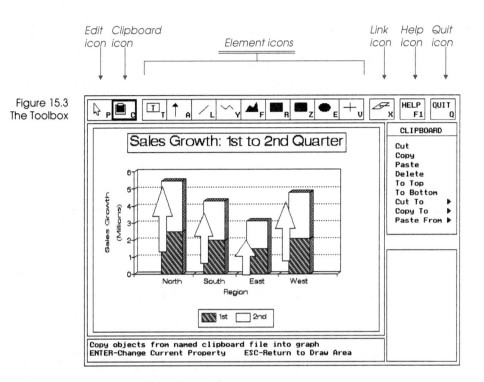

Figure 15.3
The Toolbox

The Toolbox contains the following commands, represented as icons. To choose one of these tools, click its icon or press the keystrokes associated with it, shown in parentheses in the following list:

- The **white arrow pointer** (/P) is the edit icon, which activates Edit mode. In Edit mode, you can copy, move, delete, resize, and reposition elements in the Draw Area. You can also change property settings for existing elements, including the graph title, legend, and the graph itself.

- The **Clipboard** (/C) displays a list of commands in the Property Sheet area that you can use to cut and paste elements in and out of temporary memory (the Clipboard) or in and out of a file. You can also move drawn elements in front of or in back of other elements.

- The **elements** (the group of nine icons in the middle) let you create graphic design elements in the Draw Area.

- The **link icon** (*/X*) lets you connect one or more elements to a particular point in the graph, so that when the value represented by that point changes, the annotation elements move along with it.

- **Help** (*F1*) activates Quattro's online help facility. The first screen displayed describes the Annotation screen. You can also display other help screens that describe all aspects of Quattro.

- **Quit** (*/Q*) exits the Annotator and returns you to the zoomed graph or to the **Graph** menu, depending on where you were when you activated the Annotator.

Note   If you have a CGA graphics card, you won't see the white arrow or link icons. In their place, you'll see the words `Pick` and `Link`.

The graphic design elements

Quattro offers a variety of design elements to add to your graph: rectangles, ellipses, lines, arrows, polylines, and polygons. You can also add text to a graph, either in a box or "floating."

The Annotator Toolbox shows all the types of elements you can create (see Figure 15.3, top). To create an element, choose it from the Toolbox, then draw it directly in the Draw Area. The Property Sheet always shows the properties available for the selected element.

The Toolbox contains nine design element icons. To activate a design tool, click its icon or press the keystrokes associated with it, shown in parentheses in the following list. From left to right, they are as follows:

- The **boxed T** (*/T*) is the text icon, which you can use to add text to your graph. After you select this icon, you can position the cursor (or mouse pointer) in the Draw Area and begin typing to enter text. Using the Property Sheet, you can change the color, justification, and font Quattro uses to display the text. You can also change the type of box, the pattern used to fill the box, and the colors of the box. If you don't want a box around the text, set the box type to **None**.

- The **arrow** (*/A*) draws a line with an arrowhead at the end. You can use it to point out areas of the graph. You can change the color of the arrowhead, and the color and style of the line.

- The **line** (/L) lets you draw a straight line anywhere in the Draw Area. You can change the color and style of the line.

- The **jointed line**, or **polyline** (/Y), lets you create a line that is anchored in more than two places. After you select this element, position the cursor (or mouse pointer) at the point in the Draw Area where you want the line to begin. Press the Period key (or press and hold the mouse button) and move the pointer to the next point; press *Enter* (or release the mouse button), move to the next point, and so on. When you've finished drawing the line, press *Enter* twice or double-click the mouse. You can change the color and style of the line used. If you have a mouse, you can also use this element to draw a curved line (see page 401). A polyline can have no more than 1000 points.

- The **polygon** (/F) creates a multisided shape in the Draw Area. Each side can be a different length. This works just like the polyline element except that when you press *Enter* twice (or double-click the mouse), Quattro connects the beginning point with the end point to create a closed shape. You can change the color and pattern used to fill the polygon and the color and style of its border. If you have a mouse, you can also use this element to draw freehand shapes (see page 401). A polygon can have no more than 1000 points.

- The **rectangle** (/R) creates a rectangle of whatever dimensions you specify. You can change the color and pattern used to fill it and the color and style of its border.

- The **rounded rectangle** (/Z) creates a rectangle with rounded corners. The rectangle can be any dimension, and you can change the color and pattern used to fill it and the color and style of its border.

- The **ellipse** (/E) creates a circle (or elongated circle), the exact shape of which you determine. You can change the color and pattern used to fill the ellipse and the color and style of its border.

- The **vertical/horizontal line** (/V) creates a perfectly vertical or horizontal line, depending on which way you move the pointer. After choosing this element, point to the place in the Draw Area where you want the line to begin, press the Period key (or press and hold the mouse button), and move the pointer. If you move the pointer up or down, Quattro creates a vertical line; if you move it right or left, Quattro creates a horizontal line. When the line is the length you want, press *Enter* (or release the mouse button).

Creating design elements

To create a design element in your graph, begin by choosing the specific element icon from the Toolbox. If you want to set properties for the element before you create it, use the Property Sheet and Gallery. Then return to the Draw Area to draw it. The procedure is as follows:

1. Select the icon you want to create from the Toolbox. If you have a mouse, just click the icon you want. To select an icon using the keyboard, press the Slash key (/) then press the letter assigned to the icon you want, or use the arrow keys to highlight (with a dark border) the icon and press *Enter*. Quattro moves you to the Draw Area and displays a graph pointer (a plus sign or, if you have a mouse, an arrow). The Property Sheet changes to display properties for that element.

2. If you want to set any properties for the element before you create it (for example, to change the color it will be drawn in), press *F3* and use the Property Sheet and Gallery to make changes, then press *Esc* to return to the Draw Area (or if you have a mouse, click the property and option, then click the Draw Area). See "Setting design properties" later in this chapter for details.

3. Now press *Esc* to return to the Draw Area or click in the Draw Area if you have a mouse.

4. In the Draw Area, there's a pointer that looks like a large plus sign or, if you have a mouse, an arrow. Position the pointer (the tip of the arrow or the center of the plus sign) where you want to anchor the design element. If you're creating an arrow element, move to the place where you want the arrow to point from. If you're creating text, move to where you want the text to begin.

5. If you're creating text, begin typing. If you want to add bullets to your text, use the \bullet #\ syntax described on page 167. To wrap the text onto a new line, press *Ctrl-Enter*. When you're finished, press *Enter*. (*Esc* removes any text you've typed.) If you added bullet codes to your text element, Quattro replaces them with actual bullets when you press *Enter*.

6. If you're creating a line or shape, press the Period key (or press and hold the mouse button), then move the pointer to extend the line or shape to where you want it and press *Enter* (or release the mouse button). To create a polygon or polyline with smooth curves instead of or in combination with straight edges, see the next section.

Note No graph can have more than approximately 800-900 objects.

Drawing curves

If you have a mouse, you can use Quattro's special Curve Draw mode to create curved lines or shapes:

1. In the Toolbox, click either the polygon icon (for a curved line) or polyline icon (for a closed shape).
2. Turn *Scroll Lock* on or hold down the *Shift* key to enter Curve Draw mode.
3. Position the pointer in the Draw Area, hold down the mouse button, and drag to draw curves. As you drag, Quattro places points along the mouse's path; the slower or curvier you drag the mouse, the more closely Quattro spaces the points.
4. If you want both curves and straight edges, hold down the *Shift* key or turn *Scroll Lock* on while you draw curves, then release it or turn *Scroll Lock* off to draw straight edges.
5. To allow you to draw small curves or objects with fine details, Quattro will not finish a polyline or close a polygon while you are in Curve Draw mode, regardless of whether you double-click or how close you place points in the element. If you are in Curve Draw mode and want to finish a polyline or close a polygon, do either of the following:

   a. Click the polyline or polygon element in the Toolbox.
   b. Release the *Shift* key or turn *Scroll Lock* off to exit Curve Draw mode, then double-click to finish the polyline or close the polygon normally.

Drawing multi-loop polygons

Quattro also lets you create a polygon element with an empty area inside of it. A simple example of this type of object, called a *multi-loop polygon*, is a doughnut shape or a frame.

To create a multi-loop polygon,

1. Click the polygon element in the Toolbox.
2. Position the pointer in the Draw Area and draw the outer polygon loop, which can be straight, curved, or a combination of both. Instead of finishing off the polygon with a double-click or double-*Enter*, close off the shape yourself by connecting the beginning and ending points and click or press *Enter* once.
3. Move the pointer inside the polygon to where you want the inside loop to begin and draw it. A line should connect the outside loop with the beginning of the inside loop.
4. When you finish the inside loop, connect the last point of the inside loop to the first point of the inside loop. You can place as many loops within loops as you wish.
5. When you have finished your multi-loop polygon, double-click or press *Enter* twice, just as you would with a single-loop polygon.

Quattro fills in the space between the two loops and leaves the inside of the inner loop blank. If there is anything underneath the inner loop (another element or part of the graph), you'll be able to see through to it. If your multi-loop polygon is filled oddly, or if the line between the two loops remains, you didn't close the loops exactly. Delete the shape and try again, taking more care to connect the beginning and ending points.

Making changes

There are many kinds of changes you can make to an annotated graph, both before and after you create elements. You can

- reposition selected elements, including the graph title, the legend, and the graph itself
- adjust the size of selected elements, including the graph itself
- delete selected elements
- change property settings for elements either before or after you create them
- make changes to the graph itself; for example, change the background color or the size of x-axis labels
- make changes to the graph title or legend, including text font and colors

- store elements you've created in temporary memory (the Clipboard) or in a file for use in a different graph
- paste in elements stored in the Clipboard or in a file
- move an element in front of or behind another element

Selecting elements

Before you can make changes to an existing design element in an annotated graph, you must select it. The way you select an annotation design element depends on whether you have a mouse.

To select an element using the keyboard,

1. From within the Draw Area, press */P* to choose the edit icon from the Toolbox. Quattro activates the Draw Area so you can select elements.

2. Use the *Tab* and *Shift-Tab* keys to move to the element you want to select. *Tab* moves you clockwise around the elements; *Shift-Tab* moves you counterclockwise. To select more than one element, press *Shift-F7* to select the ones you want as you move from element to element with the *Tab* or *Shift-Tab* keys. To "de-select" an element, move to it and press *Shift-F7* again.

To select an element with a mouse,

1. Click the edit icon (the white arrow) in the Toolbox.

2. In the Draw Area, click the element you want to select. To select more than one element in an area, drag from one corner of the area to the opposite corner so that a box encloses the area, then release. To select several disjointed elements, hold down the *Shift* key (on the keyboard) and click each element.

Quattro adds little boxes, called *handles*, to the selected element(s).

With an element or group of elements selected, you can change properties for the elements and move, delete, or resize the elements. You can also store selected *drawn* elements (not the titles, legend, and graph itself) in the Clipboard or a file.

As well as design elements, you can also select graph elements including the graph title, the legend, and the graph itself. You can move, resize, and change certain properties for a selected graph. You can change properties for or reposition a selected title or legend.

Deleting elements

To delete an element or group of elements, just select it, then press the *Del* key. Quattro removes the element(s) from the Draw Area.

You can also delete an element without selecting it by moving the pointer to it and then pressing *Del*. This is very useful when you make a mistake while drawing an element. Instead of going into Edit mode, selecting and deleting the element, then choosing the icon for the element you were drawing, you can just point to the element you want to delete, press *Del*, and continue drawing.

You can delete selected graph titles and legends, but not the graph itself. If you delete graph titles, Quattro clears the / Graph I Text I 1st Line and / Graph I Text I 2nd Line commands. If you delete the legend, Quattro sets the / Graph I Text I Legend I Position command to None.

Repositioning elements

You can move both design elements and graph elements anywhere in the Draw Area. In fact, this is a great way to reorganize your graph. The following figure shows the graph in Figure 15.1 on page 393 with the title underneath and the legend and boxed text on the left:

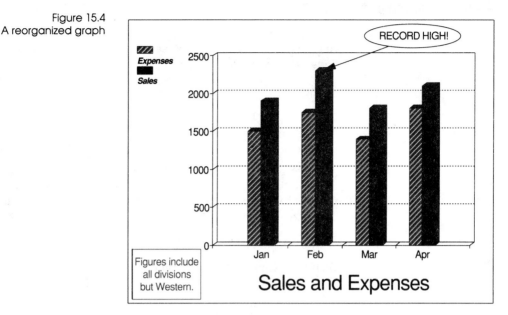

Figure 15.4
A reorganized graph

The way you move a design element depends on whether you have a mouse.

To move an element using the keyboard,

1. Select the element you want to reposition (see page 403). If you select a group, elements in the group will move in a cluster, maintaining the same distance between them.
2. Use the arrow keys to reposition an outline of the selected element(s).
3. When the outline is where you want it, press *Enter*.

To move an element with a mouse,

1. Select the element you want to reposition (see page 403). If you select a group, elements in the group will move together, maintaining the same distance between them.
2. Point to inside the selected element or group.
3. Drag to move the outline of the element or group.
4. When the outline is where you want the element(s) to be, release.

Resizing elements

You can change the size of any element you create. You can also change the size of the graph itself. The procedure you use depends on whether you have a mouse.

To resize an element using the keyboard,

1. Select the element you want to resize (see page 403). If you select a group, Quattro will resize elements in the group together (see the following section for details).
2. Press the Period key to enter Resize mode. Quattro highlights the bottom right corner, indicating that it's the one Quattro uses to resize the element. Handles are not visible during the resize operation, but the corners beneath the handles are what you'll use to resize the element. Press the arrow keys to resize the selected corner.
3. If you want to use a different corner to resize, press the Period key until the corner you want to use is highlighted.
4. Use the arrow keys to move the highlighted corner. An outline of the element follows the corner, showing you what the element would look like with the corner in that position. (Use the *Home, End, PgUp,* and *PgDn* keys to move the corner diagonally.)
5. When the element outline is where you want it, press *Enter.*

To resize an element with a mouse,

1. Select the element you want to resize (see page 403). If you select a group, Quattro will resize elements in the group together (see the following section for details).
2. Quattro adds little boxes, called *handles,* to the movable parts of the elements you select. Point to the handle you want to use to resize the element. The handles are not visible as you resize an element; instead, you use the corners to guide you as you resize it. With a rectangle, you can use side handles to move one side of the rectangle or corner handles to move two sides at once.
3. Drag the corner or side handle. An outline of the element follows the corner, showing you what the element would look like with the corner in that position.
4. When the element outline is where you want it, release.

Note If you change the size of a boxed text element, only the box is adjusted, not the size of the text. Use the Font property to change text size (see "Text properties" later in this chapter).

Warning If you size a group of elements down to almost zero and then zoom it back again, the objects in the group will lose their spatial relationships with each other. In Proportional Resize mode (see the following section), the effect is even more dramatic. In general, try to avoid shrinking any group of objects down to almost zero and then expanding it again; Quattro loses the ability to distinguish spatial relationships when groups lose resolution.

Resizing elements as a group

When you resize a group of elements, Quattro equally adjusts their sizes and keeps each element anchored in its original position. In most cases, this is the desired effect, but sometimes you may want to adjust the *space* in between the elements as well as their size.

For example, imagine that you've drawn a simple picture of a car using one polygon and two ellipses for wheels. You want to make the car smaller. If you resize the car elements as a group, the wheels stay where they were and may end up somewhere near the car's bumper. If you resize each element separately, you'll have to work hard to make the wheels the same size.

An easy solution to this problem is Proportional Resize mode. This allows you to resize a group of elements and, at the same time, adjust the space in between the elements proportionally. With Proportional Resize mode, you could adjust the size of your car just as if it were a single element.

To activate Proportional Resize mode, just select your group of elements and press *F7*. Quattro removes the resize handles from each element and replaces them with one set of handles for the group. When you move one of the handles, the whole group moves proportionally.

To select a group of elements in Proportional Resize mode with the mouse, hold down the *Alt* key while you drag to select an area that encloses the group, release the mouse button, and release the *Alt* key.

Editing text elements

With text elements, you can change not only the size and position of the element, but you can edit the text it contains as well.

To edit a text element,

1. Select the text element you want to edit (see page 403). Don't select more than one element. Note that you can't use this method to edit graph titles or other text entered with commands on the **Graph** menu. To change those items, you must go back to the command you used to create them.

2. Type new text to overwrite the old, or press *F2* to edit existing text. An edit cursor appears at the end of the text. If the text element includes a bullet, the bullet display reverts to bullet code so you can edit it.

If you delete all characters in a text element, the element disappears when you press Enter.

3. Just as in spreadsheet Edit mode, use the arrow keys to position the cursor in front of any characters you want to delete. Press *Del* to delete the character to the right and *Backspace* to delete the character to the left. Type to insert characters in front of the cursor. Use *Ctrl-Enter* to insert a carriage return.

4. Press *Enter* to complete the changes. To discard the changes, press *Esc*. When you press *Enter*, Quattro replaces any bullet codes in your text with actual bullets.

Note To join two lines of a text element together, press *Backspace* at the beginning of the second line.

Graph Annotator keys

The following tables list keys used in the Annotator: Table 15.1 lists function keys and Table 15.2 lists other special keys. Note that function keys work differently in the Annotator.

Table 15.1
Function keys in the Graph
Annotator

Key	Function
F2	When a text element is selected, enters Edit mode.
F3	Activates the Property Sheet.
F7	With a group of elements selected, enters Proportional Resize mode so you can adjust the size of the elements *and* the space between them at once.
Shift-F7	Retains current element selection, so that pressing *Tab* or *Shift-Tab* selects an *additional* element without removing the previous selection.
F10	Redraws the Annotator screen. If the graph was only partially drawn (to avoid delays in annotating complex graphs), Quattro redraws it in full.

Table 15.2
Other Graph Annotator keys

Key	Function
Tab	Selects the next element in the Draw Area.
Shift-Tab	Selects the previous element in the Draw Area.
Shift	If you have a mouse, hold down the *Shift* key as you click elements in the Draw Area to select multiple elements. If you're drawing a polygon or polyline, *Shift* puts you in Curve Draw mode so you can use a mouse to draw curves.
Del	Deletes a selected element or group of elements. (If you have a mouse, point and press *Del* to delete one element.)
Period key (.)	With an element or group of elements selected, anchors the selected area and lets you resize it (Resize mode). The lower right-hand corner is the default corner, which will extend or contract the element as you press the arrow keys or move the pointer (if you have a mouse). If you want to resize the area using a different corner, press the Period key repeatedly to cycle around the corners of the selected area. Press *Enter* to accept the resize or *Esc* to cancel it.
Home, End PgUp, PgDn	Move the corners of a selected area diagonally.
Arrow keys	Move or resize a selected element or group of elements.
Ctrl-Enter	In Text or Edit mode, starts a new line.

Table 15.2: Other Graph Annotator keys (continued)

Key	Function
Backspace	In Edit mode, deletes the character to the left of the cursor. *Backspace* at the beginning of a line joins it with the line above.
Slash key (/)	Activates the Toolbox.
Esc	In the Draw Area, cancels the current operation without making the change. In a menu, *Esc* exits the menu. You can always get to the Draw Area by pressing *Esc* one or more times.
Enter	Accepts and ends a Draw Area operation, such as moving an element.
Alt	If you have a mouse, you can select a group of elements in Proportional Resizing mode using the *Alt* key. Hold down the *Alt* key while you drag to enclose a group of elements in a selection box, then release the mouse button.

Setting design properties

Each design element has properties connected to it that determine how Quattro displays it. For example, the properties for a rectangle determine

- the color inside the rectangle
- the color of the rectangle's border
- the pattern that fills the rectangle
- the line style of the rectangle's border

You can change the property settings for any element you create—either before you draw it or after you create it. You can also set properties for the graph title, the legend, and the graph itself.

```
┌─ Rectangle ─┐
│             │
│ Fill        │
│   Color     │
│   Pattern   │
│   Bkgrd Color│
│ Border      │
│   Drawn     │
│   Color     │
│   Style     │
│             │
└─────────────┘
```

The Property Sheet, located in the upper right area of your screen, lists properties for the currently selected element. The items in this menu change as you select different elements from the Toolbox. For example, when you highlight a rectangle element, the Property Sheet lists properties for the rectangle border and the inside of the rectangle.

When you choose a command from the Property Sheet, the Gallery changes to show the options available for that property.

The following figure shows the Gallery when the **B**ox Type command is chosen for a selected text element. The Gallery displays the different box types you can use to outline a text element.

You can set properties for an element either before or after you create it. If you've already created the element, you must select it first before editing its properties (see page 403).

Figure 15.5
The Gallery showing box
types

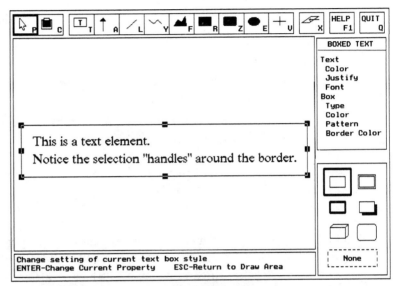

To set design properties for an element,

1. If you haven't created the element yet, select the element icon from the Toolbox. If the element has already been drawn, select it in the Draw Area (see page 403). The Property Sheet automatically changes to show options for the selected element.

2. Select the property you want to set: Press *F3* and choose the property or, if you have a mouse, click the property you want. Quattro activates the Gallery, which now contains options for the property you selected.

3. Choose the option you want from the Gallery (if you have a mouse, just click the option). Quattro moves you back into the Property Sheet.

4. If there are other properties you want to change for the selected element, choose them from the Property Sheet and choose new options for them.

5. To exit the Property Sheet and return to the Draw Area, press *Esc.*

Quattro changes any selected (existing) elements to reflect the new property settings, and any new elements you create of this type will have the new settings.

The following sections give details on the properties you can change for each type of element, including the graph itself, graph titles, and legends.

Text properties

When you select the text icon, the Property Sheet contains the following options:

- **Text Color** affects the color used for the actual text characters. It displays a gallery of colors.

- **Text Justify** determines how Quattro aligns the text in the box. It displays three options in the Options Gallery: **Left**, **Centered**, and **Right**.

- **Text Font** lets you change the typeface, point size, and style (bold, italics, and so on) of text. It displays a menu listing **Typeface**, **Point Size**, and **Style**. Choosing any one of the menu options displays a menu of possible settings for that option.

Note   If you select a text element with a special font, that font becomes the new default.

- **Box Type** determines the type of box used to surround the text. It displays a gallery of box designs, including double-line boxes, three-dimensional boxes, shadowed boxes, and none.

- **Box Color** determines the color used to fill in the box. It displays a gallery of colors.

- **Box Pattern** sets the pattern that's used to fill the text box (solid, empty, dotted, and so on). It displays a gallery of 16 patterns. Be sure to choose one that doesn't make the text hard to read.

- **Box Border Color** affects the color used for the border of the box. It displays a gallery of colors.

Shape properties

When you select a shape element (rectangle, rounded rectangle, ellipse, or polygon), the Property Sheet contains the following:

- **Fill Color** affects the color used to fill the shape. It displays a gallery of colors available with your screen.
- **Fill Pattern** affects the pattern used to fill the shape. It displays a gallery of 16 different patterns.
- **Fill Background Color** lets you change the color used behind the shape's fill pattern. (If the fill pattern is solid, this color isn't displayed.) It displays a gallery of colors.
- **Border Drawn** determines whether the shape's outline is shown in a separate color. When you choose this command, the option toggles back and forth between *Yes* and *No*.
- **Border Color** determines the color of the border (when you set Border Drawn to **Yes**). It displays a gallery of colors.
- **Border Style** determines the line pattern of the border (when you set **Border Drawn** to **Yes**). It displays a gallery of line patterns (thick, thin, dotted, dashed, and so on).

Line and arrow properties

When you select the arrow icon, the Property Sheet contains the following:

- **Arrowhead Color** determines the color of the arrowhead. It displays a gallery of colors available with your screen.
- **Line Color** determines the color of the line. It displays a gallery of colors.
- **Line Style** affects the pattern of the line. It displays a gallery of line patterns (thick, thin, dotted, dashed, and so on).

When you select a line or polyline element, the Property Sheet lists only the line properties shown here.

Graph properties

You can set properties for the graph itself as well as for elements you create. You must first select the graph (choose the edit icon, then point to the graph and press the Period key or click the mouse). The Property Sheet then changes to list the following graph properties:

```
╔══ Graph ══╗
║           ║
║ Reset Scale║
║ Grid Color ║
║ Chart Color║
║ Background ║
║ Text       ║
║  Label Font║
║  X Title Font║
║  Y Title Font║
║           ║
╚═══════════╝
```

■ **Reset Scale** returns the graph, title, and legend to their original positions. If you resized the graph, it returns to the default size. Any annotation elements you created remain in place.

■ **Grid Color** lets you change the color of grid lines. You can choose the color you want from the Gallery and see the effects immediately. This is the same as the /Graph | Overall | Grid | Color command.

■ **Chart Color** lets you use the Gallery to change the color behind the chart area of the graph (inside the graph borders). This is the same as the /Graph | Overall | Grid | Fill Color command.

■ **Background** lets you change the color of the area outside of the chart area. This is the same as the /Graph | Overall | Background Color command.

*All graph properties duplicate commands you can set within the **Graph** menu, but because any changes are displayed instantly, you should find these properties easier to set within the Annotator.*

■ **Text Label Font** lets you change the display of the axes and interior labels. When you choose this command, a menu shows three options: Typeface, Point Size, and Style. Choosing one displays another menu of options. This is the same as the /Graph | Text | Font | Data & Tick Labels command.

■ **Text X-Title Font** lets you change the typeface, point size, and style of any x-axis title. It's the same as the /Graph | Text | Font | X-Title command.

■ **Text Y-Title Font** lets you change the typeface, point size, and style of any y-axis title. It's the same as the /Graph | Text | Font | Y-Title command.

With the graph itself selected, you can also change the size and position of the graph, just as you would for any other annotation element (see pages 404 and 406). You cannot, however, delete the graph.

Legend properties

If your graph includes a legend, you can select it and set properties for it. Like the graph properties, legend properties duplicate commands available within the **Graph** menu, but are often more efficient to use.

```
╔═ Legend ═╗
║          ║
║ Text      ║
║  Color    ║
║  Font     ║
║ Box       ║
║  Color    ║
║  Type     ║
║          ║
╚══════════╝
```

■ **Text Color** affects the color of text in the legend. This is the same as the /Graph | Text | Font | Legend | Color command.

■ **Text Font** lets you change the typeface, point size, and style of legend text. This is the same as the /Graph | Text | Font | Legends command.

- **Box Color** lets you change the color of the box around the legend; colors are shown in the Gallery. This is the same as the /Graph I Outlines I Grid I Grid Color command (and the Annotator's Grid Color and Legend Box Color properties). This command also affects the color of grids, the graph outline, and any title outline.

- **Box Type** lets you change the type of box that encloses the legend. (The Gallery shows small pictures of different box types for this option.) This is the same as the /Graph I Overall I Outlines I Legend command.

With the legend selected, you can also change its position, just as you would for any other annotation element (see page 404). Pressing *Del* also removes the legend. (This, in effect, sets the /Graph I Text I Legend I Position command to **None**.) You cannot, however, resize the legend, although changing the Text I Font I Point Size command will affect the legend size.

Title properties

If your graph includes a main title and/or subtitle, you can also select it and set properties for it. When a graph title is selected, the Property Sheet contains the following:

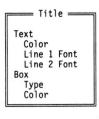

- **Text Color** lets you change the color of title text (both lines). This is the same as the /Graph I Text I Font I 1st Line/2nd Line I Color commands. (If you want the title lines to be different colors, use the Graph menu commands.)

- **Text Line 1 Font** lets you change the typeface, point size, and style of the font used for the first line of the title. It duplicates the /Graph I Text I Font I 1st Line I Typeface I Point Size I Style commands.

- **Text Line 2 Font** is the same as Line 1 Font except that it affects the second line of the title.

- **Box Type** lets you choose a different type of box to enclose the graph title. This is the same as the /Graph I Overall I Outlines I Title command.

- **Box Color** affects the color of the title box. It duplicates the /Graph I Overall I Grids I Grid Color command (and the Annotator's Grid Color and Legend Box Color properties). This command also affects the color of grids, the graph outline, and any legend outline.

Like legends, you can move or delete a selected graph title, but you cannot resize it (except with the Line I Font Size command).

Group properties

If you've selected more than one element and the elements are different types, Quattro displays a generic list of properties in the Property Sheet (called *group* properties). You can use these to change properties for all the selected elements at once.

```
┌───── Group ─────┐
│ Fill            │
│    Color        │
│    Pattern      │
│    Bkgrd Color  │
│ Line            │
│    Color        │
│    Style        │
└─────────────────┘
```

- **Fill Color** affects the color used to fill any shapes in the selected group.
- **Fill Pattern** affects the pattern used to fill any shape in the group.
- **Fill Background Color** lets you change the color used behind the shapes' fill patterns. (Quattro doesn't display this color for solid fill patterns.)
- **Line Color** determines the color of any lines in the selected group, including shape borders.
- **Line Style** determines the line pattern of any lines, including shape borders.

These properties affect selected elements (when applicable), except for the graph titles, legend, and the graph itself.

Using the Clipboard

You can use commands on the Annotator Clipboard to cut and paste annotation elements. For example, you can

- create "clip art" elements, such as company logos or special symbols, and store them in a Clipboard file for future use with any Quattro graph
- paste in "clip art" elements stored in the Quattro Clipboard
- delete selected elements from the Draw Area
- duplicate elements within a graph
- copy elements to a different graph
- move elements in front of or in back of other elements

```
┌─ Clipboard ─┐
  Cut
  Copy
  Paste
  Delete
  To Top
  To Bottom
  Cut To       ▶
  Copy To      ▶
  Paste From   ▶
└─────────────┘
```

To use **Clipboard** commands, choose the Clipboard icon from the Toolbox (press /C or click the icon).

- **Cut** removes the selected elements from the Draw Area and stores them in the Clipboard so you can insert them in a different graph.

- **Copy** stores a copy of the selected elements in the Clipboard without deleting them from the Draw Area.

- **Paste** inserts the elements stored in the Clipboard at the same place from which they were cut.

- **Delete** removes the selected elements without storing them in the Clipboard. This is the same as pressing *Del.*

- **To Top** moves the selected element(s) in front of any other elements that might be covering it up.

- **To Bottom** moves the selected element(s) in back of any other elements it might be covering up.

- **Cut To** removes selected elements from the Draw Area and stores them as clip art in the Clipboard file you name. (Quattro gives all Clipboard files the extension .CLP.)

- **Copy To** copies selected elements into the Clipboard file you specify.

- **Paste From** inserts elements stored as clip art in the specified Clipboard file into the current graph. The inserted elements are positioned just as they were in the graph from which they were taken. You can reposition them however you like.

Note   Quattro comes with a library of over 35 clip art images (from Marketing Graphics Inc.'s PicturePak series), including a U.S. map (see page 423). To use these images, choose the Clipboard icon from the Toolbox and then choose Paste From.

Cutting and pasting elements

By using the Clipboard to temporarily store selected elements, you can move or copy an element to a different graph, or duplicate an element in the current graph. The Clipboard is also a good place to store an element you want to delete temporarily.

To store a design element in the Clipboard,

1. Go into the Draw Area and select the element(s) you want to store (see page 403).

Only one element or group of elements can be stored in the Clipboard at a time. To cut and paste several elements, select them as a group, or paste each one directly after you cut it.

2. Choose the Clipboard icon from the Toolbox (press /C or click the icon).

3. Choose **Copy** from the **Clipboard** menu if you want to store a copy of the element, or choose **Cut** if you want to remove the original.

4. If you want to copy the element to a different graph, choose the Quit icon from the Toolbox (/Q). If the graph is displayed, press any key to remove it. Save the current graph, if you want, with /**Graph** | **Name** | **Create**. Then display the graph you want to insert the element in. (Use /**Graph** | **Name** | **Display** to load a different graph for the same spreadsheet or use /**File** | **Retrieve** to load a different spreadsheet.)

You cannot cut and paste graph titles, legends, or the graph itself.

5. Press /GA to activate the Annotator.

6. Choose the Clipboard icon from the Toolbox.

7. Choose **Paste** from the **Clipboard** menu. Quattro inserts the element or group of elements exactly where it was positioned in the original graph. The inserted elements remain selected so you can easily move or resize them.

You can also cut and paste within the same graph. For example, if you want to duplicate an element three times in your graph, select the element, choose **Copy** from the **Clipboard** menu (/CC), then choose **Paste** three times. Quattro copies the duplicate elements on top of the original, so that all you see is one element. However, when you select the item and move it, only the top layer moves. The other elements in the stack stay put. So once you've created a stack of duplicate elements, you can move each layer to a different part of the Draw Area.

Moving elements between files

If there's an element or group of elements you expect to use in the future, you can store it in a special clip art file that you can then use with other graphs.

To store an element or group of elements in a file, select the element(s), then choose **Copy To** (to store a copy) from the **Clipboard** menu (/CC). Quattro prompts you for a file name and displays a list of all element files in the current directory. Enter the name you want to give the file. Don't include an extension; Quattro automatically adds on a .CLP extension. When you press *Enter*, Quattro stores the element(s) in the file.

To paste an element or group of elements stored in a file in the current graph, just choose **Paste From** from the **Clipboard** menu (*/CP*). Quattro prompts you for the name of the element file you want to insert and displays a list of such files in the current directory. Enter the name by typing it or choosing it from the list. Quattro immediately inserts the element or group of elements in the same position as in the original graph. You can then move it to the position you want (see page 404).

Layering design elements

If you have elements layered, or stacked, on top of one another, you can easily change their layering order with the **To Top** and **To Bottom** commands on the **Clipboard** menu:

1. Go into the Draw Area and select the element(s) you want to rearrange (see page 403).
2. Choose the Clipboard icon from the Toolbox (press */C* or click the icon).
3. Choose **To Top** from the **Clipboard** menu if you want to move the selected element to the top of the stack, or choose **To Bottom** if you want to move it to the bottom.

Linking an element to a point in a graph

When you have an element that's directly related to a point in the graph, such as an arrow pointing to a graph bar, it's a good idea to "link" the element to that point. Then, when the graph changes to reflect new data, the element moves to follow the point. You don't have to adjust your annotation each time the graph changes.

The way Quattro links an element to a data point is to memorize the distance between the element and a point in the graph that best represents the data point.

For example, if you link an element to a point represented by a bar, Quattro memorizes the distance between the element and a point on the center of the top of the bar. If you link to a slice of a pie chart, Quattro uses the distance between the element and a point on the center of the edge of the slice. If the graph changes, Quattro maintains the positive distance between the linked element and the bar, slice, or other part of the graph that represents the data point.

In the following figure, the text element and arrow are linked as a group to the second value in the first series; that is, February sales (50) in the Southeast.

Figure 15.6
A graph with linked
annotation

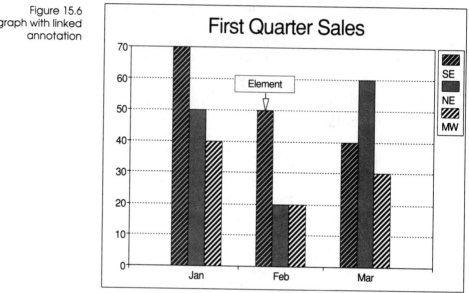

In the following figure, 50 is changed to –50. Note how Quattro preserves the positive distance between the element and a point on the center of the top of the bar representing Feburary sales in the Southeast.

Figure 15.7
A graph with linked
annotation and a negative
value

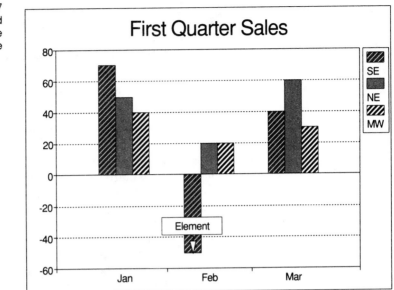

In the following figure, the graph type changes from bar to rotated bar. Note that, no matter how the graph changes, the distance between the element and the point in the graph that represents February sales in the Southeast stays the same.

Figure 15.8
A changed graph with linked
annotation

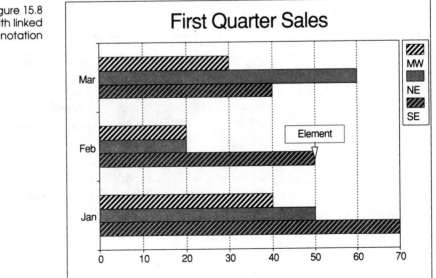

To link an element to a graph point,

1. Go into the Draw Area and select the element(s) you want to link to a graph point (see page 403). If the element is part of a group (such as an arrow connected to text inside a circle), be sure to select them all.

You can link as many elements as you like to a given point—either separately or as a group.

2. Choose the link icon from the Toolbox (press /X or click the icon).

3. Quattro displays a Link menu, listing the six graph series. Choose the series containing the value you want to link to.

4. Quattro prompts you for the *link index*, or the position of the value you want to link to in that series. Specify the value position. For example, if it's the third point in the line or the third bar for the series, enter 3.

Quattro links that element or group of elements with the given point in the series. If you change that value in the spreadsheet, the elements will follow the point wherever it moves in the graph. You can still move or edit elements that are linked to the graph.

If you remove a linked point from a graph (by resetting the series or assigning a series with fewer numbers), Quattro removes the element it's linked to as well. If you later return that point to the graph, the element reappears.

Annotating a text graph

Tip: With text graphs, you can create title screens to introduce graphs in a slide show.

The purpose of a text graph is to give you a clean slate on which to draw annotation elements. A text graph ignores any series assigned to the graph and shows only annotation. When first displayed, it appears completely blank. You can use it like a graphic scratchpad on which to draw annotation elements, just as you would on any other graph type.

You can use a text graph to create all kinds of graphics: flow charts, bulleted lists, handdrawn graphs, and other drawings. The following figures are just a few examples of what you can do with the Annotator:

Figure 15.9
Annotation example 1

*If you want to use this map
in your own annotation,
choose **C**lipboard from the
Toolbox, then choose **P**aste
From to paste it into the
Draw Area from the
USMAP.CLP file.*

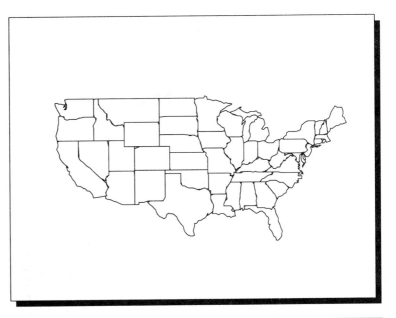

Figure 15.10
Annotation example 2

Figure 15.11
Annotation example 3

5

Advanced features

426

16

Using macros

Quattro's macro facility is a valuable accessory to the program. It is simple enough to be of use to the least experienced of users, yet its extensive vocabulary of commands offers advanced users all the tools they need to create complex macros.

In Quattro, you can use macros to customize the program to suit your requirements. You can create simple macros to automate routine tasks, such as advancing the cell selector down a column as you enter values. You can also create more complex macros to build your own application—for example, a complete expense-tracking system.

This chapter describes how to

- record macros using Quattro's Record mode
- execute macros
- edit existing macros
- debug macros using Quattro's extensive Macro Debugger utility
- delete macros
- enter macros in the spreadsheet without recording them
- change the way Quattro records macros
- use macro commands within macros
- store a set of macros in a separate spreadsheet

For detailed descriptions of each of the macro commands, see *@Functions and Macros.*

What is a macro?

A *macro* is a sequence of recorded keystrokes or commands that Quattro executes automatically. When you replay a macro, Quattro performs the actions recorded in the macro. Quattro stores macros with the spreadsheet in which you created them, so you can have a different set of macros for each spreadsheet you use.

Quattro macros can use any key on the keyboard and any command on the menus. In addition, they can include *macro commands*: special commands that perform functions beyond the scope of menu commands, such as prompting the user for input before continuing the macro. Macro commands also bring into play several programming functions, such as looping, branching, and subroutines.

Because you create your own macros, their level of complexity (and effectiveness) is up to you. If you're new to macros, you might want to begin by simply assigning the menu commands you use most often to macros, thereby reducing your keystrokes. You can also use macros to enter frequently used labels.

As you become more familiar with macros, you can automate complex command sequences, such as printing a standard report. If you're a more sophisticated user, you can build actual spreadsheet applications, which can then be used by others with little or no knowledge of Quattro.

The Macro menu

The Macro menu lets you create, execute, and delete macros—and more. There are two ways to call up this menu:

- Choose /Tools | Macro.
- Press *Alt-F2*.

 If you're using the 123-compatible menus, choose /Worksheet | Macro or press *Alt-F2*.

```
======= Macro =======

Record
Paste
Instant Replay
Macro Recording    ▶

Transcript
Clear Breakpoints
Debugger           ▶
Name               ▶
Library            ▶

Execute
```

■ **Record** puts Quattro in Record mode, during which it records all your actions as a macro. To exit Record mode, choose Record again or choose Paste to stop recording and paste your macro into the spreadsheet.

■ **Paste** stores the last recorded macro in the spreadsheet block you specify. It also prompts you for a name to give the block.

■ **Instant Replay** executes the last macro you recorded.

■ **Macro Recording** switches macro recording mode from menu-equivalent commands to literal keystrokes, if you prefer.

■ **Transcript** activates the Transcript utility, which you can use to view and work with a command history of all your work. Transcript creates the command history automatically while you work, recording all your actions in a file like a huge macro.

■ **Clear Breakpoints** removes any breakpoints set in a macro during debugging.

■ **Debugger** activates the Macro Debugger, which you can use to work out problems in your macros.

■ **Name** lets you assign a name to a cell block containing a macro or delete an assigned block name. You can use the assigned name to invoke the macro.

■ **Library** lets you specify the current spreadsheet as a macro library, or remove the library status from a spreadsheet. A macro library is simply a spreadsheet where you store macros for use within other spreadsheets.

■ **Execute** plays back the macro you specify.

This chapter explains how to use each of these commands except Transcript, which is covered in the next chapter.

The basics

The most efficient way to create a macro is with Quattro's Record mode. To enter Record mode, choose /Tools | Macro | Record or press *Alt-F2 R*. Quattro begins recording each action you take until you exit Record mode by choosing **Record** again. You can then use Instant Replay to play the macro back, or choose **Paste** to store the macro in a spreadsheet block. (Paste also exits Record mode if you're in it.) When you paste the recorded macro in a spreadsheet, Quattro writes it into the block as a set of generic menu-equivalent commands, which can be understood by any Quattro menu tree.

Once you've pasted a macro, you can execute it at any time by choosing /Tools I Macro I Execute or pressing *Alt-F2 E*. If the macro is stored in a spreadsheet you've designated as a macro library, you can execute it from within other spreadsheets.

Quattro also supports *instant macros*, macros you can execute directly with an *Alt*-letter combination. To make a macro an instant macro, just give it an alphabetic name: any letter (upper- and lowercase letters are equivalent) from *A* to *Z*, preceded by a backslash (\). To execute the macro, press *Alt* plus the letter you assigned to it.

If you're using the 123-compatible menu tree with 123-compatible defaults, you'll be able to execute Lotus macros within Quattro. You'll also be able to use macros you created in Quattro with Lotus 1-2-3.

Recording a macro

Quattro has greatly simplified the procedure for creating spread-sheet macros. Instead of requiring you to type the keystrokes needed to perform an action as a label in a cell, it lets you *record* actions *as you perform them*.

For example, in many spreadsheet programs, to create a macro that changes a cell's numeric format, you would have to step through the appropriate menu commands and prompts and write down each keystroke you make to perform the action. Then you would enter those keystrokes as a label.

In Quattro, you can enter macro Record mode, which records actions as you perform them. Record mode also lets you use Quattro macros with different menu trees because it's the *commands* that are recorded, not the keystrokes that initiated them.

If Quattro is recording your actions keystroke by keystroke instead of as menu-equivalent commands, use the **Macro** Recording command to change the way Quattro records your macros. See "Changing macro recording mode" later in this chapter.

Note   When you record a macro, you can choose menu commands either by pressing the first letter, clicking with the mouse, or using the arrow keys and pressing *Enter*. The resulting macro reads exactly the same. For example, if you use the arrow keys to choose /**Options** | **Formats** | **Align Labels** | **Center**, the macro appears as

```
{/ Publish;AlignCenter}
```

If you use first-letter keys, the same macro appears. When you specify a cell block in a macro command, be sure to type in the coordinates for the block rather than pointing it out.

To record a macro,

1. First, plan ahead for what you want the macro to do. Take notes if necessary.
2. Choose /**Tools** | **Macro** | **Record** or press *Alt-F2 R*. Quattro enters Record mode and displays the REC mode indicator on the status line.
3. Carry out whatever actions you want recorded in the macro. You can use any key on the keyboard. Quattro displays menus, prompts, and messages and moves the cell selector as usual. The only difference is that each key you enter is recorded in the macro. You can enter as many command sequences as you like.
4. When you've completed the sequence you want stored in the macro, choose **Record** again. Quattro exits Record mode and returns to the spreadsheet.

   Another way to end the macro is to choose **Paste**, which exits Record mode and prompts for a macro name and a block to paste the recorded macro into (see the following section, "Pasting a recorded macro").

If you're using the 123-compatible menus, choose /**Worksheet** | **Macro** | **Record**. If you want your Quattro macros to run with Lotus 1-2-3, make sure that /**Tools** | **Macro** | **Macro Recording** is set to **Keystroke**, which records actual keystrokes instead of menu-equivalent commands. Also, avoid using the "Quattro-only" commands on the 123-compatible menu tree, which are identified by boxes on the menus.

Once you've recorded a macro, there are two things you can do with it:

- Store, or *paste*, the macro in a spreadsheet so you can play it back at any time (see the following section).

■ Use the Instant Replay command to play the macro back (see "Instant replay" later in this chapter).

Pasting a recorded macro

After you've recorded a macro you want to save, you need to paste it into a spreadsheet. The macro is then saved with the spreadsheet, and you can access it any time the spreadsheet is open.

To paste the last recorded macro into a spreadsheet,

1. Press *Alt-F2 P* or choose /Tools | Macro | Paste. You can either use the Record command to exit Record mode before you paste the macro or simply choose the Paste command to end the macro. Quattro prompts you for a macro name.

2. Enter a name for your macro using standard rules for block names. Quattro prompts you for a macro name. (See "Naming a macro" later in this chapter for details on the name you give a macro.) You'll then be able to execute the macro by name instead of by location. If you don't want to name your macro, just press *Enter*.

3. Specify the block you want to store the macro in. It doesn't have to be in the same spreadsheet. Use standard linking rules to store it in a different spreadsheet. If there's no chance of overwriting data in cells below, specify a single cell or row, and Quattro fills the cells below as necessary. Otherwise, specify at least two rows, and Quattro writes into that block only.

Quattro writes your macro into the given location. If you specified one or more cells in a single row, it deletes data beneath those cells first. If you specified cells in two or more rows, Quattro limits the macro to those cells.

1-2-3

If you're using the 123-compatible menus, choose /Worksheet | Macro | Paste.

Instant replay

The Instant Replay command executes the last-recorded macro. You can use it to test a macro before pasting it into a cell. It's also a good way to use *temporary macros*, which are macros you don't necessarily want to save for future use.

To play back the last macro you recorded, press *Alt-F2 /* or choose /Tools | Macro | Instant Replay. Quattro immediately executes the macro.

You can use Instant Replay many times to play back the last-recorded macro, but once you exit that spreadsheet or record a different macro, that macro is erased. So if you want to use your recorded macro in the future, be sure to paste it into a spreadsheet.

 If you're using the 123-compatible menus, choose /Worksheet | Macro | Instant Replay.

Changing macro recording mode

The Macro Recording command determines how Quattro records your macros. The default is Logical, which records actions as *menu-equivalent commands* that can be read by any Quattro menu tree. If you want to use macros you record in Quattro with Lotus 1-2-3, set this command to Keystroke, which records actual keystrokes instead of menu-equivalent commands. However, you can't use keystroke-recorded macros with every menu tree you might load.

If you want to use your Quattro macros with the 123-compatible menu tree, it's a good idea to keep Macro Recording set to Logical to record menu-equivalent commands. Then, whether you're using the standard Quattro menu tree or the 123-compatible menu tree, your Quattro macros will always run correctly.

To change the way Quattro records macros,

1. Choose /Tools | Macro | Macro Recording.
2. Choose Logical to record your macros as menu-equivalent commands. Choose Keystroke if you want to use the macros you record with Lotus 1-2-3.

 If you're using the 123-compatible menus, choose /Worksheet | Macro | Macro Recording.

See "Reading macro instructions" later in this chapter for information about how menu-equivalent commands work.

Naming a macro

There are three ways to name a macro:

- Give it a name when you paste it into a cell.
- Use /Tools | Macro | Name | Create.
- Use /Edit | Names | Create.

The name you give a macro has special significance. Since you will use this name to invoke the macro, it should help identify the actions taken by the macro. For example, you could use the name "PERCENT" for a macro that changes the numeric format of the current cell to percentage.

Macro names are the same as block names and appear on the block names choice list when you press *F3* from the input line. For this reason, don't give a macro the same name as a named block. When naming macros, follow the same guidelines as those for block names (see page 127).

 If you're using the 123-compatible menus, choose /**Worksheet** | **Macro** | **Name**.

Instant macros

If the macro you're creating is one you'll use often, you can give it a special name that will make it easier to execute: Any letter of the alphabet (*A-Z*) preceded by a backslash (\). You will then be able to initiate the macro directly from the keyboard simply by pressing *Alt* and that letter (in either upper- or lowercase). Such macros are called instant macros, and they differ from standard macros only in the way they are invoked. (For information on how to invoke a standard macro, see "Executing a macro" later in this chapter.

Because there can be only 26 instant macros, it's a good idea to reserve these for the macros you'll use most often. It also helps to name macros according to their functions. For example, if you have a macro that centers data in the current cell, you might name it \C.

Autoload macros

If you assign a macro the same autoload name specified in the /**Options** | **Startup** | **Startup** Macro default setting (initially \0), Quattro automatically executes it every time you retrieve the spreadsheet. This feature is useful to invoke a special application used with all spreadsheets.

Note   To ensure that a \0 macro will run in a spreadsheet regardless of whether it's linked to another, begin the macro with {ESC}. This will back you out of the links options prompt when you retrieve a supporting spreadsheet without any adverse effect on a primary spreadsheet. You can always use the /**Tools** | **Update Links** command to access linked values or load supporting spreadsheets after you retrieve the file.

There can be only one autoload macro per spreadsheet.

If you no longer want Quattro to load a macro automatically, you can always tell Quattro to execute a different macro at startup by changing the /**Options** | **Startup** | **Startup** Macro default setting to a different macro name (see page 194). You can also change the macro name with /**Tools** | **Macro** | **Name** | **Create**, or delete the name with /**Tools** | **Macro** | **Name** | **Delete**.

Locating your macros

You can store your macros within the spreadsheet you create them in, or in a separate spreadsheet called a *macro library*. Either way, you'll be able to access them from any spreadsheet, although using a macro library simplifies linked access. It's not only easier to keep track of where the macros are, but if you execute a macro that Quattro can't find in the current spreadsheet, it automatically searches through all loaded macro libraries until it finds it.

Storing macros in the spreadsheet

If you don't expect to use the macros you're building with other spreadsheets, you may want to store them within the current spreadsheet. If you change your mind, you can always copy or move them into a macro library.

How you position macros in your spreadsheet in relation to your data is important. It would be easy to place them in the lower right corner of the spreadsheet, but this wastes memory space. Therefore, they should be near your spreadsheet data, but not in a place that would interfere with data operations.

The following figure shows a spreadsheet with data and four sets of macros:

Figure 16.1
Macros stored in a
spreadsheet

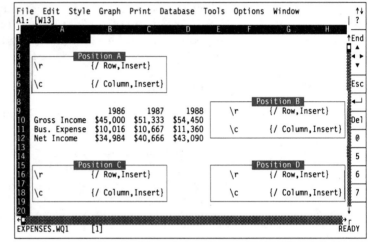

Although each of these locations has its advantages and disadvantages, the B position (to the right of the data) is not recommended. If you delete, insert, or sort rows with macros in this position, your macros will be ruined. Also, if you delete columns—a far less frequent action—you might damage macros in positions A and C (above and below spreadsheet data). Position D (below and to the right of the spreadsheet) is probably the best location, since it is not affected when you delete rows or columns of your data.

You should also leave space on either side of the macros. You can use one column for labels that identify the macros (and cells used for temporary storage) by name. In the other column, you can add comments that explain steps in the macros. If you place the names in their own column, you will be able to locate macros much more easily. The macro descriptions will help in reading and debugging macros. The following figure shows a set of macros with this layout:

User's Guide

Figure 16.2
A set of macros with
descriptions

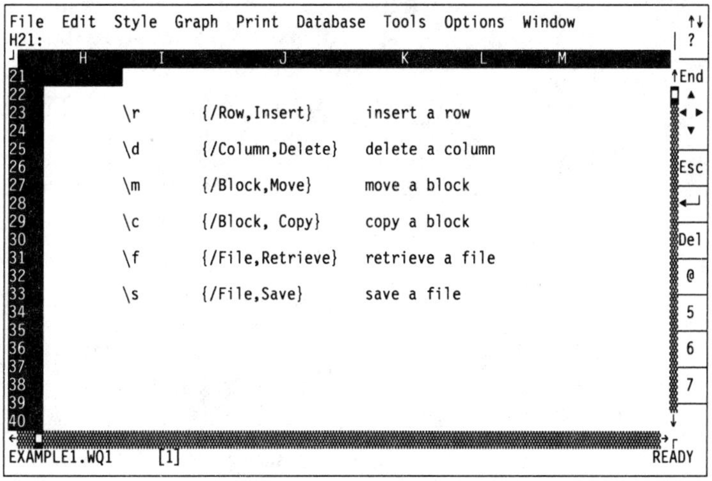

```
File  Edit  Style  Graph  Print  Database  Tools  Options  Window        ↑↓
H21:                                                                    |  ?
      H        I          J              K          L        M          ↑End
21
22
23        \r       {/Row,Insert}      insert a row                      ◄ ►
24                                                                       ▼
25        \d       {/Column,Delete}   delete a column
26                                                                      Esc
27        \m       {/Block,Move}      move a block
28                                                                       ↵
29        \c       {/Block, Copy}     copy a block
30                                                                      Del
31        \f       {/File,Retrieve}   retrieve a file
32                                                                       @
33        \s       {/File,Save}       save a file
34                                                                       5
35
36                                                                       6
37
38                                                                       7
39
40                                                                       ↓
EXAMPLE1.WQ1      [1]                                                   READY
```

When Quattro executes a macro, it begins with the first cell in the
macro block. It continues down through the column, interpreting
everything it encounters as part of the same macro, until it finds a
blank cell, a cell with a value, the {QUIT} macro command, or an
invalid macro entry. At that point, it stops reading cells and
returns control to the keyboard. For this reason, it's imperative
that you leave a blank cell (or include the {QUIT} command) after
each macro in your spreadsheet.

Macro libraries

The most efficient way to store macros is in a *macro library*, a
special spreadsheet reserved for macros. You can use it to store
macros you want to access from any spreadsheet. When you
execute a macro, Quattro first looks for it in the active spreadsheet. If it can't find it there, it searches through every open macro
library until it finds it, then executes the macro.

There are several advantages to storing macros in a library:

■ If Quattro can't find the macro you specify within the current
spreadsheet, it automatically searches through all loaded macro
libraries until it finds it. So even if you can't remember which
library you stored a macro in, you can execute it.

■ Your macros don't interfere with your spreadsheet data, and
vice versa.

■ Using one set of macros for a group of spreadsheets saves disk
space.

- If there's a set of macros you *do* want to insert into individual spreadsheets, you can store them in a library, then copy the macros into spreadsheets as you need them.
- You can have a separate set of macros for each application or type of spreadsheet you work with.

To create a macro library, open a new spreadsheet and create the macros you want to store in it (or copy them from another spreadsheet).

To designate the spreadsheet as a library,

1. Choose /Tools | Macro | Library. Quattro displays a menu with two options: Yes and No.
2. Choose Yes to make the current spreadsheet a macro library. Quattro now knows to look in that file for any macro it can't find in the active spreadsheet.

1-2-3 If you're using the 123-compatible menus, choose /Worksheet | Macro | Library.

Note It's a good idea to keep only one macro library open at a time. If two open libraries contain a macro with the same name, it's difficult to predict which macro will execute.

When you execute a macro in a macro library, it behaves as though it were stored in the active spreadsheet. In other words, block coordinates entered at command prompts refer to the active spreadsheet. However, coordinates used in macro commands, such as {BRANCH}, refer to the macro library. If you need to refer to a block in the active spreadsheet in a macro command, use the standard link syntax with empty cell brackets. For example, to branch from the macro library to cell A1 in the active spreadsheet, use the following syntax:

{BRANCH []A1}

You can use this same syntax to access other spreadsheets as well.

To remove the macro library status from a spreadsheet, choose /Tools | Macro | Library | No.

Executing a macro

To execute a standard (non-instant) macro, choose /Tools |
Macro | Execute or press *Alt-F2 E*. Quattro prompts you for the
macro to execute. Specify the macro in any of three ways:

- Press *F3* and choose it from the displayed list of block names.
- Use the arrow keys or mouse to point to the first cell in the
  macro's block.
- Type in the macro's name or block coordinates.

The MACRO mode indicator appears onscreen. Press *Enter* and
Quattro immediately executes the macro.

If you're using the 123-compatible menus, choose /**W**orksheet |
Macro | Execute.

The macro you execute doesn't have to be in the current spreadsheet. You can specify a macro in a different spreadsheet by
pointing to it or by using standard linking syntax (see "Using
linking in macros" later in this chapter). If you specify a macro
name (without link syntax) that Quattro can't find in the current
spreadsheet, it automatically searches through any open macro
library for the macro. Note that if you have two open libraries that
both contain a macro with the same name, it's difficult to predict
which macro will execute.

You can invoke instant macros (named \A through \Z) directly
from the keyboard by pressing *Alt* and the letter in the macro's
name.

You can also execute a macro as you load Quattro by specifying
its name after you enter the letter *Q* and a file name on the DOS
command line. For example,

    Q EXPENSE \F

loads Quattro, retrieves the spreadsheet named EXPENSE, and
executes the macro named \F.

If you try to execute a macro that contains an error, Quattro beeps
and displays an error message. To correct a macro that contains
an error, you can use the Macro Debugger utility (discussed later
in this chapter).

To stop a macro in mid-execution, press *Ctrl-Break*. Then, press *Esc*
to return to Ready mode.

Note If the *Ctrl-Break* key has been disabled with the {BREAKOFF} macro command, you will not be able to interrupt the macro with *Ctrl-Break*.

Reading macro instructions

When you paste a recorded macro into your spreadsheet, Quattro writes macro instructions into the specified block. When you look at the cell entry, you can see that Quattro has not recorded your actions keystroke by keystroke. Instead, it has translated keystrokes that invoked menu selections into special commands, called menu-equivalent commands.

If Quattro is recording your actions keystroke by keystroke instead of as menu-equivalent commands, use the **M**acro Recording command to change the way Quattro records your macros.

Menu-equivalent commands have two purposes:

- They make reading the macro much easier. For example, a macro to change the default numeric format to Currency with zero precision would be displayed as

  ```
  {/ Defaults;Format}C0~
  ```

  rather than as its key-equivalent sequence:

  ```
  /OFNC0~
  ```

- Menu-equivalent commands make it possible to use the macros with different menu trees because the commands themselves are recorded, not the actual keystrokes.

The menu-equivalent commands are designed to best describe the action taken, rather than simply list the keystrokes used to invoke them. They each consist of two words surrounded by curly braces and preceded by a slash and space; for example,

  ```
  {/ File;Retrieve}
  ```

or

  ```
  {/ Print;Breaks}
  ```

The first word relays the general action taken by the command. The second word (in combination with the first) pinpoints the action of the command.

Menu-equivalent commands are listed and categorized in detail in Chapter 3 of *@Functions and Macros*.

Editing a macro

If a macro contains an error, or if you want to alter it, you can change it by editing it. If it's a lengthy macro and you're not sure where the problem is, you can debug it to find the error (discussed later in this chapter).

To edit a macro, move the selector to the cell you want to change, and press the Edit key (*F2*). Quattro enters Edit mode, which is the same mode used to edit any other kind of spreadsheet entry. Make the changes you want, then press *Enter*. Be sure to leave a blank cell at the end of the macro.

When you record a macro, Quattro translates special keys you press, such as arrow keys and *Enter*, into special key-equivalent commands, and translates menu commands you choose as menu-equivalent commands. This increases both readability and flexibility (see "Reading macro instructions" on page 440). When you edit a macro, you need to use the same equivalent commands. For example, if you want to move the selector one cell to the right, you need to enter {RIGHT}. If you want to use the / Graph | Text | X-Title command, you need to enter {/ XAxis;Title}.

Table 16.1 on page 444 lists each of the key-equivalent commands required when writing or editing macros. Table 2.1 in Chapter 2 of *@Functions and Macros* lists macros in every available category. Chapter 3 of *@Functions and Macros* lists each Quattro menu-equivalent command.

Note Press the Macros key (*Shift-F3*) to enter any macro command automatically by choosing it from a list.

See "Entering macros as labels" for information about how to write macro instructions.

Deleting a macro

When you no longer use a macro, you can conserve spreadsheet space and shorten the macro name list by deleting both the macro and its name.

To delete the name assigned to a macro block, use the /Edit | Names | Delete command or /Tools | Macro | Name | Delete. Quattro displays a list of existing block or macro names. Choose one from the list or type in the name.

This command deletes the block name only. To delete the actual macro cells, choose /Edit | Erase Block and specify the block containing the macro.

Advanced macro techniques

With the information given up to here, you should be able to record, execute, edit, and delete simple macros. The rest of this chapter deals with macro techniques appropriate for more advanced users. It tells you how to

- enter macros directly into the spreadsheet as labels
- use linking in macros
- debug macros
- use macro commands
- use the Macros key (*Shift-F3*) to enter macro commands and menu-equivalent commands

Entering macros as labels

If you're an advanced macro user, you may prefer to write macros directly into cells as labels instead of using Record mode. Because this method requires a great amount of precision (one incorrect keystroke could invalidate your macro), it is not recommended for novice users.

Warning If you create macro labels that list keystrokes used to invoke menus, they may not work with alternate menu trees.

To enter a macro as a label,

1. Plan your macro well. If the macro involves menu commands, step through the commands first and write down each keystroke involved. If it involves special macro commands, make sure you know exactly what you're going to enter as the command arguments. For complex command macros, you may want to sketch out a flow chart first.

2. Move the cell selector to the first cell in the block in which you want to store the macro.

3. Enter an apostrophe (') label-prefix character to begin the label. This ensures that Quattro regards whatever follows as a label. Macros must always be entered into cells as labels.

4. Enter the keystrokes required to execute the commands you want. You can use any of the keys on the keyboard, although certain keys must be indicated with special key-equivalent commands (see Table 16.1). If you use more than one cell, be sure they proceed directly downward with no blank cells between them. Each of the cells must contain commands entered as a label. If you want to be able to use the macros you enter as labels with other menu trees, use menu-equivalent commands instead of keystroke-equivalent commands (see "Entering menu-equivalent commands," which follows this section).

5. When you're finished with the macro or want to move to the next cell to enter more of the macro, press *Enter*. Be sure to leave a blank cell at the end of the macro, or end it with {QUIT} or {RETURN}.

6. When the macro is complete, you can assign a name to the macro block. Choose /Tools | Macro | Name, enter the name, then specify the first cell of the block containing the macro.

If your macro invokes more than one command, it's a good idea to use separate cells for each command. That way, if there is a problem, it's easier to pinpoint.

The following figure shows a macro written into three cells. Descriptions of each step are included in cells to the right. The name of the macro is shown to the left. Macros set up this way are much easier to read and debug.

Figure 16.3
A macro written into three
cells

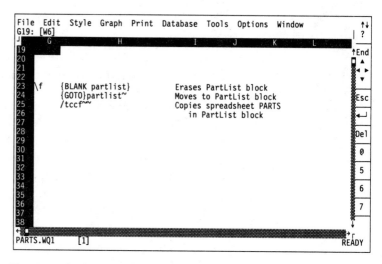

To enter the keys shown in Table 16.1 in a macro, you must use
the special key-equivalent commands shown. You can enter the
commands in either upper- or lowercase letters.

Table 16.1
Commands for entering
special keys in macros

Key	Name	Key-equivalent command
Enter		~ (tilde) or {CR}
Backspace		{BS} or {BACKSPACE}
Esc		{ESC} or {ESCAPE}
Del		{DEL} or {DELETE}
Ins		{INS} or {INSERT}
Home		{HOME}
End		{END}
PgUp		{PGUP}
PgDn		{PGDN}
Ctrl → or Tab		{BIGRIGHT} or {TAB}
Ctrl ← or Shift-Tab		{BIGLEFT} or {BACKTAB}
↑		{UP} or {U}
↓		{DOWN} or {D}
→		{RIGHT} or {R}
←		{LEFT} or {L}
Ctrl \ (backslash)		{DELEOL}
Ctrl-Backspace		{CLEAR}
Ctrl-D		{DATE}
F2	Edit	{EDIT}
Shift-F2	Debug	{STEP}
F3	Choices	{NAME}
Shift-F3	Macros	{MACROS}
Alt-F3	Functions	{FUNCTIONS}
F4	Absolute	{ABS}
F5	GoTo	{GOTO}

Key	Name	Key-equivalent command
Shift-F5 or *Alt-0*	Pick Window	{CHOOSE}
Alt-F5	Undo	{UNDO}
F6	Pane	{WINDOW}
Shift-F6	Next Window	{NEXTWIN}
Alt-F6	Zoom Window	{ZOOM}
F7	Query	{QUERY}
Shift-F7	Select	{MARK}
Alt-F7	All Select	{MARKALL}
F8	Table	{TABLE}
Shift-F8	Move	{MOVE}
F9	Calc	{CALC}
Shift-F9	Copy	{COPY}
F10	Graph	{GRAPH}
Shift-F10	Paste	{PASTE}

You can repeat most of the keys listed in Table 16.1 by specifying a repeat number with the code. For example, to move the cell selector down 5 cells from its current position, use the command {Down 5} or {Down A4} if cell A4 contains the value 5.

For descriptions of each of the function keys listed here, see Appendix D.

Entering menu-equivalent commands

The easiest and most accurate way to enter menu-equivalent commands is with the Macros key (*Shift-F3*). When you press this key, Quattro displays a menu of seven macro command categories.

The first six items on the menu are special macro categories and are described in "Entering macro commands" on page 456. The last item, / Commands, lets you enter menu-equivalent commands. When you choose it, Quattro displays a menu of general-action categories, giving the general area of the command. Use the arrow keys to highlight the area you want (scrolling the list, if necessary), and press *Enter*. Quattro then displays a menu of specific actions for that category. Choose the specific action you want to take, and Quattro automatically writes the menu-equivalent command created by the general and specific actions into your spreadsheet's input line.

To find the menu-equivalent command corresponding to the menu command you want to use, see Chapter 3 in *@Functions and Macros.*

Using linking in macros

You can use spreadsheet linking in macros just as you would in any other area. Linking macros is useful to execute a macro in a different spreadsheet, access data in another file, store user input in a different spreadsheet, and so on. The link syntax is the same: Just precede the block name or cell reference with the file specification in brackets. For example,

[BUDGET]A3

If you store the spreadsheet in a different directory, include the path name with the file name. You could also use window commands or function keys (or their key-equivalent commands) to go into the spreadsheet yourself. For details on creating spreadsheet links, see Chapter 11.

If you execute a macro that's in a different spreadsheet, such as a macro library, the macro behaves as though it were stored in the active spreadsheet, so that block coordinates entered at macro prompts refer to the active spreadsheet. However, coordinates stored in the macro as arguments to a macro command refer to the macro library. For example, {BRANCH A1} branches to cell A1 of the library spreadsheet. To refer to a block in a different spreadsheet, use the standard link syntax. For example,

{BRANCH [MACROS]A1}

branches to cell A1 of the MACROS spreadsheet. To refer to a block in whichever spreadsheet you execute the macro from, precede the block coordinates with empty brackets. For example, {BRANCH []A1} branches to cell A1 in the active spreadsheet.

Debugging a macro

Quattro contains a powerful utility for debugging macros; *debugging* is the process of isolating the specific command(s) or logical error(s) causing a problem in a macro.

With the Quattro Macro Debugger, you can

- execute macros in slow motion (step by step), pausing as long as you want between steps
- set breakpoints that "freeze" a macro when it reaches a given cell or satisfies a given condition

- execute a macro at full speed until it reaches a breakpoint, then either continue in slow motion or at full speed until the next breakpoint

- view, or *trace*, changes to a specific cell as a macro executes

Isolating a problem in a long macro is not simple at regular speed. For this reason, the Macro Debugger uses a special macro mode called Debug. In Debug mode, Quattro executes a macro step by step, pausing for a signal from the keyboard before going on to the next step. This way, you can figure out exactly what is happening in each phase of the macro.

Shift F2
Debug

To execute a macro in Debug mode, choose /Tools | Macro | Debugger | Yes or press *Shift-F2*. This activates Debug mode and displays the DEBUG indicator on the status line. Use the /Tools | Macro | Execute command or press *Alt-F2 E* to invoke the macro you want to debug. A Debug window appears in the bottom half of the screen (see the following figure). The first cell of the macro appears in the middle of the Debug window, and the DEBUG mode indicator appears on the status line.

Figure 16.4
The macro Debug window

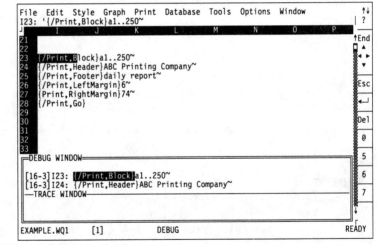

```
File  Edit  Style  Graph  Print  Database  Tools  Options  Window       ↑↓
I23: '{/Print,Block}a1..250~                                            | ?
J         I         J         K         L         M         N         O         P      ↑End
21                                                                                    □ ▲
22                                                                                    ◄ ►
23  {/Print,Block}a1..250~                                                            ▼
24  {/Print,Header}ABC Printing Company~
25  {/Print,Footer}daily report~
26  {/Print,LeftMargin}6~                                                             Esc
27  {Print,RightMargin}74~
28  {/Print,Go}                                                                       ◄┘
29
30                                                                                    Del
31
32                                                                                    @
33
┌DEBUG WINDOW                                                                         5
                                                                                     
  [16-3] I23: {/Print,Block}a1..250~                                                  6
  [16-3] I24: {/Print,Header}ABC Printing Company~
 ─TRACE WINDOW                                                                        7

EXAMPLE.WQ1    [1]              DEBUG                                   READY
```

The Debug window is divided into two sections:

- **The top (macro) section** contains at most three rows. The middle row displays the macro cell currently executing. The top row displays the previous macro cell (if any), and the third row displays the next macro cell (if any).

■ **The bottom (trace window) section** displays the contents of "trace cells" and is used to view the effects of a macro on specific cells.

To execute the first step of the macro (the first keystroke or command), press *Spacebar*. Press it repeatedly to execute each step of the macro until you pinpoint the error. To execute the rest of the actions in the macro at full speed, press *Enter*.

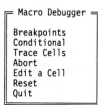 If you have a mouse, click to execute the next step of a macro in Debug mode.

To display the special Macro Debugger menu, press the Slash key (/) from within the Debug window.

```
┌─ Macro Debugger ─┐
│                  │
│ Breakpoints      │
│ Conditional      │
│ Trace Cells      │
│ Abort            │
│ Edit a Cell      │
│ Reset            │
│ Quit             │
└──────────────────┘
```

■ **Breakpoints** lets you specify up to four cells or blocks at which macro execution should be suspended.

■ **Conditional** lets you specify up to four cells that contain logical expressions, such as +A3=10. As soon as the expression returns a true value, the current macro is suspended.

■ **Trace Cells** lets you specify up to four cells whose contents you want to monitor while a macro is being debugged.

■ **Abort** stops execution of the macro and removes the Debug window from the screen.

■ **Edit a Cell** lets you make changes to the macro you're debugging without leaving Debug mode.

■ **Reset** removes any breakpoints you've set with the Breakpoints, Conditional, and Trace Cells commands.

■ **Quit** exits Debug mode and continues to execute the macro until completion.

Suspending macro execution with breakpoints

If you know that most of a macro is correct, you can use *breakpoints* to execute a macro at full speed up to a certain point, then begin Debug mode. There are two kinds of breakpoints you can set: *standard breakpoints* and *conditional breakpoints*. Standard breakpoints suspend execution when the breakpoint cell is reached. Conditional breakpoints suspend execution when the condition stored in the conditional breakpoint cell is reached.

You can set up to four standard breakpoints and four conditional breakpoints per spreadsheet.

Setting standard breakpoints

When you debug a macro containing a standard breakpoint, Quattro executes the macro at full speed until it reaches one of the breakpoints, then suspends execution. To resume, press *Spacebar* to continue in Debug mode, or press *Enter* to continue at full speed until the next breakpoint or until the end of the macro.

Breakpoints provide a means to run quickly through the parts of a macro that work correctly, but pause at the cells that contain problematic macro instructions.

You can set up to four standard breakpoints per spreadsheet. To set a standard breakpoint,

1. Press the Slash key (/) from within the Debug window.
2. Choose **Breakpoints**. Quattro displays the Macro Breakpoints menu, which lists four breakpoints.
3. Choose the breakpoint you want to set. Quattro displays a menu for that breakpoint.

```
# Breakpoint

Block
Pass Count
Quit
```

4. Choose **Block** and specify the cell or block of cells at which you want the macro to stop. If you specify a block of cells, Quattro uses the first cell as the starting point.

There are situations in which a problem appears only after many repetitions of the same macro statements in a loop macro. If this is the case, you can set a pass count to indicate how many times to pass through the breakpoint before stopping. Choose **Pass Count** and specify the number of passes. The default, 1, tells Quattro to stop every time it passes through the breakpoint.

5. Choose **Quit** to return to the Debug window.

When you execute the macro, Quattro performs each step at full speed until the specified cell is reached. It then suspends execution until you press *Spacebar* or *Enter*.

The macro in the following figure includes a loop that continuously increments a single-cell block called COUNTER:

Figure 16.5
An example macro loop

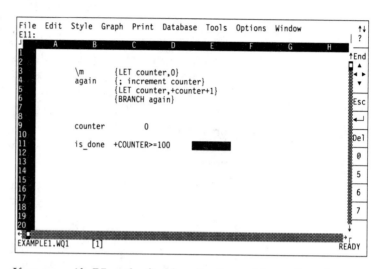

```
File  Edit  Style  Graph  Print  Database  Tools  Options  Window        ↑↓
E11:                                                                      │ ?
   A      B         C         D        E        F        G        H
1                                                                      ↑End
2
3           \m        {LET counter,0}                                    ▲
4           again     {; increment counter}                           ◄  ►
5                     {LET counter,+counter+1}                          ▼
6                     {BRANCH again}                                  Esc
7
8
9           counter        0                                         ◄┘
10
11          is_done   +COUNTER>=100        ███████                  Del
12                                                                     @
13
14
15                                                                     5
16
17                                                                     6
18
19                                                                     7
20
EXAMPLE1.WQ1     [1]                                                 READY
```

If you specify B5 as the first breakpoint and leave **P**ass Count at 0, the macro will stop at the {LET} macro command each time it goes through the loop. When you press *Enter,* Quattro executes the macro and increments the counter cell by one. In the top part of the Debug window, the selector will highlight the {LET} macro command, indicating that Quattro just executed this macro.

If you specified a pass count of 5 for the first breakpoint in this example, then every time you press *Enter,* five loops will occur. You will see the counter increment from 0 to 5, to 10, and so on.

To clear all set breakpoints (including conditional breakpoints and trace cells) choose **R**eset from the Macro Debugger menu. You can also clear breakpoints by choosing /**T**ools I **M**acro I **C**lear Breakpoints.

Setting conditional breakpoints

While standard breakpoints stop a macro when it reaches a given cell, conditional breakpoints stop the macro when a condition becomes true. In the example in the preceding figure, cell B11 contains a logical formula. (The cell containing the formula is formatted so that the formula, rather than the value calculated, appears.) B11 is false (has a value of 0) until 100 or more loops have occurred, which causes the value to become true (a value of 1). If this cell is specified as a conditional cell, the macro suspends execution when the counter reaches 100.

You can set up to four conditional breakpoints per spreadsheet. To set a conditional breakpoint,

1. Choose **C**onditional from the Macro Debugger menu. Quattro displays a menu of conditional breakpoints.

```
┌─ Conditional ─┐
│               │
│ 1st Cell      │
│ 2nd Cell      │
│ 3rd Cell      │
│ 4th Cell      │
│ Quit          │
│               │
└───────────────┘
```

2. Choose the conditional breakpoints you want to set. Quattro prompts you for a condition cell.

3. Specify the cell containing the condition.

4. To set further conditional breakpoints, repeat the steps above.

5. Choose **Q**uit to return to the Debug window.

Conditional breakpoints can be extremely valuable. Suppose you have a macro loop that writes sequential numbers into cell A5 and stops when it reaches 100. You want to pause the macro every 25 steps and check the results. Assign the **1st Cell** command to a cell that contains the formula +A5=25. Assign **2nd Cell** to a cell that contains +A5=50, and assign **3rd Cell** to a cell that contains +A5=75. The macro will then pause as the results reach 25, 50, and 75.

Setting trace cells

Macros often affect the contents of one or more specific cells. By monitoring the contents of these cells during debugging, you can see more clearly what the macro is doing.

Quattro lets you specify up to four *trace cells*, whose contents are shown during debugging in the Trace window pane. Quattro instantly updates the Debug window as the contents of the trace cells change.

To set trace cells,

1. Press / while Quattro displays the Debug window. The Macro Debugger menu appears.

2. Choose **T**race Cells to display the Macro Trace Cells menu.

```
┌─ Macro Trace Cells ─┐
│                     │
│ 1st Cell            │
│ 2nd Cell            │
│ 3rd Cell            │
│ 4th Cell            │
│ Quit                │
│                     │
└─────────────────────┘
```

3. Choose the trace cell you want to set. Quattro prompts you for a trace cell.

4. Specify the cell you want to trace.

5. To specify further trace cells, repeat the steps above.

6. Choose **Q**uit to return to the Debug window.

In the example shown in Figure 16.5, if you specified the counter cell (B9) as a trace cell, you could watch the counter incremented during each loop.

Resetting breakpoints and trace cells	To remove all breakpoints (standard and conditional) and trace cells set for the spreadsheet, choose **Reset** from the Macro Debugger menu.

To remove all breakpoints (standard and conditional) and trace cells set for the spreadsheet, choose **Reset** from the Macro Debugger menu.

You can also reset breakpoints and trace cells from within the spreadsheet (instead of the Debug window). Just choose /**Tools** | **Macro** | **Clear Breakpoints**.

Editing a cell in Debug mode

Once you've pinpointed the problem with a macro, you can use the Edit a Cell command to make corrections to the macro.

When you choose Edit a Cell from the Macro Debugger menu, Quattro prompts you for the address of the cell you want to edit. Point to the cell or type in its coordinates. Quattro then displays the contents of the cell on the input line. You can make changes to the cell just as you would in regular Edit mode. When you press *Enter*, Quattro enters the changes and returns you to the Debug window.

For details on editing macros, see "Editing a macro" on page 441.

Exiting Debug mode

When a macro is finished executing in Debug mode, the Debug window disappears and you exit from Debug mode. If the macro terminates because of an error or *Ctrl-Break* being pressed, Debug mode remains in effect. To exit Debug mode, press *Shift-F2* (the Debug key) or choose /**Tools** | **Macro** | **Debugger** and then choose No. Yet another way to exit Debug mode is to press *Alt-F2 DN*.

To abort a macro before debugging is finished, press the Slash key (/) and choose **Abort** from the Macro Debugger menu. The Debug window disappears. You can debug another macro, or press *Shift-F2* to exit Debug mode.

Using macro commands

Quattro's macro facility includes an extensive set of special commands for use within macros. These commands perform unique functions that you can't always do from the keyboard, such as sounding your computer's beep or pausing the macro and prompting for user input. Quattro's command set also includes conditional and branching commands, making it a true programming language. (Chapter 2 of *@Functions and Macros* describes each of the macro commands.)

You can use macro commands in combination with keyboard commands to create advanced macros. For example, the macro shown in the following figure uses the {GETNUMBER} command to prompt the user for a year, month, and day and stores each response in a named block. It then uses menu commands to set the column width to 10 and change the numeric format to Date 1.

Figure 16.6
A macro example

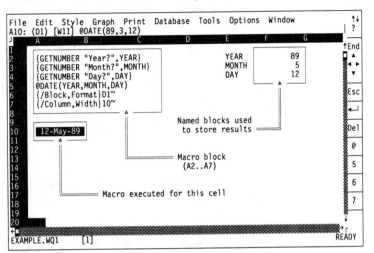

Macro commands are similar to Quattro's @functions in that they have specific grammatical rules, or *syntax*. The syntax for macros is fairly straightforward:

{COMMANDNAME *Argument1,Argument2,Argument3...*}

COMMANDNAME is the exact name of the command. The arguments are values you enter to give further instructions with the command. Not all macro commands require arguments. When they do, they require a specific type of information. (See the next section for a description of argument types used in macro commands.)

Examples   {DISPATCH D35}
{BEEP 3}
{GETNUMBER "How old are you?",AGE}
{CONTENTS E15,F15,15}

The syntax rules for Quattro macros are as follows:

Syntax rules   ■ The command must begin and end with braces { }.

   ■ There must be a space between the command name and the argument(s).

- When you use more than one argument, commas must separate the arguments. You can use a semicolon or period instead of a comma if you specify it as the international punctuation character (see page 189).
- Arguments must be the correct type. In other words, if a string is required, the argument must be a valid character string. If a number is required, it must be a numeric value. If a cell location is called for, the block coordinates must be valid.
- Quattro permits no spaces or other punctuation within the argument list, except within quoted strings. For example,

    {GETLABEL "Hello, world",A4}

    is allowed, but

    {GETLABEL Hello, world,A4}

    is not.
- You must enter the entire expression in a single cell.
- You can enter the command in either upper- or lowercase letters.
- You can include more than one macro command in a cell.

Because macros are labels, Quattro won't beep if you enter a macro command using the wrong syntax. It will beep if you try to execute an incorrect macro command, however. You can save debugging time by paying careful attention to the format of macro commands as you enter them.

Arguments in macro commands

Arguments in macro commands, like those used with @functions, require specific information to be supplied with the command. There are four different types of arguments:

- **Number**—requires any numeric value, entered as
  - an actual number (such as 2 or 0.45)
  - a formula resulting in a number (such as A3 * 15)
  - a reference to a cell containing a numeric value or formula (such as C10)
- **String**—requires a text string, entered either as an actual string or a reference to a cell containing a label. In many cases, you can use a formula that returns a string value.
- **Location**—requires a reference to either a single cell or a cell block. The reference can be

- a block name
- coordinates for a block containing one or more cells; for example, (A1) or (A1..A4)
- a formula returning a string representing any of these options; for example, +"A + "2" (for cell A2)

■ **Condition**—requires a logical expression; that is, an expression containing any cell reference, number, string, or string-valued formula that can be evaluated to be either true or false; for example, C4 > 500.

Unlike @functions, string values you enter in a macro do not always require quotes. However, strings *and block names* must be enclosed in quotes if they contain a comma or a semicolon (or a period if it's specified as the argument separator with the international punctuation setting—see page 189). For example,

{GETLABEL "Good morning; what's your name?",A10}

You must also enclose in quotes any formula you want to appear as a label and any string that is identical to a block name.

Caution! Unlike @function statements, Quattro *does not update* block references in macros when the block coordinates change. If you move a cell, or insert or delete a row or column, the macro may reference the wrong location. For this reason, you should always reference block or macro names whenever possible. Quattro always updates block names automatically to reference the correct location.

The specific values required by each macro are described in Chapter 2 of *@Functions and Macros*. Some commands accept a combination or choice of argument types. For example, {LET} stores either a label or a number in a cell, depending on the argument type. You can specifically indicate a value or label entry by including *argument suffixes* in the command. Using *:string* assures a label entry, and *:value* assures a value entry (if the entry is a valid number). For example, {LET BLOCK,3+4:value} enters a value of 7 in C3, and {LET BLOCK,3+4:string} enters 3 + 4 as a label in the block named BLOCK.

You can also use quotes around a numeric value to enter it as a label.

You can enter a macro command in a macro by typing it, but there's an easier and more accurate way—using the Macros key (*Shift-F3*). This key displays a menu of seven macro command categories.

```
Keyboard
Screen
Interactive
Program Flow
Cell
File
/ Commands
```

- **Keyboard** commands emulate the action of cursor-movement keys, function keys, status keys, plus various other keys.
- **Screen** commands affect the screen display.
- **Interactive** commands let you create interactive macros that pause for the user to enter data from the keyboard.
- **Program Flow** commands are programming commands that let you include branching and looping in your macro.
- **Cell** commands affect the data stored in specified cells.
- **File** commands work with data within files other than your current spreadsheet file.
- **/ Commands** are menu-equivalent commands—see "Entering menu-equivalent commands" on page 445.

Choose the category that contains the command you want to use. Quattro displays a list of each macro within that category. (For a list of the macros in each category, followed by detailed descriptions and examples for each, see Chapter 2 of *@Functions and Macros*.)

To insert one of the listed commands into the input line, choose it from the list. The list disappears and Quattro inserts the macro command at the cursor position on the input line. If there are any arguments required with the command, press the ← key to back up and insert the arguments.

Using subroutines

If you use many macros in your spreadsheets, you may find that you include the same command sequence in many of your macros. You can save time and memory space by storing that command sequence in a separate macro, called a *subroutine*. You can then reference the subroutine within any other macro to include the subroutine's command sequence. You do this by typing the name of the subroutine inside braces. For example, if the subroutine name is GORIGHT4, then {GORIGHT4} invokes the subroutine.

The following figure shows a main macro called MAIN referencing a subroutine called SUB. The {RETURN} command at the end of the subroutine returns control to the main macro. It then picks up where it left off.

Figure 16.7
Using a subroutine macro

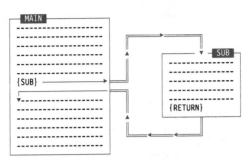

Caution! When you name your subroutines, be sure to avoid any names that duplicate macro commands. Otherwise, the macro commands become invalid. For example, if you named a subroutine READLN, then tried to read a line from a file into cell A6 ({READLN A6}), Quattro would assume that you were calling the READLN subroutine and passing it the contents of cell A6 as an argument.

When you reference a subroutine, you can "pass" the subroutine arguments to use with its commands. These arguments are stored in spreadsheet cells which are referenced by the subroutine. For example,

{SUB C10,36}

sends control to the SUB subroutine and passes two arguments (C10 and 36) along with it. In order for the subroutine to know what to do with the arguments, you must define them within the subroutine, using the {DEFINE} command. This command tells Quattro where to store the arguments and whether they should be interpreted as values or labels.

The following figure shows a main macro passing two arguments (C10 and 36) to a subroutine. These arguments are immediately defined by the subroutine's {DEFINE} command as values to be stored in cells E10 and E11, respectively. The next line of the subroutine then uses these values to calculate a third value, which is stored in E12.

Figure 16.8
Passing arguments to a
subroutine

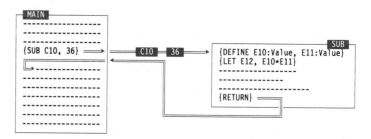

To jump from one macro to another and *stay with* the second
macro (effectively passing control to another macro) use the
{BRANCH} command.

For more information on subroutines and branching with the
{SUBROUTINE}, {DEFINE}, and {BRANCH} commands, see Chapter 2
of *@Functions and Macros*.

Using Transcript

Transcript is a useful and unobtrusive recording tool. As soon as you load Quattro, it records every keystroke you make and every command you choose.

Transcript has four main purposes. You can use it to

- undo a mistake you made
- protect your work against power failure or system crashes
- audit the changes you make to a spreadsheet
- create macros

A macro is a sequence of keystrokes or commands that Quattro executes automatically.

The Transcript utility stores your keystrokes and commands as recorded macros, using menu-equivalent commands that can work with any menu tree (see *@Functions and Macros* for descriptions of these commands). Unlike macros, however, Transcript stores your actions as you make them, in a file in your default directory called QUATTRO.LOG. You can thus restore your work by playing back sections of this file (more later).

You can store your transcripts in a spreadsheet file that contains only macros, or you can paste them into spreadsheet files directly. This lets you reuse the macros: Simply choose /Tools I Macro I Execute and move the cursor to the row containing the transcript macro. When you press *Enter*, Quattro replays the commands or keystrokes in the transcript.

Viewing your command history

You can pause at any point in Quattro to view the steps you've taken so far. To see the recorded transcript or command history, just activate the Transcript utility: Choose /Tools I Macro I Transcript or press *Alt-F2 T*. The Transcript window appears.

The Transcript window shows every step you've taken in Quattro since you opened the file. The last command you gave is highlighted. Quattro marks all actions since the last checkpoint (a /File I Save, /File I Retrieve, or /File I Erase command) with a vertical line to the left. That is, all actions *before* the vertical line have been saved to disk; the marked actions exist in memory, but haven't been saved.

Your steps are shown like macros, using menu-equivalent commands by default. If you see keystroke-by-keystroke macro recordings instead of menu-equivalent commands, choose /Tools I Macro I Recording I Logical to make Quattro record your actions as menu equivalents. See page 433 for details.

Figure 17.1
The Transcript window

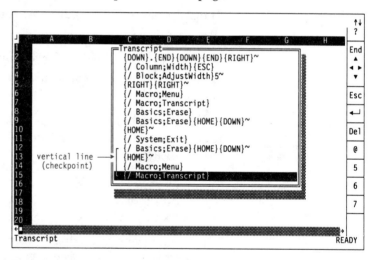

Each line of the window contains several steps, only some of which can be viewed in the window. To see *all* the steps stored on a line, use the arrow keys to highlight the line. Quattro shows its full contents on the input line at the top of the window.

If the transcript contains more lines than fit in the window, use the cursor-movement keys to scroll the window. *Home* takes you to the first command in the history; *End* takes you to the last.

Working with your command history

Besides viewing your command history, you can also

- undo the last command you issued
- restore the actions from the last /File | Save, /File | Retrieve, or /File | Erase command up to the highlighted line in the window (restores work in one file only)
- replay a marked block of the transcript
- copy a marked block of the transcript to the spreadsheet for use as a macro

To work with your transcript file, use the Transcript menu. Press /Tools | Macro | Transcript to open the Transcript window, then press the forward slash key (/) from within Transcript to display this menu.

```
====== Transcript ======

Undo Last Command
Restore to Here
Playback Block
Copy Block
Begin Block
End Block
──Settings──────
Max History Length
Single Step          ▶
Failure Protection
```

- **Undo Last Command** replays (performs each action in) the command history from the most recent checkpoint (the last time you saved, erased, or retrieved a file) to the command immediately preceding the last command.
- **Restore to Here** replays the command history from the last checkpoint to the end of the line highlighted in the Transcript window (restores work in one file only).
- **Playback Block** replays the marked block of actions.
- **Copy Block** lets you copy a block of the transcript into your spreadsheet for use as a macro.
- **Begin Block** lets you mark the beginning of a block of actions you want to replay or copy to the spreadsheet.
- **End Block** lets you mark the end of a transcript block.
- **Max History Length** determines how large the transcript file can be (in characters) before Quattro stores it in a backup file and begins a new file.
- **Single Step** plays actions back one keystroke at a time.
- **Failure Protection** determines how often (in keystrokes) your recorded actions are written to disk.

Undoing the last action

Suppose you issue a command, such as /Edit I Erase Block, and realize as you do it that you've made a grave mistake. You can press /EU or Alt-F5 to choose the /Edit I Undo command, but it must be enabled *before* you use it. You can also choose Undo Last Command, so Quattro replays all the commands in the history from the last checkpoint (when you last saved, erased, or retrieved a file) to immediately before the last command you gave (not counting the command to run Transcript). In effect, it "undoes" the last command you gave. You can then return to your spreadsheet and continue as if the mistake never happened. While Quattro plays back your actions, the WAIT mode indicator appears in the bottom right corner of the screen.

To abort actions being played back, press *Ctrl-Break*. Quattro stops at the end of the current command (unless it's in Single-Step mode—discussed later in this chapter).

Restoring actions to a point

The **Restore to Here** command replays commands in your command history from the last checkpoint to the end of the line that's highlighted. (All actions after the last checkpoint are marked with a vertical line to the left.)

Note   Transcript does not fully restore your work if you've been working in multiple file windows. If you have been working in more than one file, **Restore to Here** correctly restores the work you have done in one file only.

Suppose you made a serious mistake in your spreadsheet but didn't realize it immediately. Use the arrow keys to highlight the line before the mistake and choose **Restore to Here**. Your spreadsheet reverts to how it was before you made the mistake.

To restore a spreadsheet after system or power failure:

1. Highlight the last line of the command history.
2. Choose **Restore to Here**. Quattro restores all your work from the last checkpoint to the point of failure. While it restores your actions, the WAIT indicator appears in the bottom right corner of the screen.

To abort restoration, press *Ctrl-Break*. Quattro stops at the end of the current command (unless it's in Single-Step mode).

Note   You cannot use Transcript to restore actions that occurred *before* the last checkpoint. You can, however, use the **Playback Block** command to replay sections of your command history before the last checkpoint.

Playing back a block of actions

If you want to repeat a series of actions, or just take a closer look at what you did earlier, use the **Playback Block** command.

First, mark off the block of actions you want to replay:

1. Use the arrow keys to highlight the first line you want replayed, and choose /**Begin Block**. After you choose /**Begin Block**, an arrowhead (▸) appears beside the beginning line.
2. Highlight the last line you want replayed, and choose /**End Block**. Arrowheads appear beside each line within the marked block.

When you choose **Playback Block**, Quattro reexecutes all actions stored in that block, just as if it were a macro. While Quattro plays back your actions, the RESTORE indicator appears in the bottom right corner of the screen.

To abort playback, press *Ctrl-Break*. Quattro stops at the end of the current command (unless it's in Single-Step mode).

Copying a block of actions

Because Quattro records your actions exactly as it does macros (using a combination of menu-equivalent commands, key-equivalent commands, and exact keystrokes), your transcript is like one very long macro. In fact, you can convert part or all of the transcript into a macro, and copy it directly into your spreadsheet.

First, in the Transcript window, block off the area you want to copy (see the previous section), then choose **Copy Block**. Quattro prompts you for a name for the macro it's creating or modifying. It displays a list of existing macro names, so you can either pick one or type in a new name.

The Transcript window and menu disappear to reveal the spreadsheet, and Quattro prompts you for the destination of the block.

Use the cursor-movement keys to position the cell selector in the top left cell of the block you want to copy the transcript to. Press *Enter*. Quattro copies the actions into the spreadsheet block.

You can also choose /Tools I Macro I Name and specify a name for the macro or /Tools I Macro I Paste to copy the block.

Transcript restrictions

Transcript makes changes to your spreadsheets only; it doesn't affect actual *files*. Therefore, it cannot restore changes made at the DOS level with /File I Utilities I DOS Shell.

This restriction has no effect on Transcript's ability to restore your spreadsheet. It just means Transcript won't get bogged down with writing to files, allowing it to work faster.

Maximum history length

Transcript stores all your actions in a file called QUATTRO.LOG. Each time you load Quattro, it opens to this file and appends to it. This makes it possible for you to restore work you did days ago.

When your QUATTRO.LOG file reaches the maximum size (initially, 2000 keystrokes), Quattro renames it QUATTRO.BAK at the next checkpoint and begins a new QUATTRO.LOG file. The QUATTRO.BAK file is overwritten each time this happens.

To disable Transcript, just set Max History Length to 0.

You can change the maximum size allotted to the .LOG file with the Max History Length command. Just choose this command and enter any value from 1 to 25,000 keystrokes.

Playing back a macro in slow motion

The Single Step command lets you play back actions in your command history one step (or keystroke) at a time. This is useful when you know you made a mistake but you're not sure what it was, or if you just want to check over your actions carefully.

Single Step is initially disabled (set to No). You can change this to either Yes or Timed.

To play back a block of actions in Single-Step mode,

1. From the Transcript window, choose /Single-Step. If you want to pause between steps until you press *Spacebar* or *Enter*, choose

Yes. If you want Quattro to pause for a number of seconds between steps, then continue, choose Timed.

2. Use the /Begin Block and /End Block commands to mark the block you want to play back.

3. Choose /Playback Block, /Undo Last Command, or /Restore to Here. Quattro will step through the actions in the block just as in Debug mode in macro debugging.

4. If you set Single-Step mode to Yes, press *Spacebar* to execute the next step in the block or press *Enter* to continue execution at full speed. If you set Single-Step to Timed, Quattro pauses for a number of seconds between each step.

While your actions are executing in Single-Step mode, Quattro displays the DEBUG indicator on the status line. To exit Single-Step mode, return the setting to No.

If you press *Ctrl-Break* while replaying actions in Single-Step mode, Quattro stops the playback immediately. If it was in the middle of a command, you may have to press *Esc* several times to return to the spreadsheet.

Protecting against power outs

Normally, Transcript stores your actions on disk after every 100 keystrokes. This ensures that if there's a power failure, your work will have been saved to disk and can be fully restored.

If you find that Transcript slows down your work and you can risk possible data loss, you can set the Failure Protection command to a higher value than the default of 100 keystrokes between saves. Transcript will then store your actions in a memory buffer and write them periodically to disk at less frequent intervals. If there's a power failure, you may have to repeat some of the final steps involved in your work after restoring it.

Printing your transcript

To print a copy of your transcript, mark off the entire transcript as a block and copy the block to your spreadsheet. Then exit Transcript and print that block of the spreadsheet with /File | Print | Block.

Exiting Transcript

To close the Transcript menu, press *Esc*. The Transcript window remains onscreen. To exit the Transcript utility, press *Esc* again and you're back in the spreadsheet, where Transcript continues to record your actions.

To disable Transcript altogether, choose /**Tools** | **Macro** | **Tran**script or press *Alt-F2 T*, then press the Slash key (/) to call up the Transcript menu and set **M**ax History Length to 0 (zero).

18

Using Quattro as a database manager

The basic spreadsheet format is perfect for most accounting applications, including budget analyses, expense records, and even real estate calculations. But what if you want to sort a sales list by customer name? Or search through your budget for expenses of $1000 or more? Or build a table that automatically predicts future production rates based on an existing database, or see how many employees have salaries that fall within given ranges? For such applications, Quattro adds another dimension to the traditional spreadsheet: a *database manager*.

This chapter describes what a database is and how to set one up, as well as how to

- sort data in a database
- search through a database for records meeting specified criteria, and copy those records to a different part of the spreadsheet or delete them
- set up the spreadsheet as a form for easy data entry
- use links to access information in an untranslated Paradox database file

The Database menu

The **Database** menu contains all commands specifically geared toward a database spreadsheet setup.

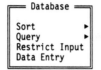

- **Sort** lets you arrange records in your database according to the entries in specified fields.
- **Query** lets you search through your database for records that meet specific requirements. Optionally, you can copy the records you find to another part of the spreadsheet, or delete them.
- **Restrict Input** restricts movement of the cell selector to only those cells that are not protected.
- **Data Entry** lets you limit the type of data permitted in a block of cells to general data, values, or dates only.

In addition, all standard spreadsheet functions (discussed in the previous chapters) apply to a database setup.

What is a database?

A database differs from a standard spreadsheet in that it separates information into sections, each containing similar information—much like a card file (see the following figure). You can use a database to keep track of all kinds of information, from simple mailing lists to detailed statistics.

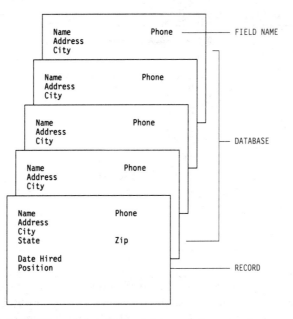

Figure 18.1
A card-file database

A traditional database program lets you set up your screen like a form, into which you then enter information. The form contains a set of entry blanks, called *fields*, each defined by *field names*. To fill in a form, you simply move the selector to each blank field and type in data relating to the field name. A filled-in form constitutes a *record*. A database is composed of many such records. To create another record, save the first, call up a blank form, then fill it in.

The following figure shows a database form designed in Paradox, Borland's relational database program. This particular form is used to store information on sales contacts.

Figure 18.2
A Paradox database form

```
Editing Contacts table with form F1: Record 1 of 1                    Edit

┌─ Form ──────────────────────────────────────────────────────────────┐
│                                                                      │
│                         PRIMARY CONTACT RECORD                       │
│                                                                      │
│    Last Name:              First:              Middle:               │
│    Title:                                                            │
│    Name of Firm:                                                     │
│    Street:                 City:       State:      Zip:              │
│    Phone Number:                                                     │
│                                                                      │
│    Birthday:                                                         │
│    Secretary's Name:                                                 │
│                                                                      │
│    Sales Rep:                                                        │
│    Most Recent Contact:                                              │
│    Total Sales Last 12 Months:                                       │
│                                                                      │
│    Comments:                                                         │
│                                                                      │
│                                                                      │
│                                                                      │
│                                                                      │
└──────────────────────────────────────────────────────────────────────┘
```

Although Quattro allows you to design a form for data entry (discussed near the end of this chapter), you can easily set up a standard Quattro spreadsheet for database use. Figure 18.3 shows a Quattro spreadsheet with the same database shown above. The field names appear as column headings with correlating field entries below them. (Additional headings are stored off the screen to the right.) Each row of the spreadsheet contains one record of the database.

Figure 18.3
A database in a Quattro
spreadsheet

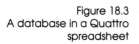

```
File  Edit  Style  Graph  Print  Database  Tools  Options  Window      ↑↓
A1: [W10]                                                            |  ?
┘     A        B        C        D         E           F          ↑End
1                    PRIMARY CONTACT RECORD                          ■  ▲
2                                                                       ◄ ►
3     LAST NAME FIRST    MIDDLE   TITLE     FIRM        STREET          ▼
4     Meyer     Jennifer A.       Writer    Matrix      319 Clinton St.
5     Hill      Kate     E.       Manager   E.R.A.      41 Cedar St.
6     Glass     Angel    W.       Sales     C.T.        1 Pacific Ave.  Esc
7     Carter    Kim      J.       Finance   B.S.P.      50 Cayuga Dr.
8     Caignon   Denise   L.       Manager   B.I.        25 Columbia     ↵
9     Moore     Claire   S.       Designer  TypaGraphix 80 Sears Crc.
10    Conger    Presley  J.       Therapist P.C.        4 Oceanview St. Del
11                                                                      @
12
13
14                                                                      5
15
16                                                                      6
17
18                                                                      7
19
20
←                                                                  →
PRIMARY.WQ1   [1]                                              READY
```

Setting up a database

Once you have an idea of the kind of data you want to include in your database, it's fairly easy to set up such a spreadsheet. Generally, you enter the field names as labels in the top row, then fill in the rows below them. Specifically, you need to adhere to these rules when setting up your database:

- The area you use for the data must be rectangular, although it can contain any number of blank cells.
- Use the same type of data throughout each column. In other words, don't mix labels (except for the field name) and numeric data in the same column.
- Do not separate the row of field names and the first record with a blank or decorative row.
- Make sure to use unique names for your field names. To avoid confusion, they should be different from any of your block names.

The tutorial in Chapter 6 of *Getting Started* contains a good example of how part of a spreadsheet can be set up like a database.

Sorting a database

A Quattro database can store as many as 8191 records. You can make it easier to locate and view information in a database by sorting it.

When you sort a database, you arrange the records (or rows) in a specific order, according to the entries in one or more fields. For example, you could alphabetize entries in the Name field and sort them chronologically using a Date field.

The fields used to sort a database are called *sort fields*. You can have up to five sort fields. Records are first sorted by the primary sort field, then the secondary, and so on. For example, if you specified City as the primary sort field and Date as the secondary, the records would be arranged alphabetically by city; then, if there were more than one record for a single city, Quattro would arrange them chronologically by date within that city group.

Caution! Formulas that reference cells outside their own row are not updated when records are resorted. If you have such formulas in your records, convert them to their end values (see page 136) before sorting them.

To sort your database,

```
═══ Sort ═══
Block
1st Key
2nd Key
3rd Key
4th Key
5th Key

Go
Reset
Sort Rules  ▶
Quit
```

1. Choose /Database | Sort to display the Sort menu.
2. Choose **Block**. Quattro prompts for a cell block. Specify (either by pointing or typing) the cell block containing all the records you want to sort. Be sure to include the entire records. *Do not include* the column headings (field names). Quattro then returns you to the Sort menu.

   Warning: Be sure to specify *all* the cells of each record you want to sort; otherwise, the fields of your database will be mismatched. You will then have to retrieve your file again or reenter the records.
3. Choose **1st Key**. Again, Quattro prompts you for a cell block. This time, specify the field on which you want the primary sort performed. (For example, the primary sort can be by Zip Code and the secondary sort by Name.) To specify a sort field, enter the address of any cell in that column or enter the field name. Quattro prompts you for the sort order: **A**scending or **D**escending.
4. Press *A* to sort the records in ascending order (*A-Z* and *0-9*), or press *Enter* to use descending order (*9-0* and *Z-A*). The Sort menu returns.
5. If you want to specify further sort keys, do so in the same way.
6. When you're ready to perform the sort, choose **Go**. The Sort menu disappears and the records are sorted as specified. To exit the menu without performing the sort, choose **Quit** or press *Esc*.

1-2-3

If you're using the 123-compatible menus, choose /Data | Sort | Data Range instead of /Database | Sort | Block, and /Data | Sort | Primary Key instead of /Database | Sort | 1st Key.

Note   If a Sort command gives you unwanted results, use the Undo command (press */EU* or *Alt-F5*) to reverse the operation. Undo must be enabled *before* you choose it. If you've performed another "undo-able" operation since the sort, or if Undo is disabled, either re-sort the data or use Transcript to undo the sort (see Chapter 17, "Using Transcript").

Records you enter after sorting your database are not automatically inserted in the sort order. Make sure to include the new records with the /Database I Sort I Block command, then choose /Database I Sort I Go again to reorder the records.

The sort order you assign to a spreadsheet remains with it when it is saved. The next time you retrieve the file, the same sort order will be in effect.

To change the current sort order, choose /Database I Sort, make the necessary changes, and choose **Go**. To erase all of the Sort menu settings, choose **Reset**.

To change the rules Quattro uses to perform the sort (such as whether numbers are put before or after labels), use the Sort Rules command (see the following section).

Sorting tip   If you want to return your database records to their original order after sorting, insert a blank column to the left of the columns to be inserted. Choose /Edit I Fill to number each record (row). To return your database to its original order, use the row of numbers as your first sort key.

Changing the sort rules

Each sort key you specify can be assigned one of two *sort directions*: **Ascending** or **Descending**. When you choose **Ascending**, Quattro sorts data in the following order:

1. blank cells
2. labels beginning with numbers (in numerical order)
3. labels beginning with letters and special characters (in ASCII order)
4. values (in numerical order)

When you choose **Descending**, Quattro sorts records in the opposite order:

1. values (in reverse numerical order)
2. labels beginning with letters and special characters (in reverse ASCII order)
3. labels beginning with numbers (in reverse numerical order)
4. blank cells

Note Quattro sorts formulas according to their end values, and dates according to their date serial numbers.

To change the order in which Quattro sorts data,

1. Choose /Database | Sort | Sort Rules. Quattro displays the **Sort Rules** menu.

```
======= Sort Rules =======

Numbers Before Labels ►
Label Order           ►
Quit
```

2. To change the default rule of labels before numbers, choose **Numbers Before Labels** and choose **Yes** to place numbers before labels.

3. To change how Quattro sorts labels, choose **Label Order**. You'll see a menu with two choices:

   ■ ASCII, the default, sorts labels according to the ASCII character code of the first letter. It sort labels alphabetically, with labels beginning with special characters at the end and all uppercase letters before lowercase.

   ■ Dictionary sorts labels as you would expect in a dictionary; it disregards case and looks at each letter of a word, so that *alarm* would precede *Alice*.

4. If you want to use the new sort rules from now on, choose /Options | Update.

1-2-3 If you're using the 123-compatible menus, choose /Data | Sort | Sort Rules.

Searching through a database

One of the more powerful features of a database manager is its ability to swiftly separate out requested information. For example, with just a few keystrokes, you can locate all Pennsylvania customers in your database or all students with a grade point average of 3.0 or above.

With the /Database | Query menu, you can specify certain criteria that you want to look for. The criteria you might use for the examples above are State=PA and +GPA>=3.0.

Once you've set up criteria, you can tell Quattro to find all records meeting the criteria, copy all records or just unique records to a different part of the spreadsheet, or delete the records.

Choose /Database | Query to display the **Query** menu.

```
╔══════ Query ══════╗
║                   ║
║ Block             ║
║ Criteria Table    ║
║ Output Block      ║
║                   ║
║ Assign Names      ║
║ Locate            ║
║ Extract           ║
║ Unique            ║
║ Delete            ║
║                   ║
║ Reset             ║
║ Quit              ║
║                   ║
╚═══════════════════╝
```

- **Block** lets you specify the block of data you want to search through.

- **Criteria Table** lets you specify the block containing search conditions. This is a table you set up beforehand to indicate which fields to search and what to search for.

- **Output Block** lets you specify a block to which you can copy the records that meet the criteria.

- **Assign Names** automatically assigns names to each cell in the second row of your database, using the field names in the first row. This makes referencing fields in your search criteria much easier.

- **Locate** highlights all records that meet your criteria.

- **Extract** copies records that match the conditions to another part of the spreadsheet.

- **Unique** works just like Extract except it eliminates duplicate records from the extracted copy.

- **Delete** erases all records that match the conditions.

- **Reset** erases all values previously entered in the menu commands.

- **Quit** returns you to the spreadsheet.

| F7 |
| Query |

To execute the last-used **Query** command, press the Query key (*F7*).

1-2-3

If you're using the 123-compatible menus, choose /**Data** I **Query**.

Entering search information

Before you can search through a database, you must enter the search information:

1. Indicate the block to search.
2. Set up a block of search criteria.
3. Set up an output block.

The following sections describe each of these steps in detail.

Indicating the block to search

The first step in setting up a search is to tell Quattro which block of your spreadsheet to search through.

To specify the block of data you want to search,

1. Choose /**Database** | **Query** | **Block**.
2. Specify your entire database, including the field names. If you want to search only part of your database, you can specify that part, but the block must include the field names you want to search through. Be sure to include, also, any fields you want copied to the output block (discussed later in this chapter).
3. If you want to specify a database block in another open spreadsheet, use standard linking syntax. For example,

   [DATA]A1..Z50

   specifies block A1..Z50 in the spreadsheet called DATA.

If you're using the 123-compatible menus, choose /**Data** | **Query** | **Input**.

You can also use linking syntax to query a database file created with Paradox, Reflex, or dBASE. This allows you to access database information without having to translate the database into a spreadsheet file first. Just include the name of the file (and directory if different) when specifying the query block. For example,

   [\PARADOX\SALES.DB]A1..A2

specifies the file called SALES in the PARADOX directory. The A1..A2 block is all you need to specify when you query a database file directly from disk without translating the file. If the file is open, you must specify the actual query block. For an example of how to query an external Paradox database file, see "Querying an outside database" later in this chapter.

Naming the first field entries

After you've specified the block to search, you can use the **Assign Names** command to assign block names to the first entry of each field. This is not a required step, but will make entering search criteria much easier. You'll then be able to reference fields by name within search formulas (for example, AMOUNT>300).

If you don't name the first field entries, you'll need to reference fields by the address of the *first* entry in the field (*not* the cell containing the field name); for example, C4>300.

To automatically name each cell in the second row of your database,

1. Choose /Database | Query | Assign Names.
2. Quattro names each cell in the second row according to the field name above it. For example, in Figure 18.4, Quattro has assigned the name LAST to cell A4, the first entry in the Last Name field, after the field name in the row above it (cell A3).

Caution! If any of your field names are more than one word or longer than 15 characters, problems may arise. You should adjust any such field names before initiating the **Assign Names** command.

1-2-3
If you're using the 123-compatible menus, choose /Data | Query | Assign Names.

Figure 18.4 shows a sample database and the block names created for it with the **Assign Names** command. (The /Edit | Names | Make Table command created the table.)

Figure 18.4
How Quattro names first field entries

```
File  Edit  Style  Graph  Print  Database  Tools  Options  Window          ↑↓
A1: [W10]                                                                    | ?
┌──────A────────B────────C────────D──────────E────────────F─────────┐     ↑End
1                          PRIMARY CONTACT RECORD                           ▲
2                                                                           ◄ ►
3  LAST      FIRST    MIDDLE   TITLE     FIRM        STREET                  ▼
4  Meyer     Jennifer A.       Writer    Matrix      319 Clinton St.
5  Hill      Kate     E.       Manager   E.R.A.      41 Cedar St.
6  Glass     Angel    W.       Sales     C.T.        1 Pacific Ave.         Esc
7  Carter    Kim      J.       Finance   B.S.P.      50 Cayuga Dr.
8  Caignon   Denise   L.       Manager   B.I.        25 Columbia            ↵
9  Moore     Claire   S.       Designer  TypaGraphix 80 Sears Crc.
10 Conger    Presley  J.       Therapist P.C.        4 Oceanview St.        Del
11                                                                          @
12
13                             CITY      G4                                 5
14                             FIRM      E4
15                             FIRST     B4                                 6
16                             LAST      A4
17                             MIDDLE    C4                                 7
18                             STREET    F4
19                             TITLE     D4
20                             ZIP       H4                                 ↓
├─■                                                                        ► ⌐
PRIMARY.WQ1   [1]                                                          READY
```

For information on how to use the block names created with the **Assign Names** command, see the following section.

Setting up the search criteria
The most important step when you perform a database search is to specify the data you want to search for. To do this, set up a table of *search criteria* in the spreadsheet. This table can be in the spreadsheet containing your database or in a different spreadsheet. If in a different spreadsheet, both spreadsheets must be open when you perform the query.

A criteria table lists the data you want to search for under the names of the fields you want to search through. If you enter more than one criterion in a single row, Quattro searches for records that match *all* of the conditions. When you enter the criteria in separate rows, Quattro searches for records that match *either* of the conditions.

The following figure shows two different criteria tables. The first searches for all records with both "Lunches" in the Expense field *and* a value greater than 500 in the Amount field. The second table searches for any record with either "Lunches" in the Expense field *or* a value of greater than 500 in the Amount field.

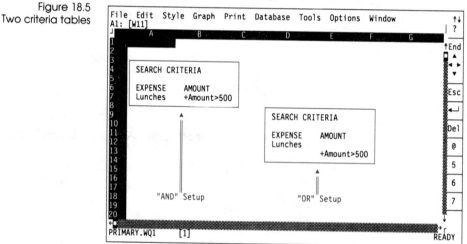

Note   The tables in the preceding figure show the conditions entered for the search. Normally, Quattro displays end values instead of the formulas you enter, but you can switch the display to show the formulas (or conditions) by changing the display format for that block to Text with the /Style | Numeric Format command.

To set up a criteria table,

1. Choose an area of the spreadsheet to use for the criteria table. It should be close enough to the database block to be easy to find.

2. In the first row of the table, copy the names of the fields you want to search through. (You could type them in, but because they must match exactly those names in the database, copying ensures accuracy.) To make future searches easier, you may

want to copy all field names from the database. The criteria table can hold up to 256 field names.

If Quattro encounters an invalid field name in the criteria table, it selects *all* records. Invalid field names include misspelled field names or field names not in the database block.

3. Below the appropriate field name, enter the data you want to search for. To search for an exact match, enter the value exactly as it appears in the database. To enter a condition, use a formula (see the next section).

4. If you want more than one criterion met by each record, enter them all in the same row, under the appropriate field names. To search for records that meet *any* of the given criteria, use a separate row for each criterion.

Note Unless you've changed the display format for your table to Text, Quattro displays a 0 or 1 in the table when you enter a search formula (0 if the first cell searched returns a false value, 1 if the first cell returns a true value). These numbers have no impact on the search and can be replaced by the actual formulas if you prefer (by specifying the Text format for the block).

Search formulas

If you're searching for an exact match, you can enter the exact value directly below the field name in your criteria table. For example, if you specify the criteria table

SALE
500

Quattro looks for all records that contain the value 500 in the Sale field.

Note Quattro searches for exact matches; therefore, if a database field name contains trailing spaces, Quattro cannot find a match for that name without trailing spaces. For example, "TEST" is not the same as "TEST " (with two trailing spaces). Also, if you have entered numbers as labels, you must search for them as labels. For example, '1 is not the same as the value 1. The first is a label, the second is a value.

To search for records that meet a *condition* (rather than an exact match), you must enter a search formula beneath the field name. It must include a cell reference, an operator, and a value. If you've named your first field entries with the **Assign Names** command (as described earlier in this chapter), you can reference the field you want to search by name; just type + (a plus sign), press *F3*, choose the field name you want from the list, and press *Enter*. If you didn't use **Assign Names**, you must reference the address of the first entry in the field (preceded by a plus sign). For example, the criteria table

SALE
+C3>500

tells Quattro to look for all records that contain a value greater than 500 in the Sale field (C3). The search formula presents a true/false statement concerning field entries. When you perform the search, Quattro starts with the first field entry in the column. It makes note of whether the statement is true or false, then moves to the next cell in the field (C4). It updates the formula internally to read +C4>500 and evaluates cell C4. It evaluates each subsequent field entry similarly—updating the formula and checking to see if the statement is true (see the following figure).

Figure 18.6
How Quattro searches
through a database

*Note how the formula adjusts
as it moves down the
column.*

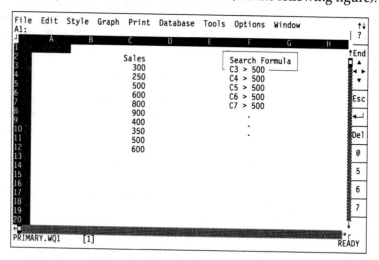

You can use any of the following operators in a search formula:

= < <= > >= <>

To tie together two search formulas under one field, use #AND#, #NOT#, or #OR#. For example,

AMOUNT>300#AND#AMOUNT<600

tells Quattro to look for all entries in the Amount field that are between 300 and 600, and

AMOUNT>300#AND#AMOUNT<600(#NOT# REP=BOB)

tells Quattro to look for all records except Bob's that have a value greater than 300 but less than 600 in the Amount field.

Wildcards

In a criteria table, you can use wildcards when searching for labels. Quattro allows three types of wildcards:

- **?** (question mark) is a single-character wildcard. It takes the place of any single character. For example, t?p would find *tip*, *top*, and *tap*, but not *tape* or *stop*. And t??p would find *trap* and *trip*, but not *tap* or *strap*.

- ***** (asterisk) is a multiple-character wildcard. It takes the place of any number of characters. For example, ten* would find *tender*, *tension*, and *tent* but not *attention*, and t*n would find *ten* but not *tender*.

- **~** (tilde) searches for all labels in a field *except* those that match the search condition. For example, CITY=~Boston searches for all records that don't contain *Boston* in the City field. And ~T* searches for all Name entries that don't begin with *T*.

The following figure shows several different criteria tables and what they search for:

Figure 18.7
Sample criteria tables

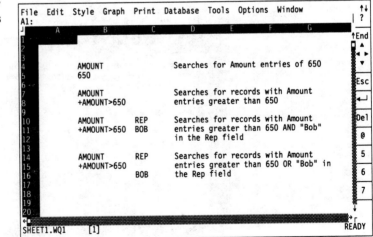

After you've set up a criteria table, you must specify its coordinates with the /Database | Query | Criteria Table command.

1-2-3

If you're using the 123-compatible menus, choose /Data | Query | Criterion.

Setting up an output block

The /Database | Query | Extract command copies all matching records your search uncovers to a designated area of your spreadsheet. The /Database | Query | Unique command copies all matching records *except duplicates*. If you intend to use either of these commands, you must first prepare the area to copy the records to (the *output block*).

To set up an output block,

1. Choose a blank area of the spreadsheet that will not overlap your spreadsheet data or criteria table.

2. In the first row of the block, copy the name of each field that you want included in the output from the database. (You could type in the names, but because they must match exactly those names in the database, copying them is more accurate.) You can include as many field names as you want, in any order. Fields that you don't include won't be included in the output.

The following figure shows an output block set up for a sample database. Notice that only some of the fields are included and the order is not the same.

Figure 18.8
A sample output block

```
File  Edit  Style  Graph  Print  Database  Tools  Options  Window          ↑↓
A1: [W10]                                                                    | ?
        A         B         C         D         E            F              ↑End
1                         PRIMARY CONTACT RECORD                               ▲
2                                                                           ◄ ► ►
3   LAST NAME FIRST     MIDDLE    TITLE     FIRM       STREET                  ▼
4   Meyer     Jennifer  A.        Writer    Matrix     319 Clinton St.
5   Hill      Kate      E.        Manager   E.R.A.     41 Cedar St.
6   Glass     Angel     W.        Sales     C.T.       1 Pacific Ave.       Esc
7   Carter    Kim       J.        Finance   B.S.P.     50 Cayuga Dr.
8   Caignon   Denise    L.        Manager   B.I.       25 Columbia          ◄┘
9   Moore     Claire    S.        Designer  TypaGraphix 80 Sears Crc.
10  Conger    Presley   J.        Therapist P.C.       4 Oceanview St.      Del
11
12                                                                           @
13
14                                                                           5
15  FIRM      FIRST     LAST NAME CITY
16                                                                           6
17
18                                                                           7
19
20
PRIMARY.WQ1    [1]                        CAP                       READY
```

The output block is A15..D15.

Once you've set up your output block, you need to specify the cell block with the /Database | Query | Output Block command. If there's any existing data below the block that the copied records might overwrite, specify the exact block you expect the output to fill. If the block is too small, Quattro displays an error message. If there's no danger of overwriting data, simply specify the top row of the block (the row containing the field names). The copied records will then fill whatever space is necessary.

1-2-3

If you're using the 123-compatible menus, use /Data | Query | Output instead of /Database | Query | Output Block.

Performing the search

With your criteria table and/or output block set up, you can begin the search operation:

1. Choose /Database | Query. Quattro prompts you for a cell block.
2. Specify the database block you want to search through. Include all the records you want to search, and be sure to include the field names. The **Query** menu returns.
3. Choose **Criteria Table** from the **Query** menu and enter the coordinates of your criteria table. The **Query** menu returns.
4. If you've set up an output block for copying the matching records to, choose **Output Block** and enter the coordinates of that block. If there's nothing below the block that might be overwritten, you can specify the top row only (the field names). If data *is* below the block, specify the exact coordinates of the block. If the matching records don't fit in the block, Quattro will copy as many as it can and display an error message warning you that there are more.
5. You're now ready to perform the search. You have four search options:

   ■ **Locate** highlights the matching records on the spreadsheet.

   ■ **Extract** copies the matching records to the output block.

   ■ **Unique** copies non-duplicate matching records to the output block.

   ■ **Delete** erases the matching records.

   Each of these options is discussed in the following sections.

6. When the operation is complete, choose **Quit** to return to the spreadsheet in Ready mode.

Query

With the spreadsheet in Ready mode, you can repeat the previous Query operation by pressing the Query key (*F7*).

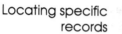

Locating specific records

To search through the database for all records that meet the conditions you specified, choose /**D**atabase I **Q**uery I **L**ocate. Quattro highlights the first record in the input block that meets the conditions (see the following figure). If there are no qualifying records, Quattro beeps and returns you to the menu.

Figure 18.9
Locating a record in a database

```
File  Edit  Style  Graph  Print  Database  Tools  Options  Window        ↑↓
A1: [W10]                                                                  | ?
J        A       B         C        D          E          F            ↑End
1                       PRIMARY CONTACT RECORD
2
3    LAST NAME FIRST     MIDDLE   TITLE      FIRM       STREET
4    Meyer     Jennifer  A.       Writer     Matrix     319 Clinton St.
5    Hill      Kate      E.       Manager    E.R.A.     41 Cedar St.
6    Glass     Angel     W.       Sales      C.T.       1 Pacific Ave.    Esc
7    Carter    Kim       J.       Finance    B.S.P.     50 Cayuga Dr.
8    Caignon   Denise    L.       Manager    B.I.       25 Columbia      ↵
9    Moore     Claire    S.       Designer   TypaGraphix 80 Sears Crc.
10   Conger    Presley   J.       Therapist  P.C.       4 Oceanview St.  Del
11
12                                                                        @
13
14   TITLE                                                                5
15   SALES
16                                                                        6
17
18                                                                        7
19
20
←
PRIMARY.WQ1     [1]                        CAP                       READY
```

The criteria table is block A14..A15.

To highlight other records that meet the criteria, press ↑ or ↓. *Home* takes you to the first record in the database (matching or not); *End* takes you to the last.

To make changes to a highlighted record, press ← or → until the column letter containing the field you want to change is highlighted, then press *F2* to enter Edit mode. The field entry appears on the input line, and you can make any changes to it. When you press *Enter*, the changes are entered.

To end the Locate operation and return to the Query menu, press *Enter* or *Esc*. To then return to the spreadsheet in Ready mode, choose **Quit**.

1-2-3

If you're using the 123-compatible menus, choose /**D**ata I **Q**uery I **F**ind.

Deleting specific records

To delete the records that match the given criteria,

1. Choose /Database | Query | Delete. Quattro asks for confirmation.

```
┌─ Delete record(s)? ─┐
│                     │
│ Cancel              │
│ Delete              │
└─────────────────────┘
```

2. Press *D* to carry out the deletion, or *C* to cancel the operation and return to the Query menu.

Quattro erases all qualifying records from the database. Records below the deleted records move up to fill in the empty rows.

Note Delete does not work when you are querying a Paradox database that has not been translated first.

If you accidentally delete records with the /Database | Query | Delete command, use the Undo command (*/EU* or *Alt-F5*) to bring them back. Undo must be enabled *before* you use it. If you've performed another "undo-able" operation since the deletion, enlist Transcript to reverse the operation.

Extracting records

To copy all records that match the given criteria to the designated output block, choose /Database | Query | Extract. Quattro searches through the database for all records that meet the criteria. It then copies the matching records into the output block specified with the /Database | Query | Output Block command. It includes only those fields whose names are written on the first row of the output block.

If you specified only the first row of the output block, the copied records take up as much space as needed.

If you specified a multiple-row output block, and the matching records do not fit in the block, Quattro copies what it can and displays a warning that there are more matching records than those copied. Press *Esc* and begin the procedure again, this time specifying a larger output block, or, if it is safe to do so, specifying only the first row of the block.

Before you can extract records from a database, you must first set up an output block in your spreadsheet (discussed earlier in this chapter), and specify the block with the /Database | Query | Block command (also discussed earlier).

Extracting unique records

The /**Database** I **Query** I **Unique** command copies only unique records that meet the criteria to the specified output block. It works exactly like the **Extract** command except that it eliminates duplicate records from the output block.

The duplicate records eliminated from the output block are identical in all fields, not just those specified in the criteria table. For example, the following figure shows an output block containing several similar records copied with the **Unique** command. Even though the entries in the field searched through (the Amount field) are the same, other fields in the record are not identical.

Figure 18.10
Records extracted with the
Unique command

```
File  Edit  Style  Graph  Print  Database  Tools  Options  Window        ↑↓
J1:                                                                       | ?
J         J      K           L           M        N      O       P
1                                                                        ↑End
2
3                              OUTPUT BLOCK                                ▲
4                                                                        ◄ ►
5                     DATE OF SALE   REP       AMOUNT                      ▼
6                     04/04/89       Bob          300
7                     04/04/89       Jane         300                     Esc
8                     04/04/89       Jane         500
9                     04/15/89       Tim          500                     ◄┘
10                    04/17/89       Tim          650
11                    04/17/89       Jane         650                     Del
12                    04/24/89       Bob          700
13                                                                        @
14
15                                                                        5
16
17                                                                        6
18
19                                                                        7
20
SALES.WQ1      [1]                                                      READY
```

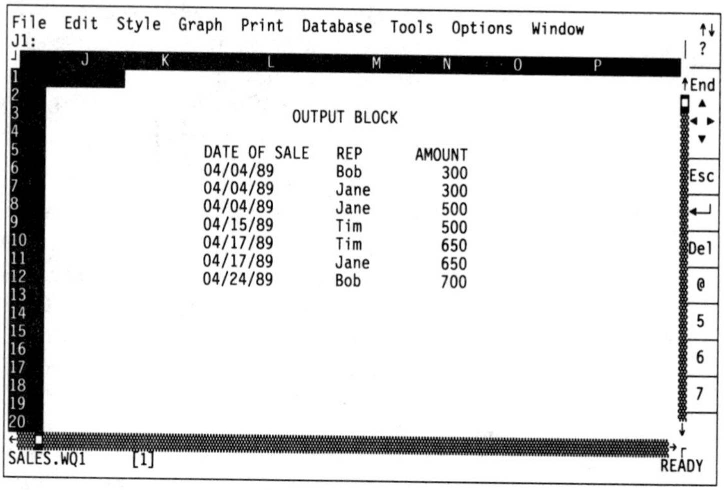

Search recap

The Quattro search procedure can be summarized as follows:

1. Choose /**Database** I **Query** I **Block** and specify the block of data you want to search.

2. If you want to reference field names instead of addresses in your search formulas, choose **Assign Names**. Quattro names each cell in the second row of your database according to the label above it.

3. Specify your search criteria by setting up a criteria table and specifying the block's coordinates with the **Criteria Table** command.

4. If you want to copy matched records to another part of the spreadsheet, set up an output block, listing the fields you want included. Then choose /Database I Query I Output Block and specify the coordinates of the block.

5. Finally, choose the search operation you want to perform from the **Query** menu: Locate, Extract, Unique, or Delete.

6. When the operation is finished, choose **Quit** to return to the spreadsheet in Ready mode.

To repeat the same **Query** operation (the one last used) from the spreadsheet, press the Query key (*F7*).

The following figure shows a spreadsheet set up for a database search and indicates which items on the Query menu identify which parts on the screen:

Figure 18.11
Preparing for a database search

```
File  Edit  Style  Graph  Print  Database  Tools  Options  Window           ↑↓
A1: [W10]                                                                    | ?
╔═══════A═══════B═══════C═══════D═══════E═══════F═══════╗                   ↑End
║                    PRIMARY CONTACT RECORD             ║
║                                                       ║                    ▲
║   LAST NAME FIRST   MIDDLE   TITLE     FIRM      STREET       ║            ◄ ►
║   Meyer     Jennifer A.      Writer    Matrix    319 Clinton St. ║          ▼
║   Hill      Kate     E.      Manager   E.R.A.    41 Cedar St.  ║
║   Glass     Angel    W.      Sales     C.T.      1 Pacific Ave. ║          Esc
║   Carter    Kim      J.      Finance   B.S.P.    50 Cayuga Dr.  ║
║   Caignon   Denise   L.      Manager   B.I.      25 Columbia    ║          ←┘
║   Moore     Claire   S.      Designer  TypaGraphix 80 Sears Crc.║
║   Conger    Presley  J.      Therapist P.C.      4 Oceanview St.║          Del
║                                                       ║
║                                                       ║                    @
║   ┌─────────────┐                                     ║
║   │ FIRM        │                                     ║                    5
║   │ Matrix      │                                     ║
║   └─────────────┘                                     ║                    6
║                                                       ║
║          ┌─────────────────────────────────────┐     ║                    7
║          │ FIRM      FIRST      LAST NAME  CITY │     ║
║          └─────────────────────────────────────┘     ║
╚═══════════════════════════════════════════════════════╝
PRIMARY.WQ1        [1]                CAP                                    READY
```

Output Block (C18..F18)
Criteria Table (A14..A15)
Query Block (A3..F10)

Querying an outside database

As mentioned previously, you can use linking with the /Database I Query I Extract command to access information in an outside database file created with Paradox, Reflex, or dBASE, so you can extract the information you need from a database file without having to translate the file first.

The procedure for this is basically the same as querying the current spreadsheet. You set up a criteria table and an output block in a spreadsheet. Use the same field names as those in the database file, even within the search conditions. Then specify the database file itself as the query block with the /Database | Query | Block command using linking syntax; for example,

[FILENAME]A1..A2

If the file is in a different directory than the current one, include the directory path as well; for example,

[\SUBDIRECTORY\FILENAME]A1..A2

The block coordinates you include after the file name can be any valid block with at least two rows. Since database files don't use blocks, they're used for Quattro syntax only.

When you choose /Database | Query | Extract, Quattro copies the specified information from the outside database file and writes it into the output block. It references only those records that pass the given criteria and extracts data from only those fields listed in the output block.

Once you've extracted the data, you can use regular spreadsheet formulas to reference the data in the output block.

Note   The link you set up with the /Database | Query | Block command is not an active link, like those used in formulas. If you make changes to the database file, Quattro does not automatically update data in the output block. But once the criteria table and output block are set up, you need only use the /Database | Query | Extract command again to update the extracted data. (If you've used a query operation since your last database extract, be sure the **B**lock, **C**riteria Table, and **O**utput Block commands reference the correct locations.)

An example   In the following example, you'll see how to use the /Database | Query menu to extract commission figures from an unopened Paradox sales database, adding them into a spreadsheet that breaks down commissions by month and sales representative. The following figure shows the Paradox database:

Figure 18.12
The Paradox database

```
Viewing Sales table: Record 1 of 22                              Main

SALES======Date======    ===Sales Rep===    ===Price===    ===Commission===
    1     11/22/88       Hanover            12,000.41        1,200.00    St
    2     12/24/88       Matthews           12,995.13        1,299.00    Mo
    3      5/31/88       Simms              14,354.25        1,435.00    Lo
    4      8/01/88       Ranier             38,400.56        3,840.00    Ri
    5     12/16/88       Hanover            14,452.43        1,445.00    Da
    6      7/27/88       Hanover             4,995.76          499.00    Da
    7      6/04/88       Ranier             12,000.95        1,200.00    Pa
    8      6/24/88       Matthews           14,999.45        1,499.00    Sa
    9      4/22/88       Matthews           38,495.95        3,849.00    Al
   10      4/30/88       Hanover            14,354.00        1,435.00    Sa
   11      1/14/88       Simms              50,000.95        5,000.00    Se
   12      9/04/88       Ranier             12,995.95        1,299.00    Kl
   13     10/27/88       Ranier             14,365.45        1,436.00    Kl
   14      3/04/88       Simms              16,375.37        1,637.00    To
   15      2/28/88       Simms              12,264.47        1,264.00    Da
   16      1/13/88       Matthews           16,854.95        1,685.00    Sa
   17      5/30/88       Matthews           34,543.84        3,454.00    Da
   18      7/22/88       Ranier             67,342.65        6,734.00    Lo
   19      8/01/88       Simms              43,369.94        4,336.00    So
   20     10/10/88       Hanover            75,943.57        7,594.00    Ne
   21      8/04/88       Hanover            35,325.43        3,532.00    Lo
   22      9/16/88       Simms              56,435.56        5,643.00    Sa
```

The first step is to specify the untranslated Paradox database as the file you want to query. Choose /Database I Query I Block and use linking syntax to specify the Paradox sales database as the block to search through:

[C:\PARADOX\SALES.DB]A1..A2

The block coordinates you specify after the file specification can be any valid block of at least two rows; as long as the Paradox file isn't translated into a spreadsheet file, a two-row block is all that Quattro requires. However, if the file is open, you must specify the entire block to query.

The following figure shows the Quattro spreadsheet that will use the data you extract from the Paradox database. You will create the criteria table and output block for the query operation in the same spreadsheet (1988.WQ1), below the block you see in the figure.

Figure 18.13
The Quattro spreadsheet

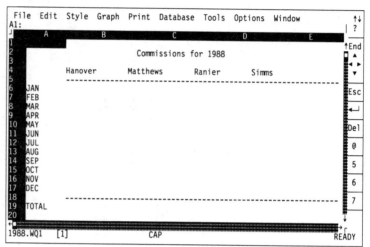

Now set up the criteria table for records you want to access. In cell A21, enter the name of the Commission field. Since you're concerned with all records that contain a commission amount, type

```
+[C:\PARADOX\SALES.DB]COMMISSION>0
```

as the search condition in cell A22. This accesses the Commission field in the database called SALES in the PARADOX directory. The following figure shows this criteria set up as a table in block A21..A22 of the Quattro spreadsheet:

Figure 18.14
The criteria table

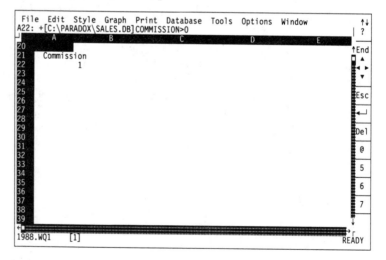

The "1" in cell A22 is the value returned by the formula you entered as your search criteria. See the input line for the actual formula you entered.

Next, set up the output block in A24..C24. This is the area to which the database information will be written. It should include only those fields you want to access data from—in this case, Date, Sales Rep, and Commission. The following figure shows this output block:

Figure 18.15
The output block

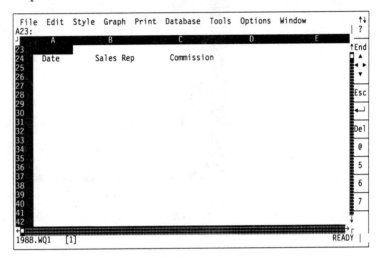

Now specify the coordinates of the criteria table (A21..A22) with the /Database | Query | Criteria Table command and the coordinates of the output block (A24..C24) with the Output Block command on the same menu.

Finally, choose Extract on the Query menu. Quattro searches through the Paradox database for all records with a Commission entry greater than zero. It then copies the Date, Sales Rep, and Commission entries for each of those records below the appropriate headings in the output block. The next figure shows most of the output block with the extracted data (A24..C46):

Figure 18.16
The extracted data

```
 File  Edit  Style  Graph  Print  Database  Tools  Options  Window       ↑↓
A43: (D1) [W16] 32356                                                     | ?
J        A              B              C              D            |
24   Date            Sales Rep     Commission                          ↑End
25   22-Nov-88        Hanover       1200                                 ▲
26   24-Dec-88        Matthews      1299                               ◄ ►
27   31-May-88        Simms         1435                                 ▼
28   01-Aug-88        Ranier        3840
29   16-Dec-88        Hanover       1445                               Esc
30   27-Jul-88        Hanover        499
31   04-Jun-88        Ranier        1200                               ↵
32   24-Jun-88        Matthews      1499
33   22-Apr-88        Matthews      3849                               Del
34   30-Apr-88        Hanover       1435
35   14-Jan-88        Simms         5000                                @
36   04-Sep-88        Ranier        1299
37   27-Oct-88        Ranier        1436                                5
38   04-Mar-88        Simms         1637
39   28-Feb-88        Simms         1264                                6
40   13-Jan-88        Matthews      1685
41   30-May-88        Matthews      3454                                7
42   22-Jul-88        Ranier        6734
43   01-Aug-88        Simms         4336
◄                                                                    ►
1988.WQ1     [1]                                                     READY
```

To plug the extracted data into the existing spreadsheet data, you
would sort the output block by Date and Sales Rep, then use
formulas to access data in those cells. Or, you could treat the
output block as a database and use database statistical functions
to access the data you need (see @*Functions and Macros* for
information about database statistical functions). The following
figure shows the final spreadsheet with the new commission
figures:

Figure 18.17
The spreadsheet with new
database figures

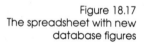

```
 File  Edit  Style  Graph  Print  Database  Tools  Options  Window       ↑↓
A1:                                                                      | ?
J        A         B            C            D            E        |
1                                                                     ↑End
2                        Commissions for 1988                          ▲
3                                                                    ◄ ►
4              Hanover     Matthews     Ranier       Simms              ▼
5
6   JAN                   $1,685                     $5,000           Esc
7   FEB                                              $1,264
8   MAR                                              $1,637           ↵
9   APR        $1,435     $3,849
10  MAY                   $3,454                     $1,435           Del
11  JUN                   $1,499       $1,200
12  JUL        $499                    $6,734                          @
13  AUG        $3,532                  $3,840        $4,336
14  SEP                                $1,299        $5,643            5
15  OCT        $7,594                  $1,436
16  NOV        $1,200                                                  6
17  DEC        $1,445     $1,299
18                                                                     7
19             $15,705    $11,786      $14,509       $19,315
20
◄                                                                    ►
1988.WQ1     [1]                                                     READY
```

To update the commission figures after you've made changes to the Paradox database, you would simply perform the /Database | Query | Extract operation again. Make sure the Criteria Table and Output Block commands reference the tables you set up here and that the Block command still references

[C:\PARADOX\SALES.DB]A1..A2

Then choose /Database | Query | Extract.

Setting up a form for data entry

The /Database | Restrict Input command lets you set up all or part of your spreadsheet like a data-entry form. It limits movement of the cell selector only to those cells in a block that are not protected. All other cells remain visible but inaccessible.

When you restrict access in a spreadsheet with the Restrict Input command, you can only move the cursor to unprotected cells in the specified block and input or change data. You cannot use the menus.

To set up the spreadsheet for data entry,

1. Remove protection from those cells you want access to with the /Style | Protection | Unprotect command.
2. Choose /Database | Retrict Input.
3. Specify the block you want to use for data entry. (All cells outside of this block will be inaccessible.)
4. After you press *Enter*, you can move the cell selector only to those cells in the block that are unprotected.
5. To remove the restricted access and return selector access to all cells, press *Esc* or *Enter*.

The /Database | Restrict Input command is used mostly in macro applications, to limit unauthorized access to the Quattro spreadsheet.

1-2-3

If you're using the 123-compatible menus, choose /Range | Input.

Quattro includes other commands that supplement the Restrict Input command:

- Shading and line-drawing commands let you emphasize the input cells by boxing or shading them, or by shading all areas not used for input.
- The **Data Entry** command lets you set a cell or block of cells to accept only entries of a specific data type.

The /Database | Data Entry command is covered in the next section. For information on the shading and box layout commands, see pages 160 and 162.

Restricting the type of data entry

With the **Data Entry** command, you can force a cell or block of cells to accept only labels or dates:

1. Choose /Database | Data Entry. Quattro displays a menu with three options: General, Labels Only, and Dates Only.
2. Choose Labels Only to force all entries to be labels; choose Dates Only to allow only date entries for the block.
3. Specify the block you want to restrict data entry in.

To return to allowing any kind of data entry, choose /Database | Data Entry | General and specify the cell block you previously restricted.

The /Database | Data Entry command can help increase accuracy during data entry. If someone enters a date or number in a label-only cell, Quattro converts it automatically to a label. If someone attempts to enter a label or number into a date-only cell, Quattro beeps and enters Edit mode.

If you're using the 123-compatible menus, choose /**Range** | Data Entry.

Working with statistics and analyzing data

Quattro offers a special group of commands that perform intricate mathematics on your spreadsheet data. With these commands, you can gain a much deeper perspective on your data. For example, you could build a table that automatically predicts future production rates based on an existing database, or see how many employees have salaries that fall within given ranges.

This chapter describes how to

- create a sensitivity table that shows what would happen if certain factors in your database changed
- create a frequency distribution table that shows how often values within specified ranges appear in your data
- multiply and invert matrices
- create a regression analysis table that shows how certain variables in your data can affect a set of other variables
- find the best set of variable values when more than one set satisfies the constraints (limitations) on your system

Performing a sensitivity analysis

The /Tools I What-If menu lets you see how varying a value affects the rest of your data. With it, you can substitute one or two values with a range of values and see how the new values affect other cells. It asks, in essence, "What if this value were different?" Quattro creates a table, separate from your spreadsheet data, that shows both the substitutions and the effects they have on other cells.

These tables, called sensitivity or what-if tables, display a whole range of possibilities given different circumstances. For example, "What if my company's business expenditures were to increase 10%? 15%? 20%? And what if, at the same time, production increased 10-25%?"

Choose /Tools I What-If to display the **What-If** menu.

```
┌──── What-If ────┐
│                 │
│  1 Variable     │
│  2 Variables    │
│  Reset          │
│  Quit           │
│                 │
└─────────────────┘
```

- **1 Variable** lets you create a one-way sensitivity table showing the effects of altering one variable.

- **2 Variables** lets you create a two-way sensitivity table that alters the values of two variables and shows how they affect each other.

- **Reset** clears the information entered with either of the **What-If** commands.

- **Quit** returns you to the spreadsheet.

Press *Esc* to back out of the **What-If** menu to the **Tools** menu.

To recreate the last-specified sensitivity (what-if) table, press the Table key (*F8*).

1-2-3

If you're using the 123-compatible menus, chose /Data I Table.

One-way sensitivity tables

Choose the **1 Variable** command from the /Tools I **What-If** menu to build a table of formula results based on varying a value referenced by one or more formulas. You can create a basic one-way table that uses only the data you supply. You can also build a table that refers to data already entered in the spreadsheet.

1-2-3

If you're using the 123-compatible menus, choose /Data I Table I 1.

A basic one-way table

A basic one-way sensitivity table simply substitutes values for a variable in one or more formulas. You set up a column of figures to use as substitutions, set up one or more formulas that reference a blank cell, then use the **1 Variable** command to calculate the formulas repeatedly, inserting a new substitution value in the blank cell each time. The table is completely independent from any other data you might have in the same spreadsheet.

The best way to show this is through an example. Suppose you want to set up a table that shows commissions earned for a range of sales amounts. Your employees receive three different commission rates: 12%, 15%, and 18%.

The first thing you need to do is create a column of figures that reflect the sales range you want to show. Choose any empty area of your spreadsheet. (Don't use cell A1, however, because the top left cell of the table must be blank.) If the figures increase at regular intervals, you can use the /Edit I Fill command to enter the numbers (see "Filling a block with sequential values" on page 134). In this case, you'll enter a range of 100 to 1000 with intervals of 50 (see the following figure).

The next step is to enter the formulas you want to use to calculate the commissions. You'll use three different formulas, one for each commission rate. The formulas are entered above and to the right of the substitution values—in this case in cells B1, C1, and D1 (see the following figure). (The format for these cells has been changed to Text in order to display the actual formulas.)

Figure 19.1
Preparing data for a what-if table

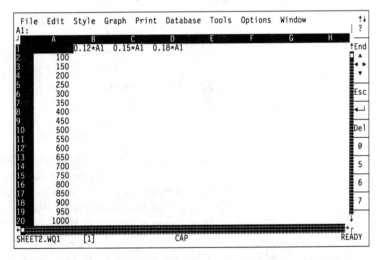

Each of these formulas references a blank cell (A1). This is the input cell; each of the substitution values will be input in this cell, one by one, to create the table. The input cell can be any cell outside of the table.

Now you're ready to use the What-If menu,

1. Choose /Tools I What-If, then choose 1 Variable. Quattro prompts you for the block of cells to use as a data table.

2. Specify the entire block, including formulas and substitution values; in this case, A1..D20. Quattro then prompts for an input cell.
3. Enter A1, the blank cell referenced by the formulas. The table is instantly created (see the following figure). You can see exactly what commissions would be given for each value in the range.

Figure 19.2
The finished commission table

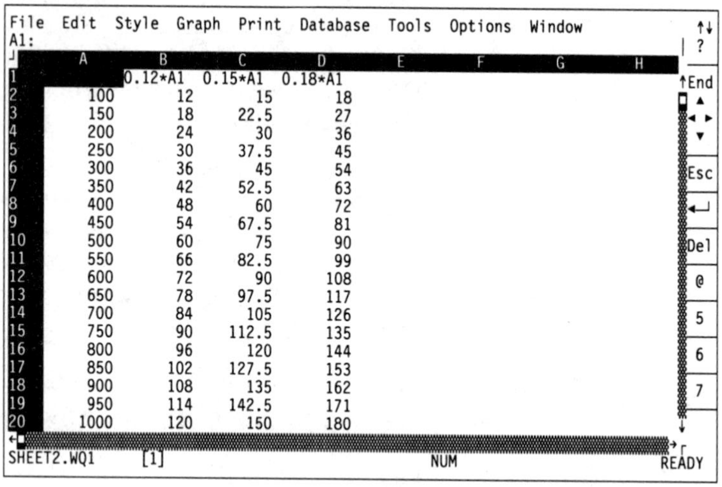

	A	B	C	D
1		0.12*A1	0.15*A1	0.18*A1
2	100	12	15	18
3	150	18	22.5	27
4	200	24	30	36
5	250	30	37.5	45
6	300	36	45	54
7	350	42	52.5	63
8	400	48	60	72
9	450	54	67.5	81
10	500	60	75	90
11	550	66	82.5	99
12	600	72	90	108
13	650	78	97.5	117
14	700	84	105	126
15	750	90	112.5	135
16	800	96	120	144
17	850	102	127.5	153
18	900	108	135	162
19	950	114	142.5	171
20	1000	120	150	180

To fill in the values of the table, Quattro moves down each column of the table. For each cell, Quattro inputs that row's substitution value in the input cell, recalculates the formula at the top of that column, and places the results in the cell.

If you change any of the formulas in the first row or any of the substitution values in the first column, you must use the **1** Variable command again to see the results. The Calc key (*F9*) does not recalculate the formulas. If this was the last sensitivity table you created, just press the Table key (*F8*) to update the results.

Using a one-way table with a database

A sensitivity table can be a helpful supplement to existing database information. You can create a data table that uses information in a database without ever affecting the database itself.

The most common way a sensitivity table is used with a database is to create what-if situations. Suppose you want to determine what your net income might be in 1992. Your boss has promised you a yearly 10% raise, and the current inflation rate is 6.5%. You've created a database projecting yearly gross income (based on a yearly 10% increase), expenses (based on a 6.5% yearly increase), and net income (subtracting expenses from gross income) as shown in the next figure:

Figure 19.3
A database projecting yearly income

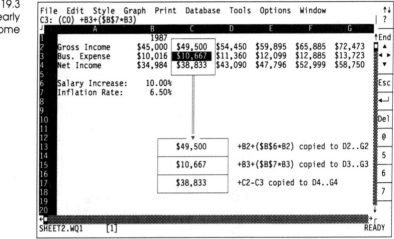

You'd like to see what happens to your projected income should the inflation rate rise or drop. You could experiment with entering different values in the Inflation Rate cell (B7) and recording how it changes the values in the Net Income field. But creating a sensitivity table would be much more efficient. Not only would it be quicker; it would also show all the possibilities at once.

To create a table showing how different inflation rates would affect your net income, do the following:

1. Underneath the database, enter a range of inflation rates you want to experiment with. Use the /Edit I Fill command for quick entry (see "Filling a block with sequential values" on page 134).

2. Above and to the right of the list, enter +G4, the address of the cell that shows net income in 1992.

3. If you'd like to also see the effects of inflation on expenses, enter +G3 in the cell to the right.

4. Choose /Tools I What-If, then choose 1 Variable. Quattro prompts you for the block to use as the data table.

5. Specify the data table either by pointing or entering a cell block or block name. Quattro prompts you for the input cell.

6. Enter B7 as the input cell. This is the cell you want to put the range of substitution values into. Quattro automatically

creates the table, showing different expense and net income values for 1992, given the various inflation rates.

The following figure shows such a table. It lists different 1992 projections for inflation rates from 5% to 10%.

Figure 19.4
A table showing net income
at different inflation rates

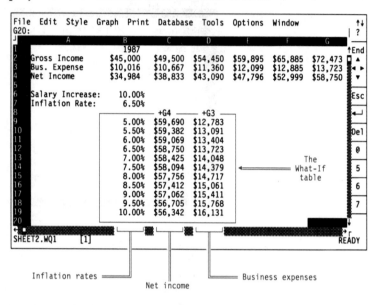

Using database functions in a one-way table

When you set up a sensitivity table using information in an existing database, you can use database @functions to calculate values in the table. Consider the database shown in the following figure. It shows a list of employees, their departments, salaries, and years with the company.

User's Guide

Figure 19.5
An employee database

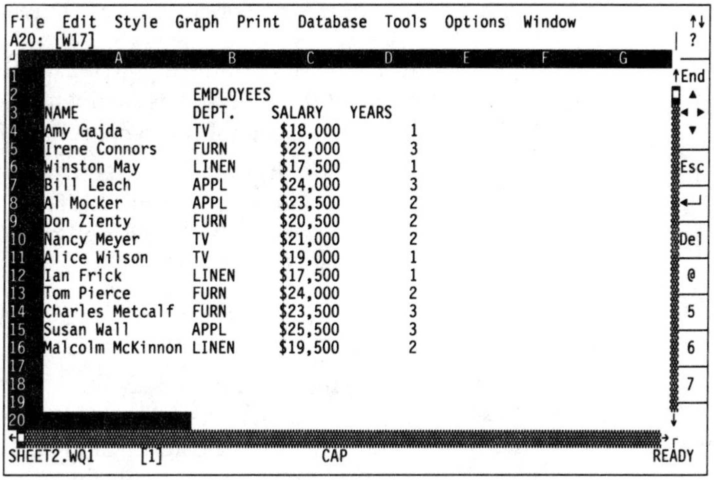

```
File  Edit  Style  Graph  Print  Database  Tools  Options  Window        ↑↓
A20: [W17]                                                              |  ?
┌─────────A──────────B──────────C──────────D──────────E──────────F──────────G──── ↑End
1                                                                               ▲
2                      EMPLOYEES                                              ■ ◄ ►
3   NAME             DEPT.    SALARY    YEARS                                   ▼
4   Amy Gajda        TV       $18,000     1
5   Irene Connors    FURN     $22,000     3
6   Winston May      LINEN    $17,500     1                                   Esc
7   Bill Leach       APPL     $24,000     3
8   Al Mocker        APPL     $23,500     2                                    ↵
9   Don Zienty       FURN     $20,500     2
10  Nancy Meyer      TV       $21,000     2                                   Del
11  Alice Wilson     TV       $19,000     1
12  Ian Frick        LINEN    $17,500     1                                    @
13  Tom Pierce       FURN     $24,000     2
14  Charles Metcalf  FURN     $23,500     3                                    5
15  Susan Wall       APPL     $25,500     3
16  Malcolm McKinnon LINEN    $19,500     2                                    6
17
18                                                                            7
19
20
←■─────────────────────────────────────────────────────────────────────→┌
SHEET2.WQ1     [1]                      CAP                              READY
```

Suppose you wanted to see the number of employees and average salary within each department. You would need to set up the spreadsheet as shown in the following figure:

Figure 19.6
Preparing the spreadsheet
for a table

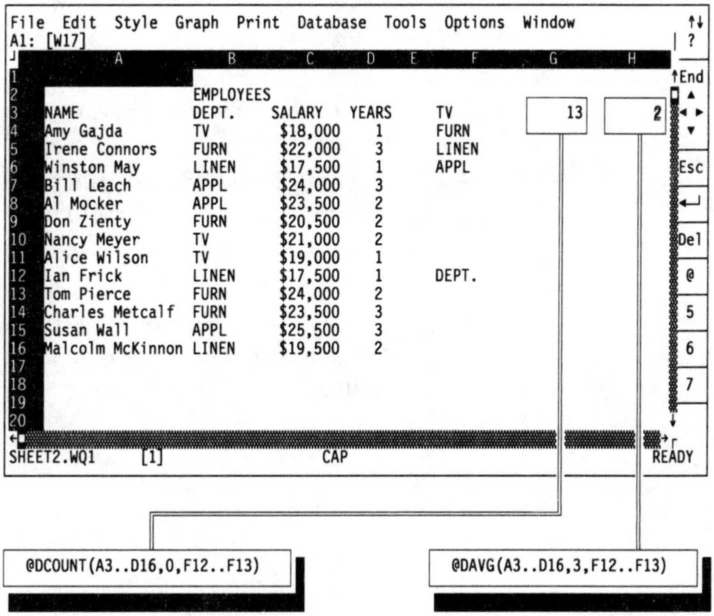

```
File  Edit  Style  Graph  Print  Database  Tools  Options  Window        ↑↓
A1: [W17]                                                               |  ?
┌─────────A──────────B──────────C──────────D──────E──────F──────G──────H──── ↑End
1                                                                               ▲
2                      EMPLOYEES                                              ■ ◄ ►
3   NAME             DEPT.    SALARY    YEARS        TV        │ 13  │ │ 2 │  ▼
4   Amy Gajda        TV       $18,000     1          FURN
5   Irene Connors    FURN     $22,000     3          LINEN
6   Winston May      LINEN    $17,500     1          APPL                     Esc
7   Bill Leach       APPL     $24,000     3
8   Al Mocker        APPL     $23,500     2                                    ↵
9   Don Zienty       FURN     $20,500     2
10  Nancy Meyer      TV       $21,000     2                                   Del
11  Alice Wilson     TV       $19,000     1
12  Ian Frick        LINEN    $17,500     1          DEPT.                     @
13  Tom Pierce       FURN     $24,000     2
14  Charles Metcalf  FURN     $23,500     3                                    5
15  Susan Wall       APPL     $25,500     3
16  Malcolm McKinnon LINEN    $19,500     2                                    6
17
18                                                                            7
19
20
←■─────────────────────────────────────────────────────────────────────→┌
SHEET2.WQ1     [1]                      CAP                              READY
```

```
@DCOUNT(A3..D16,0,F12..F13)            @DAVG(A3..D16,3,F12..F13)
```

To prepare the spreadsheet as shown,

1. To the right of the employee database, in cells F3..F6, enter a list of the different departments as the first column of the data table (instead of the usual range of values).
2. Outside the data table, set up a mini-criteria table. Enter the field name Dept. in cell F12. The blank cell in F13 will serve as the input cell. Both cells will be referenced by the formulas in the data table.
3. In cell G2, enter the following formula:

    ```
    @DCOUNT(A3..D16,0,F12..F13)
    ```

    The first parameter (A3..D16) refers to the entire database. The second parameter (0) specifies an offset of 0, telling Quattro to refer to the first column of data. The third parameter (F12..F13) refers to the criteria table you set up in step 2. This formula tells Quattro to count the number of employees listed in the Name column in relation to the department shown in the criteria table.
4. In cell H2, enter the following formula:

    ```
    @DAVG(A3..D16,2,F12..F13)
    ```

    This tells Quattro to average the values in the third column of the database (Salary) in relation to the department shown in the criteria table.
5. Choose /Tools I What-If, then choose 1 Variable. Quattro prompts you for the block to use as the data table.
6. Specify cells F2..H6 as the data table. Quattro prompts you for the input cell.
7. Specify F13 as the input cell. When you press *Enter,* Quattro immediately creates the data table shown in the following figure:

Figure 19.7
A table showing number of
employees and average
salary per department

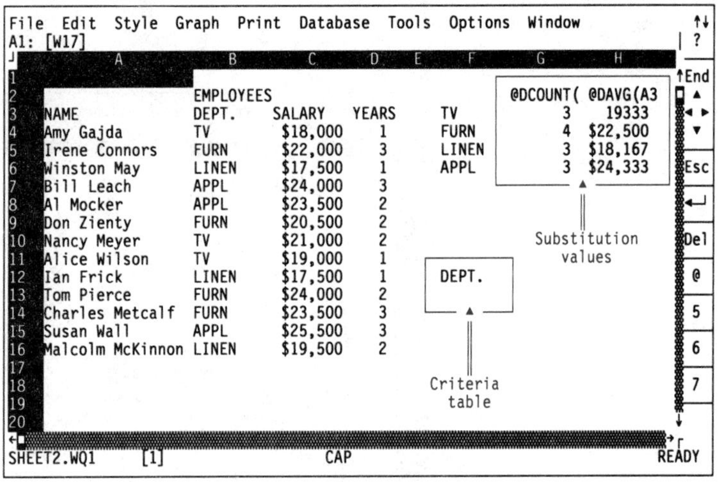

```
 File  Edit  Style  Graph  Print  Database  Tools  Options  Window          ↕
 A1: [W17]                                                                   │ ?
 J          A         B        C       D   E    F        G          H       ↑End
 1                                                                          ▯ ▲
 2                   EMPLOYEES                      @DCOUNT(  @DAVG(A3       │◄ ►
 3    NAME          DEPT.    SALARY   YEARS     TV     3      19333           ▼
 4    Amy Gajda      TV      $18,000    1      FURN    4     $22,500
 5    Irene Connors  FURN    $22,000    3      LINEN   3     $18,167         Esc
 6    Winston May    LINEN   $17,500    1      APPL    3     $24,333
 7    Bill Leach     APPL    $24,000    3                     ▲              ↵
 8    Al Mocker      APPL    $23,500    2                     ‖
 9    Don Zienty     FURN    $20,500    2                     ‖              Del
 10   Nancy Meyer    TV      $21,000    2              Substitution
 11   Alice Wilson   TV      $19,000    1                values             @
 12   Ian Frick      LINEN   $17,500    1     ┌─────────┐
 13   Tom Pierce     FURN    $24,000    2     │ DEPT.   │                    5
 14   Charles Metcalf FURN   $23,500    3     │         │
 15   Susan Wall     APPL    $25,500    3     └──┐  ▲  ┌─┘                    6
 16   Malcolm McKinnon LINEN $19,500    2        │  ‖  │
 17                                             ‖                            7
 18                                          Criteria
 19                                           table
 20
 ←▯▮▮▮▮▮▮▮▮▮▮▮▮▮▮▮▮▮▮▮▮▮▮▮▮▮▮▮▮▮▮▮▮▮▮▮▮▮▮▮▮▮▮▮▮▮▮▮▮▮▮▮▮▮▮▮▮▮▮▮▮▮↕▸r
 SHEET2.WQ1     [1]                      CAP                       READY
```

For more information on database @functions, see "Using
@functions" on page 67 and the *@Functions and Macros* manual.

Building a two-way sensitivity table

A two-way sensitivity table shows values computed by varying
two variables in a formula. Unlike a one-way table, you cannot use
more than one formula in a two-way table. You can create a two-
way table in conjunction with a database or completely separate
from the other information in the spreadsheet.

A basic two-way table

A basic two-way table uses only the data you supply it to
calculate values. It is completely separate from any other
information in the spreadsheet.

Suppose you own a health club and you want to try an innovative
fee schedule. You're going to implement a sliding scale. You've
come up with a formula to figure out individual yearly fees:

Family Income – (No. of Dependents * 1000) / 100

Now you want to build a lookup table to make it easy to pinpoint
fees. The following figure shows such a table, created with the
/Tools I What-If I 2 Variables command. It shows a fee range of
$140 to $370.

Figure 19.8
A sliding scale lookup table

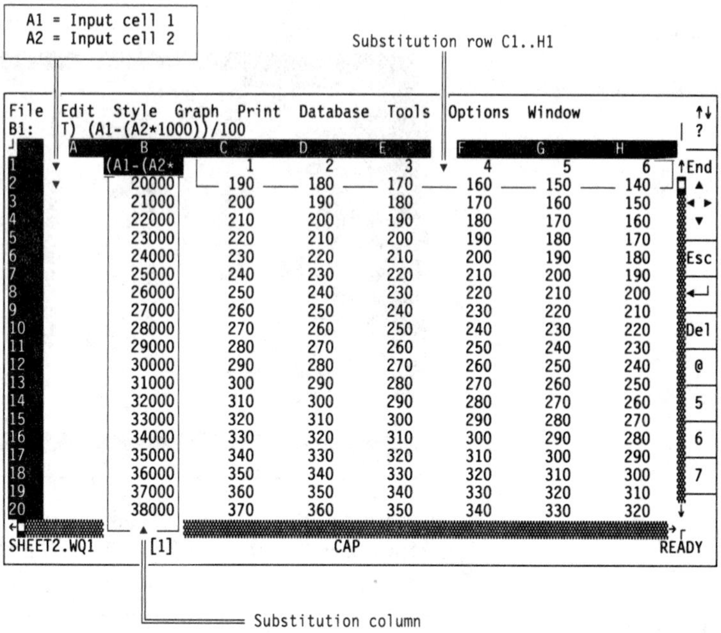

```
A1 = Input cell 1
A2 = Input cell 2
```

Substitution row C1..H1

```
File  Edit  Style  Graph  Print  Database  Tools ‖Options  Window          ↑↓
B1:   T) (A1-(A2*1000))/100                                                 | ?
   A       B          C       D       E       F       G       H      ↑End
1          (A1-(A2*   1       2       3       4       5       6
2          20000      190     180     170     160     150     140    ▲
3          21000      200     190     180     170     160     150    ◄ ►
4          22000      210     200     190     180     170     160    ▼
5          23000      220     210     200     190     180     170
6          24000      230     220     210     200     190     180    Esc
7          25000      240     230     220     210     200     190
8          26000      250     240     230     220     210     200    ↵
9          27000      260     250     240     230     220     210
10         28000      270     260     250     240     230     220    Del
11         29000      280     270     260     250     240     230
12         30000      290     280     270     260     250     240    @
13         31000      300     290     280     270     260     250
14         32000      310     300     290     280     270     260    5
15         33000      320     310     300     290     280     270
16         34000      330     320     310     300     290     280    6
17         35000      340     330     320     310     300     290
18         36000      350     340     330     320     310     300    7
19         37000      360     350     340     330     320     310
20         38000      370     360     350     340     330     320
SHEET2.WQ1      [1]              CAP                          READY
```

Substitution column

To create a table like this one,

1. Create a column of figures showing the salary range you want to include. Use the /Edit | Fill command to enter the values automatically.

2. Above and to the right of this column, create a row showing the number of dependents.

3. In the top left cell of the table, enter the formula to calculate fees. In the sample, A1 is the input cell for the salary amount and A2 is the input cell for the number of dependents. The formula is entered as

    `(A1-(A2*1000))/100`

4. Choose /Tools | What-If, then choose 2 Variables. Quattro prompts you for the block to use as the data table.

5. Specify the entire block, including both substitution ranges. Quattro prompts you for the input cell for the column of values.

6. Enter A1, or whatever cell you referenced in the formula as the salary value. The cell must be outside of the data table. Quattro prompts you for the input cell for the row of values.

7. Enter A2, or whatever cell you referenced in the formula as the number of dependents value. When you press *Enter*, Quattro displays the WAIT status indicator while it creates the table.

If you're using the 123-compatible menus, choose /Data I Table I **2**.

You can build similar tables showing all kinds of information—for example, a mileage chart listing miles per gallon for different amounts of gas used and numbers of miles driven, or profit amounts for a range of prices and costs.

Using a two-way table with a database

A two-way table can help draw out and analyze information in an existing database. When you create a two-way table in conjunction with a database, you can make use of any of the database statistical @functions offered with Quattro. (See *@Functions and Macros* for descriptions of these functions.)

Reconsider the example of @functions in a one-way table discussed on page 500. A one-way table was created to show the number of employees and average salary for each of the departments. Using that same database, let's suppose you now want to check to see how long people have been employed in each department.

Figure 19.9 shows such a table. A criteria table (F12..G13) has been set up with two fields: Dept. and Years. The empty cells below these field headings are used as input cells. The first column of the data table (F3..F6) lists each department. The first row shows a range of years employed. The formula in cell F3,

@DCOUNT(A3..D16,0,F12..G13)

tells Quattro to count the number of employees listed for each department and employment length shown in the criteria table.

Figure 19.9
A table showing
employment lengths in each
department

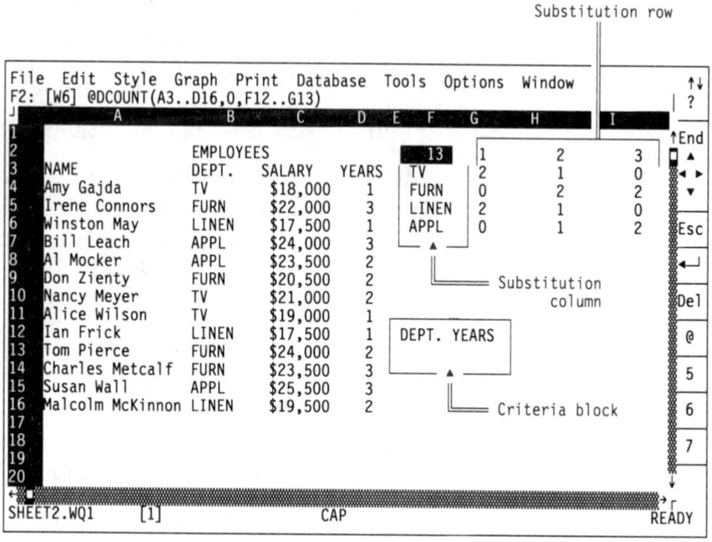

Substitution row

```
 File  Edit  Style  Graph  Print  Database  Tools  Options  Window        ↑↓
 F2: [W6] @DCOUNT(A3..D16,0,F12..G13)                                       | ?
J         A            B        C        D    E    F     G       H      I
1                                                                        ↑End
2                   EMPLOYEES                      13   1     2       3    □ ▲
3  NAME             DEPT.    SALARY    YEARS   TV       2     1       0    ◄ ►
4  Amy Gajda        TV       $18,000     1     FURN     0     2       2      ▼
5  Irene Connors    FURN     $22,000     3     LINEN    2     1       0
6  Winston May      LINEN    $17,500     1     APPL     0     1       2    Esc
7  Bill Leach       APPL     $24,000     3         ▲
8  Al Mocker        APPL     $23,500     2                                 ↵
9  Don Zienty       FURN     $20,500     2              Substitution
10 Nancy Meyer      TV       $21,000     2                   column       Del
11 Alice Wilson     TV       $19,000     1
12 Ian Frick        LINEN    $17,500     1     DEPT. YEARS                  @
13 Tom Pierce       FURN     $24,000     2
14 Charles Metcalf  FURN     $23,500     3         ▲                        5
15 Susan Wall       APPL     $25,500     3
16 Malcolm McKinnon LINEN    $19,500     2              Criteria block      6
17
18                                                                         7
19
20
←
 SHEET2.WQ1    [1]                     CAP                         READY
```

Creating a frequency distribution table

The /Tools | Frequency command calculates the number of values
that fall within given value ranges and displays the results in a
frequency distribution table.

To create a frequency distribution table, you need two things:

- **a block of values** on which to perform the frequency
  distribution.

- **a bin block** listing the value ranges you want to check the block
  of values for. The results of the distribution analysis appears to
  the right of this block.

The following figure includes a database that shows students' test
scores and a frequency distribution table that shows how many
scores fell within each bin block:

Figure 19.10
A table showing test score
distribution

```
File  Edit  Style  Graph  Print  Database  Tools  Options  Window        ↑↓
A20: [W20]                                                              | ?
J        A          B          C        D        E        F           ↑End
1         Test Scores                                                   □ ▲
2  STUDENT NAME    ┌ SCORE ┐            ┌ 60      0 ┐                    ◄ ►
3  Howard Smith        89                 70      3                      ▼
4  Sandy Whiting       78                 80      4
5  Marianne Balin      67                 90      5
6  Joni Beard          92                100      3                     Esc
7  Colleen Connors     85                └         0 ┘                    ↵
8  Richard Meyer       79                  ▲       ▲
9  Heidi Zienty        64                                               Del
10 Mark Mann           84
11 Ray Reed            95                                                @
12 Tom Pierce          62
13 Lorraine Fischer    84                         └── Results           5
14 Nadine Baron        96
15 Kate Hill           78                                               6
16 Toby Goncharoff     81                └── Bin block
17 Tony Ramirez        75                                               7
18                      ▲
19                 └───── Values block
20
←                                                                      ► ┌
TEST.WQ1    [1]                                                        READY
```

To create a frequency distribution table,

1. Set up a bin showing the range intervals you want analyzed. The block must be a single column with a column of blank cells to the right (where the results will be written). You can use the /Edit I Fill command to create the bin. The numbers must appear in ascending order.

2. Choose /Tools I Frequency. Quattro prompts you for the coordinates of the values block.

3. Specify the block of values you want to analyze, either by pointing or entering a cell block or block name. The values block can be any valid block; labels and blank cells will be assigned a value of zero. In Figure 19.10, the values block is B3..B17. Quattro prompts you for a bin block.

4. Specify the bin block you set up showing the range intervals for which you want to display results. In Figure 19.10, the bin block is D2..D6. When you press *Enter*, the results are displayed to the right of the bin block, overwriting any data previously stored there.

1-2-3

If you're using the 123-compatible menus, choose /Data I Distribution.

Each value in the bin block represents all values from it down to the previous value. (The first value represents any value less than or equal to itself.) Notice that the result block is one cell longer than the bin block. Its last cell contains the number of values found that were greater than the final number in the bin.

Frequency results are not automatically updated. If you change the data in either the values block or the bin, you will have to re-execute the Frequency command to receive correct results.

Values in a frequency distribution table can be easily and effectively displayed in an XY graph. Simply specify the bin block as the x-axis values and the results as the 1st Series of values (see "Assigning values to a graph" on page 338). The following figure shows an XY graph showing the test score distribution results found earlier.

Figure 19.11
An XY graph showing
frequency distribution

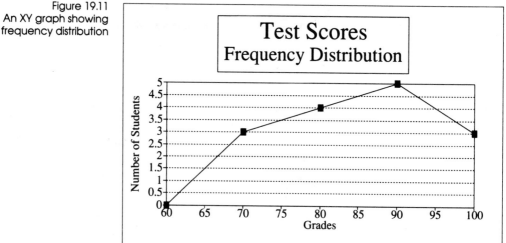

Advanced mathematics

The /Tools I Advanced Math menu contains commands that solve linear problems. In other words, these commands find values for certain unknowns, or *variables*, subject to the condition that those values satisfy certain *linear constraints* on the variables.

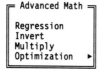

- **Regression** shows how one set of values is influenced by other sets of values.

- **Invert** creates a matrix of the inversion numbers for an existing matrix.

- **Multiply** multiplies the values in two matrices and displays the results in a third matrix.

- **Optimization** maximizes (or minimizes) some combination of variable values while keeping within certain limitations.

Generally, one of three possible situations can represent each linear problem:

- *Variables = Constraints*: In problems where the number of variables is equal to the number of constraints, the Invert command finds a solution. In such circumstances, the variable values are unique; there is one and only one solution.

- *Constraints > Variables*: If there are more constraints than variables, it's usually impossible to find values for the variables that satisfy all the constraints. But there are unique values that come closest to satisfying all of the constraints. The **Regression** command solves for these unique values.

- *Variables > Constraints*: If there are more variables than constraints, there are usually many possible values for the variables that satisfy the constraints. You must use some other criterion to select a *best* solution. The **Optimization** command allows you to find the solution that is best in the sense that it maximizes or minimizes some linear function of the variables.

In each of these three situations, you specify the constraints with a *matrix*. Each column in the matrix corresponds to one variable, and each row corresponds to one of the linear constraints. (In the case of **Optimization**, you can also specify constraints as a formula.)

Using matrix arithmetic

A *matrix* is a rectangular array of numbers. Using matrices enables you to systematize linear formulas and equations. For example, suppose you had these four unique equations describing your variables w, x, y, and z:

$$1w + 1x + 2y + 3z = 10$$
$$3w + 2x + 2y + 1z = 20$$
$$1w + 0x + 3y + 4z = 15$$
$$1w + 1x + 0y + 1z = 6$$

You could express the coefficients of these equations (the numbers multiplying the variables w, x, y, and z) in this "4 by 4" matrix:

$$\begin{bmatrix} 1 & 1 & 2 & 3 \\ 3 & 2 & 2 & 1 \\ 1 & 0 & 3 & 4 \\ 1 & 1 & 0 & 1 \end{bmatrix}$$

And you could express the variables themselves in this "4 by 1" matrix:

$$\begin{bmatrix} w \\ x \\ y \\ z \end{bmatrix}$$

(For detailed information about matrices, refer to any textbook on linear algebra.)

Matrix multiplication

With the /Tools I Advanced Math I Multiply command, you multiply the values in two matrices to obtain a third matrix. For example, to express this pair of linear equations,

$$2x + 3y = 31$$
$$x + 2y = 19$$

in terms of matrix multiplication, you simply say that multiplying the matrix of *coefficients* on the left by the matrix of *variables* on the right,

results in this matrix of *constants*:

$$\begin{bmatrix} 31 \\ 19 \end{bmatrix}$$

To use the matrix **Multiply** command, you need two multiplication blocks (the coefficient matrix and the variables matrix) and an output block (the matrix where Quattro writes the results).

The number of columns in the first multiplication block (matrix) and the number of rows in the second multiplication block must be equal. In other words, if the first matrix has four columns, the second matrix must have four rows.

The results of the matrix multiplication overwrite any data already in the output block.

The output block can be any valid cell block; you only need to specify the top left cell. The size of the output block is determined by the sizes of the two multiplication blocks. For example, if you multiply a 5 (row) by 4 (column) matrix by a 4 by 1 matrix, the output block will be 5 rows by 1 column.

To multiply two matrices,

1. Choose /Tools I Advanced Math I Multiply. Quattro prompts you for the first matrix block.

2. Specify the first of the matrices you want to multiply. Quattro prompts you for the second matrix block.

3. Specify the second matrix. Quattro prompts you for a destination block.

4. Enter the top left cell of the area where you want the resulting matrix entered. Quattro multiplies the two matrices and displays the results in a new matrix.

🌸 *1-2-3*   If you are using the 123-compatible menu trees, choose /Data I Matrix I Multiply.

The following figure shows three matrices; a 3 by 1, a 1 by 3, and a 3 by 3. The third is the result of multiplying the first two.

Figure 19.12
A multiplied matrix

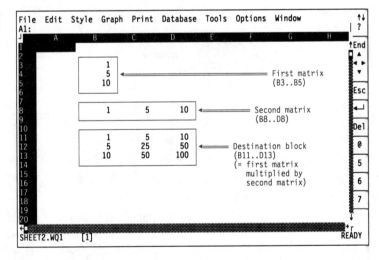

Matrix inversion
With the /Tools I Advanced Math I Invert command, you can find the inverse of a matrix. (When you multiply a matrix by its inverse, the resultant matrix is an *identity matrix*: all 1s and 0s, with only a single diagonal of 1s.) For instance,

$$\begin{bmatrix} 3 & 4 \\ 5 & 6 \end{bmatrix} \text{ times } \begin{bmatrix} -3 & 2 \\ 2.5 & -1.5 \end{bmatrix} \text{ equals } \begin{bmatrix} 1 & 0 \\ 0 & 1 \end{bmatrix}$$

A matrix   Its inverse   An identity matrix

You can only use the Invert command with "square" matrices (those with the same number of rows as columns), and you can't invert matrices larger than 90 rows by 90 columns.

You use Invert to solve linear systems of equations. For example, you can apply matrix inversion to solve the linear equations mentioned previously in the section "Matrix multiplication." Here's how to solve those equations:

1. First, you invert the coefficient matrix (on the left, following) to get the *invert matrix* (on the right):

$$\begin{bmatrix} 2 & 3 \\ 1 & 2 \end{bmatrix} \text{ inverts to } \begin{bmatrix} 2 & -3 \\ -1 & 2 \end{bmatrix}$$

A matrix   Its inverse

2. Then you multiply the invert matrix (on the left, following) by the constant terms (on the right):

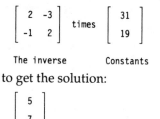

$$\begin{bmatrix} 2 & -3 \\ -1 & 2 \end{bmatrix} \text{ times } \begin{bmatrix} 31 \\ 19 \end{bmatrix}$$

The inverse   Constants

to get the solution:

$$\begin{bmatrix} 5 \\ 7 \end{bmatrix}$$

Solution

3. The solution is a matrix that gives the values for x and y that satisfy the original matrix multiplication problem:

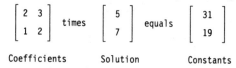

$$\begin{bmatrix} 2 & 3 \\ 1 & 2 \end{bmatrix} \text{ times } \begin{bmatrix} 5 \\ 7 \end{bmatrix} \text{ equals } \begin{bmatrix} 31 \\ 19 \end{bmatrix}$$

Coefficients   Solution   Constants

Thus, the solution to the pair of linear equations is $x = 5$, $y = 7$.

To invert a matrix,

1. Choose /**Tools** I **Advanced Math** I **Invert**. Quattro prompts you for a source block.

2. Specify the matrix block you want to invert. Quattro prompts you for a destination block.

3. Specify the upper left cell of the block where you want to write the inverted matrix. If you specify the same block as the invert block, the inverted matrix overwrites the existing matrix.

    Quattro inverts the matrix and writes the results into the output block. Any existing data in the output block is overwritten.

 If you are using the 123-compatible menu trees, choose /**Data** I **Matrix** I **Invert**.

The following figure shows two matrices. The second is the inverted version of the first.

Figure 19.13
An inverted matrix

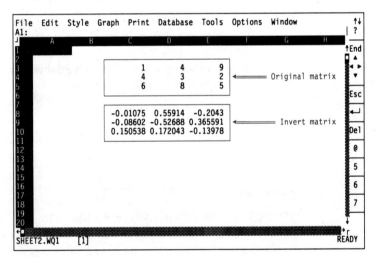

To return an inverted matrix to its original condition, use the /**Tools** I **Advanced Math** I **Invert** command again.

Note There are some square matrices that can't be inverted; for example,

$$\begin{bmatrix} 1 & -2 \\ -1 & 2 \end{bmatrix} \qquad \begin{bmatrix} 1 & 2 & 2 \\ 2 & 4 & 4 \\ -1 & 2 & 3 \end{bmatrix}$$

These are called *singular matrices*, and you'll get an error message if you try to invert one. Singular matrices can't be inverted because the corresponding system of linear equations would have redundancies or inconsistencies in it and would not be truly square.

A *redundancy* is when one equation is just a variation on another equation or is a combination of equations. For example, the following system of linear equations has a redundancy because the third equation is actually the sum of the first two, and so it is not unique:

$$1x + 2y + 3z = 10$$
$$2x + 3y + 5z = 15$$
$$3x + 5y + 8z = 25$$

An *inconsistency* is when two equations are essentially identical, but give different (conflicting) results. For example, this system has an inconsistency because the second and third equations give conflicting results for the variables (to see this, divide the third equation by 10):

$$1x + 2y + 3z = 10$$
$$2x + 3y + 5z = 15$$
$$20x + 30y + 50z = 250$$

Regression analysis

The /Tools I Advanced Math I Regression menu creates a regression analysis table that shows how other sets of variables can affect a certain set of variables. Regression analysis is especially helpful when you need to determine the relationship between variables; for example, how does number of hours worked affect production? Or, how does advertising expenditure affect total sales?

Choose /Tools I Advanced Math I Regression to display the Regression menu.

```
╔══ Regression ══╗
║                ║
║ Independent    ║
║ Dependent      ║
║ Output         ║
║ Y Intercept  ► ║
║                ║
║ Go             ║
║ Reset          ║
║ Quit           ║
║                ║
╚════════════════╝
```

■ **Independent** is where you specify the columns of independent data (x), or the data you think might be affecting the dependent data. You can specify more than one column, but they must be in a block (adjacent columns, with the same number of rows).

■ **Dependent** is where you specify the column of dependent data (y); in other words, the data you think might be affected by other variables.

■ **Output** is where you specify the area where you want the regression results written.

■ **Y Intercept** forces the y-intercept value to zero. The **Y** Intercept default requires Quattro to calculate the y-intercept value.

■ **Go** begins the regression operation.

■ **Reset** returns the values entered in the **Regression** menu to the defaults.

■ **Quit** returns to the spreadsheet.

Press *Esc* to back out of the **Advanced Math** menu.

 If you're using the 123-compatible menus, use the / **Data** I **Regression** menu.

To create a regression analysis table,

1. Make sure the columns you want to compare are the same length. If you're going to compare more than two columns, the dependent variables must be in adjacent columns.

2. Choose / **Tools** I **Advanced Math** I **Regression**. Quattro displays the **Regression** menu.

3. Choose **Dependent** and specify the column that contains the dependent data.

4. Choose **Independent** and specify the block containing the independent data. Remember, this can be more than one column.

5. Choose **Output** and specify the upper left cell of the block where you want Quattro to write the regression information. This block, nine rows deep, will be three columns wider than the number of columns in the independent block. Make sure to leave enough blank space, or the information block overwrites underlying data.

6. If you want to force the y-intercept value to zero, choose **Y** Intercept, then **Zero**.

7. Choose **Go**. Quattro builds a regression analysis table based on data in the independent and dependent blocks and displays it in the output block.

If you are using the 123-compatible menus, choose **/Data I Regression** instead of **/Tools I Advanced Math I Regression**. On the 123-compatible **Regression** menu, **Y-Range** is the equivalent of **Dependent**, **X-Range** is the equivalent of **Independent**, **Output Range** is the equivalent of **Output**, and **Intercept Range** is the equivalent of **/Data I Regression I Y Intercept I Zero**.

Quattro does not automatically update regression tables. If you alter the values in the independent and dependent blocks, you must initiate the **/Tools I Advanced Math I Regression** command again to see the new results.

Regression table

The following figure shows a sample database and regression table. The database tracks the amount of money spent per week on advertising and the total sales per week. The regression analysis shows the relationship between advertising expenditures and total sales. Total sales are given as the dependent variable; advertising money is the independent variable. The question is, how does the number of sales per week depend on advertising dollars spent per week?

Figure 19.14
A regression analysis table

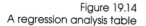

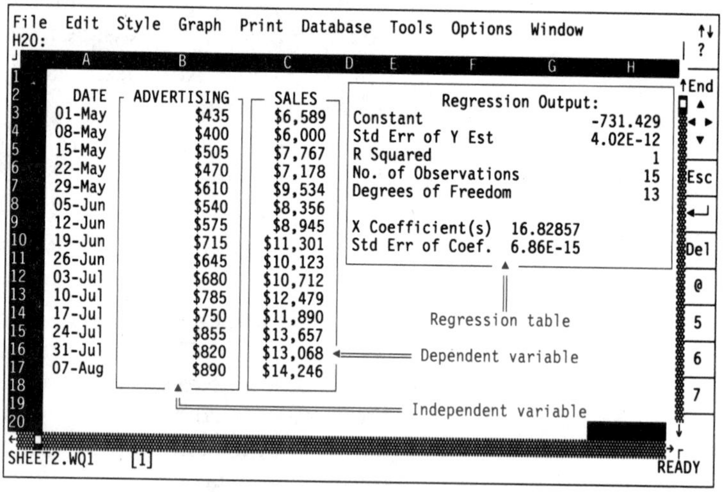

The regression table includes seven different values. This method of analysis finds a model in which the dependent variable (*y*) is approximated by a linear combination of the independent variables (x), either with or without a constant term. Mathematically speaking, regression analysis finds values of $A_1, \ldots, A_k$ and C for each y such that the values of

$$A_1 x_1 + \ldots + A_k x_k + C$$

are as close to the values of y as possible in a least squares sense. These values of $A_1, \ldots, A_k$ and C are the values that minimize SSE for each y (see SSE under R $Squared$, following).

$$(A_1 x_1 - y_1)^2 + \ldots + (A_k x_k - y_k)^2 + C \rightarrow 0$$

These are the pieces of information given in the regression output:

Constant is the y-axis intercept of the regression. It is zero if you specified **Zero** as the **Y** **Intercept**. Otherwise, it is the value of C, the constant term in the linear model.

Std Err of Y Est is the estimated standard error of the y values and represents the deviation of the observed y values from the values of the linear combinations,

$$A_1 x_1 + \ldots + A_k x_k + C$$

Quattro computes this standard error in three steps:

1. It takes the sum of the squares of the differences
   $$(A_1 x_1 - y_1)^2 + \ldots + (A_k x_k - y_k)^2$$
2. It divides this sum by the number of *Degrees of Freedom* (see following).
3. It takes the square root of the result.

R Squared is a statistic that measures the validity of the model. It ranges up to 1, with 1 being optimal. This statistic is useful for comparing different models that have the same number of independent variables. R $Squared$ is defined like this:

Let B be the average of the y observations, and let

$$SSR = \text{sum of squares of } A_1 x_1 + \ldots + A_k x_k + C - B$$
$$SSE = \text{sum of squares of } A_1 x_1 + \ldots + A_k x_k + C - y$$
$$SST = \text{sum of squares of } y - B$$

Then

$$R \ Squared = 1 - \frac{SSE}{SST}$$

In the case where the y-intercept (C) is computed rather than forced to zero, then

$$SST = SSR + SSE$$

and *R Squared* can also be defined as *SSR/SST*. In this case, *R Squared* is actually the square of something meaningful, and it ranges from 0 to 1.

No. of Observations is the total number of dependent (y) values, or, equivalently, the number of values for any of the independent (x) variables.

Degrees of Freedom is the number of observations minus the number of independent values being computed by the regression.

- If you have specified the y-intercept constant (C) to be zero, *Degrees of Freedom* equals

    (number of observations)
        – (number of independent x variables)

- If Quattro must compute the y-intercept, C, then *Degrees of Freedom* equals

    (number of observations)
        – (number of independent x variables + 1)

If *Degrees of Freedom* is less than 0, Quattro displays an error message.

X Coefficient(s) are the coefficients $A_1, ..., A_k$ of the independent (x) variables in the model.

Std Err of Coef. gives an error estimate of the coefficients (the A_n values in the $A_n x_n$ terms), assuming that

1. The model is valid.
2. You can attribute the observed values' deviations from the model to a Gaussian distribution of errors.

You should interpret each coefficient as the given *X Coefficient* value *plus or minus* the corresponding standard error of coefficient. There is one value of *X Coefficient*(s) and one value of *Std Err of Coef.* corresponding to each Independent (x) variable.

You can use these statistics to calculate projected sales. Using the same example, you could project future sales on the basis of advertising money with the following formula:

*Constant + X Coefficient(s) * Advertising Money*

First, set up a column of projected advertising figures, as shown in Column A of the following figure. You can use whatever numbers you want. Then create a column of projected sales figures based on the figures in the Advertising column. Set up the Sales heading, then enter the following formula in cell B23:

```
$H$3+$G$9*A23
```

Copy the formula into block B24..B37. The following figure shows the results:

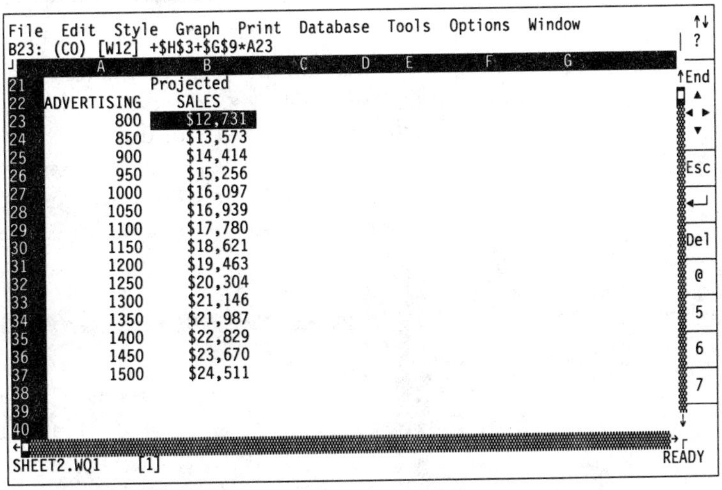

Figure 19.15
Projected sales predicted
with a regression table

```
File  Edit  Style  Graph  Print  Database  Tools  Options  Window          ↑↓
B23: (C0) [W12] +$H$3+$G$9*A23                                              | ?
J         A           B         C      D      E       F        G        ↑End
21             Projected
22  ADVERTISING    SALES
23        800    $12,731
24        850    $13,573
25        900    $14,414
26        950    $15,256                                                  Esc
27       1000    $16,097
28       1050    $16,939
29       1100    $17,780
30       1150    $18,621                                                  Del
31       1200    $19,463
32       1250    $20,304                                                  @
33       1300    $21,146
34       1350    $21,987                                                  5
35       1400    $22,829
36       1450    $23,670                                                  6
37       1500    $24,511
38                                                                        7
39
40
SHEET2.WQ1    [1]                                                      READY
```

By adding further independent variables to the analysis, you can increase its accuracy. The following figure shows the same database with two added columns—Reps/Day and Hours Open:

Figure 19.16
Two columns added to the
sales database

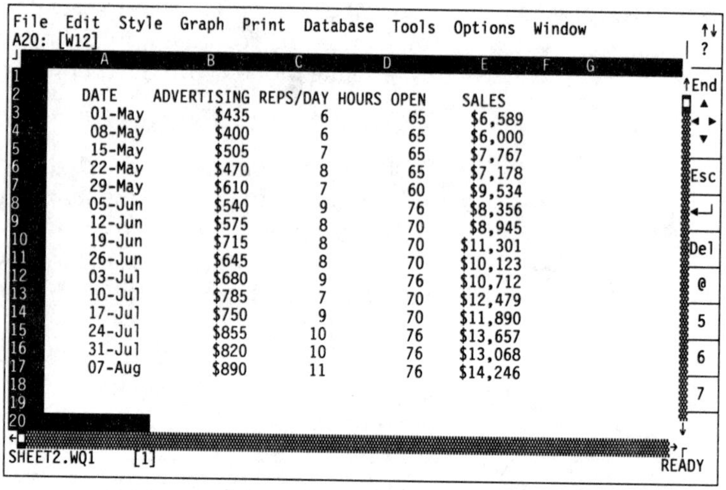

```
File  Edit  Style  Graph  Print  Database  Tools  Options  Window          ↑↓
A20: [W12]                                                                  | ?
J        A          B        C      D        E      F    G                 ↑End
1                                                                          ▲
2     DATE     ADVERTISING REPS/DAY HOURS OPEN   SALES                    ◄ ►
3     01-May      $435        6       65        $6,589                     ▼
4     08-May      $400        6       65        $6,000
5     15-May      $505        7       65        $7,767
6     22-May      $470        8       65        $7,178                    Esc
7     29-May      $610        7       60        $9,534
8     05-Jun      $540        9       76        $8,356                     ↵
9     12-Jun      $575        8       70        $8,945
10    19-Jun      $715        8       70       $11,301                    Del
11    26-Jun      $645        8       70       $10,123
12    03-Jul      $680        9       76       $10,712                     @
13    10-Jul      $785        7       70       $12,479
14    17-Jul      $750        9       70       $11,890                     5
15    24-Jul      $855       10       76       $13,657
16    31-Jul      $820       10       76       $13,068                     6
17    07-Aug      $890       11       76       $14,246
18                                                                         7
19
20
SHEET2.WQ1    [1]                                                      READY
```

By creating a regression table that includes these two new factors,
you can see how all three variables affect the total sales. To do so,
include the two new columns in the Independent block (B3..D17)
and specify the Sales column (E3..E17) as the Dependent block.
The following figure shows the resulting table. The regression
table gives coefficient results for each independent variable.

Figure 19.17
A regression table with three
independent variables

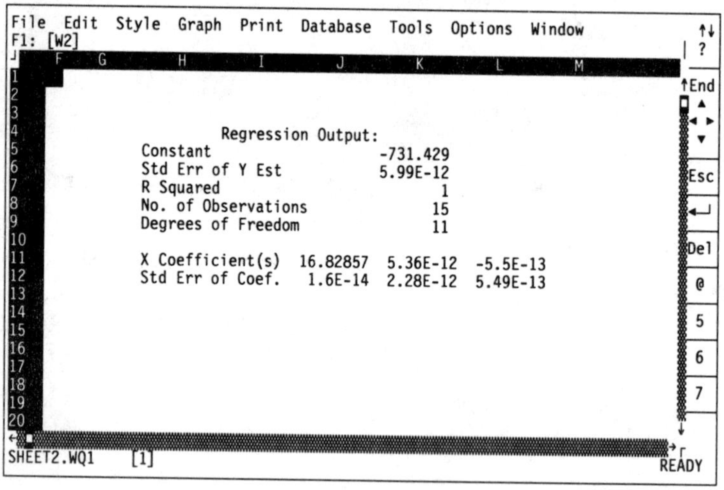

```
File  Edit  Style  Graph  Print  Database  Tools  Options  Window          ↑↓
F1: [W2]                                                                    | ?
J     F   G        H        I        J       K       L        M            ↑End
1                                                                          ▲
2                                                                          ◄ ►
3                     Regression Output:                                   ▼
4     Constant                        -731.429
5     Std Err of Y Est                5.99E-12
6     R Squared                              1                            Esc
7     No. of Observations                   15
8     Degrees of Freedom                    11                             ↵
9
10    X Coefficient(s)  16.82857   5.36E-12  -5.5E-13                     Del
11    Std Err of Coef.   1.6E-14   2.28E-12  5.49E-13
12                                                                         @
13
14                                                                         5
15
16                                                                         6
17
18                                                                         7
19
20
SHEET2.WQ1    [1]                                                      READY
```

Using the data in this regression table, you could expand your
Projected Sales table to include projected Reps/Day and Hours
Open. First, add these two columns with projected figures to
columns B and C of the Projected Sales table. Then, in the first cell
under Sales (D23), enter the following formula:

```
$K$5+A23*$J$11+B23*$K$11+C23*$L$11
```

This formula is based on the following format:

Constant
*   + (1st Indep. Value * 1st X Coefficient)*
*   + (2nd Indep. Value * 2nd X Coefficient)*
*   + (3rd Indep. Value * 3rd X Coefficient)*

All references to the regression table must be absolute; others must be relative.

Copy this formula to other cells in the column (D24..D37). The results are calculated automatically (see the following figure):

Figure 19.18
Projected sales based on
three independent variables

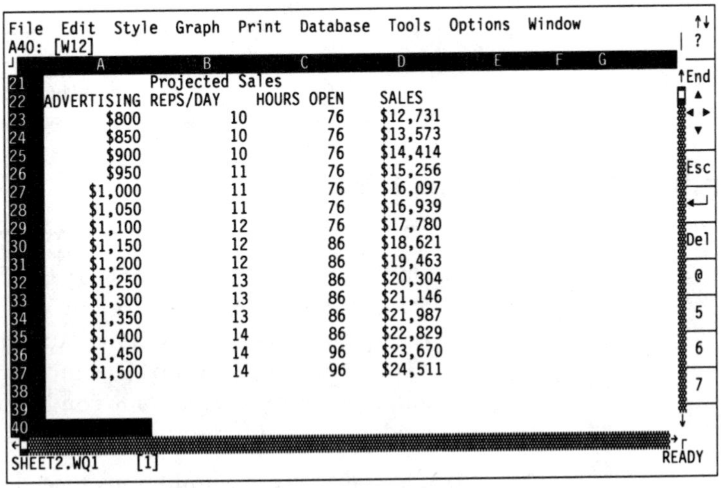

```
File  Edit  Style  Graph  Print  Database  Tools  Options  Window        ↑↓
A40: [W12]                                                                | ?
J──────A──────────B──────────C─────────D─────────E──────F──────G──────  ↑End
21           Projected Sales                                              ▪ ▲
22 ADVERTISING REPS/DAY   HOURS OPEN     SALES                            ◄ ►
23      $800        10         76    $12,731                              ▼
24      $850        10         76    $13,573
25      $900        10         76    $14,414
26      $950        11         76    $15,256                            Esc
27    $1,000        11         76    $16,097
28    $1,050        11         76    $16,939                            ↵
29    $1,100        12         76    $17,780
30    $1,150        12         86    $18,621                            Del
31    $1,200        12         86    $19,463
32    $1,250        13         86    $20,304                            @
33    $1,300        13         86    $21,146
34    $1,350        13         86    $21,987                            5
35    $1,400        14         86    $22,829
36    $1,450        14         96    $23,670                            6
37    $1,500        14         96    $24,511
38                                                                       7
39
40
SHEET2.WQ1    [1]                                                      READY
```

You can now see what your weekly sales totals might be if you increase your advertising, sales representatives, and store hours. You can experiment with these results by adjusting the values in the first three columns.

A regression table is also a good way to set up an XY graph showing projected values. In the following figure, projected advertising figures were assigned to the x-axis, and projected sales figures calculated with the regression table were assigned to the first series.

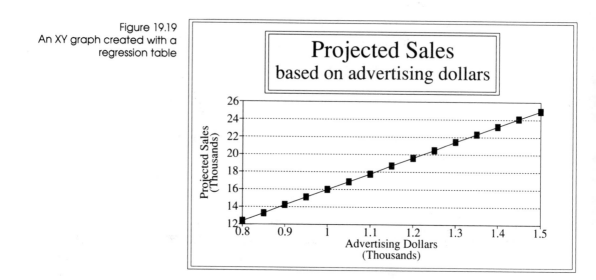

Figure 19.19
An XY graph created with a
regression table

Optimization: The best solution

Optimization is another tool for analyzing data in the context of a linear model. With optimization, which does *linear programming,* you specify a linear model in your spreadsheet. Then you use the /Tools | Advanced Math | Optimization | Go command to minimize or maximize some combination of variables in your model—subject to various constraints.

Constraints are the limitations placed on your variables. If you're trying to optimize a manufacturing operation, for example, the amount of resources available is a constraint; you don't have endless supplies, or an infinite number of human-hours per month. Capacity is also a constraint; you can't manufacture an unlimited number of products.

Choose /Tools | Advanced Math | Optimization to display the Optimization menu.

```
┌─════════ Optimization ═══════┐
│                              │
│ ─Input Values──────────────  │
│  Linear Constraint Coefficients
│  Inequality/Equality Relations
│  Constant Constraint Terms   │
│  Bounds for Variables        │
│  Formula Constraints         │
│  Objective Function          │
│  Extremum                    │
│                              │
│ ─Output Values───────────    │
│  Solution                    │
│  Variables                   │
│  Dual Values                 │
│  Additional Dual Values      │
│                              │
│ ─Commands──────────          │
│  Go                          │
│  Reset                       │
│  Quit                        │
└──────────────────────────────┘
```

The **O**ptimization menu is divided into three logical sections:

- Input Values
- Output Values
- Commands

In the first section of the menu, Input Values, you specify certain individual cells or blocks of cells as input; these are the cells on which Quattro performs the linear programming operation. In Output Values, the second section, you specify the cells and cell blocks where Quattro places the results of the optimization. (We cover the first two sections of the **O**ptimization menu in the following pages.)

The third section consists of three commands:

- **Go** starts Quattro's search for the optimal solution; you must define the input value blocks and output value blocks before choosing this command.

- **Reset** clears the settings in the input and output values sections of the **O**ptimization menu so you can start over.

- **Quit** leaves the **O**ptimization menu and returns to the spreadsheet. Any blocks you've defined in the input and output sections remain defined for future use.

1-2-3

If you are using the 123-compatible menu trees, choose /Data | **O**ptimization.

Setting input values

Before running **O**ptimization on your system, you need to designate certain cells of data in your spreadsheet. You do this with the items in the Input Values section of the **Optimization** menu.

The variables in your system can be any real numbers as long as they satisfy certain constraints (real-world limitations) and fall within certain bounds. With the Linear Constraint Coefficients menu item, you define the block of cells that contains the linear constraints on your system's variables. This matrix consists of one row for each constraint and one column for each variable.

Maximum size for the coefficient matrix is 90 constraints (rows) by 254 variables (columns). Note that Quattro requires 500K of expanded memory to solve an optimization problem of this magnitude.

What are constraints?

Constraints are limitations placed on the variables in your system; these limitations can be expressed as algebraic statements. For example, if a car factory that builds hatchbacks, sedans, jeeps, and station wagons can produce no more than 1000 vehicles per month, this is a constraint:

(# hatchbacks) + (# sedans) + (# jeeps) + (# wagons) ≤ 1000

Likewise, if the factory *must* produce at least 500 vehicles per month, this is another constraint:

(# hatchbacks) + (# sedans) + (# jeeps) + (# wagons) ≥ 500

Having only 900 tons of steel to work with per month is also a constraint:

(hatchback stl) + (sedan stl) + (jeep stl) + (wagon stl) ≤ 900 tons

And, because human-hours are limited by the number of employees and how many hours they can each work per month, the time that can be allotted to manufacturing the vehicles is a fourth constraint:

(hatchback hrs) + (sedan hrs) + (jeep hrs) + (wagon hrs)
≤ 150,000 hrs

Constraints are *linear* when the algebraic statements express relationships where the variables are being *added* (or subtracted) in various combinations. For instance, if W is the number of hatchbacks, X is the number of sedans, Y the number of jeeps, and Z the number of wagons, these are some additive relationships:

$$W + X + Y + Z \leq 1000$$

$$0.76W + X + 0.72Y + 1.5Z \leq 900$$

$$80W + 130X + 110Y + 140Z \leq 150,000$$

Here is the matrix of coefficients for this system of linear equations:

$$\begin{bmatrix} 1 & 1 & 1 & 1 \\ 0.76 & 1 & 0.72 & 1.5 \\ 80 & 130 & 110 & 140 \end{bmatrix}$$

These are the system's linear constraint coefficients.

Constraints are *nonlinear* when the relationships between the variables are not just additive. For example, if an algebraic statement includes components like (x times y) or ($5/x$) or (w^2), the relationship is nonlinear and can't be solved directly with linear programming techniques. For example, here are some nonlinear constraints:

$$WX + X + Y + XY/2 \leq 200$$

$$3(XY) + X^2 + 4/Y \leq 5000$$

Inequality/equality relations

The constraints on your system can be *equality* constraints, such as,

$$2W + 5X + 3Y + Z = 1000$$

Or they can be *inequality constraints*, as in these formulas:

$$W + X + Y + Z \leq 100$$

$$W + X + Y + Z \geq 50$$

If your system incorporates inequality constraints, choose Inequality/Equality Relations to specify a column of M labels, where M is the number of constraints (rows) in the matrix of linear constraint coefficients.

Type <= to express ≤, and type >= for ≥.

You can use the symbols <, >, >=, <=, and <> to express inequality. As with any labels, you can precede the symbol with a single quote—although this isn't necessary. And you can right-justify the symbol with a double quote, or center it with a caret (^). You can also precede the symbol with spaces, and can place any character (including spaces) after it. So " < " is an acceptable way of saying *less than*.

If you don't specify a column of Inequality/Equality Relations labels, Quattro assumes all your system's constraints to be equality constraints.

Constant constraint terms

Each of the linear constraints within your system states that some combination of the variables is equal to (or greater than or less than) some constant value. With the Constant Constraint Terms menu item, you define a column with M entries, where M is the number of constraints in your system (the number of rows in the matrix of coefficients). Each of the entries in this column is the constant term for one of the linear constraints in your system.

Formula constraints

Instead of specifying your system's constraints as a matrix of coefficients, you can specify them as formulas, which are required to be nonnegative. For example, this constraint

$$2 * A + 3 * B \le 10$$

is essentially equivalent to this formula

$$10 - (2 * A + 3 * B)$$

To use the Formula Constraints menu item, you specify a block of cells that includes all of the formulas you want treated as constraints. Quattro must then find values for the variables such that the formula, when evaluated, is nonnegative.

The formulas must all be linear in the unknown variables. Here are some examples of linear formula constraints—the unknowns in these examples are A and B:

$$10 - (2 * A + 3 * B)$$

$$A * P + B * Q + R$$

$$R - @\text{SUMPRODUCT}(P1..Q1, A1..B1)$$

if P, Q, and R are values, not formulas. But, given the same unknowns, these are nonlinear formulas:

$$A * B$$

$$@\text{EXP}(1) * A + B\text{^}2$$

Extremum
: This item calls up a menu, from which you select either a **Largest** or **Smallest** optimal value for the objective function. In other words, you specify whether you want Quattro to *maximize* the objective function, such as the profit (choose **Largest**), or to *minimize* a function, such as the cost of goods (choose **Smallest**).

Default
: If you don't specify a value with this item, Quattro automatically chooses **Smallest**, minimizing the objective function.

Objective function
: In a system where there are more variables than constraints, there is usually more than one set of variable values that satisfies all the constraints. The objective of linear programming is to find the *best* solution among these sets.

Generally, the best solution—the best set of variable values—is one that yields some optimal value when plugged into a specific function. This specific function is called the *objective function*, and it is this function that Quattro optimizes when you choose /**Tools** I **Advanced Math** I **Optimization** I **Go**. Quattro allows you to define one objective function. If you define multiple objective functions, Quattro generates an "Objective function is invalid" error message.

For example, there might be three or four different combinations of hatchbacks, sedans, jeeps, and wagons produced in the previously mentioned factory that meet the monthly production constraints (more than 500, less than 1000) and don't exhaust the monthly resources (900 tons of steel, 150,000 human-hours, and so on). But the factory manager must also consider another factor: the total profit per month. This profit is a linear function of the number of vehicles produced each month:

Total Profit = (hatchback profit) + (sedan profit)
+ (jeep profit) + (wagon profit)

$$\begin{aligned}
(\text{number of hatchbacks produced}) &= W \\
(\text{number of sedans produced}) &= X \\
(\text{number of jeeps produced}) &= Y \\
(\text{number of wagons produced}) &= Z
\end{aligned}$$

$$\begin{aligned}
(\text{profit per hatchback}) &= \$625 \\
(\text{profit per sedan}) &= \$825 \\
(\text{profit per jeep}) &= \$600 \\
(\text{profit per wagon}) &= \$1200
\end{aligned}$$

Objective Function = 625(W) + 825(X) + 600(Y) + 1200(Z)

With the **O**bjective Function menu item, you specify a single row of cells containing the coefficients for the variables of your objective function. This row must have N entries, where N is the number of variables in your system. For example, in the hatchbacks/sedans/jeeps/wagons example, the **O**bjective Function row would be

625	825	600	1200

You can omit the **O**bjective Function block of cells if a suitable formula is in the **S**olution cell. To be suitable, the formula must be linear in the variables. In this case, the formula would be

@SUMPRODUCT(*Objective Function Row, Variables Row*)

Bounds for variables

Just as the variables that represent the "best" solution to your system must satisfy certain constraints, they might also be required to fall within certain upper and lower bounds. For example, perhaps variable A must be at least 10 but no more than 50, while variable B must be at least 20 but no more than 100, and variable C must be at least 5 but no more than 80. In this case, the lower bounds for A, B, and C, respectively, are 10, 20, and 5; the upper bounds for these same variables are 50, 100, and 80.

You specify the bounds by selecting a block with two rows, the first row being the lower bounds and the second being the upper. The number of columns is the same as the number of variables.

Going back to the case of the car factory, dealer commitments require the manufacturer to produce at least 100 of each vehicle per month. In addition, since the factory's monthly capacity is 1000 vehicles, there can be no more than 700 of any one model manufactured in any given month. To represent these bounds, you would select a block of cells with the following values:

100	100	100	100
700	700	700	700

The variables don't *have* to be bounded. For instance, the only restriction on a particular variable might be that it must be nonnegative ($x \geq 0$). This means the variable's lower bound is 0, but it has no upper bound. If the car manufacturers had no dealer commitments, the only lower bound would be zero; they can produce none of a particular model, but they can't produce a negative number of cars.

You specify nonnegative bounds by putting 0 in the lower-bound cell and leaving the upper-bound cell blank (or putting a label in it). Likewise, a blank or a label in a lower-bound cell means that the corresponding variable has no lower bound. Quattro treats a label or blank in an upper bound cell as infinity, and a label or blank in a lower bound cell as negative infinity.

Default If you don't specify any **B**ounds for Variables, Quattro restricts all variables to the nonnegative real numbers.

Setting output values

Once you've specified the input data for the optimization, you need to designate the blocks where Quattro will place the output values—the results of the optimization. You do this with the items in the Output Values section of the **O**ptimization menu.

Variables The row that you specify with the **V**ariables command is where Quattro places the set of variable values that represents the "best" solution. This row must have N entries, where N is the number of variables in your system. These output values, when plugged into the objective function, yield the optimal value for that function.

Solution With the **S**olution command, you specify a single cell where Quattro places the calculated value of the objective function. This optimal value is either a maximum or minimum, as you specified with the Input Values menu item Extremum.

You can also obtain the optimal value by leaving the **O**bjective Function block unspecified and entering this formula in the solution cell:

```
@SUMPRODUCT(Objective Function, Variables Row)
```

where *Objective Function* and *Variables Row* have these meanings:

- *Objective Function* is the row of cells containing the function that Quattro will maximize or minimize.

- *Variables Row* is the row of output variable values you've specified with **V**ariables in the Output Values section of the **O**ptimization menu.

Constraints and bounds dual values

Dual values allow you to determine how much the optimal value depends on the individual linear constraints and on the bounds for the variables. A dual value is the amount by which the optimal value of the objective function would be increased (or decreased) if one constant term or one bound were relaxed (or tightened) by one unit. Dual values are for sensitivity analysis; generally, only advanced users should use them. (In a real-world sense, a dual value tells you how much that constraint's or bound's value is restricting your profit or adding to your total cost.)

In the Output Settings section of the **O**ptimization menu, you can specify two types of dual values: for constraints and bounds. **D**ual Values is a column containing as many entries as there are constant terms in your system. **A**dditional Dual Values, on the other hand, is a row containing as many entries as there are variables in your system.

Default

If you don't specify any dual values blocks, Quattro omits these calculations.

Note

As with the other Advanced Math operations, Quattro does not automatically recalculate the dual value results. If you change any of the input data, you will have to choose /**T**ools I **A**dvanced Math I **O**ptimization I **G**o again to get the correct solution and its related values.

Dual Values

With the **D**ual Values command, you specify a column of M entries, where M is the number of constraints in your system. Quattro places the dual values corresponding to the individual constraints in this column.

A small change in the constant term, multiplied by the dual value for that constraint, gives the resultant small change in the optimal value of the objective function. If the dual value corresponding to a constraint is 0, a small change in the constant term of that constraint will cause no change in the optimal value. If the dual value for a given constraint is D (not 0), changing the constant term by 1 will change the optimal value by D.

Additional Dual Values

With the **A**dditional Dual Values menu item, you specify a row of N entries, where N is the number of variables in your system. Quattro will place the additional dual values corresponding to the individual variables' bounds in this row.

Interpreting these additional dual values can be a little tricky: Only one additional dual value is associated with each variable, but each variable can have two bounds. You need to be able to tell which bound of a variable—upper or lower—is affecting the optimal value of the objective function.

If a variable's value is equal to one of its bounds, that bound is said to be *active*, and the additional dual value relates to that active bound. A small change in the active bound, multiplied by the corresponding additional dual value, gives the resultant small change in the optimal value. If a variable's additional dual value is D, changing the active bound by 1 will change the optimal value of the objective function by D. If, on the other hand, the variable's value does not equal either of its bounds, its additional dual value will be 0, and a small change in the bounds for that variable won't affect the optimal value.

Sample optimization

Suppose you're in charge of the previously mentioned factory that manufactures hatchbacks, sedans, jeeps, and station wagons. Each month, you must deliver at least 100 of each vehicle to dealers, but you can only produce a total of 1000 vehicles. You've got 1000 employees, and each works 150 hours per month. You can only obtain 900 tons of steel per month. Your materials used and profit per model are as follows:

Model	Steel tons	Human hours	Profit dollars
Hatchback	0.76	80	625
Sedan	1.00	130	825
Jeep	0.72	110	600
Station Wagon	1.50	140	1200

You want to produce the combination of vehicles that yields the most profit, satisfies the limitations of time, capacity, and steel, and meets your dealer commitments. Therefore,

- The resource limitations are your *constraints*.

- The amounts of each model manufactured are your *variables*.

- The dealer commitments and factory capacity are the *lower and upper bounds* on your variables.

- The sum of the individual profits (total profit, which you want to maximize) is your *objective function*.

- The unique combination of vehicles that yields the largest total profit is the *solution*.

- The most profit you can get (in terms of dollars) is the *optimal value*. This is calculated as the solution times the objective function.

The following figure shows one way to arrange the spreadsheet so you can use optimization to find the best solution:

Figure 19.20
Vehicle factory spreadsheet

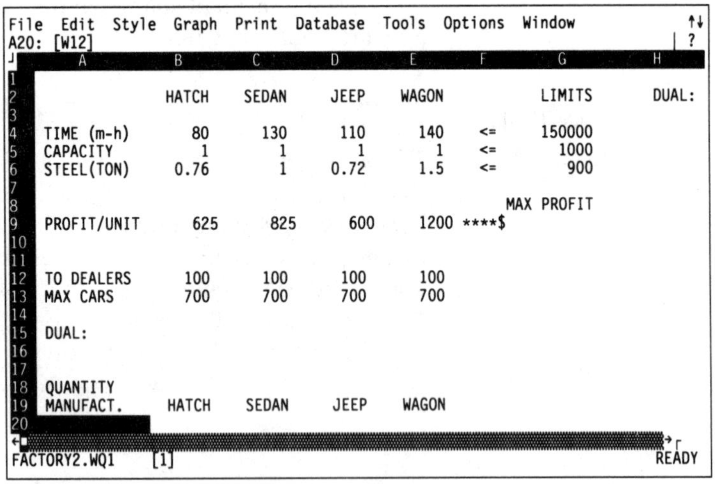

```
File  Edit  Style  Graph  Print  Database  Tools  Options  Window        ↑↓
A20: [W12]                                                                 | ?
  ⌐     A          B       C       D       E      F        G          H
  1
  2               HATCH   SEDAN   JEEP    WAGON           LIMITS     DUAL:
  3
  4   TIME (m-h)    80     130     110     140    <=      150000
  5   CAPACITY       1       1       1       1    <=        1000
  6   STEEL(TON)   0.76      1     0.72     1.5   <=         900
  7
  8                                               MAX PROFIT
  9   PROFIT/UNIT   625     825     600    1200  ****$
 10
 11
 12   TO DEALERS   100     100     100     100
 13   MAX CARS     700     700     700     700
 14
 15   DUAL:
 16
 17
 18   QUANTITY
 19   MANUFACT.    HATCH   SEDAN   JEEP    WAGON
 20
←⊡                                                                      →⌐
FACTORY2.WQ1    [1]                                                    READY
```

With your spreadsheet set up as in the preceding figure, the next step is to designate the input settings:

1. Choose /Tools I Advanced Math I Optimization. From that menu choose **Linear Constraint Coefficients**, then mark the block of constraints you want to satisfy. In this example, the resource limitations are the constraints. (In mathematical parlance, this block is the *matrix of linear constraint coefficients*, sometimes referred to as the $A_{m,n}$ terms.) The columns of this block represent your system's variables, while the rows represent the linear constraints. In this example, the Linear Constraint Coefficients block is B4..E6.

2. The next input block to mark in this example is Inequality/Equality Relations, the column of <= symbols (one for each constraint). In this example, the **Inequality/Equality Relations** block is F4..F6.

3. After that, mark the block of **Constant Constraint Terms**; the constant values that the linear equations relate to: 150000, 1000, and 900. In this example, the **Constant Constraint Terms** block is G4..G6.

4. Use **Objective Function** to mark the profit function: a single row that contains one cell for each variable in your system (in this case, there are four variables—hatchbacks, sedans, jeeps, and wagons). In this example, the **Objective Function** block is B9..E9.

5. Because you want to maximize the total profit, choose **Extremum**, then choose **Largest** from the pop-up menu. (The default value is **Smallest**.)

6. Since there are limitations on both the minimum and maximum number of vehicles your factory can produce (at least 100 of each but no more than 700 of any one model), you must specify both lower and upper bounds for your variables. Choose **Bounds for Variables**, then mark off the two rows labeled To Dealers and Max Cars. In this example, the **Bounds for Variables** block is B12..E13.

The following figure shows the location of the input settings blocks in the spreadsheet illustrated in Figure 19.20, as well as the settings in the Input Values section of the Optimization menu after you've specified these blocks.

Figure 19.21
Designating input values

```
┌─Input Values──────────────────────────┐
║                                       ║
║  Linear Constraint Coefficients   B4..E6  ║
║  Inequality/Equality Relations    F4..F6  ║
║  Constant Constraint Terms        G4..G6  ║
║  Bounds for Variables            B12..E13 ║
║  Formula Constraints              B9..B12 ║
║  Objective Function               B9..E9  ║
║  Extremum                         Largest ║
║                                       ║
└───────────────────────────────────────┘
```

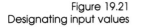

```
┌──────────────┐   ┌──────────────┐   ┌──────────────┐
│   Linear     │   │ Inequality/  │   │  Constant    │
│  Constraint  │   │  Equality    │   │  Constraint  │
│ Coefficients │   │  Relations   │   │   Terms      │
└──────────────┘   └──────────────┘   └──────────────┘
```

```
File  Edit  Style  Graph  Print  Database  Tools  Options  Window        ↑↓
A20: [W12]                                                               | ?
J      A        B       C       D       E      F      G            H
1
2             HATCH   SEDAN   JEEP    WAGON        LIMITS       DUAL:
3                     ▼                           ▼
4  TIME (m-h)    80     130     110     140   <=   150000
5  CAPACITY       1       1       1       1   <=     1000
6  STEEL (ton) 0.76       1    0.72     1.5   <=      900
7                                             MAX PROFIT
8
9  PROFIT/UNIT  625     825     600    1200   ◄───────────── Objective
10                                                           Function
11
12 TO DEALERS   100     100     100     100   ◄───────────── Bounds for
13 MAX CARS     700     700     700     700                  Variables
14
15 DUAL:
16
17
18 QUANTITY
19 MANUFACT.   HATCH   SEDAN   JEEP    WAGON
20
FACTORY2.WQ1   [1]                                                    READY
```

After you've designated the input settings, you need to specify where Quattro will place the results of the optimization. Go back to the Output Values section of the **O**ptimization menu.

1. Choose **S**olution, then designate one cell where the maximum profit will display (in this case, it's G9).

2. With **V**ariables, specify a row where Quattro will place the solution to the objective function—the "best" set of variable values. The **V**ariables block in this example is B18..E18.

3. Dual values are an optional, advanced user's calculation, but we include them in this example anyway to show how to implement them. Choose **D**ual Values, then mark a block one column wide with the same number of entries as there are linear constraints. The **D**ual Values block in this example is H4..H6.

4. Use **A**dditional Dual Values to mark a row with as many entries as there are variables in your system. In this example, the **A**dditional Dual Values block is B15..E15.

The following figure shows the location of the output values blocks in the spreadsheet illustrated in Figure 19.20, as well as the Output Values section of the **O**ptimization menu after you've specified these blocks.

Figure 19.22
Designating output values

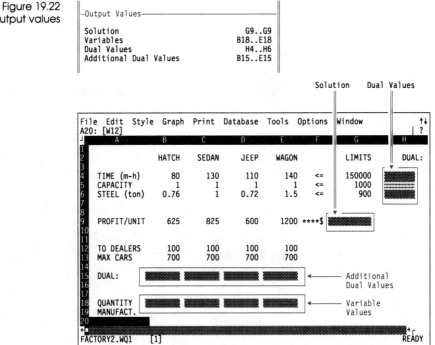

Once you've specified all the input and output settings, all you need to do is choose **O**ptimization | **G**o. Quattro will run through its linear programming optimization, find the unique set of variable values that yields the "best" value for your objective function (in this case, the largest total profit), then display the calculated values in the blocks you designated with the **O**utput Settings menu items.

The following figure shows the result of optimizing the system in this example:

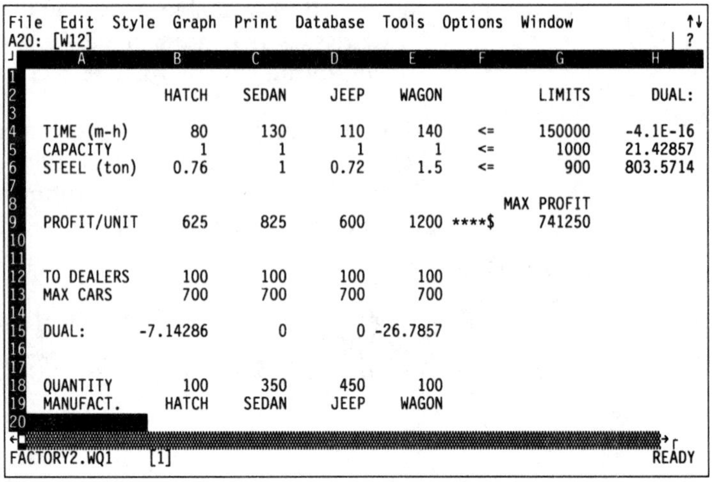

Figure 19.23
The factory spreadsheet
after optimization

```
File  Edit  Style  Graph  Print  Database  Tools  Options  Window          ↑↓
A20: [W12]                                                                 | ?
J        A         B        C        D        E       F        G        H
1
2                  HATCH    SEDAN    JEEP     WAGON            LIMITS    DUAL:
3
4   TIME (m-h)     80       130      110      140     <=       150000   -4.1E-16
5   CAPACITY       1        1        1        1       <=       1000     21.42857
6   STEEL (ton)    0.76     1        0.72     1.5     <=       900      803.5714
7
8                                                          MAX PROFIT
9   PROFIT/UNIT    625      825      600      1200  ****$    741250
10
11
12  TO DEALERS     100      100      100      100
13  MAX CARS       700      700      700      700
14
15  DUAL:          -7.14286 0        0       -26.7857
16
17
18  QUANTITY       100      350      450      100
19  MANUFACT.      HATCH    SEDAN    JEEP     WAGON
20
←■
FACTORY2.WQ1    [1]                                                       READY
```

From this result, you can see that producing 100 hatchbacks, 350 sedans, 450 jeeps, and 100 wagons will yield the maximum profit ($741,250.00). In addition, the bounds dual values show that you could increase your profits if you could make less than 100 each of the hatchbacks and wagons. Also, the constraints dual values show that the human-hours available aren't affecting your profitability, but that the constraints on both steel and capacity are limiting your objective function. In particular, if you had more steel, you could increase your profits.

6

Appendixes and glossary

A

Help and hints

Problems and solutions

This appendix lists common problems encountered in Quattro and possible solutions. The problems are listed in the order you would ordinarily encounter difficulties while learning or working with Quattro. If you need to contact Borland's Technical Support staff for further assistance, see "How to contact Borland" on page 6.

The basics

Program won't load.
Make sure you are logged on to the directory containing the Quattro program files. If you get the message "Not enough memory to run Quattro," your computer doesn't have enough system memory. If you have RAM-resident programs (such as SideKick Plus or SuperKey) loaded, unload them and try again.

If you know you have enough memory, but still get this message, perhaps you've somehow exited to DOS with the Quattro /File | Utilities | DOS Shell command. Just type EXIT to return to Quattro.

It could also be that Quattro is set to a video mode that is incompatible with your computer. Try installing again with Q /I.

If your computer has expanded memory, it may be incompatible with Quattro. Try removing the EMS driver from your CONFIG.SYS file and loading Quattro again.

No help messages.
In order for Quattro to display help messages, it must be able to access the help file (QUATTRO.HLP). Make sure this file is present in the directory that contains Quattro program files.

Parts of my screen are hard to read.
If you have a black-and-white screen with a color graphics card, Quattro treats it as if it were color and translates the colors into shades of black and white. Some of the shades may be hard to distinguish onscreen. To switch to black-and-white display, choose **Black & White** from the /**Options** I **Colors** I **Palettes** menu.

My spreadsheet just disappeared!!
If the DOS prompt is displayed onscreen below a message that says "Type EXIT and press Enter to return to Quattro," you accidentally chose the /**File** I **Utilities** I **DOS** Shell command. Simply do as the message says: Type EXIT and press *Enter*. You'll return to the spreadsheet exactly as you left it.

If there's a spreadsheet on the screen, but it's not the one you were working with, you probably opened a new spreadsheet window by accident or jumped into another open window. Choose /**Windows** I **Pick** and pick the spreadsheet you were working with from the list.

I'm having trouble pointing to blocks.
Remember the following guidelines:

- The edit cursor must be after an operator or open parenthesis.
- Press the Period key (.) to anchor a cell. Move the cell selector to extend the selection from that anchor cell.
- Press *Esc* to unanchor a cell. You can then move the cell selector without extending the selection.
- Press *Backspace* to unanchor a cell and return to the cell that was current before you began pointing.
- Press *Enter* to end pointing and enter the selected block on the input line.
- Press *End* before pressing an arrow key to move the cell selector to the last (or next) filled-in cell in that direction.

I can't move the selector into a cell.
Probably the cell is part of a column or row that is locked on the screen as a title. Use the GoTo key, *F5*, to go to a cell in a locked title. To unlock the titles, choose /**Window** I **Options** I **Locked Titles** I **Clear**.

If the cell is not part of a locked title, it's possible that the spreadsheet has been set up for data entry with the /Database I Restrict Input command. This command limits selector access to only the unprotected cells in a given block. To remove the movement restrictions, press *Esc* or *Enter*.

Entering data

Quattro beeps when I try to enter data.
Quattro rejects data that doesn't meet its expectations. Follow these guidelines when you enter data in the spreadsheet:

- If you start a label with a number, precede it with a label-prefix character: ' (an apostrophe), " (double quotation marks), or ^ (a caret).
- Don't include commas in numbers.
- Press *Ctrl-D* before you enter a date.
- If a formula begins with a cell reference, precede it with a plus sign.

When you enter data that doesn't make sense to Quattro, it beeps and enters Edit mode so you can correct your mistake.

You can't enter data in a protected cell. If the cell is protected, you'll see PR on the input line when you select it. To remove the cell's protection, use /Style I Protection I Unprotect. To remove protection from the whole spreadsheet, choose /Options I Protection I Disable.

If you restrict data entry to a certain data type with the /Database I Data Entry command, you'll only be able to enter data of that type. If you're not sure whether a cell's data type has been restricted, highlight the cell and look at the input line at the top of the screen. If it's restricted, you'll see the data type (Date or Label) at the beginning of the input line.

If the beep drives you crazy, turn it off with /Options I Startup I Beep.

Quattro won't accept my @function formula.
Make sure you've entered the formula with the correct syntax (see the *@Functions and Macros* book). There should be no spaces between @ and the function name. Arguments must be entered in the correct order, enclosed in parentheses, and should meet the required data type and any other restrictions. If the syntax is

perfectly correct, check /**Options** | International | **Punctuation** to make sure the argument separator is set to whatever you're using.

Some of my cell entries appear as asterisks.
The value in the cell is too wide to fit in the column. Widen the column with the /**Style** | Column Width command or change the numeric format to one that uses fewer decimal places or mathematical symbols.

Quattro won't calculate my formula.
If the formula begins with text, such as a cell address or block name, you must precede it with a plus sign (+).

Make sure the /**Options** | Recalculation | **Mode** command is set to **Automatic** or **Background**. Otherwise, Quattro will only calculate your formulas when you press *F9*.

Quattro calculates my formulas incorrectly.
This might seem to happen if the display format for your numbers does not show all the digits actually stored in the cells. For example, if you have the values 2.4, 3.3, and 4.4 stored in cells and your display format is set to show no decimal places, you'll see only 2, 3, and 4. These values would appear to add up to 9, but Quattro takes the hidden decimal places into account and comes up with 10.1, which displays as 10. If you want, tell Quattro to round off figures to a certain decimal precision with the @ROUND function.

Quattro isn't displaying numbers or dates as I entered them.
Quattro always stores numbers, including dates, as a series of numerals (up to 16 significant digits). How Quattro *displays* your numbers and dates in the spreadsheet depends on the numeric format. Use numeric format to add currency symbols, restrict decimal places, use scientific notation, change date format, and so on. To change the global numeric format (for the whole spreadsheet), use /**Options** | Formats | Numeric Format. This affects all cells *except* those that have been formatted individually. To change numeric for a block of cells, use /**Style** | Numeric Format.

If you enter a number that's longer than the cell is wide, Quattro displays a string of asterisks in its place. Widen the column to see the number in the spreadsheet.

If you're entering a date in standard date format (rather than using a date @function), remember to press *Ctrl-D* first.

When I enter phone numbers, Quattro calculates them.
Quattro assumes a phone number is a formula and subtracts the suffix from the prefix, then displays the result. Precede the phone number with a label-prefix character: ' (an apostrophe), " (double quotation marks), or ^ (a caret) to enter it as a label.

If you have a lot of phone numbers to enter, set the data entry mode for the block to Labels Only (/Database I Data Entry I Labels Only). Then Quattro turns anything you enter into a label, with or without a label-prefix character.

/Edit Fill won't fill my block with dates.
Quattro stores dates as numbers that equal the number of days between the date and December 30, 1899. The default stop value for Fill is 8192, which is lower than the numbers of current dates. Try again, this time increasing the stop value for Fill to 99999. Also, press *Ctrl-D* before entering the beginning and ending dates. If you haven't preformatted the block to display dates, the filled dates appear as numbers. Use /Style I Numeric Format I Date to change their display format to date.

When I enter a bullet code, the code gets repeated across the cell and doesn't show up as a bullet when I preview or print.
When the bullet code is the first thing you enter in a spreadsheet cell, you must precede it with a label-prefix character; otherwise, Quattro interprets the first backslash as a repeat command. The correct bullet code syntax is \bullet #\, where # is a number from zero to six.

When I enter a zero value, nothing shows up in the cell.
Your /Options I Formats I Hide Zeros command has been set to Yes. Set it back to No to display zero values in the spreadsheet.

Editing data

I can't get the GoTo key (*F5*) to work.
The GoTo key doesn't work in Edit mode or Point mode. You must be in Ready mode.

I can't point to a block in Edit mode.
To initiate pointing in Edit mode, the cursor must be at the end of the entry, and must be preceded by a mathematical operator (+, –, *, or /), an open parenthesis [(], or a comma.

I can't make changes to a cell entry.
The cell is protected. Remove protection from the cell with the /Style I Protection I Unprotect command. To remove protection

from the entire spreadsheet, choose /**Options** I **Protection** I **Disable**.

Nothing appears on the input line for the cell I'm trying to edit.
You're probably trying to edit spillover text from a cell to the left. If text doesn't fit in a cell, and if cells to the right are empty, the text runs over into adjacent cells. These cells are used for display only. To edit the entry, go to the cell where you made the entry.

I changed the global label alignment, but my labels are still aligned as they were.
Global label alignment affects only new entries, not labels you entered before.

When I copied a formula, the formula changed.
Quattro automatically changes references in a formula to refer to the same position as the original references. If you don't want Quattro to do this, use the Abs key (*F4*) to make the references absolute before copying the formula (see "Relative vs. absolute addresses" on page 65).

One of my formulas just turned to ERR after I deleted or moved data.
You probably deleted or moved data into a cell referenced by the formula or a corner cell of a block referenced by the formula. You can also get an ERR value if you inserted a column or row that pushed a named block or formula reference "over the edge" of the spreadsheet. If you just did this and Undo was enabled, press */EU* or *Alt-F5* to reverse the operation; otherwise, reenter the formula or use Transcript to undo the action.

When I moved some data, one or more of my formula references changed.
You must have moved one of the corner anchors of a referenced cell block. When you do this, Quattro automatically adjusts references to the block to include the new area. You can edit the cell references if you don't want this, or use **Undo** to move the data back.

If you transpose columns and rows of data that contain formulas with cell references, the references will refer to the original cell positions, which usually causes problems. Use **Undo** or Transcript to reverse the operation, then rearrange the columns individually with the /**Edit** I **Move** command.

The coordinates of one of my named blocks just changed by itself.
If you have two block names referencing the same block and change the coordinates of one of the names, the other name changes automatically. For this reason, it's best to only use one block name per block.

After I sorted my data, all my formulas were messed up.
If formulas in your sort block reference cells outside their own row, they'll end up referencing the wrong cells when you sort the block. Undo the sort (either with Undo or Transcript), then convert formulas in the block to end values (with /Edit I Values), and try again.

Every time I make a change to the spreadsheet, Quattro pauses to recalculate formulas.
Change the /Options I Recalculation command to Background (to recalculate formulas in between your keystrokes), or to Manual (to recalculate only when you press *F9*).

Whenever I retrieve my spreadsheet, the line drawing, inserted graphs, graph colors, or linked formulas I added before are gone.
You must be saving the file to a format that can't handle these features. Change the default file-name extension to .WQ1 (the QUATTRO PRO extension). If you need to use the file with another program, save a copy of it with the file-name extension for that program. (See page 233 for a list of the types of files that Quattro translates automatically.)

I'm having trouble translating my spreadsheets into dBASE II format.
dBASE II and dBASE III use the same file-name extension (.DBF) but have different file formats. To save files in dBASE II format, use the .DB2 extension, then change the extension of the translated file to .DBF before retrieving it in dBASE II.

Menu commands

I can't get the Undo command (or key) to work.
You must enable the Undo command first with /Options I Other I Undo I Enable. Then you can use Undo, but it only works for actions you take while Undo is enabled. If you make a big mistake, then realize Undo is disabled, all is not lost. You can still use Transcript to redo your work up to the mistake. If you want to

play it safe, keep the Undo command enabled: Choose /Options I
Update after you set Undo to Enable.

How do I undo a command using Transcript?
Choose /Tools I Macro I Transcript (or press *Alt-F2 T*). Choose
/Undo Last Command, or, if you made the mistake a while back,
use the arrow keys to highlight the action you took right before
the mistake (on the displayed command history), then choose
/Restore to Here. If the mistake was back before the last checkpoint (the last time you saved, erased, or retrieved a file), you'll
have to use /Playback Block to restore the spreadsheet. Use the
arrow keys and the /Begin Block and /End Block commands to
mark off the block of command history you want to replay, then
choose /Playback Block.

The Undo key reversed something I didn't want it to.
The Undo key reverses only certain types of operations and
overlooks others. When you try to undo an operation that Undo
doesn't reverse (such as drawing a line in a spreadsheet), Quattro
instead undoes the last "reversible" operation. To reverse an
operation that the Undo key doesn't recognize, use the Restore to
Here command in Transcript.

I can't insert a column or row.
You have data stored in the last column or row of the spreadsheet. Delete the data or move inward.

I can't open a second window pane.
Opening a second window pane splits the screen at the position of
the cell selector. You cannot open a horizontal pane if the cell
selector is in the first or last row of the screen. You can't open a
vertical pane if the selector is in the first or last column of the
screen.

I can't delete a column or row.
There is a protected cell within the column or row. Find the cell
and unprotect it (using the /Style I Protection I Unprotect
command) or turn off default protection with the /Options I
Protection I Disable command.

**When I change the default column width, some columns are
unaffected.**
Those columns have been individually adjusted with the /Style I
Column Width command. To include them in default width
adjustments, use the /Style I Reset Width command to return
them to the default width.

The /Database | Query command doesn't work.
Make sure you've followed these rules for querying a database:

- When indicating which field to search through, reference the cell containing the first entry in that field, *not* the field name.
- In the criteria table, include field names in the block to search.
- In the criteria table, include the reference to the first entry cell underneath the field name (unless you're searching for an exact entry). For example, in the criteria table shown below, the reference isn't required in the first condition because it's an exact entry. The cell address in the second condition refers to the first cell containing an entry (underneath the field name):

NAME	SALARY
Smith	+C4>25000

I can't get wildcards to work in searching.
If you're using the /Edit | Search & Replace command, choose Match and set it to Part. Wildcards should always work with the /Database | Query command.

Printing

Printing spreadsheets

Make sure the printer is securely connected and turned on. If so, check the following:

- The **Device** setting on the /Options | Hardware | Printers | 1st/2nd Printer menus should be set to the port used to connect your printer (see "Defining printers" on page 176).
- The /Print | Block setting should include the data you want to print (see "Specifying the block to print" on page 82).
- The /Print | Destination setting should be set to Printer or Graphics Printer (see "Specifying print destination" on page 84).

Drawn lines appear as unconnected dashes when printed.
When you print drawn lines in draft mode, they appear as –, |, and + characters. To print higher-quality, solid lines, choose /Print | Destination | Graphics Printer before you choose Spreadsheet Print.

If you created horizontal lines with repeating hyphens (\–), they'll print with slight gaps between the columns on a graphics printer. Use the /Style | Line Drawing command instead to produce a solid line.

My spreadsheet doesn't start at the top of the page.
Adjust the paper in the printer so that it's at the beginning of the page (the exact placement depends on your printer). Then choose /Print | Adjust Printer | Align.

Special fonts and shading don't show up when I print.
To print special fonts and shading, you must have a graphics printer and the /Print | Destination must be set to Graphics Printer.

My column or row headings appear twice on the first page.
If you specify row or column headings with the /Print | Left Heading or /Print | Top Heading command, don't include the headings in the block to print.

I've set the /Print | Layout | Break Pages command to No, but there are still page breaks in my printed spreadsheet.
The Break Pages command doesn't affect hard page breaks (set with /Style | Insert Break or the | :: code). You have to delete these individually from within the spreadsheet.

I'm using the default margin settings, but my right margin is wrong.
The default right margin (76) is correct for printers that print 10-pitch characters on 8½-inch paper. If your paper size or character pitch is different, or if you've assigned a special font with a size larger than 10 characters per inch to the spreadsheet, you'll need to adjust the right margin accordingly.

Page breaks are off.
The default page length (66 lines) assumes that you're using a dot-matrix printer that prints 6 lines per inch (the standard setting) on 11-inch paper. If your printer is set to a different lines-per-inch value, if your paper is a different length, or if it is a laser printer, you need to adjust the /Print | Layout | Margins | Page Length setting accordingly.

When I print, the spreadsheet columns are too wide or too narrow.
Column widths are measured by character spaces (1 to 254), and character spaces are measured by the point size of the default spreadsheet font (Font 1). If you've changed the point size of this font, it could make the columns appear unexpectedly wide or narrow when you print. It's best to keep this font at the default size of 12 points, and use other fonts to print text in different sizes.

Quattro doesn't print my text in the fonts I specified.
Make sure the /Options | Graphics Quality command is set to
Final. If set to Draft, it won't use any Bitstream fonts it hasn't
already built.

The text in my spreadsheet printed in unexpectedly large, small,
or different type.
You must have changed the definition of Font 1. Quattro uses this
font as the default for all spreadsheet text that you don't assign a
special font to. Change this font back to the default definition (12-
point Bitstream Dutch), then use one of the other fonts to print
text in other typefaces or sizes.

I can't get bullets to print.
The correct bullet code syntax is \bullet #\, where # is a number
from zero to six. When you enter a bullet code as the first thing in
a spreadsheet cell, be sure to start the code with a label-prefix
character. Number Two bullets (\bullet 2\, checked boxes)
require a minimum column width of three in order to print.

Printout is double-spaced.
Change the Auto LF command on the /Options | Hardware |
Printers menu to Yes.

Printer won't advance after each line.
Change the Auto LF command on the /Options | Hardware |
Printers menu to No.

My printer doesn't advance to the next page automatically.
If you have continuous-feed paper, make sure the /Options |
Hardware | Printers | Single Sheet command is set to No. Other-
wise, Quattro pauses printing after each page and waits for you to
insert a new page.

Headers and footers aren't positioned correctly.
Make sure you align the printer each time you print a new block
so that Quattro knows to start printing at the top of the page.

Printing graphs   My graph won't print.
You must have a graphics printer in order to print graphs. Make
sure the printer is securely connected and turned on. If so, check
the following:

■ The /Print | Graph Print | Destination command should be set
  to the printer you're using (see "Specifying print destination"
  on page 84).

- All information about the printer you're using should be specified with the /Options I Hardware I Printers I 1st or 2nd Printer command. Make sure the **Device** command for that printer is set to the port connected to that printer. And make sure the make, model, and mode are set correctly for that printer with the **Type of Printer** command. See "Defining printers" on page 176 for more information.

Quattro ignores my Height and Width settings when I print a graph.
By default, Quattro preserves the rectangular shape of a graph, so that no matter what height and width you specify, it keeps a basic aspect ratio of 4:3 (4 inches of width for every 3 inches of height). If you want to stretch a graph to fit the height and width you specify, set the /Print I Graph Print I Layout I **4:3 Aspect** command to **No**.

Also, **Width** must be a value from 1 to 8 inches and **Height** must be between 1 and 10 inches. If you set values for these commands outside of these ranges, Quattro prints the graph full size.

Graph margins are off when I print horizontally (landscape).
When you print a graph with Landscape orientation, the graph shifts sideways on the printed page, but the margins stay the same. So if you hold the printed page sideways, the left margin is the space from the top of the page to the top of the graph, and the top margin now measures the space from the right of the graph to the right edge of the paper. The **Height** and **Width** settings exchange places, too.

How can I speed up graph printing?
At 300 dots per inch, a typical laser printer requires no fewer than one million bytes of information to define a full page of graphics. (In contrast, a full page of text typically requires 2000 bytes.) To speed things up, reduce the number of bytes required to image your document. For example, print at a lower dots per inch setting, don't print an outline around the graph, use a smaller layout, and use printer fonts when possible.

The text in my graphs isn't printing in the exact point size I specified.
Quattro automatically scales your graph fonts to fit the space you allocate for the graph. For example, if you use a 50-point font for a graph title, then print that graph in a 3x4-inch space, Quattro scales down the font accordingly so it can fit in the new space. If you don't want Quattro to do this, set /Options I Hardware I

Printers I Fonts I Autoscale Fonts to **No**. Then your graph will print with the exact point sizes you specified, no matter what size graph you specify.

Graphs

I can't get graphs to display on my screen.
You must have a graphics card to display graphs onscreen. If you don't have a graphics card, you can still create, save, and print graphs, but you won't be able to see them onscreen.

Why don't my graphs show up in color?
If you have a CGA graphics card, Quattro displays your graphs in black and white for maximum resolution (color graphics on a CGA has pretty poor resolution). If your color monitor isn't a CGA, check the /Graph I Overall I Color/B&W command and make sure it's set to **C**olor.

The graph I inserted in my spreadsheet just shows up blank.
You must have an EGA or VGA display adapter to view graphs in a spreadsheet, and the /Options I Display Mode command must be set to **G**raphics. If you don't have an EGA or VGA card or are working in text mode, press *F10* with the cursor inside the graph block to view the inserted graph.

My pie charts look oblong on the screen.
You need to adjust the aspect ratio for your screen. Choose /Options I Hardware I Screen I Aspect Ratio and use the arrow keys to adjust the onscreen circle. When it looks right, press *Enter*.

My text graph is sitting on top of the graph I just made.
The annotation you create in a text graph is part of the current graph, just as any annotation is. If you create a text graph, then want to create, for example, a bar graph, choose /Graph I Customize Series I Reset I Graph first to clear all graph settings. (Save the text graph first if you want, with /Graph I Name I Create.) If you've just spent a lot of time creating this new graph and don't want to reset it, go into the Annotator and delete the text graph annotation.

Sections of my pie graph are exploded, colored, or patterned differently than specified on the menus.
For compatibility, Quattro allows you to explode, color, or pattern pie slices using numbers in a second series. If you don't intend to use this feature, don't include the second series in the pie graph

assignment; otherwise, the numbers in the second series may have an unexpected effect.

My x-axis labels overlap each other.
If the labels don't all fit on the x-axis, they overlap. There are three things you can do to remedy this:

- Use the /Graph | X-Axis | Alternate Ticks command to display the labels on alternate lines.
- Use the /Graph | X-Axis | No. of Minor Ticks command to display only some of the labels.
- Change the size of the labels with the /Graph | Text | Font | Data & Tick Labels command.

How do I change the color of the outlines around the graph legend, title, bars, pie and column slices, areas, and the overall graph?
Use the /Graph | Overall | Grid | Grid Color command.

How do I change the background color inside the graph area?
Use the /Graph | Overall | Grid | Fill Color command.

My inserted graph doesn't fill the space I allotted for it.
When Quattro inserts a graph in a spreadsheet, it maintains the original graph proportions of 4:3 (3inches of height for every 4 inches of width). If the space you allot for the inserted graph has different proportions, Quattro floats the graph in the space. If you'd rather Quattro stretch the graph to fill the space, set the /Print | Graph Print | Layout | 4:3 Aspect command to **No**.

How do I make changes to an inserted graph that isn't the current graph?
Move the cell selector into the inserted graph block, then choose /Graph. Settings on the Graph menu will reflect and affect the inserted graph.

Whenever I try to logarithmically scale my graph, I get an error message saying it can't logarithmically scale zero or negative values, but the series doesn't include any zero or negative values.
Even if the series doesn't include any zero or negative values, the y-axis scale Quattro sets up for a graph often starts with a zero. If this is the case, you need to rescale the axis manually to begin at 1 (or 10 or .00001 or any positive number) first.

I resized a group of objects in the Graph Annotator and now they're too close together or too far apart.

If you want to adjust the size between objects along with the size of a group of objects, resize the group in Proportional Resize mode. Just select the group of elements, then press *F7*. Quattro replaces the individual handles for the objects with one set of handles for the group. When you move one of the handles, the whole group moves proportionally.

For problems with printing graphs, see the previous section.

For problems with fonts in graphs, see the next section.

Fonts

I ran out of memory when building a font, and from then on Quattro used a different font. What happened?

Quattro requires 125K bytes of free memory to build a font, and each font file requires from 5 to 500K of disk space. If Quattro doesn't have enough system memory or disk space to build a font, it won't attempt to build any more fonts for the rest of that session. Instead, it will substitute one of the Hershey fonts for unbuilt Bitstream fonts. (Any prebuilt Bitstream fonts will still be available.) To build Bitstream fonts again, exit Quattro, correct the problem (for example, free up disk space), and rerun Quattro.

Can I delete .FON files?

Yes. You can delete some or all of the .FON files in your Quattro directory to free up disk space. Since fonts made for printing tend to be much larger than screen fonts, you can free up a lot of space with relatively few deletions. However, if Quattro needs the deleted fonts for printing or previewing again, it will have to rebuild them. You should always get rid of any unnecessary .FON files if you switch printers. (Be careful, however, not to delete the INDEX.FON file unless you delete *.FON. See the next question for information about INDEX.FON.)

What is the file INDEX.FON used for?

Quattro uses INDEX.FON to keep track of .FON files. INDEX.FON and the .FON files are matched sets; don't delete the INDEX.FON file unless at the same time you delete every .FON file in your Quattro directory (DEL *.FON is always safe). Don't copy .FON files built on another computer without copying their associated INDEX.FON as well. Similarly, if you delete INDEX.FON without deleting *.FON, the .FON files in your

Quattro directory have no meaning, and Quattro will act as if they aren't there; new fonts will be built as needed, and existing files will be overwritten.

Why does Quattro build so many fonts when previewing?
In previewing a spreadsheet or graph, Quattro goes through the motions of preparing it for printing, building any .FON files required. The previewing module then requests bitmaps for the screen; each zoom factor will require additional fonts to be built if they aren't already available. See the next question to find out how to turn off font building, if you prefer.

How do I stop font building?
You can turn off Quattro's font-building activity with the /Options I Graphics Quality I Draft command. You gain speed in Draft mode because Quattro never pauses to build fonts, substituting Hershey fonts instead of building Bitstream or printer-specific fonts when you print or preview a spreadsheet or print, preview, display, annotate, or insert a graph. When you're ready to print your final version, choose /Options I Graphics Quality I Final, which allows Quattro to build the higher-quality fonts that you have chosen for your graph or spreadsheet.

Quattro prints using different fonts than those I see on the screen.
When you choose a typeface for some element of a graph, Quattro stores your pick along with the other information defining the graph (series selections, colors, title text, and so on). At print time, Quattro retrieves the font selection and prints your graph. Circumstances can arise that cause Quattro to substitute a different font when displaying or printing a graph. For example, when reproducing a graph using PostScript's Palatino typeface on the screen, Quattro must substitute a font that works on the screen; namely, a Hershey or Bitstream font. Therefore if you choose a PostScript font, what you see when drawing that graph on the screen is an approximation of what you'll get when you print it out on a PostScript printer. The same is true for page previewing.

A similar situation can exist when exchanging files with another Quattro user. If a spreadsheet or graph file that specifies a PostScript font is printed or previewed by someone with a non-PostScript printer, Quattro will substitute a font that is available on his or her printer. At any time, either user is free to set his or her copy of the file's fonts to something else.

In addition, certain types of output devices can only take certain fonts. For example, PostScript devices can print only PostScript fonts, and plotters can print only Hershey fonts.

I chose the italic style for a font and didn't get it. Why?
The bold and italic font styles can't be applied to certain typefaces. In general, the Bitstream fonts will have the best performance relative to font styles. Of the Hershey fonts, only Roman can be italicized.

Quattro isn't displaying (or printing) the fonts I chose.
If font building is turned off (/**Options** | **Graph Quality** is set to **Draft**), and the exact font you asked for doesn't exist, Quattro substitutes another Bitstream font of the same size. If it cannot find a font of the right size, it substitutes a Hershey font with similar characteristics.

How can I use my special LaserJet fonts?
Quattro needs to know which cartridge fonts you have installed in your LaserJet printer. Specify this with the /**Options** | **Hardware** | **Printers** | **Fonts** | **LaserJet Fonts** command. Then those special fonts should appear on the **Typeface** menu for you to choose from.

Quattro won't let me change the size or style of my font.
LaserJet typefaces are preset to specific sizes and styles. If you choose one of these, you won't be able to change the font's point size or style.

While in graphics display mode, I inserted a graph in my spreadsheet. Why did font building occur, even though I had already built the fonts when viewing the graph?
To accurately represent an inserted graph, Quattro may require a Bitstream font in a size that isn't already constructed. Moreover, resizing an inserted graph may require additional font building. To prevent font building, set the /**Options** **Graph Quality** command to **Draft**, or choose Hershey fonts for your graph.

Using windows and linking

The macros I created in one spreadsheet don't work in another spreadsheet.
In the spreadsheet that contains the macro, set the /**Tools** | **Macro** | **Library** command to **Yes**. Then, as long as that spreadsheet is open, you can access macros in it without linking. To execute a macro in a spreadsheet that isn't a library, make sure the

spreadsheet is open, then use standard linking syntax to execute it; for example, [FILENAME]MACRONAME.

My autoload (\0) macro doesn't work in a linked spreadsheet.
Begin the \0 macro with {ESC}. Then, if you retrieve a linked spreadsheet, the autoload macro backs out of the linking prompt menu. You can still use the macro in an independent spreadsheet because *Esc* has no effect on a spreadsheet in Ready mode.

My macros won't run in a different menu tree.
If you created your macros in Lotus 1-2-3, you can use them in Quattro as long as the 123-compatible menu tree is loaded.

If you created the macros in Quattro, you probably recorded them in Keystroke mode, or typed them in yourself. Re-create the macros, this time recording them in Logical mode. Then you can use them with any menu tree.

Memory use and disk space

Quattro requires at least 512K of system memory (RAM), but 640K is recommended. If you have many or very large spreadsheets open, are creating Bitstream fonts, or have RAM-resident programs loaded, you may run short of system memory. (The /Options I Hardware menu tells you how much memory you have left.) If this happens, you can do several things:

- Save and reload any spreadsheets you've been working on.
- Exit Quattro, unload any RAM-resident programs, and load Quattro again.
- If you have expanded memory, set the /Options I Other I Expanded Memory option to **B**oth to utilize more expanded memory (there might be a trade-off with speed, however).
- Use a few unzoomed windows sharing the screen at once rather than a lot of full-sized windows.
- If you're using an 80x43 display mode, switch back to 80x25.
- If you're working with a large spreadsheet, break it down into two or more linked ones. Then load only one of them at a time.
- If your spreadsheet contains a lot of formulas whose results you don't expect to change, convert the formulas to end values with the /Edit Values command.
- Don't preformat large areas of the spreadsheet. For example, don't set half the spreadsheet to Currency display format when you've only entered data in a fourth of it. Better yet, set global

formats to reflect what you'll use most and use the **S**tyle format commands only on those areas that differ.

■ Use non-Bitstream fonts (Quattro needs 125K of free memory to create Bitstream fonts).

What if I run out of disk space?
If you run out of disk space, you won't be able to save new files on your hard disk. Here's what you can do to prevent this:

■ Look through your directories and delete old or duplicate files.

■ Compress your files as you save them by adding a compress extension to the file name (.WQ! for QUATTRO PRO files).

■ Delete the Bitstream font files Quattro has created (*.FON). It will create more as you use them.

■ Delete your Transcript log and backup log files (QUATTRO.LOG and QUATTRO.BAK).

■ Decrease the /**M**ax History Length setting in Transcript to create smaller command history files, or turn it off altogether by setting this command to zero.

■ Cut down on individual spreadsheet size by converting unnecessary formulas to end values (with /**E**dit I **V**alues) and avoiding preformatted blocks.

Speeding up Quattro

If it seems like Quattro isn't running as fast as it should, it could be because you're running out of system memory or disk space (see the previous sections). Apart from these, there are a few other things you can do to speed up Quattro:

■ Use a text display mode rather than graphics display mode (/**O**ptions I **D**isplay Mode).

■ Don't use conditional colors in your spreadsheets. This requires more calculation time.

■ Disable Undo (choose /**O**ptions I **O**ther I **U**ndo).

■ If you have expanded memory and seem to have plenty of system memory available, set the /**O**ptions I **O**ther I **E**xpanded Memory command to **N**one or **F**ormat to store less in EMS. This gives better performance but may limit your ability to work with very large or very many spreadsheets.

The /X option is ideal for computers that have a total of 1M memory available with no EMS driver installed. (When more than 1M of memory is available, an EMS driver should be used because Quattro can use the additional memory for storing more spreadsheet data and/or executable modules.)

■ Start Quattro with the /X option (type Q /X). This lets Quattro use up to 512K of extended memory to store additional executable modules in memory.

Warning: Don't use disk cache drivers, RAM disk drivers, or RAM-resident programs when using Quattro with this option.

■ Use "Normal" mode printing for most printing jobs on PostScript printers (choose /Options | Hardware | Printers). Normal Mode printing is much faster because it uses shades of gray for filled objects instead of patterns.

■ Increase the /Failure Protection setting in Transcript so that Transcript writes your actions to disk less frequently, or if you feel confident working with Transcript for backup, disable it altogether by setting the /Max History Length command in Transcript to 0.

■ To increase macro speed, make sure the /Options | Other | Macro command is set to Both to suppress redrawing of windows and menus during macros.

Handy hints

Taking a quick look.
To momentarily view a different part of the spreadsheet without losing your place, press the GoTo key (*F5*), then instead of entering a cell address, move the cell selector to the area you want to see (you can even go to a different window), then press *Esc* to jump right back to your original position.

Using the *End* key to point out a block.
The easiest way to point out a block of filled-in cells is with the *End* key. From any corner cell of the block, press the Period key to anchor the block (if it's not already anchored), then press *End* and an arrow key to move to another corner of the block. Press *End* and an arrow key again to move to the opposite corner of the anchored cell.

Checking the boundaries of an existing block.
If a Quattro command has been previously assigned to a block of cells, that block appears as the default when Quattro prompts you for a block. If part of the block is offscreen, you can easily check its boundaries by pressing the period key (.). This moves you to each corner of the block. You can use the arrow keys to move the current corner, expanding or contracting the block.

Setting up a spreadsheet template.
If you have a set of formulas, macros, or spreadsheet headings that you use often, copy them into a separate file to use as a spreadsheet template. Then, when you want to create a new spreadsheet, simply retrieve the template, add your data, and save the spreadsheet under a new name.

Experimenting with changes.
If you want to see the effects of a change to your spreadsheet without committing to it, make the change then use the Undo command (/Edit Undo or *Alt-F5*) to reverse it. This is especially handy for changing a key cell, such as Interest Rate, to see the effects on different areas, such as Loan Payment and Future Value.

For more complex what-if situations, you can create an entire spreadsheet model based on estimated figures in a linked file. Store several sets of estimates in different files. Then to see the effects of different estimates, just change the links from file to file with the /Tools I Update Links I Change command.

For example, you could have a spreadsheet model that figures your interest, monthly payments, required down payment, and estimated closing costs for a house loan. For each house you're considering buying, create a separate spreadsheet with cost information and any special requirements. Make sure you set up each spreadsheet in the same way, with related figures in the same cells. Link the spreadsheet model to cells in one of the house spreadsheets to calculate loan information for it. To plug in figures from the other house spreadsheets, just use the Change command to switch all linked references to another spreadsheet.

Unveiling columns whose widths have been individually adjusted.
The default column width doesn't affect columns that have been individually adjusted. If you want to easily spot these columns, temporarily set the default column width to something minuscule, like two. The unaffected columns will then stand out like sore thumbs.

Creating "drop shadows."
You can use a combination of line-drawing techniques and shading to create a "drop shadow" effect in your spreadsheet. First, draw the box or lines on the screen (with /Style I Line Drawing). In a blank row below the bottom line, draw a shadow under the box. The shadow will be as large as the row, but you

can adjust its thickness by changing the height of the row. A row's height is determined by the point size of the largest font used on the row. So enter a blank label somewhere on the row (type ' and press *Enter*), then assign a very small point size to the label with /**Style** | **Font**. (You may need to edit a font first, to create a font with a point size of six or so.) The size of the row (and the shadow) adjusts to reflect the point size you use. To create the same effect with a vertical shadow, adjust the width of its column.

Using the current directory as the default directory.
If you have several directories that you store spreadsheets in, you may want to set up the default directory to be the current directory. Then, when you go into whatever directory you expect to use the most and load Quattro, Quattro uses that directory as the default. To tell Quattro to use the current directory as the default, choose /**Options** | **Startup** | **Directory** and enter a period (.) at the prompt.

Tracking circular cells.
Sometimes, by accident, your spreadsheet will contain formulas that reference cells that eventually loop back and reference the original formula. These are called "circular cells" and can often cause miscalculations. If your spreadsheet doesn't seem to be calculating formulas correctly, choose /**Options** | **Recalculation** and look at the Circular Cell setting. If your spreadsheet contains a circular cell, it's listed here. Only one cell can be listed at a time, so after you fix the circular reference, check this menu again to see if another one has popped up. If you suspect several circular cells, put your spreadsheet in Map mode (choose /**Window** | **Options** | **Map View** | **Yes**) and search for the letter *c* (the mapping code for circular cells).

Entering the contents of a spreadsheet cell in response to a command prompt.
Anytime Quattro prompts you to enter text (for a graph title, for example), you can enter the contents of a spreadsheet cell as a response. Just type a backslash followed by the cell's address; for example, \B3.

Adjusting a graph with the Annotator.
Even if you don't want to annotate your graph, you'll find the Graph Annotator an easy way adjust your graph. You can use it instead of the **Graph** menu to adjust colors, fonts, title and legend display, and outlines.

Using graphic "clip art."
You can store any graphic element created with the Graph Annotator in a clip art file for use with graphs in any spreadsheet. Quattro Clipboard files are perfect for storing and reusing a company logo or standard illustrations. If you've created a text graph, you can use this method to copy the entire graph to another spreadsheet.

Creating a macro using Transcript.
If you find yourself repeating an action while you work on a spreadsheet, you might benefit from turning the action into a macro. An easy way to do this is to copy the action from your Transcript command history into your spreadsheet and naming it as a macro.

Breaking down a large spreadsheet.
If you have a large, complex spreadsheet, you can easily break it down into two or more spreadsheets. When you copy part of the spreadsheet into a new spreadsheet, Quattro automatically links any related formulas. See page 290 for an example of breaking a large spreadsheet down into several smaller ones.

B

A DOS primer

If you are new to computers or to DOS, you may have trouble understanding certain terms used in this manual. This appendix provides you with a brief overview of the following DOS concepts and functions:

- what DOS is and does
- directories, subdirectories, and the path command
- using AUTOEXEC.BAT files

This information is by no means a complete explanation of the DOS operating system. If you need more details, please refer to the MS-DOS or PC-DOS user's manual that came with your computer system.

Quattro runs under the MS-DOS or PC-DOS operating system, version 2.0 or later.

What is DOS?

DOS is shorthand for Disk Operating System. MS-DOS is Microsoft's version of DOS, while PC-DOS is IBM's rendition. DOS is the traffic coordinator, manager, and operator for the transactions that occur between the parts of the computer system and the computer system and you. DOS operates in the background, taking care of the menial computer tasks you wouldn't want to have to think about—for instance, the flow of characters between your keyboard and the computer, between the computer and your printer, and between your disk(s) and internal memory (RAM).

Other transactions are ones that you initiate by entering commands on the DOS command line; in other words, immediately after the DOS prompt. Your DOS prompt looks like one of the following:

```
A>
B>
C>
```

The capital letter refers to the active disk drive (the one DOS and you are using right now). For instance, if the prompt is A>, it means you are working with the files on drive A, and that commands you give DOS will refer to this drive. When you want to switch to another drive, making it the active drive, all you do is type the letter of the drive, followed by a colon and *Enter*. For instance, to switch to drive B, just type B: and press *Enter*.

There are a few commands that you will use often with DOS, if you haven't already, such as

DEL or ERASE	Erases a file
DIR	Lists files on the logged disk
COPY	Copies files from one disk or directory to another
Q	Loads Quattro

DOS doesn't care whether you type in uppercase or lowercase letters, or a combination of both, so you can enter your commands however you like.

We'll assume you know how to use the first three commands listed; if you don't, refer to your DOS manual.

Directories

A *directory* is a convenient way to organize your floppy or hard disk files. Directories allow you to subdivide your disk into sections, much the way you might put groups of manila file folders into separate file boxes. You might want to put all your file folders having to do with finance—for instance, a bank statement file, an income tax file, or the like—into a box labeled "Finances."

When you organize your hard disk into directories, you don't have to wade through hundreds of file names looking for the file you want every time you type DIR on the command line. You'll get a listing of only the files on the directory you're currently logged onto.

For example, the Quattro installation program automatically creates a directory named QPRO off the root to hold all your Quattro files unless you specify another name. It also automatically creates a FONTS directory off the QPRO directory to hold all your font files.

Although you can make directories on either floppy or hard disks, they are used most often on hard disks. This is because they can hold a greater volume of data, so there is a greater need for organization and compartmentalization.

When you're at the DOS level, rather than in Quattro or another program, you can tell DOS to create directories, move files around between directories, and display which files are in a particular directory.

Subdirectories

If you are someone who really likes organization, you can further subdivide your directories into subdirectories. You can create as many directories and subdirectories as you like—just don't forget where you put your files!

A subdirectory is created the same way as a directory. To create a subdirectory from the Quattro directory (for instance, for storing your spreadsheet files), do the following:

1. Be sure you are in the Quattro directory.
2. Type MD SPREAD *Enter.*
3. Type CD SPREAD. You are now in the SPREAD subdirectory.
4. Copy your spreadsheet files to the new subdirectory.

Where am I? The $P $G prompt

You probably have noticed that, when you change directories, you still see the C> prompt; there is no evidence of what directory or subdirectory you are in. This can be confusing, especially if you leave your computer for a while. It's easy to forget where you were when you left.

DOS gives you an easy way to find out. Just type

```
PROMPT=$P $G
```

and from now on (until you turn your computer off or reboot), the prompt will show you exactly where you are. Try it. If you are still in the SPREAD subdirectory, your DOS prompt should look like

```
C:\QPRO\SPREAD >
```

The AUTOEXEC.BAT file

To avoid typing the prompt command (discussed in the previous section) to see "where you are" every time you turn on your computer, you can set up an AUTOEXEC.BAT file to do it for you each time you turn on your computer.

The AUTOEXEC.BAT file is a useful tool to get your computer to do things automatically. There are many more things it can do, but rather than go into great detail here, we suggest referring to your DOS manual for more information. We will show you how to create an AUTOEXEC.BAT file that automatically changes your prompt so you know where you are in your directory structure and sets a path to the Quattro directory.

Note   The Quattro installation program sets a path to your Quattro directory automatically, if you let it. You can also do it yourself, as we describe shortly.

The DOS PATH command tells your computer where to look for commands it doesn't recognize. DOS only recognizes programs in the current (logged) directory, unless there is a path to the directory containing pertinent programs or files.

In the following example, we'll set a path to the Quattro directory.

If you have an AUTOEXEC.BAT file in your root directory, your computer will do everything in that file when you first turn your computer on. (The root directory is where you see the C> or C:\ prompt, with no directory names following it.)

Here's how to create an AUTOEXEC.BAT file:

1. Type `CD\` to get to the root directory.
2. Type `COPY CON AUTOEXEC.BAT` *Enter*. This tells DOS to copy whatever you type next into a file called AUTOEXEC.BAT.
3. Type

   ```
   PROMPT=$P $G Enter
   PATH=C:\QPRO
   ```
   Ctrl-Z Enter

The *Ctrl-Z* sequence saves your commands in the AUTOEXEC.BAT file.

To test your new AUTOEXEC.BAT file, reboot your computer by holding down the *Ctrl* and *Alt* keys and then pressing *Del*. You should see

```
C:>
```

on the command line. You should now be able to load Quattro from any directory on your disk.

Changing directories

How do you get from one directory to another? It depends on where you want to go. The basic DOS command for changing directories is CD. Use it like this:

- *To move from one directory to another*: For example, to change from the Quattro directory to one called WP, type the following at the Quattro directory prompt (`C:\QPRO>`):

  ```
  CD \WP
  ```

  and then press *Enter*. Notice the backslash (\) before the directory name. Whenever you are moving from one directory to another unrelated directory, type the name of the directory, preceded by a backslash.

- *To move from a directory to its subdirectory*: For example, to move from the Quattro directory to the SPREAD subdirectory, type the following at the Quattro directory prompt (`C:\QPRO>`):

  ```
  CD SPREAD
  ```

  and then press *Enter*. In this case, you did not need the backslash because the SPREAD directory is a direct offshoot of the Quattro directory. In fact, DOS would have misunderstood what you meant if you had used the backslash in this case. If you had included the backslash, DOS would have thought that SPREAD was a directory off the main (root) directory.

■ *To move from a subdirectory to its parent directory*: For example, to move from the SPREAD subdirectory to the Quattro directory, type the following at the SPREAD subdirectory prompt (C:\QPRO\SPREAD>):

    CD..

and then press *Enter*. DOS moves you back to the Quattro directory. Any time you want to move back to the parent directory, type two periods after the CD command.

■ *To move to the root directory*: The *root directory* is the original directory. It is the parent (or grandparent) of all directories (and subdirectories). When you are in the root directory, you see this prompt: C:\ >.

To move to the root directory from any other directory, simply type

    CD \

and press *Enter*. The backslash without a directory name signals DOS that you want to return to the root directory.

This appendix has presented only a quick look at DOS and some of its functions. Once you're familiar with the information given here, you may want to study your DOS manual and discover the many things you can do with your computer's operating system.

C

Networking with Quattro

A special version of Quattro is available for use on a local area network. If this is the version you've bought, you'll find included in your Quattro package the *Network Administrator's Guide.* Refer to this for information on setting up and maintaining Quattro on your network.

If you haven't bought the network version of Quattro, you can still use Quattro on a network, but only one person will be able to use the program at a time. If more than one person tries to use a non-network version of Quattro, an error message states that the resource files cannot be shared (unless, of course, you have more than one copy of the program in separate directories). Then one person can use each copy at a time. In this case, Quattro uses the following rules concerning file access:

■ The first person to open a given spreadsheet has full read/write access to that spreadsheet until it is closed.

■ All subsequent users who open an already opened spreadsheet have read-only access to the spreadsheet. The spreadsheet will appear as it was when last saved. That is, changes made to the spreadsheet since the last time a user chose the /File | Save command will not appear.

■ A user with read-only access to a spreadsheet can make changes and recalculate the spreadsheet but cannot save it under its original name. The spreadsheet can, however, be saved under a different name, which will give the user who named it full read/write access.

If your group is connected to a local area network, you really should consider purchasing the network version. Then any number of people can use Quattro on the network at the same time. It's also more economical than buying numerous copies and takes up much less disk space.

D

Quattro keys and indicators

This appendix describes the spreadsheet mode and status indicators that appear on the status line, and the function of various keys in Quattro.

See page 28 for a list of Quattro's preassigned control-key shortcuts.

Note that certain keys function differently in the File Manager and Graph Annotator than in a spreadsheet window.

- Refer to page 254 for a list of window keys in the File Manager. Pages 259, 263, and 267 list special keys in the File Manager control, file list, and tree panes, respectively.

- For descriptions of special keys in the Graph Annotator, see "Graph Annotator keys" on page 408.

For a list of Quattro's key-equivalent macro commands, see page 444.

Table D.1: Spreadsheet mode and status indicators

Indicator	Description
CALC	At least one formula in the spreadsheet needs to be recalculated. Press *F9* to recalculate the formula(s).
CAP	The *Caps Lock* key is on.
CIRC	A formula in the spreadsheet contains a circular reference (it refers to itself or to another formula that refers back to it).
DEBUG	Quattro is in Debug mode. If you execute a macro in Debug mode, the macro Debug window appears and Quattro debugs your macro one step at a time.
EDIT	The spreadsheet is in Edit mode, which allows you to make changes to the contents of the current cell. To enter Edit mode, press *F2*.
END	The *End* key is on. Any arrow keys you press will move to the end of an area in the spreadsheet instead of scrolling.
ERROR	An error has occurred. Press *Esc* to go back to what you were doing before the error, or correct the error.
EXT	You are extending a block selection. When you are finished, choose a command that operates on a block.
FIND	The system is searching for entries that match the conditions you specified with the Query command.
FRMT	You are editing a format line during a Parse operation.
HELP	A help screen is displayed. To display help, press *F1*. To exit, press *Esc*.
LABEL	The entry you are making is text (a label).
MACRO	Quattro is executing a macro.
MENU	The Quattro menus are active. To choose a menu item, use the arrow keys to highlight it and press *Enter*, or press the highlighted key letter in the menu command name. To remove a menu, press *Esc*.
NUM	The *Num Lock* key is on.
OVLY	Quattro is loading an overlay file.
OVR	The *Insert* key is on.
POINT	The spreadsheet is in Point mode, allowing you to specify a cell or block with the cell selector or to view a choice list of block names with *F3*.
READY	Quattro is ready for the next entry or command.
REC	Macro recording is in progress.
REP	The value you enter (in a menu command) will replace the existing value.
SCR	The *Scroll Lock* key is on.
VALUE	The entry you are making is a number or formula.
WAIT	An action is in progress. You must wait before proceeding.

Table D.2: The cursor-movement keys in a spreadsheet

Key	Description
←	Moves left one cell.
→	Moves right one cell.
↑	Moves up one cell.
↓	Moves down one cell.
Ctrl ← or *Shift-Tab*	Moves left one screen.
Ctrl → or *Tab*	Moves right one screen.
PgUp	Moves up one screen.
PgDn	Moves down one screen.
End	Must be used with another direction key.
End Home	Moves to lower right corner of the filled-in part of the spreadsheet.
End ↑	If the current cell contains an entry, moves up to the next filled-in cell beneath an empty one. If the current cell is blank, moves up to the next filled-in cell encountered.
End ↓	If the current cell contains an entry, moves down to the next filled-in cell above an empty one. If the current cell is blank, moves down to the next filled-in cell encountered.
End →	If the current cell contains an entry, moves right to the next filled-in cell followed by an empty one. If the current cell is blank, moves to the next filled-in cell to the right.
End ←	If the current cell contains an entry, moves left to the next filled-in cell preceded by an empty one. If the current cell is blank, moves to the next filled-in cell to the left.
GoTo (*F5*)	Moves to any cell you specify.

Table D.3: The Quattro function keys

Key	Name	Description
F1	Help	Displays information about the current area; for example, a highlighted menu item or active Quattro function. Press *Esc* to exit help.
F2	Edit	Puts Quattro into Edit mode so you can make changes to a cell entry. In the File Manager, renames a file. In a file prompt box, locates the last file beginning with the characters you type. If a text element is selected in the Graph Annotator, *F2* activates Edit mode.
Shift-F2	Debug	Puts Quattro in Debug mode so you can execute a macro step by step.
Alt-F2	Macro Menu	Displays the Macro menu.
F3	Choices	Whenever Quattro prompts you for a block, or in Edit mode with your cursor positioned after an operator, press *F3* to display a list of block names for the spreadsheet. Press + (plus on the numeric keypad) to show coordinates and – (minus) to remove them. Press *F3* again to toggle the display to full screen. Selecting a block name enters it on the input line. In the Graph Annotator, *F3* activates the Property Sheet.
Shift-F3	Macros	Displays a list of macro commands for the spreadsheet. Choosing a command enters it on the input line.
Alt-F3	Functions	Displays a list of functions for the spreadsheet. Specifying a function enters it on the input line.
F4	Abs	Makes the cell address to the left of the cursor absolute. Press repeatedly to cycle through the possible absolute combinations; for example, $B$4, B$4, $B4, B4.
F5	GoTo	Moves the cell selector to a specified cell address.
Shift-F5	Pick Window	Displays a list of open windows. Choose a window from the list to activate it.
Alt-F5	Undo	If enabled, lets you "undo" erasures, edits, deletions, and file retrievals.
F6	Pane	Moves the cell selector to the inactive window pane when the window is split into two panes. In the File Manager, moves from control pane to file list pane to tree pane.
Shift-F6	Next Window	Displays the next open window.
Alt-F6	Zoom	Expands the active window so that it fills the screen. If the window is already expanded, shrinks it back to its previous size.

Table D.3: The Quattro function keys (continued)

Key	Name	Description
F7	Query	Repeats the previous **Query** command. In the Graph Annotator, press *F7* with a group of objects selected to enter Proportional Resize mode.
Shift-F7	Select	In the spreadsheet, press *Shift-F7* and use the arrow keys to select a block of text in Ext mode. In the File Manager, selects the highlighted file in the active file list for copying or moving.
Alt-F7	All Select	Selects all files in the active File Manager file list. If some files were already selected, deselects all files in the list.
F8	Table	Repeats the last **What-If** command.
Shift-F8	Move	Removes the files marked in the active File Manager file list and stores them in temporary memory so you can insert them somewhere else.
F9	Calc	In Ready mode, calculates any formulas that have been entered or changed since you turned off automatic recalculation or last pressed the Calc key. In Value or Edit mode, converts the formula on the input line to the end result. In a File Manager window, rereads the current directory. In graphics display mode, *F9* repaints the screen.
Shift-F9	Copy	Copies the files marked on the active File Manager file list into temporary memory so you can insert them somewhere else.
F10	Graph	Displays the current graph. Press *Esc* to return to the spreadsheet. In the Graph Annotator, redraws the graph.
Shift-F10	Paste	Inserts any files stored in temporary memory into the directory displayed in the active File Manager file list.

Table D.4: Special keys in Quattro

Key	Description
+ (Expand on numeric keypad)	If you are in a menu, displays the command settings for the menus. If you are in a choice list, displays the block coordinates.
– (Contract on numeric keypad)	If you are in a menu, shrinks the menus so that settings no longer appear. If you are in a choice list with block coordinates displayed, removes them.
Alt	Press with the number of any open window to jump to that window; Alt-0 displays a pick list of open windows. Press with certain function keys to invoke commands.
Backspace	Used in typing or editing an entry to erase the character to the left of the cursor. If pressed within a help screen, returns you to the previous level of help. If pressed while pointing out a cell block, returns you to the cell that was current before you entered Point mode.
Caps Lock	Enters Caps mode, in which all letters you enter are displayed in capital letters. Press again to exit Caps mode.
Ctrl-Backspace	Clears any existing entry in a prompt line, or on the input line in Edit mode.
Ctrl-Break	Exits from a menu and returns to the spreadsheet's Ready mode. If pressed while a macro is executing, it terminates the macro.
Ctrl-D	Press before entering a value to to insert a date into a cell.
Ctrl-Enter	Lets you assign the highlighted menu command to a special key as a "shortcut."
Del	Erases the contents of the current cell.
/ (Slash)	In the spreadsheet or File Manager, activates the pull-down menu bar. In a displayed graph, activates the Graph Annotator. In the Graph Annotator, activates the Toolbox. In a Macro Debugger window, activates the Macro Debugger menu. In a Transcript window, activates the Transcript menu.
\ (Backslash)	Lets you enter one or more characters to repeat across an entire cell width.
Ctrl \	Delete to end of line
Enter	In the spreadsheet, writes the entry on the input line into the current cell and returns to Ready mode. In a menu or choice list, chooses the highlighted item. Also used with Ctrl to store a menu command in a special key as a "shortcut."
Esc	Cancels whatever you are doing; for example, backs you out of a menu, erases any changes you made to an entry on the input line, or removes a system prompt from the screen without invoking a command. If pressed within a Help screen, returns you directly to the spreadsheet. In the Graph Annotator, activates the Draw Area.

Table D.4: Special keys in Quattro (continued)

Key	Description
Num Lock	Lets you use the numeric keypad on the right of the keyboard to enter numbers. Press again to use these keys as direction keys.
Scroll Lock	Lets you switch from Move to Size mode after you choose /Window I Move/Size.
PrtSc	Prints the contents of the current screen exactly as displayed (in character mode only).
Shift	Pressed with alphanumeric keys, enters an uppercase character.
Tab or *Ctrl* →	In the spreadsheet, moves right one screen. In the File Manager, moves from pane to pane. In the Graph Annotator, selects the next element in the Draw Area.
Shift-Tab or *Ctrl* ←	In the spreadsheet, moves left one screen. In the File Manager, moves the cursor to the File Name prompt in the control pane. In the Graph Annotator, selects the previous element in the Draw Area.

E

Printer setup strings

See page 97 for information about how to send a setup string to your printer.

When you print a spreadsheet to a text printer, you can send it special formatting instructions with a *setup string* command. In a setup string, you can specify line spacing, print mode, typeface, and so on.

A setup string consists of one or more ASCII *character codes*, which are translated from the printer control commands listed in your printer's manual. Each printer recognizes its own set of control commands. The following tables list the ASCII codes for control printer commands for selected printers.

To enter a command for a printer other than these, refer to your printer's manual for the control or escape commands. To translate your printer's escape (*Esc*) command, type \027, then enter the letter or number that follows *Esc* in the print command.

To enter a control command (a key combination that uses the *Ctrl* key, such as *Ctrl-N*), look up the letter to be entered after *Ctrl* on an ASCII table (see Appendix G). Type \0 and the corresponding Hex code shown on the table.

You can enter more than one code in a setup string, as long as the printer supports it. For example, you can enter \027X1\027G\027M to have your Epson FX 85 print near letter-quality, double-strike, elite-pitch characters, but it cannot print italicized characters in near letter-quality mode if you enter \027X1\0274. When you enter multiple codes, don't insert spaces between them.

Be careful to distinguish between a lowercase letter *l* (el) and the number 1 (one), and between a capital letter *O* (oh) and the number 0 (zero).

See page 94 for general information about the margin and page length settings for your spreadsheet.

See page 94 for general information about the margin and page length settings for your spreadsheet.

Table E.1
C.Itoh 8510

Code	Instruction
Print mode:	
\027Q	Select compressed mode
\027E	Select elite pitch (12 cpi)
\027N	Select pica pitch (10 cpi)
\027!	Select emphasized mode
\027\034	Cancel emphasized mode
\027X	Select underlining
\027Y	Master reset
Page formatting:	
\027T48	Double-space text (3 lines per inch)
\027A	Single-space text (6 lines per inch)
\027B	8 lines per inch

Table E.2
DEC LA100

Code	Instruction
Print mode:	
\027[4w	Select compressed mode
\027[2w	Select elite pitch (12 cpi)
\027[0w	Select pica pitch (10 cpi)
\027[5w	Select expanded mode
\027[2"z	Select emphasized mode
Page formatting:	
\027[3z	Double-space text (3 lines per inch)
\027[0z	Single-space text (6 lines per inch)
\027[2"z	8 lines per inch

Code	Instruction
Print mode:	
\015	Select compressed mode
\018	Cancel compressed mode
\014	Select expanded mode (one line)
\020	Cancel expanded mode (one line)
\027x1	Select near letter-quality mode
\027x0	Select draft mode
\027$W$1	Select expanded mode
\027W0	Cancel expanded mode
\027M	Select elite pitch (12 cpi)[1]
\027P	Select pica pitch (10 cpi)
\027E	Select emphasized mode
\027F	Cancel emphasized mode
\027G	Select double-strike mode
\027H	Cancel double-strike mode
\027S0	Select superscript
\027$S$1	Select subscript
\027T	Cancel superscript/subscript
\027-1	Select underlining
\027-0	Cancel underlining
\0274	Select italic mode
\0275	Cancel italic mode
\027$R(n)$	Select international character set
\027p1	Select proportional mode
\027p0	Cancel proportional mode
\027(space)(n)	Select character space
\027$a(n)$	Near letter-quality justification[2]
\027@	Master reset
Page formatting:	
\027$Q(n)$	Set right margin
\027$I(n)$	Set left margin
\027$N(n)$	Select skip-over perforation
\027O	Cancel skip-over perforation
\0272	Single-space text (6 lines per inch)
\027$J$24 or \027\026\024	Double-space text (3 lines per inch)
\027$C(n)$	Set page length in number of lines
\027C0(n)	Set page length in number of inches

1. Except for Epson MX series.

2. The justification values for (n) are as follows:

   0 = left justification; 1= centering; 2 = right justification; 3 = full justification

Table E.4
Epson LQ1500

Code	Instruction
Print mode:	
\027x1	Select letter-quality (or near letter-quality) mode
\027x0\015	Select compressed mode
\027M	Select elite pitch (12 cpi)
\027P	Select pica pitch (10 cpi)
\027w\001	Select expanded mode
\027E	Select emphasized mode
\027-\001	Select underlining
\027+(s1S	Select italic mode
\027@	Master reset
Page formatting:	
\027\065\020	Double-space text (3 lines per inch)
\0272	Single-space text (6 lines per inch)
\0270	8 lines per inch

Table E.5: HP LaserJet

Page setup		Page length	Right margin
PORTRAIT			
Letter-size paper			
60 lines per page			
10 cpi	\027E	60	80
16.66 cpi	\027(s16.66H	60	132
66 lines per page			
10 cpi	\027&l7.27C	66	80
16.66 cpi	\026&l7.27C\027(s16.66H	66	132
Legal-size paper (legal tray)			
78 lines per page			
10 cpi	\027E	78	80
16.66 cpi	\027(s16.66H	78	132
104 lines per page			
10 cpi	\027&l8D	100	80
16.66 cpi	\027&l8D\027(s16.66H	100	132
Legal size paper (manual feed)			
78 lines per page			
10 cpi	\027&l84p2H	78	80
16.66 cpi	\027&l84p2H\027(s16.66H	78	132
104 lines per page			
10 cpi	\027&l84p2h0o8D	100	80
16.66 cpi	\027&l84p2h0o8D\027(s16.66H	100	132

Table E.5: HP LaserJet (continued)

Page setup		Page length	Right margin
LANDSCAPE			
Letter size paper			
45 lines per page			
10 cpi	\027&*l*1O	45	106
16.66 cpi	\027&*l*1O\027(*s*16.66H	45	176
66 lines per page			
10 cpi	\027&*l*1*o*5.45C	66	106
16.66 cpi	\027&*l*1*o*5.45C\027(*s*16.66H	66	176
Legal size paper (legal tray)			
45 lines per page			
10 cpi	\027&*l*1O	45	136
16.66 cpi	\027&*l*1O\027(*s*16.66H	45	226
66 lines per page			
10 cpi	\027&*l*1*o*5.45C	66	136
16.66 cpi	\027&*l*1*o*5.45C\027(*s*16.66H	66	226
Legal size paper (manual feed)			
45 lines per page			
10 cpi	\027&*l*84*p*2*h*1O	45	136
16.66 cpi	\027&*l*84*p*2*h*1O\027(*s*16.66H	45	226
66 lines per page			
10 cpi	\027&*l*84*p*2*h*1*o*5.45C	66	136
16.66 cpi	\027&*l*84*p*2*h*1*o*5.45C\027(*s*16.66H	66	226

Table E.6
HP ThinkJet[1]

Code	Instruction
Print mode:	
\016	Select compressed mode
\014	Select expanded mode
\027E	Select emphasized mode
\027-1	Select underlining
Page formatting:	
\0270	8 lines per inch

1. DIP switch 5 must be in the *On* position (IBM mode) for the printer to read these setup strings.

Code	Instruction

Print mode:

Code	Instruction
\027*I*2	Select letter-quality (or near letter-quality) mode[1]
\015	Select compressed mode
\018	Cancel compressed mode
\027\058	Select elite pitch (12 cpi)[2]
\014 or 027\087\001	Select expanded mode (one line)
\020	Cancel expanded mode (one line)
\027*W*1	Select expanded mode
\027*W*0	Cancel expanded mode
\027\069	Select emphasized mode[3]
\027*F* or 027\070	Cancel emphasized mode[4]
\027*G*	Select double-strike mode
\027*H*	Cancel double-strike mode
\027*S*0	Select superscript
\027*S*1	Select subscript
\027*T*	Cancel superscript/subscript
\027\045\001	Select underlining
\027\045\000	Cancel underlining[5]
\0276	Select international character set
\0277	Select standard character set
\024	Master reset[6]

Page formatting:

Code	Instruction
\027*X*(*n*1)(*n*2)	Set margins (1=left; 2=right)
\027*N*(*n*)	Select skip-over perforation
\027*O*	Cancel skip-over perforation
\0272 or \027\050	Single-space text (6 lines per inch)[7]
\027*A*24	Double-space text (3 lines per inch)
\027\048	8 lines per inch
\027*C*(*n*)	Set page length in lines
\027*C*0(*n*)	Set page length in inches

1. For IBM Proprinter only; for Color Jetprinter, use \027\073\002.

2. Except for IBM Color Jetprinter.

3. For IBM Proprinter, use \027*E*.

4. Except for IBM Proprinter.

5. Except for IBM 5182 Color Printer and Proprinter.

6. For IBM 5182 Color Printer only.

7. Except for IBM Proprinter.

Code	Instruction
Print mode:	
\015\027\073\000	Select compressed mode[1]
\027\087\001	Select expanded mode
\027\045\001	Select underlining
Page formatting:	
\027\065\024\027\050	Double-space text (3 lines per inch)
\027\048	8 lines per inch

1. If 15-pitch font is in A slot; use \015\027\073\001 if 15-pitch font is in alternate slot.

Code	Instruction
Print mode:	
\031	Select compressed mode
\030	Select elite pitch (12 cpi)
\029	Select pica pitch (10 cpi)
Page formatting:	
\027,*B*,16,$	Double-space text (3 lines per inch)
\027,*B*,8,$	Single-space text (6 lines per inch)
\027,*B*,6,$	8 lines per inch

1. Many of the print modes available are DIP-switch selectable and do not require setup strings.

Code	Instruction
Print mode:	
\027*Q*	Select compressed mode
\027*E*	Select elite pitch (12 cpi)
\027*N*	Select pica pitch (10 cpi)
\027!	Select emphasized mode
\027"	Cancel emphasized mode
\027*X*	Select underlining
\027*Y*	Cancel underlining
Page formatting:	
\027\,*T*,48	Double-space text (3 lines per inch)
\027*A*	Single-space text (6 lines per inch)
\027*B*	8 lines per inch

Code	Instruction
Print mode:	
\027\049	Select letter-quality (or near letter-quality) mode
\029	Select compressed mode
\028	Select elite pitch (12 cpi)
\030	Select pica pitch (10 cpi)
\030\031	Select expanded mode
\029\031	Select emphasized mode
\027\067	Select underlining
\027\068	Cancel underlining
\027\024	Master reset
Page formatting:	
\027\037\057\048	Double-space text (3 lines per inch)
\027\054	Single-space text (6 lines per inch)
\027\056	8 lines per inch

Code	Instruction
Print mode:	
\027\055	Select letter-quality (or near letter-quality) mode
\027\066	Select compressed mode
\027\065	Select elite pitch (12 cpi)
\027\054	Select pica pitch (10 cpi)
\027\054\027\067	Select expanded mode
\027\066\027\067	Select emphasized mode
\027\090\027\054	Cancel emphasized mode
\027\085	Select underlining
\027\086	Cancel underlining
Page formatting:	
\027\037\057\048	Double-space text (3 lines per inch)
\027\052	Single-space text (6 lines per inch)
\027\053	8 lines per inch

Code	Instruction
Print mode:	
\027\073\003	Select letter-quality (or near letter-quality) mode
\015	Select compressed mode
\027\058	Select elite pitch (12 cpi)
\018	Select pica pitch (10 cpi)
\027\087\049	Select expanded mode
\015\027\087\049	Select emphasized mode
\027\087\048\018	Cancel emphasized mode
\027\045\001	Select underlining
\027\045\000	Cancel underlining
Page formatting:	
\027A0\0272	Double-space text (3 lines per inch)
\027A0\024\0272	Single-space text (6 lines per inch)
\027\048	8 lines per inch

Code	Instruction
Print mode:	
\015	Select compressed mode
\027\066\002	Select elite pitch (12 cpi)
\018	Select pica pitch (10 cpi)
\027\087\001	Select expanded mode
\027\069	Select emphasized mode
\027-1	Select underlining
\027\045\000	Cancel underlining
\027\052	Select italic mode
\027\053	Cancel italic mode
\027\064	Master reset
Page formatting:	
\027065\024	Double-space text (3 lines per inch)
\0272	Single-space text (6 lines per inch)
\0270	8 lines per inch

Code	Instruction
Print mode:	
\027q	Select letter-quality (or near letter-quality) mode
\027P	Select compressed mode
\027z	Select elite pitch (12 cpi)
\027y	Select pica pitch (10 cpi)
\027F	Select expanded mode[1]
\027G	Select emphasized mode
\027H	Cancel emphasized mode
\027@	Master reset
Page formatting:	
\027\028\049	Double-space text (3 lines per inch)
\0272	Single-space text (6 lines per inch)
\0270	8 lines per inch

1. DIP switch 4 must be in the *Off* position for the 855 and 856 to read setup strings.

2. Must be set at the beginning of each line.

Code	Instruction
Print mode:	
\027\091	Select compressed mode
\027*1\027E10	Select elite pitch (12 cpi)
\027!	Select expanded mode
\027K2	Select emphasized mode
\027\077	Cancel emphasized mode
\027\018	Select italic mode[1]
\027\020	Cancel italic mode[1]
\027\0261	Master reset
Page formatting:	
\027L16	Double-space text (3 lines per inch)

[1] For Toshiba P351 only.

For more information about any of these printer commands, see the owner's manual for your printer.

F

Working with fonts

A *font* is a complete set of type of one point size, typeface, and style. Quattro uses fonts to display and print characters in both spreadsheets and graphs. You can use up to eight different fonts in a spreadsheet (see page 164) and innumerable fonts in a graph (see page 347).

This appendix describes

- how Quattro handles different types of fonts
- how Quattro builds special bitmap files for each Bitstream font you use
- how to use a macro to build several bitmap files at once
- how different printers handle Quattro fonts
- how to use your own, separately purchased Bitstream typefaces with Quattro

Types of fonts

Quattro supports three classes of fonts: Hershey fonts, Bitstream fonts, and printer-specific fonts:

- **Hershey fonts** are basic type fonts that can be instantly output in all sizes on any screen and on most printers.
- **Bitstream fonts** are more attractive than Hershey fonts, especially at larger point sizes and on high-resolution output

devices. Quattro comes with three Bitstream typefaces for building fonts, and you can buy more separately.

- **Printer-specific fonts** are special fonts used only by PostScript or LaserJet printers. If you have one of these printers, you can use printer-specific fonts in graphs or spreadsheets.

Hershey fonts

QUATTRO PRO comes with nine Hershey fonts, each stored in a file with the .CHR file-name extension. They are the same basic fonts that earlier versions of Quattro provide, although their names are different. Table F.1 lists each of the available Hershey fonts and their equivalents in earlier versions of Quattro.

Table F.1
Hershey Fonts

Hershey Font in QUATTRO PRO	Earlier Quattro equivalent
Roman	Triplex
Roman Light	Complex
Roman Italic	Triplex Script
Sans Serif	San Serif
Sans Serif Light	Simplex
Script	Script
Monospace	Small
Old English	Gothic
EuroStyle	EuroStyle

Bitstream fonts

In addition to the Hershey fonts, Quattro uses the state-of-the-art Fontware system from Bitstream, Inc., a leader in digital typography. Your Quattro package includes the following Bitstream typefaces:

- Dutch (similar to Times Roman)
- Swiss (similar to Helvetica)
- Courier

The fonts produced from Bitstream typefaces are of higher quality than Hershey fonts. Unlike Hershey fonts, however, they do not come prebuilt. Before Quattro can use a Bitstream font, it needs to build a unique "bitmap" font file for a particular combination of typeface, style, and point size for your particular screen or printer.

Therefore, when you display, annotate, and print graphs or spreadsheets with Bitstream fonts, Quattro will, from time to time, pause and display the message "Now building font" while it creates a bitmap file. Because printing, previewing, and annotation often require different sizes of a given typeface, Quattro may build separate bitmap files in each instance. Once a bitmap file is built, Quattro can reference it without hesitation.

When you first start out, all this font building makes using Bitstream fonts a bit cumbersome. But after several days of graph drawing or previewing presentation-quality graphics in your spreadsheet, you will build up a customized library of Bitstream fonts, and the "Now building font" message will appear less and less often. And once built, you'll actually find Bitstream fonts faster to use than other fonts.

Note   If you find the font-building pause objectionable and don't require the highest-quality typography, stick to using Hershey fonts (see page 590). These fonts, while not as aesthetically pleasing as Bitstream fonts, require no building. Or, if you prefer, you can turn off font building temporarily (set the /Options Graphics Quality command to **D**raft), then turn it back on for printing.

Quattro also supports Bitstream typefaces you've purchased separately. (See the brochure included with your Quattro package.) First, you must install them for use with Quattro with the BSINST.EXE program. (See page 594 for more information.)

For details on how Quattro builds Bitstream fonts, see page 592.

Printer-specific fonts

Quattro takes full advantage of cartridge fonts available in the HP LaserJet family of printers and the 37 most popular fonts in printers that use Adobe's PostScript page-description language. If you have either of these types of printers, additional printer-specific fonts will be listed at the bottom of the **T**ypeface menu you access through /**S**tyle I **F**ont I **E**dit Fonts.

When you display a graph that uses printer-specific fonts, Quattro substitutes a reasonable facsimile onscreen; at print time, however, it uses the real thing.

Note: LaserJet typefaces are preset to specific sizes and styles. If you choose one of these typefaces, you won't be able to change its point size or style.

If you assign special PostScript or LaserJet fonts to a spreadsheet block or graph title, then switch to a different printer setting (with /**O**ptions I **H**ardware I **P**rinters), Quattro will still show that font assigned to the text, even though it's no longer available on the **T**ypeface menu. When you print the graph, Quattro substitutes a similar font.

Building Bitstream fonts

Bitstream typeface files in Quattro's format (with an .SFO file extension) contain the master definition of a particular typeface and text style; for example, the file SWSI.SFO contains a master description of each character in the Bitstream Swiss Italic typeface. Bitmap font files (with the .FON file extension) are a particular expression of one of these masters, created by Quattro from an .SFO file.

.FON file names consist of a four- or five-letter prefix indicating the typeface, followed by an underline character and a three-letter suffix indicating when it was built relative to other fonts of the same typeface. For example,

SWSI_003.FON

is the fourth font (counting begins at zero) to be built from the Swiss Italic .SFO master file, and

DTBI_000.FON

is the first font built from the Dutch Bold Italic .SFO master file. You can't tell from the file name which point size the file is for, although file size is a general indicator. Screen fonts range from 2 to 25K for 6- to 72-point files, respectively; printer-specific fonts, depending on resolution, range from 5 to 500K.

Important! In addition to the disk space you need for the files themselves, you also need 125K bytes of free memory (RAM) to *build* the files.

Quattro stores each .FON file it builds in the FONT subdirectory, where Quattro can access it the next time you use that font. If you ever find yourself running out of disk space, you can always delete the contents of the FONT subdirectory and let Quattro start over building fonts as you use them. Or, just delete the files you use infrequently or the larger printer fonts.

For answers to common questions about using Bitstream fonts, see Appendix A, "Help and hints."

Building Bitstream fonts with a macro

Rather than waiting for Quattro to build Bitstream fonts individually while you work with them, you can use the

User's Guide

{/ Hardware;PreRender} macro to build a whole set of fonts at once. (You can use fonts built this way for screen display only, not for printing.)

To build fonts with a macro:

1. To create the macro, just type {/ Hardware;PreRender} into any spreadsheet cell. If you want, you can assign it a macro name with the /Tools I Macro I Name command (see Chapter 16).

2. Before you use the macro, you need to set up a spreadsheet block that indicates the fonts you want to build. Each cell in the block should contain a string specifying a Bitstream typeface and size. The syntax for each string is

   <typeface> <size>

   where *<typeface>* is a three-to-four character string that identifies the master typeface (.SFO) file, and *<size>* is a point size from 6 to 72. For example, SWSB 34 builds a 34-point Swiss bold .FON file, and DUTI 14 builds a 14-point Dutch italic .FON file.

   To best take advantage of Quattro's font-sizing logic, you'll probably want to build continuous ranges of fonts; for example, from 6 through 36 points rather than a few individual sizes.

3. Before you execute the macro, we recommend that you delete all existing font files. Go into the FONTS subdirectory and type DEL *.* *Enter*.

4. Execute the macro (using /Tools I Macro I Execute). Quattro prompts you for a block of cells.

5. Specify the cells you stored the font strings in.

Tip   If you're short on disk space, periodically delete all *.FON files from your disk and use the font-building macro to build only those fonts you use most often. Or, to save even more space, set up a separate macro for each spreadsheet that builds only the fonts you need for that spreadsheet. Then erase font files and rebuild them whenever you begin working with a new spreadsheet.

Printing fonts

Not all printers can print all the fonts available with Quattro. For example, plotters (and some printers) can print only Hershey fonts. Conversely, PostScript printers can print beautiful text, but they can't output Hershey fonts. Most other printers, including all dot-matrix machines and the popular LaserJet series from Hewlett Packard, can print both Bitstream and Hershey fonts. Still, even on these printers, font substitutions can occur.

If your printer won't accept a font in your spreadsheet or graph, Quattro uses a comparable font. This may cause confusion sometimes when your printer output doesn't match your screen display. For best results, design your graphs and spreadsheets using the same fonts your printer will use to print them. If you're not sure what fonts your printer will accept, experiment.

Important! Quattro has to build separate Bitstream fonts for printing; it can't use the ones it built while displaying your data. And because printer fonts tend to be large, Quattro doesn't pre-install any as it does with screen fonts. So be sure that font building is turned on (with **/O**ptions **G**raphics Quality Final) before you print. Otherwise, Quattro will substitute Hershey fonts for any Bitstream fonts it hasn't yet built. Occasionally, the font substitution can cause minor changes between the viewed and printed forms of a graph or spreadsheet.

Installing additional Bitstream fonts

If you have additional Bitstream typefaces you've purchased separately (either through Bitstream or with another program), you can use them to create type fonts in Quattro. First, you must copy the typeface outline file and convert it to Quattro format. Quattro includes a special typeface conversion program that makes this easy:

1. Place the disk containing your Bitstream typefaces (.BCO files) in drive A.

2. Go into the subdirectory that contains your Quattro program files. (For example, type `CD \QPRO` and press *Enter.*)

3. Type BSINST and press *Enter.* The BSINST program copies and converts all typeface files on the disk in drive A. When it's done, it asks if you want to install more typefaces.

4. If you want to convert more typeface files on another disk, press *Y* and insert the disk in drive A. If you're done, press *N.*

The BSINST.EXE program creates new Bitstream typeface files with the file-name extension .SFO. It also modifies other Quattro program files to take these new typefaces into account. So if you reinstall Quattro, or recopy the Quattro program files onto your hard disk, you'll need to reinstall any Bitstream typefaces you converted.

The next time you use Quattro, the typefaces you installed will be listed on the Typeface menu along with the other typefaces.

G

ASCII codes

The American Standard Code for Information Exchange (ASCII) is the accepted standard for translating the first 128 alphabetic and numeric characters, symbols, and control instructions into 7-bit binary code. Table G.1 shows both printable characters and control characters with their decimal and hexadecimal equivalents (decimal numbers 0 to 31). The characters higher than 128 are the IBM graphics screen characters.

The caret in ^@ means to press the Ctrl key and type @.

Dec	Hex	Char		Dec	Hex	Char	Dec	Hex	Char	Dec	Hex	Char
0	0	^@	NUL	32	20		64	40	@	96	60	'
1	1	☺	SOH	33	21	!	65	41	A	97	61	a
2	2	●	STX	34	22	¬	66	42	B	98	62	b
3	3	♥	ETX	35	23	#	67	43	C	99	63	c
4	4	♦	EOT	36	24	$	68	44	D	100	64	d
5	5	♣	ENQ	37	25	%	69	45	E	101	65	e
6	6	♠	ACK	38	26	&	70	46	F	102	66	f
7	7	•	BEL	39	27	'	71	47	G	103	67	g
8	8	◘	BS	40	28	(	72	48	H	104	68	h
9	9	○	TAB	41	29	)	73	49	I	105	69	i
10	A	◙	LF	42	2A	*	74	4A	J	106	6A	j
11	B	♂	VT	43	2B	+	75	4B	K	107	6B	k
12	C	♀	FF	44	2C	,	76	4C	L	108	6C	l
13	D	♪	CR	45	2D	※	77	4D	M	109	6D	m
14	E	♫	SO	46	2E	.	78	4E	N	110	6E	n
15	F	☼	SI	47	2F	/	79	4F	O	111	6F	o
16	10	►	DLE	48	30	0	80	50	P	112	70	p
17	11	◄	DC1	49	31	1	81	51	Q	113	71	q
18	12	↕	DC2	50	32	2	82	52	R	114	72	r
19	13	‼	DC3	51	33	3	83	53	S	115	73	s
20	14	¶	DC4	52	34	4	84	54	T	116	74	t
21	15	§	NAK	53	35	5	85	55	U	117	75	u
22	16	▬	SYN	54	36	6	86	56	V	118	76	v
23	17	↨	ETB	55	37	7	87	57	W	119	77	w
24	18	↑	CAN	56	38	8	88	58	X	120	78	x
25	19	↓	EM	57	39	9	89	59	Y	121	79	y
26	1A	→	SUB	58	3A	:	90	5A	Z	122	7A	z
27	1B	←	ESC	59	3B	;	91	5B	[	123	7B	{
28	1C	∟	FS	60	3C	<	92	5C	\	124	7C		
29	1D	↔	GS	61	3D	=	93	5D	]	125	7D	}
30	1E	▲	RS	62	3E	>	94	5E	^	126	7E	~
31	1F	▼	US	63	3F	?	95	5F	_	127	7F	⌂

Table G.1: ASCII table (continued)

Dec	Hex	Char	Dec	Hex	Char	Dec	Hex	Char	Dec	Hex	Char
128	80	(	160	A0	á	192	C0	└	224	E0	α
129	81	)	161	A1	í	193	C1	┴	225	E1	β
130	82	\	162	A2	ó	194	C2	┬	226	E2	Γ
131	83	â	163	A3	ú	195	C3	├	227	E3	π
132	84	ä	164	A4	ñ	196	C4	─	228	E4	Σ
133	85	à	165	A5	Ñ	197	C5	┼	229	E5	σ
134	86	å	166	A6	a	198	C6	╞	230	E6	μ
135	87	ç	167	A7	o	199	C7	╟	231	E7	τ
136	88	ê	168	A8	¿	200	C8	╚	232	E8	Φ
137	89	ë	169	A9	⌐	201	C9	╔	233	E9	θ
138	8A	è	170	AA	¬	202	CA	╩	234	EA	Ω
139	8B	ï	171	AB	½	203	CB	╦	235	EB	δ
140	8C	î	172	AC	¼	204	CC	╠	236	EC	∞
141	8D	ì	173	AD	i	205	CD	=	237	ED	φ
142	8E	Ä	174	AE	«	206	CE	╬	238	EE	∈
143	8F	Å	175	AF	»	207	CF	╧	239	EF	∩
144	90	É	176	B0	░	208	D0	╨	240	F0	≡
145	91	æ	177	B1	▒	209	D1	╤	241	F1	±
146	92	Æ	178	B2	▓	210	D2	╥	242	F2	≥
147	93	ô	179	B3	│	211	D3	╙	243	F3	≤
148	94	ö	180	B4	┤	212	D4	╘	244	F4	ü
149	95	ò	181	B5	╡	213	D5	╒	245	F5	é
150	96	û	182	B6	╢	214	D6	╓	246	F6	÷
151	97	ù	183	B7	╖	215	D7	╫	247	F7	≈
152	98	ÿ	184	B8	╕	216	D8	╪	248	F8	°
153	99	Ö	185	B9	╣	217	D9	┘	249	F9	•
154	9A	Ü	186	BA	║	218	DA	┌	250	FA	·
155	9B	¢	187	BB	╗	219	DB	█	251	FB	√
156	9C	£	188	BC	╝	220	DC	▄	252	FC	n
157	9D	¥	189	BD	╜	221	DD	▌	253	FD	²
158	9E	Pt	190	BE	╛	222	DE	▐	254	FE	■
159	9F	ƒ	191	BF	┐	223	DF	▄	255	FF	

H

Error messages

This appendix lists, alphabetically, each error message that could possibly display on your screen except those that concern running Quattro on a local area network. (For network error messages, see the *Network Administrator's Guide*.) It briefly describes the error that caused the message and offers resolutions. To remove an error message from the screen, press *Esc*.

A system error has occurred.
Please report to Borland if you get this error (see "How to contact Borland" on page 6).

Access denied.
You tried to access a network file or directory that you didn't have the required privileges for. Quattro cannot open, delete, or write to a file you're not allowed access to. **Note:** If you are using DOS version 4.0, all files are treated as network files if your hard disk has more than 32 megabytes. Try increasing the FILES parameter in the CONFIG.SYS file (on your root directory) to 40 so you can open more files.

All links are opened or no link to other spreadsheet.
You chose /**T**ools I **U**pdate Links I **O**pen to open supporting spreadsheets, but the current spreadsheet contains no links to other spreadsheets (or all supporting spreadsheets are already open).

Attempt to write on write-protected disk.
If a floppy disk is write-protected, you won't be able to store information on it, or delete information from it. First, see what's

on the disk and make sure it doesn't contain data you don't want to lose. If you still want to use it, remove the metallic adhesive from the corner (for $5\frac{1}{4}$-inch disks) or push the write-protect switch to the other side (for $3\frac{1}{2}$-inch disks).

Bad memory image of FAT.
Your file allocation table has been corrupted. Refer to the explanation for CHKDSK in your DOS manual for further assistance.

Bad metakey.
You used an unassigned metakey in a macro. Check the metakey number assignment.

Bad offset.
The macro you just executed included a PUT command for which the offset argument is outside the block specified for PUT. Respecify the block.

Block is in an unopened spreadsheet.
The cell block you referenced (with link syntax) is in a closed spreadsheet. You can't copy, move, or modify data in an unopened file. Open the spreadsheet first, then try again.

Block is out of boundary.
You are attempting to save a spreadsheet that has more than 2048 rows to a format that is limited to 2048 rows. If you save the file to that format, you will lose all data below row 2048. To preserve this data, save the spreadsheet as a .WQ1 file.

Break.
You pressed *Ctrl-Break* to halt execution of a macro. Press *Esc* to remove the error message.

Calculation interrupted.
Quattro was executing a macro and was making a calculation when you pressed *Esc* or *Ctrl-Break*. If the macro is not working as planned, try using Quattro's Macro Debugger.

Cannot accept a block here.
You entered a block in a formula at a point where only a cell is appropriate—for example, 1+A1..A10.

Cannot create: *File* or *Dir*.
In the File Manager, Quattro could not create the file or directory you specified. Check the file operation you were trying to perform.

Cannot cut or copy title, graph, or legend.
You can cut or copy graph text elements created with the text icon in the Graph Annotator Toolbox. You cannot cut or copy graph text created in the **Graph** menu. If you select a graph title or legend and press *Del*, Quattro erases the title or legend, but does not put a copy in the Clipboard. If you go back to the /Graph | Text menu, you will see that the title or legend text has been erased from that menu, as well.

Cannot delete it.
You tried to erase a file and the operation failed, perhaps because it was a shared file on a network.

Cannot delete this directory, it is open in another window.
Close the File Manager window that lists the files in this directory and try again.

Cannot do this to directories.
You tried to perform an illegal operation on a directory in the File Manager.

Cannot do this until you Paste or Undo.
You must select the name of a file in the file list with *Shift-F7*, the Plus key, or the /Edit | Select File command you can copy or move that file in the File Manager. See Chapter 10 for information about the File Manager.

Cannot Duplicate to same file.
In the File Manager, you cannot choose /Edit | Duplicate to duplicate a file and then specify the same file name in the same directory.

Cannot execute: *macro*.
Quattro was unable to execute the macro. Check the syntax and try again. See Chapter 16 for information about writing and recording macros.

Cannot find font file.
Quattro cannot find the font file it needs for a font operation. Go through the installation procedure again to make sure that Quattro has copied all the files it needs to the directory containing the Quattro program files.

Cannot hide all columns.
You attempted to hide all columns of the spreadsheet, which is impossible. Respecify the columns you want to hide.

Cannot initialize graphics.
You lack sufficient memory to initialize graphics. Free up or get more memory and try again. See the "Insufficient memory" entry.

Cannot insert any more graphs.
You can insert only eight graphs in any one spreadsheet.

Cannot insert graphs in other spreadsheets.
You can't choose /Graph I Insert and switch to another spreadsheet to point out a block. Insert only works in the current spreadsheet.

Cannot link a graph to itself.
You selected the graph and then chose the link icon from the Graph Annotator Toolbox. Since Quattro cannot link a graph to itself, you must select some other object to link to a series.

Cannot link objects to a text graph.
You selected an object in a text graph and then chose the link icon from the Graph Annotator Toolbox. Since a text graph has no series defined, there is nothing for Quattro to link the object to.

Cannot link to an undefined series or point.
You selected an object in a graph, chose the link icon from the Graph Annotator Toolbox, and then tried to link to a series or point that does not exist in that graph. For example, if a graph has only one series defined, you cannot link to a second series. Similarly, if the series want to you link to has only three values, you cannot specify a link index of four.

Cannot load graphics driver.
Quattro can't load its graphics driver files, or your computer's video display card doesn't support graphics. If you do have a graphics card, make sure that all files with the .BGI extension are in the directory containing the Quattro program files. If not, go through the installation procedure again to make sure that Quattro has copied all the files it needs to the directory containing the Quattro program files.

Cannot load graphics font.
Quattro can't find or open the file that contains the font you assigned to text. You might not have enough memory to load the specified font file. Free up or get more memory and try again. See the entry for "Insufficient memory."

Cannot open: *file.*
The file you specified either doesn't exist or is in a different disk or directory.

Cannot open/create a database file.
Quattro was not able to perform the translation you requested.

Cannot open Clipboard file.
You tried to open a Clipboard (.CLP) file whose name is also a directory name. For example, Quattro cannot open a file named QUATTRO.CLP if a directory by that name exists.

Cannot open LASERJET.BGI.
The LASERJET.BGI file is missing from the directory with the Quattro program files or is damaged or corrupted. Go through the installation procedure again to make sure that Quattro has copied all the files it needs to the directory containing the Quattro program files.

Cannot open memo field.
The database file you're trying to access contains a memo field. Quattro cannot open memo fields. Go into the program that created the database and change the memo field to a text field, then try again.

Cannot open or error in FONTS.BGI file.
The FONTS.BGI file is missing from the directory with the Quattro program files or is damaged or corrupted. Go through the installation procedure again to make sure that Quattro has copied all the files it needs to the directory containing the Quattro program files.

Cannot open POSTSCRP.BGI.
The POSTSCRP.BGI file is missing from the directory with the Quattro program files or is damaged or corrupted. Go through the installation procedure again to make sure that Quattro has copied all the files it needs to the directory containing the Quattro program files.

Cannot open QUATTRO.HLP.
The QUATTRO.HLP file is missing from the directory with the Quattro program files or is damaged or corrupted. Go through the installation procedure again to make sure that Quattro has copied all the files it needs to the directory containing the Quattro program files.

Cannot Paste to the same directory.
You selected a file for moving or copying in the File Manager and then pressed the Paste key, *Shift-F10*, or chose /Edit I Paste while

still in the same directory. You must move to a different directory to paste the file.

Cannot perform file operation: *???*.
A file operation you attempted has failed. Check the message for more detailed information on why it failed (for example, the disk drive door might be open).

Cannot perform log scaling on negative or zero data.
It's impossible to logarithmically scale negative or zero values. If your graph's y-axis scale begins with zero, set the scale manually to begin at 1 (or 10 or .00001 or any positive number) first. You must also adjust the upper end of the graph scale.

Cannot pull graph over linked objects.
You selected the graph in the Draw Area and then chose **To Top** from the Clipboard menu to move the graph in front of a linked object. Before you can do this, you must unlink the object.

Cannot push linked objects below graph.
You selected a linked object in the Draw Area and then chose **To Bottom** from the Clipboard menu to move the object in back of the graph. Before you can do this, you must unlink the object.

Cannot read an encrypted database file.
You are attempting to read a database file that is encrypted (saved with a password). Quattro cannot decrypt all database formats.

Cannot read text in the Clipboard file.
You attempted to read text from a Clipboard file that is either corrupted or created with a program that Quattro does not support.

Cannot redraw. The second window is cleared.
You resized a window that was split into two panes; the size is too small to show both panes. Resize the window larger or clear the window split.

Cannot rename to existing file name.
You chose /Edit | **Rename** or pressed *F2* and then specified the existing file name. Specify a different name.

Cannot save without destroying family files.
You've modified a Paradox database file (.DB) in Quattro and attempted to save it with the Paradox file format. Specify another file name to save to.

Cannot write Clipboard file.
The disk you are trying to write to is full. Specify another disk to save the Clipboard file to.

Column hidden.
You attempted to go to a hidden column. Expose the hidden column first with the /Style I Hide Column I Expose command, then try again.

Could not load graphics driver.
You do not have enough memory available to load the graphics driver. Free up or get more memory and try again.

Could not load graphics font.
You do not have enough memory available to load the graphics font. Free up or get more memory and try again.

Could not load printer driver.
You do not have enough memory available to load the printer driver. Free up or get more memory and try again.

Could not read: *file.*
The file you are trying to open is probably corrupted.

Could not write: *file.*
The disk you are trying to save to is full, or there are too many entries in the directory.

Desktop settings are removed.
You are attempting to save a spreadsheet that has blocks with line drawing, shading, fonts, data entry restrictions, or number alignment to a file format that does not support them. To preserve these settings, save the spreadsheet as a .WQ1 file.

Directory does not exist.
Make sure you typed the exact path name of the directory (See Appendix B, "A DOS primer," for more information about directories.)

Disk failure.
Your disk most likely has bad sectors. Consult the owner's manual for your computer.

Disk full.
Your hard disk is too full to store the spreadsheet you're saving, or the new font file Quattro has created. Use the File Manager to delete unnecessary files from the disk, or move some files to floppy disks.

Drive not ready.
The disk drive specified is not ready for I/O. Make sure the proper floppy drive has a disk, and that the drive door is closed.

Duplicate field names.
You are trying to perform a database operation where two fields have the same name. The fields must have unique names. Rename the matching fields, then try again.

Error accessing device: ???.
Quattro was not able to access a device. Check the message for more information.

Error during printing: ???.
An error has occurred during printing. Check the message for more information.

Error in opening printer/file.
You attempted to print to a file on a disk with zero bytes free.

Error in reading a file.
You attempted to load a corrupted spreadsheet file.

Error in reading or writing a database file.
You attempted to load or save to a corrupted database file.

Error loading Bitstream font index.
The INDEX.FON file is missing or corrupted. Quattro uses INDEX.FON to keep track of .FON files. INDEX.FON and the .FON files are matched sets; don't delete the INDEX.FON file unless at the same time you delete every .FON file in your Quattro directory (DEL *.FON is always safe). Don't copy .FON files built on another computer without copying their associated INDEX.FON as well. Similarly, if you delete INDEX.FON without deleting *.FON, the .FON files in your Quattro directory have no meaning, and Quattro will act as if they aren't there; new fonts will be built as needed, and existing files will be overwritten.

Error validating font information, probably low memory.
Quattro ran out of memory while trying to initialize for a graphic operation. Free up or get more memory and try again.

Field name too long.
A field name in the data you're trying to export from your spreadsheet to a database is too long for the database format. Try a shorter field name.

File not found.
Quattro can't find the file you specified. Check your file name for correct spelling and location. You can use the File Manager to search through your entire hard disk for a file. Just type the name after the File Name prompt and press the GoTo key, *F5*. If file name and location are correct, check for possible disk error.

Font bld error: Out of memory.
You must have 125K of free memory (RAM) to build a font file, apart from the disk space the new font file requires.

Formula computation error.
Too many strings were used in a formula, and Quattro ran out of memory. Try breaking the formula into several simpler formulas.

Formula is not linear.
The optimization formula constraints must depend linearly on the variables. There may be non-obvious nonlinearities such as +A1*B1, which is nonlinear in A1 if B1 is given by a formula depending on A1. Try using a formula

@SUMPRODUCT(*block1*, *block2*)

where *block1* is the variables block and *block2* has cells which don't depend on the variables.

Formula too long.
The formula you entered is too long. Try breaking it into several shorter formulas.

Formula with link translated to value.
You are attempting to save a spreadsheet with formula links to a file format that does not support them. To keep the formula from being translated to a value, save the spreadsheet as a .WQ1 file.

Formulas are too complicated.
The optimization formula constraints depend on too many cells for Quattro to handle. This can happen if the formulas have a circular reference. Try simplifying the formulas.

General disk failure.
There has been a DOS general disk failure. If you tried to save to a floppy disk, make sure that the disk is formatted for DOS.

Graph contains information that won't translate.
You are attempting to save a spreadsheet with special graph settings to a file format that does not support them. To preserve the graph settings, save the spreadsheet as a .WQ1 file.

Graph error.
You have inserted a graph that has a problem. To find out what the problem is, put the cursor in the inserted graph block and press *F10*. Quattro then displays the specific error message for the situation. However, if you don't have enough memory to insert the graph in the spreadsheet, no message appears.

Graph too complex.
There are too many data points in your graph; Quattro cannot work with a graph that requires more than 400K of memory.

Graph too large.
The inserted graph is too large for Quattro to display in the spreadsheet. You can't see it on the screen, but it will print out as you specified.

Import file format error.
A database operation failed because of an error in the database file. Go into the program that created the database, correct any errors you find in the file's data or format, and try again.

Import implementation and file version don't match.
You attempted to load a Reflex 2.0 file that was not created with a valid 2.0 release version. Quattro's file translation works only with .R2D files created with the official release of Reflex 2.0.

Incomplete formula.
The formula you typed is incomplete. For example, 1+ is missing an operand following +. When you press *Esc*, Quattro will be in Edit mode so you can edit the formula.

Input block must start with a format line.
You didn't include the format line with your parse block. Respecify the input block (with /Tools | Parse | Block), this time with the parse line as the first row of it.

Input line too long.
You tried to import a file containing a line longer than 254 characters. If it is an ASCII text file, shorten the line.

Inserted graph block too large.
The block you specify to insert a graph into cannot be larger than 12 columns by 32 rows.

Insufficient memory.
Your computer's memory is full. Free up or get more memory and try again. To free up memory space, do any of the following: Split your spreadsheet into separate files, close some of your open

spreadsheet files, or remove a memory-resident program. You can also use the /Options | Other | Expanded Memory command to optimize any expanded memory you have. See page 200 for details.

Invalid /X command.
A macro tried to execute a /X command that does not exist.

Invalid argument type.
You used the wrong argument type in a macro command. Check the @*Functions and Macros* book for the correct syntax.

Invalid block.
You tried to play back an invalid block of your command history in the Transcript window. Mark the block you want to replay with **B**egin Block and End Block and try again. See page 463 for more information about Playback Block.

Invalid cell or block address.
The address you entered doesn't exist. If it's a single cell, make sure its column coordinate is between A and AZ and its row coordinate is between 1 and 256. If it's a block address, reenter the block coordinates, separated by one or two periods. You can also use pointing to specify the cell or block.

Invalid character.
You used an invalid character in a formula—for example, you ended a formula with a comma.

Invalid character in file name.
Do not use spaces in file names. (You can use an underline character to simulate a space; for example, 89_SALES.) Nor can you use DOS wildcard characters * and ?.

Invalid constraint coefficients.
No optimization constraints have been specified, or the constraint coefficient matrix has cells which are not numbers (the matrix must not contain a label, blank, ERR, or NA).

Invalid constraint constants.
This block must be a column with the same number of rows as the constraint coefficient block. Each cell must have a number (not ERR, NA, a label, or blank).

Invalid constraint relations.
This block need not be specified, but if it is, it must be a column with the same number of rows as the constraint coefficient block. Each cell must have a number (not ERR, NA, a label, or blank).

Invalid database file.
The file you specified is not a file of the required database format.

Invalid date or time.
You entered a date or time in an invalid format. You must enter dates in any of the following formats:

DD-MMM-YY (4-Jul-89)
DD-MMM (4-Jul—assumes current year)
MMM-YY (Jul-89—assumes first day of month)
Long International format—initially MM/DD/YY (7/4/89)
Short International format—initially MM/DD (7/89)

You must enter time in any of the following formats:

HH:MM:SS AM/PM (2:36:15 PM)
HH:MM AM/PM (2:36 PM)
Long International format (14:26:15)
Short International format (14:26)

You can change the numeric format of a cell to display a date or time in a different format.

Invalid directory name or format.
You entered a directory name or path that Quattro does not recognize. Reenter and try again.

Invalid drive or path.
Quattro cannot locate the drive or path you specified. Specify a different one and try again.

Invalid drive was specified.
You gave an invalid drive letter as part of a file name or path.

Invalid field name.
The field name you specified is not a valid name for the database file format.

Invalid field type.
The field type you specified is not a valid type for the database file format.

Invalid ForBreak.
The macro you executed used a {FORBREAK} command outside the procedure called by the {FOR} loop.

Invalid format line.
A format line for parsing is invalid. Check to see that there is a " | " at the beginning of the parse line and that there are no invalid characters.

Invalid input block.
An input block is either unspecified, the wrong size, or has nonnumeric data in it such as a string or ERR.

Invalid matrix sizes.
In a matrix multiply operation, the number of columns in the first matrix must be the same as the number of rows in the second.

Invalid number.
Quattro expected you to enter a number and got something else. If you're entering a label that begins with a number, precede it with an apostrophe.

Invalid number or expression.
A Quattro macro command expected a number and got something else.

Invalid objective function.
This optimization objective function block must be a row with the same number of columns as the constraint coefficient block, and the cells must all have numbers in them (not ERR, NA, a label, or a blank). If the objective function is expressed as a formula, the formulas must be linear in the variables.

Invalid or damaged Clipboard file.
You attempted to paste to or from an invalid or damaged Clipboard (.CLP) file. Specify a different file name and try again.

Invalid output block.
You've executed a command, such as /Database I Query I Extract, without first defining the block in which to store the output. Specify the output block, then try again.

Invalid password.
The password you entered is not correct; try again. If you can't supply the correct password, you won't be able to retrieve the file.

Invalid spreadsheet file.
You tried to retrieve a file that cannot be translated by Quattro. Quattro automatically translates the following types of files: Reflex, Paradox, Surpass, Lotus 1-2-3, dBASE II, III, III+, and IV, Symphony, VisiCalc, and Multiplan. To work with a file created by a program not listed here, translate it first into an ASCII text file, then import the file with /Tools I Import.

Invalid string.
You entered a number or date when Quattro expected a string of text.

Invalid use of Menu macro command.
The menu you tried to create with macros is not properly defined.

Invalid variable bounds.
You need not specify this block, but if you do it must consist of two rows and must have the same number of columns as the constraint coefficient block. Strings and blanks cells are allowed and are interpreted as the lack of a bound on the corresponding variable.

Invalid X block.
The independent values specified for regression are invalid. Make sure the number of values is less than 17. Alternatively, you are trying to draw an XY graph with no block defined.

Invalid Y block.
The dependent values specified for regression are invalid. Make sure that there are an equal number of dependent and independent values.

Joining these lines would make a line too long.
You attempted to join two lines in a boxed text element into one, but Quattro cannot fit a line that long in the graph. The maximum length is approximately twice the width of the Annotator screen. To join the two lines successfully, decrease the number of characters they contain.

Key column outside of sort block.
You specified a sort key that was not part of the sort block. Specify a different sort key or respecify the sort block.

LaserJet font selected. Choose size with Typeface menu.
You have a LaserJet font selected with the **Typeface** menu. Because each LaserJet font includes a specific type size, you can't adjust size with the **Point Size** menu. If you want to change the size of the type, choose a different LaserJet font (with the size you want), or choose a regular font, then adjust the size with the **Point Size** command.

Link is removed.
You are attempting to save a spreadsheet that contains links with block name references to a file format that does not support them. To preserve these links, save the spreadsheet as a .WQ1 file.

Macro block is full.
The block you tried to paste your macro into is too small to hold the text. You must specify a larger block.

Matrices incompatible for multiplication.
The number of columns in the first matrix must be the same as the number of rows in the second matrix and neither matrix can be over 90 rows or columns.

Matrix is singular.
You attempted a matrix operation that failed because one of its pivots is zero. (For detailed information about matrices, refer to any textbook on linear algebra.)

Missing arguments.
The @function you just entered is missing one or more required arguments. Refer to the syntax for that @function in the *@Functions and Macros* book.

Missing Define command.
You called a macro subroutine with parameters but it has no {DEFINE} command to receive the parameters.

Missing operator.
The formula you tried to enter is missing a required operator. Check the syntax and edit the formula.

Missing or invalid PRINTERS.BGI file.
The PRINTERS.BGI file is missing from the directory with the Quattro program files or is damaged or corrupted. Go through the installation procedure again to make sure that Quattro has copied all the files it needs to the directory containing the Quattro program files.

Missing right parenthesis.
The @function you tried to enter is missing an ending parenthesis. Check the syntax and edit the formula.

Mouse not supported for this display mode.
Most mouse software supports only three display modes: 80x25, graphics mode, and EGA 80x43. If you choose a display mode not supported by your mouse, Quattro displays this error message and disables your mouse.

Named block not found in file.
The block name you specified does not exist. Make sure the block name you specified is valid and is spelled correctly. If you're referring to a block name in another spreadsheet, make sure your link syntax is correct: [*path/filename*]*blockname*.

No Bitstream font files (.SFO extension) located.
Quattro cannot find any .SFO files, which are the Bitstream typeface files in Quattro's format. Each .SFO file contains the master definition of a particular typeface, which Quattro needs to create a bitmap font file (with the .FON file extension) for a particular expression of one of these masters. (See Appendix F for more information about working with Bitstream fonts.) To restore the files, go through the installation procedure again to make sure that Quattro has copied all the files it needs to the directory containing the Quattro program files.

No block defined.
You attempted an operation that works on a block of cells (for example, /Print | Spreadsheet Print), but you haven't defined that block. Specify the block you want to affect (usually with the /Print | Block command), then try again.

No font selected.
You attempted an operation that requires a font selection, but you haven't specified a font. Specify a font, then try again.

No graph defined.
You tried to view a graph, but no graph series is defined for this spreadsheet. Quattro saves the current graph for each spreadsheet and any named graphs as well. If you can't find a graph you created, perhaps you reset the graph settings and erased it. If you named the graph, you can redisplay it with /Graph | Name | Display.

No graphics hardware.
Your display card or printer doesn't support graphics. Without a graphics display card, you can't view Quattro graphs on your screen. You must have a graphics printer to print graphs.

No Hershey font files (.CHR extension) located.
Quattro cannot find the Hershey font files it needs to perform the operation you attempted. Bitstream typeface files in Quattro's format. To restore the files, go through the installation procedure again to make sure that Quattro has copied all the files it needs to the directory containing the Quattro program files. (See Appendix F for more information about working with Hershey fonts.)

No objects are currently selected.
You attempted to perform an operation on a graph annotation object without first selecting an object or group of objects.

No printer selected.
You haven't told Quattro what kind of printer you have. Use the /Options I Hardware I Printers command to define your printer first, then try printing (or screen preview) again.

No room for text. Please change margins.
The combination of values you specified for the margin settings is invalid. Respecify them. The left margin setting cannot be greater than the right, and the top margin setting cannot be greater than the bottom. The valid ranges for each are Left and Right (0-240); Top and Bottom (0-32).

No series selected.
You tried to view the current graph, but no series have been defined yet. Use the Series menu or the Fast Graph command to define your graph series and try again.

No unprotected cells.
You can't use the /Database I Restrict Input command unless there are cells that have been explicitly unprotected. Choose /Style I Protection I Unprotect, then disable protection for the block of cells you want access to.

No X block defined for XY graph.
To create an XY graph, you must assign at least the 1st Series and X-Axis Series of values.

Not a square matrix.
Quattro can only invert matrices where the number of rows is the same as the number of columns.

Not enough memory for graphics mode.
You are in graphics mode, but you do not have enough memory for certain operations like redrawing a graph inserted in the spreadsheet. Choose another display mode.

Not enough memory for that operation.
Your computer's memory is full. To free up memory space, do any of the following: Split your spreadsheet into separate files, close some of your open spreadsheet files, or remove a memory-resident program.

Not enough memory to undo. Undo is disabled.
In order to complete the operation you just executed, Quattro had to use memory that is normally required by the Undo command. Therefore, Quattro disabled the Undo key. To re-enable it, choose /Options I Other I Undo I Enable.

Not found. Change to: ???
Quattro couldn't find the spreadsheet you attempted to link to. Choose a file from the list to switch the link over to a different spreadsheet.

Not found.
Quattro could not find the search string you were looking for. Check your search string. Make sure the **Look In** option is set to search the right place (Formulas for actual formulas, Values for formula results, or Conditions to interpret your search string as a search condition). If you're not sure of capitalization, make sure the **Case Sensitive** option is set to **Any Case**. To search through the entire spreadsheet, move to cell A1 and choose **Next**.

Nothing in Clipboard.
You attempted to paste from the Clipboard to a graph, but no object was cut or copied to the Clipboard for you to paste. Select the object that you want to cut or copy, choose **Cut** or **Copy** from the Clipboard menu in the Graph Annotator, move to the place you want to paste the object in this or any other graph, and choose **Paste** from the Clipboard menu.

Nothing to Paste.
In the File Manager, you attempted to copy or move a file or files from one directory to another without selecting them for moving or copying first. You need to select the files you want to copy or move with *Shift-F7* or the Plus key, then press *Shift-F9* to copy or *Shift-F8* to move, before you can move to another directory and press *Shift-F10* to paste the files.

Objective function is invalid.
You defined an invalid objective function or multiple objective functions. Choose **/Tools | Advanced Math | Optimization | Objective Function** and respecify the function to optimize.

Only one data point selected.
You attempted to define a series with only one value in it. Quattro cannot graph a series unless it contains more than one value.

Out of memory.
You do not have enough memory for Quattro to continue. Free up or get more memory and try again.

Out of spreadsheet boundary.
The rows or columns you attempted to insert would push some cells off the edge of the spreadsheet. Erase or move the data near the edge, then try again. Alternatively, you're trying to import a

file that has more than 8192 rows. You need to split up the file in its parent program before you can import it to Quattro.

Overflow occurred.
A floating-point overflow or divide by zero occurred during the course of computation.

Passwords do not match.
Quattro asks you to type the password twice to verify that it got the correct password. You typed two different passwords.

Path is too long.
The directory path you typed is longer than the maximum 63 characters. If you're saving or retrieving a file, use the file list to go into the directory you want to access. (Press *Backspace* to go into the parent directory, or choose a subdirectory from the list to access it.)

Polygon or polyline is too complex, close object.
A polygon or polyline can only have 1000 points. You have drawn 999, so close the object now.

Print block and headings in different spreadsheets.
The columns or rows that you specified as headings with the /Print | Headings command are not in the same spreadsheet as your print block. Copy the headings you want into the same spreadsheet as the print block and try again.

Print block is completely hidden.
All columns in the specified print block have been hidden with the /Style | Hide Columns command. Redisplay them with the same command or change the print block.

Printer error.
The printer is unable to print your spreadsheet or graph. Make sure the printer is turned on, securely connected to your computer, and online.

Printer I/O errors.
Your printer is not ready to print. Perhaps the printer is offline or out of paper. Choose **Abort** to stop printing, or correct the situation and choose **Continue** to try printing again.

Printer out of paper.
Choose **Abort** to stop printing, or correct the situation and choose **Continue** to try printing again.

Problem is infeasible.
There are no values for the optimization variables which satisfy the constraints.

Problem is unbounded.
There is no finite optimum for the problem. Usually, the solution is too good to be true, such as maximizing profits and finding they are infinite. Most likely, the problem is formulated incorrectly.

Protected cell or block.
You attempted to enter information into or change data in a protected cell or block of cells. You can use the /Style | Protection | Unprotect command to remove protection from the block so you can make changes.

Record too large.
You attempted to write a database record that was too large for the database format.

Reformat block is full.
The block you specified with the /Tools | Reformat command is too small to hold the text. You must specify a larger block.

Search String is not a condition, Look In is changed Formula.
You tried to perform a conditional search, but the search string was not a valid formula. Change it to a formula and set the Look In option back to Condition.

Series 1 undefined.
You tried to create a pie chart without assigning a block of values to the first series. Define 1st Series and try again.

Shortcut key is already in use.
You tried to assign a menu command to an illegal shortcut key. Reassign it, this time to a *Ctrl*-key and letter combination, such as *Ctrl-P*.

Size is too large.
The Advanced Math operations require memory. Besides being limited by available memory, matrix inverses are limited to 90 rows and columns, regressions are limited to 90 columns, and optimizations are limited to 90 constraints.

Spreadsheet is already open.
You attempted to open a spreadsheet file that is already loaded into Quattro. You can't load the same spreadsheet into two windows. If the window containing the spreadsheet you want

isn't visible, choose /Window | Pick and choose the spreadsheet name from the list.

Spreadsheet was opened.
See the previous message.

String is too long to replace.
Replacing the search string you've defined with the defined replace string would cause the cell entry to be longer than 254 characters. Reduce the length of the replace string.

Syntax error.
The syntax of your formula is incorrect. Check the syntax (in the *@Functions and Macros* book) and edit the formula.

That file is already open.
You attempted to open a file that is already open. If it's not displayed on your screen, choose /Window | Pick to see a list of open windows. Choose the file from the list to display it.

That would make this label too wide.
You attempted to insert a character in a boxed text element that would make the label too wide. The maximum width is approximately twice the width of the Annotator screen.

That would make this line too long.
Inserting this character would put too many characters in this line of the boxed text element. The maximum number of characters is approximately 250 per line.

Too few observations.
There are not enough rows in the X and Y blocks to calculate a regression. Add more rows of data to the independent and dependent blocks. The number of *Degrees of Freedom*, which is the number of observations (rows of X) minus the number of independent variables (columns of X plus one if the intercept is computed), must be positive.

Too many arguments.
You entered too many arguments in an @function. Refer to the syntax for that @function in the *@Functions and Macros* book.

Too many constraints.
There are more constraints than variables, so the variables are overdetermined. Optimization is not possible.

Too many fields.
The records you are appending to an outside database file contain more fields than the database can handle.

Too many iterations.
Optimization is performed by an iterative algorithm, which can take a very large number of iterations in bizarre special cases. Execution is terminated in such cases. Please report to Borland if you get this error (see "How to contact Borland" on page 6).

Too many nested subroutine calls.
You can only nest eight levels of {FOR} loop commands or 32 levels of subroutine calls.

Too many open files.
No more file handles are available because too many network spreadsheets are open. A network spreadsheet with read/write access uses one file handle. Close one or more network spreadsheets to continue, or move the spreadsheet to a local drive.

Too many open windows.
You cannot have more than 32 windows open at any one time. Close any of the files you are not using now.

Too many records.
You are exporting too many records to the database.

Too many records for output block.
The Query output block you specified is not large enough to hold all the records that match the criteria. Respecify the block so that it's larger. Or specify only the first row of the block and Quattro will use as many rows below as are necessary.

Too many retries.
The number you specified for Paradox network retries is too high. Choose /**O**ptions | **O**ther | **P**aradox | **R**etries and enter a lower number.

Too many spreadsheets loaded.
You tried to load one or more spreadsheets that would make the total open spreadsheets more than 32. Put away one or more open spreadsheets, then try again.

Too many subdirectories: ???.
The File Manager cannot handle this many subdirectories. Reduce the number and try again.

Two or more series must be selected for this graph type.
You attempted to create a high-low graph with less than two series. A high-low graph uses the first two series to create a set of vertical lines—one for each pair of values. Any other series are optional. See Chapter 13 for more information.

Undo is disabled. Cannot undo it.
To undo actions, the Undo command must be enabled with /Options I Other I Undo. If you want to undo an action and the Undo command was disabled during the action, you can use Undo Last Command in the Transcript utility to undo it. (Choose /Tools I Macro I Transcript to activate Transcript.)

Unknown @function.
Quattro doesn't recognize this @function. See the *@Functions and Macros* book for a list of valid @functions.

Unknown function translated to value.
The file format you are saving to does not support one or more @functions contained in your spreadsheet. If you choose Yes to save the file, Quattro converts any unknown functions to their resulting values. If you don't want this to happen, choose No to stop the save.

Unknown key or block name.
You gave an unrecognized key or block name in a macro.

Unsupported database file format.
Quattro cannot translate a file in that format. You need to translate the file in its parent program into a format that Quattro recognizes before you can open the file in Quattro. (See page 233 for a list of file formats Quattro translates automatically.)

X, Y blocks have different number of rows.
You need to use the same number of rows for the X and Y blocks.

123-compatible menu tree commands

This appendix contains one long table that lists commands on the 123-compatible menus and their corresponding commands on the standard Quattro menus. You can use it to track down information in the documentation, which is oriented toward the Quattro menus. You can also use it to help you switch over to the Quattro menus. For example, if you know where a command is on the Lotus 1-2-3 menus, but don't know where to find it in the Quattro menus, you can use this table to look it up.

Table I.1 lists all 123-compatible commands except those on submenus that are identical to the corresponding Quattro submenu. In other words, if a 123-compatible submenu contains the same commands (given a few terminology variations) as the equivalent Quattro submenu, those commands are not listed here.

Note If you see a menu item followed by a box symbol (■), whether in the 123-compatible menu tree or in Table I.1, this means that the item is unique to Quattro and therefore not compatible with Lotus 1-2-3. If you are writing macros in Quattro to run later under Lotus 1-2-3, avoid choosing these non-compatible menu commands.

Table I.1
123-compatible commands
and their Quattro menu
equivalents

123-compatible command	Quattro command
In a spreadsheet window:	
WORKSHEET	
Global	
Format	/Options I Formats I Numeric Format
Label Prefix	/Options I Formats I Align Labels
Column Width	/Options I Formats I Global Width
Recalculation	/Options I Recalculation
Natural	/O I R I Order I Natural
Columnwise	/O I R I Order I Columnwise
Rowwise	/O I R I Order I Rowwise
Automatic	/O I R I Mode I Automatic
Manual	/O I R I Mode I Manual
Background	/O I R I Background
Iteration	/O I R I Iteration
Protection	/Options I Protection
Default	
Printer	
Interface	/Options I Hardware I Printers I 1st (or 2nd) Printer I Device
Auto LF	/Options I Hardware I Printers I Auto LF
Left	/Print I Layout I Margins I Left
Right	/Print I Layout I Margins I Right
Top	/Print I Layout I Margins I Top
Bottom	/Print I Layout I Margins I Bottom
Page Length	/Print I Layout I Margins I Page Length
Wait	/Options I Hardware I Printers I Single Sheet
Setup	/Print I Layout I Setup String
Name	/Options I Hardware I Printers I Default Printer
Quit	
Directory	/Options I Startup I Directory
Status (display only—commands indicated will change these settings)	
—Interface	/Options I Hardware I Printers I 1st (or 2nd) Printer I Device
—Auto LF	/Options I Hardware I Printers I Auto LF
—Left	/Print I Layout I Margins I Left
—Right	/Print I Layout I Margins I Right
—Top	/Print I Layout I Margins I Top
—Bottom	/Print I Layout I Margins I Bottom
—Page Length	/Print I Layout I Margins I Page Length
—Wait	/Options I Hardware I Printers I Single Sheet
—Setup	/Print I Layout I Setup String
—Name	/Options I Hardware I Printers I Default Printer
—Directory	/Options I Startup I Directory

Table I.1: 123-compatible commands and their Quattro menu equivalents (continued)

123-compatible command	Quattro command
/Worksheet I Global I Default I Status…	
—Clock	/Options I Other I Clock
—Punctuation	/Options I International I Punctuation
—Currency	
—Date	
—Time	
Update	/Options I Update
Other	
International	/Options I International
Punctuation	/Options I International I Punctuation
Currency	/Options I International I Currency
Date	/Options I International I Date
Time	/Options I International I Time
Quit	
Help	
Clock	/Options I Other I Clock
Undo ■	/Options I Other I Undo
Macro ■	/Options I Other I Macro
Expanded Memory ■	/Options I Other I Expanded Memory
Beep ■	/Options I Startup I Beep
Hardware ■	/Options I Hardware
Colors ■	/Options I Colors
Mouse Palette ■	/Options I Mouse Palette
Files ■	
Autoload File	/Options I Startup I Autoload File
Startup Macro	/Options I Startup I Startup Macro
File Extension	/Options I Startup I File Extension
Menu Tree	/Options I Startup I Menu Tree
Graphics Quality	/Options I Graphics Quality
Quit	
Zero	/Options I Formats I Hide Zeros
Insert	
Column	/Edit I Insert I Columns
Row	/Edit I Insert I Rows
Delete	
Column	/Edit I Delete I Columns
Row	/Edit I Delete I Rows
Column	
Set Width	/Style I Column Width
Reset Width	/Style I Reset Width
Hide	/Style I Hide Column I Hide
Display	/Style I Hide Column I Expose

Table I.1: 123-compatible commands and their Quattro menu equivalents (continued)

123-compatible command	Quattro command
/Worksheet...	
Erase	/File I Erase
Titles	/Window I Options I Locked Titles
Window	/Window I Options
Horizontal	/Window I Options I Horizontal
Vertical	/Window I Options I Vertical
Sync	/Window I Options I Sync
Unsync	/Window I Options I Unsync
Clear	/Window I Options I Clear
Row & Col Borders ■	/Window I Options I Row & Col Borders
Map View ■	/Window I Options I Map View
Status (display only—commands listed will change these settings)	
—Normal Memory	/Options I Hardware
—Expanded Memory	/Options I Hardware
—Co-Processor	/Options I Hardware
—Recalc Mode	/Options I Recalculation I Mode
—Recalc Order	/Options I Recalculation I Order
—Iterations	/Options I Recalculation I Iteration
—Circular Reference	/Options I Recalculation I Circular Cell
—Cell Format	/Options I Formats I Numeric Format
—Label Prefix	/Options I Formats I Align Labels
—Column Width	/Options I Formats I Global Width
—Suppress Zero	/Options I Formats I Hide Zeros
—Protection	/Options I Protection
—Macro Library	/Tools I Macro I Library
—Undo	/Options I Other I Undo
Page Break	/Style I Insert Break
Macro ■	/Tools I Macro
Undo ■	/Edit I Undo
RANGE	
Format	/Style I Numeric Format
Label	
Left:	
Right:	
Center:	
Erase	/Edit I Erase Block

Table I.1: 123-compatible commands and their Quattro menu equivalents (continued)

123-compatible command	Quattro command
/Range...	
Name	/Edit I Names
Create	/Edit I Names I Create
Delete	/Edit I Names I Delete
Labels	/Edit I Names I Labels
Reset	/Edit I Names I Reset
Table	/Edit I Names I Make Table
Justify	/Tools I Reformat
Protect	/Style I Protection I Enable
Unprotect	/Style I Protection I Disable
Input	/Database I Restrict Input
Value	/Edit I Values
Transpose	/Edit I Transpose
Column ■	/Style I Block Widths
Search & Replace ■	/Edit I Search & Replace
Alignment ■	/Style I Alignment
Data Entry ■	/Database I Data Entry
Output Style ■	
Line Drawing	/Style I Line Drawing
Shading	/Style I Shading
Font	/Style I Font
COPY	/Edit I Copy
MOVE	/Edit I Move
FILE	
Retrieve	/File I Retrieve
Save	/File I Save

Table I.1: 123-compatible commands and their Quattro menu equivalents (continued)

123-compatible command	Quattro command
/File...	
Combine	/Tools	Combine
Copy	/Tools	Combine	Copy
Entire File	/Tools	Combine	Copy	File
Named Range	/Tools	Combine	Copy	Block
Add	/Tools	Combine	Add
Entire File	/Tools	Combine	Add	File
Named Range	/Tools	Combine	Add	Block
Subtract	/Tools	Combine	Subtract
Entire File	/Tools	Combine	Subtract	File
Named Range	/Tools	Combine	Subtract	Block
Xtract	/Tools	Xtract
Erase	/Edit	Erase (in a File Manager window)
Worksheet	
Print	
Graph	
Other	
List	/Sort (in a File Manager window)
Worksheet	
Print	
Graph	
Other	
Import	/Tools	Import
Text	/Tools	Import	ASCII Text File
Numbers	/Tools	Import	Comma & "" Delimited File
Comma	/Tools	Import	Comma & "" Delimited File
Directory	/File	Directory
New ■	/File	New
Open ■	/File	Open
Workspace ■	/File	Workspace
!SQZ! ■	/File	Utilities	SQZ
Update Links ■	/Tools	Update Links

Table I.1: 123-compatible commands and their Quattro menu equivalents (continued)

123-compatible command	Quattro command

PRINT

Draft-Mode Printing
Printer /Print I **Destination** I **Printer**
  Range /Print I **Block**
  Line /Print I **Adjust Printer** I **Skip Line**
  Page /Print I **Adjust Printer** I **Form Feed**
  Options /Print I **Page Layout**
    Header /Print I **Layout** I **Header**
    Footer /Print I **Layout** I **Footer**
    Margins /Print I **Layout** I **Margins**
      Left /Print I **Layout** I **Margins** I **Left**
      Right /Print I **Layout** I **Margins** I **Right**
      Top /Print I **Layout** I **Margins** I **Top**
      Bottom /Print I **Layout** I **Margins** I **Bottom**

      Dimensions ■ /Print I **Layout** I **Dimensions**
    Borders /Print I **Headings**
      Columns /Print I **Headings** I **Top Heading**
      Rows /Print I **Headings** I **Left Heading**
    Setup /Print I **Layout** I **Setup String**
    Pg Length /Print I **Layout** I **Margins** I **Page Length**
    Other
      As Displayed /Print I **Format** I **As Displayed**
      Cell Formulas /Print I **Format** I **Cell Formulas**
      Formatted /Print I **Layout** I **Break Pages** I **Yes**
      Unformatted /Print I **Layout** I **Break Pages** I **No**

      Direction ■ /Print I **Layout** I **Orientation**
    Update /Print I **Layout** I **Update**
    Quit
  Clear /Print I **Layout** I **Reset**
    All /Print I **Layout** I **Reset** I **All**
    Range /Print I **Layout** I **Reset** I **Print Block**
    Borders /Print I **Layout** I **Reset** I **Borders**
    Format /Print I **Layout** I **Reset** I **Layout**
  Align /Print I **Adjust Printer** I **Align**
  Go /Print I **Spreadsheet Print**
  Quit

File /Print I **Destination** I **File**
  same options as /Print I Printer

Table I.1: 123-compatible commands and their Quattro menu equivalents (continued)

123-compatible command	Quattro command

/Print...

Final-Quality Printing

Binary File   /Print I Destination I Binary File
     same options as /Print I Printer

Graphics Printer   /Print I Destination I Graphics Printer
     same options as /Print I Printer

Screen Preview   /Print I Destination I Screen Preview
     same options as /Print I Printer

Chart Print   /Print I Graph Print

GRAPH

Type	/Graph I Graph Type
X	/Graph I Series I X-Axis Series
A – F	/Graph I Series I 1st – 6th Series
Reset	
Graph	/Graph I Customize Series I Reset I Graph
X	/G I C I Reset I X-Axis
A – F	/G I C I Reset I 1st – 6th Series
Quit	
View	/Graph I View
Save	/Print I Graph Print I Write Graph File
Options	
Legend	/Graph I Text I Legends
A – F	/Graph I Text I Legends I 1st – 6th Series
Position ■	/Graph I Text I Legends I Position
Typeface ■	/Graph I Text I Font I Legend I Typeface
Format	/G I C I Markers & Lines I Formats
Graph	/G I C I M I Formats I Graph
A – F	/G I C I M I Formats I 1st – 6th Series
Line Styles ■	/G I C I M I Line Styles
A-F	/G I C I M I Line Styles I 1st – 6th Series
Quit	

Table I.1: 123-compatible commands and their Quattro menu equivalents (continued)

123-compatible command	Quattro command
/Graph I Options I Format…	
Markers	/G I C I Markers & Lines I Markers
A-F	/G I C I M I Markers I 1st – 6th Series
Quit	
Quit	
Titles	/Graph I Text
First	/Graph I Text I 1st Line
Second	/Graph I Text I 2nd Line
X-Axis	/Graph I Text I X-Title
Y-Axis	/Graph I Text I Y-Title
2nd Y-Axis ■	/Graph I Text I Secondary Y-Axis
Typeface ■	/Graph I Text I Font
Grid	/Graph I Overall I Grid
Scale	
Y-Scale	/Graph I Y-Axis
Automatic	/Graph I Y-Axis I Scale I Automatic
Manual	/Graph I Y-Axis I Scale I Manual
Lower	/Graph I Y-Axis I Low
Upper	/Graph I Y-Axis I High
Format	/Graph I Y-Axis I Format of Ticks
Indicator	/Graph I Y-Axis I Display Scaling
Tick Increment ■	/Graph I Y-Axis I Increment
No. of Minor Ticks ■	/Graph I Y-Axis I No. of Minor Ticks
Scaling Mode ■	/Graph I Y-Axis I Mode
Quit	
X-Scale	/Graph I X-Axis
Automatic	/Graph I X-Axis I Scale I Automatic
Manual	/Graph I X-Axis I Scale I Manual
Lower	/Graph I X-Axis I Low
Upper	/Graph I X-Axis I High
Format	/Graph I X-Axis I Format of Ticks
Indicator	/Graph I X-Axis I Display Scaling
Tick Increment ■	/Graph I X-Axis I Increment
Scaling Mode ■	/Graph I X-Axis I Mode
Draw Alternating Ticks ■	/Graph I X-Axis I Alternate Ticks
Quit	

Table I.1: 123-compatible commands and their Quattro menu equivalents (continued)

123-compatible command	Quattro command
/Graph I Options I Scale...	
Skip	
2nd Y-Scale	/Graph I 2nd Y-Axis
Automatic	/Graph I 2nd Y-Axis I Scale I Automatic
Manual	/Graph I 2nd Y-Axis I Scale I Manual
Lower	/Graph I 2nd Y-Axis I Low
Upper	/Graph I 2nd Y-Axis I High
Format	/Graph I 2nd Y-Axis I Format of Ticks
Indicator	/Graph I 2nd Y-Axis I Display Scaling
Tick Increment ■	/Graph I 2nd Y-Axis I Increment
No. of Minor Ticks ■	/Graph I 2nd Y-Axis I No. of Minor Ticks
Scaling Mode ■	/Graph I 2nd Y-Axis I Mode
Quit	
Color	/Graph I Overall I Color/B&W I Color
B&W	/Graph I Overall I Color/B&W I B&W
Data Labels	/Graph I Customize Series I Interior Labels
A – F	/G I C I Interior Labels I 1st – 6th Series
Quit	
Range Customize ■	/Graph I Customize Series
Colors	/Graph I Customize Series I Colors
A-F	/G I C I Colors I 1st – 6th Series
Quit	
Fill Patterns	/Graph I Customize Series I Fill Patterns
A-F	/G I C I Fill Patterns I 1st – 6th Series
Quit	
Override Type	/Graph I Customize Series I Override Type
Y-Axis	/Graph I Customize Series I Y-Axis
Pies	/Graph I Customize Series I Pies
Bar Width	/Graph I Customize Series I Bar Width
Quit	
Overall ■	/Graph I Overall
Outlines	/Graph I Overall I Outlines
Background Color	/Graph I Overall I Background Color
Three-D	/Graph I Overall I Three-D
Annotate ■	/Graph I Annotate
Insert ■	/Graph I Insert
Hide ■	/Graph I Hide
Update	/Graph I Customize Series I Update
Quit	

Table I.1: 123-compatible commands and their Quattro menu equivalents (continued)

123-compatible command	Quattro command
/Graph...	
Name	/Graph | Name
Use	/Graph | Name | Display
Create	/Graph | Name | Create
Delete	/Graph | Name | Erase
Slide	/Graph | Name | Slide
Reset	/Graph | Name | Reset
Instant Graph ■	/Graph | Fast Graph
Quit	
DATA	
Fill	/Edit | Fill
Table	/Tools | What-If
1	/Tools | What-If | **1** Variable
2	/Tools | What-If | **2** Variables
Reset	/Tools | What-If | Reset
Sort	/Database | Sort
Data Range	/Database | Sort | Block
Primary Key	/Database | Sort | 1st Key
Secondary Key	/Database | Sort | 2nd Key
3rd Key ■	/Database | Sort | 3rd Key
4th Key ■	/Database | Sort | 4th Key
5th Key ■	/Database | Sort | 5th Key
Reset	/Database | Sort | Reset
Go	/Database | Sort | Go
Order	/Database | Sort | Sort Rules
Quit	
Query	/Database | Query
Input	/Database | Query | Block
Criterion	/Database | Query | Criteria Table
Output	/Database | Query | Output Block
Assign Names	/Database | Query | Assign Names
Find	/Database | Query | Locate

Table I.1: 123-compatible commands and their Quattro menu equivalents (continued)

123-compatible command	Quattro command
**/Data	Query...**	
Extract	/Database	Query	Extract
Unique	/Database	Query	Unique
Delete	/Database	Query	Delete
Reset	/Database	Query	Reset
Quit	
Distribution	/Tools	Frequency
Matrix	
Invert	/Tools	Advanced Math	Invert
Multiply	/Tools	Advanced Math	Multiply
Regression	/Tools	Advanced Math	Regression
X-Range	/T	A	Regression	Independent
Y-Range	/T	A	Regression	Dependent
Output Range	/T	A	Regression	Output
Intercept	/T	A	Regression	Y Intercept
Reset	/T	A	Regression	Reset
Go	/T	A	Regression	Go
Quit	
Parse	/Tools	Parse
Format Line	
Create	/Tools	Parse	Create
Edit	/Tools	Parse	Edit
Input Column	/Tools	Parse	Input
Output Range	/Tools	Parse	Output
Reset	/Tools	Parse	Reset
Go	/Tools	Parse	Go
Quit	
Optimization ■	/Tools	Advanced Math	Optimization
VIEW	
Zoom ■	/Window	Zoom
Tile ■	/Window	Tile
Stack ■	/Window	Stack

Table I.1: 123-compatible commands and their Quattro menu equivalents (continued)

123-compatible command	Quattro command
/View…	
Move/Size ■	/Window I Move-Size
Pick ■	/Window I Pick
Close ■	/File I Close
Close All ■	/File I Close All
Exit ■	/File I Exit
SYSTEM	
OS	/File I Utilities I DOS Shell
Display Mode ■	/Options I Display Mode
File Manager ■	/File I Utilities I File Manager
QUIT	/File I Exit

In a File Manager window: Exactly the same as in the default Quattro menu tree.

J

Menu maps

This appendix illustrates the standard Quattro menu tree, broken up according to the chapters of this manual.

The top-level menus (those that pull down from the menu bar) are shown with drop shadows so you can spot them quickly.

All menus appear in double-line boxes; any text in single-line boxes is informational only and does not represent an onscreen element.

1-2-3   To find the Quattro command that corresponds to the 123-compatible command you might be looking for, refer to Appendix I, which lists the 123-compatible menu tree commands.

Menus for Chapter 4

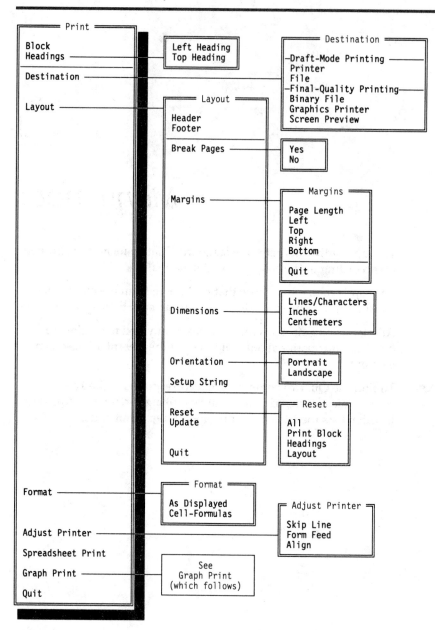

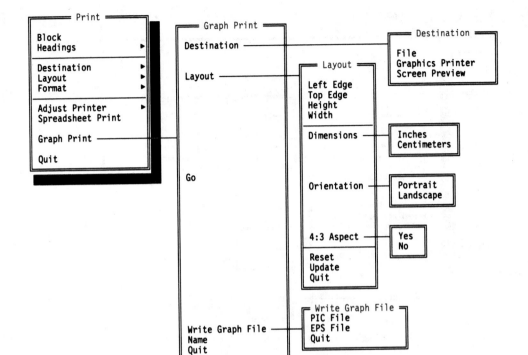

Menus for Chapter 5

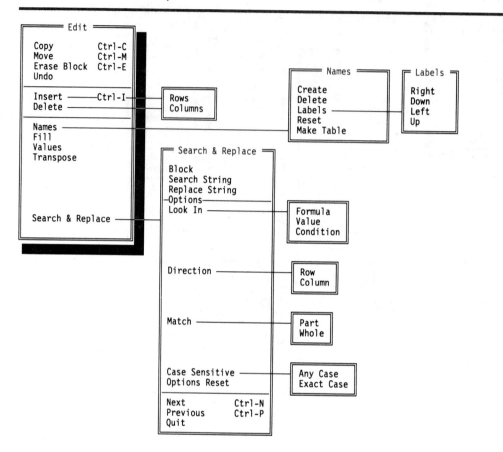

Menus for Chapter 6

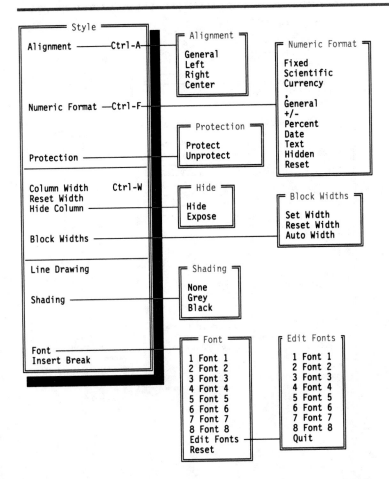

Menus for Chapter 7

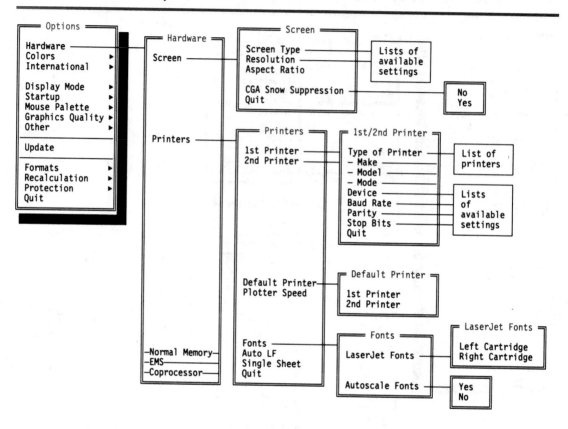

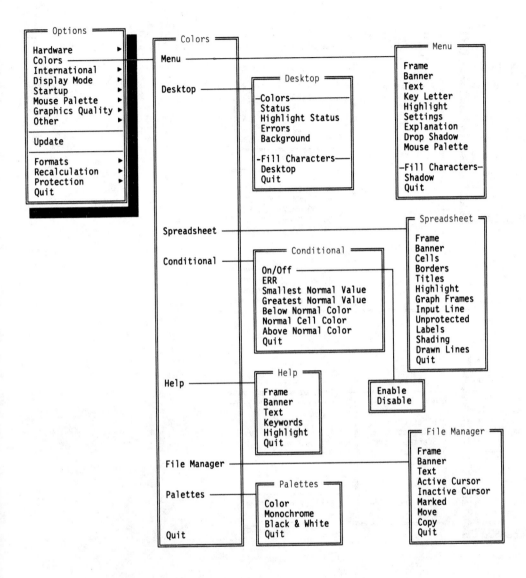

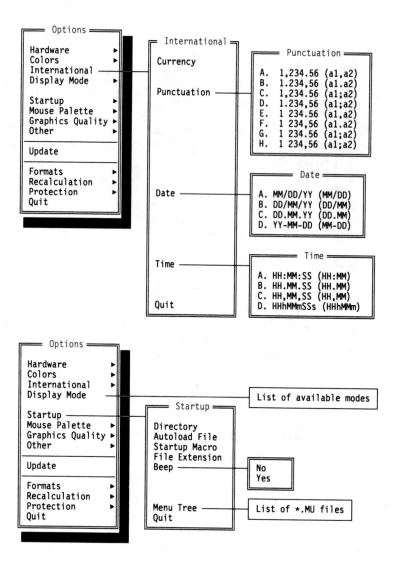

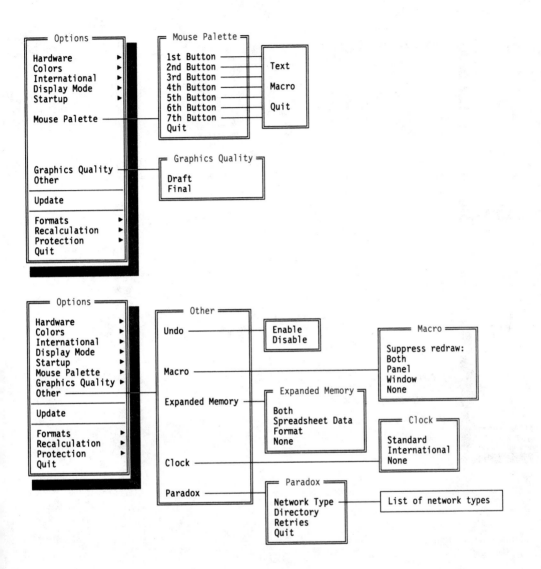

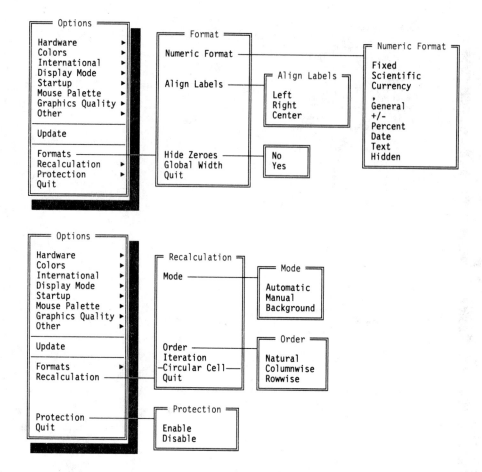

Menus for Chapter 8

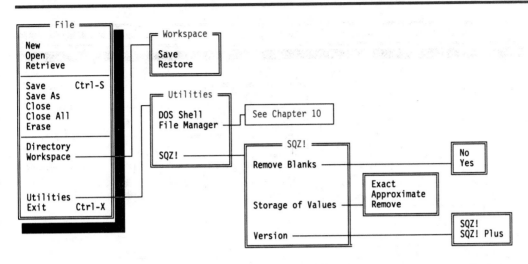

Menus for Chapter 9

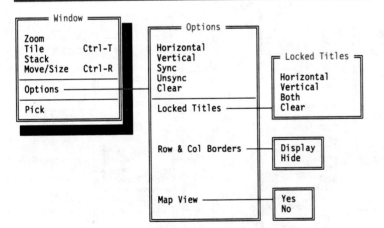

Menus for Chapter 10

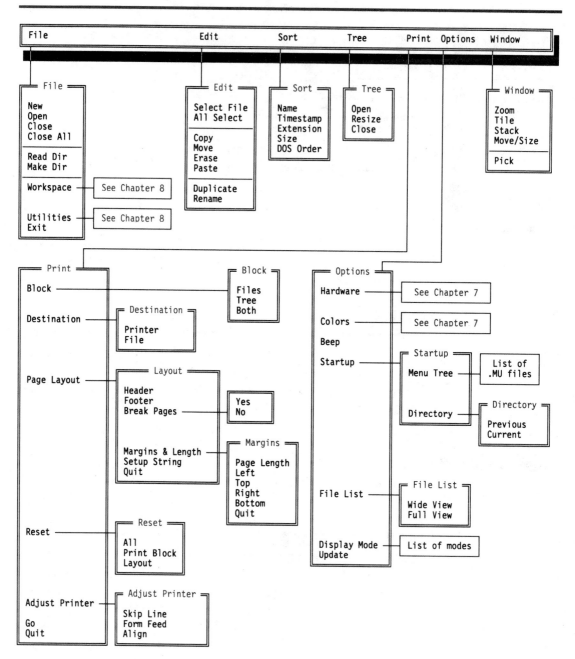

Menus for Chapters 11 and 12

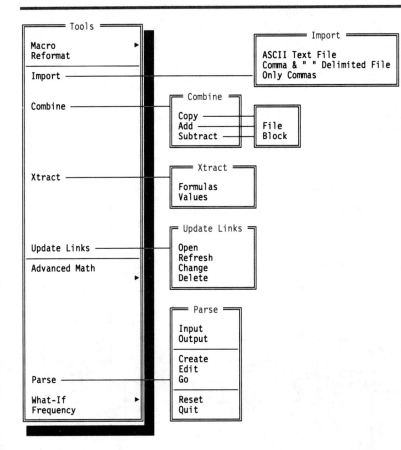

Menus for Chapter 13

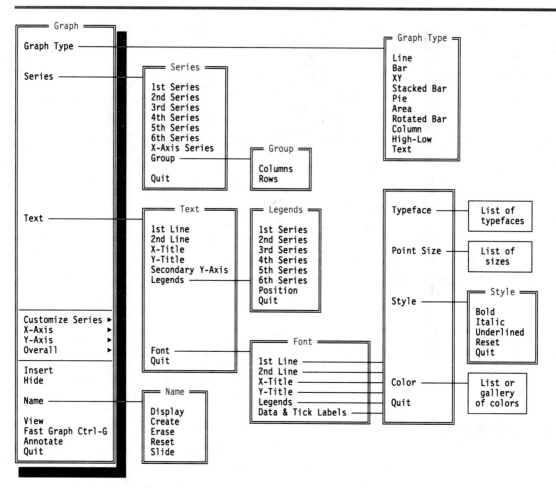

Menus for Chapter 14

The following two pages show an overview of the menu tree discussed in Chapter 14.

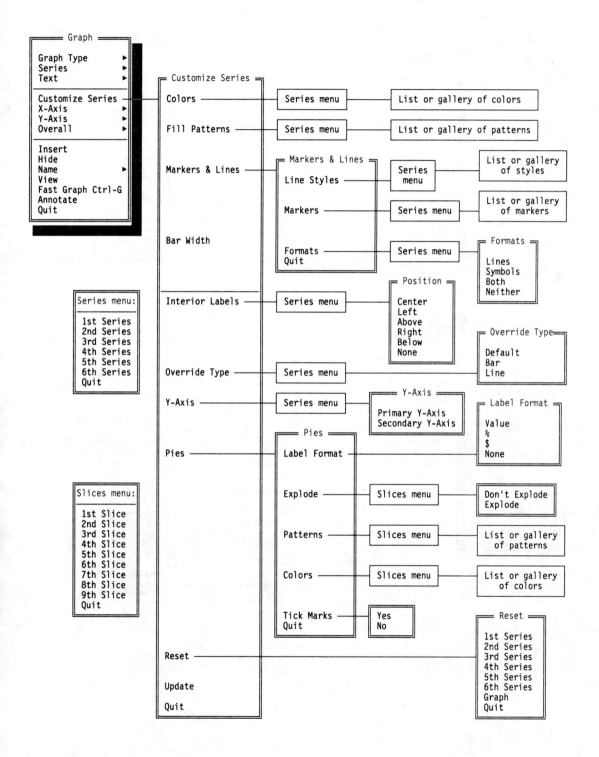

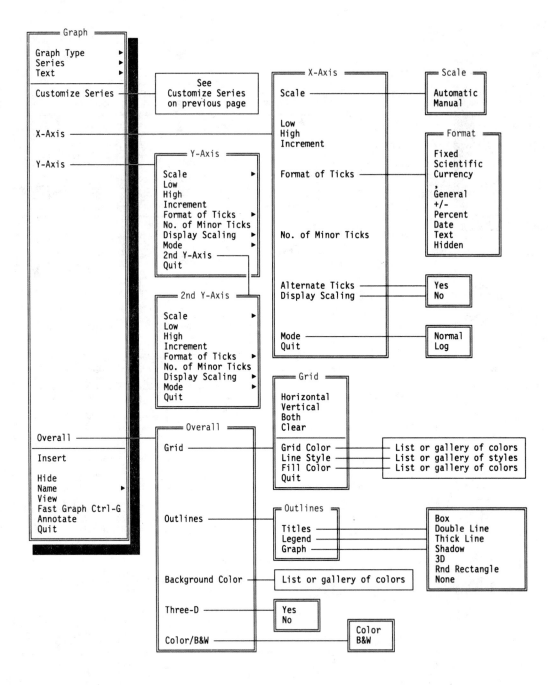

Menus for Chapters 16 and 17

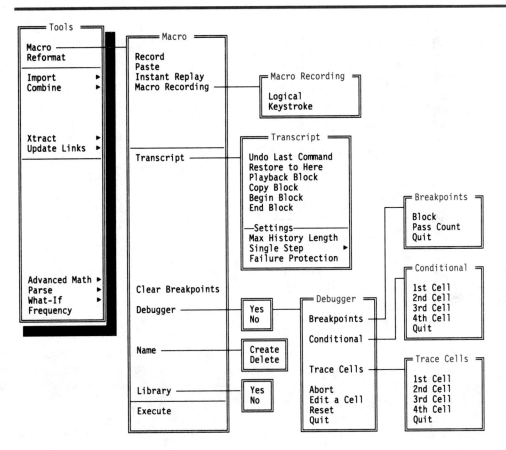

Tools
- Macro
- Reformat
- Import ▶
- Combine ▶
- Xtract ▶
- Update Links ▶
- Advanced Math ▶
- Parse ▶
- What-If ▶
- Frequency

Macro
- Record
- Paste
- Instant Replay
- Macro Recording
- Transcript
- Clear Breakpoints
- Debugger
- Name
- Library
- Execute

Macro Recording
- Logical
- Keystroke

Transcript
- Undo Last Command
- Restore to Here
- Playback Block
- Copy Block
- Begin Block
- End Block
- —Settings—
- Max History Length
- Single Step ▶
- Failure Protection

Debugger
- Yes
- No

Name
- Create
- Delete

Library
- Yes
- No

Debugger
- Breakpoints
- Conditional
- Trace Cells
- Abort
- Edit a Cell
- Reset
- Quit

Breakpoints
- Block
- Pass Count
- Quit

Conditional
- 1st Cell
- 2nd Cell
- 3rd Cell
- 4th Cell
- Quit

Trace Cells
- 1st Cell
- 2nd Cell
- 3rd Cell
- 4th Cell
- Quit

Menus for Chapter 18

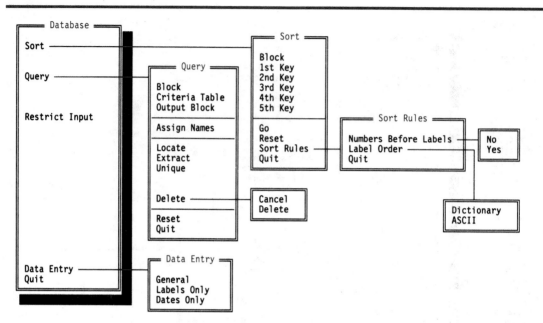

Menus for Chapter 19

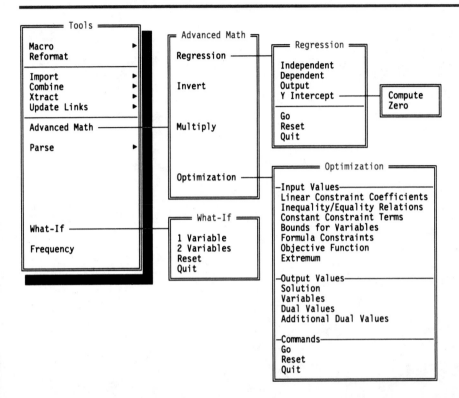

658

G L O S S A R Y

@function   See *function*.

absolute cell reference   A cell reference in a formula that will always reference the same cell, even if the formula is copied to a different part of the spreadsheet. To make a cell reference absolute, use the Abs key (*F4*) to insert dollar signs in its address—for example, $A$5.

active window   The window that contains the cursor and that is affected by commands you issue. In Quattro, the active window is indicated by a double-line border. See also *window*.

address   The location of a cell in a spreadsheet, defined by the letter of its column followed by the number of its row. For example, D5 is the address of the cell in column D and row 5.

annotation   Explanatory text or art added to a graph. Types of Quattro graph annotation include lines, arrows, polylines, polygons, rectangles, round rectangles, ellipses, and text.

argument   A variable required by many @function and macro commands. It supplies additional information used by the command. For example, in the @function command @SUM(A4..A10), the block address A4..A10 is the argument; it tells Quattro what values to add together.

aspect ratio   The ratio of a screen's width to its height, used to display graphics.

background recalculation   The method of calculating formulas in a spreadsheet in between user keystrokes, so that the user never has to pause for recalculation.

Bitstream typefaces   Typefaces designed by Bitstream, Inc. Quattro comes with several Bitstream typeface files in Quattro's format (with an .SFO extension) that it converts into device-specific fonts. You can use these fonts for printing spreadsheet and graph text. Examples of Bitstream typefaces include Dutch Bold and Dutch Italic: Dutch is the name of the *typeface family*, and bold and italic are names of *styles* that are part of the individual typeface designs. You can also use Bitstream typefaces that you purchase separately from Bitstream.

block Any rectangular group of cells, indicated by the addresses of the top left and bottom right cells.

borders The lettered row at the top of the spreadsheet and the numbered column to the left used to identify cell addresses. See also *headings*.

cell A box in the spreadsheet used to store data. A spreadsheet is made up of thousands of cells, ordered by rows and columns.

cell identifier The left part of the *input line* (or the *status line* in Edit mode) that displays information about the current cell. It includes the cell's address and contents and (if different from the default) column width and display format.

cell selector The highlighted rectangle that indicates the current cell.

coordinates The two points of reference that define a cell or block. The address of a cell is the letter of the column followed by the number of the row containing it. The coordinates of a block are the addresses of the top left and bottom right cells in the block.

criteria table The block of data in your spreadsheet that tells Quattro what field(s) to search and what data to search for. Quattro looks for all database records that match search criteria in the specified criteria table.

cursor-movement keys Keys on the numeric keypad (usually on the right side of the keyboard) used to move the cursor or cell selector. Usually marked with arrows: ↑, ↓, ←, →.

database An organized collection of information. In Quattro, a database is organized as rows, or *records*, of information, divided into separate columns, or *fields*.

date/time serial number A number assigned to a date or time, counting the number of days since December 30, 1899, and the number of seconds from midnight. The integer portion is used for the date; the fractional portion is used for time.

default A standard setting used when no other is specified. For example, the default column width is nine. You can change a default value temporarily or permanently. And you can depart from the default value for specified areas of the spreadsheet (for example, changing the width of an individual column).

destination block See *source block*.

directory	A section of a disk created with the DOS MKDIR or MD command. Directories are often further broken down into *subdirectories*.
DOS	The computer operating system required in order to run Quattro.
element (annotation)	The specific type of annotation art. Quattro annotation elements include lines, arrows, polylines, polygons, rectangles, round rectangles, ellipses, and text.
encryption	A method of protecting access to your files with a password.
expanded memory	An optional computer card that extends the computer's system memory (RAM).
extension	A code of up to three letters attached to the end of a file name and separated from the rest of the name by a period. A file's extension often identifies the type of file it is. For example, Quattro menu files have the extension .MU.
field	A category of information in a database. In a Quattro database, fields are set up as columns of information.
field names	Field names define the columns of information that make up a database.
file	A section of a disk used to store data.
font	A complete set of type used to print or display text. In Quattro, you can assign different fonts to blocks of a spreadsheet and to different parts of a graph. You can change the fonts by choosing a different typeface, point size, and style (bold, italics, or underlined).
format line	A line used to parse data. Symbols on the line tell Quattro how to break down and interpret the data.
frequency distribution	A table showing how many times numbers within given ranges are found in a block of data.
frozen titles	See *locked titles*.
function	One of a set of special commands that you can enter in a spreadsheet cell, either alone or in a formula. They perform advanced calculations and provide the resulting value. Also called @functions, because they all begin with an @.
function keys	The keys labeled *F1* through *F10* at the top or left of the keyboard, used to perform special Quattro functions.

gallery	A pictorial menu that displays available options visually. In Quattro, if your screen is in graphics mode, you see several menus as galleries instead of the standard menu of command names. For example, rather than listing graph types by name, Quattro shows a gallery with pictures of each graph type.
hard disk	Part of a computer used to store data in files; required to run QUATTRO PRO.
hardware	The physical equipment used to run Quattro: your computer, disk drives, screen, and printer.
headings	Columns or rows that contain text defining data below or to the right.
indicator	A highlighted word on the *status line* that indicates a special status condition or spreadsheet mode. For example, CAP indicates that the *Caps Lock* key is on.
input line	The line above the spreadsheet where Quattro displays information about the current cell in Ready mode. In Edit mode, the current cell information moves to the *status line* and the input line shows the data you're entering or editing. System prompts for cell block coordinates also appear on the input line.
iteration (recalculation)	The number of times the program recalculates formulas before it considers the spreadsheet correct.
label	Any textual cell entry.
label-prefix character	A character preceding a label entry that indicates how to align the entry. A single quote (') left-aligns a label entry, a double quote (") right-aligns it, and a caret (^) centers it.
link index	The link index determines to which value in the series Quattro links a selected annotation element or element(s). Choose Index 1 to link to the first value in a series, Index 2 to link to the second value in a series, and so on.
linking	The ability to pass information between spreadsheets. In Quattro, you can create permanent links, which are active references to other spreadsheet cells. You can also create temporary links to create a momentary bridge between spreadsheets—for example, when you copy data from one spreadsheet to another.
locked titles	Columns or rows that have been fixed on the screen. They remain in place even when you scroll the rest of the spreadsheet.

macro	A sequence of keystrokes or commands, recorded and stored in a spreadsheet, that Quattro can execute automatically.
macro commands	A set of special commands that can be used within macros.
macro library	A separate spreadsheet where sets of macros are stored. When you execute a macro, if it's not stored in the current spreadsheet, Quattro automatically looks for it in the loaded macro library.
matrix	A rectangular array of numbers used to systematize linear formulas and equations.
menu-equivalent commands	Special commands that correspond to menu items, used in macros and command history transcripts.
mode indicator	A highlighted word on the bottom line of the spreadsheet that indicates the current state, or *mode*, of the program. For example, when you're in Edit mode, the EDIT indicator appears.
mouse	A hand-operated pointing device attached to your computer. In Quattro, you can use a mouse to select cells, blocks, and menu commands, and to adjust window boundaries.
named block	A block of cells that has been assigned a name. You can then reference the block by name instead of by coordinates.
numeric format	The format in which Quattro displays a value or date.
operating system	The base software your computer uses to run the hardware and other programs. For example, Quattro requires DOS as a base in order to run.
operator	A mathematical symbol used in a formula to express a relationship between two values. For example, both + and / are operators in the formula A6+10/B2.
output block	A separate area of the spreadsheet where Quattro copies the records that match the specified search criteria. The output block must include the names of the fields you want copied for those records.
palette	A visual representation of options that you can choose from. Quattro includes a color palette that you can use to change screen colors. It also displays a mouse palette that you can use with a mouse to enter common commands.
pane	Part of a window. In Quattro, you can break a spreadsheet window into two panes and view different parts of the spread-

sheet in each. A File Manager window includes up to three panes, each offering a different function. See also *windows*.

parse
: To break down a column of long labels (such as those created by importing a text file) into two or more columns of data.

paste
: To insert something from the paste buffer, or Clipboard, into the current area. In the File Manager, you can "paste" files into a different directory.

permanent link
: A formula reference to a cell or block of cells in a different spreadsheet. See also *linking*.

plotter
: A computer printing device that uses interchangeable colored ink jets, or pens, to print multicolored text and graphs.

pointing
: The method of indicating a cell block by moving the cell selector to its coordinates.

protection
: A security function that prevents the contents of a cell block or the entire spreadsheet from being changed.

query
: To find specific information in a database. In Quattro, you use the Query command to look for and separate out information in a database.

RAM (random access memory)
: A temporary storage area within your computer, used for storing your work until you save it to disk. If you turn off your power before saving, you'll lose everything in RAM.

recalculation
: The act of calculating formulas again in a spreadsheet.

record
: A set of information in a database. In a Quattro database, records are rows of data.

regression analysis
: A table of figures that indicate how one set of variables is affected by other sets of variables.

resolution
: The number of pixels used by a screen to display graphics and text. The greater the resolution, the sharper the screen display.

scale
: The range of values assigned to an axis and used for plotting data on a graph. Quattro scales each numeric axis of a graph automatically to best display the data plotted on it, but you can adjust the scale manually if you prefer.

scroll bars
: Highlighted bars along the left and bottom edges of the spreadsheet window. If you have a mouse, use these bars to scroll the active area of the spreadsheet: Click on the scroll box, drag until the window is where you want it, then release the button.

sensitivity analysis	A table that shows the results of varying one or two essential values. Also called a what-if table, because it shows what would happen to other figures if certain values were to be changed.
series	A series of values plotted as a group on a graph.
shortcut	A menu command programmed into a *Ctrl*-key sequence. To create a shortcut, highlight the menu command you want to program and press *Ctrl* and *Enter* at the same time. Then press *Ctrl* and the letter you want to assign to the command. To execute a shortcut, press *Ctrl* and the letter assigned to the shortcut.
sort key	The key element used in sorting. In Quattro, you can sort records in a database by the entries in a given field, such as Date. Each field you specify sorting by is called a sort key.
source block	When a menu command prompts for two blocks, it might first prompt for a source block, then a destination block. For example, when you copy or move a block, the source block is the original location of the block, and the destination block is the place in that spreadsheet or any other where you want Quattro to paste the block.
spillover	Part of a long label displayed in empty cells to the right of the cell in which the label was entered.
status line	The bottom line of the spreadsheet screen, showing file name, window number, spreadsheet mode, and any status conditions. If you press *F2* to enter Edit mode , the status line shows information about the current cell (and any error messages).
temporary links	Temporary bridges between spreadsheets that let you pass information back and forth. When you copy or move data into different spreadsheets, you're creating a soft link. As soon as the operation is over, the link disappears. See also *linking*.
tick mark	A small line on an axis indicating a value in the axis scale.
typeface	A design of a set of type. Bitstream Swiss Italic and Bitstream Swiss Bold are examples of related but individual typefaces. A typeface is one attribute of a *font*. Style (bold, italic, or underlined) and point size are other attributes. Each combination of typeface, style, and size makes up a different font.
value	Any numeric value in the spreadsheet, entered either as a number, a date, or a formula that calculates a number.

VROOMM™	A Virtual Real-Time Object-Oriented Memory Manager that allows QUATTRO PRO to deliver many new functions and features without requiring additional hardware beyond a hard disk, and without compromising capacity or performance. VROOMM™ uses memory dynamically; it loads small modules of QUATTRO PRO program code into memory only as needed to perform different tasks. Data occupies the rest of memory, so you can load very large spreadsheets without affecting program function.
what-if table	See *sensitivity analysis*.
wildcard	A special code that allows substitution of any character. In Quattro, you can use wildcards in search conditions when querying a database and in the File Manager for displaying files. There are two types of wildcards: * allows substitution of any number of characters in its place, and ? allows substitution of a single character.
window	The part of the spreadsheet screen used to view and work with data. In Quattro, you can open and display up to 32 spreadsheet or File Manager windows at a time. The windows can all be displayed on the screen at once or can be layered, so you can see one or a few at a time. Spreadsheet windows let you create and work with spreadsheets; File Manager windows access the File Manager for working with files on your disk. You can divide a spreadsheet window into two panes to view different parts of your spreadsheet at the same time. A File Manager window can have three panes.
workspace	An arrangement of windows and open files in Quattro, which includes the position and size of all windows and the files contained in each window. If, after creating a workspace that includes various files and windows, you want to leave Quattro but don't want to have to build your workspace all over again when you return, use the /File I **W**orkspace command to save it. When you restore a workspace, Quattro opens and arranges all of the files and windows that you saved as a workspace.
x-axis	The horizontal line at the bottom of a graph, used to plot values.
y-axis	The vertical line at the left of a graph, used to plot values.
zoom	To focus in on something. In Quattro, you can "zoom" a window to make it fill the screen, then "zoom" out of it to return it to its previous size. You can also zoom in and out of choice lists, such

as a block name list. To zoom a choice list, press *F3* when the list is displayed.

I N D E X

User's Guide

cells 72, 76
    formula references 64
Proportional Resize mode and 407
resizing
    columns 155
    windows 242
selecting blocks and 280
stacking windows 241
zooming windows 238
Mouse Palette command
    Colors | Menu 181
    Options 45, 172, 197
Move command
    Edit 39, 119, 290, 309
    File Manager | Edit 268, 270
    Options | Colors | File Manager 186
MOVE indicator 241
Move key (Ctrl-M) 120
move operations, reversing 121
Move/Size command 46, 241
Move/Size key (Ctrl-R) 241
multiplication blocks 510
Multiply command 508, 510, 511

N

NA values 284
Name command
    File Manager | Sort 261
    Graph 41, 352
    Tools | Macro 429, 443, 464
named blocks *See* block names
Names command 39, 129
NEC 8023A printer setup strings 585
negative file filters (File Manager) 257
negative numbers 55
    descending sequential values and 136
    in pie and column charts 328, 331
Neither command 364
nesting
    formulas 61
    @functions 69, 70
Network Type command 202
networks *See* local area networks
New command 38, 272
Next command 139
Next key (Ctrl-N) 140
Next Window key (Shift-F6) 73, 238

No. of Minor Ticks command 378, 381
No. of Observations (regression analysis) 518
None command
    Customize Series | Pies | Label Format 371
    Options | Other | Expanded Memory 201
    Style | Line Drawing 161
nonlinear constraints 524, *See also* linear
    programming, optimization
nonnegative bounds 529, *See also* linear
    programming, optimization
Normal Cell Color command 184
Normal command 178
Normal Memory command 173
notation, scientific *See* scientific notation
number argument (macros) 454
number sign (#) in headers and footers 93
numbers 149, *See also* numeric values
    calculating 52
    display formats *See* numeric display formats
    entering 55-56
        automatically 134
        in bin blocks 507
        in labels 53
        problems with 542
        telephone 53
        zip code 53
    fractional 153
    negative *See* negative numbers
    plotting in graphs 338-343
    scientific *See* scientific notation
    searching 138
    serial, converting to dates 543
    sorting 474
    window 221
Numbers Before Labels command 474
numeric display formats 150, *See also* specific
    type
    display options 204, 205
    input line and 14, 151
    International options 187-191
    negative numbers and 55
    types 56, 152
    viewing changes to 244
Numeric Format command
    Options | Formats 203, 204
    Style 40, 150, 244
        search conditions and 478

R

R Squared (regression analysis) 517
RAM 215, *See also* memory
range of cells *See* blocks
Read Dir command 272
read-only access, local area networks and 569
READY indicator 51
Ready mode 126
   input line in 14
   locked titles and 246
   repeating query operations and 484
   status line display in 15
REC indicator 431
recalculation 48, *See also* arithmetic operations;
   calculation
   complex formulas 210
   options 65, 207-210
   problems with 542, 545
   resetting order of 209
   sensitivity tables 498
   single cell 66, 208
Recalculation command 45, 173, 207
Record command 428, 429
Record mode 429, 430, 442
   exiting 431
recorded keystrokes and commands *See*
   keystrokes, recording; macros; Transcript
   utility
records in databases 469
   eliminating duplicate 486
   linking to other database files 488
   matching 484
      copying 482, 485
      deleting 485
   searching for 474
   sorting 471-474
rectangles (graph design element) 399
redundancy (linear regression) 514
references
   absolute 116
   block
      macro command arguments and 454, 455
      names 70, 128, 130
         copying files and 299
         parsing files and 308
   cell 74
      ERR values in 144

moving formulas and 120, 305
   problems with 544, 545
   sorting databases and 472
ERR 71
fields in search criteria 476, 480
formula
   circular 210
   extracted data from other files and 488
   in specified blocks 65
   links as 275
   pointing to 64
   recalculation and 66
   sensitivity tables and 496, 503
   tracking 65
link 281, 340
moving data and 121
number argument in macro commands 454
regression table 521
relative 115
   transposing columns and rows and 145
Reflex files 233
   querying 476
Reformat command 43, 140
reformatting blocks 141, 142
Refresh command 287, 288
regression analysis 514-521
   constants 517
   output 517
   used to forecast data 519
      with a database 516, 519
      with XY graphs 521
Regression command 508, 514
relative cell address 65
   absolute vs. 115
Remove Blanks command 228
Rename command 268, 271
repeat numbers 445
repeating characters 54
Replace String command 138
requirements, system 5
Reset command
   Database | Query 475
   Database | Sort 473
   Edit | Names 129
   Graph
      Customize Series 340, 361, 376
      Name 352

displaying as time 152
dual 530
effects of varying 495
entries
  alignment 149
  asterisks in cells 542
  comments in 66
  illegal 30, 48, 53
ERR *See* ERR values
executing macros and cell 437
formulas and 58, 60
graph *See* data points; series
input, in linear programming 523
International options and 187
label alignment and 205
linked 285
NA, in linked spreadsheets 284
nonnumeric characters 59
output 529
plotting *See* graphs, plotting data
range of 319
search conditions and 138
solving unknowns 508
subtracting from other spreadsheets 304
true/false 63
  conditional search and 480
  macros and 450, 455
  search criteria tables and 479
updating in linked spreadsheets 275, 285, 287
variables *See* variables
y-intercept 515
Values command
  Edit 39, 137
  Tools I Xtract 305
variables 514, 519
  concatenation and 62
  linear programming and 523, 527, 529, 531
  linear regression and 508
Variables command 529
Version command 228
version differences, Quattro *See Getting Started*
vertical bars *See* I (vertical bars)
vertical borders 13
Vertical command
  Graph I Overall I Grid 385
  Style I Line Drawing 161
  Window I Options 244, 246

vertical lines *See also* lines
  drawing 161, 399
  in Transcript utility 460
videos *See* monitors
View command 41
View Structure command 234
viewing graphs and spreadsheets
  simultaneously 315
VROOMM™ memory manager 215, 233

W

WAIT indicator 81, 309, 462
warning beeps *See* beeps
What-If command 44, 496
what-if models 559
what-if tables *See* sensitivity analysis
Wide View command 261
Width command 104
widths
  bars in graphs 323, 365
  block 156, 157
  column 155, 158
    changing 206
    input line and 14
    problems with 546, 548
    restoring default 156
    setting 154
    viewing changes to 244, 559
  graph 105
wildcards
  directory lists and 219, 258
  DOS 256
  file prompts and 220
  link references and 281
  problems with searching and 547
  querying a database with 481
  search conditions and 138
Window command 200
Window menu 46, 237, 255
windows 215, 235-250, *See also* Window menu
  arranging
    as stacks 240
    as tiles 239
  changing background colors 182
  closing 230
  copying files between directories and
    multiple 270

Zoom command 46, 238
zoom icon (mouse) 24
Zoom key (Alt-F6) 238

zooming
  Screen Previewer 88
  windows 238, 253